Next-Generation AI Methodologies in Education

Eriona Cela
University of New York, Tirana, Albania

Narasimha Rao Vajjhala
University of New York, Tirana, Albania

Mathias Mbu Fonkam
Pennsylvania State University, USA

IGI Global
Scientific Publishing
Publishing Tomorrow's Research Today

Vice President of Editorial	Melissa Wagner
Managing Editor of Acquisitions	Mikaela Felty
Managing Editor of Book Development	Jocelynn Hessler
Production Manager	Mike Brehm
Cover Design	Phillip Shickler

Published in the United States of America by
IGI Global Scientific Publishing
701 East Chocolate Avenue
Hershey, PA, 17033, USA
Tel: 717-533-8845
Fax: 717-533-8661
E-mail: cust@igi-global.com
Website: https://www.igi-global.com

Library of Congress Cataloging-in-Publication Data

Names: Çela, Eriona, 1992- editor. | Vajjhala, Narasimha, 1978- editor. | Fonkam, Mathias Mbu, 1964- editor.
Title: Next-generation AI methodologies in education / Edited by Eriona Çela, Narasimha Rao Vajjhala, Mathias Fonkam.
Description: Hershey, PA : IGI Global Scientific Publishing, 2025. | Includes bibliographical references and index. | Summary: "This book aims to inform educational professionals about AI technologies and their practical applications in teaching. This book will also provide empirical evidence and case studies from schools and colleges to showcase how AI can be integrated effectively"-- Provided by publisher.
Identifiers: LCCN 2024053108 (print) | LCCN 2024053109 (ebook) | ISBN 9798369372203 (hardcover) | ISBN 9798369372210 (paperback) | ISBN 9798369372227 (ebook)
Subjects: LCSH: Artificial intelligence--Educational applications. | Education--Effect of technological innovations on. | Curriculum planning--Technological innovations.
Classification: LCC LB1028.43 .N52 2025 (print) | LCC LB1028.43 (ebook) | DDC 370.285/63--dc23/eng/20241218
LC record available at https://lccn.loc.gov/2024053108
LC ebook record available at https://lccn.loc.gov/2024053109

British Cataloguing in Publication Data
A Cataloguing in Publication record for this book is available from the British Library.

Dr. Eriona Çela

I would like to extend my heartfelt gratitude to my family. Its unwavering support and belief in me have been my guiding light throughout this journey. Thank you for standing by me, for your patience, and for always reminding me of the importance of this work. I am truly fortunate to have you in my life.

Assoc. Prof. Narasimha Rao Vajjhala

I want to thank my family members, particularly my mother, Mrs. Rajeswari Vajjhala, for her blessings and for instilling in me the virtues of perseverance and commitment.

Assoc. Prof. Mathias Fonkam

I would like to express my sincere gratitude to my beloved wife Antonia and our 2 younger ones – my 10-year old princess, Noella, and my 8-year old son, Asobo, for their endless love, patience, understanding and support as I have had to steal time off the dad schedule for this and other work. I also owe much gratitude to the many in this field who have structured and charted the course and on whose shoulders we mostly stand.

Editorial Advisory Board

Lori Annette Slater, *American InterContinental University, USA*
Vijender Kumar Solanki, *CMR Institute of Technology, India*
Zhaohao Sun, *PNG University of Technology, Papua New Guinea*
Thenmozhi T., *KGISL Institute of Technology, India*
George Salu Thandekkattu, *American University of Nigeria, Nigeria*
Jelena Vucetic, *Alpha Mission, Inc., USA*
Denise Wright, *Howard University USA*
P. B. Zirra, *Federal University of Kashere, Nigeria*

Table of Contents

Detailed Table of Contents

This chapter explores the transformative role of artificial intelligence (AI) in education, focusing on secondary and higher education contexts. This chapter provides a comprehensive overview of how AI technologies are reshaping educational practices through personalized learning, adaptive curriculum design, and enhanced student engagement. By examining current trends, such as AI-driven assessment tools, learning analytics, and adaptive learning systems, the chapter highlights both the opportunities and challenges AI presents for educators and institutions. Key ethical considerations, including algorithmic bias, data privacy, and equitable access, are addressed, emphasizing the need for responsible AI deployment in educational settings. The chapter also examines the evolving role of educators in AI-enhanced classrooms, where traditional teaching roles are augmented by AI's ability to support personalized learning experiences.

This chapter explores the transformative impact of artificial intelligence (AI) on the education sector, highlighting how AI technologies enhance teaching quality, streamline assessment processes, and support both physical and virtual learning environments. By facilitating innovative methods of lecture delivery and interactive learning, AI tools benefit educators and students alike, enabling a more engaging and efficient educational experience. The chapter provides a comprehensive review of various AI techniques and methodologies used within educational contexts, illustrating practical applications that support personalized learning, efficient evaluations, and adaptive teaching strategies. Additionally, it examines the benefits and challenges

This chapter investigates undergraduate students' perceptions of the potential of artificial intelligence (AI) in higher education. Using a descriptive survey method, data were collected from 322 undergraduate students in West Bengal through random sampling and analyzed using perception scales. Additionally, unstructured interviews were conducted to explore the reasons behind low levels of perception. The study employed Mean, Standard Deviation, Kruskal-Wallis test, Mann-Whitney U test, post-hoc analysis, and percentage calculations to analyze data and test hypotheses. Findings indicate that students generally have a moderate perception of AI's potential in higher education, with significant variation observed across academic streams (Arts, Science, and Commerce) but no notable differences based on gender, caste, location, or semester. The study also uncovers factors contributing to the low perception levels among undergraduates regarding AI's role in higher education.

This chapter examines AI’s transformative role in educational assessment and feedback, focusing on enhancing teaching and learning through technology. As AI reshapes traditional practices, the chapter emphasizes that AI in assessment should extend beyond automation, advocating for designs that encourage deep learning and student engagement. Using adaptive feedback, educators can support skill development and promote meaningful engagement with the material. The chapter presents a framework for AI-integrated assessments, stressing clear guidance, ethical considerations, and the active roles of both educators and students. It discusses tools like plagiarism detectors and adaptive learning platforms, underscoring the need to align AI with learning objectives and integrity standards. The framework also emphasizes the collaborative nature of AI in assessment—educators mentor students in using AI responsibly while students engage critically with technology. This approach balances AI’s benefits with human insight, offering a model for inclusive, adaptive assessments.

This chapter examines the rapid adoption of artificial intelligence (AI) technologies in higher education, focusing specifically on students' perceptions and attitudes toward AI writing tools within the Department of English Studies, Faculty of Letters and Humanities Ben M'sik, Morocco. Grounded in the Technology Acceptance Model (TAM), this study addresses a significant research gap in the Moroccan context, where few quantitative studies have explored factors influencing technology acceptance. To fill this gap, Partial Least Squares Structural Equation Modeling (PLS-SEM) was used to analyze survey data from 253 participants. The results reveal strong, positive relationships among TAM variables, identifying perceived usefulness and attitudes towards AI writing tools as primary predictors of actual usage. The findings suggest that educational institutions should highlight the potential benefits of AI tools, design accessible and user-friendly systems, and offer training to enhance student engagement and adoption of AI technologies.

This chapter examines the application of artificial intelligence techniques for multimodal classification of the Arabic alphabet across three key domains: handwriting, sign language, and braille. Each modality employs a specialized methodology tailored to its unique requirements. For handwritten Arabic character recognition, a hybrid model combining particle swarm optimization and a support vector classifier achieves a test accuracy of 90.20%. Arabic sign language alphabet classification utilizes MediaPipe for hand landmark detection alongside Inception ResNet v2 for feature extraction, followed by a custom neural network, achieving a test accuracy of 93.77%. Arabic braille character recognition employs EfficientNet B3 for feature extraction with a simple neural network for classification, resulting in a macro-average F1-score of 81.33%. These AI-driven approaches underscore

This chapter explores the expanding role of artificial intelligence (AI) in education, focusing on future projections and emerging trends shaping the next generation of learning. AI has already transformed educational landscapes, fostering personalized learning experiences, adaptive technologies, and automated administrative processes. This chapter examines upcoming AI-driven innovations poised to enhance educational outcomes further. Key trends, including intelligent tutoring systems, AI-powered assessments, and data-driven learning analytics, are analyzed for their potential impact. The chapter also addresses the ethical and practical challenges posed by AI in education, such as algorithmic bias and privacy concerns. By understanding these evolving dynamics, educators and policymakers can better prepare for a future where AI contributes positively to global learning environments.

This concluding chapter synthesizes the integration of Artificial Intelligence (AI) in education, underscoring its transformative potential across learning, teaching, and administrative domains. The authors examine pivotal AI applications, such as personalized learning, automated assessment, and enhanced classroom management, emphasizing how these innovations boost student engagement and learning outcomes. Alongside these advancements, the chapter critically addresses ethical challenges associated with AI in education, including algorithmic bias, data privacy issues, and the risk of reducing human interaction. The chapter illustrates AI's practical applications and effectiveness through case studies and examples, such as AI-driven tools like DreamBox and Georgia State University's student success platform. To support the ethical use of AI, the authors highlight the need for strategies to mitigate biases, ensure diverse and representative datasets, and uphold stringent data privacy standards.

In the rapidly evolving fields of education, entrepreneurship, and artificial intelligence, understanding the applications of AI in educational entrepreneurship is essential. This chapter adopts an applied research approach, using qualitative methods such as a systematic literature review and semi-structured interviews with 14 experts from education, entrepreneurship, and AI. Through thematic analysis, 1830 initial themes were distilled into 42 first-level themes, categorized into 20 second-level themes, and ultimately consolidated into three overarching themes. These global themes reveal AI's impact on enhancing learning productivity, streamlining instructional methods, and advancing educational administration and leadership. The findings underscore AI's transformative potential in educational entrepreneurship, providing a comprehensive framework highlighting AI's diverse contributions to the education system.

Foreword

The merge of artificial intelligence and education is more than just a section in a new textbook; it is the beginning of a completely new narrative in teaching and learning. Reflecting on the changes that I have witnessed in education, it's evident that AI is transforming what we originally thought were constant aspects of education. I recollect my own early days of investigating educational technology, feeling both excited and anxious about how digital tools could transform the learning experience. Moving forward to today, we're not merely integrating computers to regular classrooms; we're also experiencing settings where AI personalizes education and technology is geared toward each student's need. This book, Next-Generation AI Methodologies in Education, provides an exceptional insight into this evolution. Through a variety of case studies and theoretical ideas, it provides readers with an honest look at what it requires to integrate AI effectively into educational settings. The authors have not shied away from describing both the benefits and the real challenges, ensuring that this book remains an invaluable tool not only to those actively involved in AI, but also for educators, administrators, and policymakers with different levels of experience and technological comfort.

I particularly like the book's emphasis on practical AI applications. The book puts together theory and practice by sharing examples from educational settings where AI tools, such as adaptive learning systems or AI-powered tutors, are already in use. I recall conversations I've had with educators who were rather reluctant to use AI in their classrooms. They were concerned about implications for their roles or unclear about how AI tools could be incorporated into conventional educational environments. This book, on the other hand, guides readers through real-world applications while providing comfort by illustrating the human dimension of technology in education.

One of the most thought-provoking topics involves ethical issues. In our desire to embrace AI, we often ignore challenges such as data privacy and algorithmic biases. However, if AI in education is to fulfill its full potential, we must be cautious regarding these issues. The book provides a balanced approach, highlighting possible challenges and suggesting how educators could address these issues to create a more comparable learning environment.

This book encourages educators and academic professionals to consider the broader potential of teaching and learning, alongside the immediate impact of AI. It is evident that AI cannot replace educators; rather, it transforms the ways we engage with students. AI enables us to reach students who might otherwise struggle, personalizing their learning experiences in ways that were unthinkable a generation ago. This change encourages us to view AI as a partner in education, rather than a new "tool" one which enables for more personalized, versatile, and inclusive learning experiences.

I propose you to approach this book with curiosity and a sense of purpose. Whether you are an educator, an administrator at your institution, or an education policymaker, there is much to gain here. Appreciate its findings, reflect on its case studies, and, most importantly, explore how such approaches might fit into your own vision for the future of education. At last, it is in our hands and minds to realize AI's full potential in education.

Vasileios Paliktzoglou
Bahrain Polytechnic, Bahrain

Vasileios Paliktzoglou, an academic and industry professional, holds a Ph.D. in Computer Science from the University of Eastern Finland. He is an active contributor to academia, serving as a guest and associate editor for prestigious journals like the Journal of Information Systems Education (JISE) and IAFOR Journal of Education. He has been a keynote speaker at several academic and industry events, sharing his insights on social computing, collaborative learning, and emerging technologies in higher education. Dr. Paliktzoglou also actively participates in international research projects, highlighting his commitment to advancing knowledge and innovation as the Book Series Editor for the "Emerging Technologies in Education" at Vernon Press and "AI and Education" at STAR Scholars Press. His expertise continues to shape the academic and research landscape at Bahrain Polytechnic

Preface

INTRODUCTION

We are proud to present this volume as a testament to the exceptional international collaboration that brought together 65 authors from 20 countries, culminating in a comprehensive collection of 28 chapters. This global perspective has infused the book with a diversity of insights and approaches, reflecting the many ways AI methodologies are being explored and applied across educational settings worldwide. The contributions span various disciplines and contexts, showcasing both innovative ideas and practical applications that speak to the universal challenges and opportunities presented by AI in education. The journey to this final collection was marked by a rigorous selection process that reflects the high standards we set for this project. Out of an impressive 267-chapter proposals received, 91 were chosen for full submission. Following a thorough double-blind peer-review process, only 28 chapters were ultimately accepted, resulting in a final acceptance rate of approximately 10.5%. This rigorous curation ensures that each chapter provides valuable, evidence-based insights, setting a new benchmark for research and practice in the field of AI-driven education.

Chapter Overview

In Chapter 1 - Artificial Intelligence in Education: Foundations, Trends, and Implications, Eriona Çela, Mathias Fonkam, and Narasimha Rao Vajjhala explore the transformative potential of artificial intelligence (AI) within educational settings, emphasizing its impact across secondary and higher education. This chapter provides an in-depth examination of how AI technologies—such as adaptive learning systems, data analytics, and virtual assistants—are reshaping educational practices by enabling personalized learning, refining curriculum design, and fostering enhanced student engagement. It also addresses key ethical considerations, including algorithmic bias, data privacy, and equitable access, advocating for responsible AI deployment to ensure inclusivity and fairness in education. Through a critical analysis of current practices and literature, the chapter offers valuable insights for educators, policymakers, and researchers on the implications and future directions of AI in education. By highlighting both the opportunities and challenges presented by AI integration, the authors underscore the importance of interdisciplinary collaboration and continuous research in navigating this evolving landscape, ultimately aiming to create an adaptive and inclusive educational environment.

In Chapter 2 - Applications of Artificial Intelligence in Education, Aravindh K. and Brijendra Singh examine the diverse applications of artificial intelligence (AI) within educational environments, emphasizing its role in transforming both teaching and learning processes. The chapter explores how AI technologies, such as adaptive learning platforms, chatbots, virtual classrooms, and automated assessments, are reshaping education by enabling personalized learning and enhancing teaching quality. By analyzing various AI tools and their applications, the authors highlight the benefits of AI for educators in creating more efficient and engaging learning experiences, as well as for researchers in assessing student performance and adapting instructional methods. Additionally, the chapter addresses challenges in implementing AI in educational settings, such as data privacy concerns, technological access, and the need for ethical guidelines. To maximize AI's potential in education, the authors propose strategies for overcoming these challenges, promoting a future where AI facilitates a dynamic, accessible, and inclusive educational landscape. This chapter provides critical insights into the opportunities and limitations of AI in education, paving the way for future innovations and improvements in learning methodologies.

In Chapter 3 - Emerging Trends of AI Technologies in the Higher Education Sector: A Case of India and Kazakhstan, Rajasekhara Mouly Potluri and Madhavi Kilaru examine the transformative impact of artificial intelligence (AI) on higher education in India and Kazakhstan. This chapter explores how AI applications like data analytics, language learning tools, virtual assistants, and collaborative learning platforms are reshaping educational practices in these regions. Through a comparative analysis, it highlights both commonalities and unique approaches in AI adoption, focusing on the regulatory frameworks and ethical considerations needed for responsible AI use in education. This chapter provides valuable insights for educators and policymakers, addressing opportunities and challenges in integrating AI technologies to enhance learning experiences and operational efficiencies across diverse educational landscapes.

In Chapter 4 - Key Drivers of Artificial Intelligence on Learner Engagement and Experience, Shankar Subramanian Iyer explores the factors that influence the adoption of artificial intelligence (AI) in education and how they impact student engagement and experience. This chapter examines cognitive, emotional, and behavioral dimensions of student engagement, analyzing how AI-driven technologies like adaptive learning systems, real-time feedback, and personalized learning environments can enhance or hinder educational outcomes. Through a detailed literature review and empirical analysis, the author identifies critical factors driving AI integration in education, including technology design, ethical considerations, and organizational support. Additionally, the chapter addresses challenges such as data privacy, algorithmic bias, and infrastructure limitations, particularly in under-resourced regions, providing a holistic perspective on AI's transformative potential in education. This chapter offers valuable insights for educators, policymakers, and developers on leveraging AI to create inclusive, engaging, and personalized educational experiences while addressing essential ethical considerations.

In Chapter 5 - Exploring Undergraduate Students' Perceptions of Artificial Intelligence in Higher Education: A Study in West Bengal, India, Mazhar Shamsi Ansary, Indrajit Mahato, Jayashree Mahanti, Nupur Gorai, and Santosh Kumar Behera investigate the perceptions of undergraduate students in West Bengal regarding the potential of artificial intelligence (AI) in higher education. Using a descriptive survey method, data were gathered from 322 students and analyzed to explore how academic stream (Arts, Science, and Commerce) impacts AI perception, while also considering variables like gender, caste, location, and semester. The study reveals a moderate overall perception of AI's potential in higher education, with significant differences among academic streams but no notable disparities based on gender, location, caste, or semester. Additionally, the chapter identifies factors contributing to low perception levels, such as digital divide, economic constraints, and language barriers, offering insights for educators and policymakers aiming to improve AI adoption and accessibility in educational settings.

In Chapter 6 - AI in Assessment and Feedback, Smitha Shivshankar and Nirmal Acharya explore the transformative role of artificial intelligence (AI) in enhancing assessment and feedback processes in education. The chapter emphasizes that AI's role in assessment should go beyond automation, advocating for designs that foster deep learning and active student engagement. By utilizing adaptive feedback, AI can help support skill development and improve learning outcomes. The authors present a framework for AI-integrated assessments, which includes clear guidance and ethical considerations, alongside tools such as plagiarism detectors and adaptive learning platforms. The framework underscores the collaborative nature of AI in assessment, with educators guiding students in responsible AI usage while promoting critical engagement with technology. This approach balances AI's capabilities with human insight, offering a model for inclusive and adaptive assessments that aim to support students' academic success and lifelong learning.

In Chapter 7 - Integrated Use of AI Educational Platforms, Melissa Li Sa Liow addresses a significant gap in educational psychology by examining the integrated use of Artificial Intelligence Educational Platforms (AIEPs) within educational settings. This chapter presents four primary research objectives: evaluating the effectiveness of AIEPs in supporting educators, administrators, and students (collectively termed "AI users"); analyzing potential risks associated with AIEP usage; exploring how AIEPs affect users' sense of relatedness, autonomy, and competence, framed through the Technology Acceptance Model (TAM) and Self-Determination Theory (SDT); and investigating factors that impact users' perceived utility and sustained adoption of AIEPs. Through this comprehensive analysis, the chapter offers critical insights for educators, policymakers, and AIEP developers, providing a forward-looking perspective on the role of AI in shaping future educational practices.

In Chapter 8 - An Analysis of Cloud Computing in Game Theory, Dibyanshu Mohanty and Vishal Jain discuss the convergence of artificial intelligence (AI) and cloud computing in optimizing resource allocation, enhancing user Quality of Experience (QoE), and minimizing latency in educational environments. This chapter introduces an AI-driven model using game-theoretic techniques to manage resources in cloud-based educational systems. By conceptualizing the educational cloud ecosystem as a multi-agent environment, the model enables intelligent adaptation to user needs, thus minimizing resource wastage and ensuring equitable access. Initial findings reveal significant improvements in content loading speeds, latency reduction, and adaptability to user demands, highlighting the model's potential to support scalable, learner-centric educational technologies. This chapter offers valuable insights into sustainable cloud resource management, advancing digital education for diverse user needs.

In Chapter 9 - Student Adoption of AI Writing Tools Using a PLS-SEM and TAM-Based Analysis in Moroccan Higher Education, Mouad Malmous and Said Zaidoune investigate the adoption of AI writing tools among students in Moroccan higher education. Focusing on the Department of English Studies at the Faculty of Letters and Humanities Ben M'sik, this chapter applies the Technology Acceptance Model (TAM) alongside Partial Least Squares Structural Equation Modeling (PLS-SEM) to analyze the factors influencing student acceptance of AI technologies. Through a survey of 253 students, the authors examine key TAM variables, including perceived usefulness, perceived ease of use, and attitudes, as predictors of actual usage. Findings indicate strong relationships among these factors, highlighting that perceived usefulness and positive attitudes are significant drivers of adoption. The chapter emphasizes the importance of creating accessible and user-friendly AI systems while addressing ethical concerns like data privacy and algorithmic bias. These insights offer valuable guidance for educators and policymakers aiming to enhance student engagement with AI tools in educational settings.

In Chapter 10 - Multimodal Classification of the Arabic Alphabet: An Artificial Intelligence Approach for Handwriting, Sign Language, and Braille, Sarra Rouabhi and Redouane Tlemsani present AI techniques for classifying the Arabic alphabet across three modalities: handwriting, sign language, and Braille. Each modality utilizes a unique methodology tailored to its specific requirements. For handwritten characters, a hybrid model of particle swarm optimization (PSO) and a support vector classifier (SVC) achieves high accuracy. Arabic sign language classification combines MediaPipe for hand landmark detection with Inception ResNet v2, yielding impressive results. Arabic Braille recognition leverages EfficientNet B3 for feature extraction with a neural network, supporting diverse learning needs and accessibility. This chapter highlights the potential of AI in Arabic language education, emphasizing inclusivity for learners with varied abilities.

In Chapter 11 - Generative Artificial Intelligence and the 4C Learning Skills for the 21st Century, Pınar Mıhcı Türker and Mücahit Öztürk examine the relationship between generative artificial intelligence (AI) and the development of critical thinking, creativity, collaboration, and communication—referred to as the 4C skills essential for the 21st century. This chapter examines how generative AI tools, such as ChatGPT and Canva, foster these competencies by providing interactive and personalized learning experiences that stimulate cognitive engagement and collaborative work. Through a comprehensive review of current research, the authors analyze the transformative potential of AI in education, alongside the ethical and practical challenges it presents, including issues of data privacy, over-reliance on AI, and algorithmic bias. The chapter emphasizes the balanced integration of generative AI to support educational outcomes, offering educators, technologists, and policymakers insights on effectively harnessing these tools to enhance student learning and prepare them for complex social and professional environments.

In Chapter 12 - Transforming Hybrid Service-Learning with Generative AI: The LivePBL Ada-Rob Communication Skills Design Approach, Ying Liu, Joy Dsouza, Yuanyuan Li, and Ting Zhao introduce the Ada-Rob Skill Communication Design Approach. This innovative framework leverages generative AI to address communication challenges within service-learning environments. The Ada-Rob approach enhances engagement through two main components: 'Ada' for adaptive and personalized learning, and 'Rob' for role-based, structured interactions. This dual approach supports expertise-specific interactions and general communicative abilities, creating a scalable solution that fosters dynamic, collaborative learning experiences in hybrid environments. Through real-world use cases, the authors illustrate how generative AI can facilitate meaningful communication and collaboration, addressing the critical needs of diverse educational and community settings. This chapter provides valuable insights for educators and community leaders seeking to implement hybrid service-learning programs that integrate AI tools for enhanced communication and skill development.

In Chapter 13 - The Future of AI in Education: Predictions and Emerging Trends, Mustafa Kayyali explores the expanding role of artificial intelligence (AI) in education, focusing on future projections and trends shaping the next generation of learning. This chapter reviews how AI has already transformed educational landscapes through personalized learning experiences, adaptive technologies, and automated administrative processes. Key upcoming innovations, including intelligent tutoring systems, AI-powered assessments, and data-driven learning analytics, are analyzed for their potential impact on educational outcomes. The chapter also addresses ethical and practical challenges, such as algorithmic bias and privacy concerns, offering insights for educators and policymakers on preparing for a future where AI positively contributes to global learning environments.

In Chapter 14 - Artificial Intelligence in Education: Emerging Trends, Ethical Considerations, and Future Directions, Houda Boumediene and Mustapha Bouakkaz synthesize the integration of artificial intelligence (AI) across educational contexts, highlighting its transformative role in learning, teaching, and administration. The chapter discusses pivotal AI applications, including personalized learning, automated assessments, and enhanced classroom management, which contribute to increased student engagement and improved learning outcomes. Alongside these advancements, the authors critically address ethical challenges, such as algorithmic bias, data privacy issues, and the potential reduction of human interaction in education. Through case studies, including tools like DreamBox and Georgia State University's student success platform, the chapter emphasizes the need for ethical frameworks to mitigate biases, ensure data security, and foster equitable AI usage. This chapter offers comprehensive insights and recommendations for responsibly implementing AI in education, aiming to enhance the learning experience while upholding ethical standards.

This book represents a pivotal contribution to the evolving landscape of artificial intelligence in education, reflecting the collective expertise and diverse perspectives of contributors from around the world. The rigorous selection and review process that led to these 28 chapters ensures that the insights presented here are both cutting-edge and robust, addressing a broad spectrum of AI applications and their impact on learning environments. Each chapter has been crafted to serve as a valuable resource for educators, researchers, policymakers, and technologists, offering actionable strategies and thought-provoking discussions that bridge theory with practice. As AI continues to redefine the educational experience, we hope this book provides readers with a comprehensive foundation on current methodologies, ethical considerations, and future directions for AI in education. By capturing the innovations and challenges shared by a global community, this volume aspires to inspire further research, collaboration, and responsible implementation of AI technologies. We are excited to contribute to this transformative journey, equipping readers with the knowledge and insights needed to navigate and shape the future of AI-enhanced education.

In Chapter 15- Identifying the Applications of Artificial Intelligence in Educational Entrepreneurship Development: A Qualitative Research Based on Thematic Analysis, Mahnaz Zolfaghar, Aidin Salamzadeh, and Omid Afsharpour adopt an applied research approach, using qualitative methods such as a systematic literature review and semi-structured interviews with 14 experts from education, entrepreneurship, and AI. Through thematic analysis, 1830 initial themes were distilled into 42 first-level themes, categorized into 20 second-level themes, and ultimately consolidated into three overarching themes. These global themes reveal AI’s impact on enhancing learning productivity, streamlining instructional methods, and advancing educational administration and leadership. The findings underscore AI's transformative potential in educational entrepreneurship, providing a comprehensive framework highlighting AI's diverse contributions to the education system.

Editors

Dr. Eriona Çela is a renowned researcher in artificial intelligence, deep learning, machine learning, and natural language processing, with a distinguished academic career that bridges AI innovation with educational and public administration reforms. Renowned for her expertise in European integration and policy negotiation, Dr. Çela holds prestigious roles at the Academy of European Integration and Negotiations (AIEN), the Albanian School of Public Administration (ASPA), and the Business Academy College. Her influential research in AI applications for educational technology and governance is widely published, contributing to her reputation as a leading expert in advancing AI within Albania and across Europe. As a Jean Monnet Chair at the Institute of European Studies, University of Tirana, she has driven high-impact projects like the European Integration School 2023, shaping educational strategies that integrate AI to address complex policy challenges. Her academic work has appeared in premier journals, including the European Journal of Arts, Humanities and Social Sciences, the European Journal of Contemporary Education, and the International Journal of Balkan Studies. She also serves as an Associate Editor for the International Journal of Risk and Contingency Management (IJRCM), where she promotes research at the cutting edge of AI and risk management. Dr. Çela's collaborative efforts extend to the OSCE Academy in Bishkek, Vytautas Magnus University, and the Università degli Studi di Bari Aldo Moro, Dipartimento di Studi Umanistici, where she fosters AI-centered research on a European scale. Her leadership at Shkolla e Drejtorëve (CSL) and the AADF reflects her dedication to nurturing the next generation of AI-savvy leaders and administrators. A sought-after keynote speaker, Dr. Çela's work continues to set a standard for integrating AI-driven strategies within educational and administrative frameworks, solidifying her role as a cornerstone in Albania's technological and educational advancement.

Dr. Narasimha Rao Vajjhala is working as the Dean of the Faculty of Engineering and Architecture at the University of New York Tirana, Albania. He had previously worked as the Chair of Computer Science and Software Engineering programs at the American University of Nigeria. He is a senior member of ACM and IEEE. He is the Editor-in-Chief (EiC) of the International Journal of Risk and Contingency Management (IJRCM). He is also a member of the Risk Management Society (RIMS), and the Project Management Institute (PMI). He has over 23 years of experience teaching programming and database-related courses at both graduate and undergraduate levels in Europe and Africa. He has also worked as a consultant in technology firms in Europe and has experience participating in EU-funded projects. He has completed a Doctorate in Information Systems and Technology (United States); holds a Master of Science in Computer Science and Applications (India), and a Master of Business Administration with a specialization in Information Systems (Switzerland).

Dr. Mathias M. Fonkam is an Associate Professor at Penn State University with extensive experience in both academia and industry. He has previously served as Dean and Associate Professor at the American University of Nigeria (AUN), where he played a pivotal role in establishing and leading the School of Information Technology and Computing (SITC). Dr. Fonkam has a rich academic background, having taught at various esteemed institutions such as Albany State University, St. Joseph's University, and the Federal University of Maranhao in Brazil. With over 20 years of teaching experience, Dr. Fonkam specializes in computer science and engineering, focusing on areas such as open-source software development, object-oriented and functional programming, AI, data science, blockchain, cybersecurity, and system dynamics. He has published more than 50 scientific papers in international journals, conferences, and book chapters, and has authored multiple books. Dr. Fonkam's industry experience includes roles as a software engineer, web consultant, and technical director at various tech companies in the USA and Brazil. He has been actively involved in developing educational technologies, including the creation of a Cyber Security Lab at the University of Computer Studies in Yangon, Myanmar, and implementing AI-powered learning management systems at AUN. An advocate for integrating technology in education, Dr. Fonkam has contributed to the development of several innovative educational programs and policies. His research interests span across computational thinking, systems dynamics, AI applications, and blockchain technologies. He is fluent in English, Portuguese, and French, with a reasonable command of Spanish.

Eriona Çela
University of New York Tirana, Albania

Narasimha Rao Vajjhala
University of New York Tirana, Albania

Mathias Mbu Fonkam
Penn State University, USA

Chapter 1
Artificial Intelligence in Education: Foundations, Trends, and Implications

Eriona Çela
https://orcid.org/0000-0003-2710-5489
University of New York, Tirana, Albania

Mathias M. Fonkam
https://orcid.org/0000-0002-2776-1462
Pennsylvania State University, USA

Narasimha Rao Vajjhala
https://orcid.org/0000-0002-8260-2392
University of New York, Tirana, Albania

Alexey Vedishchev
https://orcid.org/0009-0009-3840-7440
American University of Nigeria, Nigeria

ABSTRACT

This chapter explores the transformative role of artificial intelligence (AI) in education, focusing on secondary and higher education contexts. This chapter provides a comprehensive overview of how AI technologies are reshaping educational practices through personalized learning, adaptive curriculum design, and enhanced student engagement. By examining current trends, such as AI-driven assessment tools, learning analytics, and adaptive learning systems, the chapter highlights both the opportunities and challenges AI presents for educators and institutions. Key ethical considerations, including algorithmic bias, data privacy, and equitable access,

DOI: 10.4018/979-8-3693-7220-3.ch001

are addressed, emphasizing the need for responsible AI deployment in educational settings. The chapter also examines the evolving role of educators in AI-enhanced classrooms, where traditional teaching roles are augmented by AI's ability to support personalized learning experiences.

INTRODUCTION

Artificial Intelligence (AI) has emerged as a transformative force in various sectors, with education being one of the most significantly impacted domains. The integration of AI technologies into educational settings has the potential to revolutionize teaching and learning processes, offering personalized experiences, enhancing administrative efficiency, and fostering innovative pedagogical approaches. AI encompasses a range of technologies, including machine learning, natural language processing, and data analytics, which can be leveraged to improve educational outcomes and streamline operations within educational institutions (Hinojo-Lucena et al., 2019; Popenici & Kerr, 2017; Selwyn, 2022). As AI continues to evolve, its applications in education are becoming increasingly sophisticated, prompting educators and policymakers to explore its implications for both secondary and higher education. The importance of AI in secondary and higher education cannot be overstated. In secondary education, AI can facilitate personalized learning experiences that cater to the diverse needs of students. For instance, intelligent tutoring systems can adapt to individual learning styles and paces, providing tailored feedback and resources that enhance student engagement and achievement (Davies et al., 2021; Utomo et al., 2017). Moreover, AI-driven analytics can help educators identify at-risk students early, allowing for timely interventions that support academic success (Bearman et al., 2023; Schönberger, 2023). In higher education, AI technologies are being utilized to optimize administrative processes, such as enrollment management and academic advising, thereby improving institutional efficiency and student satisfaction (Fowler, 2023; Kromydas, 2017). Furthermore, AI is playing a crucial role in the development of innovative curricula that incorporate emerging technologies, preparing students for a rapidly changing job market (Akinwalere & Ivanov, 2022).

The purpose of this chapter is to provide a comprehensive overview of the role of AI in education, with a particular focus on its applications in secondary and higher education. This exploration will encompass the historical context of AI in educational settings, current trends and innovations, and the potential future trajectories of AI technologies in education. Additionally, the chapter will address the ethical considerations and challenges associated with the implementation of AI in educational contexts, including issues of equity, privacy, and the evolving role of educators (Hannan & Liu, 2023; Karimi & Khawaja, 2023). By synthesizing existing literature and empirical studies, this chapter aims to offer a nuanced understanding of how AI is reshaping educational landscapes and the implications for stakeholders at all levels. As we examine the significance of AI in education, it is essential to recognize the multifaceted nature of its impact. AI technologies are not merely tools for efficiency; they represent a paradigm shift in how education is conceptualized and delivered. For instance, the rise of AI has led to the emergence of new educational models that prioritize learner agency and adaptability (Rienties et al., 2020; Watanabe, 2023). These models challenge traditional notions of teaching and learning, prompting educators to rethink their roles in the classroom. The integration of AI into educational practices also raises critical questions about the nature of knowledge, assessment, and the skills required for success in an increasingly automated world.

This chapter explores the socio-political dimensions of AI in education, examining how various stakeholders—including policymakers, educators, and technology developers—interact within this evolving landscape. The discourse surrounding AI in education is often characterized by a tension between optimism and skepticism, with proponents highlighting the potential for enhanced learning experiences and critics cautioning against the risks of over-reliance on technology (Chembe et al., 2023; Zawacki-Richter et al., 2019). This chapter critically engages with these perspectives, drawing on a diverse range of scholarly sources to illuminate the complexities of AI's role in education.

In addition to examining the benefits and challenges of AI in education, this chapter also considers the implications for educational equity. As AI technologies become more prevalent, there is a risk that disparities in access to technology may exacerbate existing inequalities in educational outcomes (Khare et al., 2018; Lepori, 2022). It is crucial to address these concerns by exploring strategies for ensuring that AI is implemented in ways that promote inclusivity and equitable access to educational resources (Butow & Hoque, 2020). This includes examining the role of policy frameworks and institutional practices in mitigating the risks associated with AI adoption in education. The integration of AI into education presents both opportunities and challenges that warrant careful consideration. As educational institutions navigate this complex landscape, it is essential to engage in ongoing dialogue about the ethical implications, pedagogical practices, and policy frameworks that will shape the future of AI in education. This chapter seeks to contribute to that dialogue by offering a comprehensive overview of the current state of AI in education, its significance for secondary and higher education, and the pathways forward for educators and policymakers alike.

BACKGROUND

AI has become a pivotal element in the evolution of educational practices, reshaping how educators and learners interact with content, each other, and the educational environment itself. The foundational overview of AI technologies in education reveals a landscape characterized by diverse applications, from intelligent tutoring systems to predictive analytics, all aimed at enhancing the learning experience. AI technologies leverage machine learning, natural language processing, and data analytics to create adaptive learning environments that cater to individual student needs, thereby fostering personalized education (Harry, 2023; Lin et al., 2023). Key AI technologies and tools in education include intelligent tutoring systems (ITS), which provide personalized feedback and support to students, and learning analytics platforms that analyze student data to inform instructional strategies (Kucirkova & Leaton Gray, 2023). These tools utilize algorithms to assess student performance and engagement, enabling educators to tailor their teaching methods accordingly. For instance, predictive learning analytics can identify students who may be struggling and require additional support, while also recognizing high-performing students who may benefit from more challenging material (Herodotou et al., 2019; Murtaza et al., 2022). AI-driven chatbots and virtual assistants are increasingly being integrated into educational settings, providing on-demand assistance and facilitating communication between students and educators (Taddeo et al., 2019).

The applications of AI in personalized learning are particularly noteworthy, as they allow for a more tailored educational experience. Personalized learning, which adapts content and instructional methods to meet the unique needs of each learner, has been shown to significantly enhance student engagement and academic performance (Shemshack & Spector, 2020). AI systems can analyze vast amounts of data related to students' learning patterns, preferences, and progress, enabling the development of customized learning pathways. This level of personalization not only supports individual learning styles but also fosters a sense of ownership and agency among students, motivating them to take charge of their educational journeys (Charmet et al., 2022; Lin et al., 2023). In addition to enhancing personalized learning, AI plays a crucial role in curriculum development. By analyzing data on student performance and engagement, AI can inform the design of curricula that are more aligned with learners' needs and interests (Akgun & Greenhow, 2022). For example, AI can identify gaps in knowledge and skills, allowing educators to create targeted interventions and resources that address these deficiencies. Moreover, AI can facilitate the integration of interdisciplinary approaches, encouraging the development of curricula that reflect the interconnected nature of knowledge in the 21st century (Harry, 2023). This adaptability is essential in a rapidly changing educational landscape, where the relevance of content is paramount.

Enhancing student engagement through AI is another critical aspect of its application in education. AI technologies can create immersive and interactive learning experiences that capture students' attention and foster deeper understanding (Murtaza et al., 2022). For instance, gamification strategies powered by AI can transform traditional learning activities into engaging challenges that motivate students to participate actively (Bennani et al., 2022; Bulathwela et al., 2021). Additionally, AI can facilitate collaborative learning environments by connecting students with peers and resources that complement their learning objectives, thereby promoting a sense of community and shared purpose (Bulathwela et al., 2021; Rienties et al., 2020). The integration of AI into educational practices also raises important ethical considerations. As AI technologies become more prevalent, issues related to data privacy, algorithmic bias, and the potential for over-reliance on technology must be addressed (Akgun & Greenhow, 2022). Educators and policymakers must ensure that AI applications are designed and implemented in ways that promote equity and inclusivity, rather than exacerbating existing disparities in educational access and outcomes (Akgun & Greenhow, 2022; Shemshack & Spector, 2020). The role of educators in this new landscape must be redefined, as they transition from traditional knowledge transmitters to facilitators of learning who leverage AI tools to enhance student experiences (Popenici & Kerr, 2017). The foundational overview of AI technologies in education highlights their transformative potential across various dimensions, including personalized learning, curriculum development, and student engagement. As educational institutions continue to explore and implement AI solutions, it is essential to remain mindful of the ethical implications and the need for equitable access to these technologies. By harnessing the power of AI, educators can create more dynamic, responsive, and effective learning environments that meet the diverse needs of today's learners.

CURRENT TRENDS IN AI INTEGRATION IN EDUCATION

The integration of AI in education is rapidly evolving, reflecting current trends that emphasize personalized learning, adaptive systems, and data-driven pedagogical strategies. As educational institutions increasingly adopt AI technologies, they are reshaping traditional teaching methodologies and enhancing the overall learning experience. The integration of AI in education has gained momentum due to its potential to enhance learning outcomes and streamline educational processes. One significant trend is the shift towards personalized learning environments, where AI technologies tailor educational experiences to meet individual student needs. This approach recognizes that learners have diverse backgrounds, learning styles, and paces, necessitating a more customized educational framework (López-Chila et al.,

2023). Furthermore, the growing familiarity of students with technology, particularly digital natives, has facilitated the acceptance and implementation of AI tools in educational settings (López-Chila et al., 2023).

Another trend is the increasing use of AI in administrative functions, such as enrollment management and resource allocation, allowing educators to focus more on teaching and less on bureaucratic tasks. AI applications are also being utilized to enhance student engagement through interactive learning experiences, gamification, and intelligent tutoring systems that provide real-time feedback and support. As these trends continue to evolve, educational institutions are challenged to adapt their curricula and teaching methodologies to incorporate AI effectively while addressing ethical considerations and ensuring equitable access to technology (Slimi & Carballido, 2023). Adaptive learning systems represent a cornerstone of AI integration in education. These systems utilize algorithms to assess student performance and adjust the learning content accordingly, providing a personalized learning experience. For instance, adaptive assessments dynamically modify the difficulty of questions based on a student's previous answers, ensuring that learners are neither bored with material that is too easy nor overwhelmed by content that is too challenging (Chan & Zary, 2019). This tailored approach not only enhances student engagement but also promotes mastery of concepts by allowing learners to progress at their own pace.

The effectiveness of adaptive learning systems has been supported by research indicating that personalized learning can significantly improve academic outcomes (Gligorea et al., 2023). By leveraging AI, educators can create individualized learning pathways that cater to the unique strengths and weaknesses of each student, fostering a more inclusive educational environment. Moreover, adaptive learning systems can provide valuable insights into student behavior and learning patterns, enabling educators to make informed decisions about instructional strategies and interventions (Gligorea et al., 2023). AI-driven assessment tools are another critical component of AI integration in education. These tools employ machine learning algorithms to evaluate student performance, providing immediate feedback and insights that can inform instructional practices. For example, automated grading systems can assess written assignments and quizzes, allowing educators to focus on more complex tasks such as providing personalized support and guidance. Additionally, AI-driven assessments can help identify learning gaps and recommend targeted resources to address these deficiencies, thus enhancing the overall learning experience (Chan & Zary, 2019).

The use of AI in assessments also extends to formative evaluations, where ongoing feedback is provided to students throughout their learning journey. This approach encourages a growth mindset and promotes continuous improvement, as students receive timely insights into their progress and areas for development (Chan

& Zary, 2019). Furthermore, AI-driven assessment tools can facilitate programmatic assessments, which are designed to optimize learning outcomes by aligning assessments with specific curricular goals (Chan & Zary, 2019). Data analytics plays a pivotal role in supporting pedagogy through the integration of AI in education. By analyzing vast amounts of data generated by students' interactions with learning platforms, educators can gain valuable insights into learning behaviors, preferences, and outcomes. This data-driven approach enables educators to make informed decisions about curriculum design, instructional strategies, and resource allocation.

For instance, learning analytics can identify trends in student performance, allowing educators to tailor their teaching methods to better align with student needs. Additionally, predictive analytics can help identify at-risk students who may require additional support, enabling timely interventions that can improve academic success (Khater et al., 2023). The ability to harness data analytics not only enhances the effectiveness of teaching practices but also fosters a culture of continuous improvement within educational institutions. The integration of AI in education is characterized by current trends that emphasize personalized learning, adaptive systems, and data-driven pedagogical strategies. Adaptive learning systems and AI-driven assessment tools are transforming the educational landscape, enabling educators to provide tailored learning experiences that meet the diverse needs of students. Furthermore, the use of data analytics supports informed decision-making and continuous improvement in teaching practices. As educational institutions continue to embrace AI technologies, it is essential to address ethical considerations and ensure equitable access to these innovations, ultimately enhancing the learning experience for all students.

OPPORTUNITIES AND BENEFITS OF AI IN EDUCATIONAL PRACTICES

AI technologies facilitate personalized learning experiences by analyzing individual student data to tailor educational content and delivery methods. Research indicates that AI algorithms can effectively analyze students' learning patterns, cognitive styles, and performance histories, thereby customizing educational experiences to meet individual needs. For instance, adaptive learning systems powered by AI can modify the difficulty of tasks based on real-time assessments of student performance, ensuring that learners are neither overwhelmed nor under-challenged (Gligorea et al., 2023). This personalized approach not only enhances engagement but also fosters a deeper understanding of the material, as students can progress at their own pace. The use of AI in educational settings has been shown to improve academic self-efficacy among students. A study highlighted the correlation between self-directed learning and academic performance, suggesting that AI tools can empower students to take charge of their learning journeys (Zhang et al., 2018). By providing immediate feedback and resources tailored to their specific needs, AI fosters an environment conducive to self-directed learning, ultimately enhancing students' problem-solving abilities and academic outcomes (Namjoo et al., 2023).

AI technologies also play a crucial role in enhancing student engagement and retention. The incorporation of AI-driven gamification strategies has been found to significantly boost student motivation and participation in learning activities (Alenezi, 2023). By integrating game-like elements into educational content, AI can create a more interactive and enjoyable learning experience, which is essential for maintaining student interest and commitment (Almusaed et al., 2023). For example, AI can analyze student interactions and adapt gamified elements to better suit their preferences and learning styles, thus fostering a more engaging educational environment (Oliveira et al., 2023). AI chatbots and virtual assistants have emerged as effective tools for providing real-time support to students, addressing their queries, and guiding them through learning materials (Wu & Yu, 2024). This immediate access to assistance not only enhances the learning experience but also contributes to higher retention rates, as students feel more supported in their educational endeavors (Gual-Montolio et al., 2022). The ability of AI to facilitate continuous engagement through personalized interactions is a key factor in promoting student persistence and success in their studies. The integration of AI in curriculum development and assessment processes can lead to more efficient and effective educational practices. AI can assist educators in analyzing large datasets related to student performance, enabling them to identify trends and areas for improvement within the curriculum (Ouyang et al., 2023). This data-driven approach allows for the continuous refinement of educational programs, ensuring that they remain relevant and effective in meeting the needs of students (Kadaruddin, 2023).

AI can automate various assessment processes, such as grading and feedback provision, which can save educators significant time and resources (Schiff, 2021). By utilizing AI to handle routine assessment tasks, educators can focus more on instructional quality and student interaction, ultimately enhancing the overall educational experience (Randhawa & Jackson, 2020). Moreover, AI can provide insights into student performance that go beyond traditional assessment methods, offering a more comprehensive understanding of individual and group learning outcomes. The opportunities and benefits of AI in educational practices are vast and multifaceted. From improved learning personalization and enhanced student engagement to streamlined curriculum development and assessment processes, AI has the potential to transform the educational landscape. As educators and institutions increasingly adopt AI technologies, it is essential to consider the ethical implications and ensure that these tools are used to complement, rather than replace, the invaluable role of human educators. The future of education lies in the harmonious integration of AI, fostering an environment where both students and educators can thrive.

TRENDS AND THEMES IN AI FOR EDUCATION

The integration of AI in education has emerged as a significant trend, reshaping pedagogical practices and enhancing learning experiences. AI's role in education is characterized by several key trends, including personalized learning, adaptive learning environments, and the use of AI-driven analytics to inform educational practices. Personalized learning, facilitated by AI, allows for the customization of educational experiences based on individual student needs, preferences, and learning styles. This trend is supported by the findings of Gocen and Aydemir (2020), who emphasize that AI provides robust technical support for personalized learning, making it a central theme in contemporary educational discourse. Adaptive learning systems, which utilize AI algorithms to adjust content delivery in real-time, have gained traction, as they cater to the varying pace and comprehension levels of student (Akavova et al., 2023). Another significant trend is the increasing reliance on data analytics in education. AI technologies enable the collection and analysis of vast amounts of educational data, which can be leveraged to enhance learning outcomes. Rienties et al. highlight the need for coherence among various educational technologies, including AI, learning analytics, and educational data mining, to foster a more integrated approach to educational improvement (Rienties et al., 2020). This trend underscores the importance of data-driven decision-making in educational settings, allowing educators to tailor their approaches based on empirical evidence.

Numerous studies have explored the implications of AI in educational contexts, providing valuable insights into its effectiveness and challenges. For instance, Aghaziarati's research on teacher attitudes towards AI reveals a correlation between educators' awareness of AI technologies and their willingness to adopt them in their teaching practices (Aghaziarati et al., 2023). This finding underscores the necessity for ongoing professional development to equip educators with the knowledge and skills needed to effectively integrate AI into their classrooms. The work of Bozkurt et al. offers a comprehensive review of AI studies in education over the past fifty years, identifying three primary research clusters: artificial intelligence, pedagogical issues, and technological challenges (Bozkurt et al., 2021). The study by Miao investigates the effectiveness of individualized learning trajectories in smart sports education classrooms, demonstrating how AI can facilitate personalized learning experiences by adjusting content delivery based on real-time data (Miao et al., 2023). This research exemplifies the potential of AI to enhance student engagement and learning outcomes through tailored educational experiences. The integration of AI in education raises several themes that warrant attention. Firstly, technology adoption remains a critical theme, as educators grapple with the implications of incorporating AI into their teaching practices. The research indicates that while there is enthusiasm for AI's potential, there are also significant barriers to adoption, including lack of training and resources (Aghaziarati et al., 2023). This highlights the need for institutions to invest in professional development and infrastructure to support AI integration.

Secondly, the pedagogical impacts of AI are profound. AI technologies can facilitate more engaging and interactive learning experiences, as evidenced by studies that demonstrate improved student outcomes in personalized learning environments (Bombardelli, 2020). However, the pedagogical shift necessitated by AI integration also raises questions about the role of educators in the learning process. As AI takes on more instructional responsibilities, educators must adapt their roles to focus on mentorship and facilitation rather than traditional content delivery (Triplett, 2023). Ethical considerations surrounding AI in education are paramount. The rapid advancement of AI technologies presents challenges related to data privacy, algorithmic bias, and the potential for inequitable access to educational resources. As highlighted by Britton, educational institutions must navigate these ethical dilemmas while implementing AI solutions, ensuring that they uphold principles of equity and inclusivity (Britton & Vallis, 2023). The need for ethical frameworks to guide AI use in education is increasingly recognized, as institutions seek to balance innovation with responsibility.

Despite the growing body of literature on AI in education, several gaps remain that warrant further investigation. One notable gap is the lack of large-scale studies that assess the long-term impacts of AI integration on student learning outcomes across diverse educational contexts. Most existing research is localized or context-specific, limiting the generalizability of findings (Rienties et al., 2020). Future research should aim to conduct longitudinal studies that evaluate the effectiveness of AI interventions in various educational settings. There is a need for more comprehensive studies that explore the intersection of AI and social-emotional learning. While AI can enhance academic outcomes, its impact on students' emotional and social development remains underexplored. Investigating how AI can support holistic education, including social-emotional learning, could provide valuable insights into its broader implications for student well-being (Miao et al., 2023). Finally, as AI technologies continue to evolve, research must address the ethical implications of their use in education. This includes examining issues related to data privacy, algorithmic transparency, and the potential for bias in AI systems. Establishing ethical guidelines for AI use in educational contexts will be crucial to ensuring that these technologies are implemented responsibly and equitably (Britton & Vallis, 2023). The integration of AI in education presents significant opportunities for enhancing learning experiences, personalizing education, and improving pedagogical practices. However, it also raises important questions regarding technology adoption, ethical considerations, and the role of educators. As research continues to evolve, it is essential to address existing gaps and explore the multifaceted impacts of AI on education.

FUTURE RESEARCH DIRECTIONS

Future research in the field of Artificial Intelligence (AI) in education should focus on several key areas to enhance the understanding and application of AI in learning environments. A primary direction is to investigate the longitudinal effects of AI on student outcomes, such as academic performance, retention, and engagement. Given the rapid adoption of AI in educational settings, examining the sustained impact of AI tools over extended periods could provide critical insights into whether these tools contribute to long-term improvements in learning or if their effects diminish over time. This line of research would benefit from multi-year studies that track cohorts of students through various stages of their educational journeys, comparing those with AI-enhanced learning experiences to those without.

Another promising research direction is the development and testing of highly individualized learning pathways enabled by AI. Current AI systems in education offer some degree of personalization, but future advancements could focus on refining these systems to respond dynamically to students' cognitive, emotional, and behavioral cues. Research in this area could explore how AI might adapt in real-time to fluctuations in a learner's understanding, motivation, or engagement, creating a more responsive and supportive learning environment. The outcomes of such studies could pave the way for AI tools that not only tailor content but also actively foster a student's growth mindset and resilience by adapting based on real-time learner data. Ethical and responsible AI usage in education is another crucial avenue for research. As AI technologies continue to evolve, the potential for unintended consequences, such as biases in algorithms or privacy concerns, grows alongside. Investigating methods to ensure that AI applications in education are transparent, fair, and secure is essential for building trust in these technologies among educators, students, and parents. Research could explore best practices for designing ethical AI systems in educational settings and examine regulatory approaches that protect students' data privacy while fostering innovation. By establishing frameworks for responsible AI use, future studies could set a foundation that addresses both the risks and rewards of AI in education.

Interdisciplinary collaboration is also a significant area for future exploration, as it can facilitate the integration of diverse perspectives and expertise in developing AI tools that are educationally sound and technologically robust. Collaboration between educators, AI developers, cognitive scientists, and policymakers could lead to the creation of systems that are not only effective but also relevant to classroom realities. Researching successful models of interdisciplinary partnerships in AI for education may provide valuable insights into how these collaborations can best be structured and sustained. Such studies would also reveal the practical challenges and benefits of integrating cross-disciplinary knowledge into AI-driven educational tools. Additionally, future research could examine the role of AI in addressing educational inequities and enhancing accessibility for students with disabilities or from under-resourced communities. AI holds the potential to level the educational playing field by providing tailored support and resources to those who might otherwise face barriers to learning. Research in this domain could investigate how AI can be effectively harnessed to create inclusive learning environments and what specific features are most beneficial for students with diverse needs. Understanding these factors could help optimize AI tools to ensure they serve as effective resources for all learners, regardless of their backgrounds or abilities.

Finally, exploring AI's impact on teacher roles and professional development is essential for maximizing the technology's benefits. As AI becomes more embedded in education, teachers' roles will likely evolve to accommodate new modes of teaching and learning facilitated by AI tools. Future research could investigate how teachers perceive these changes and what professional development programs are most effective in equipping them to use AI in the classroom confidently and creatively. Understanding teachers' evolving needs and the support they require can contribute to more effective AI implementation strategies, ensuring that AI serves as an enhancement to, rather than a replacement for, skilled educators.

CONCLUSION

The integration of AI in education is transforming traditional learning environments by enabling personalized learning, enhancing curriculum design, and fostering student engagement. This chapter has explored the foundational elements of AI technologies in education, highlighting both the opportunities and the ethical challenges that accompany their implementation. AI's role in adapting to diverse learning needs and providing data-driven insights offers substantial benefits for both students and educators. However, the ethical implications, including concerns around data privacy, algorithmic fairness, and equitable access, underscore the necessity for responsible deployment of these technologies. As educational institutions increasingly adopt AI-driven solutions, it is essential to prioritize inclusivity, transparency, and accountability in their application. Furthermore, fostering a culture of ongoing research and interdisciplinary collaboration will be key to addressing the complex challenges posed by AI while maximizing its potential benefits. The future of AI in education holds promising avenues for research and practice, including long-term studies on AI's impact on learning outcomes, the development of ethically grounded AI frameworks, and the role of AI in enhancing educational accessibility. AI in education is not just a tool for efficiency but a catalyst for reimagining pedagogical practices. By embracing AI thoughtfully and ethically, educators and policymakers can create a more adaptive, engaging, and inclusive educational landscape that meets the diverse needs of learners in an evolving digital age.

REFERENCES

Aghaziarati, A., Nejatifar, S., & Abedi, A. (2023). Artificial Intelligence in Education: Investigating Teacher Attitudes. *AI and Tech in Behavioral and Social Sciences*, 1(1), 35–42. DOI: 10.61838/kman.aitech.1.1.6

Akavova, A., Temirkhanova, Z., & Lorsanova, Z. (2023). Adaptive learning and artificial intelligence in the educational space. E3S Web of Conferences, Akgun, S., & Greenhow, C. (2022). Artificial intelligence in education: Addressing ethical challenges in K-12 settings. *AI and Ethics*, 2(3), 431–440.

Akinwalere, S. N., & Ivanov, V. (2022). Artificial intelligence in higher education: Challenges and opportunities. *Border Crossing*, 12(1), 1–15. DOI: 10.33182/bc.v12i1.2015

Alenezi, A. (2023). Teacher perspectives on AI-driven gamification: Impact on student motivation, engagement, and learning outcomes. *Information Technologies and Learning Tools*, 97(5), 138–148. DOI: 10.33407/itlt.v97i5.5437

Almusaed, A., Almssad, A., Yitmen, I., & Homod, R. Z. (2023). Enhancing student engagement: Harnessing "AIED"'s power in hybrid education—A review analysis. *Education Sciences*, 13(7), 632. DOI: 10.3390/educsci13070632

Bearman, M., Ryan, J., & Ajjawi, R. (2023). Discourses of artificial intelligence in higher education: A critical literature review. *Higher Education*, 86(2), 369–385. DOI: 10.1007/s10734-022-00937-2

Bennani, S., Maalel, A., & Ben Ghezala, H. (2022). Adaptive gamification in E-learning: A literature review and future challenges. *Computer Applications in Engineering Education*, 30(2), 628–642. DOI: 10.1002/cae.22477

Bombardelli, O. (2020). Inclusive education and its implementation: International practices. *Education and Self Development*, 15(3), 37–46. DOI: 10.26907/esd15.3.03

Bozkurt, A., Karadeniz, A., Baneres, D., Guerrero-Roldán, A. E., & Rodríguez, M. E. (2021). Artificial intelligence and reflections from educational landscape: A review of AI Studies in half a century. *Sustainability (Basel)*, 13(2), 800. DOI: 10.3390/su13020800

Britton, B., & Vallis, C. (2023). *Digital facelift: Emerging tools and typologies for educational media*. ASCILITE Publications. DOI: 10.14742/apubs.2023.552

Bulathwela, S., Pérez-Ortiz, M., Holloway, C., & Shawe-Taylor, J. (2021). Could AI democratise education? Socio-technical imaginaries of an edtech revolution. *arXiv preprint arXiv:2112.02034*.

Butow, P., & Hoque, E. (2020). Using artificial intelligence to analyse and teach communication in healthcare. *The Breast*, 50, 49–55. DOI: 10.1016/j.breast.2020.01.008 PMID: 32007704

Chan, K. S., & Zary, N. (2019). Applications and challenges of implementing artificial intelligence in medical education: Integrative review. *JMIR Medical Education*, 5(1), e13930. DOI: 10.2196/13930 PMID: 31199295

Charmet, F., Tanuwidjaja, H. C., Ayoubi, S., Gimenez, P.-F., Han, Y., Jmila, H., Blanc, G., Takahashi, T., & Zhang, Z. (2022). Explainable artificial intelligence for cybersecurity: A literature survey. *Annales des Télécommunications*, 77(11), 789–812. DOI: 10.1007/s12243-022-00926-7

Chembe, C., Nasilele, N. B., & Msendo, R. (2023). The Fuss about Artificial Intelligence in Education Sector: Should we Worry? *Zambia ICT Journal*, 7(2), 30–35. DOI: 10.33260/zictjournal.v7i2.269

Davies, H. C., Eynon, R., & Salveson, C. (2021). The mobilisation of AI in education: A Bourdieusean field analysis. *Sociology*, 55(3), 539–560. DOI: 10.1177/0038038520967888

Fowler, D. S. (2023). AI in Higher Education: Academic Integrity, Harmony of Insights, and Recommendations. *Journal of Ethics in Higher Education*, (3), 127–143. DOI: 10.26034/fr.jehe.2023.4657

Gligorea, I., Cioca, M., Oancea, R., Gorski, A.-T., Gorski, H., & Tudorache, P. (2023). Adaptive learning using artificial intelligence in e-learning: A literature review. *Education Sciences*, 13(12), 1216. DOI: 10.3390/educsci13121216

Gocen, A., & Aydemir, F. (2020). Artificial intelligence in education and schools. *Research on Education and Media*, 12(1), 13–21. DOI: 10.2478/rem-2020-0003

Gual-Montolio, P., Jaén, I., Martínez-Borba, V., Castilla, D., & Suso-Ribera, C. (2022). Using artificial intelligence to enhance ongoing psychological interventions for emotional problems in real-or close to real-time: A systematic review. *International Journal of Environmental Research and Public Health*, 19(13), 7737. DOI: 10.3390/ijerph19137737 PMID: 35805395

Hannan, E., & Liu, S. (2023). AI: New source of competitiveness in higher education. *Competitiveness Review*, 33(2), 265–279. DOI: 10.1108/CR-03-2021-0045

Harry, A. (2023). Role of AI in Education. [INJURITY]. *Interdiciplinary Journal and Hummanity*, 2(3), 260–268.

Herodotou, C., Hlosta, M., Boroowa, A., Rienties, B., Zdrahal, Z., & Mangafa, C. (2019). Empowering online teachers through predictive learning analytics. *British Journal of Educational Technology*, 50(6), 3064–3079. DOI: 10.1111/bjet.12853

Hinojo-Lucena, F.-J., Aznar-Díaz, I., Cáceres-Reche, M.-P., & Romero-Rodríguez, J.-M. (2019). Artificial intelligence in higher education: A bibliometric study on its impact in the scientific literature. *Education Sciences*, 9(1), 51. DOI: 10.3390/educsci9010051

Kadaruddin, K. (2023). Empowering education through Generative AI: Innovative instructional strategies for tomorrow's learners. *International Journal of Business, Law, and Education*, 4(2), 618–625. DOI: 10.56442/ijble.v4i2.215

Karimi, H., & Khawaja, S. (2023). The Impact of Artificial Intelligence on Higher Education in England. *Creative Education*, 14(12), 2405–2415. DOI: 10.4236/ce.2023.1412154

Khare, K., Stewart, B., & Khare, A. (2018). Artificial intelligence and the student experience: An institutional perspective.

Khater, A. S., Zaaqoq, A. A., Wahdan, M. M., & Ashry, S. (2023). Knowledge and attitude of Ain Shams University Medical Students towards Artificial Intelligence and its application in Medical Education and Practice. *Educational Research and Innovation Journal*, 3(10), 29–42. DOI: 10.21608/erji.2023.306718

Kromydas, T. (2017). Rethinking higher education and its relationship with social inequalities: Past knowledge, present state and future potential. *Palgrave Communications*, 3(1), 1–12. DOI: 10.1057/s41599-017-0001-8

Kucirkova, N., & Leaton Gray, S. (2023). Beyond Personalization: Embracing Democratic Learning Within Artificially Intelligent Systems. *Educational Theory*, 73(4), 469–489. DOI: 10.1111/edth.12590

Lepori, B. (2022). The heterogeneity of European Higher Education Institutions: A configurational approach. *Studies in Higher Education*, 47(9), 1827–1843. DOI: 10.1080/03075079.2021.1968368

Lin, Y., Luo, Q., & Qian, Y. (2023). Investigation of Artificial Intelligence algorithms in education. *Applied and Computational Engineering*, 16(1), 180–184. DOI: 10.54254/2755-2721/16/20230886

López-Chila, R., Llerena-Izquierdo, J., Sumba-Nacipucha, N., & Cueva-Estrada, J. (2023). Artificial Intelligence in Higher Education: An Analysis of Existing Bibliometrics. *Education Sciences*, 14(1), 47. DOI: 10.3390/educsci14010047

Miao, F., Zhang, Q., & Yan, J. (2023). Exploring the Effectiveness of Individualized Learning Trajectories in University Smart Sports Education Classrooms: A Design and Implementation Study. *Journal of Social Science Humanities and Literature*, 6(5), 67–73. DOI: 10.53469/jsshl.2023.06(05).10

Murtaza, M., Ahmed, Y., Shamsi, J. A., Sherwani, F., & Usman, M. (2022). AI-based personalized e-learning systems: Issues, challenges, and solutions. *IEEE Access : Practical Innovations, Open Solutions*, 10, 81323–81342. DOI: 10.1109/ACCESS.2022.3193938

Namjoo, F., Liaghat, E., Shabaziasl, S., Modabernejad, Z., & Morshedi, H. (2023). Students Experience on Self-Study through AI. *AI and Tech in Behavioral and Social Sciences*, 1(3), 35–42. DOI: 10.61838/kman.aitech.1.3.6

Oliveira, W., Hamari, J., Shi, L., Toda, A. M., Rodrigues, L., Palomino, P. T., & Isotani, S. (2023). Tailored gamification in education: A literature review and future agenda. *Education and Information Technologies*, 28(1), 373–406. DOI: 10.1007/s10639-022-11122-4

Ouyang, F., Wu, M., Zheng, L., Zhang, L., & Jiao, P. (2023). Integration of artificial intelligence performance prediction and learning analytics to improve student learning in online engineering course. *International Journal of Educational Technology in Higher Education*, 20(1), 4. DOI: 10.1186/s41239-022-00372-4 PMID: 36683653

Popenici, S. A., & Kerr, S. (2017). Exploring the impact of artificial intelligence on teaching and learning in higher education. *Research and Practice in Technology Enhanced Learning*, 12(1), 22. DOI: 10.1186/s41039-017-0062-8 PMID: 30595727

Randhawa, G. K., & Jackson, M. (2020). The role of artificial intelligence in learning and professional development for healthcare professionals. Healthcare management forum, Rienties, B., Køhler Simonsen, H., & Herodotou, C. (2020). Defining the boundaries between artificial intelligence in education, computer-supported collaborative learning, educational data mining, and learning analytics: A need for coherence. Frontiers in Education, Schiff, D. (2021). Out of the laboratory and into the classroom: the future of artificial intelligence in education. *AI & Society*, 36(1), 331–348. PMID: 32836908

Schönberger, M. (2023). ChatGPT in higher education: the good, the bad, and the University.

Selwyn, N. (2022). The future of AI and education: Some cautionary notes. *European Journal of Education*, 57(4), 620–631. DOI: 10.1111/ejed.12532

Shemshack, A., & Spector, J. M. (2020). A systematic literature review of personalized learning terms. *Smart Learning Environments*, 7(1), 33. DOI: 10.1186/s40561-020-00140-9

Slimi, Z., & Carballido, B. V. (2023). Navigating the Ethical Challenges of Artificial Intelligence in Higher Education: An Analysis of Seven Global AI Ethics Policies. *TEM Journal, 12*(2).

Taddeo, M., McCutcheon, T., & Floridi, L. (2019). Trusting artificial intelligence in cybersecurity is a double-edged sword. *Nature Machine Intelligence*, 1(12), 557–560. DOI: 10.1038/s42256-019-0109-1

Triplett, W. J. (2023). Artificial intelligence in STEM education. *Cybersecurity and Innovative Technology Journal*, 1(1), 23–29. DOI: 10.53889/citj.v1i1.296

Utomo, H. P., Bon, A. T., & Hendayun, M. (2017). Modeling of academic information system in higher education institution toward education 3.0: A literature review. *International Journal of Information and Education Technology (IJIET)*, 7(10), 738–742. DOI: 10.18178/ijiet.2017.7.10.964

Watanabe, A. (2023). Exploring totalitarian elements of artificial intelligence in higher education with Hannah Arendt. [IJT]. *International Journal of Technoethics*, 14(1), 1–15. DOI: 10.4018/IJT.329239

Wu, R., & Yu, Z. (2024). Do AI chatbots improve students learning outcomes? Evidence from a meta-analysis. *British Journal of Educational Technology*, 55(1), 10–33. DOI: 10.1111/bjet.13334

Zawacki-Richter, O., Marín, V. I., Bond, M., & Gouverneur, F. (2019). Systematic review of research on artificial intelligence applications in higher education–where are the educators? *International Journal of Educational Technology in Higher Education*, 16(1), 1–27. DOI: 10.1186/s41239-019-0171-0

Zhang, X.-H., Meng, L.-N., Liu, H.-H., Luo, R.-Z., Zhang, C.-M., Zhang, P.-P., & Liu, Y.-H. (2018). Role of academic self-efficacy in the relationship between self-directed learning readiness and problem-solving ability among nursing students. *Frontiers of Nursing*, 5(1), 75–81. DOI: 10.1515/fon-2018-0011

ADDITIONAL READING

Ayeni, O. O., Al Hamad, N. M., Chisom, O. N., Osawaru, B., & Adewusi, O. E. (2024). AI in education: A review of personalized learning and educational technology. *GSC Advanced Research and Reviews*, 18(2), 261–271. DOI: 10.30574/gscarr.2024.18.2.0062

Ivanashko, O., Kozak, A., Knysh, T., & Honchar, K. (2024). The role of artificial intelligence in shaping the future of education: Opportunities and challenges. *Futurity Education*, 4(1), 126–146.

Onesi-Ozigagun, O., Ololade, Y. J., Eyo-Udo, N. L., & Ogundipe, D. O. (2024). Revolutionizing education through AI: A comprehensive review of enhancing learning experiences. *International Journal of Applied Research in Social Sciences*, 6(4), 589–607. DOI: 10.51594/ijarss.v6i4.1011

Pawar, G., & Khose, J. (2024) Exploring the Role of Artificial Intelligence in Enhancing Equity and Inclusion in Education. *International Journal of Innovative Science and Research Technology (IJISRT)*, 2180-2185.

Sappaile, B. I., Vandika, A. Y., Deiniatur, M., Nuridayanti, N., & Arifudin, O. (2024). The Role of Artificial Intelligence in the Development of Digital Era Educational Progress. *Journal of Artificial Intelligence and Development*, 3(1), 1–8.

KEY TERMS AND DEFINITIONS

Adaptive Learning Systems: AI-powered educational tools that adjust content delivery and assessments based on real-time student performance to meet individual learning needs.

Algorithmic Bias: A phenomenon where AI systems produce unfair outcomes due to biases in the algorithms, potentially affecting student equity and inclusivity in education.

Artificial Intelligence (AI): The simulation of human intelligence in computers, enabling them to perform tasks such as learning, reasoning, and problem-solving within educational settings.

Curriculum Development: The process of designing educational content and structures that align with student needs, enhanced by AI's ability to analyze and recommend improvements based on performance data.

Data Analytics: The use of computational techniques to analyze educational data, providing insights into student behavior, performance, and learning trends to inform teaching strategies.

Ethical Considerations: A set of moral principles guiding the responsible implementation of AI in education, addressing issues like privacy, transparency, and fairness.

Learning Analytics: The collection and analysis of student data to enhance learning experiences, often using AI to provide insights and personalize education.

Personalized Learning: An educational approach that tailors learning experiences to individual students' needs, preferences, and abilities, made possible through AI technologies.

Student Engagement: The level of interest and involvement a student shows in learning, which AI can enhance through personalized content and interactive tools.

Virtual Assistants: AI-based digital tools that assist students by answering questions and guiding them through learning materials, contributing to a supportive learning environment.

Chapter 2
Applications of Artificial Intelligence in Education

K. Aravindh
https://orcid.org/0009-0007-6436-585X
Vellore Institute of Technology, India

Brijendra Singh
https://orcid.org/0000-0003-2608-3388
Vellore Institute of Technology, India

ABSTRACT

This chapter explores the transformative impact of artificial intelligence (AI) on the education sector, highlighting how AI technologies enhance teaching quality, streamline assessment processes, and support both physical and virtual learning environments. By facilitating innovative methods of lecture delivery and interactive learning, AI tools benefit educators and students alike, enabling a more engaging and efficient educational experience. The chapter provides a comprehensive review of various AI techniques and methodologies used within educational contexts, illustrating practical applications that support personalized learning, efficient evaluations, and adaptive teaching strategies. Additionally, it examines the benefits and challenges of AI from the perspectives of both educators and students, shedding light on the potential improvements AI can bring to learning outcomes. Future directions and opportunities for AI in education are also discussed, offering insights into the next steps for integrating AI into educational systems for enhanced adaptability and impact.

DOI: 10.4018/979-8-3693-7220-3.ch002

INTRODUCTION

AI is a branch of computer science that builds machines and software with similar human capabilities, as they can perform tasks such as thinking, problem-solving ideas, and decision-making in a situation like a human. In simpler words, we can say that the ability given by humans to machines to think, judge, and decide reduces the work of humans. AI in education is about using computational intelligence and logic to help educators and students make the education system in a very efficient manner. The main motive of AI in education is to assist the learners with flexible and personalized learning which makes students easily learn the concepts. In the book chapter, we will see various applications of AI in education systems, their potential benefits, and the drawbacks of using AI in the education sector. Figure 1 represents the requirements to implement AI.

Figure 1. Requirement to implement AI in education

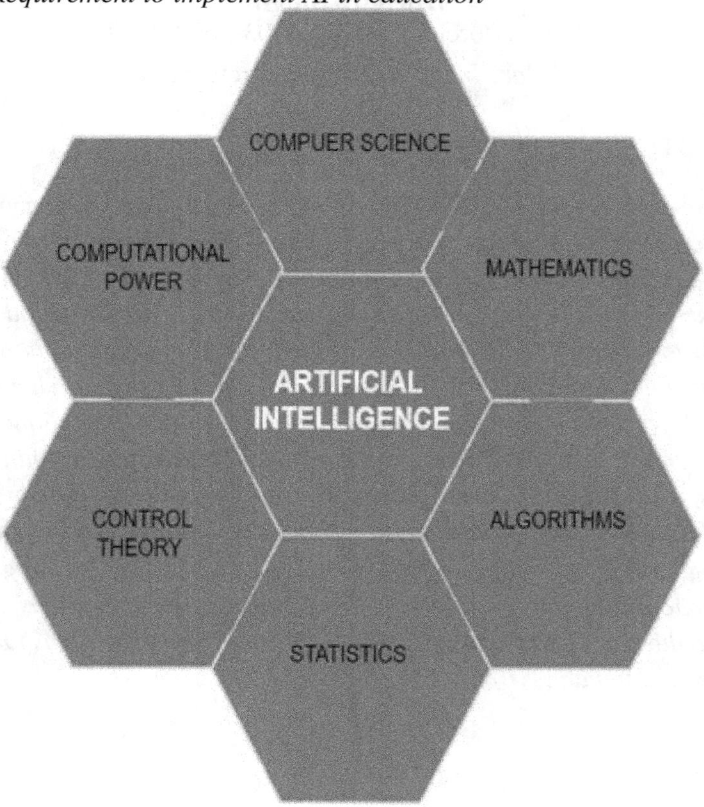

Implementing AI in education is one of challenging task in education system. From 2015 to 2024 the usage of AI in education in the world experienced rapid growth in universities and institutes. Mainly during post COVID in world (after 2021) the emergence of AI in education has grown significantly in India. The utilization of AI in education mainly in universities has many benefits such as better teaching and understanding of the concepts that lead to smooth learning. The development of generative AI has rebuilt a few education practices in our country. AI implementation in education is an expeditiously growing field which has obtained awareness for educators as well as learners. The development of AI technology will improve in the future and its implementation in education will rise in the future which will reform the entire education system in the upcoming days. In this chapter, we can see the implementation of AI in education including application, supremacy, a few drawbacks to using AI in the education sector, about the future of the education system using AI in it.

RECENT APPLICATION OF AI IN UNIVERSITIES

In recent years implementing AI in education has achieved rapid growth in universities and institutes. In a few institutes they have assisted their student in using AI tools to prepare for their exams where 97% of students scored good grades, students who have used AI projects completed their projects as early as possible and received appreciation for their projects. Universities have guided their students to AI for writing purposes. The technology helps students for writing purposes in which this technology uses few algorithms, students who have used this technology have completed their articles, and projects and got reviews for their articles and projects. In 2018, there was a development of learning AI in universities that started using, with the help of Google an online tutor for learning concepts, where this software allows learning concepts and gaining knowledge wherever, whenever (24/7) they want. In recent years universities have invented an AI-powered chatbot to assist students in their academic programs. This chatbot has shown its efficiency by giving 93% of correct answers to the asked questions. Using this chatbot staff can free up the time they usually spend responding to queries to do other tasks. The universities have created and given access to a chatbot (a type of generative AI) where students can give prompts and get answers to their prompts, which is widely used in that university.

AI technology has been developed that uses logic and specific algorithms. AI tool is used for students who have difficulty in their traditional teaching learning. AI tools help them study well and achieve their academic goals. In a few institutes faculty found that many students did not utilize material and share new ideas, with low creativity. Instead, they were writing questions and responses that repeated what was in their textbook or assignment. So they have started using an instructional AI platform for writing and getting new ideas, which helped them to present examinations with new ideas and deliver their best in exams. We can see the different types of users in percentage using AI technology, where college students use the AI tools more than other users represented in Figure 2.

Figure 2. Percentages of different AI tools users

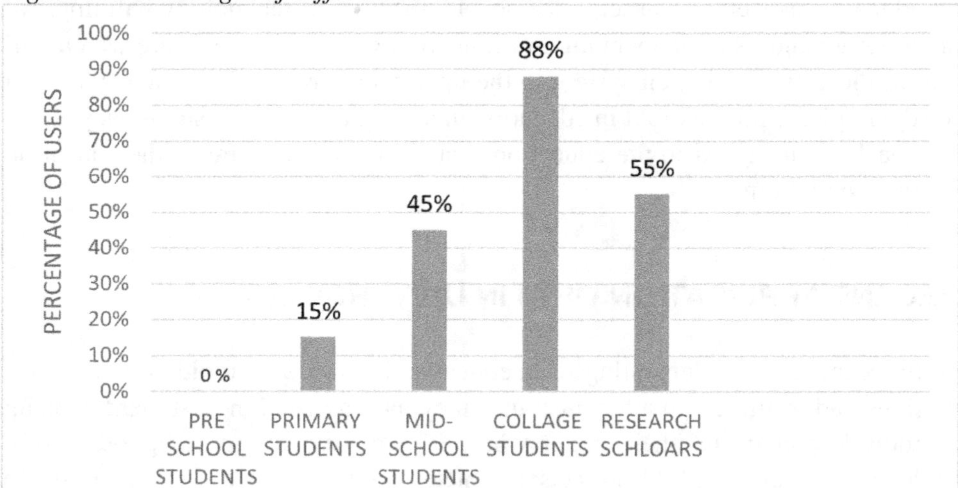

APPLICATIONS OF AI IN EDUCATION

The emergence of AI in education has brought a significant change in the entire education system, which the help of AI technology many applications were used in the education sector to provide the best education. This session lets us see how AI technology has been applied to education systems.

Personalized learning

AI in education has encouraged every student to learn their concepts and chapters without any distractions; understand concepts easily will examine the student's previous performance on tests and assessments where teacher comes to know about the student's difficulty and deliver the perfect solution to improve their performance in upcoming tests and assessments. Personalized learning can give customized help and assist every student to improve their academic performance. In addition, AI can be used to monitor students so that teachers can make needed adjustments to the teaching methods and curriculum, which saves time to the teachers on evaluating, and making feedback on the students' assessments, teachers easily understand every student's knowledge based on the feedback provided by the AI technology (Harry, A., & Sayudin, 2023.)

Lecture Bot

AI uses many technologies to give its best efficiency to improve education systems, one of the major technologies is "robotics" (Yin, Robert K.& Gwendolyn B,2020) where with the help of a few algorithms those robots are used in education systems. "Lecture bot" is a small-sized robot that has a display screen on it where it teaches concepts to students with the help of its screen; it is a tutor that monitors the students in the absence of teachers, acts as a substitute for the teachers (Catlin & Blamires, 2019).

Performance Evaluation

It is the process of AI systems that reviews the performance of students in their assessments, tests and assignments submitted., AI helps teachers prepare exam questions it also provides feedback for their submission of the tests, exams, and assessments. Using automated evaluation system, and automated feedback service system. (Zawacki-Richter et al., 2019),It reduces the work also helps teachers to know about the particular student's knowledge and performance, improves accuracy and provides a good level of efficiency which is essential to provide time to the teachers.

Virtual Classroom

In the era of the technology world, the education system uses a virtual technology program called Virtual Classroom, the technology used by educators to teach concepts to learners, where educators and learners communicate with each other with required learning materials (Encalada & Sequera, 2017; Krumm, 2018). Virtual classroom helps the learning process by engaging students to communicate with the educators. Learners and educators can connect to this virtual classroom wherever in the world with the help of internet-connected devices (Nagao&Katashi,2019).

With the help of virtual classrooms, educators can:

- Display learning material in the form of PowerPoint presentation (PPT), portable document format (PDF)
- Educators can enrich the learning process by sharing their screen and virtual board features; with the help of these features, they can teach the concepts easily.
- Engage the students in quizzes, polls and another assignment.

Voice Assistance

The emergence of voice assistance in education had an impact on learning, which allows students to get materials by themselves, without a teacher and learners can interact with voice assistance to learn concepts and gain extra knowledge without the teacher's help. Voice assistance such as:

- Amazon's Alexa
- Apple's Siri
- Google's assistance

Are the voice assistants that are popularly used around the world? Mainly voice assistance is used for learning a new language, for reading practices, making online tests and for revision purposes (Fitria, T. N. et al.,2021).

AI as a Reminder

When learners or teachers forget their work this AI system sends a remainder using popup messages (Liu Yufeia, Salmiza Salehb, Huang Jiahuic, Syed Mohamad Syed Abdullah,2020). Apps such as: Google Keep, Microsoft to do, Any. Do, and ClickUp.

These are the apps that use AI systems to give reminders to the users. At first, we must set the remainder in the app, corresponding with work respect with to the time. When the time gets nearer the apps gives a prior alert to the work that has to be completed. Let's take an example a teacher's work is to evaluate students' assessment in online mode, the teacher has updated the app with their work corresponding to the time that they have to complete it, but the teacher forgets the work to do, the app sends the remainder message to the teacher that he/she has to complete the work and shows the deadline.

Chatbots

Chatbots in education are AI conversational agents that assist and facilitate learning for the users. They have gained significant growth in the education sector due to their ability to offer personalized support to the users and help them to do their work related to academics. 24/7 Availability. Supporting Teachers, Administrative Support, in these ways, chatbots help users for education purposes.

Curriculum Design

Designing a curriculum is not an easy task for the curriculum designers. Where AI can provide lesson plans to schools and universities. AI can progress huge data on students' participation, interest, progress, results, and issues faced by students, by using these data curriculum designers have ideas on how to improve the curriculum and designers design curriculum plans accordingly, schools and universities follow this curriculum and implement this curriculum to follow in their institutes and schools.

Adaptive Learning

Adaptive learning platforms such as 360 Learning, LinkedIn Learning, and Dreambox customize the learning activities. In these platforms, users learn concepts from video lectures, write assessments, and get immediate results with feedback on the assessments by the platform, which uses AI technology (Zhai, X., Chu, X., Chai, et al2021.)

In recent years the usage of AI has increased a lot in education sectors. In Figure 3 we can see the growth of users (in millions) from 2012 to 2024 .

Figure 3. Growths of users from 2012 to 2024

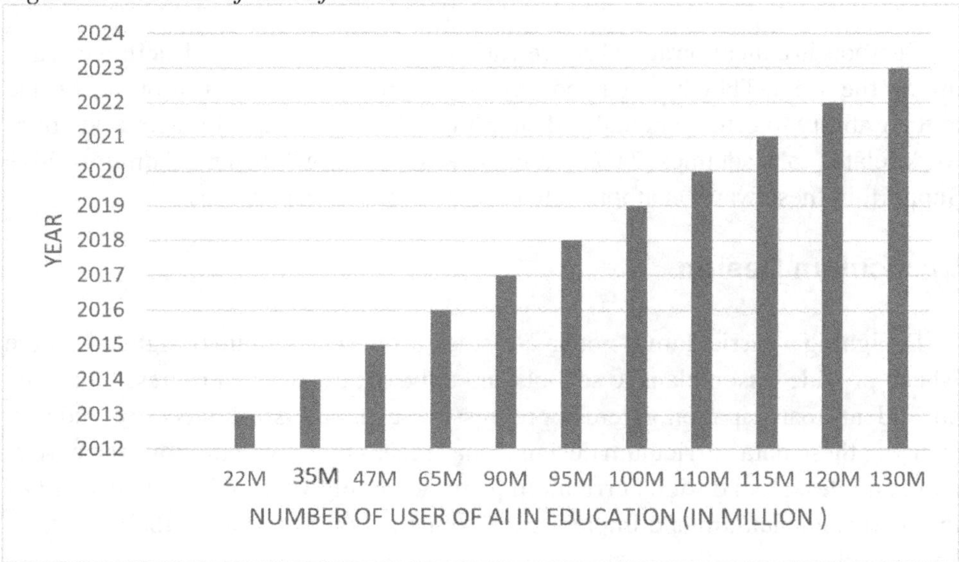

BENEFITS OF AI IN UNIVERSITIES

AI provides various guidelines to learners, educators, and to overall education system. Among all one of the biggest remarkable benefits is providing education is very flexible and in customizable manner, which makes learners learn concepts more simply in an easily understandable manner (Verma A, Kumar et al,2021) There is a complete change in teacher's work where there is a decrease in workload, work pressure and stress towards teaching and examining the students. AI usage in education sector has many advantages, mainly increasing student's learning and helping them to complete their works by themselves. The other one is giving personalized and flexible teaching methods to the teachers through some outlook to the educators to provide successive and smooth teaching. Teachers use AI in order to prepare a few education materials, conduct exams, quizzes and assignments also they can provide grades for the students based on their work (submission). AI systems save teachers time and energy which helps them to concentrate on student's intelligence instead of spending time in preparing materials and other academic works.

In universities, a few systems of AI technology are used to evaluate Automated Evaluation System (AES) where this system evaluates the student's performances in the examination, for providing feedback Automated Feedback System (AFS) where this system provides feedback for the student's performances, for providing scores Automated Scoring System (ASS), this system of AI is used for providing scores for quizzes which have been submitted by the student. Same as educators, learners also use AI for their education purposes mainly for developing their projects, and assignments and for other learning purposes. where AI system gives 97% accuracy and gives the expected results, especially students who use generative AI such as “GPT 3.4,4” and “COPILOT” for their projects to get perfect results in their work. With the help of AI students get knowledge about various topics which helps them to have a better intelligence where they can increase their performance in their academics.

Generative AI gives several benefits in the education sector, where it provides a personalized and interactive experience to the users, where the generative AI cracks the complex topics and makes the lecture materials for the same topic in multiple languages. Also, generative AI helps the users to work with coding, improve their writing skills, generate ideas for brainstorming, and in the visual arts. AI technologies such as Payroll management systems (PMS), face recognition and fingerprint verification provide significant technical support for the development of education institutes. These technologies provide safety to campus which includes the safety of the university, classroom monitoring, access to the library and tracking attendance. As an outcome of those features students and teachers have quality education and learning, which also saves the university's time and reduces costs which help in financial management. The graphical representation of the usage of AI tools that have been given in Figure 4, such as AES, AFS, ASS and PMS are given in the pie chart for reader's reference.

Figure 4: Graphical representation AI tools usage

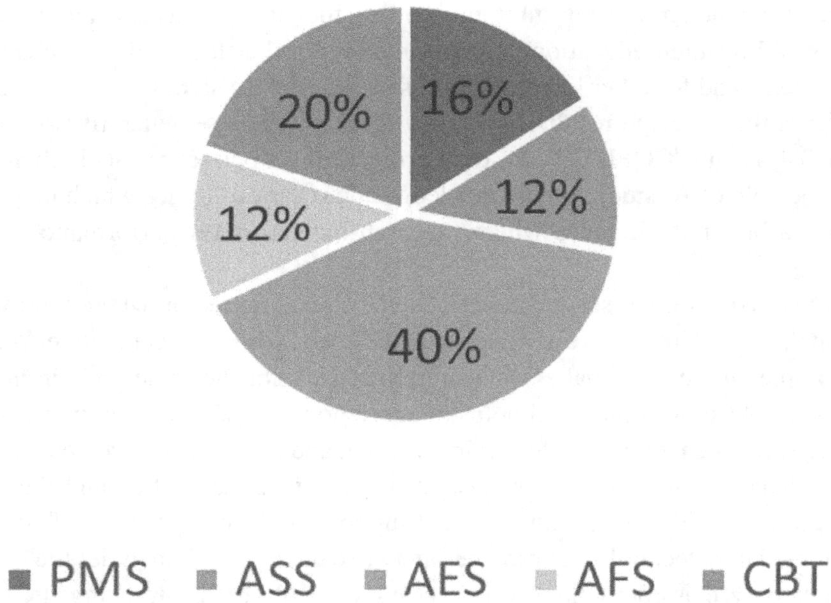

The implementation of AI technology in education has reformed traditional education practices with modern education methods such as:

- Physical classroom to virtual classroom.
- Pen and paper mode of examination (offline exams) to Computer-Based Test (CBT) (online exams).
- Physical evaluation of exam paper to automated evaluation of exam paper using Automated Evaluation System (AES) technology.

Figure 5 represents the usage of AI tools in the education sector.

Figure 5. Usage of AI tools in the education sector

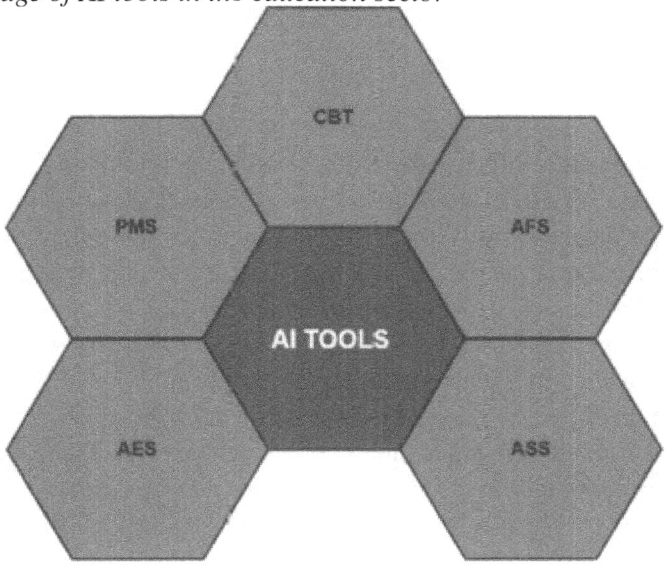

This is the era of AI, computation, and automation rules everywhere, where in the current scenario usage of AI in universities has been, increased consequentially which has brought a change in the education system. In this chapter we will further discuss application of artificial intelligence in education and its drawbacks.

CHALLENGES OF USING AI IN EDUCATION

AI is a rapidly growing technology that faces many challenges in all fields; these challenges become very complex when it comes to the education field (Xeusong Zhai, Xiaoyan et al., 2021).AI assures enhancing the educational experience, but when we implement it in the academic sector, it brings a few concerns and challenges. In this session, let us explore the impacts of using AI in education and a few drawbacks and challenges in it, the potential risks and challenges faced, and how they can be solved in the future when AI is used in the education field (TTahiru, F., 2021). A reproving challenge in AI in education is the uncertainty in the procedure and algorithm developed to implement it, those uncertainties are the design of the algorithm and the data which is used to train the algorithm used must be related to the education sector as it is going to be used for the education purposes. Clearness and liability are the most important ethical challenges in AI systems (Akgun, B., & Greenhow, 2022). The clearness in the design of the AI system is critical during the implementation period; the liability mechanism in the AI must ensure that it takes responsibility for the outcomes given by it.

Security Threat

One of the topmost challenges in using AI in education is data privacy. AI technology needs access to personal data to log in and use its feature, in this case, we are not sure that the data will be secured, and it will not be revealed to some unauthorized organization or person. In case the data is revealed to some unauthorized person can lead to identity theft, fraud, and targeted attacks such as spear phishing, malware, spoofing and some other security threats to the users. AI in education is not only implemented in higher education institutes and universities; it is also implemented for medical education purposes. It is used by medical institutes, which involve a large amount of medical data into the databases, and there is a chance of cyber-attacks, issues regarding confidentiality, and other threats to the data stored.

Technological Framework

To implement AI technology in the education sector we need the hardware and software resources, which is very difficult in small and less developed universities, as that hardware and software are expensive to install and run in entire universities, so the universities do not use such resources, where technology framework acts a barrier to use AI technology in the education sector such as universities and institutes (Blodgett, Su Lin et al,2021).

Skillset to use AI in Education

To implement AI in education, the users must have the skills to handle the technology especially the educators must be well trained to use AI technology, if not using AI in education is useless. Students must know how to use AI technology for their academic purposes mainly learning concepts, doing their projects, taking tests and submitting their assignments in AI technology. Without knowing the basics of AI applications users are unable to use those AI tools related to education, where those skills are pre-required for the users to use AI for education purposes (Pedro, F., Subosa, M et al., 2019).

Balance Between AI And Human

AI can only be efficient in performing education tasks, but it does not replace the human effort of teaching such as motivating the student to study, giving emotional support, and helping the student personally. When students over depend on AI can reduce their creativity, imagination skills and problem-solving skills, finally, the student's IQ level, where AI must be used as a tool that supports education, one must not depend on AI completely as it destroys student's intelligence completely(De la Vall, & Araya, F. G. 2023).

Costs

Implementing AI for education purposes is not an easy job it requires lots of investment to implement, we require advanced technology resources to implement where small, scaled universities require a large amount of investment to implement AI tools in their universities and institutes, where Costs play a major role to install and implement AI tools in the education sector. This factor makes it difficult to implement AI in the education sector (Grassini, 2023).

Fake Information and Errors

AI can make mistakes, AI is designed to provide accurate information, but in the worst cases, it can provide fake information, incorrect statements and some misunderstood responses (Owac et aL,2019).When AI is delivering the complex lectures AI may not delivery the lecture exactly and correctly, this is really a problem when a student fully depend on the AI tools to the lectures with complex topics. In few complex topics these tools make few logical and computational errors.

Accessibility Issues

AI technology in some cases is not accessible by every user, this AI technology acts as a technical barrier to differentially abled users such as auditory and visual impairments, users from rural areas are not developed they face a few technology issues. The availability of this technology to learners has crucial challenges due to physical abilities, geographical locations, and other challenges to use the AI technology in education purposes.

Job Fear

The active use of AI in the education sector and the significant use of AI by students has a potential risk of reducing the need for teachers and replacing the teacher's job, with the help of AI students can learn wherever and whenever they want (De Cremer et al.,2021). Where the major drawback for teachers is fear of their jobs, will AI replace the teachers in the future is questionable?

Over Dependent on AI Tools

The users will be over-dependent on the AI tools, which is not recommended, which causes addition to the AI tools where users are dependent on AI tools for the simpler works, those simple works are not done by themselves. Education institutions depend on AI-driven tools for teaching, assessment, and other education tasks, there is a risk of becoming overly dependent on these technologies. It may also diminish the development of critical thinking and problem-solving skills among students, as they may become dependent on AI systems providing answers and solutions. Challenges of using AI in education sector are represented in Figure 6.

Figure 6. Challenges of using AI in education sector

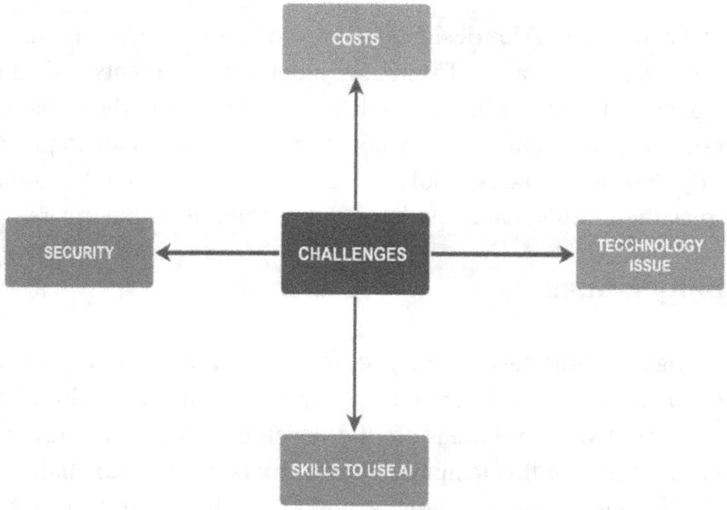

SUCCESSFUL IMPLEMENTATION OF AI TOOLS

Implementing AI successfully for education purposes requires a prudent approach that involves a collaboration of technological ideas, human intelligence, and prior objectives. In this section, we will see the steps on how to implement AI in the education sector successfully.

Investment in Technological Framework

It is imperative to invest in modern technological infrastructure, including hardware, software, and other necessary frameworks that support the use of AI tools for education purposes, prior to adopting AI tools at the institutes. When the necessary technology services are available, AI tools perform as intended and produce the best results. AI tools have several problems when used without proper technology; they perform poorly and are less accurate in their activities. As a result, education institutions must invest in modern technology in order to use AI tools.

Train the Educators Towards AI Tool

Training the educators to use AI tools is a must-required one for making the AI tools to use in the learning process. If the educators are not well trained, they feel difficult using the tools in the process of teaching. Well-trained educators know how to integrate AI tools in teaching as well as monitor the impact of AI tools on the students. Without training, educators may not use the AI tools efficiently, and there is a chance of misusing the AI tools. Training the educators makes sure that education is given in an efficient, correct, as well as best way to the learners.

Agreement with AI Founders

Before implementing AI in education institutions, it is necessary that the institutes make a prior agreement that is clear and legal with the AI developers and founders regarding the safety issues. This agreement makes the guarantee about the data security and that the data is not accessed by the unauthorized users. AI developers as well as institutes must mutually work together to implement and use the AI tools to run smoother in the future.

Choosing the right AI Tools

When we use AI tools in education institutes, selecting the right AI tools is very important to ensure the required education need. There are many AI tools that support education where every tool is made with different functions to serve different needs. Educators must check the functions of AI tools based on their requirements. The selected AI tools must be user-friendly for the teachers, and they must be working efficiently so that the teaching and learning process will be easy.

Track and Monitor

After implementing AI tools in education institutes, it is necessary for the institutes to monitor the impact of the AI tools on student's performance as well as teacher's work. Also, the institutes must ensure the tool is providing the expected benefits and is also very efficient to the level expected by them. If the AI tool is not working as expected, the institutes must make the necessary changes as per the requirements. By tracking and monitoring the AI tool regularly, the institutes can ensure the AI tool is working efficiently and safely, and it supports the learning process in the right way.

Ethical Guidelines

Establishing clear social frameworks AI use in education is essential to promote ethical practices and minimize diagonal. Institutions should create guidelines that ensure data security, equity, and accountability in AI algorithms. These policies should address concerns such as privacy protection, fairness, and algorithmic transparency, helping to foster the responsible and balanced integration of AI in learning environment. When the institutes follow these guidelines before and after implementing the AI tools in their institutes, it would be safe, efficient, as well as a best education practice in the universities.

FUTURE RESEARCH DIRECTIONS

The usage of AI technology in the education sector has been grown in recent years which has many potential benefits and makes teacher's job easier, although having many potential benefits and drawbacks. The rapid growth of AI technology in the recent years makes the implementation of AI in education sectors better; it will overcome the challenges faced by current education system. The development of AI technology and associated tools for education will allow the users to use the

AI tools more efficiently and easily. The development of AI technology towards generative AI will have an impact on the generative AI such as G and copilot will produce an extensive development where generative AI will produce the content which includes images, video, graphs and other required contents. In the future, AI in the education sector will revolutionize the current teaching methodologies and the way that teachers teach, and students learn the subjects.

The current correctness of AI usage in education is 60 to 70 percent, in a few years the correctness of AI usage will be 95 to 97 percent, and every institute will use AI tools for education purposes. In the future all the students will be using AI tools for their education purposes, they will get personalized support and the best learning opportunity and gain extra knowledge about their domain field, as there will not be any challenges about the usage of AI in education sectors. In a few years AI will be developed as it will be easily accessed by all learners in any part of the world, AI tools will be easily available to all learners and educators. Technology tools will be used efficiently such that there will be no challenges due to technology-wise. Not only the college students use AI for their academic purposes even AI tools will be used by all school students for their academic purposes in the schools by all the students.

CONCLUSION

The implementation of AI in education sectors has revolutionized the method of learning and teaching concepts. This chapter focused on the various AI technologies and methodologies used in the education sector, various applications of AI in the education sector have been explored. We also analyzed the potential risks and drawbacks faced by academicians, and learners and also steps to avoid a few drawbacks have also been discussed during the implementation of AI system in education sectors. AI applications in different fields have simplified our work in all the tasks, but when it comes to education purposes it has simplified our tasks and work significantly. As this is the era of AI and computation, education is partially dependent on AI tools and technology, this dependency will not stop here rather this will continue to evolve as AI technology evolves and develops in the future. As the outcome of efficient implementation and usage of AI tools in education produces a high academic performance to the learners but one should keep it in mind that there is a limit for everything even AI tools have a lot of advantages, there are few disadvantages also. AI must be used in a limited manner; there should not be any over-dependence of AI in education practices. AI has the power to revolutionize education; it is our responsibility to keep in mind about the risks and drawbacks, and using the AI tools must be handled responsibly in education.

REFERENCES

Akgun, S., & Greenhow, C. (2022). Artificial intelligence in education: Addressing ethical challenges in K-12 settings. *AI and Ethics*, 2(3), 431–440. DOI: 10.1007/s43681-021-00096-7 PMID: 34790956

Blodgett, S. L., & Madaio, M. (2021). Risks of AI foundation models in education. *arXiv preprint arXiv:2110.10024.*

Catlin, D., & Blamires, M. (2019). Designing robots for special needs education. Technology, knowledge and learning, 24(2), 291-313.

De la Vall, R. R. F., & Araya, F. G. (2023). Exploring the benefits and challenges of AI-language learning tools. *International Journal of Social Sciences and Humanities Invention*, 10(01), 7569–7576. DOI: 10.18535/ijsshi/v10i01.02

Fitria, T. N. (2021, December). Artificial intelligence (AI) in education: Using AI tools for teaching and learning process. In *Prosiding Seminar Nasional & Call for Paper STIE AAS* (Vol. 4, No. 1, pp. 134-147).

Grassini, S. (2023). Shaping the future of education: Exploring the potential and consequences of AI and ChatGPT in educational settings. *Education Sciences*, 13(7), 692. DOI: 10.3390/educsci13070692

Harry, A. (2023). Role of AI in Education. [INJURITY]. *Interdiciplinary Journal and Hummanity*, 2(3), 260–268.

Nagao, K., & Nagao, K. (2019). Artificial intelligence in education. *Artificial Intelligence Accelerates Human Learning: Discussion Data Analytics*, 1-17.

Owoc, M. L., Sawicka, A., & Weichbroth, P. (2019, August). Artificial intelligence technologies in education: benefits, challenges and strategies of implementation. In *IFIP International Workshop on Artificial Intelligence for Knowledge Management* (pp. 37-58). Cham: Springer International Publishing.

Pedro, F., Subosa, M., Rivas, A., & Valverde, P. (2019). Artificial intelligence in education: Challenges and opportunities for sustainable development.

Tahiru, F. (2021). AI in education: A systematic literature review. [JCIT]. *Journal of Cases on Information Technology*, 23(1), 1–20. DOI: 10.4018/JCIT.2021010101

Verma, A., Kumar, Y., & Kohli, R. (2021). Study of AI techniques in quality educations: Challenges and recent progress. *SN Computer Science*, 2(4), 238. DOI: 10.1007/s42979-021-00635-3

Yin, R. K., & Moore, G. B. (1987). The use of advanced technologies in special education: Prospects from robotics, artificial intelligence, and computer simulation. *Journal of Learning Disabilities*, 20(1), 60–63. DOI: 10.1177/002221948702000111

Zawacki-Richter, O., Marín, V. I., Bond, M., & Gouverneur, F. (2019). Systematic review of research on artificial intelligence applications in higher education–where are the educators? *International Journal of Educational Technology in Higher Education*, 16(1), 1–27. DOI: 10.1186/s41239-019-0171-0

Zhai, X., Chu, X., Chai, C. S., Jong, M. S. Y., Istenic, A., Spector, M., Liu, J.-B., Yuan, J., & Li, Y. (2021). A Review of Artificial Intelligence (AI) in Education from 2010 to 2020. *Complexity*, 2021(1), 8812542. DOI: 10.1155/2021/8812542

ADDITIONAL READING

Judijanto, L., Atsani, M. R., & Chadijah, S. (2024). Trends In The Development Of Artificial Intelligence-Based Technology In Education. *International Journal of Teaching and Learning*, 2(6), 1722–1723.

Lai, T., Zeng, X., Xu, B., Xie, C., Liu, Y., Wang, Z., Lu, H., & Fu, S. (2024). The application of artificial intelligence technology in education influences Chinese adolescent's emotional perception. *Current Psychology (New Brunswick, N.J.)*, 43(6), 5309–5317. DOI: 10.1007/s12144-023-04727-6 PMID: 37359676

Suresh Babu, S., & Dhakshina Moorthy, A. (2024). Application of artificial intelligence in adaptation of gamification in education: A literature review. *Computer Applications in Engineering Education*, 32(1), e22683. DOI: 10.1002/cae.22683

Venkateswaran, P. S., Ayasrah, F. T. M., Nomula, V. K., Paramasivan, P., Anand, P., & Bogeshwaran, K. (2024). Applications of artificial intelligence tools in higher education. In *Data-Driven Decision Making for Long-Term Business Success* (pp. 124–136). IGI Global.

Wardat, Y., Tashtoush, M., AlAli, R., & Saleh, S. (2024). Artificial intelligence in education: Mathematics teachers' perspectives, practices and challenges. *Iraqi Journal for Computer Science and Mathematics*, 5(1), 60–77.

KEY TERMS AND DEFINITIONS

Adaptive Learning: An educational method using AI to personalize content delivery based on individual learning needs, enabling more effective learning experiences.

Algorithmic Bias: A tendency of AI algorithms to produce skewed results due to biases in data or design, potentially affecting fairness and equity in educational applications.

Artificial Intelligence (AI): The simulation of human intelligence in machines, allowing them to perform tasks like learning, reasoning, and problem-solving, which are increasingly applied in education.

Automated Assessment: A process where AI systems evaluate and score student work, offering instant feedback and freeing educators to focus on personalized teaching.

Chatbot: An AI-driven conversational tool that provides real-time assistance and information to students and staff, often available 24/7 for support.

Curriculum Design: The process of structuring educational content, which can be enhanced by AI through analysis of student data to tailor curriculum effectively.

Personalized Learning: An approach enabled by AI, where educational experiences are customized to meet the specific needs, pace, and preferences of each learner.

Predictive Analytics: The use of data analysis by AI to forecast student performance trends, helping educators identify at-risk students early for intervention.

Virtual Classroom: A digital learning environment powered by AI, enabling remote education through interactive tools that facilitate real-time teaching and learning.

Voice Assistance: AI-powered applications, such as Siri or Alexa, that aid in learning by responding to voice commands, helping students access information hands-free.

Chapter 3
Emerging Trends of AI Technologies in the Higher Education Sector:
A Case of India and Kazakhstan

Rajasekhara Mouly Potluri
https://orcid.org/0000-0002-6935-1373
Kazakh-British Technical University, Kazakhstan

Madhavi Kilaru
VNR Vignana Jyothi Institute of Engineering and Technology, India

ABSTRACT

This chapter explores the transformative integration of artificial intelligence (AI) in education, examining how AI methodologies have reshaped teaching and learning practices in India and Kazakhstan. By analyzing trends such as data analytics for informed decision-making, language learning and translation tools, virtual assistants, and collaborative learning platforms, this chapter provides insights into the evolving applications of AI across these diverse educational landscapes. Through comparative analysis, it highlights both the similarities and unique approaches in AI adoption within the educational systems of India and Kazakhstan. Additionally, the chapter discusses the opportunities and challenges associated with implementing AI in education, focusing on ethical considerations and the regulatory mechanisms needed to ensure responsible and effective use of AI technologies in educational settings.

DOI: 10.4018/979-8-3693-7220-3.ch003

INTRODUCTION

The COVID-19 pandemic, which started in March 2020, made many changes in the Indian education system, including suspending face-to-face teaching for months. During this period, millions of students have shifted to online platforms for learning, which have gained importance as an effective educational tool. Even in rural areas with minimal internet facilities, millions of students are pushed to the source of online platforms. In the dynamic landscape of higher education, the integration of AI technologies is rapidly gaining momentum. In India, AI technologies have become a transformative catalyst in higher education institutes to personalize student learning practices. From AI-powered virtual tutors that provide personalized feedback to intelligent learning management systems that evaluate student performance data, AI is transforming education delivery.

Moreover, Indian institutions are utilizing AI in administrative processes such as student admissions, counseling, and alums engagement, streamlining operations to improve efficiency and increase productivity. One of the critical trends in India's education sector is the implementation of AI-powered personalized learning platforms, which can analyze student learning patterns, preferences, and progress using machine learning algorithms. Chatbots that employ various AI technologies, from machine learning to natural language processing capabilities, are being deployed to provide instant support to students and faculty, enhancing communication and accessibility within educational institutions. Students' performance and intellectual ability levels vary inside a classroom, and it is complicated to provide adequate attention to each student, particularly in institutes with limited budgets and insufficient faculty. AI applications will help fill the gap by providing customized teaching, adaptive learning, and personalized education. These features of AI applications will help each learner learn according to their mental abilities (Mislevy et al., 2020). For any country, higher education is crucial; there, new ideas and knowledge are generated, political and economic leaders and entrepreneurs of the future are brought up, and opportunities are given for students of all social groups to raise their social status.

BACKGROUND

Significance of Education Sector

The education sector in India and Kazakhstan plays a vital role in shaping the countries' future by providing knowledge, skills, and opportunities for personal and societal growth. According to the latest records, India is currently the largest-populated country in the world. India's education system is vast and diverse, providing for the needs of students from different cultures and regions. The education sector is mainly linked with other sectors to improve productivity; providing quality education and training to citizens is a must to enter and work with other sectors. A well-educated human capital is essential for establishing industries, attracting investments, and driving sustainable growth (Baah-Boateng, 2013). By providing equal access to education to all individuals in the country regardless of socio-economic background, education enables people to break poverty, improve their standard of living, and contribute to society at large (Rieser, 2012). For achieving professional and personal success, education acts as a potent weapon for developing knowledge, contemplation, and social mobility. For countries like India and Kazakhstan, education is vital in equipping students with the skills and capabilities required to flourish in a competitive global environment. For the development of a nation, education acts as a cornerstone, and it is necessary to promote values such as diversity and social harmony. With the introduction of ChatGPT, Google Bard, Midjourney, and Canvas magic features, artificial intelligence (AI) is swiftly becoming an integral part of today's human lives, transforming businesses and reshaping the current process of work, learning, and communication. This rapid technological advancement highlights the significance of incorporating AI education into the curriculum not only to ensure that all students are well-equipped for their academic futures.

The education sector can stimulate a sense of unity among the citizens. Education inculcates a sense of social responsibility, fairness, and equity in interpersonal and academic relationships (Resh & Sabbagh, 2014).In developing countries like India, which has a vast population, education is one of the backbones that will help change a developing nation's status into a developed one. Moreover, we observed that from generation to generation, there is a lot of enhancement in literacy rates, superior infrastructure, and advanced technology compared to other countries (Haque, 2002). Hence, global organizations such as UNESCO and UNICEF are developing educational projects in India to help the nation develop progressively. The education sector collaborates with different sectors, which is required to address industry needs and drive economic growth (Arshed et al., 2022). It can closely work with industries to meet the emerging demands of the job market, ensuring that young graduates are equipped with new skills and knowledge that must be implemented practically in their respective fields.

INDIAN EDUCATION SYSTEM: AN OVERVIEW

The education system is the step-by-step process of obtaining knowledge developed by a learning process in training a child (Kirschner & Van Merrienboer, 2008). The term education is associated with mental and physical training, a combination of formal and informal learning. Informal learning means learning with daily experiences like communicating with family members, peers, and people in society. In contrast, in formal learning, learning should occur with structured training classes and the need to follow specific rules, regulations, assessments, and grades. Education involves not only information but also experiences, skills, and the development of attitudes, in addition to inculcating customs and beliefs (Serpell & Hatano, 1997). This will all help in the development of the personality of an individual throughout their life journey. One of the primary objectives of education is to help build the character of an individual as well as that of society as a whole. In the words of Mahatma Gandhi, if a person can succeed in building character, society will take care of them. Education should help individuals understand and cultivate their understanding of real society and their own potential within the framework of the economic development of society, and this will help identify the skills required to get a profession.

The Indian education system has different stages, like nursery, primary, secondary, senior secondary, graduation, and post-graduation. Education is the process of learning, teaching, and training human capital. It stimulates and increases knowledge, consequently leading to better skill development and improving individuals' quality. In India, the government always values the importance of education. The schools in India are controlled by different boards like the Center Board of Secondary Education (CBSE), the Council for the Indian School Certificate Examinations (CISCE) Board, the state government boards, the national open schools, and the International schools. At the kindergarten stage, the children recognize and read consistent letter-sound correspondences (Huang et al., 2014). Secondary school education occurs between the ages of eleven and fifteen, and the classes are organized from six to ten. After this stage, the students are between the ages of sixteen and seventeen, and the higher secondary classes are organized into different streams. Universities, colleges, professional schools, and other institutions provide higher education in India. It focuses on in-depth learning in specific fields of study, facilitating individuals to develop expertise and progressive knowledge in their chosen areas (Aithal & Aithal, 2019).

KAZAKHSTAN EDUCATION SECTOR SYSTEM

The education sector system in Kazakhstan is structured into three levels: Primary education, basic secondary education, and senior secondary education. Primary school begins at the age of 6 years. There is a shift-wise system in schooling; two groups of children attend morning and afternoon shifts, respectively, in order to share facilities. The courses, standards, and policies prescribed by the Ministry of

Education and Science of the Republic of Kazakhstan are introduced and applied to private and public schools. The education system in Kazakhstan is highly centralized, which allowed it to effectively implement a response to the COVID-19 pandemic, with local governments moving quickly to online learning platforms. Most higher education institutions already had online infrastructure, and secondary schools were 90% ready. Technical and vocational colleges were less prepared for the transition. Despite 78% internet coverage nationwide and access to cheap cellular data, some rural areas, without access, trusted on TV and radio to transmit material to students. The government will persist to seek digital learning content from sources abroad to be designed to local standards, with over 7,000 schools operating online in 2020. Lack of learning devices was mentioned as a critical issue, especially in rural areas; lack of technical skills and cyber-pedagogy is a potential opportunity for U.S. education training providers. All webinars, education fairs, and promotion events have moved to virtual venues, but face-to-face communication remains critical for creating partnerships in Kazakhstan. Local agents are willing to speak with institutional representatives online. Skype and Zoom are the most popular communication platforms. At the same time, Facebook, Instagram, TikTok, and YouTube are the best alternatives for promotional purposes and are widely used to promote overseas education. LinkedIn and Head Hunter are popular sites for finding career opportunities. Networks are critical tools for entering the country and recruiting effectively and successfully. These include education agents and institutional partnerships that collaborate with school guidance counselors. This is an agent-driven sector, and several qualified educational agencies operate in Kazakhstan. Proper due diligence is recommended before establishing partnership relations. An essential segment of the market to target is parents. Marketing materials need to be created to speak to parents. Internet and social networks are rapidly growing in Kazakhstan. The number of national users is approaching 10 million people.

Digital technologies have found the most outstanding applications in the media, business, and many other industries—the same thing is required for the higher education system. Institutes will remain, but digital technologies will transform education delivery and access. Online education as a form of introduction of new technologies has existed since the 1990s, but over the past few years, the rate of its use rapidly enhanced. The so-purported Massive Open Online Courses (MOOCs) are an exciting example of finding new models. Some of these models have substantial economic value. Countries like India and Kazakhstan must also use Cloud-based technology because it can offer administrators benefits in terms of cost savings. At the same time, the classroom provides students with straightforward access to a broader range of educational resources.

Every country, particularly developing and underdeveloped parts of the world, must review its present education system based on the current new generation's requirements. These must introduce necessary changes to meet the industry requirements and improve public living standards. These changes the higher education system and develop its relations with the industry, which plays several roles as a client and partner of higher education institutions and a competitor. To survive and succeed, universities must establish a much deeper relationship with the industry in the next decade. For example, the scale and depth of training and internships will become an increasingly important source of competitive advantage for academies with a partnership branch. One of the most essential functions of the higher education system in Kazakhstan is to produce graduates who meet the industry's requirements. This involves a strong partnership between the higher education sector and the organizations that employ graduates. This partnership will gradually help us understand the industry's requirements and the economy. Higher education institutes must maintain the proper databases on graduates' employability to help monitor career paths, strengthen relationships with graduates, and inform job-seeking graduates about vacancies.

REQUIREMENTS OF AI TECHNOLOGIES IN THE HIGHER EDUCATION SECTOR

AI tremendously transforms learning methods by fostering personalized, competent, and engaging everyday educational experiences. Artificial intelligence (AI) is revolutionizing how humans live their lives, and similar to other domains, the education field will also identify a paradigm shift through this technology. A new era of AI-powered education started in the world of higher education with the emergence of ChatGPT in November 2022 (Kebritchi, 2024) and identified notable challenges like framing policies and guidelines, adaptability, evaluation, and ethics. The development of artificial intelligence (AI), precisely AI generative tools, has spread anxiety across the education field in recent months, and institutions have one primary concern that AI adoption would challenge the existence of valuable academic paradigms like assessment, course design, activities, and more (Nguyen, 2023). Artificial intelligence can be applied in the education sector to unleash insights about understanding how students learn, how to personalize the learning experience of students, how to get more information to help in the decision-making process, and how to model the complex interaction between student learning, the knowledge domain and the tools that enable students to interact with the domain? (Ahmed et al., 2023). AI can help address academic challenges primarily related to teaching, assessment criteria, etc. In different ways, AI-powered tools are capable of meeting the individual needs of students by tailoring academic content in a faster way. For example, platforms like Coursera, Udemy, and Khan Academy engage students by using AI algorithms to adapt creative coursework based on the student's skills and knowledge, and they offer different assignments and exercises. Many of the reputed higher education institutions understood that the role of AI was significant in both the present and future education systems and the world's economic development. Artificial intelligence (AI) offers numerous education opportunities, but it also has some disadvantages. These technology systems are designed to simulate the cognitive knowledge of an individual with the information received from this source, precisely reasoning, problem-solving, learning, perception, understanding natural language, and making decisions. Artificial intelligence (AI) assists the teaching community in preparing lesson plans and teaching material and generating projects with the quickest possible time, personalization, context, and individualization.

Modern technology, like AI, provides students an interactive and advanced experience (Kuleto et al.,2021). As educational environments become increasingly complex, the ability to collect, analyze, and act upon data is crucial for institutional improvement, and Internet of Things (IoT) technologies offer opportunities for educational leaders to optimize various aspects of campus operations, enhance student experiences, and improve admin efficiency (Çela et al., 2025). The application of AI in higher education fundamentally redefines the teacher's role from knowledge provider to facilitator of personalized learning experiences. This shift is steered by AI's power to automate administrative tasks and provide data-driven insights into student performance. Hence, the numerous powers of AI in higher education are personalized learning experiences, improved educational outcomes, increased efficiency, and diverse learning styles (Zawacki-Richter et al., 2019). The role of AI in higher education is not only in engaging students with different activities but also in achieving quality education, free from the constraints of location and time, and promoting creativity, problem-solving ability, and collaboration. Instead of passive learning, many institutions want to personalize the learning environments for better student engagement. Personalized learning ensures that students get better knowledge and work better with teachers. Hence, students effectively working with teachers can help define and reach learning goals (Akyuz, 2020). Using AI as a complementary tool may improve students' learning while stimulating their critical thinking abilities. Encouraging man-machine collaboration reinforces students' ability to adapt technology to any environment or job role. There is a need to prepare the future users, designers, and shapers of these technologies to keep up with the pace of change because change is inevitable. An essential part of teaching students to use AI is introducing them to new platforms and functionalities as these innovations arise. The New Educational Policy (NEP) 2020 also highlights the role of AI in the teaching-learning process to address the various issues through advancing AI core research, which would enable the maximum intervention of AI in this process. It is also proposed in NEP-2020 that various PG and PhD programs in artificial intelligence in various multidisciplinary fields be offered.

ISSUES, CONTROVERSIES, AND PROBLEMS IN THE IMPLEMENTATION OF ARTIFICIAL INTELLIGENCE (AI) IN EDUCATION

We all know how the COVID-19 pandemic has been highly disruptive in educational settings and how educational content delivered by major academic institutions changed over to online learning to follow social distance guidelines (Alio et al., 2024). The pandemic effectively interrupted the traditional teaching and learning system, which means a significant transition and exceptional digital drive were required in the teaching and learning process. People must accept online platforms such as Zoom, Google Classroom, Microsoft Teams, JioMeet, etc. Hence, the introduction of different virtual learning platforms has transformed the delivery of education, which has had to become more agile in order to invite the participation of students from various areas. In the process of virtual learning, learners require independent learning, understanding, and self-motivation. Artificial Intelligence and generative models such as ChatGPT play an essential role in virtual learning, and these tools also help users make learning convenient. However, this AI transition has expanded many academic issues related to implementing digital technology for those who can access advanced technology and those who can't.

Other drawbacks of AI generative models are restricted interaction, inadequate academic readiness, and some issues related to ethics and accountability (Farrelly & Baker, 2023). An essential understanding of technology integration in human disciplines is human interaction, which is very important in the learning process. Still, ChatGPT does not offer the idea of a human instructor. Learners found that online courses received poorer outcomes than traditional learning methods. Adopting advanced technologies may create infrastructure problems and economic burdens for many academic institutions. For example, The growing demand for sophisticated technology in educational institutions has increased costs. The model needs continuous maintenance, i.e., software updates, bug fixes, performance optimization issues, etc. This could require skilled people, while it is expensive and time-consuming.

Further, problems like copyright and plagiarism infringement are another significant challenge that educational institutions will need to address before the application is implemented practically. Sustainability is one of the essential factors for any academic institution because it is the ability to maintain over time. It is categorized into three types: economic, social, and environmental. Many organizations focus on reducing their ecological footprints and conserving resources. The sustainable practices are at VNR Vignana Jyothi Institute of Engineering & Technology, Hyderabad. It is one of the leading educational institutions in Hyderabad. The campus has adequate infrastructure facilities spread over 21.13 acres. The sustainable initiatives are saving water, reducing waste, reducing energy consumption (Electricity) in terms of regular maintenance and check-ups to identify unnecessary power usage, conserving greenery, and constructing and maintaining eco-friendly building technology.

Eco-friendly Brands:

Students and staff are motivated to minimize paper cups and use their own cups/ mugs. At the college canteen, stainless steel tumblers are promoted. The total campus strictly prohibits the usage of plastic by conducting awareness programs for students and staff. Course end surveys, student feedback, leave forms, and payrolls are done online to minimize paper usage. Waste segregation bins were maintained with different waste bins, such as green, biodegradable, and non-degradable

Noise Management:

No horn boards are provided inside the campus. Vehicles contributing to noise and air pollution should be banned from entering the premises. Soundproof generators are used in the institute. Civil works and works producing noise levels beyond the limits are encouraged after working hours.

Soil management:

Harmful or waste is not dumped into the soil surface, and proper provisions are made to prevent soil erosion. Students and staff are involved in various awareness-related campaigns for environmental protection. The institute has a canopy of trees and plants that makes the environment carbon dioxide-free and maintains inmates' health.

Water Management:

The college has initiated rainwater harvesting to conserve water; for this, rainwater harvesting rooftops have been designed and implemented at different blocks. Pipelines, taps, and other sources of water discharge are well maintained without any leakages. Likewise, a significant number of rainwater harvesting pits are maintained.

Energy Conservation:

The buildings at the campus with different blocks, namely A, B, C, and D, have solar power plants established on the top. There is a center for "Renewable Energy Sources" in the institute. Street lights are powered by solar panels, and unnecessary usage of power is reduced by maintaining signboards that savage the electricity that is put across the institute.

Ethical Guidelines in the usage of ChatGPT and Online Tools:

The constructive effort of all the stakeholders and policymakers should be considered when formulating the ethical guidelines.

Encourage Responsible Use:

These days, both faculty and students are using online tools, especially ChatGPT, which provides information in different ways in terms of academics, like course notes, mini and major project content, and software programs. Some students do not adequately use this tool for academic purposes. For this, the institution conducts awareness programs in the usage of ChatGPT for both staff and students. This will help in sustainable use over time and will not be socially and environmentally harmful. Faculty also encourage students by providing alternative education solutions and pedagogical practices instead of using ChatGPT. Faculty members also have bad experiences with student academics regarding submitting assignments and projects. Some students copied content, directly submitted without further modifications, and even made meaningful sentences.

Finally, for any educational sector, maintaining sustainability requires consolidated efforts of teachers, students, institutions, policymakers, and administrators, which should aim to reduce this technology's immediate and long-term impact on ecological and environmental grounds. The actions must be aimed at maintaining the application and its technical derivatives for their sustained and ethical implications in the classroom (Kasneci et al., 2023). Artificial intelligence and its diverse tools can change the current higher education system by offering numerous advantages. Klutka et al. (2018) listed the following objectives for AI in higher education. These are increased outcomes and access, enhanced retention, lower cost, and decreased time to completion. Many researchers identified four key areas of AI applications for teaching and learning: profiling and prediction, intelligent tutoring systems, assessment and evaluation, and adaptive systems and personalization (Bates et al., 2020). The application of AI deals with big data, statistics, and machine learning in higher education institutions to tackle many challenges of student admissions, add or drop for courses, group behavior tendencies, teaching, and research-related support, and services directing entire academics to deliver the best to enhance the quality of knowledge earning process initiated by the educational institutions. Researchers Hannan and Liu (2023) emphasized the successful applications of AI technologies in three main areas of college operations: student learning experience, student support, and enrollment management. As highlighted by Davenport and Ronanki (2018) throughout their research, three types of AI are used in higher education: process automation, cognitive insight, and cognitive engagement.

Process automation is the form of AI that automates back-end tasks such as updating records or administrative filing in higher education institutions. This automation can lead to a high return on investment (ROI) by saving institutions or organizations time and money on repetitive tasks. The second category of AI is cognitive insight, where computers learn from data in real-time, mimic the human brain by recognizing patterns, and perform predictive analytics. Cognitive insight can be seen in a software system predicting which products customers will likely purchase. Cognitive engagement, the last category, is primarily seen in chatbots that engage in 24/7 customer support by using natural language processing and machine learning capabilities. Compared to AI applications in manufacturing, finance, banking, and healthcare, implementing AI in higher education is very slow and highly significant.

SOLUTIONS AND RECOMMENDATIONS

For effective implementation of AI technologies in the education sectors of India and Kazakhstan, provide ultimately pledged training programs for faculty and administrators to enhance skill and knowledge in understanding and implementing AI technologies effectively in the process of the curriculum. Developing the necessary infrastructure is vital to integrating AI technologies in educational institutions, procuring AI-enabled devices, recruiting skilled people to build algorithms, and using the proper data storage and management data process frameworks to implement AI effectively. Collaboration between educational institutions with AI experts, industry professionals, and stakeholders facilitates effective resource allocation and also gains insights, guidance, and support in adopting AI technologies in academic institutions. Monitoring AI usage has become an essential aspect for institutions; it requires continuous monitoring and analysis of the impact of technology on student learning outcomes, resource allocation and efficiency, teacher effectiveness, and overall quality of educational institutions. By focusing on these requirements, both countries can successfully integrate AI technologies in academic institutions to transform their education sectors and provide superior learning experiences to students.

CONCLUSION

AI-driven innovations in higher education have the ability to modernize the way education is given, and research has an effective and efficient educational experience for both faculty and students (Mohamed Hashim et al., 2022). There are impending benefits of AI in higher education institutions, such as personalized learning, accessibility, improved student feedback system, efficient administrative tasks, and enhanced student engagement and research capabilities; however, there are challenges that must be addressed for technology to be used productively, and responsibly.AI can improve administrative procedures, resource allocation and so on. Still, there are ethical consequences that must be carefully addressed. Regarding integrating AI in educational institutions, policymakers must guide the people involved in implementing technology, formulate strategic approaches, and implement best practices to use AI responsibly. Collaboration between academic institutions, AI developers, and stakeholders is crucial in addressing the threats and opportunities connected with artificial intelligence.

Fairness, data protection, transparency, and security are essential aspects of implementing technology. AI-driven transformation in educational institutions heavily relies upon faculty, thus providing training and appointing effective administrators to implement artificial intelligence. Educators must have the requisite skills and knowledge to incorporate AI into their teaching practices effectively, and administrators need to be familiar with the ethical, legal, and workforce implications of AI in university administration and operations (Shiohira, 2021). The impact of AI on education and learning, as well as university administration and operations, can be transformative, nonetheless accountable in implementation. Finally, implementing AI in higher education is complex and critical to recognize the disadvantages of using AI. By taking a proactive and attentive approach, educational institutions can identify the positive transformation of AI. As AI continues to evolve, higher education stakeholders must stay informed, collaborate, and adapt to the changing landscape of AI-driven revolutions in higher education. With responsible implementation, AI has the potential to enhance the quality, accessibility, and effectiveness of higher education institutions, benefitting the students, faculty, and stakeholders involved. Both countries understand the challenges and the need for transformations aimed at a radical restructuring of the existing system and awareness of responsibility to the citizens of the country - these factors are present; hence the constant desire for reforms, steps forward, sometimes throwing in search of creative solutions will definitely help for the growth.

REFERENCES

Ahmad, K., Iqbal, W., El-Hassan, A., Qadir, J., Benhaddou, D., Ayyash, M., & Al-Fuqaha, A. (2023). Data-driven artificial intelligence in education: A comprehensive review. *IEEE Transactions on Learning Technologies.*

Aithal, P. S., & Aithal, S. (2019). Analysis of higher education in Indian National Education Policy Proposal 2019 and its implementation challenges. [IJAEML]. *International Journal of Applied Engineering and Management Letters*, 3(2), 1–35. DOI: 10.47992/IJAEML.2581.7000.0039

Akyuz, Y. (2020). Effects of intelligent tutoring systems (ITS) on personalized learning (PL). *Creative Education*, 11(06), 953–978. DOI: 10.4236/ce.2020.116069

Ali, O., Murray, P. A., Momin, M., Dwivedi, Y. K., & Malik, T. (2024). The effects of artificial intelligence applications in educational settings: Challenges and strategies. *Technological Forecasting and Social Change*, 199, 123076. DOI: 10.1016/j.techfore.2023.123076

Arshed, N., Ahmad, W., & Hanif, U. (2022). A spatial, temporal exploration of factors motivating academia-industry collaboration. *Journal of the Knowledge Economy*, 13(1), 521–540. DOI: 10.1007/s13132-021-00729-6

Baah-Boateng, W. (2013). Human Capital Development: The Case of Education as a Vehicle for Africa's Economic Transformation.

Bates, T., Cobo, C., Mariño, O., & Wheeler, S. (2020). Can artificial intelligence transform higher education? *International Journal of Educational Technology in Higher Education*, 17(1), 1–12. DOI: 10.1186/s41239-020-00218-x

Çela, E., Potluri, R. M., & Vajjhala, N. R. (2025). A Comprehensive Meta-Analysis of IoT Integration for Data-Driven Decision Making in Education. In Thandekkattu, S., & Vajjhala, N. (Eds.), *Designing Sustainable Internet of Things Solutions for Smart Industries* (pp. 27–50). IGI Global., DOI: 10.4018/979-8-3693-5498-8.ch002

Davenport, T. H., & Ronanki, R. (2018). Artificial intelligence for the real world. *Harvard Business Review*, 96(1), 108–116.

Farrelly, T., & Baker, N. (2023). Generative artificial intelligence: Implications and considerations for higher education practice. *Education Sciences*, 13(11), 1109. DOI: 10.3390/educsci13111109

Hannan, E., & Liu, S. (2023). AI: New source of competitiveness in higher education. *Competitiveness Review*, 33(2), 265–279. DOI: 10.1108/CR-03-2021-0045

Haque, M. S. (2002). E-governance in India: Its impacts on relations amongcitizens, politicians and public servants. *International Review of Administrative Sciences*, 68(2), 231–250. DOI: 10.1177/0020852302682005

Huang, F. L., Tortorelli, L. S., & Invernizzi, M. A. (2014). An investigation of factors associated with letter-sound knowledge at kindergarten entry. *Early Childhood Research Quarterly*, 29(2), 182–192. DOI: 10.1016/j.ecresq.2014.02.001

Kasneci, E., Seßler, K., Küchemann, S., Bannert, M., Dementieva, D., Fischer, F., & Kasneci, G. (2023). ChatGPT for good? On opportunities and challenges of large language models for education. *Learning and Individual Differences*, 103, 102274. DOI: 10.1016/j.lindif.2023.102274

Kebritchi, M. (2024). The implications of AI in higher education. https://evolllution.com/the-implications-of-ai-in-higher-education

Kirschner, P., & Van Merrienboer, J. J. (2008). *Ten steps to complex learning: A new approach to instruction and instructional design. In 21st century education: A reference handbook*. SAGE Publications Ltd.

Kuleto, V., Ilić, M., Dumangiu, M., Ranković, M., Martins, O. M., Păun, D., & Mihoreanu, L. (2021). Exploring opportunities and challenges of artificial intelligence and machine learning in higher education institutions. *Sustainability (Basel)*, 13(18), 10424. DOI: 10.3390/su131810424

Mislevy, R. J., Yan, D., Gobert, J., & Sao Pedro, M. (2020). Automated scoring in intelligent tutoring systems. In *Handbook of automated scoring* (pp. 403–422). Chapman and Hall/CRC. DOI: 10.1201/9781351264808-22

Mohamed Hashim, M. A., Tlemsani, I., & Matthews, R. (2022). Higher education strategy in digital transformation. *Education and Information Technologies*, 27(3), 3171–3195. DOI: 10.1007/s10639-021-10739-1 PMID: 34539217

Morze, N., Varchenko-Trotsenko, L., Terletska, T., & Smyrnova-Trybulska, E. (2021, March). Implementation of adaptive learning at higher education institutions by means of Moodle LMS. [). IOP Publishing.]. *Journal of Physics: Conference Series*, 1840(1), 012062. DOI: 10.1088/1742-6596/1840/1/012062

Nguyen, N. (2023). Opportunities and challenges of AI in higher education. https://feedbackfruits.com/blog/opportunities-and-challenges-of-ai-in-higher-education

Resh, N., & Sabbagh, C. (2014). Sense of justice in school and civic attitudes. *Social Psychology of Education*, 17(1), 51–72. DOI: 10.1007/s11218-013-9240-8

Rieser, R. (2012). *Implementing inclusive education: a Commonwealth guide to implementing Article 24 of the UN Convention on the Rights of Persons with Disabilities*. Commonwealth Secretariat.

Serpell, R., & Hatano, G. (1997). *Education, schooling, and literacy* (Vol. 2). Handbook of cross-cultural psychology.

Shiohira, K. (2021). Understanding the Impact of Artificial Intelligence on Skills Development. [*UNESCO-UNEVOC International Centre for Technical and Vocational Education and Training*.]. *Education*, •••, 2030.

Syzdykbayeva, A., Baikulova, A., & Kerimbayeva, R. (2020). Introduction of artificial intelligence as the basis of modern online education on the example of higher education. In *2021 IEEE International Conference on Smart Information Systems and Technologies (SIST)* (pp. 1-8). IEEE.

Zawacki-Richter, O., Marín, V. I., Bond, M., & Gouverneur, F. (2019). Systematic review of research on artificial intelligence applications in higher education–where are the educators? *International Journal of Educational Technology in Higher Education*, 16(1), 1–27. DOI: 10.1186/s41239-019-0171-0

ADDITIONAL READING

Batista, J., Mesquita, A., & Carnaz, G. (2024). Generative AI and Higher Education: Trends, Challenges, and Future Directions from a Systematic Literature Review. *Information (Basel)*, 15(11), 676. DOI: 10.3390/info15110676

Chu, H. C., Hwang, G. H., Tu, Y. F., & Yang, K. H. (2022). Roles and research trends of artificial intelligence in higher education: A systematic review of the top 50 most-cited articles. *Australasian Journal of Educational Technology*, 38(3), 22–42.

Msekelwa, P. Z. (2024). The Impact of AI on Education: Innovative Tools and Trends. *Journal of Artificial Intelligence General science (JAIGS) ISSN: 3006-4023, 5*(1), 227-236.

Ruchi, K. C., & Ganguly, S. (2024). Revolutionizing Higher Education with AI: Opportunities, Challenges, and Future Trends. *Library Progress International*, 44(3), 9834–9844.

KEY TERMS AND DEFINITIONS

Artificial Intelligence: AI is the technology that enables computers and machines to simulate human learning, comprehension, problem-solving, decision-making, creativity, and autonomy.

AI in Higher Education: AI is the impending technology that addresses many of the biggest challenges or issues in education, such as innovative teaching and learning practices, research, and other support services that are essential to accelerate knowledge transformation.

AI Application in Education: Artificial intelligence in education is applied to improve learning outcomes and support teachers in developing better educational practices. From automatic assignment grading to tailored curriculums, AI solutions can be used in academic institutions in many ways.

Challenges of AI in Education: Educators should be involved in defeating the challenges that AI presents, such as technical expertise, cost, ethical concerns, quality concerns, and human-AI collaboration.

Higher Education in India: Higher education in India is reported in recognized universities, specialized institutions, and colleges affiliated with recognized universities. The disciplines cover various subjects, including literature, basic sciences, computer engineering, and space research. Most universities and colleges of higher learning and research are autonomous in function along with private and public sector-controlled ones.

Higher Education in Kazakhstan: Higher Education in Kazakhstan is at the stage of dynamic development; keep in mind the scientific and technological progress requirements of the country by undertaking global measures to upgrade and reform the teaching methods, infra development, and research support by providing full-fledged student support. In the context of the Bologna process parameters, the Kazakhstani higher education system is of the following structure: baccalaureate, magistrate, and doctoral programs.

Chapter 4
Key Drivers of Artificial Intelligence on Learner Engagement and Experience

Shankar Subramanian Iyer
https://orcid.org/0000-0003-0598-9543
Westford University College, UAE

ABSTRACT

This chapter explores the intricate relationship between artificial intelligence (AI) and student engagement within educational settings. As AI technologies become increasingly integrated into education, educators, policymakers, and technology developers must understand the factors driving AI adoption and its effects on student engagement and experience. This chapter identifies critical elements influencing AI use in education through a comprehensive literature review and empirical analysis. This chapter investigates their impact on student engagement's cognitive, emotional, and behavioral dimensions. The findings offer valuable insights into how AI can enhance the student experience, supporting the development of more effective, AI-driven educational strategies tailored to foster engagement.

INTRODUCTION

Artificial Intelligence (AI) has rapidly become a transformative force in education, offering innovative tools to enhance learner engagement and improve educational outcomes. While AI's potential to revolutionize traditional learning approaches is well-established, recent interdisciplinary research highlights the importance of un-

DOI: 10.4018/979-8-3693-7220-3.ch004

derstanding AI's socio-technical dimensions in diverse global contexts. This chapter explores the key drivers of AI that influence learner engagement, focusing on how AI technologies—such as machine learning, adaptive learning platforms, and real-time analytics—can provide personalized, interactive, and inclusive learning experiences (Rane et al., 2023). AI addresses traditional education's limitations by aligning content with students' needs and offering instant feedback, particularly its one-size-fits-all model. These technologies enhance cognitive, emotional, and behavioral engagement, fostering a more immersive and supportive learning environment. However, challenges such as data privacy, algorithmic biases, and infrastructural limitations in low-income regions must also be considered. By incorporating emerging studies on AI's ethical implications and long-term effects on learning, this research provides a comprehensive understanding of how AI can be effectively leveraged in education while addressing critical concerns that shape its adoption and integration. This study aims to inform educators, policymakers, and technologists, offering practical insights for harnessing AI to create more equitable, engaging, and personalized educational experiences for learners worldwide (Alqahtani et al., 2023). For researchers and developers in educational technology, this study provides valuable insights into the factors driving the adoption of artificial intelligence in educational settings. Understanding these drivers can help in designing and implementing AI-driven tools and platforms that effectively enhance student engagement.

Educators and instructional designers can benefit from understanding the impacts of AI on student engagement. By knowing how AI interventions influence cognitive, affective, and behavioral aspects of engagement, educators can leverage AI tools more effectively to design innovative teaching and learning experiences that cater to individual student needs (Aggarwal, 2023). Given the interdisciplinary nature of the topic, the collaboration between researchers from diverse fields such as education, computer science, psychology, and human-computer can foster a deeper understanding of the complex interactions between AI and student engagement and lead to the development of more holistic approaches to leveraging AI in education (Kaswan et al., 2024).The exploration of AI's impact on learner engagement can be extended to various interdisciplinary areas, further enriching the understanding of its potential in education. For instance, integrating insights from psychology can deepen the analysis of how AI-driven personalized learning affects cognitive development, motivation, and emotional well-being. Additionally, collaboration with experts in human-computer interaction (HCI) can enhance the design of AI tools that are more intuitive and accessible, fostering better student interaction and engagement. The field of ethics is also critical, as addressing issues related to data privacy, algorithmic biases, and fairness can ensure that AI is deployed in ways that promote equity and inclusiveness. Furthermore, the inclusion of sociological perspectives can help in understanding how AI adoption might differ across cultural and socio-economic contexts, revealing how the digital divide and varying levels of technological access influence educational outcomes. Extending the research to these interdisciplinary areas would provide a more holistic framework for understanding how AI can transform education while ensuring it remains inclusive, ethical, and effective across diverse global settings (Modi, 2023).

Research Scope

This research focuses on identifying and analyzing the key drivers of AI that enhance learner engagement in educational settings, exploring the impact of various AI technologies in both formal and informal learning environments. It aims to examine how these technologies influence different dimensions of learner engagement, including cognitive, emotional, and behavioral aspects. The study will cover several key areas: Personalized Learning, where AI-driven customization is explored to understand its effect on learner motivation and engagement; Adaptive Learning Systems, analyzing their influence on student performance and retention rates; and Interactive Learning Environments, investigating the role of AI in creating immersive and engaging educational experiences. Additionally, the research will assess the impact of AI-powered real-time feedback mechanisms on learner satisfaction and engagement, providing insights into how timely and targeted support can enhance the learning process. Finally, it will address the challenges and ethical considerations associated with the use of AI in education, identifying potential risks and ethical implications that need to be managed to ensure the responsible and effective integration of AI technologies in learning environments.

Research Questions

1. How do AI-driven personalized learning systems influence learner motivation and engagement across cognitive, emotional, and behavioral dimensions?
2. How do adaptive learning technologies affect student performance and retention rates?
3. How do AI-enabled real-time feedback and support improve learner satisfaction and engagement?
4. What are the key challenges and ethical issues of using AI in education?

Research Objectives

1. To examine how AI-powered personalized learning systems impact learner engagement in terms of cognitive, emotional, and behavioral aspects.

2. To analyze the effect of adaptive learning technologies on student performance and retention.
3. To evaluate the impact of AI-facilitated real-time feedback and support on learner satisfaction and engagement.
4. To identify the challenges and ethical issues involved in implementing AI in education.

LITERATURE REVIEW

This review explores how AI is transforming the learning landscape by examining its key drivers on learner experience. This chapter focuses on personalized learning, adaptive learning technologies, real-time feedback and support, and ethical considerations.

Personalized Learning

Personalized learning leverages AI to tailor educational content and experiences to individual learners' needs, preferences, and abilities. AI systems analyze data from various sources like learner interactions, assessments, and behavior patterns to create customized learning paths. Studies by Luckin et al. (2022) and Jaiswal et al. (2021) highlight benefits like dynamically adjusted content difficulty and increased engagement with relevant and interesting materials. Srinivasa et al. (2022) demonstrate that personalized learning models significantly improve student achievement compared to traditional methods. Platforms like Knewton and DreamBox Learning, and intelligent tutoring systems like Carnegie Learning, exemplify personalized instruction and feedback powered by AI.

Adaptive Learning Technologies

Adaptive learning technologies use AI to modify learning materials in response to a learner's performance in real-time. These systems aim to optimize learning efficiency and effectiveness by providing the right level of challenge and support. Research by Graf (2023) and Li et al. (2021) suggests that adaptive learning can significantly improve outcomes by tailoring pace and content to individual needs. Additionally, El-Sabagh (2021) reports on enhanced learner satisfaction and engagement through continuous adjustment of learning activities with adaptive systems like ALEKS (Assessment and Learning in Knowledge Spaces) and Smart Sparrow.

Real-Time Feedback and Support

Real-time feedback and support systems powered by AI provide immediate, actionable insights to learners, helping them understand their performance and areas for improvement. This timely feedback is crucial for maintaining learner engagement and fostering a growth mindset. Research by Wilkinson et al. (2023) and Afzaal et al. (2024) emphasizes the importance of real-time, formative feedback for enhanced understanding and addressing misconceptions. Naseer et al. (2024) report that AI-driven feedback systems can reduce educator workload, allowing them to focus on more complex student needs. Grammarly and platforms like Coursera and edX exemplify real-time feedback on writing, quizzes, and assignments.

Ethical Considerations

The implementation of AI in education raises several ethical considerations that must be addressed to ensure equitable and fair learning experiences. These include data privacy, algorithmic transparency, bias and fairness, and accountability. Faccia et al. (2024) highlight the risks of bias in AI systems, while Chaika (2023) stresses the importance of algorithmic transparency and explainability for trust and accountability. Kamalov et al. (2023) emphasize the need for ethical guidelines and frameworks to govern the use of AI in education, ensuring data privacy and learner autonomy are protected. The IEEE Global Initiative on Ethics of Autonomous and Intelligent Systems and data governance frameworks adopted by educational institutions address these concerns.

The Road Ahead

The successful integration of AI in education requires careful consideration of ethical issues. The successful integration of AI in education requires careful consideration of ethical issues, including data privacy, security, bias mitigation, transparency, and accountability mechanisms. Studies by Udvaros et al. (2023) and George et al. (2023) emphasize the importance of robust data protection for learner acceptance, while Schwartz et al. (2022) and Ferrara (2023) underscore the need for fairness in AI systems. Transparency in AI algorithms, as discussed by Hassija et al. (2024) and Nakashima et al. (2024), builds trust, and establishing clear accountability, as suggested by Novelli et al. (2023) and Díaz-Rodríguez et al. (2023), is crucial for responsible AI implementation. Research exploring the socio-technical dimensions of AI reveals its potential to enhance inclusivity and shape long-term learning outcomes, especially in diverse educational contexts like the UAE and India. AI can create personalized learning environments that accommodate different needs, such as language barriers or learning disabilities, promoting inclusivity. However, AI also poses risks, such as reinforcing biases or unequal access due to technological disparities, particularly in under-resourced regions. While AI can improve cognitive skills through personalized feedback, over-reliance may hinder critical thinking and problem-solving skills. Addressing ethical concerns such as data privacy and algorithmic transparency is vital as AI becomes more integrated into global educational systems (Slimi et al., 2023).

Educators and policymakers must understand the key drivers of AI's impact on learner experience to harness its benefits while mitigating risks. This review provides a comprehensive overview of current research, offering valuable insights into future AI-driven education developments (Ng et al., 2023). Factors influencing learner experiences with AI-powered education include learner characteristics such as learning styles, motivation, interest levels, and competencies (Sethi et al., 2024; Mosleh et al., 2024). Technological factors, including ease of use, system quality, user interface design, content quality, and data management, are essential for a seamless and engaging learning experience (Umali, 2024). Institutional elements, such as assessment scores, policies, organizational culture, government directives, and management support, also shape the effectiveness of AI in education (Owan et al., 2023).

Learner engagement can be significantly enhanced by incorporating interdisciplinary insights from cognitive science, educational psychology, human-computer interaction, ethics, and data science. Cognitive science highlights how AI-driven platforms, like those used in UAE institutions such as Abu Dhabi University, can personalize learning and boost cognitive and emotional engagement. Educational psychology emphasizes AI's role in recognizing emotional cues and providing timely feedback, while human-computer interaction research stresses the importance of intuitive user interfaces, as seen in UAE schools adopting AI-powered tools. Ethical considerations, such as fairness and bias mitigation, are critical in building trust, particularly in diverse UAE classrooms. Learning analytics, demonstrated by the Mohammed Bin Rashid Smart Learning Program, further enhances engagement by offering real-time insights into learner progress (Rajest et al., 2023).

AI's potential to create equitable educational experiences for marginalized or differently-abled learners is significant. Tools like speech-to-text applications and adaptive learning platforms support students with disabilities, offering engagement opportunities that traditional methods may lack. However, AI's role in fostering creativity and critical thinking remains underexplored, and research on its ability to nurture these skills is necessary. Financial and infrastructural barriers, particularly in low-income regions, hinder AI adoption, as many schools lack the resources or technical infrastructure needed to leverage AI fully. Addressing these gaps, alongside AI's ethical concerns such as data privacy and algorithmic fairness, is crucial to ensuring that AI enhances education equitably and does not exacerbate existing inequalities. Ethical and infrastructural challenges must be addressed to ensure AI's transformative potential is realized in education globally, without reinforcing disparities (Farahani et al., 2024).

The Literature Gap

The current literature on AI-powered education offers a strong foundation in core drivers like personalized learning and ethical considerations, but a gap exists in comprehensively examining how learner characteristics, technology factors, and implementation context interact with these drivers. This gap opens the door for a conceptual model that explores how individual learning styles, motivation, and knowledge levels are interwoven with user-friendly interfaces, high-quality content, and robust data management to create a personalized experience. Additionally, the model could explore how factors like assessment practices, supportive policies, and leadership influence the effectiveness of AI in education. By bridging this gap, the model can provide a more holistic understanding of the factors that truly optimize the learner's experience with AI-driven education.

Emerging issues related to AI adoption, such as data privacy, algorithmic biases, and the digital divide, are increasingly critical topics gaining attention in both academic and policy circles. Addressing these complexities is essential for a more robust discussion of AI's integration into education. Concerns over data privacy arise as AI systems require extensive personal data to function effectively, while algorithmic biases can reinforce existing inequalities, particularly among marginalized groups. The digital divide further complicates AI adoption, with under-resourced schools and regions struggling to access the necessary infrastructure, which exacerbates educational inequities. A forward-looking section on future trends, such as AI's role in lifelong learning and its potential to evolve in meeting future educational needs, would enhance the chapter's relevance. Expanding the discussion on ethical considerations, especially regarding algorithmic fairness and data privacy, is crucial, as these issues will likely become more pressing as AI becomes more integrated into educational systems. Providing real-world examples of AI successes and failures in addressing ethical concerns—such as cases where AI-driven tools have either mitigated or perpetuated bias—along with practical suggestions for how educational institutions can better navigate these challenges, would make the chapter more comprehensive. Emphasizing the balance between innovation and ethical responsibility ensures that AI's transformative potential is harnessed in a way that benefits all learners, fostering both technological advancement and equity in education. Figure-1 describes the conceptual model.

CONCEPTUAL MODEL USING KOLB'S EXPERIENTIAL LEARNING CYCLE AND TOE THEORIES

Figure 1. Conceptual model

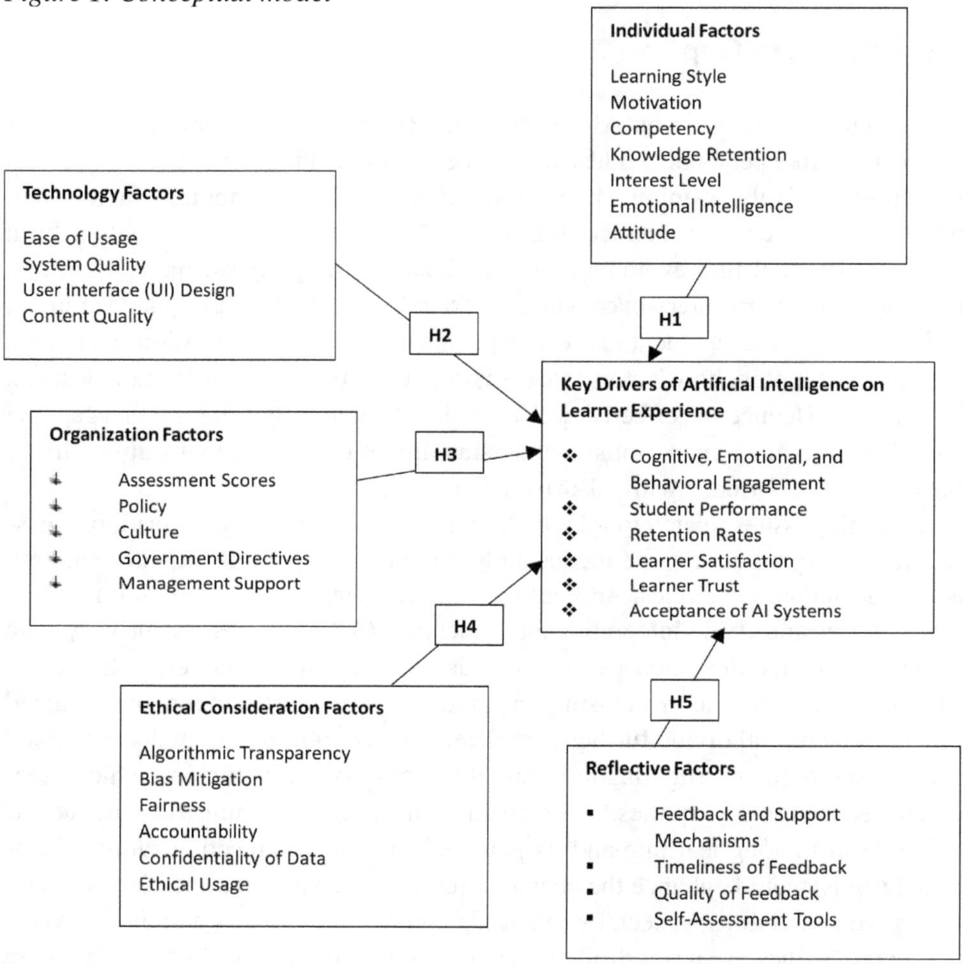

Hypotheses

H1: There is a significant relationship between the Individual Factors and the Key Drivers of Artificial Intelligence on Learner Experience

H2: Technology Factors Significantly Influence the Key Drivers of Artificial Intelligence on Learner Experience

H3: There is a significant relationship between the Organization Factors and the Key Drivers of Artificial Intelligence on Learner Experience

H4: The Ethical Consideration Factors Significantly Influence the Key Drivers of Artificial Intelligence on Learner Experience

H5: There is a significant relationship between the Reflective Factors and the Key Drivers of Artificial Intelligence on Learner Experience

METHODOLOGY

This study employs a mixed methods approach to investigate the key drivers of AI on learner experience, using cross-sectional sampling to capture data from 395 stakeholders at a single point in time. The quantitative component involves a structured survey administered to all stakeholders, measuring aspects such as engagement, performance, satisfaction, and ease of use, with statistical analysis identifying significant predictors and relationships. Complementing this, the qualitative component includes semi-structured interviews with a representative subset of around 15 experts, exploring their experiences and perceptions in depth. The cross-sectional sampling method ensures representation across students, educators, administrators, and AI developers, with data collected through electronic surveys and scheduled interviews. Quantitative data will be analyzed using statistical software for descriptive statistics, correlation analysis, and regression modeling, while qualitative data will be transcribed and thematically analyzed to uncover common themes and patterns (Iyer et al, 2024). The integration of quantitative and qualitative findings will provide a comprehensive understanding of the key drivers of AI on learner experience. The study will culminate in a detailed report, disseminated through presentations, workshops, and academic publications, providing actionable insights for educational institutions, policymakers, and AI developers (Iyer et al, 2022).

FINDINGS AND DISCUSSIONS

The summary of the Interviews is shown in Table 1.

Table 1. Interview summary

Interviewee no, (Experience in years), Designation, Location	Main Comments on Key Drivers of Artificial Intelligence on Learner Experience (Other Interviewees agreeing to these comments)
1. (11) CEO, Banking Solutions company, Abu Dhabi	- Tailored content improves cognitive engagement and reduces frustration, boosting motivation and retention. - Personalized support fosters acceptance and satisfaction. - Intuitive interfaces enhance emotional and behavioral engagement. (Interviewees 3, 4, 8, 14) (Pinera, 2021)
2. (11), VP, Logistics in charge, Sharjah	- Personalized learning paths improve comprehension and retention. High-quality systems and user-friendly interfaces increase satisfaction, trust, and engagement. - Emotional intelligence supports positive engagement (Interviewees 3, 5, 7, 10, 13) (Lahiassi et al., 2024); (Sandhu et al., 2024).
3. (9) Head of University Administration, Abu Dubai	- Secure data handling, supportive policies, and management commitment enhance satisfaction and trust. - Personalization, clear policies, and user-friendly interfaces boost engagement and motivation (Interviewees 4, 7, 11, 13), (Kılınç et al., 2024); (Santos, 2023).
4. (10) Media Head, MNC, Dubai	- Strong infrastructure and management support increase satisfaction and trust. - Proper resource allocation, adaptive technologies, and timely feedback enhance engagement, performance, and retention (Interviewees 2, 5, 8, 9, 13) (Manna et al., 2022)
5. (11) Vice President Environmental Group, Mumbai	- Effective assessment use, supportive policies, and resource allocation enhance performance and retention. - Transparent, ethical AI systems boost engagement and trust (Interviewees 1, 4, 7, 10, 12), (Huang et al., 2023); (Akinrinola et al., 2024); (Saaida, 2023).
6. General Manager, Mall Administration, Dubai	- Management support and timely feedback increase acceptance and engagement. - Adaptive technologies and real-time feedback boost performance and satisfaction (Interviewees 3, 5, 12, 13) (Molefi et al., 2024); (Markauskaite et al., 2022); (Vattøy et al., 2021).
7. (8), CFO, Energy Private Sector, Abu Dhabi	- Metacognitive support and continuous monitoring enhance engagement and performance. - Transparent, fair, and ethical AI systems foster trust and positive engagement (Interviewee 2, 7,11, 14), (Sheffler et al., 2022); (Anwar et al., 2022); (Miao et al., 2021)
8. (12), HR Manager, Restaurant, Dubai	- AI tools improve engagement through autonomy, social interaction, and real-time feedback. Personalized content reduces dropout rates, and ethical AI use supports trust and acceptance (Interviewees 2, 3, 6, 7,11, 12, 13), (Marantika, 2021); (El-Sabagh, 2021); (Nguyen et al., 2023)
9. (9), CEO, HSE Company, RAK	- Timely, personalized feedback and metacognitive support improve engagement and retention. - Transparent, fair AI systems foster trust and satisfaction (Interviewees 1, 4, 6, 9,10, 12), (Williams, 2024); (Muijsenberg et al., 2023); (Balasubramaniam et al., 2023)

continued on following page

Table 1. Continued

Interviewee no, (Experience in years), Designation, Location	Main Comments on Key Drivers of Artificial Intelligence on Learner Experience (Other Interviewees agreeing to these comments)
10. (11), Senior Manager in Airport Administration, Sharjah	- Learning analytics and real-time feedback enhance engagement and performance. - Clear communication on data use and ethical practices fosters trust and satisfaction (Interviewee 2, 7,11, 14), (Alam, 2023); (Yousef et al., 2023); (Deeva et al., 2021)
11. (12), HR Manager, Restaurant, Dubai	- Providing metacognitive support fosters learner independence and acceptance. - Fairness in content and assessments promotes equal opportunities, reduces bias, and creates an inclusive environment that encourages active participation. - Timely, high-quality feedback and personalized insights significantly enhance student performance, retention, and commitment to their educational journey (Interviewees 1, 5, 7, 8, 10, 11); (Saxena et al., 2023).
12. (9), CEO, HSE Company, RAK	- Continuous, adaptive feedback boosts confidence, helps learners overcome challenges, and reduces dropout rates. - Ensuring fairness, transparency, and ethical considerations in AI systems promotes positive perceptions and high satisfaction levels by meeting individual learning styles and preferences (Interviewees 1, 3, 5, 7, 9, 12, 13); (Siddiqi, 2024)
13. (11), Senior Manager in Airport Administration, Sharjah	- Learning analytics enhances cognitive engagement by addressing specific learning needs, helping learners identify and close gaps. - Impartial AI leads to equitable assessments and personalized learning, improving student outcomes and increasing acceptance of AI technologies. - Immediate responses and tailored support increase motivation, emotional investment, and satisfaction. (Interviewee 1, 4, 7, 10, 11, 14); (Wu et al., 2023)
14. (12) General Manager, Oil and Gas Company, Oman	- Clear communication about data usage, privacy, and consent builds trust and fosters a positive learning experience. - User-friendly, adaptive systems keep learners cognitively stimulated, encouraging participation and sustained effort while providing real-time feedback that enhances overall learning effectiveness - Equitable access to learning resources through AI enhances cognitive engagement for all students, addressing diverse learning needs and contributing to overall success. (Interviewees 2, 5, 8,10,12); (Zhao et al., 2023)
15. (13) Consultant – Education Sector, Dubai	- Ethical use of learning analytics is vital for maintaining trust and satisfaction, as these systems tailor content and pacing to individual needs, making learning more relevant and engaging. - Transparent, unbiased AI algorithms ensure equitable treatment while safeguarding learner data contributes to positive perceptions. - Robust infrastructure minimizes disruptions and enhances engagement, while open communication about system operations builds trust (Interviewees 3, 9,11, 14); (Udeozor et al., 2023)

Experts emphasize the importance of establishing Generative AI and planning for the future. AI technology is pivotal in fostering innovation, enhancing products and services, and optimizing operations. As a result, businesses must stay abreast of the latest technological developments and proactively explore new technologies to harness their benefits. However, it is equally important for the industry to remain vigilant about the ethical implications of technology use, ensuring alignment with core values. While technology presents numerous opportunities, thoughtful implementation is crucial to address potential risks and impacts.

Demographic Profile

Table 2. Demographic profile

Age		
16-25 Years	18.71%	74
26-35 Years	35.91%	141
36-50 Years	21.73%	86
51-65 Years	13..88%	54
> 65 years	9.77%	40
Total	**100%**	**395**
Income Level		
< 6000 AED	37.34%	148
6001 – 11000 AED	32.80%	129
11001- 21000 AED	21.45%	84
> 21001 AED	8.41%	34
Total	**100%**	**395**

Gender		
Male	49.30%	195
Female	50.35%	198
Don't want to reveal	0.35%	2
Total	**100%**	**395**
Education Level		
Undergraduate	20.33%	80
Bachelors	37.40%	147
Masters	14.78%	58
Professional	11.14%	44
Doctorate	16.35%	66
Total	**100%**	**395**

Profession	
Self Employed	28
Trader	47
Salesman	43
Startup Entrepreneur	34
Housewife	134
Student	328
Teacher	298
Advertiser	65
Social Media User	324

QUANTITATIVE ANALYSIS USING ADANCO OUTPUT

In addition to utilizing the Dijkstra-Henseler's rho (ρA) coefficient and AVE values, the study incorporated discriminant validity analysis to ensure the distinctiveness of the constructs. The findings from this analysis indicated that the correlations within each construct were higher than those with other constructs, thereby confirming good discriminant validity. Furthermore, the study employed structural equation modeling (SEM), a well-established statistical technique, to test hypotheses and explore the relationships among the constructs. SEM's capability to handle complex models and examine multiple relationships simultaneously made it an appropriate and fruitful choice for this study, providing a comprehensive understanding of the connections between the constructs. In summary, the study implemented sound and established methods to assess construct validity, convergent validity, and discriminant validity. The use of SEM facilitated a thorough investigation into the relationships among the constructs, yielding valuable insights into the Big Data Model (Iyer et al., 2024).

Table 3. Analysis of measurement model

Latent Variables	Convergent Validity		Construct reliability	
	AVE >0.50	**ρA reliability >0.70**	**Pc reliability >0.70**	**Cronbach's alpha(α) >0.70**
Individual Factors	0.5267	0.7453	0.8067	0.8341
Technology Factors	0.5678	0.7257	0.7543	0.7659
Organization Factors	0.5621	0.7981	0.8543	0.7896
Ethical consideration Factors	0.6231	0.8125	0.8245	0.8125
Reflective Factors	0.6432	0.7765	0.7982	0.7651
Key Drivers of Artificial Intelligence on Learner Experience Factors	0.5129	0.8187	0.8432	0.8098

In PLS path modeling, determining construct validity often involves the use of indicator variables and their outer loading values. This approach is widely acknowledged and accepted within the field. Typically, a standardized outer loading value of 0.70 or higher is considered acceptable as an indication of a quality measure. This value signifies that the indicator variable effectively represents the construct being measured. To present the outer loading values for each indicator variable, Table 3 is employed in this study. This presentation method offers a clear and concise overview, which facilitates easy comprehension and interpretation of the data. It significantly contributes to the effectiveness of construct validity assessment. In general, the appropriate and successful application of indicator variables and their outer loading values is demonstrated in this study, as the results indicate that the indicator variables served as reliable measures for their respective constructs, surpassing the threshold of 0.7 (Sarstedt et al., 2023).

Table 4. Discriminant validity heterotrait-monotrait ratio

Construct	Individual Factors	Technology Factors	Organization Factors	Ethical consideration Factors	Reflective Factors	Key Drivers of Artificial Intelligence on Learner Experience Factors
Individual Factors						
Technology Factors	0.7411					
Organization Factors	0.6874	0.7653				
Ethical consideration Factors	0.6323	0.7547	0.7754			
Reflective Factors	0.6145	0.7234	0.7653	0.7964		
Key Drivers of Artificial Intelligence on Learner Experience Factors	0.6023	0.6876	0.7541	0.7765	0.8120	

All p-values indicating the validity of the relationships are well below the significance level of 0.05, providing strong support for the hypotheses. The results not only support but also validate all the hypotheses, as noted by Sarstedt et al. (2023).

Table 5. Discriminant validity

Construct	Individual Factors	Technology Factors	Organization Factors	Ethical consideration Factors	Reflective Factors	Key Drivers of Artificial Intelligence on Learner Experience Factors
Individual Factors	**0.5881**					
Technology Factors	0.5761	**0.6321**				
Organization Factors	0.5656	0.6134	**0.7765**			
Ethical consideration Factors	0.5460	0.5805	0.7213	**0.8118**		
Reflective Factors	0.5223	0.5563	0.7012	0.7543	**0.7753**	
Key Drivers of Artificial Intelligence on Learner Experience Factors	0.5120	0.5365	0.6876	0.7461	0.7611	**0.8478**

Source: ADANCO results, 2024

Table 5 presents the discriminant validity measures, assessing the degree of correlation between variables in the structural model. These measures are evaluated using the Fornell-Larcker criterion and cross-loadings. The diagonal bold figures in the table represent the highest values in both the rows and columns, providing strong evidence of discriminant validity. The analysis was conducted using ADANCO 2.3 output, as described by Sarstedt et al. (2023).

Table 6. Loadings of indicator loadings

Indicator	Individual Factors	Technology Factors	Organization Factors	Ethical consideration Factors	Reflective Factors	Key Drivers of Artificial Intelligence on Learner Experience Factors
(IF1)	0.7157					
(IF2)	0.7145					
(IF3)	0.6761					
(IF4)	0.7321					
(IF5)	0.7459					
(IF6)	0.7654					
(IF7)	0.7354					

continued on following page

Table 6. Continued

Indicator	Individual Factors	Technology Factors	Organization Factors	Ethical consideration Factors	Reflective Factors	Key Drivers of Artificial Intelligence on Learner Experience Factors
(TF1)		0.7276				
(TF2)		0.6943				
(TF3)		0.7321				
(TF4)		0.6897				
(TF5)		0.7349				
(TF6)		0.75654				
(OF1)			0.6760			
(OF2)			0.6698			
(OF3)			0.7123			
(OF4)			0.7564			
(OF5)			0.6389			
(OF6)			0.6865			
(OF7)			0.7065			
(ECF1)				0.7532		
(ECF2)				0.7457		
(ECF3)				0.7076		
(ECF4)				0.6761		
(ECF5)				0.6981		
(ECF6)				0.7213		
(ECF7)				0.7543		
(ECF8)				0.7765		
(RF1)					0.7348	
(RF2)					0.7478	
(RF3)					0.7432	
(RF4)					0.6654	
(RF5)					0.7321	
(RF6)					0.7097	
(RF7)					0.6789	
(KDAILE1)						0.7321
(KDAILE2)						0.7653
(KDAILE3)						0.7324
(KDAILE4)						0.6565
(KDAILE5)						0.7634
(KDAILE6)						0.7611
(KDAILE7)						0.7093

Table 7 displays the cross-loadings to examine the impact of variables on each other. The coefficient of determination (R^2) explains the relationship between the construct and all the constructs in the research study. The minimum requirement for R^2 was 0.25, indicating that a construct is relevant and significant if its R^2 value exceeds this threshold (Guenther et al., 2023). Based on the results, the R^2 value for the Resilient Supply Chain was 0.704, demonstrating that the construct is relevant, significant, and highly explanatory of all the variables in the research.

Table 7. R- squared

Construct	Coefficient of determination (R^2)	Adjusted R^2
Individual Factors	0.432	0.405
Technology Factors	0.00	0.00
Organization Factors	0.324	0.289
Ethical consideration Factors	0.378	0.343
Reflective Factors	0.563	0.537
Key Drivers of Artificial Intelligence on Learner Experience Factors	0.704	0.687

Figure 2 shows the PLS-SEM Validation framework given by the ADANCO software.

Figure 2. PLS-SEM validation framework

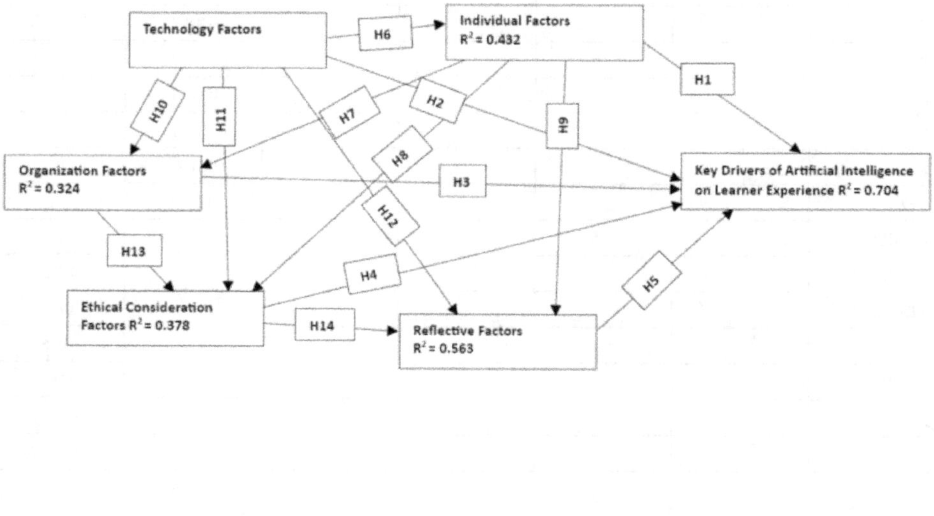

So, the above research framework was developed and tested for validity and reliability using PLS-SEM has been a useful contribution to this research paper and getting a consensus of 395 respondents- stakeholders of the Education sector. The methodology followed goes a long way in addressing the scarcity of relevant data for future researchers and lays the path for further research by developing this model or similar models. The above-cited theories have their importance in a particular situation in stable economies, equal education opportunities, and infrastructure availability. However, in recession, COVID, and sanction regimes, these above theories seem lacking to explain many factors. Hence some concrete, sound research-based framework has been developed to contribute to further work (Sarstedt et al., 2023).

Table 8. Direct relationships

Hypotheses no	**Construe Description**	**β-value**	**t-value**	**p-value**	**Significance t ≥2.59 1.96 ≤ t ≤2.59**	**Hypotheses Supported or not supported**
H1	Individual Factors -> Key Drivers of Artificial Intelligence on Learner Experience Factors	0.311	5.564	0.001	Strong	Yes
H2	Technology Factors -> Key Drivers of Artificial Intelligence on Learner Experience Factors	0.456	5.431	0.000	Strong	Yes
H3	Organization Factors -> Key Drivers of Artificial Intelligence on Learner Experience Factors	0.543	7.843	0.000	Strong	Yes
H4	Ethical Consideration Factors -> Key Drivers of Artificial Intelligence on Learner Experience Factors	0.389	13.245	0.001	Strong	Yes
H5	Reflective Factors -> Key Drivers of Artificial Intelligence on Learner Experience Factors	0.419	14.872	0.000	Strong	Yes

Table 9. Indirect relationships

Hypotheses No	Construe Description	β-value	t-value	p-value	Significance t ≥1.96	Hypotheses Supported or not supported
H61	Technology Factors -> Key Drivers of Artificial Intelligence on Learner Experience Factors through Individual Factors	0.067	4.987	0.001	Strong	Yes
H73	Individual Factors -> Key Drivers of Artificial Intelligence on Learner Experience Factors through Organization Factors	0.074	6.232	0.000	Strong	Yes
H84	Individual Factors -> Key Drivers of Artificial Intelligence on Learner Experience Factors through Ethical Consideration Factors	0.186	6.576	0.000	Strong	Yes
H95	Individual Factors -> Key Drivers of Artificial Intelligence on Learner Experience Factors through Reflective Factors	0.171	5.677	0.001	Strong	Yes
H103	Technology Factors -> Key Drivers of Artificial Intelligence on Learner Experience Factors through Organization Factors	0.076	8.563	0.000	Strong	Yes
H114	Technology Factors -> Key Drivers of Artificial Intelligence on Learner Experience Factors through Ethical Consideration Factors	0.182	7.568	0.001	Strong	Yes
H125	Technology Factors -> Key Drivers of Artificial Intelligence on Learner Experience Factors through Reflective Factors	0.098	4.875	0.000	Strong	Yes
H134	Organization Factors -> Key Drivers of Artificial Intelligence on Learner Experience Factors through Ethical Consideration Factors	0.082	6.587	0.000	Strong	Yes
H145	Ethical Consideration Factors -> Key Drivers of Artificial Intelligence on Learner Experience Factors through Reflective Factors	0.176	5.776	0.001	Strong	Yes

The third-level relationships are not relevant as the β value tends to be below the 0.01 levels hence not considered for this study (Sarstedt et al., 2023). The hypotheses are well supported by both methodologies so; it is validated, and reliability tested to a greater extent (Cheung et al., 2023)

Hypotheses

H1: Individual Factors -> Key Drivers of Artificial Intelligence on Learner Experience Factors (H1), $\beta_{IF-KDAILE}$ = 0.311, t=5.564, indicates a Strong relationship. The significant influence of technology factors such as ease of usage, system quality, user interface (UI) design, content quality, data management, and personalization capabilities on the key drivers of AI on learner experience is well-supported by the study's objectives. These objectives include analyzing the impact of AI-driven interactive personalized learning systems on cognitive, emotional, and behavioral engagement; assessing how adaptive learning technologies affect student performance and retention; evaluating the role of AI-powered real-time feedback and support in enhancing learner satisfaction and engagement; and identifying challenges and ethical considerations in the implementation of AI in education. By examining how these technological attributes enhance or hinder the learning experience, the study offers a comprehensive understanding of how well-designed and effectively managed AI systems can optimize learner outcomes, foster trust and acceptance, and address ethical concerns, thereby ensuring holistic improvements in educational practices.

H2: Technology Factors -> Key Drivers of Artificial Intelligence on Learner Experience Factors (H2), $\beta_{TF-KDAILE}$ = 0.456, t=6.431, indicates a Strong relationship. The effective influence of technology factors such as ease of usage, system quality, user interface (UI) design, content quality, data management, and personalization capabilities on the key drivers of AI on learner experience is significantly supported by the research objectives. User-friendly interfaces and high system quality ensure that learners can interact with AI-driven personalized learning systems effortlessly, enhancing cognitive, emotional, and behavioral engagement; superior content quality and data management facilitate accurate and adaptive learning, positively impacting student performance and retention rates; robust personalization capabilities cater to individual learner needs, driving satisfaction and trust in AI systems; and ethical considerations, addressed through these technological factors, foster acceptance and responsible use of AI in education. Together, these elements create a cohesive framework where AI can be maximally leveraged to improve educational outcomes, align with learner preferences, and maintain ethical standards, thereby achieving the research objectives.

H3: Organization Factors -> Key Drivers of Artificial Intelligence on Learner Experience Factors (H3), $\beta_{OF-KDAILE}$ = 0.543, t=7.843, indicates a Strong relationship. The hypothesis that organizational factors such as assessment scores, policy culture, government directives, management support, infrastructure, and resource allocation significantly influence the key drivers of AI on learner experience—including cognitive, emotional, and behavioral engagement, student performance, retention rates, learner satisfaction, learner trust, acceptance of AI systems, and ethical perceptions—is well-supported by the study's objectives. These objectives include analyzing the impact of AI-driven interactive personalized learning systems on cognitive, emotional, and behavioral engagement; assessing the influence of adaptive learning technologies on student performance and retention; evaluating the role of AI-powered real-time feedback and support in enhancing learner satisfaction and engagement; and identifying challenges and ethical considerations in the implementation of AI in education. By examining how these organizational factors support or hinder the deployment and effectiveness of AI applications in educational settings, the study provides a comprehensive understanding of how robust policies, adequate infrastructure, strong management support, and strategic resource allocation can optimize AI-driven educational outcomes, enhance learner trust and satisfaction, and ensure ethical use of AI in educational practices.

H4: Ethical Consideration Factors -> Key Drivers of Artificial Intelligence on Learner Experience Factors (H4), $\beta_{ECF\text{-}KDAILE}$ = 0.389, t=13.245, indicates a Strong relationship. The hypothesis that ethical consideration factors such as algorithmic transparency, bias mitigation, fairness, accountability, confidentiality of data, ethical usage, inclusive design, consent, and opt-out options significantly influence the key drivers of AI on learner experience—including cognitive, emotional, and behavioral engagement, student performance, retention rates, learner satisfaction, learner trust, acceptance of AI systems, and ethical perceptions—is well-supported by the study's objectives. These objectives aim to analyze the impact of AI-driven interactive personalized learning systems on the cognitive, emotional, and behavioral engagement of learners; assess how adaptive learning technologies impact student performance and retention; evaluate the role of AI-powered real-time feedback and support in enhancing learner satisfaction and engagement; and identify challenges and ethical considerations in the implementation of AI in education. By examining how these ethical factors ensure transparency, mitigate biases, uphold fairness, and protect data confidentiality while promoting ethical usage and inclusive design in AI applications, the study provides a comprehensive framework for understanding how ethical practices in AI can enhance learner trust, acceptance, satisfaction, and overall educational outcomes.

H5: Reflective Factors -> Key Drivers of Artificial Intelligence on Learner Experience Factors (H5), $\beta_{RF\text{-}KDAILE}$ = 0.419, t=14.872, indicates a Strong relationship. The hypothesis that reflective factors such as feedback and support mechanisms, timeliness and quality of feedback, self-assessment tools, peer interaction and collaboration, metacognitive support, learning analytics, and insights significantly influence the key drivers of AI on learner experience—including cognitive, emotional, and behavioral engagement, student performance, retention rates, learner satisfaction, learner trust, acceptance of AI systems, and ethical perceptions—is strongly supported by the study's objectives. These objectives aim to analyze the impact of AI-driven interactive personalized learning systems on cognitive, emotional, and behavioral engagement; assess the influence of adaptive learning technologies on student performance and retention; evaluate how AI-powered real-time feedback and support enhance learner satisfaction and engagement; and identify challenges and ethical considerations in AI implementation in education. By examining how these reflective factors enhance feedback efficacy, promote collaborative learning environments, support metacognitive development, and utilize learning analytics to provide actionable insights, the study contributes to a deeper understanding of how AI can optimize educational outcomes, foster learner trust, and satisfaction, and address ethical concerns in educational settings.

Research Objectives Met

The research study successfully addressed its objectives through a comprehensive analysis of AI-powered personalized learning systems. First, the examination of how these systems impact learner engagement revealed significant enhancements across cognitive, emotional, and behavioral dimensions. Participants reported increased motivation and active participation due to tailored learning experiences that aligned with their individual needs. The personalized nature of the content provided by AI systems not only captivated students' interest but also encouraged deeper intellectual engagement, thereby fostering a more dynamic learning environment. Additionally, the study analyzed the effect of adaptive learning technologies on student performance and retention. The findings indicated a positive correlation between the use of these technologies and improved academic outcomes. Students benefited from customized content that matched their learning pace and style, which facilitated a deeper understanding of the material. This adaptive approach not only helped learners grasp complex concepts more effectively but also contributed to higher retention rates, demonstrating the potential of AI to enhance educational effectiveness.

The evaluation of AI-facilitated real-time feedback and support further illustrated the study's objectives. Results showed a marked increase in learner satisfaction and engagement as students received instant feedback that provided timely insights and support. This immediate response mechanism enabled learners to identify and address their learning gaps effectively, contributing to higher retention levels and a more fulfilling educational experience. The sense of support and guidance offered by real-time feedback systems was a crucial factor in maintaining student motivation and commitment to their studies. Lastly, the research identified several challenges and ethical issues involved in implementing AI in education. Concerns about data privacy, algorithmic bias, and the need for transparency in AI systems emerged as significant obstacles. These findings underscored the importance of ensuring ethical practices in AI applications to foster trust among users. By addressing these ethical considerations, educational institutions can maximize the benefits of AI technologies while safeguarding the interests and rights of learners. Overall, the study provided valuable insights into the transformative role of AI in education, highlighting both its potential benefits and the challenges that must be navigated for effective implementation.

RECOMMENDATIONS AND FUTURE RESEARCH DIRECTIONS

AI's ability to personalize learning paths is particularly transformative for students. Personalized learning caters to individual needs by identifying strengths and weaknesses, providing targeted resources, and adapting to learning paces. This personalized approach not only enhances engagement but also improves learning outcomes, as students receive tailored support that addresses their specific challenges. Furthermore, AI-driven adaptive assessments play a crucial role in enhancing the learner's experience. These assessments dynamically adjust to student performance, offering immediate feedback and targeted interventions. This real-time adaptability helps students understand their progress and areas for improvement, fostering a more effective and engaging learning process. AI's ability to automate routine administrative tasks, such as grading and attendance tracking, significantly reduces the workload for educators, allowing them to focus more on teaching and direct student interaction. AI also promotes improved accessibility in education. Assistive technologies powered by AI, such as speech-to-text and text-to-speech tools, support students with disabilities, ensuring they have access to the same educational opportunities as their peers. Additionally, AI-driven virtual assistants provide 24/7 learning support, answering queries, and guiding students through their learning journeys outside of regular classroom hours. This constant availability of support helps students overcome challenges promptly, further enhancing their learning experience.

From a managerial perspective, the integration of AI in education necessitates strategic planning and policy formulation. AI provides actionable insights through data analytics, enabling educational leaders to make informed decisions regarding curriculum design, resource allocation, and student support services. For instance, predictive analytics can identify students at risk of falling behind, allowing for timely interventions that can prevent dropout and improve retention rates. Training and development of staff are essential for the successful implementation of AI in educational institutions. Educators and administrative staff need to be proficient in using AI tools to maximize their benefits. Continuous professional development programs are crucial to keep staff updated on the latest AI advancements and their applications in education. This ongoing training ensures that the potential of AI is fully realized, leading to improved teaching and administrative efficiency. Organizational culture and change management are also critical factors in the successful adoption of AI. Promoting a culture that embraces technological advancements and AI integration is essential for gaining acceptance and support from all stakeholders. Effective change management strategies are needed to address resistance and ensure a smooth transition to AI-driven processes. This includes clear communication of the benefits and addressing any concerns related to job displacement or changes in work practices.

The social implications of AI in education are profound and multifaceted. AI has the potential to bridge educational gaps by providing quality educational resources to underserved communities and promoting equity and inclusivity. By democratizing access to education, AI can help level the playing field, ensuring that all students, regardless of their background, have the opportunity to succeed. However, the integration of AI also raises ethical considerations, particularly regarding data privacy and algorithmic accountability. Protecting student data privacy is paramount, and ethical guidelines must be established to govern data collection, storage, and usage. Ensuring transparency and accountability in AI algorithms is essential to build trust among students, parents, and educators. This involves regular audits and assessments of AI systems to detect and mitigate biases that could lead to unfair educational outcomes. Furthermore, AI can play a significant role in preparing students for the future workforce. By developing critical 21st-century skills such as problem-solving, critical thinking, and digital literacy, AI equips students with the tools needed for future job markets. AI-driven personalized learning encourages lifelong learning habits, enabling individuals to continuously update their skills and knowledge, which is crucial in a rapidly changing world.

One significant constraint is the generalizability of findings. The impact of AI on learner experience may vary widely across different educational contexts, including primary, secondary, and higher education, as well as across diverse cultural and socio-economic backgrounds. The specific cohort used in the study may not fully represent these varied contexts, potentially limiting the applicability of the findings to broader educational settings. Another limitation is the rapidly evolving nature of AI technology. As AI tools and applications are continuously being developed and improved, the study's findings may quickly become outdated. This presents a challenge in ensuring that the research remains relevant and reflective of the current state of AI in education. Additionally, the study's focus on six months may not capture the long-term effects and sustainability of AI interventions on learner experience, performance, and engagement. The research also faces challenges related to ethical and privacy concerns. While the study aims to explore the positive impacts of AI, it must also acknowledge the potential risks, including data privacy issues and algorithmic bias. These ethical considerations can affect the implementation and acceptance of AI in educational settings and addressing them comprehensively within the study's scope is difficult.

Future research should aim to address these limitations and expand the understanding of AI's impact on learner experience. Longitudinal studies are needed to examine the long-term effects of AI on learner outcomes. Such studies would provide valuable insights into how AI-driven educational interventions influence student performance, retention, and satisfaction over extended periods. Understanding these long-term impacts can help in designing sustainable AI integration strategies in education. Additionally, future research should explore the variability of AI's impact across different educational contexts. Comparative studies across various educational levels, cultural settings, and socio-economic backgrounds can offer a more comprehensive understanding of how AI influences learner experience in diverse environments. This can help in developing tailored AI solutions that address specific needs and challenges in different educational contexts. To stay relevant in the face of rapidly evolving technology, future research should adopt a dynamic and adaptive approach. This includes continuously monitoring and evaluating new AI tools and applications as they emerge. Collaborative efforts between researchers, educators, and AI developers can facilitate the timely integration of cutting-edge AI technologies into educational research. Ethical considerations must remain a central focus in future research. Studies should investigate strategies for mitigating data privacy concerns and algorithmic biases. This involves developing robust frameworks for ethical AI use in education, ensuring transparency, accountability, and fairness in AI-driven educational interventions. Researchers should also explore the effectiveness of policy measures and guidelines designed to safeguard student data and promote ethical AI practices. Another promising area for future research is the examination of AI's role in fostering skills for the future workforce. Investigating how AI can enhance the development of critical skills such as problem-solving, critical thinking, and digital literacy can provide valuable insights for educators and policymakers. Research should also explore the potential of AI-driven personalized learning to promote lifelong learning habits and continuous skill development. Finally, interdisciplinary research collaborations are essential for advancing the understanding of AI's impact on learner experience. Engaging experts from education, technology, ethics, and policy can lead to more holistic and comprehensive insights. Such collaborations can help in designing AI systems that are not only effective but also aligned with educational goals and societal values.

The primary contribution lies in its comprehensive framework for understanding the multifaceted impacts of AI on learner experience. By examining individual, technological, organizational, ethical, and reflective factors, this research provides a holistic view of how AI influences various aspects of the educational process, from cognitive and emotional engagement to student performance and ethical perceptions. Another original aspect of this research is its focus on mixed methodology. By utilizing both qualitative and quantitative methods over a reasonable period, the study captures a more nuanced understanding of AI's effects on learner experience. This methodological rigor allows for a richer, more detailed analysis that can identify both immediate and longer-term impacts, setting a precedent for future research in this domain. The research also contributes by identifying specific individual factors (such as learning style, motivation, and emotional intelligence) and technology factors (such as system quality and personalization capabilities) that significantly influence the effectiveness of AI in educational settings. This granular level of analysis provides valuable insights for educators and technology developers, helping them to design and implement AI-driven tools that are tailored to meet diverse student needs and enhance learning outcomes. Furthermore, the study's exploration of ethical considerations in AI applications in education is particularly original and timely. By addressing issues like algorithmic transparency, bias mitigation, and data confidentiality, the research highlights the importance of ethical AI use and provides a framework for developing guidelines and policies that ensure fair and responsible AI implementation. This focus on ethics adds a critical dimension to the discourse on AI in education, emphasizing the need to balance innovation with ethical responsibility.

The value of this research is multifaceted, benefiting various stakeholders including educators, policymakers, technology developers, and students. One of the key values lies in its practical implications for educators and institutions. By providing detailed insights into how AI can be leveraged to enhance personalized learning, adaptive assessments, and overall learner engagement, the research offers actionable recommendations that can be implemented to improve educational practices and outcomes. For policymakers, the study provides a data-driven foundation for developing policies and frameworks that support the ethical and effective use of AI in education. The research's findings on the importance of transparency, accountability, and fairness in AI applications can inform the creation of regulations and guidelines that protect student data privacy and promote equitable access to AI-driven educational tools. Technology developers can also derive significant value from this research. By identifying key factors that influence the success of AI in education, the study offers valuable insights for designing user-friendly, high-quality AI systems that cater to the diverse needs of learners. The emphasis on personalization capabilities and adaptive learning environments can guide developers in creating more effective and engaging AI-driven educational tools. Students stand to benefit the most from the findings of this research. By highlighting the positive impacts of AI on personalized learning, cognitive and emotional engagement, and learning outcomes, the study underscores the potential of AI to transform the learning experience. The focus on ethical considerations also ensures that the benefits of AI are realized fairly and responsibly, fostering a safe and supportive learning environment for all students.

CONCLUSION

This chapter provides a comprehensive and nuanced understanding of AI's multifaceted impact on education by examining individual characteristics, technological aspects, organizational dynamics, ethical considerations, and reflective practices. Utilizing a mixed-methodology and cross-sectional sampling of 395 stakeholders, the study captures both immediate and sustained effects of AI-driven interventions on learner experience. It achieves its objectives by identifying how personal attributes influence engagement, highlighting the technological features that enhance learner satisfaction and performance, assessing organizational factors that facilitate AI implementation, emphasizing the need for ethical frameworks to ensure responsible AI use, and exploring reflective practices that enhance engagement and satisfaction. The findings offer actionable insights and practical recommendations for educators, policymakers, technology developers, and students, providing strategies for personalized learning, data-driven policy development, effective AI tool creation, and supportive learning environments. This chapter also suggests future research directions, including longitudinal studies, comparative analyses, and continuous monitoring of emerging AI technologies, with a focus on robust ethical frameworks. Ultimately, this research advances academic discourse on AI in education and provides a practical roadmap for its responsible and effective integration, benefiting all stakeholders involved.

REFERENCES

Afzaal, M., Zia, A., Nouri, J., & Fors, U. (2024). Informative feedback and explainable AI-based recommendations to support students' self-regulation. *Technology. Knowledge and Learning*, 29(1), 331–354. DOI: 10.1007/s10758-023-09650-0

Aggarwal, D. (2023). Integration of innovative technological developments and AI with education for an adaptive learning pedagogy. *China Petroleum Processing and Petrochemical Technology*, 23(2), 709–714. https://zgsyjgysyhgjs.cn/index.php/reric/article/pdf/02-709.pdf

Akinrinola, O., Okoye, C. C., Ofodile, O. C., & Ugochukwu, C. E. (2024). Navigating and reviewing ethical dilemmas in AI development: Strategies for transparency, fairness, and accountability. *GSC Advanced Research and Reviews, 18*(3), 050-058. DOI: DOI: 10.30574/gscarr.2024.18.3.0088

Alam, A. (2023). Harnessing the Power of AI to Create Intelligent Tutoring Systems for Enhanced Classroom Experience and Improved Learning Outcomes. In Rajakumar, G., Du, K. L., & Rocha, Á. (Eds.), *Intelligent Communication Technologies and Virtual Mobile Networks* (pp. 571–591). Springer Nature Singapore., DOI: 10.1007/978-981-99-1767-9_42

Alqahtani, T., Badreldin, H. A., Alrashed, M., Alshaya, A. I., Alghamdi, S. S., bin Saleh, K., Alowais, S. A., Alshaya, O. A., Rahman, I., Al Yami, M. S., & Albekairy, A. M. (2023). The emergent role of artificial intelligence, natural learning processing, and large language models in higher education and research. *Research in Social & Administrative Pharmacy*, 19(8), 1236–1242. DOI: 10.1016/j.sapharm.2023.05.016 PMID: 37321925

Anwar, A., Haq, I. U., Mian, I. A., Shah, F., Alroobaea, R., Hussain, S., & Umar, F. (2022). Applying Real-Time Dynamic Scaffolding Techniques during Tutoring Sessions Using Intelligent Tutoring Systems. *Mobile Information Systems*, 2022(1), 6006467. DOI: 10.1155/2022/6006467

Balasubramaniam, N., Kauppinen, M., Rannisto, A., Hiekkanen, K., & Kujala, S. (2023). Transparency and explainability of AI systems: From ethical guidelines to requirements. *Information and Software Technology*, 159, 107197. DOI: 10.1016/j.infsof.2023.107197

Chaika, O. (2023). The role of artificial intelligence in higher education. *Молодь і ринок*, (6/214), 69-74. DOI: DOI: 10.24919/2308-4634.2023.287898

Cheung, G. W., Cooper-Thomas, H. D., Lau, R. S., & Wang, L. C. (2023). Reporting reliability, convergent and discriminant validity with structural equation modeling: A review and best-practice recommendations. *Asia Pacific Journal of Management*, •••, 1–39. DOI: 10.1007/s10490-023-09871-y

Deeva, G., Bogdanova, D., Serral, E., Snoeck, M., & De Weerdt, J. (2021). A review of automated feedback systems for learners: Classification framework, challenges and opportunities. *Computers & Education*, 162, 104094. DOI: 10.1016/j.compedu.2020.104094

Díaz-Rodríguez, N., Del Ser, J., Coeckelbergh, M., de Prado, M. L., Herrera-Viedma, E., & Herrera, F. (2023). Connecting the dots in trustworthy Artificial Intelligence: From AI principles, ethics, and key requirements to responsible AI systems and regulation. *Information Fusion*, 99, 101896. DOI: 10.1016/j.inffus.2023.101896

El-Sabagh, H. A. (2021). Adaptive e-learning environment based on learning styles and its impact on development students' engagement. *International Journal of Educational Technology in Higher Education*, 18(1), 53. DOI: 10.1186/s41239-021-00289-4

Faccia, A., Ridon, M., & Cavaliere, L. P. L. (2024). The AI Application for an Automated Education System. In *Innovation in the University 4.0 System based on Smart Technologies* (pp. 176–199). Chapman and Hall/CRC. DOI: 10.1201/9781003425809-12

Farahani, M. S., & Ghasemi, G. (2024). Artificial intelligence and inequality: challenges and opportunities. *Qeios, 7*, 1-14. https://radensa.ru/wp-content/uploads/2024/05/Artificial_Intelligence_and_Inequality_Challenges_.pdf

Ferrara, E. (2023). Fairness and bias in artificial intelligence: A brief survey of sources, impacts, and mitigation strategies. *Sci*, 6(1), 3. DOI: 10.3390/sci6010003

George, B., & Wooden, O. (2023). Managing the strategic transformation of higher education through artificial intelligence. *Administrative Sciences*, 13(9), 196. DOI: 10.3390/admsci13090196

Graf, A. (2023). Exploring the role of personalization in adaptive learning environments. *International Journal Software Engineering and Computer Science (IJSECS), 3*(2), 50-56. https://journal.lembagakita.org/ijsecs/article/view/1200

Guenther, P., Guenther, M., Ringle, C. M., Zaefarian, G., & Cartwright, S. (2023). Improving PLS-SEM use for business marketing research. *Industrial Marketing Management*, 111, 127–142. DOI: 10.1016/j.indmarman.2023.03.010

Hassija, V., Chamola, V., Mahapatra, A., Singal, A., Goel, D., Huang, K., & Hussain, A. (2024). Interpreting black-box models: a review on explainable artificial intelligence. *Cognitive Computation, 16*(1), 45-74. https://doi.org/DOI: 10.1007/s12559-023-10179-8

Huang, A. Y., Lu, O. H., & Yang, S. J. (2023). Effects of artificial Intelligence–Enabled personalized recommendations on learners' learning engagement, motivation, and outcomes in a flipped classroom. *Computers & Education*, 194, 104684. DOI: 10.1016/j.compedu.2022.104684

Iyer, S. S. (2022). Application of Digital Technologies Integrated Blockchain with Emerging Technologies. In *Handbook of Research on Supply Chain Resiliency, Efficiency, and Visibility in the Post-Pandemic Era* (pp 267-294). IGI Global. DOI: DOI: 10.4018/978-1-7998-9506-0.ch014

Iyer, S. S., Malhotra, S., Reyes, F. E.Jr, Subramanian, R., Singh, R., & Anwar, S. (2024). Strategy For Business Recovery In Novo Cinemas. *Educational Administration: Theory and Practice*, 30(4), 7923–7942. DOI: 10.53555/kuey.v30i4.1621

Jaiswal, A., & Arun, C. J. (2021). Potential of Artificial Intelligence for transformation of the education system in India. *International Journal of Education and Development Using Information and Communication Technology*, 17(1), 142–158. https://eric.ed.gov/?id=EJ1285526

Kamalov, F., Santandreu Calonge, D., & Gurrib, I. (2023). New era of artificial intelligence in education: Towards a sustainable multifaceted revolution. *Sustainability (Basel)*, 15(16), 12451. DOI: 10.3390/su151612451

Kaswan, K. S., Dhatterwal, J. S., & Ojha, R. P. (2024). AI in personalized learning. In *Advances in Technological Innovations in Higher Education* (pp. 103–117). CRC Press. DOI: 10.1201/9781003376699-9

Kılınç, A. Ç., Polatcan, M., Savaş, G., & Er, E. (2024). How transformational leadership influences teachers' commitment and innovative practices: Understanding the moderating role of trust in principal. *Educational Management Administration & Leadership*, 52(2), 455–474. DOI: 10.1177/17411432221082803

Lahiassi, J., Elwarraki, O., Aammou, S., & Jdidou, Y. (2024). Pedagogical Innovations in Personalized Learning. In *Fostering Pedagogical Innovation Through Effective Instructional Design* (pp. 329–341). IGI Global., DOI: 10.4018/979-8-3693-1206-3.ch015

Li, F., He, Y., & Xue, Q. (2021). Progress, challenges and countermeasures of adaptive learning. *Journal of Educational Technology & Society*, 24(3), 238–255. https://www.jstor.org/stable/27032868

Luckin, R., Cukurova, M., Kent, C., & Du Boulay, B. (2022). Empowering educators to be AI-ready. *Computers and Education: Artificial Intelligence*, 3, 100076. DOI: 10.1016/j.caeai.2022.100076

Manna, M. S., Balusamy, B., Sood, K., Chilamkurti, N., & George, I. R. (Eds.). (2022). Edutech Enabled Teaching: Challenges and Opportunities. DOI:DOI: 10.1201/9781003254942

Marantika, J. E. R. (2021). Metacognitive ability and autonomous learning strategy in improving learning outcomes. [EduLearn]. *Journal of Education and Learning*, 15(1), 88–96. https://eric.ed.gov/?id=EJ1299455

Markauskaite, L., Marrone, R., Poquet, O., Knight, S., Martinez-Maldonado, R., Howard, S., & Siemens, G. (2022). Rethinking the entwinement between artificial intelligence and human learning: What capabilities do learners need for a world with AI? *Computers and Education: Artificial Intelligence*, 3, 100056. DOI: 10.1016/j.caeai.2022.100056

Miao, F., Holmes, W., Huang, R., & Zhang, H. (2021). *AI and education: A guidance for policymakers*. Unesco Publishing.

Modi, T. B. (2023). Artificial Intelligence Ethics and Fairness: A study to address bias and fairness issues in AI systems, and the ethical implications of AI applications. *Revista Review Index Journal of Multidisciplinary*, 3(2), 24–35. DOI: 10.31305/rrijm2023.v03.n02.004

Molefi, R. R., Ayanwale, M. A., Kurata, L., & Chere-Masopha, J. (2024). Do in-service teachers accept artificial intelligence-driven technology? The mediating role of school support and resources. *Computers and Education Open*, 6, 100191. DOI: 10.1016/j.caeo.2024.100191

Mosleh, S. M., Alsaadi, F. A., Alnaqbi, F. K., Alkhzaimi, M. A., Alnaqbi, S. W., & Alsereidi, W. M. (2024). Examining the association between emotional intelligence and chatbot utilization in education: A cross-sectional examination of undergraduate students in the UAE. *Heliyon*, 10(11), e31952. Advance online publication. DOI: 10.1016/j.heliyon.2024.e31952 PMID: 38868023

Muijsenberg, A. J., Houben-Wilke, S., Zeng, Y., Spruit, M. A., & Janssen, D. J. (2023). Methods to assess adults' learning styles and factors affecting learning in health education: A scoping review. *Patient Education and Counseling*, 107, 107588. DOI: 10.1016/j.pec.2022.107588 PMID: 36502561

Nakashima, H. H., Mantovani, D., & Machado, C.Junior. (2024). Users' trust in black-box machine learning algorithms. *Revista de Gestão*, 31(2), 237–250. DOI: 10.1108/REGE-06-2022-0100

Naseer, F., Khalid, M. U., Ayub, N., Rasool, A., Abbas, T., & Afzal, M. W. (2024). Automated Assessment and Feedback in Higher Education Using Generative AI. In *Transforming Education With Generative AI: Prompt Engineering and Synthetic Content Creation* (pp. 433-461). IGI Global. DOI: DOI: 10.4018/979-8-3693-1351-0.ch021

Ng, D. T. K., Lee, M., Tan, R. J. Y., Hu, X., Downie, J. S., & Chu, S. K. W. (2023). A review of AI teaching and learning from 2000 to 2020. *Education and Information Technologies*, 28(7), 8445–8501 DOI: 10.1007/s10639-022-11491-w

Nguyen, A., Ngo, H. N., Hong, Y., Dang, B., & Nguyen, B. P. T. (2023). Ethical principles for artificial intelligence in education. *Education and Information Technologies*, 28(4), 4221–4241. DOI: 10.1007/s10639-022-11316-w PMID: 36254344

Novelli, C., Taddeo, M., & Floridi, L. (2023). Accountability in artificial intelligence: What it is and how it works. *AI & Society*, •••, 1–12. DOI: 10.1007/s00146-023-01635-y

Owan, V. J., Abang, K. B., Idika, D. O., Etta, E. O., & Bassey, B. A. (2023). Exploring the potential of artificial intelligence tools in educational measurement and assessment. *Eurasia Journal of Mathematics, Science and Technology Education*, 19(8), em2307. Advance online publication. DOI: 10.29333/ejmste/13428

Pinera, J. M. (2021). Adaptive Delivery as a Means to Increase Student Engagement and Learning Outcomes. https://digitalcommons.fiu.edu/etd/4727/

Rajest, S. S., Singh, B., Obaid, A. J., Regin, R., & Chinnusamy, K. (Eds.). (2023). *Advances in artificial and human intelligence in the modern era*. IGI Global., DOI: 10.4018/979-8-3693-1301-5

Rane, N., Choudhary, S., & Rane, J. (2023). Education 4.0 and 5.0: Integrating artificial intelligence (AI) for personalized and adaptive learning. *Available atSSRN* 4638365. DOI: 10.2139/ssrn.4638365

Saaida, M. B. (2023). AI-Driven transformations in higher education: Opportunities and challenges. *International Journal of Educational Research and Studies, 5*(1), 29-36. ISSN: 2664-6811

Sandhu, R., Channi, H. K., Ghai, D., Cheema, G. S., & Kaur, M. (2024). An Introduction to Generative AI Tools for Education 2030. *Integrating Generative AI in Education to Achieve Sustainable Development Goals*, 1-28. DOI: DOI: 10.4018/979-8-3693-2440-0.ch001

Santos, O. C. (2023). Beyond cognitive and affective issues: Designing smart learning environments for psychomotor personalized learning. In *Learning, Design, and Technology: An International Compendium of Theory, Research, Practice, and Policy* (pp. 3309–3332). Springer International Publishing., DOI: 10.1007/978-3-319-17461-7_8

Sarstedt, M., Hair, J. F.Jr, & Ringle, C. M. (2023). "PLS-SEM: Indeed a silver bullet"–retrospective observations and recent advances. *Journal of Marketing Theory and Practice*, 31(3), 261–275. DOI: 10.1080/10696679.2022.2056488

Saxena, A. K., García, V., Amin, M. R., Salazar, J. M. R., & Dey, S. (2023). Structure, Objectives, and Operational Framework for Ethical Integration of Artificial Intelligence in Educational. *Sage Science Review of Educational Technology, 6*(1), 88-100. https://journals.sagescience.org/index.php/ssret/article/view/139

Schwartz, R., Schwartz, R., Vassilev, A., Greene, K., Perine, L., Burt, A., & Hall, P. (2022). *Towards a standard for identifying and managing bias in artificial intelligence* (Vol. 3, p. 00). US Department of Commerce, National Institute of Standards and Technology.

Sethi, S. S., & Jain, K. (2024). AI technologies for social emotional learning: recent research and future directions. *Journal of Research in Innovative Teaching & Learning*. DOI: 10.1108/JRIT-03-2024-0073

Sheffler, P., Rodriguez, T. M., Cheung, C. S., & Wu, R. (2022). Cognitive and metacognitive, motivational, and resource considerations for learning new skills across the lifespan. *Wiley Interdisciplinary Reviews: Cognitive Science*, 13(2), e1585. DOI: 10.1002/wcs.1585 PMID: 34783458

Siddiqi, M. M. (2024). Future of Digital Education: Inclusive, Immersive, Equitable. *MediaSpace: DME Media Journal of Communication*, 5(01), 8–24. DOI: 10.53361/dmejc.v5i01.02

Slimi, Z., & Carballido, B. V. (2023). Navigating the Ethical Challenges of Artificial Intelligence in Higher Education: An Analysis of Seven Global AI Ethics Policies. *TEM Journal, 12*(2). https://www.ceeol.com/search/article-detail?id=1122977

Srinivasa, K. G., Kurni, M., & Saritha, K. (2022). Harnessing the Power of AI to Education. In *Learning, teaching, and assessment methods for contemporary learners: pedagogy for the digital generation* (pp. 311–342). Springer Nature Singapore., DOI: 10.1007/978-981-19-6734-4_13

Udeozor, C., Chan, P., Russo Abegão, F., & Glassey, J. (2023). Game-based assessment framework for virtual reality, augmented reality and digital game-based learning. *International Journal of Educational Technology in Higher Education*, 20(1), 36. DOI: 10.1186/s41239-023-00405-6 PMID: 36644670

Udvaros, J., & Forman, N. (2023). Artificial intelligence and Education 4.0. In *INTED2023 proceedings* (pp. 6309-6317). IATED. DOI: 10.21125/inted.2023.1670

Umali, J. N. D. (2024). Artificial Intelligence Technology Management of Teachers, Learners Motivation and Challenges Encountered. [IJMCER]. *Educational Research*, 6(3), 821–880. https://www.ijmcer.com/wp-content/uploads/2024/06/IJMCER_MM0630821880.pdf

Vattøy, K. D., Gamlem, S. M., & Rogne, W. M. (2021). Examining students' feedback engagement and assessment experiences: A mixed study. *Studies in Higher Education*, 46(11), 2325–2337. DOI: 10.1080/03075079.2020.1723523

Wilkinson, S., Pullen, R., Rutledge, P., & Schmid, S. (2023). Digital Formative Assessments for Learning. DOI: 10.1039/9781839167942-00301

Williams, A. (2024). Delivering Effective Student Feedback in Higher Education: An Evaluation of the Challenges and Best Practice. *International Journal of Research in Education and Science*, 10(2), 473–501. https://eric.ed.gov/?id=EJ1426687. DOI: 10.46328/ijres.3404

Wu, Y., & Schunn, C. D. (2023). Passive, active, and constructive engagement with peer feedback: A revised model of learning from peer feedback. *Contemporary Educational Psychology*, 73, 102160. DOI: 10.1016/j.cedpsych.2023.102160

Yousef, A. M. F., & Khatiry, A. R. (2023). Cognitive versus behavioral learning analytics dashboards for supporting learner's awareness, reflection, and learning process. *Interactive Learning Environments*, 31(9), 5460–5476. DOI: 10.1080/10494820.2021.2009881

Zhao, F., Liu, G. Z., Zhou, J., & Yin, C. (2023). A learning analytics framework based on human-centered artificial intelligence for identifying the optimal learning strategy to intervene in learning behavior. *Journal of Educational Technology & Society*, 26(1), 132–146. https://www.jstor.org/stable/48707972

ADDITIONAL READING

Ayanwale, M. A., Frimpong, E. K., Opesemowo, O. A. G., & Sanusi, I. T. (2024). Exploring Factors That Support Pre-service Teachers' Engagement in Learning Artificial Intelligence. *Journal for STEM Education Research*, •••, 1–31. DOI: 10.1007/s41979-024-00121-4

Castro, G. P. B., Chiappe, A., Rodríguez, D. F. B., & Sepulveda, F. G. (2024). Harnessing AI for Education 4.0: Drivers of Personalized Learning. *Electronic Journal of e-Learning, 22*(5), 01-14.

Iweuno, B. N., Orekha, P., Ojediran, O., Imohimi, E., & Adu-Twum, H. T. (2024). Leveraging Artificial Intelligence for an inclusive and diversified curriculum. *World Journal of Advanced Research and Reviews*, 23(2), 1579–1590. DOI: 10.30574/wjarr.2024.23.2.2440

Nguyen, A., Kremantzis, M., Essien, A., Petrounias, I., & Hosseini, S. (2024). Enhancing student engagement through artificial intelligence (AI): Understanding the basics, opportunities, and challenges. *Journal of University Teaching & Learning Practice*, 21(06). Advance online publication. DOI: 10.53761/caraaq92

KEY TERMS AND DEFINITIONS

Adaptive Learning Systems: AI-based platforms that adjust learning content and pathways based on individual student performance to optimize engagement and comprehension.

Algorithmic Transparency: The clarity and openness with which AI algorithms are designed and operate, allowing users to understand how decisions are made, fostering trust in educational settings.

Artificial Intelligence (AI): The use of computer systems to simulate human intelligence, enabling applications that support personalized learning, adaptive assessments, and automated feedback.

Behavioral Engagement: A learner's active participation in educational activities, influenced by AI tools that promote motivation through interactive content and real-time support.

Cognitive Engagement: The intellectual investment learners make in understanding concepts, which AI enhances by providing tailored content based on cognitive needs.

Emotional: Engagement: The affective aspect of learning that AI can influence by creating supportive and interactive learning environments, thereby enhancing motivation and satisfaction.

Learning Analytics: The collection and analysis of data on student behavior and performance to inform and personalize learning experiences through AI.

Personalized Learning: Tailoring educational content to individual learners' needs, preferences, and pace, which AI achieves by analyzing user data and providing targeted recommendations.

Reflective Feedback: Real-time AI-generated insights that allow students to evaluate and adjust their learning approaches, enhancing engagement and understanding.

Virtual Classroom: An online learning environment facilitated by AI technologies that enables interactive, collaborative, and flexible learning experiences across different locations.

Chapter 5
Exploring the Potentiality of Artificial Intelligence in the Higher Education System:
Perceptions of Undergraduate Students in West Bengal, India

Mazhar Shamsi Ansary
Netaji Nagar College for Women, India

Indrajit Mahato
https://orcid.org/0000-0003-3719-2627
Mahatma Gandhi College, India

Jayashree Mahanti
https://orcid.org/0000-0002-3083-7819
Central University of Jharkhand, India

Nupur Gorai
https://orcid.org/0000-0001-9467-672X
Bankura University, India

Santosh Kumar Behera
Kazi Nazrul University, India

ABSTRACT

This chapter investigates undergraduate students' perceptions of the potential of artificial intelligence (AI) in higher education. Using a descriptive survey method,

DOI: 10.4018/979-8-3693-7220-3.ch005

data were collected from 322 undergraduate students in West Bengal through random sampling and analyzed using perception scales. Additionally, unstructured interviews were conducted to explore the reasons behind low levels of perception. The study employed Mean, Standard Deviation, Kruskal-Wallis test, Mann-Whitney U test, post-hoc analysis, and percentage calculations to analyze data and test hypotheses. Findings indicate that students generally have a moderate perception of AI's potential in higher education, with significant variation observed across academic streams (Arts, Science, and Commerce) but no notable differences based on gender, caste, location, or semester. The study also uncovers factors contributing to the low perception levels among undergraduates regarding AI's role in higher education.

INTRODUCTION

'Quest for knowledge' is one of the salient characteristics of human beings from the inception. Knowledge is power. Education empowers us. We may observe evolution in many facets of our lives as a result. In particular, the technology side is evolving daily, and we don't know where it will be stopped. Now technology is an inseparable part of our education system so whichever is invented, we grab those things and try to cope up these. The term Artificial Intelligence (AI) emerged two decades before but very recently, it surfaced on majority of people's mind who are attached with Smartphone, Tab, Laptop, PC's etc. Even students are more curious about Artificial Intelligence. After pandemic they are always tried to grab new technological inventions, because these are interesting, personalized, relatively safe, and can learned at anytime and anywhere. John McCarthy described the term Artificial Intelligence (AI) as "the science and engineering of making intelligent machines" (as cited in Amisha et al., 2019; Hamet& Tremblay, 2017). AI has been defined as "the ability of a digital computer or computer-controlled robot to perform tasks commonly associated with intelligent beings" (Remian, 2019). Artificial intelligence (AI) can be defined briefly as the branch of computer science that deals with the simulation of intelligent behavior in computers and their capacity to mimic, and ideally improve, human behavior (Naqvi, 2020). According to Encyclopedia Britannica, AI is the ability of digital computers or computer-controlled robots to solve problems that are normally associated with the higher intellectual processing capabilities of Humans.

The term "Artificial Intelligence" was initially used in the 1950s. Since then, scientists have worked to create machines that can carry out intellectually demanding jobs and function somewhat autonomously (Sheikh et al., 2023). In 1956, Artificial Intelligence came into view in a laboratory for the first time. A group of scientists arranged a conference that specifically focuses on Artificial Intelligence and the project is known as "the Dartmouth Summer Research Project on Artificial Intelligence". It was a 6-week brainstorming session where several founders of this related area were present. The organizers were very optimistic about the team's outcome, which was largely predicated on their proposal from the Rockefeller Foundation (Bostrom, 2016). McCarthy and Minsky organized this project and the AI project lab in M.I.T. (McCarthy, et al., 1973). In the same year, McCarthy coined the term 'Artificial Intelligence' (Broussard, 2019).

Renowned scientists who were presented in the summer project Herbert Simon, John Nash and Arthur Samuel responsible for bringing AI into the laboratory (Sheikh et al., 2023). Many of those summer project meeting attendees went on to create Artificial Intelligence research groups at some of the most important universities in the United States. Those early methods sought to reproduce some of the parts of human reasoning that seemed most advanced at the time. Such as proving theorems, organizing action sequences and playing games like chess or checkers (Sousa et al., 2024). Again, in the same year a program called 'Logic Theorist' was written by A. Newell and H. Simon, which was able to prove several mathematical theorems, including some found in the seminal Principia Mathematica by Whitehead and Russell (Newell & Simon, 1956). Arthur Samuel developed a program in 1959 that could play checkers well enough to beat its creator (Samuel, 1959). Several artificial intelligence-related concepts were integrated into the program to find solutions to large and complicated research areas (Sousa et al., 2024). Another significant milestone was the "General Problem Solver". This program can be applied to solve any problem in principle. It was able to determine the correct answer by converting issues into goals, subgoals, actions, and operators. An example of this is the river crossing puzzle (Boden, 2018). Natural Language Processing attempts to enable computers to perform tasks such as translating and even understanding written sentences.

In the early stages of Artificial Intelligence studying, it was a complex process. Despite the inherent difficulties of this processing, mainly because of the great ambiguity in the way people use language, systems that handle simple conversation in plain English have been designed, the most famous of which is ELIZA (Weizenbaum, 1966). A notable advance was the introduction of expert systems in symbolic AI in the 1970s. These are a form of rule-based AI where human experts in a particular field are asked to formulate rules for a program, an example of which is MYCIN, a program trained by medical experts to help doctors diagnose infectious conditions and prescribe proper medicines. The project was used to analyze organic chemistry molecules (Sheikh et al., 2023). The Macsyma system was developed in the 1960s due to research by MITs AI group. It was developed to solve complex mathematical problems and plan manufacturing processes. At various times in the 1970s, Macsyma worked on one such computer, one of the most popular nodes on the ARPANET (Moses,2012). Some were also developed in the Netherlands in the

1980s and tested in pilot studies. These address issues such as social security and criminal sentencing policy implementation (Hage&Verheij, 1999).

The Japanese government invested in a Prolog-based AI system through the Fifth-Generation Computer Systems Project in 1982 (Russell, 2019). In 1989, YannLeCun used convolutional neural networks (CNNs), to broken down complex images into small parts for making image recognition more efficient. It was a crucial contribution to contemporary AI programs (Marcus &Davi, 2019). The Bayesian network was developed in the 1990s.It enables us to answer questions and offer a comprehensive form of causal representation that extends to counterfactual reasoning (Pearl, 1985; 1988). the first Robot World Cup Soccer Games conference known as RoboCup-97, was held at the fifteenth International Joint Conference on Artificial Intelligence in 1997 (Noda et al., 1998). It was an initiative to enhance robotics and artificial intelligence research by giving various theories, Procedures, and agent architectures (Kitano et al., 1997). Chess matches between IBM's Deep Blue software and chess grandmaster Garry Kasparov are played in the same year (Newborn & Newborn, 2003). Deep Blue succeeded due to its more powerful computer system. Furthermore, this software provided insightful ideas by several chess champions. This achievement is regarded as a collective consisting of a computer program and multiple human players rather than a single grandmaster (Ihde, 2010). In the late 1980s, neural networks became a Mainstream issue in Machine Learning (ML) Along with Artificial Intelligence (AI), due to the invention of various efficient learning methods and network structures (Karhunen et al., 2015). Multilayer perceptron networks trained by "Backpropagation" type algorithms, self-organizing maps, and radial basis function networks were such innovative methods (Du &Swamy,2013; Han et al., 2011; Haykin, 2010). While neural networks have been effectively used in a variety of applications, interest in investigating this issue has waned over time. In 2006, Hinton and others presented "Deep Learning" (DL) to colleges and universities (Hinton et al., 2006). This was founded on the concept of artificial neural networks (ANN). Deep learning became a significant matter after that, resulting in a rebirth in neural network research, thus, sometimes referred to as "new generation neural networks". It's because deep networks, when properly trained, have produced Remarkable accomplishments in a variety of classification and regression challenges (Karhunen et al., 2015).

In 2011 Watson beat two human champions on the television game show Jeopardy. Watson understands natural language and quickly answers difficult questions (Ertel, 2018). According to Chang et al. (2016), AlphaGo's unexpectedly convincing victory over the current world go champion Lee Sedol in Seoul in March 2016. From 2000 to 2015 there was an upward trend in the growth of Artificial Intelligence (Liu et al, 2018). DARPA financed the "Explainable AI (XAI) program" in April 2017, to increase the explainability of AI decisions (Turek, 2017). "The General Data

Protection Regulation" (GDPR) was issued, in which the European Union offers their citizens the "right to explanation" if they are affected by algorithmic decision-making (Goodman & Flaxman, 2017). Explainable AI will become more important for all groups of stakeholders, including users, affected individuals, and AI system developers (Xu et al., 2019). A highlight of 2019 in natural language processing was the introduction of the BERT text association model, which can produce accurate results in many automated word processors. In one way or another, the publication of this novel model in 2019 sparked the majority of scientific studies on the subject of word processing in natural languages, and its authors have since grown to become highly cited machine learning researchers (Koroteev,2021). In 2018, developers of OpenAI first proposed the GPT-1 model. It automatically learns existing text corporeal with grammar, semantics, idioms and context information by using the transformer model. The goal of this technology was to achieve an algorithmic model of language that closely matches the expression of human thought (Finnie-Ansley et al., 2022). In 2019 OpenAI released GPT-2 model based on the core concept of GPT-1 model and employs more transformer decoders and rich corpora to improve training efficiency and accuracy (Henrickson & Meroño-Peñuela, 2022). GPT-3 (Generative Pre-trained Transformer) is a third-generation autoregressive language model that uses deep learning to generate human-like text. Using GPT-3 is simple, no more complex than searching for information through a search engine. In the same manner that Google "reads" our requests without understanding them and delivers relevant results, thus, GPT-3 writes a text continuing the sequence of our words (the prompt), without any understanding (Floridi & Chiriatti, 2020). The introduction of these models has influenced the development of NLP(Natural Language Processing) and brought new Possibilities and challenges for the improvement of future natural language processing (Chan & Hu, 2023). Chat GPT was launched on November 30, 2022, and was considered an unparalleled technological development. Chat GPT (Generative Pre-trained Transformer) is a new generation of artificial intelligence, propelling the innovative development of intelligent technology into a new historical stage. This technology not only substantially influences and shapes the production, life, and communication patterns of the entire civilization, but it also fundamentally reshapes society and mankind itself (Hill-Yardin et al., 2023).Artificial intelligence is rapidly used in a variety of industries, including higher education. It has become critical for personalized learning and supporting instructional staff. It has also become necessary for universities and colleges (Gill et al., 2024).

The remarkable advancement of technology has brought about its influence in various domains, including education, healthcare, and industry. These fields now have distinct dimensions thanks to AI, the latest iteration of this technology. Generally, we can say Artificial Intelligence uses machines and computers to simulate how the human mind makes decisions and solves problems. It has some enchanted features, like- language processing is very natural, it will recognize anybody's speech, accessible, learner centered, relatively secure. Humans are becoming almost insane because the only thought they have is how rapidly we can access everything in our hand. Since higher education is a highly delicate phase of any nation's educational system, if we neglect it, our biggest problems won't be resolved. Accordance with the needs of the moment, National Education Policy 2020, India, is also pressing light on uses of technology in higher education and we also need to consider how the teaching-learning process will develop in the future. The many AI tools have simplified the tasks of educators and pupils, particularly in the sphere of education. In addition to bridging the digital divide in the field of education, AI is also serving the demands of students West Bengal, who live in a developing nation alongside India. It is now crucial to understand how West Bengal UG students' perception about AI. This study has attempted to understand UG students' perceptions on the potentiality of AI I the lens of West Bengal, which is anticipated to be highly beneficial and fruitful in the field of education as well in social context.

LITERATURE REVIEW

To demonstrate the value of utilizing generative AI techniques in higher education today, Yusuf et al. (2024) gathered information from 1271 individuals across 76 nations. The respondents in this study showed a high degree of awareness regarding generative artificial intelligence. But there are still unanswered concerns about ethical standards and academic dishonesty. Damiano et al. (2024) tried to find out how beneficial ChatGPT is thought to be in higher education. Most respondents provide incorrect results. They concluded that faculty members and students in higher education require data literacy. Teaching requires critical thought if Gen-AI is to be used to support learning. Chan and Hu (2023) investigated the attitudes, advantages, and difficulties associated with generative AI in higher education by surveying 399 students in Hong Kong. Students in higher education exhibit a positive willingness to employ artificial intelligence (AI) in the areas of writing, research, analysis, and personalized learning, but they also raise concerns about privacy, accuracy, and ethical concerns. Mandal and Mete (2023) surveyed West Bengal board CBSE students in Class IX and X to see how they felt about the inclusion of AI in the curriculum. There, they made the point that joyful learning would be feasible if AI was included into the curriculum and the educational system took a student-centric approach.

Along with helping teachers with instruction and assessment, students will be at the forefront of technical education. Obenza et al. (2023) gathered data from 500 students at various universities in region XI to learn about the application of GAI in higher education and students' perceptions. According to their findings, pupils have a good level of comprehension, knowledge, and perception of the benefits and drawbacks of GAI. A survey conducted by Kumar and Raman (2022) gathered information about the application of artificial intelligence in higher education from 682 students. The findings indicate that while AI can be useful in academic administration during the teaching-learning process, it cannot be applied to admissions, exams, or placement. Agarwal and Lahoti (2022) demonstrated the widespread usage of AI in feedback, evaluation, and content distribution. Positive attitudes on the application of AI technology in higher education have also been noted.

However, several difficulties have also surfaced, including inadequate resources, a lack of formal training, infrastructure constraints, etc. It is also stated that to include AI into the educational process, infrastructure, institutional support and a policy framework are required. A qualitative review of the benefits and drawbacks of AI learning in the education of students in the twenty-first century was carried out by Channa et al. (2021). Because of the amazing progress in technology, AI learning tools will be of enormous assistance to students both now and in the future. Additionally, AI tools will be crucial in helping students develop their advanced skills in social, exploratory, and ubiquitous learning. Artificial Intelligence in Education, or AIED, should be highlighted in this study, along with its drawbacks and ethical considerations. Compton and Song (2021) draw attention to the advantages of implementing AI in several higher education contexts, including customized learning, cooperation through intelligent tutoring systems, automatic grading systems, etc. Encouragement of faculty members is necessary so they can explain to students the various advantages of the various AI tools. Sit et al. (2020) investigated the educational landscape in the United Kingdom as well as the career goals of medical students pursuing radiology. 89% of the 484 students in the sample said they would use AI to further their careers, and 78% said they had used it to earn their medical degrees. 45 of them studied AI, however the subject was not covered in their required curriculum. However, a lot of students lack the confidence and comprehension to apply AI critically in their education

Although the concept of AI dates to the late 20thcentury, research on it has grown rapidly. We can see that, after the COVID-9, AI takes an enormous speed for its development. However, from 2020 to 2024, the impact of AI in higher education has been studied extensively. However, several studies have raised questions about ethical standards, academic honesty, data literacy, etc. At the same time, students and educators have agreed in various studies about the benefits of using AI in higher education. Some studies have been conducted in developed countries about the impact of AI in higher education. But West Bengal, one of India's developing states, where the digital divide is at its extreme, we saw that very few research has been carried out till now. We have started a study with the UG students of this area, where an attempt has been made to know the potentiality of AI in Higher education system from the perspective of some new variables. It is hoped that this study will open a new perspective on the impact of AI in higher education, which will be very beneficial to current and future students, educators as well as social context.

OBJECTIVES OF THE STUDY

1. To determine the perception of Undergraduate students on the potentiality of Artificial Intelligence in Higher Education System of West Bengal.
2. To find out the difference in the perception of Undergraduate students on the potentiality of Artificial Intelligence in Higher Education System with respect to their gender.
3. To find out the difference in the perception of Undergraduate students on the potentiality of Artificial Intelligence in Higher Education System with respect to their location.
4. To investigate the difference in the perception of Undergraduate students on the potentiality of Artificial Intelligence in Higher Education System with respect to their caste.
5. To explore the difference in the perception of Undergraduate students on the potentiality of Artificial Intelligence in Higher Education System with respect to their semester.
6. To explore the difference in the perception of Undergraduate students on the potentiality of Artificial Intelligence in Higher Education System with respect to their stream.
7. To seek the reasons behind the negative or low perception of Undergraduate students on the potentiality of Artificial Intelligence in Higher Education System in West Bengal.

HYPOTHESES

To analyze the objectives five null hypotheses have been formulated and stated as-

H_1: There is a low level of the perception of Undergraduate students on the potentiality of Artificial Intelligence in Higher Education System of West Bengal.
H_2: There is no significant difference in the perception of Undergraduate students on the potentiality of Artificial Intelligence in Higher Education System with respect to their gender.

H_3: There is no significant difference in the perception of Undergraduate students on the potentiality of Artificial Intelligence in Higher Education System with respect to their location.

H_4: There is no significant difference in the perception of Undergraduate students on the potentiality of Artificial Intelligence in Higher Education System with respect to their caste.

H_5: There is no significant difference in the perception of Undergraduate students on the potentiality of Artificial Intelligence in Higher Education System with respect to their semester.

H_6: There is no significant difference in the perception of Undergraduate students on the potentiality of Artificial Intelligence in Higher Education System with respect to their stream.

Research Question: What are the reasons behind the negative or low perception of Undergraduate students on the potentiality of Artificial Intelligence in Higher Education System in West Bengal?

METHOD

A descriptive survey method was used in this study. Therefore, naturally different tools, techniques, strategies and methods of descriptive survey type research were used to analysis and interpret the data. Population of any study means total collection of elements or participants which the researcher makes some inference. As this study conducted on Undergraduate students in West Bengal state, all the Undergraduate students in West Bengal are identified as population of the study. Sample of the study means the representative part of the whole population. In this study 322 Undergraduate students of West Bengal were taken as representative sample for the whole population. Simple Random Sampling was followed for selecting the sample. To recognize the perception of Undergraduate students on the potentiality of AI in higher education system, a Perception Scale was used (constructed by the researchers). The scale consists of 20 items. The tool was standardized through process of reliability and validity. For reliability, test-retest method was opted and for validation, face validity (two experts) was opted. The score procedure of the tool was- for positive item, strongly agree- 5, agree-4. nutral-3, disagree-2, strongly disagree-1 and from negative items- strongly agree- 1, agree-2, nutral-3, disagree-4, strongly disagree-5.

Data Collection

In the first phase, data is collected with the help of Google form, from various districts colleges of West Bengal state to know the perception of UG students on the potentiality of AI in higher education system. In the later phase, to know the reasons of UG students having decidedly low perception on the potentiality of AI in higher education system, data was gathered with the help of telephonic calls.

Statistical Techniques

Mean, S.D, Shapiro-Wilk, Kolmogorov-Smirnov, Mann-Whitney U, Kruskal Wallis Test, Post-hoc test and Percentage (%) were used to analyze the collected data and verify the hypotheses.

RESULTS and DISCUSSIONS

To understand the nature of the existing data, a normality test has been performed. As the nature of the data determines which type of statistical technique can be implemented to analyze the data and draw interpretation.

Table 1. Test of normality

Shapiro-Wilk		
Statistic	**df**	**Sig.**
0.879	322	0.000

In Shapiro Wilk test of normality expressing that the table value (0.000) is below the significance value i.e., below 0.05. Hence, we can interpret that the data does not follow normal probability curve. Normality test is important to determine whether to apply parametric or non-parametric tests to analyze the data. Here the data is non- normal, so we used nonparametric test.

H_1: There is a low level of the perception of Undergraduate students on the potentiality of Artificial Intelligence in Higher Education System of West Bengal.

To understand the level of perception of students on AI, among the students of West Bengal, the cut-off point should be determined. Here the cut-off point is $M \pm 1\sigma$. With the help of this cut-off point, the level of the perception of students on AI will be determined.

Table 2. Descriptive data of the entire results

N	Mean	S.D.
322	57.96	11.69

Table 3. The level of the perception of undergraduate students on AI

Cut-Off Point	Scores	Frequency	Percentage	Level of Perception
Above M+ 1σ	Above 69.65	44	13.66%	High
Between M- 1σ - M+ 1σ	46.27 to 69.65	211	65.53%	Moderate
Below M- 1σ	Below 46.27	67	20.81%	Low

From the above table it can be concluded that most students (211 in number) i.e., 65.53% of Students were lies between 46.27 to 69.65 scores. This result signifies that there is a moderate level of perception is found on the potentiality of UG students on Artificial Intelligence in West Bengal. Therefore, the hypothesis is rejected.

Table 4. Results of Mann-Whitney U tests

Variables	Groups	Mean	SD	Level of Significance
Gender	Male	58.125	11.78082	**0.592**
	Female	57.47	11.48077	
Locality	Rural	58.43	11.75357	**0.156**
	Urban	56.55	11.45862	

Testing H_2

From Table 4, it is found that there is no significant difference found between male and female Undergraduate students as the Man-Whitney U test value is 0.592 (>p=0.05). That ensures there is no significant difference found in relation to their gender in the students' perception on the potentiality of UG students on Artificial Intelligence in West Bengal. Thus, the H_2 is retained. It is expected that the reason behind of this kind of result because of nowadays male and female both students have smart phone or digital devices, so they are quite easily accessing mobile devices. In UG level, all students have mobile devices, so male or female both can easily access AI tools.

Testing H_3

The data shown in Table 4, demonstrated that there is no significant difference found between rural and urban UG students as the Man-Whitney U test value is 0.156 (>p=0.05). That ensures there is no significant difference found in relation to their locality in the potentiality of UG students on Artificial Intelligence in West Bengal. Thus, the H_3 is retained. As we know that, the wave of digitalization is disseminated everywhere (urban and rural areas too). So UG students of West Bengal are eagerly using mobile devices or AI tools.

Testing H_4

Table 5. Kruskal Wallis test for caste

Variable	Groups	Mean	SD	Level of Significance
Caste	UR	58.76	12.20862	0.541
	SC	56.56	12.4249	
	ST	59.43	11.50728	
	OBC	57.9	10.57235	

Table 5 interprets there is no significant difference found between UR, SC, ST and OBC students as the Kruskal Wallis test value is 0.156 (>p=0.05). That signifies there is no significant difference found between UR, SC, ST and OBC students' the potentiality of UG students on Artificial Intelligence in West Bengal. Thus, the H_{04} is retained. As the Govt. of West Bengal provided scholarship to Higher Secondary students to buy Smart Phone, so all categories' students are overcome from the economic burdens. They are using the internet or mobile devices from higher secondary level. So, it is expected that this is the reason for this type of result.

Testing H_5

Table 6. Kruskal Wallis test for semester

Variable	Groups	Mean	S.D.	Level of Significance
Semester	Second	57.55	11.96699	**0.133**
	Fourth	60.5	10.7769	
	Sixth	56.9	11.11099	

From Table 6, it can be established that there is no significant difference found between second, fourth and sixth semester students as the Kruskal Wallis test value is 0.156 (>p=0.05). That indicates there is no significant difference found on the potentiality of UG students on Artificial Intelligence in West Bengal in relation to their semester. Thus, the H_5 is retained. As we can see that the previous result, students of all semesters are quite mature to access mobile devices or internet or AI tools since Higher secondary level. That is why semester variable does not differ significantly.

Testing H_6

Table 7. Kruskal Wallis test for stream

Variable	Groups	Mean	S.D.	Level of Significance
Stream	Arts	54.4	11.47084	**0.000**
	Science	54.54	8.915842	
	Commerce	57.31	5.760342	

Table7validates, there is a significant difference found between arts, science and commerce students as the Kruskal Wallis test value is 0.000 (<p=0.05). That designates there is significant difference found in the potentiality of UG students on Artificial Intelligence in West Bengal in relation to their stream. Thus, the H_{05} is vetoed. These three streams have different subject content and syllabus. UG students from these streams utilize differently, because maybe science and commerce students utilize much more than arts students. Because still now AI does not develop subject contents of some linguistics subjects. So, it can be the possible reason for this type of result.

To determine the exact difference among the three groups post-hoc test have been employed.

Table 8. Results of post-hoc test in relation to stream

Pairs	Test Statistics	Std. Error	Std. Test Statistic	Sig	Adj Sig
Arts-Science	-85.009	12.173	-6.983	0.000	0.000
Arts- Commerce	-106.990	19.307	-5.541	0.000	0.000
Science-Commerce	-21.981	20.997	-1.047	0.295	0.885

From the above table (Table-8) the pair wise differences can be visible, and it can be concluded that there is significant difference is seen between arts and science students and arts and commerce students as the calculated value 0.000 is less than p=0.05. However, there is no significant difference observed between science and commerce students with respect to their perception on AI as the calculated value 0.295 is greater than p=0.05.

Research Question- 1: what are the reasons behind the negative or low perception of Undergraduate students on the potentiality of Artificial Intelligence in Higher Education System in West Bengal?

From table 3 it is observed that out of 322 UG students, 67 students (20.81%) showed low level of perception on the potentiality of Artificial Intelligence in higher education. To know the causes of low level of perception of UG students on the potentiality of Artificial Intelligence in higher education system, the researchers made contact of certain students through phone calls. All the key problems that embarked by 67 students are discussed below.

Table 9. Percentages of problems related to low level of perception of undergraduate students on the potentiality of AI in higher education system in West Bengal

Sl. No.	Causes of Low Level of Perception	Total Students	No of Students Responded	Percentages	Ranks
1	Accessibility related problem	67	40	59.70%	5
2	Creates Digital Divide	67	55	82.09%	2
3	Language related problem	67	31	46.27%	8
4	Privacy and data security related problem	67	50	74.63%	3
5	Teacher-student relationship related problem	67	33	49.25%	7
6	Content quality related problem	67	25	37.31%	9
7	Problem in fostering creativity	67	32	67%	4
8	Problem in linguistic subject	67	37	55.22%	6
9	Become Self-centric	67	25	37.31%	9
10	Economy related problem	67	67	100%	1

Only 67 (20.81%) out of total 322 students showed low level of perception towards AI in higher education system, the specific reasons are discussed in table 9, such as - 1) Out of 67 (100%), 40 (59.70%) students attributed their low perception to accessibility. According to them, it is not possible for them to fully access all the tools that AI has, and they are ignorant of how to use the tools. 2) 55 (82.09%) students are victims of the digital divide. They think that most of the students in West Bengal live in rural areas and are quickly cut off from internet services, which make them unable to properly utilize AI in education. 3) Out of 67 (100%) students 31 (46.27%)

students feel that they are not proficient in languages other than Bengali and since the main language of AI is English, they have shown low perception regarding the use of AI in higher education. 4) 50 (74.63%) students think that privacy of various personal information will not be secure in connection with internet system and use of AI in higher education. 5) 33 students i.e. 49.25% students think that the use of AI in higher education will destroy the traditional teacher-student relationship. Since student success largely depends on teacher-student relationships, AI will create problems for students in higher education. 6) 25 (37.31%) students raised questions on digital content quality. They think that digital content is very inferior to printed books or copies. Another reason is they also embarked on a question on the validity of the content. 7) 32 (67%) students reported a decrease in their creativity level. According to them, solving all the content and problems of higher education with the help of AI will hamper the creativity of students, which will play a negative role in higher education. 8) The result shows that 37 people i.e. 55.22% of students expressed linguistic subject as their problem. That is, all these students are studying languages other than English in higher education. Apart from English, the benefits of AI tools are not available in other languages such as Bengali, Sanskrit, Santali etc. So, it has become a big factor for students associated with all these languages. 9) Another major problem is that the use of AI in higher education will lead to students' inclination towards personalized learning. For which most of the students tend to become self-centric, the problem is highlighted by 25 students (37.31%) as the main problem. They also mention that this will hinder the development of social attitudes like cooperation, sympathy etc. 10) 67 out of 67 students (100%) mentioned economic problems as their major problem. According to them, they have mobile devices but all the internet recharge, plans tools and software required to subscribe. These are very expensive, which is not possible for them to access.

IMPACT OF AI ON HIGHER EDUCATION SYSTEM

Students need to be mature enough to use the various tools of AI properly in their education. Hence, AI is particularly influential in higher education. The impact of AI in higher education is discussed below as –

- AI helps in personalized learning by analyzing the learning style. In higher education, since students can study in various fields, the role of personalized learning is important here. AI helps individualized learning by identifying students' problems (Annus, 2023).
- Administration plays an important role in the smooth running of the educational system in higher education. AI is very useful in all the work from

admission process of students to evaluation of current MCQ is done by the people associated with the administration (Slimi, 2023).

- It promotes inclusivity. In today's education, the concept of inclusive education has spread a lot. AI has considerable impact on inclusion of disadvantaged students in higher education by giving due importance to them (Kwapinska, 2024).
- AI gives an opportunity to get doubt clear and support from teachers outside the four walls. This support and advice is especially needed for students who need 24/7 support and advice outside of traditional education (Duggal, 2024).
- Research and Innovation is closely related to higher education. From literature review to data collection, data analysis, chart creation, references, plagiarism check, AI has had an important impact on all tasks, which are difficult for researchers to do manually. AI also has a special role in providing researchers with up-to-date information, thereby enabling innovative research (U.S. Department of Education, Office of Educational Technology, 2023).
- AI is especially helpful for the students to continue online distance learning. So students can be a lifelong learner.
- AI helps create an environment of practical and hands-on-experiences suitable for higher education students. AI determines the course content based on current job opportunities, market trends etc.
- AI also provides opportunities to learn other languages of the world (Baidya& C, 2024).
- AI has an impact on the ethical issue of data security of students in higher education (Sidiropoulos & Anagnostopoulos, 2024).
- AI promotes global collaboration among students across all over the World. The most significant advantage of this collaboration is that it allows them to familiarize themselves with different educational systems and cultures.

The present study aims to explore the perception level of UG students on the potentiality of AI in West Bengal context. The majority of UG students are inclined to embrace AI as their new educational weapon. Very few students have shown a negative or low level of perception on the potentiality of AI. However, the results indicate that UG students are familiar with the different AI tools. Since AI is accessible to all types of learners, it has been noted that UG students fervently supported the idea that it can increase educational inclusivity. So UG students from every region, caste, and semester can easily use AI for their educational tool. It is also found that AI helps to promote personalized learning, so students can learn their own styles and abilities. Another notable thing is that while learners use AI tools, learners get immediate feedback from it. So, learners have not to wait for their mistakes, they can modify their mistakes promptly. AI enables UG students to global access of any kind of educational resources; by which UG students are also get significant benefit. Another impact of AI is that UG students break down various barriers of language learning and they can increase language learning substantially. Another remarkable impact of AI, it can reduce human biasness in any kind of educational tasks. So, it can promote equal educational opportunity. AI has left a remarkable impression on collaborative learning. It promotes learners for global collaboration which makes a global identity for learners. Apart from some positive impacts, AI has several challenges like-data privacy and security problems, lack of quality content, reduced teacher-students' interactions, reduced creativity level, creates digital device, problems for linguistics subjects, economy related problems etc. National Policy on Education (NEP 2020) is also focusing on the utilization of technology in the Higher Education system. Therefore, we cannot diminish the significance of this study's findings considering the demands of the present scenario. We can also see that AI has an incredible potentiality in West Bengal context. But if we want to access AI in the field of educational context, we should have followed the ethical rules and regulations of AI. Otherwise, it leads to offensive activities which are not the cord of conduct of any nation as well as World.

CONCLUSION

The main aim of this study is to know the perception of UG students of West Bengal in the potentiality of Artificial Intelligence in higher education. From the analysis of the data, it can be concluded that the level of perception on AI among Students of West Bengal is moderate (65.53%). That implies a good awareness exists on AI among the students of West Bengal. However, on detailed analysis the researchers did not find any significant differences between male-female, rural-urban students on the perception of AI. Moreover, no significant difference has been found in relation to students' caste category and with respect to their semester (2nd, 4th and 6th) also in which they are studying. The only factor that contributes a significant difference on the perception of AI is student's stream of study. It is observable that there is no significant difference found between science and commerce students, but when these two groups of students are compared with the arts students, then the clear difference has been observed. Hence, it can be concluded that arts student's perception on AI is quite different with respect to science and commerce students. Also, out of 322 students, 67 students i.e. 20.80% students showed low perception towards the potentiality of AI in higher education. For which they expressed various reasons, such as digital divide, economic problem, language problem, content quality related problem etc. However, it is hoped that the rapid advancement of science and technology will solve all these problems and students in developing states like West

Bengal will also be able to enjoy the benefits of AI in their higher education, while at the same time aligning themselves with students from sectors.

REFERENCES

Agarwal, B., & Lahoti, Y. (2022). Harnessing Artificial Intelligence in higher education: Perspective and practices among educators. *NeuroQuantology : An Interdisciplinary Journal of Neuroscience and Quantum Physics*, 20(13), 4340–4351. DOI: 10.48047/nq.2022.20.13.NQ88529

Amisha., Malik, P., &Pathania, M., &Rathaur, V. K. (2019). Overview of artificial intelligence in medicine. *Journal of family medicine and primary care, 8*(7), 2328-2331. .DOI: 10.4103/jfmpc.jfmpc_440_19

Annus, N. (2023). Weigh the pros and cons of using Artificial Intelligence in education. *International journal of science, engineering and technology, 11*(3), 2-5.

Baidya, M., & C, A. K. (2024). Artificial Intelligence in education: Understanding benefits, limitations, and prospects for the future. *International journal for multidisciplinary research, 6*(2), 1-9.

Boden, A. M. (2018). *Artificial intelligence: A very short introduction*. Oxford University Press. DOI: 10.1093/actrade/9780199602919.001.0001

Bostrom, N. (2016). *Superintelligence: Paths, Dangers, Strategies*. Oxford University Press.

Broussard, M. (2019). *Artificial Unintelligence: How computers misunderstand the world*. The Mit Press.

Chan, Y. K. C., & Hu, W. (2023). Students' voices on generative AI: Perceptions, benefits, and challenges in higher education. *International Journal of Educational Technology in Higher Education*, 20(1), 43. DOI: 10.1186/s41239-023-00411-8

Chang, H. S., Fu, M. C., Hu, J., & Marcus, S. I. (2016). Google DeepMind'sAlphaGo: operations research's unheralded role in the path-breaking achievement. *Or/ Ms Today, 43*(5), 24-30.

Channa, F. R., Sarhandi, P. S. A., Bugti, F., & Pathan, H. (2021). Harnessing Artificial Intelligence in Education for Preparing Learners for the 21st Century. *Elementary Education Online, 20*(5), 3186–3192. Retrieved from https://ilkogretim-online.org/index.php/pub/article/view/5747

Crompton, H., & Song, D. (2021). The potential of Artificial Intelligence in higher education. *Revista Virtual Universidad CatólicadelNorte*, 1-4(62), 1–4. Advance online publication. DOI: 10.35575/rvucn.n62a1

Damiano, A. D., Lauria, E. J. M., Sarmiento, C., & Zhao, N. (2024). Early perceptions of teaching and learning using generative AI in higher education. *Journal of Educational Technology Systems*, 52(3), 346–375. DOI: 10.1177/00472395241233290

Du, K. L., & Swamy, M. N. (2013). *Neural networks and statistical learning*. Springer Science & Business Media.

Duggal, N. (2024). Incredible advantages of AI: Notable 23 benefits of AI. Retrieved from-https://www.simplilearn.com/advantages-and-disadvantages-of-artificial -intelligence-article

Ertel, W. (2018). *Introduction to artificial intelligence*(2nded.). Springer.

Finnie-Ansley, J., Denny, P., Becker, A. B., Luxton-Reilly, A., & Prather, J. (2022). The robots are coming: Exploring the implications of openai codex on introductory programming. In *Proceedings of the 24th Australasian Computing Education Conference*, 10-19.https://doi.org/DOI: 10.1145/3511861.3511863

Floridi, L., & Chiriatti, M. (2020). GPT-3: Its nature, scope, limits, and consequences. *Minds and Machines*, 30(4), 681–694. DOI: 10.1007/s11023-020-09548-1

Gill, S. S., Xu, M., Patros, P., Wu, H., Kaur, R., Kaur, K., & Buyya, R. (2024). Transformative effects of ChatGPT on modern education: Emerging Era of AI Chatbots. *Internet of Things and Cyber-Physical Systems*, 4, 19–23. DOI: 10.1016/j.iotcps.2023.06.002

Goodman, B., & Flaxman, S. (2017). European Union regulations on algorithmic decision-making and a "right to explanation". *AI Magazine*, 38(3), 50–57. DOI: 10.1609/aimag.v38i3.2741

Hage, J., & Verheij, B. (1999).Rechtsinformatica: de stand van zaken in de wetenschap. *A. Oskamp and A. Lodder (reds.), Informatietechnologievoorjuristen. Handboekvoor de jurist in de 21e eeuw*, Kluwer, 65-92.http://www.metajur.unimaas.nl/~bart/

Hamet, P., & Tremblay, J. (2017).Artificial intelligence in medicine. *metabolism, 69*, S36-S40.DOI: 10.1016/j.metabol.2017.01.011

Han, J., Pei, J., & Kamber, M. (2011). *Data mining: concepts and techniques*. Elsevier.

Haykin, S. (2010). *Neural networks and learning machines*. Pearson Education.

Henrickson, L., & Meroño-Peñuela, A. (2022). The hermeneutics of computer-generated texts. *Configurations*, 30(2), 115–139. DOI: 10.1353/con.2022.0008

Hill-Yardin, E., Hutchinson, M. R., Laycock, R., & Spencer, S. J. (2023). A Chat(GPT) about the future of scientific publishing. *Brain, Behavior, and Immunity*, 110(2), 152–154. Advance online publication. DOI: 10.1016/j.bbi.2023.02.022 PMID: 36868432

Hinton, G. E., Osindero, S., & Teh, W. Y. (2006). A fast learning algorithm for deep belief nets. *Neural Computation*, 18(7), 1527–1554. DOI: 10.1162/neco.2006.18.7.1527 PMID: 16764513

Ihde, D. (2010). *Embodied technics*.Automatic Press/vip.

Karhunen, J., Raiko, T., & Cho, K. (2015). Unsupervised deep learning: A short review. *Advances in independent component analysis and learning machines*, 125-142.DOI: 10.1016/B978-0-12-802806-3.00007-5

Kitano, H., Asada, M., Kuniyoshi, Y., Noda, I., & Osawa, E. (1997).Robocup: The robot world cup initiative. In *Proceedings of the first international conference on Autonomous agents*, 340-347.DOI: 10.1145/267658.267738

Koroteev, M. V. (2021). BERT: a review of applications in natural language processing and understanding. *arXiv preprint arXiv:2103*. https://doi.org//arXiv.2103.11943DOI: 10.48550

Kumar, V. V. R., & Raman, R. (2022). *Student perceptions on Artificial Intelligence (AI) in higher education.2022 IEEE Integrated STEM Education Conference*. ISEC., DOI: 10.1109/ISEC54952.2022.10025165

Kwapinska, M. (2024). AI in education: Benefits, challenges, and use cases. Retrieved from- https://www.nomtek.com/blog/ai-in-education

Liu, J., Kong, X., Xia, F., Bai, X., Wang, L., Qing, Q., & Lee, I. (2018). Artificial intelligence in the 21st century. *IEEE Access : Practical Innovations, Open Solutions*, 6, 34403–34421. DOI: 10.1109/ACCESS.2018.2819688

Mandal, R., & Mete, J. (2023). Teachers' and students' perception towards integration of Artificial Intelligence in school curriculum: A survey. *International journal of multidisciplinary educational research, 127*(5), 95-103.

Marcus, G., & Davi, E. (2019). *Rebooting AI: Building Artificial Intelligence we can trust. Vintage*. Pantheon Books.

McCarthy, J., Feigenbaum, E., & Lederberg, J. (1973). *Artificial Intelligence Project* (No. 4).Progress Report.

Moses, J. (2012). Macsyma: A personal history. *Journal of Symbolic Computation*, 47(2), 123–130. DOI: 10.1016/j.jsc.2010.08.018

Naqvi, A. (2020). *Artificial intelligence for audit, forensic accounting, and valuation: a strategic perspective*. John Wiley &Sons. DOI: 10.1002/9781119601906

Newborn, M., & Newborn, M. (2003). *Deep Blue: an artificial intelligence milestone*. Springer Science & Business Media. DOI: 10.1007/978-0-387-21790-1

Newell, A., & Simon, H. (1956). The logic theory machine—A complex information processing system. *IEEE Transactions on Information Theory*, 2(3), 61–79. DOI: 10.1109/TIT.1956.1056797

Noda, I., Suzuki, J. S., Matsubara, H., Asada, M., & Kitano, H. (1998). RoboCup-97: The first robot world cup soccer games and conferences. *AI Magazine*, 19(3), 49–49.

Obenza, B. N., Salvahan, A., Rios, A. N., Solo, A., Alburo, R. A., & Gabila, R. J. (2023). University students' perception and use of ChatGPT: Generative Artificial Intelligence (AI) in higher education. *International Journal of Human-Computer Studies*, 5(12), 1–15. DOI: 10.5281/zenodo.10360697

Pearl, J. (1985). Bayesian networks: a model of self-activated memory for evidential reasoning. *In:Proceedings of the 7th conference of the cognitive science society*, 329–334.

Pearl, J. (1988). *Probabilistic reasoning in intelligent systems: networks of plausible inference*. Morgan Kaufmann.

Remian, D. (2019).Augmenting education: ethical considerations for incorporating artificial intelligence in education, 52.https://scholarworks.umb.edu/instruction_capstone/52

Russell, S. (2019). *Human compatible: Artificial Intelligence and the problem of control*. Penguin.

Samuel, A. L. (1959). Some studies in machine learning using the game of checkers. *IBM Journal of Research and Development*, 3(3), 210–229. DOI: 10.1147/rd.33.0210

Sheikh, H., Prins, C., & Schrijvers, E. (2023). Artificial intelligence: definition and background. In Mission, A. I. (Ed.), *The new system technology* (pp. 15–41). Springer International Publishing., DOI: 10.1007/978-3-031-21448-6_2

Sheikh, H., Prins, C., & Schrijvers, E. (2023). Artificial Intelligence: Definition and Background. In Mission, A. I. (Ed.), *Research for Policy* (pp. 15–41). Springer., DOI: 10.1007/978-3-031-21448-6_2

Sidiropoulos, D., & Anagnostopoulos, C. N. (2024).Applications, challenges and ethical issues of AI and ChatGPT in education. Retrieved from- https://arxiv.org/pdf/2402.07907

Sit, C., Srinivasan, R., Amlani, A., Muthuswamy, K., Azam, A., Monzon, L., & Poon, D. S. (2020). Attitudes and perceptions of UK medical students towards artificial intelligence and radiology: Amulticentre survey. *Insights Into Imaging*, 11(1), 14. Advance online publication. DOI: 10.1186/s13244-019-0830-7 PMID: 32025951

Slimi, Z. (2023). The Impact of Artificial Intelligence on higher education: An empirical study. *European journal of educational sciences, 10*(1), 17-33.0p

Sousa, A. (2024). Multidisciplinary Perspectives on Artificial Intelligence and the Law. *Springer Nature*, 456. Advance online publication. DOI: 10.1007/978-3-031-41264-6

Turek, M. (2017). *Explainable Artificial Intelligence (XAI) Program*. Defence Advanced Research Project Agency (DARPA).

U.S. Department of Education. Office of Educational Technology, (2023). Artificial Intelligence and Future of Teaching and Learning: Insights and Recommendations, Washington, DC.

Weizenbaum, J. (1966). Eliza- A computer program for the study of natural language communication between man and machine. *Computational Linguistics*, 9(1), 36–45.

Xu, F., Uszkoreit, H., Du, Y., Fan, W., Zhao, D., & Zhu, J. (2019). Explainable AI: A brief survey on history, research areas, approaches and challenges. In *Natural language processing and Chinese computing: 8th CCF international conference, NLPCC 2019, dunhuang, China, October 9–14, 2019, proceedings, part II 8*,563-574. Springer International Publishing. DOI: 10.1007/978-3-030-32236-6_51

Yusuf, A., Pervin, N., & Roman-Gonzalez, M. (2024). Generative AI and the future of higher education: A threat to academic integrity or reformation? Evidence from multicultural perspectives. *International Journal of Educational Technology in Higher Education*, 21(1), 1–29. DOI: 10.1186/s41239-024-00453-6

ADDITIONAL READING

Almaiah, M. A., Alfaisal, R., Salloum, S. A., Hajjej, F., Thabit, S., El-Qirem, F. A., Lutfi, A., Alrawad, M., Al Mulhem, A., Alkhdour, T., Awad, A. B., & Al-Maroof, R. S. (2022). Examining the impact of artificial intelligence and social and computer anxiety in e-learning settings: Students' perceptions at the university level. *Electronics (Basel)*, 11(22), 3662. DOI: 10.3390/electronics11223662

Monib, W. K., Qazi, A., & Mahmud, M. M. (2024). Exploring learners' experiences and perceptions of ChatGPT as a learning tool in higher education. *Education and Information Technologies*, •••, 1–23. DOI: 10.1007/s10639-024-13065-4

Obenza, B., Salvahan, A., Rios, A. N., Solo, A., Alburo, R. A., & Gabila, R. J. (2024). University Students' Perception and Use of ChatGPT: Generative Artificial Intelligence (AI) in Higher Education. *International Journal of Human-Computer Studies*, 5(12), 5–18.

Sila, C., William, C., Yunus, M., & Rafiq, K. (2023). Exploring Students' Perception of Using ChatGPT in Higher Education. *International Journal of Academic Research in Business & Social Sciences*, 13(12), 4044–4054. DOI: 10.6007/IJARBSS/v13-i12/20250

ală, M. L., Müller, C. N., Năstase, I. A., & Gheorghe, G. (2024). Exploring university students' perceptions of generative artificial intelligence in education. *Amfiteatru Economic*, 26(65), 71–88. DOI: 10.24818/EA/2024/65/71

KEY TERMS AND DEFINITIONS

Artificial Intelligence (AI): A branch of computer science that creates systems capable of performing tasks that require human intelligence, such as reasoning, problem-solving, and learning.

Data Privacy: Measures taken to protect personal and sensitive information in digital systems, ensuring that it is not accessed or shared without authorization.

Digital Divide: The gap between individuals or communities with access to digital technologies and those without, often due to socioeconomic, geographical, or infrastructural factors.

Higher Education: The level of education that follows secondary school, typically provided by universities and colleges, aimed at delivering advanced knowledge and skills.

Inclusivity: An educational principle that ensures all students, regardless of background, have equal access to learning opportunities and resources.

Perception Scale: A tool used to measure individuals' attitudes, beliefs, or opinions about a specific topic, often used in research to quantify subjective responses.

Personalized Learning: An educational approach that uses technology to tailor learning experiences to an individual's strengths, needs, and interests.

Statistical Analysis: A set of mathematical techniques used to interpret, summarize, and infer patterns from collected data.

Undergraduate Students: Students enrolled in a college or university program leading to a bachelor's degree.

Virtual Assistant: An AI-powered tool that assists users by performing tasks, answering questions, and providing guidance in an educational or organizational setting.

Chapter 6
AI in Assessment and Feedback

Smitha Shivshankar
Australian International Institute of Higher Education, Australia

Nirmal Acharya
https://orcid.org/0000-0002-2132-5184
Australian International Institute of Higher Education, Australia

ABSTRACT

This chapter examines AI's transformative role in educational assessment and feedback, focusing on enhancing teaching and learning through technology. As AI reshapes traditional practices, the chapter emphasizes that AI in assessment should extend beyond automation, advocating for designs that encourage deep learning and student engagement. Using adaptive feedback, educators can support skill development and promote meaningful engagement with the material. The chapter presents a framework for AI-integrated assessments, stressing clear guidance, ethical considerations, and the active roles of both educators and students. It discusses tools like plagiarism detectors and adaptive learning platforms, underscoring the need to align AI with learning objectives and integrity standards. The framework also emphasizes the collaborative nature of AI in assessment—educators mentor students in using AI responsibly while students engage critically with technology. This approach balances AI's benefits with human insight, offering a model for inclusive, adaptive assessments.

DOI: 10.4018/979-8-3693-7220-3.ch006

INTRODUCTION

Artificial Intelligence (AI) attempts to simulate the natural intelligence of human into machines. According to Alan Turing's imitation game, if you cannot tell whether you are in a conversation with a human or a machine then it is intelligent machines or AI. The ability of computing systems to engage in human (processes) like learning, adaptation, synthesis, self-correction, and data use for complex computation duties can be defined as AI. AI has the potential to make humans better at their tasks and activities by educating, training and improving the performance (Stephen, Hiroaki, Tatsunori, Nian-Shing, 2021). AI based applications have become an integral part of our daily life, making it clear that technology is becoming increasingly important. AI systems can learn from past experiences or outcomes and make decision based on these experiences and recently applied in every field as agriculture, industries, medical, and education. The future of higher education is inevitably linked to this new technology. There are new possibilities and challenges for the higher education teaching and learning from the application of AI and the industry is already experiencing significant alteration in education services by the rapid advancement of AI.

A growing number of AI applications have emerged in the last few years focussing on the key business areas of education involving the key stakeholders. For students, AI can customize educational content to fit individual student preferences and learning styles. This aims at improving engagement and effectiveness in learning outcomes, making education more relevant to each student. For educators, AI systems can be used to modify the difficulty and type of assessments based on a student's performance. This provides a more accurate evaluation of a student's understanding and skills, thereby enhancing the assessment process. For governance and policy makers, it stresses the importance of establishing clear guidelines and standards for the ethical use of AI in educational contexts. This includes promoting transparency, accountability, and involving diverse stakeholders in the development of AI systems to ensure fairness and equity in education.

AI and Education

The unprecedented rate of technological advancements led AI is transforming teaching and learning (Post-pandemic Education Strategy, 2022). AI applications in education is constantly expanding and the new concepts and methods have a significant contribution in reforming the education industry (Liang, 2020). Machine learning (ML) algorithms, a subsystem of AI helps in systematic monitoring of student's performance and take preventive measures to support struggling students and thereby improve quality of education by improving student outcomes. AI applications assist education academically and administratively and enhance their effectiveness helping teachers in various tasks through Learning Analytics (LA), Virtual Reality (VR), Grading/Assessments (G/A), and Admissions (Ahmad et.al.,2022).

However, there is a concern on the consequences this new technology will have for teachers' working practices and students' knowledge acquisition (Morduchowicz & Suasnábar, 2023). ChatGPT is one such example today, which shows us the benefits and challenges of AI in education. The educator community agrees that ChatGPT, for example, presents a notable transformation for education—and has forced the educators to re-examine fundamental questions about their profession: Why do we teach, what we teach? What does it mean to learn?, What do educators mean by terms like 'rigor' and 'assessment'? (Myers, 2023). While the online education during the COVID-19 pandemic has transformed the role of assessment and feedback, ChatGPT's invasion has shook the educational systems once again (K. A. Tan, 2013; Chan and Luo, 2020).

According to the reports from Capgemini (Capgemini Australia, 2023) education systems around the world are already making moves to either accommodate or exclude Gen-AI tools such as ChatGPT from students' daily learning activities. Nearly half (48%) of secondary school teachers, for example, report that their schools have either blocked or restricted the tools' use in one form or another. Some have been less restrictive, with 19% saying that such tools have been allowed for specific use-cases and 18% noting that they are still evaluating it for its applicability and usefulness in the classroom setting. Overall, over half (56%) of secondary school teachers agree that curriculums and assessments needed to be adapted to account for student use of AI-generated content and a similar proportion (52%) believe AI tools will change the teaching profession for the better. On the other hand, 78% of secondary school teachers globally share concerns about the negative impact of Gen-AI tools on student learning outcomes, including the perception that the tool will limit the value of writing skill by 66%. Despite these concerns, teachers globally believe that the benefits of AI tools outweigh the risks. The key uses highlighted include using it interact and understand AI models (60%), aid critical thinking (56%) and Of the perceived benefits that AI tools could bring, key use cases highlighted by teachers include using it to teach how to interact with and understand AI models (60%), to aid critical thinking exercises (56%) and as a tool to help suggest edits to students' work (52%), among others. The sentiment towards generative AI varies significantly across different geographies: teachers in the United States, the United Kingdom, Germany and Finland recognise the importance and potential of generative AI, much more than Singapore, Japan or France.

AI and Student Learning Outcomes

Education industry base their policies, diagnosis and program design by assessing the students' performance against a set of standards based on the learning outcomes. This enables them to identify the gaps used as feedback to improve program quality, teaching effectiveness, and students' learning experience. Student performance-based evaluations of learning outcomes are foundations for evidence based continuous improvement which needs to be conducted regularly with or without interventions. With the increasing prevalent use of Gen-AI tools that allows students to generate highly precise original texts and essays without any effort calls into the questions of how assessment-based performance evaluation models with serve the purpose in higher education industry. If without the similarity checking tools, ChatGPT will give students an unfair advantage over those who do their own work without the use of the tool, not scoring best on assessments but still developing the necessary skills for future work roles. Students' achievement in their assignments will no longer reflect their learning. The goal of education to challenge and develop students' knowledge, technical expertise and soft skills, is undermined by the availability of AI solutions decreasing the value of educational systems. Therefore, it is time to revisit existing performance evaluation approaches as well as the design of assessments adopted by the higher education industry to monitor and ensure students' learning and skills development in a new era of AI.

It is imperative for the academia to leverage the era of intelligent learning tools. The educators should be responsible for adapting to the new technologies and continuing to find ways to ensure the development of students' technical and soft skills for their lifelong learning and career success while ensuring honesty and integrity in their academic conduct (Pascale, Bourgain; 2023). It is time to look at how human tutors and machines could work together by implementing AI tools within teaching practices. The transformation to online learning has changed the structure and nature of teaching and learning and the student community's prevalent use of AI bots has forced the need for restructuring the assessments and feedback methodologies. It is vital to rethink as to how the parameters of the assessment should be changed to make it more powerful to enhance student learning outcomes in a digital learning environment (Giray, 2021).

This chapter proposes a framework for the effective use of AI in assessment design and feedback process by placing the ChatGPT in the context of current AI in Education research (Carlos et.al., 2023). The rest of the chapter is organised as follows: Section 2 starts with a discussion on the assessments and feedback and its purpose in the educational environment. The section then presents the various types of assessments currently predominant in the educational setting and the need for rethinking assessments and learning outcomes in the AI era and the strategies for mitigating AI use in assessments and incorporating the use of AI in assessments. Section 3 provides insights on the application of AI in student evaluation starting with the core values of the learning outcomes that need to be considered while integrating AI in assessments. The section also includes discussion on the AI application in assessment strategies and various tools that can be leveraged for the same. Section 4 presents the insights from the different frameworks and guidelines presented from different educational settings in understanding what needs to be addressed while integrating AI into assessment design. Section 5 details the proposed framework for developing AI-based assessment integrated with the student resources to incorporate AI ethically in assessment preparation. The framework leverages the components of the prominent frameworks and highlights the inclusive role of educators and students in the efficient and ethical use of AI in assessment design and preparation and evaluation of student performance. Section 6 presents the challenges that disrupts the efficient use of AI in educational settings. Section 7 concludes the findings of the paper.

ACHIEVING LEARNING OUTCOMES THROUGH ASSESSMENTS AND FEEDBACK

Assessment is evidence of learning initiated through a continuous cycle of improvement. Teachers spend a significant amount of time in the assessment and feedback process. This is an important factor of focus as it influences all the stakeholders (S. Lynam and M. Cachia, 2018; Umar and Majeed, 2018; Pereira et.al., 2016). Assessment methods are used by teachers to provide feedback to students to adjust ongoing teaching and learning to improve their achievement of intended learning outcomes through a set of instructions. Assessment can take multiple forms such as diagnostic, formative, summative, e-assessment, self-assessment and peer assessment. The types of assessments are determined by the learning outcomes. Formative assessment - "assessment for learning" occurs throughout the learning process, whereas summative assessment - "assessment of learning" is frequently performed at the end (Wyatt-Smith, 2014). The web-based learning climate gives a platform to more execution-based assessment through real time and timely feedback, open doors for individual practice, and assistance. It also helps instructors to track cognitive activity of students in real-time and provides opportunity for students to participate as well as adapt instruction to enhance their academic achievement.

Purpose of Assessment and Feedback

The questions "Why assess?" does not only focus on the purposes of assessment but also on issues related to assessment while supporting student success. Assessment serves various purposes such as: (i) Motivation of students (ii) Feedback to students (iii) Feedback to teachers (iv) Measure students' performance and progress in the course (vi) Course design (vii) Diagnosis (viii) Support student's collaboration. For long, the main purpose of assessment has been considered as "feedback on learning"; however, why assessment cannot also be observed as "feedback on teaching"? The attention should be shifted toward "examining," consistent action of assessing learner's dialog, intelligence, and performance to inform teacher knowledge, methods, and skills that help learners during the classroom practice (Yimer, 2020).

Assessment is the process of information gathering and intervention involving a combination of criteria to perform a judgement. While assessments take a major role in measuring the student performance, feedback is an essential part of the learning and teaching process and two-fold: For student community, in helps to identify gaps, self-assess, and act upon the provided insights and for educator community, it inform instructors about the effectiveness of their teaching strategies and how to adjust these strategies according to student's needs (Faulconer, 2021). Both assessment and feedback has always remained a significant element for successful learning outcomes and high student satisfaction and have been a crucial part of the educational process. The diversity of student bodies in the higher education demands the need for inclusive assessment practices and effective feedback practices for enhancing student learning outcomes through self-regulation of learning, identifying gaps, increasing student engagement and performance, addressing accountability issues and provide information to teachers on the changes required to the assessment practices. Literature presents a variety of assessment practices across the higher education as presented in Table 1.

Table 1. Regular assessment practices in higher education

Assessment Type	Description
Summative Assessment	Sum up both teaching and learning process. Students are assessed at the end of the course module helping the instructors in knowing what the students achieve throughout the learning process. Supports the instructor in avoiding errors; provides reliable data and can be used for accountability. The transformation to online learning, the learning management systems and other e-learning technologies makes summative assessment approaches hard to detect students learning activities and assess these activities (Perera-Diltz, 2014)
Formative Assessment	Formative assessment happens throughout the learning process helping through the learning and enhances students learning outcomes (Kliej et.al., 2015). The use of formative assessment tool with automated feedback helps both teachers and students to improve the learning process (Bourke, 2018)
Self-Assessment	Students take part in their own evaluation process and evolve as independent learners (Yan and Brown, 2017). Studies shows that self-assessment improves student's motivation, engagement, and their outcomes in any forms of e-learning based education environment (Nikou and Economides, 2016; Yan and Brown 2020)
Peer Assessment	These assessments focus on improving the self-sufficiency of student learning and enhances their learning ability. Oral presentation, portfolios, articles, test performances, online discussions, quizzes, etc., are the most common types (Montagner,2019). These forms of assessment encourage students to reflect, reduce marking load to teachers, increase student evaluation skills and enhances students' retention rate through reflection (Li and Gao, 2016)

Rethinking Assessment and Learning Outcomes

The transition to the online learning environment and the transformation of educational teaching and learning into online platforms has created a shift from traditional assessments and examination methods forcing the instructors and learners to uproot themselves to new forms and means of assessment and feedback. Some approaches include qualitative, quantitative, and mixed-method approaches. Additionally, there is no doubt that AI has impacted higher education and is a game changer in academic assessment. It is vital to realise the significance of including AI to enhance the learning outcomes. The benefit of AI needs to be thoughtfully leveraged for improved operational efficiency, gaining real-time, practicable insight into student performance (Garc´ıa-Peñalvo, 2021)

However, the key focus is how is it changing the student learning and to what extent it is imperative to consider redesigning assessment and how? With the rise of Gen-AI tools, it has become a requirement to re-evaluate traditional assessment tools and develop strategies to prevent the misuse of AI tools. While technology attempts to significantly enhance the learning process, undermining academic integrity is presented as a risk for the educational community. Educational organisations must grapple with this challenge by developing strategies to prevent the misuse of AI tools (Swiecki et al., 2022 as cited in CSU, Division of Learning and Teaching, 2024) while at the same time leveraging the benefits.

There are two approaches to this: Re-evaluating assessment tools and define strategies to prevent the misuse of AI tools and redesign the assessment to include the use of AI in a way that aligns with the learning outcomes. While the first approach focuses assessment strategies to mitigate the use of AI as presented in Table 2, the later strategy focuses on the modifying the assessments to incorporate the use of AI as applicable discussed in detail in the next Section.

Table 2. Assessment strategies to mitigate the use of AI

Strategy	Benefits
Emphasise the Learning Process	Shift the focus from grades to learning outcomes Assessments viewed as opportunities for growth rather than means to score high Focus on assessing student actions and tactics throughout the learning journey
Incorporate Authentic Assessment	Students expected to apply their knowledge to contemporary real-world scenarios or problems Focus on demonstrating the ability to apply knowledge in practical situations
Promote Critical Thinking	Encourage critical thinking and problem-solving Students analyse information, draw connections, evaluate arguments, or propose solutions, encouraging critical thinking and problem solving
Individualised or Personalised Assessments	Unique parameters for each student that may involve student input or choice in developing the assessment topics
Live or Recorded Interviews or Presentations	Type of assessments making it difficult for students to use external resources
Peer Assessments	Include peer evaluations – students assessing each other's work
Frequent Low-Stake Assessments	Small assessments throughout the teaching period

continued on following page

Table 2. Continued

Strategy	Benefits
Integrate real-life situations and practical experiences	Create avenues for students engage in work-integrated learning and interact with experts in relevant fields to gain experience. Inviting industry professionals to impart their knowledge, real-life encounters, and viewpoints fosters a lively exchange of thoughts and perspectives

(CSU, Division of Teaching and Learning, 2023)

To compete with the implications of GenAI it is important to rethink what needs to be learned and how the learning should be assessed and validated. To ensure the required elements of learning are addressed, the learning outcomes needs to be redesigned to include the key attributes as presented in Table 3.

Table 3. Categories of learning outcomes

Category	Description
Values	Clearly define the values that detail the relation between education and technology. The assessment of learning outcomes and their validation need to be iteratively updated to respond to the increasing use of AI
Foundational knowledge and skills	To reflect the AI-rich environments, the foundational skills need to be regularly revisited
Higher-order thinking skills	Include skills that support higher-order thinking and problem solving based on human-AI collaboration and the use of GenAI-generated outputs in the learning outcomes
Vocational skills needed to work with AI	The use of AI requires learners to nurture new skills that enable them to develop, operate and work with GenAI tools. The redesign of learning outcomes and educational assessment will need to reflect the vocational skills required for the new jobs created by AI
(Valentine, 2023)	

STUDENT EVALUATION AND AI: AI IN ASSESSMENT AND FEEDBACK PROCESS

In the era of generative AI, evaluating students requires innovative approaches that leverage AI's capabilities while addressing its limitations. The integration of AI in education has transformed traditional assessment methods, necessitating a shift towards more dynamic and competency-based evaluations. While generative AI tools offer substantial benefits, concerns regarding academic integrity and ethical usage persist, necessitating clear guidelines for their responsible integration in education. The ethical concern of unintentional plagiarism is imposed in the widespread use of GenAI tools in higher education. The tools may inadvertently include borrowed content, posing challenges to academic integrity complicating evaluations of originality. To address these concerns, it is imperative to establish clear guidelines and educational programs for responsible use of GenAI applications. Educators need to update themselves and be proficient in the use of latest technologies and educate students on how to use them ethically.

Application of AI in Educational Assessment and Feedback

The application of AI-based tools encompassing purposes of formative and summative feedback, training and instruction, evaluating constructs of knowledge, promote the evaluation of students in the era of AI. By incorporating the dimensions of Bayesian statistics, machine learning, and natural language processing these systems effectively evaluate students in the time of generative AI, guiding learning and instruction efficiently. Tabe 4 presents the specific ways in which AI can be applied in educational assessment.

Table 4. Application of AI in assessments

Activity	Description
Personalised Learning	AI tools have the potential to customise learning with personalised learning plans by analysing data from multiple sources such as assessment and quizzes. AI tools can assist in preparing individualised instructions. Ex., DreamBox and Knewton
Automated Grading	AI can automate assessment grading, saving time for the educators enabling them to focus more on lesson planning and supporting students, and providing immediate feedback to students. Ex., Turnitin's AI powered software
Formative assessment tools	These tools enable educators to monitor students' learning in real-time, provide feedback, and adjust instruction based on their performance. Ex., Mentimeter, Nearpod, and Socrative
Digital portfolios	Enable students to collect and showcase their work, reflect on their learning, and receive feedback from educators and peers. Ex., Google Sites, Seesaw, and WordPress

continued on following page

Table 4. Continued

Activity	Description
Digital assessment tools	Enables educators to assess student knowledge and skills using a variety of question types, including multiple-choice, short answer, and essay. Ex., Edulastic, ExamView, and Google Forms.
AI-Enhanced Feedback and Grading Competency-Based Assessments	The system exemplifies the grading process by providing scalable, accurate and verifiable feedback ensuring transparency and reliability in student evaluations. AI's role in assessments extends to evaluating competencies across various disciplines. A competency-based analysis of AI language models reveals their proficiency in language, critical analysis, and reasoning, highlighting the need for assessments that measure these competencies effectively. This approach aligns with the shift towards higher-order learning, where assessments focus on students' ability to apply knowledge creatively and critically.
AI-Based Assessment Frameworks	These offer a structured approach to evaluating students, encompassing various dimensions, including summative and formative feedback, knowledge and skills assessment, and the use of multimodal data. By framing assessments within these dimensions, educators can better understand and implement AI tools, ensuring comprehensive evaluations that address both cognitive and emotional aspects of learning.
Automated Feedback Systems	The Automated Feedback Generator (AFG) streamlines feedback offering consistent and constructive feedback.
Intelligent Diagnostic Feedback	Intelligent systems analyse student responses to multiple-choice questions (MCQs) to deliver customized feedback, guiding students toward a better understanding of concepts leveraging neural network analysis providing insights into learning behaviors and enhancing the learning experience.
Semi-Automatic Assessment in Mathematics	Intelligent Assessment tools combine human and electronic assessments, offering individual feedback boosting student confidence and engagement. These tools categorise solutions and identify errors, forwarding complex cases to educators for further assessment (Bescherer et al., 2012).

(Valentine, 2023)

AI Tools for Assessment Design

The integration of AI in teaching effectively realises learner-centered learning. AI-powered tools and applications improve educational measurement, providing valuable insights into student performance, learning outcomes and instructional effectiveness. AI-powered assessment tools as presented in Table 5 have the potential to analyse student responses and provide personalised feedback to help students identify areas of strengths and weaknesses (Valentine, 2023).

Table 5. AI tools for assessment design

Tools	Area of Application
Web-Based AI Systems	Tools like WebCADET support designers in navigating vast knowledge bases, improving decision-making in assessment design
Modeling Tools	AI modeling tools enable intuitive visual authoring, allowing designers to convey complex decision logic effectively, which can be applied in creating assessment frameworks
Assessment for Learning (AfL):	AI solutions, such as Expert Control Systems, enhance AfL by minimizing human bias and involving self and peer assessments, thus promoting autonomy in learning
Student Assessment Systems	These systems utilize a comprehensive student model to diagnose learning paths, leveraging AI to provide real-time insights into student progress

(Valentine, 2023)

Role of Teachers in AI Based Assessments

In an education setting, teachers have a critical role in ensuring that the potential of AI is leveraged for measurement and evaluation purposes and transform their role in the classroom in educating students the appropriate use of AI. The ability to provide a fast and efficient evaluation of student learning has resulted in an AI-based assessment gaining popularity in recent years. However, the role of teachers in AI-based assessments is still critical and cannot be undermined. According to (Dillenbourg, 2016) the shift from traditional education to digital education does not necessarily mean that teachers will become obsolete in the future. Table 6 presents the role of educators in such assessments. Some of these roles include:

Table 6. Role of educators in AI-assisted assessment design

Roles	
Designing AI-Resilient Assignments with a Clear Context	To counteract potential misuse of AI, assignments should emphasise skills that AI cannot easily replicate, such as creative thinking, communication, and collaboration. The 4C model of learning suggests designing tasks that require these skills, such as problem-solving with incomplete information and oral presentations. This approach encourages students to engage deeply with the material and develop skills essential for the modern workforce.
Interpreting Results and Continuous Improvement	Teachers should combine the immediate feedback results from AI and their professional judgement to evaluate student responses and provide personlised feedback. Teachers need to identify the area of weakness and adapt their teaching strategies to better meet the student needs.
Promote Critical Thinking	While AI-based assessments are designed to evaluate student knowledge, teachers can use them to foster critical thinking skills. Teachers can assist students to develop critical thinking ability by asking them to reflect on their responses and analyse the feedback.
Ensuring Accuracy of AI based Assessments	Teachers need to hold responsible for the accuracy of the AI based assessments by ensuring that data is reliable and valid and the assessment measures the intended learning outcomes and if required identifying and correcting the inaccuracies in the assessment

Frameworks for Authentic Assessments

While generative AI offers numerous benefits in student evaluation, it also presents challenges that require careful consideration. Ethical dilemmas, such as the potential for AI to undermine learning, must be addressed through responsible use and strategic assessment design. Frameworks for authentic assessments, guided by Bloom's taxonomy, can help educators evaluate the capabilities of generative AI tools. These frameworks emphasise higher cognitive skills, such as creation and critical analysis, which AI tools struggle to replicate. By focusing on these skills, educators can design assessments that prepare students for a rapidly evolving professional environment. Hence, it is imperative to apply an appropriate framework to leverage the benefits of AI tools in the assessment design and feedback process. Literature presents a few frameworks for AI integration in education.

According to Glenn Kleiman, "if we don't rethink writing instruction… we are in danger of writing assignments, from students' responses to teachers' grading, being untouched by human hands and unseen by human eyes" (Glen, 2023). According to the author, students should incorporate a few steps into the writing process to effectively write with the assistance of AI.

- **Set directions** for the intended learners – specify goals, contents and audience
- **Prompt** AI to produce the specific required outputs
- **Assess** the AI output and validate the accuracy, completeness, bias and quality of the information
- **Curate** the AI-generated text to decide what information is required and organise it coherently
- **Edit** the combined human and AI input to produce a well-written report

According to the tertiary qualification standards two principles serve to underpin five ways in which assessment can be designed to mitigate misuse of AI at the same time leveraging the benefits of AI to help students develop the skills to use AI tools effectively and ethically.

Principle 1: Educate the students on the ethical use of AI and understand its limitations and impacts

Principle 2: Multiple, inclusive, contextualised assessments for trustworthy judgements about student learning

The five "propositions" the assessment should emphasis are:

1. Appropriate, authentic engagement with AI
2. A systematic approach to assessment aligned with values of discipline and qualification
3. The process of learning (rather than the output)
4. Opportunities for students to work with AI and each other, and
5. Security at meaningful points across a program

According to Hamza Aoun (Hamza Aoun), comprehensive framework is essential for teachers, students and assessments to achieve the pedagogy of AI integration in education. The author presents a framework emphasising the need for AI to align with pedagogical practices focusing on two major dimensions.

AI-assisted Learning Environments: Focussing on ethics, accountability and prioritising safety and well-being

AI Techniques and Models: Focusing on the use of AI in creating lesson plans and assessments, for enhancing LMS by providing adaptive learning experiences, assisting in personalised learning and guidance, to evaluate and provide feedback on student performance.

The first dimension emphasizes the ethical considerations and governance surrounding AI's integration into teaching and learning practices, ensuring that technology supports pedagogy in a responsible and balanced way. Meanwhile, the second-dimension shifts focus on how AI can be embedded into assessment design and enhance the overall learning experience through adaptive feedback mechanisms.

PROPOSED FRAMEWORK FOR AI INTEGRATION IN ASSESSMENTS AND STUDENT PERFORMANCE EVALUATION

In this chapter, our primary attention is on one of the components of the second dimension discussed in Hamza's framework — exploring how AI can be thoughtfully integrated into assessments and feedback processes to foster more meaningful and personalized learning outcomes. To develop a robust framework for assessment design and feedback, we draw inspiration from the foundational ideas of Hamza Aoun's framework, and the SPACE framework proposed by Glen (2023). These frameworks offer valuable insights into AI-enabled education, providing principles that align technology use with sound pedagogy. Our goal is to build on these ideas to develop a new framework that is actionable and practical for both educators and students.

For educators, it provides clear guidelines, on what aspects needs to be included while designing an AI-based assessment. These are presented as rubrics providing a clear guideline for their assessment design that align with the learning objectives while ensuring to address the ethical criteria that promote the responsible use of AI. For students, the framework aims to encouraging them to engage with AI-based assessments as active participants in their learning journey, fostering a deeper understanding of both content and process. This framework aims to offer a comprehensive and ethically sound approach to AI-based assessment design by bridging the gap between technology and pedagogy and benefitting all the stakeholder involved in the educational process.

Figure 1 presents the AI-enabled assessment design framework, that emphasis the interconnected roles of educators and students. The framework places effective student evaluation at its core, recognising the evolving role of technology in education that goes beyond merely incorporating AI into assessments, also ensure that AI tools are thoughtfully integrated into assessments to support the learning objectives. This includes defining the assessment criteria on when and how students are expected to use AI, helping them navigate the balance between independent thinking and the appropriate application of AI tools. However, successful student assessment isn't just about evaluating final performance; it requires guiding students on the proper and ethical use of AI throughout the learning process. The chances for the students to misuse or underutilise AI and missing opportunities are higher when explicit instructions are not provided to enhance their understanding. To ensure that students fully benefit from AI-enabled assessments, they need to be equipped with practical strategies such as those outlined in the SPACE framework on how to engage with AI efficiently and responsibly.

Educators must take an active role not only in crafting AI-integrated assessments but also in mentoring students on how to leverage AI as a learning tool. The synergy between the SPACE framework's strategies and the educator's involvement ensures that students receive the guidance they need to complete assessments effectively. This holistic approach to assessment and feedback promotes a deeper understanding of subject matter while fostering students' ability to use AI as a valuable educational resource.

Impact on Educators and Students

With the inevitable change with the integration of GenAI in education, educators will become facilitators of learning, nevertheless vital for the knowledge acquisition, skills and experience and AI should enable educator capabilities. Educators will need to facilitate human connection, role modelling and promoting skills critical for student development, wellbeing and learning outcomes (AAIN). The educators play a vital role in teaching students to critically assess the AI outputs considering the bias and inaccuracy. There are differing views about whether there will be a place for traditional components of education. "The core fundamental of good education will remain crucial including literacy and numeracy, as well as critical thinking, computational thinking and ethical reasoning" (AAIN; Professor Leslie Loble AM, 2024). It is worth mentioning that GenAI entirely depends on the creation of knowledge by humans, in the absence of which GenAI will limit their evolution and development.

Gen AI tools are imperfect in their interpretation of knowledge and described as 80 per cent accurate / 20 per cent inaccurate. Hence, the critical role on humans to verify GenAI created content will continue to be critical. There is and will continue to be a critical role for humans to verify Gen AI created content. It is likely that this emerging human skill set will continue to grow in significance as Gen AI moves further and further into daily life. Bloom's taxonomy provides a useful framework to explore the teaching and learning in the K-12 context is likely to be refined using GenAI. While at one end, the Bloom's scale, Knowledge, Recall, Understanding and Comprehension is likely to be blown out by Gen AI, at the same time Analysis, Synthesis and Evaluation skills will become more and more important as Gen AI moves further into the classroom settings. There will always be a starvation for great teaching and learning to unpack what the current and future technologies can provide [Education Horizons, 2024].

Figure 1. AI-enabled assessment design and feedback framework

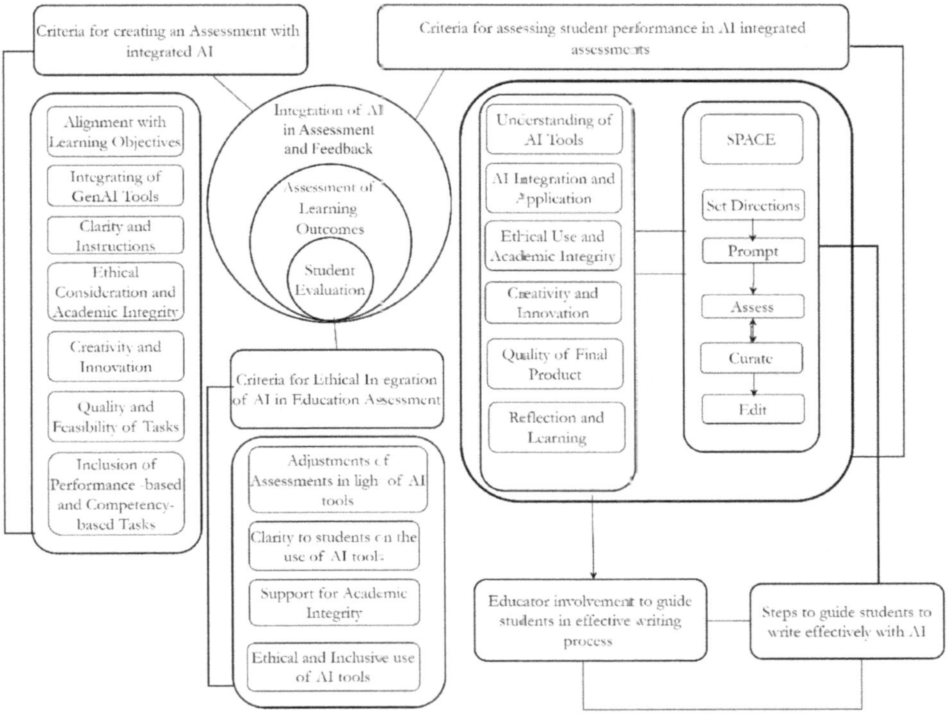

CHALLENGES OF USING AI POWERED TOOLS IN EDUCATIONAL ASSESSMENT

While generative AI tools may be seen as constructive assets and can be beneficial in various ways, including enhancing the assessment process's accuracy, speed, and efficiency, there are risks and challenges with its use in education systems. While this technology can be used at its best to enhance teaching and learning, it cannot replace the role of human interaction which should remain at the heart of education. It should not undermine the authority and status of teachers Some of these challenges include:

1. **Lack of stakeholders' involvement in business requirements:** For the AI tools to meet the specific needs of the education system, it needs to be developed with inputs from the educators, students, and other stakeholders. If otherwise, leads to the irrelevance or adoption of tools in the learning space. As developers have

minimal knowledge on the pedagogical understanding for successful integration, they tend to overlook the expectations of teachers and students who are end uses of the AI tools. Educators play a vital role in AI-based teaching and therefore essential to include to their opinions, past experiences and expectations (Seufert et al., 2020; Holmes et al., 2019).

2. **Lack of human interaction and transparency:** The use of AI in educational assessment can lead to a lack of human interaction, which can be detrimental to students' learning experiences. The underlying principle is that it should always be possible to find out why a particular decision was made by an autonomous system. AI is considered an opaque technology infused into computing systems influencing interactions, decisions without us being aware of it. Another reason for considering it opaque is due to the black box nature of the ML algorithms and the large datasets generating outputs that are not neutral and can be biased. It is challenging to understand how AI algorithms arrive at their conclusions as these algorithms can be biased, leading to inaccurate and unfair assessments due to the data on which they have been trained on. It is imperative that these issues are addressed making it fair, inclusive and provides equal opportunities for all students.
3. **Limited scope:** AI-powered tools are typically designed to focus on specific assessment areas, and therefore, sometimes may not be suitable to assess other types of learning such as critical thinking, creativity, and problem-solving. Therefore, the teacher must cover up in these areas and provide the relevant feedback to the AI model. There is always a need to combine the educator's feedback along with automated feedback generated from the AI tools.
4. **Ethical concerns:** The issues around data privacy and ownership and replacing human educators raises ethical concerns with the use of AI. The high reliance of these tools on large data sets to train the technology and optimise the individual user experience creates a range of privacy risks with the increased prevalence of cyberattacks. It is imperative to ensure that the AI tools are adopted only when the concerns related to data privacy and security are considered and addressed. Clear guidelines need to be established to protect student data, place access limits to sensitive information and the measures for security and privacy measures are in place. [Australian Human Rights Commission, 2023]
5. **Training and Awareness:** The pillar of awareness reflects a human rights approach to participation, empowerment and legality. Educators having a limited understanding of how technology works and lacking technical expertise to fully comprehend the working of the AI tools and what challenges are imposed in the integration of AI. The AI tools should be used in ways to harness the benefits while mitigating the risks. Educational institutions should develop foundational knowledge about AI so that all stakeholders can understand what

AI is, what it can and cannot do. They must consider developing an ongoing education program to raise awareness and approach taken to ensure strong informed consent especially for students with lower literacy and digital literacy skills. Without adequate training, educators and students may be unable to use the tools, leading to inaccurate assessments. Adequate training and professional development should be provided allowing them to effectively engage with these tools in responsible and ethical ways [Australian Human Rights Commission, 2023].

6. **Resistance to change:** Lack of trust in the technology or preferring to use traditional assessment methods may lead to facing resistance from educators and students, thereby resulting in experiencing challenges in introducing these new tools in educational assessment process. Digital literacy training should be prioritised to empower students and educators on the benefits and risks associated with the use of these tools. It is imperative that students should be able to critically evaluate AI-generated content, recognise the limitations and potential biases (Southgate, E. 2020)
7. **Student motivation and engagement:** The ease with which AI generates essays and reports creates risks of plagiarism or intellectual dishonesty. Additionally, the over reliance on AI leads to lack of motivation in contributing to their assessments and lack of effort in their learning. This creates an opportunity to educate students on how to responsibly use new technologies and develop the necessary skills for the future while understanding the importance of the need for originality in student work and academic integrity.
8. **Feedback and support:** AI-powered assessment tools can provide quick feedback on students' performance but may not offer the personalised feedback and support students need to improve their learning. Educators need to balance the benefits automated feedback and the importance of providing feedback that support student learning and development.

DIGITAL EQUITY

While we look at the potential benefits of Ai to improve the learning outcomes, and student participation and engagement through assessment and feedback, it is vital to ensure that all students experience equal opportunities by addressing the digital divide. The student groups with low levels of income, those living in regional areas and disability are identified of particular risk of being left behind. The Australian education Union's research revealed "a long-term gap in digital access, affordability and ability experienced by many public-school students". According to the authors () two key principles of digital equity are removing access barriers and encouraging community engagement. Additionally, it is vital to have policies in place to include them in the educational setting.

1. **Removing access barriers:** One potential solution to overcome digital divide is ensuring equal access to technology. Collaborations between government agencies, educational institutions, private sector, is vital to ensuring access to resources to benefit disadvantaged groups through resourcing in public schools and community facilities. Some of the resources that can be considered are adaptive learning platforms, AI-powered tutoring systems, content tailored to diverse learning abilities.
2. **Training and capacity building:** Education providers should focus on providing training on AI tools, building their capacity in effectively integrating these tools in their teaching environment, encouraging a technology-enabled learning. Additionally, community workshops, awareness campaigns and digital literacy programs can also significantly contribute in promoting the benefits of AI and equipping parents with the literacy to support their children's learning journey.

AI REGULATIONS AND POLICIES

With the speed the AI innovation has significantly outstripped, there is a need to draw on a combination of deep technical and ethical expertise to adequately assess, the impacts of the systems on students and staff from the perspective of digital equity. According to the authors in (AHRC), "the global survey of UNESCO in 2023 of over 450 schools and universities found that less than 10% have institutional policies and guidance in place for the use of AI application". There is a need for commitment to equity and educate ourselves on the technical and ethical-legal aspects of AI to portrait as experts in guiding the implementation and governance of AI tools in educational setting. We point the readers to some of the key resources that act as a starting point to build knowledge about the legal, regulatory and procedural approaches to guide the use of AI. The Table 7 provides the contributions towards the AI regulations and ethical guidelines (Southgate, E. 2020):

Table 7. Contributions to AI regulations and ethical guidelines

Organisation	Contribution
UNESCO	The UNESCO recommendations provide guidelines for institutions around a range of ethical issues of AI Guidance for policy makers guides on the adoption of AI in education and advocates a human-centered approach: "AI and Education" Developed policy guidelines on the use of AI in education and research and frameworks for AI competencies
UK Department of Education	Engaged in an open consultation about generative AI in education Published a statement with a key message that "education sector should make the most of the opportunities provided by technology however to be ensured that is "effectively, safely and appropriately" used". The Russel Group representing 24 leading UK universities published the "principles on the use of generative AI tools in education" to recognise the risk and opportunities of AI focussing on supporting students and staff to be AI-literate, equip staff to support students in using gen-AI tools, adapt teaching and assessment to incorporate the ethical use of generative AI, ensure to uphold academic rigour and integrity, work collaboratively to share best practice as technology evolves.
Academic Integrity Network (AAIN) Gen-AI Working Group and **Tertiary Education Quality and Standards Agency (TEQSA)**	Developed the Generative Artificial Intelligence Guidelines developed and a range of resources to address the potential impact of the AO tools.
Australian Universities	Individual universities have their guidelines and policies to address the use of AI tools by students and staff
Department of Education and	Developed guidelines regarding the use of gen-AI for department staff who has access to gen-AI tools
South Australian Certificate of Education	Developed guidelines for parents and carers and use of AI in SACE assessments
Australian Human Rights Commission (AIHRC)	Produced a discussion paper on the governance of AI
Commonwealth Ombudsman	Practice guide to automated decision-making covering areas around the suitability of automated systems, legal compliance, privacy and governance and ensuring transparency and accountability

CONCLUSION

This chapter has explored the integration of AI into the assessment and feedback process, showing how technology can enhance the way we teach, learn, and evaluate progress. The chapter begins with an introduction to AI's growing role in education and significantly reshaping various processes. The focus of this chapter remains on remains on using it thoughtfully to create assessments that not only evaluate performance but also foster meaningful learning through personalized feedback and adaptive strategies. Throughout the chapter, we examined different types of assessments and their importance in guiding students toward achieving specific learning outcomes. We also introduced various AI tools currently being used in education, helping educators save time, provide more consistent feedback, and offer students tailored learning experiences. The chapter also discusses how it is imperative it is to align with clear learning goals and ethical practices. This ensures that AI is used in ways that benefit students while maintaining fairness and transparency. By drawing on insights from existing literature and frameworks, this chapter offers a blended model that balances the benefits of AI with the irreplaceable value of human expertise. This framework combines insights from established models, recognizing that using AI effectively requires more than just adopting tools—it involves designing assessments with intention and care. The goal is to create assessments that are more engaging, inclusive, and adaptive, while ensuring that ethical considerations remain at the forefront. AI is not meant to replace educators but to act as a powerful support system, enabling them to provide more personalized guidance and feedback to their students.

A key part of this framework emphasises the importance of clear instructions, ensuring that students understand how AI tools should be used in their learning journey. Without this guidance, students might struggle to engage with AI meaningfully or miss opportunities to enhance their understanding. The framework also highlights the dual responsibility of educators and students to ensure that technology supports and not replaces the essential human elements of education. In conclusion, integrating AI into assessment and feedback offers a tremendous opportunity to enhance the learning experience, but it requires intentional design and careful implementation. Educators need to take an active role in guiding students, ensuring assessments are aligned with learning goals and ethical standards. At the same time, students must be equipped with the knowledge and skills to use AI responsibly and effectively. The framework proposed in this chapter offers a practical way forward, helping both educators and students navigate the evolving educational landscape with confidence. With thoughtful integration, AI can unlock new possibilities for teaching and learning, creating a future where assessments are not just a means to measure knowledge but a pathway to deeper understanding and growth.

REFERENCES

AAIN, *Submission 58*, pp. 6–7; Monash University *Submission 3*, pp. 2–3

Ahmad, S. F., Alam, M. M., Rahmat, Mohd. K., Mubarik, M. S., & Hyder, S. I. (2022). Academic and Administrative Role of Artificial Intelligence in Education. Sustainability, 14(3), 1101. MDPI AG. Retrieved from http://dx.doi.org/]DOI: 10.3390/su14031101

AI for T&L in Education. AI and assessment design. (2024) https://libraryguides.vu.edu.au/c.php?g=966085&p=7019124

Australian Human Rights Commission. (2023) "Utilising ethical AI in the Australian education System", Submission to the Standing Committee on Employment, Education and Training. Available at https://humanrights.gov.au/sites/default/files/inquiry_into_the_use_of_generative_artificial_intelligence_in_the_australian_education_system_14_july_2023_0.pdf

Bourke, R. (2018). Self-assessment to incite learning in higher education: Developing ontological awareness. *Assessment & Evaluation in Higher Education*, 43(5), 827–839. DOI: 10.1080/02602938.2017.1411881

Carlos, R.-C. (2023). Artificial Intelligence and Education. *South Florida Journal of Development*, 4(2), 641–655. DOI: 10.46932/sfjdv4n2-001

Chan, C. K. Y., & Luo, J. (2020). Towards an inclusive student partnership: Rethinking mentors' disposition and holistic competency development in near-peer mentoring. *Teaching in Higher Education*, •••, 1–18.

Dillenbourg, P. (2016). The evolution of research on digital education. *International Journal of Artificial Intelligence in Education*, 26(2), 544–560. DOI: 10.1007/s40593-016-0106-z

Faulconer, E., Griffith, J., & Gruss, A. (2021). The impact of positive feedback on student outcomes and perceptions. *Assessment & Evaluation in Higher Education*, 47(2), 1–10.

Garc'ıa-Peñalvo, F. J., Corell, A., Abella-Garc'ıa, V., & Grande-de-Prado, M. (2021). *"Recommendations for mandatory online assessment in higher education during the COVID-19 pandemic," in Radical Solutions for Education in a Crisis Context*. Springer.

Garc'ıa-Peñalvo, F. J., Corell, A., Abella-Garc'ıa, V., & Grande-de-Prado, M. (2021). *"Recommendations for mandatory online assessment in higher education during the COVID-19 pandemic," in Radical Solutions for Education in a Crisis Context*. Springer.

Giray, G. (2021). An assessment of student satisfaction with e-learning: An empirical study with computer and software engineering undergraduate students in Turkey under pandemic conditions. *Education and Information Technologies*, 26(6), 1–23. DOI: 10.1007/s10639-021-10454-x PMID: 33686329

Kleij, F. M. V. D., Vermeulen, J. A., Schildkamp, K., & Eggen, T. J. H. M. (2015). Integrating data-based decision making, assessment for learning and diagnostic testing in formative assessment. *Assessment in Education: Principles, Policy & Practice*, 22(3), 324–343. DOI: 10.1080/0969594X.2014.999024

Kleiman, G. 2023, Teaching Students to Write with AI: The SPACE Framework Hamza Aoun, AI in Education https://media.licdn.com/dms/document/media/D4E1FAQFDyGd4zKH0LA/feedshare-document-pdf-analyzed/0/1718894249107?e=1729728000&v=beta&t=yOTdRvHrenhzJCDcJC4WCYhYMAlb7JAH-sgmluf-8O0

Li, L., & Gao, F. (2016). The effect of peer assessment on project performance of students at different learning levels. *Assessment & Evaluation in Higher Education*, 41(6), 885–900. DOI: 10.1080/02602938.2015.1048185

Liang, W. (2020). *Development Trend and Thinking of Artificial Intelligence in Education. 2020 International Wireless Communications and Mobile Computing*. IWCMC., DOI: 10.1109/IWCMC48107.2020.9148078

Lynam, S., & Cachia, M. (2018). 2018 "Students' perceptions of the role of assessments at higher education,". *Assessment & Evaluation in Higher Education*, 43(2), 223–234. DOI: 10.1080/02602938.2017.1329928

Montagner, I. S. (2019, October). An experience with peer assessment in the context of a Computer Systems course. In *2019 IEEE Frontiers in Education Conference (FIE)* (pp. 1-5). IEEE.

Morduchowicz, A., & Suasnábar, J. (2023). ChatGPT and Education: Op portunity, Challenge, or Threat? Retrieved from https://blogs.iadb.org/educacion/en/chatgpt-education/

Myers, A. (2023). Provocations and possibilities: Stanford seminar examines the future of ChatGPT in education. Retrieved from https://acceleratelearning.stanford.edu/story/provocations-and-possibilitiesstanford-seminar-examines-the-future-of-chatgpt-in-education/]

Nikou, S. A., & Economides, A. A. (2016). The impact of paper-based, computer-based and mobile-based self-assessment on students' science motivation and achievement. *Computers in Human Behavior*, 55, 1241–1248. DOI: 10.1016/j.chb.2015.09.025

Papamitsiou, Z., Lunde, M., Westermoen, J., & Giannakos, M. N. (2021). *"Supporting learners in a crisis context with smart self-assessment," in Radical Solutions for Education in a Crisis Context, Lecture Notes in Educational Technology*. Springer.

Pascale, B. (2023). 22. Time to Revisit Existing Student's Performance Evaluation Approach in Higher Education Sector in a New Era of ChatGPT — A Case Study. *Cogent Education*, 10(1), 2210461. Advance online publication. DOI: 10.1080/2331186X.2023.2210461

Pereira, D., Flores, M. A., & Niklasson, L. (2016). Assessment revisited: A review of research inAssessment and evaluation in higher education. *Assessment & Evaluation in Higher Education*, 41(7), 1008–1032. DOI: 10.1080/02602938.2015.1055233

Perera-Diltz, D. M., & Moe, J. L. (2014). Formative and summative assessment in online education. *Journal of Research in Innovative Teaching*, 7(1).

Professor Leslie Loble, A. M. 2024]Industry Professor, University of Technology Sydney (UTS), *Committee Hansard*, 20March 2024, p. 8

Southgate, E. (2020). Artificial intelligence, ethics, equity and higher education: A 'beginning-of-the-discussion' paper. National Centre for Student Equity in Higher Education, Curtin University, and the University of Newcastle.

Tan, K. (2013). A Framework for Assessment for Learning: Implications for Feedback Practices within and beyond the Gap. *International Scholarly Research Notices*, 2013(1), 640609.

Umar, A. M. A.-T., & Majeed, A. (2018). The impact of assessment for learning on students' achievement in English for specific purposes A case study of pre-medical students at khartoum university: Sudan. *English Language Teaching*, 11(2), 15–25. DOI: 10.5539/elt.v11n2p15

Wyatt-Smith, C., Klenowski, V., & Colbert, P. (2014). *"Assessment understood as enabling," in Designing Assessment for Quality Learning, 7e Enabling Power of Assessment*. Springer.

Yan, Z., & Brown, G. T. L. (2017). A cyclical self-assessment process: Towards a model of how students engage in self-assessment. *Assessment & Evaluation in Higher Education*, 42(8), 1247–1262. DOI: 10.1080/02602938.2016.1260091

Yan, Z., Brown, G. T. L., Lee, J. C.-K., & Qiu, X.-L. (2020). Student self-assessment: Why do they do it? *Educational Psychology*, 40(4), 509–532. DOI: 10.1080/01443410.2019.1672038

Yang, S. J. H., Ogata, H., Matsui, T., & Chen, N.-S. (2021). Human-centered artificial intelligence in education: Seeing the invisible through the visible. *Computers and Education: Artificial Intelligence*, 2, 100008. DOI: 10.1016/j.caeai.2021.100008

Yimer, Amedie, Muhie., Abeselom, Befekadu, Woldie. (2020). *Integration of Artificial Intelligence Technologies in Teaching and Learning in Higher Education.* 10(1):1-7.

ADDITIONAL READING

Darvishi, A., Khosravi, H., Sadiq, S., & Gašević, D. (2022). Incorporating AI and learning analytics to build trustworthy peer assessment systems. *British Journal of Educational Technology*, 53(4), 844–875. DOI: 10.1111/bjet.13233

Guo, K., Pan, M., Li, Y., & Lai, C. (2024). Effects of an AI-supported approach to peer feedback on university EFL students' feedback quality and writing ability. *The Internet and Higher Education*, 63, 100962. DOI: 10.1016/j.iheduc.2024.100962

Hooda, M., Rana, C., Dahiya, O., Rizwan, A., & Hossain, M. S. (2022). Artificial intelligence for assessment and feedback to enhance student success in higher education. *Mathematical Problems in Engineering*, 2022(1), 5215722. DOI: 10.1155/2022/5215722

Venter, J., Coetzee, S. A., & Schmulian, A. (2024). Exploring the use of artificial intelligence (AI) in the delivery of effective feedback. *Assessment & Evaluation in Higher Education*, •••, 1–21. DOI: 10.1080/02602938.2024.2415649

KEY TERMS AND DEFINITIONS

AI Integration: The process of incorporating artificial intelligence technologies into existing systems or practices, such as educational assessments, to enhance functionality and user experience.

Assessment Design: The systematic approach to creating assessment tools and methods that accurately measure student learning and skills aligned with specific learning objectives.

Automated Feedback: Feedback generated by AI systems that provides students with insights on their performance, allowing for real-time adjustments and learning enhancements.

Ethical: Standards: Guidelines ensuring that AI tools in education are used responsibly, protecting student data privacy, maintaining fairness, and avoiding biases.

Learning Outcomes: Clearly defined educational goals that students are expected to achieve through instruction, assessed to measure student progress and effectiveness of teaching strategies.

Personalized Learning: An approach where AI tailors educational content to meet individual student needs, preferences, and learning pace, enhancing engagement and achievement.

Plagiarism Detection Systems: AI-driven tools that identify similarities between a student's work and existing sources to maintain academic integrity by preventing unauthorized copying.

Real-Time Assessment: Immediate evaluation of student work or performance through AI, allowing educators to promptly address learning gaps and provide feedback.

Student Engagement: The level of interest, motivation, and active participation students exhibit in their learning processes, crucial for meaningful educational experiences and improved outcomes.

Transparency: In the context of AI, the clarity with which AI systems operate and make decisions, allowing users to understand and trust the technology in educational assessments.

Chapter 7
Integrated Use of AI Educational Platforms

Melissa Li Sa Liow
https://orcid.org/0000-0003-3794-733X
PSB Academy, Coventry University, Singapore

ABSTRACT

This chapter addresses a critical gap in educational psychology concerning the integrated use of Artificial Intelligence Educational Platforms (AIEPs) and presents four key research objectives. Firstly, it investigates the effectiveness of AIEPs in supporting educators, school administrators, and students—collectively termed "AI users"—who work collaboratively on these platforms within educational settings. Secondly, the chapter analyzes the potential risks of AIEP usage among these users. Thirdly, it examines how AIEPs influence users' sense of relatedness, autonomy, and competence, developing a research framework informed by the Technology Acceptance Model (TAM) and Self-Determination Theory (SDT). Lastly, the chapter explores factors impacting users' perceived use and sustained adoption of AIEPs, expanding the existing literature. This chapter provides essential insights for educators, policymakers, and AIEP developers, offering a forward-looking perspective on the evolving role of AI in education and fostering a new generation of proficient users.

INTRODUCTION

This chapter aims to address a gap in educational psychology regarding the integrated use of Artificial Intelligence Educational Platforms (AIEPs). There are four primary research objectives. First, it discusses the efficacy of AIEPs for educators, school administrators, and students, collectively referred to as "AI users," as they collaborate using these platforms in educational institutions. Second, it explores

DOI: 10.4018/979-8-3693-7220-3.ch007

the risks associated with AIEPs that these users may encounter. Third, it examines the impact on users' relatedness, autonomy, and competence, developing a research framework based on the Technology Acceptance Model (TAM) and Self-Determination Theory (SDT). Fourth, it extends the literature review on how AIEPs influence perceived usefulness and the continued use of these platforms by the users.

BACKGROUND

In an era of rapid technological advancement, AI integration across various societal domains is increasingly prevalent, promising transformative changes. Education is a pivotal area where AI can revolutionize traditional teaching methodologies. Generative AI (GenAI) offers opportunities to reimagine educational practices through personalized, adaptive, and innovative learning experiences. In Obaid et al.'s (2023) book discusses on GenAI's integration in education that includes applications such as content creation, student assessment, and intelligent tutoring systems. Unlike conventional educational technologies that rely on predetermined algorithms, GenAI can autonomously create novel content, mimicking human creativity. This capability allows for personalized learning tailored to individual students' diverse needs and learning styles. A primary benefit of GenAI in education is its potential to enhance teaching and learning efficiency and effectiveness. By analyzing vast amounts of data—such as students' learning preferences, performance patterns, and feedback—GenAI systems can generate tailored learning materials and adapt instructional strategies in real-time, fostering a more engaging learning environment.

GenAI also facilitates interactive and immersive learning experiences beyond traditional classroom boundaries. GenAI-powered chatbots and virtual assistants can provide immediate feedback and support to students, promoting self-directed learning and problem-solving skills. Additionally, AI can manage administrative tasks like grading and scheduling, easing the burden on teachers and administrators, increasing student engagement, developing self-regulatory skills, and enhancing interactions between students, peers, and teachers. Despite its potential, integrating GenAI in education presents challenges. Scholars (Malik & Aslam, May 2024; Slimi & Carballid, 2023) highlight that data privacy and security are significant issues due to the gathering and examination of sensitive student information, leading to ethical and legal concerns. Robust data protection safeguards are essential. Ethical considerations surrounding algorithmic biases and fairness pose significant challenges, as AI algorithms could exacerbate existing inequalities in student assessment and decision-making, underscoring the need for transparency, accountability, and diversity in AI development.

Walter (2024) emphasizes that effective GenAI integration in education necessitates extensive teacher training and professional development. Educators must be equipped with the knowledge and skills to effectively use AI technologies and critically evaluate their impact on student outcomes. Balancing technological innovation with human-centered pedagogy is crucial to ensure that GenAI integration aligns with educational goals, fostering collaboration, critical thinking, and creativity among students. This balance directly impacts users' relatedness, autonomy, and competency when using AI Educational Platforms (AIEPs). Self-Determination Theory (SDT) is applied in this chapter to address the limitations of the Technology Acceptance Model (TAM). SDT, widely used in research on motivating behavior, focuses on the connections between the social environment, psychological needs, motivation, and outcomes. Therefore, SDT is adopted to examine the social and psychological factors influencing the perceived use and continued use of AIEPs.

LITERATURE REVIEW

Technology Acceptance Model (TAM) and Self Determination Theory (SDT)

The Technology Acceptance Model (TAM) is recognized for its efficacy, adaptability, understandability, and simplicity (Šumak et al., 2011). It has been validated across various fields, including clinical information systems (Melas et al., 2011), smartphone usage (Joo & Sang, 2013), mobile hotel booking (Ozturk et al., 2016), mobile parking services (Liang et al., 2017), blogs (Ifinedo, 2017), construction (Park & Park, 2020), mobile banking (Purwanto et al., 2020), mobile libraries (Rafique et al., 2020), autonomous vehicles (Yuen et al., 2021), and e-Word of mouth for destination management (Madi et al., 2024). In education, TAM has been applied to digital libraries (Miller & Khera, 2010), Moodle learning management systems (Rabaa'i, 2016), mobile learning (Kim & Lee, 2016; Li et al., 2021), e-learning (Saleh et al., 2022), massive open online courses (Tao et al., 2022), and administrative apps (Nuha et al., 2024).

However, TAM does not account for factors influencing the perceived and continued use of AI Educational Platforms (AIEPs) (Dishaw & Strong, 1999; Hamidi & Chavoshi, 2018). While TAM allows for the inclusion of external elements (Teo et al., 2019), Self-Determination Theory (SDT) is applied to address these limitations. SDT is extensively used in motivation research due to its focus on contextual support, psychological needs, motivation, and outcomes, making it suitable for examining the social and psychological factors influencing AIEP use.SDT has been applied across various contexts, including online learning (Chen & Jang, 2010), music education (Evans, 2015), social networking (Wang et al., 2016), video game enjoyment (Rogers, 2017), physical education (Sun et al., 2017), politics (Cho & Yang, 2018), mobile-based assessment (Stupniskya et al., 2018), virtual learning environments (Huang et al., 2019), healthcare (Hagger & Protogerou, 2020), and AI in education (Merhi & Meisami, 2024).

Rosli et al. (2022) suggests incorporating SDT factors such as intrinsic motivation, amotivation, identified regulation, external regulation, autonomy, competence, and relatedness in online education. Xia et al. (2022) found that K-12 students in SDT-based programs had positive views of AI learning, with needs satisfaction engaging both high and low achievers and males and females. Chiu et al. (2023) noted that student expertise and educator support influenced competence and intrinsic motivation in AI learning. Sharma et al. (2024) highlighted generative AI's potential for personalized learning and inclusivity in K-12 education in India.

Merhi and Meisami (2024) found that technology-related factors influence undergraduate business students' motivation and engagement. Hmoud et al. (2024) identified that GenAI ChatGPT enhances students' motivation and learning achievement through interaction, perceived relevance, reported effort, result assessment, and task enjoyment. Wood and Moss (2024) reported that integrating GenAI in master's-level courses impacts students' learning experiences and perceptions. Venkateswaran et al. (2024) noted that AI tools improve administrative efficiency in higher education, allowing educators to focus more on instructional design and student support. Guided by SDT, this chapter explores how AIEP efficacy and risks influence perceived and continued use by educators, administrators, and students.

Machine Learning and Artificial intelligence (AI)

Yildirim et al. (2021) advocates before exploring AI's potential in education, it is crucial to understand the subdivisions of machine learning and types of AI. Machine learning has three primary algorithm types: supervised, semi-supervised, and unsupervised. Supervised algorithms use labeled data for tasks like classification, requiring human-labeled training data. Semi-supervised algorithms blend supervised and unsupervised methods, utilizing a small, labeled dataset with a larger unlabeled dataset. Unsupervised algorithms analyze unlabeled data to identify patterns or make predictions. AI can be categorized into weak, general, and strong AI. Weak AI, or narrow AI, performs specific tasks without broader autonomy. General AI exhibits human-level intellect across various tasks, while strong AI surpasses human capabilities in all intellectual activities. Narrow AI is prevalent today in applications such as autonomous vehicles, e-commerce algorithms, and speech recognition systems. Advancing to general or super AI requires significant resources, budgets, and human effort. Understanding these concepts is essential for exploring AI's educational contributions.

AI Users in the Education Field

AI-learning has become crucial in both informal and formal education (Cheon et al., 2012), significantly enhancing students' attitudes and perceptions of easily accessible learning activities in higher education (O'bannon & Thomas, 2014). Defining AI is challenging due to its multidisciplinary nature, encompassing biology, mathematics, economics, linguistics, neuroscience, philosophy, and psychology. In computer science, AI is often understood through machine learning, which involves systems analyzing and learning from data to make predictions (Luckin et al., 2016). AI-learning has shifted traditional educator-centered methods towards student-centered approaches (Herring et al., 2016). Mobile technology supports various educational stages and needs, making AI-learning readily adoptable by college and university students (Almaiah & Almulhem, 2018; Diacopoulos & Crompton, 2020; Neffati et al., 2021; Reddy et al., 2023). Its convenience and flexibility have made AI-learning increasingly popular among students (Dahal et al., 2022; Jurayev, 2023). For this book chapter, AI is defined within educational psychology, focusing on technologies designed for educators, administrators, and students, collectively known as "AI users." These AI entities interact independently and mimic human behavior through machine learning algorithms. Despite significant investments in technology, education often receives limited emphasis, a gap that this chapter aims to address.

AI in the Education Field

Machine learning and AI offer transformative benefits in education, improving administrative tasks, personalizing content delivery, and enhancing student engagement (LearnDash Collaborator, 2018). Educational institutions leverage student data to monitor academic progress and address learning gaps, efficiently adapting to market needs. Companies like UBTech Robotics use advanced technologies to establish AI Labs, providing comprehensive AI education resources and training (UBTech Robotics Pte. Ltd., 2012-2023). AI applications in education enhance classroom management, parent-educator communication, professional development, gamification, and more (University of San Diego Senior College and University Commission, 2024). For example, Singapore's Ministry of Education is introducing AI-powered automated marking systems, reducing teachers' grading workload and allowing more focus on lesson design and student relationships (Government

Technology Agency of Singapore, 2023). The AI@NIE plan will enhance teacher training in AI, integrating AI education topics by 2026.

A survey of 500 U.S. educators found that 60% plan to use AI in classrooms, with tools like AI-powered educational games and adaptive learning platforms being popular. Concerns include academic dishonesty and reducing human interaction, highlighting the need for ethical AI education (Hamilton & Swanston, 2024). OpenAI's ChatGPT Edu addresses these concerns with enhanced security and education-specific features. The World Economic Forum (2024) showcases global AI integration in education:

- South Korea plans to introduce AI-powered digital textbooks to address educational inequality and personalize learning.
- The UAE aims to enhance academic performance with AI-powered personalized learning.
- West Africa's Kabakoo Academies upskills youth with AI-based virtual mentors.
- Brazil's Letrus program improves literacy with AI for personalized learning.
- UNICEF uses AI to create accessible digital textbooks for children with disabilities, aiming to bridge the digital divide.

Despite challenges, AI-powered educational platforms provide personalized learning experiences, flexible due dates, and reduced workloads for educators, fostering self-paced and independent learning (Dahal et al., 2022; Jurayev, 2023).

AIEP EFFICACY BENEFITS IN THE EDUCATIONAL FIELD

AIEPs reducing Grading Workload for Educators

AI and machine learning are revolutionizing education by automating administrative tasks, personalizing content, and enhancing student engagement (LearnDash Collaborator, 2018). AI grading systems, such as Blackboard, Canvas, Mentimeter, and Schoology, save educators time and provide consistent grading, reducing biases (Murphy, 2019). Gradescope, an AI-driven grading tool, is widely used in higher education (Yildirim et al., 2021). AI can also effectively detect cheating and plagiarism through tools like Turnitin. AI grading systems were discussed at the International Conference on Machine Learning, highlighting their ability to handle large-scale grading of computer-based assignments, reducing the need for teaching assistants (True Interaction, n.d.). Intellimetric, launched in the early 1990s, is a pioneer in automated essay scoring and is used by companies for tasks like certification testing and job applicant screening (Zupanc & Bosnic, 2016). Competitors such as Graide, Peergrade, and Real Learning also provide automated scoring services. Educational platforms like Coursera, EdX, Skillshare, and Udemy use AI for grading massive open online courses, offering feedback and writing improvement suggestions.

AI-driven tools like Chegg's Writelab, Copyleaks AI Grader, and Turnitin's Revision Assistant offer diverse feedback types, aiding students in improving their writing (Murphy, 2019). While AI-generated scores may sometimes exceed educator expectations, these tools still provide valuable support. Toprak-Yildix (2024) notes that NLP advancements, such as automated speech recognition, enhance language testing and assessment by maintaining scoring objectivity and reliability and offering personalized feedback. NLP, used since the 1950s, powers tools like automated essay scoring, text-to-speech applications, and virtual assistants (Murphy, 2019). NLP-driven AIEPs analyze text elements to provide detailed feedback, requiring significant initial effort but offering substantial time savings and student support benefits. NLP applications extend to medical records, drug formulation, legal document analysis, and financial research, enhancing independent learning outside classroom time (Thomas, 2020; Kot et al., 2024). Obadi et al. (2024) highlight the impact of advanced algorithms and large datasets in AI education, improving communication and bridging language gaps with conversational agents like BERT and GPT.

AIEPs significantly aid educators in creating formative and summative online tests, enhancing the efficiency and integrity of assessments (Bisen et al., 2021). These platforms can randomly select questions from a question bank to prevent cheating and adjust question difficulty based on student performance. AIEPs also detect cheating by analyzing variables such as word usage, time, and submission dates, improving testing administration. 6sense (2024) highlights its Revenue AITM platform, which helps businesses optimize revenue generation through data-driven insights. One example is Pymetrics, which uses AI to identify suitable job candidates and group productive teams by analyzing behavior. In educational settings, Pymetrics could assist in hiring suitable educators and administrators and enhance student collaboration by grouping students with complementary skills. Other similar AIEPs for educational institutions include AON, HireRight, Kaggle, and Pearson VUE. These tools can streamline administrative tasks, boost efficiency, and enhance educational outcomes.

AIEPs completing Routine School Administrative Tasks

Yildirim et al. (2021) advocate integrating AI through AIEPs to handle routine administrative tasks, saving time and costs for educational institutions. As AI technology advances and costs decrease, it becomes inefficient to retain staff for jobs that AI can automate. While automation may raise job displacement concerns, it ultimately benefits institutions by relieving educators and administrators of repetitive tasks, allowing them to focus on teaching and student services. AI's involvement in administrative tasks would not threaten educator-student communications but rather support educators, enhancing their roles and effectiveness.

AIEPs help School Administrators in Class Scheduling

Scheduling is a highly repetitive administrative task that AI technology can ease (Bisen et al., 2021). Creating student schedules is challenging, especially in smaller schools where meeting each student's preferences is difficult. In larger schools, the sheer number of students complicates assigning preferred teachers. AIEPs can streamline this process, making it more efficient and satisfactory. AI scheduling software like ServiceMax, Skeludo, Oracle Field Service Cloud, IFS, and Dynamics 365 Field Service can analyze various class scheduling permutations to match students and educators based on compatible personalities and interests, enhancing relationships. This automation saves administrators time, allowing them to focus on supporting students in other areas.

AIEPs handle Non-Course Queries reducing School Administrators' and Educators' Workload

AIEPs can handle frequently asked, non-course-related queries, typically managed by school administrators, such as fee payment procedures, course applications, school events, and graduation information. Similar to virtual assistants in banking and e-commerce, educational institutions could implement chatbots or virtual assistants to save money and free up administrators' time for more critical tasks (Thomas, 2020, August 17). For example, the Common App's AI chatbot, Oli, assists students with college admissions, addressing the decline in applications during COVID-19 by enabling remote consultation. Schoolinks, a college and career readiness AIEP, has a chatbot for course applications and career searches, using machine learning to match students with suitable careers and schools (Schoolinks, n.d.). Schoolinks also offers personalized student volunteering and internship opportunities. Other similar AIEPs include Adobe Captivate, HubSpot Academy, Nearpod, and Lynda.com (part of LinkedIn Learning) (TrustRadius, 2013-2024).

Advanced virtual assistants can address more complex queries, allowing educators to focus on curriculum development and ensuring all student questions are answered promptly (Bisen et al., 2021; Kim et al., 2022). This supports personalized education by enabling students to get answers at their own pace. Additionally, virtual assistants can handle common course management questions, such as test submission requirements and due dates. Chheang et al. (2024) introduced a virtual reality environment with a GenAI-embodied assistant to help students with complex anatomy questions and improve verbal communication.

Personalizing Education with AI for Students

Scholars such as Ilić et al. (2021), Saxena et al. (2023), and Kot and Nykyporets (2024) advocate that AI significantly advances education through personalization. AIEPs can model student knowledge, enhancing adaptability and efficiency by tailoring learning experiences to individual needs and recognizing knowledge gaps. This customization accommodates different learning preferences—auditory, visual, or repetitive—allowing students to focus on areas needing the most support and reducing the need for standardized courses. AIEPs enable students to progress at their own pace, promoting personalized learning paths. AI has the potential to revolutionize education by creating a more flexible and individualized learning environment.

AIEPS as Intelligent Tutoring Systems for Students

AIEPs play a crucial role in personalizing education, particularly through intelligent tutoring systems, which offer personalized and scalable tutoring experiences akin to one-on-one human tutoring (Holmes et al., 2018). Systems like Carnegie Learning's Cognitive Tutor and Andes Physics Tutoring System have significantly improved student achievement across various courses (Holmes et al., 2018), suggesting broader AIEP integration could optimize study time and free up students' schedules for other activities. These intelligent tutoring systems utilize meta-cognitive frameworks to boost student engagement and motivation, employing Socratic dialogues and narratives that actively involve students in their learning (Luckin et al., 2016). Such systems support adaptive learning environments and deepen understanding of the learning process (Luckin et al., 2016). By modeling cognitive and emotional states, AIEPs tailor feedback to enhance learning outcomes, significantly improving performance (Grawemeyer et al., 2015).

Exploratory learning environments foster hands-on, student-driven learning, allowing students to delve deeply into course material with guided support as needed (Holmes et al., 2018). AIEPs guide students with personalized tutorials based on their understanding level, drawing from the domain model (course knowledge), pedagogical model (teaching strategies), and learner model (student behavior and competency) (Holmes et al., 2019). Overall, AIEPs advance education by personalizing learning experiences, increasing engagement, an enhancing academic performance. As these systems evolve with technologies like neural networks, their ability to personalize and improve education is expected to grow, reducing educators' workloads both in and out of the classroom.

AIEPs aids Students because of its Educational Data Mining Features

AIEPs have significantly benefited schools through educational data mining features, allowing educators to evaluate teaching efficacy and experiment with instructional techniques based on their impact on student engagement and performance. This technology replaces traditional pen-and-paper assessments, enabling detailed observation of student progress (Hill et al., 2014). Continuous assessment through data mining reduces disruptions from formal tests and provides insights into student behaviors, helping forecast dropout risks (Luckin et al., 2016). Learning analytics reveals when students need support, highlighting their achievements, motivations, and challenges (Luckin et al., 2016; Swiecki et al., 2022). These capabilities personalize learning and foster a motivational, conducive environment.

AIEPs facilitate Student Involvement

AIEPs enhance online education by providing options to gauge student involvement and success. Hussain et al. (2018) used machine learning algorithms on data from a Virtual Learning Environment to measure engagement and performance. They found a correlation between assessment scores and participation, indicating AIEPs can identify engaged students, aiding educators in supporting those needing more attention. Vacalopoulou et al. (2014) highlighted AI's role in transforming education through tools like TA-bot, Dawebot, Rexy, and Kwame, which offer personalized assistance and foster self-regulated learning. GenAI technologies like ChatGPT promise interactive, real-time learning, revolutionizing student involvement and making education more effective and accessible.

AIEP RISKS IN THE EDUCATIONAL FIELD

Risks of AI Integration

The integration of AI into education through AIEPs presents several risks that need to be addressed for successful adoption. Slimi and Carballid (2023) highlight algorithmic biases and discrimination as significant concerns, where AI can perpetuate existing biases in training data, leading to unfair outcomes in admissions and grading. Mitigating these risks requires accountability, transparency, and fairness in AIEP development, including bias detection, regular audits, and inclusive dataset collation (Malik & Aslam, May 2024).

Another risk is the complexity of implementing AI across diverse educational contexts, as educational environments vary widely in pedagogical approaches and infrastructure. A customizable approach to AIEP implementation is crucial to address these unique needs (Malik & Aslam, May 2024). Over-dependency on AIEPs is also a concern, as it can reduce the human-centric elements of education. While AI can automate tasks and personalize learning, it cannot replace the creativity, empathy, and insights of human teachers. Balancing technological innovation with human-centric pedagogy is essential (Malik & Aslam, May 2024). Salloum (2024) addresses legal and ethical concerns related to the collection, accessibility, and protection of student data. AIEPs rely on large amounts of data, raising issues about data privacy and security. Ensuring compliance with regulations such as General Data Protection Regulation (GDPR) and implementing encryption protocols and data governance frameworks can help manage these risks (Proton AG., 2024; UNCTAD, n.d.).

Walter (2024) emphasizes the importance of educator training for effective AI integration. Many educators may lack the skills to use AI tools in teaching. Providing support networks, training resources, and professional development can help educators harness AI's potential. Overall, addressing ethical concerns such as accountability, algorithmic bias, data privacy, and educational inequalities is crucial for successful AI integration in education (Gaur et al., 2024).

Non-Authenticity Risks

Bailey (2023) notes that the widespread use of GenAI content in AIEPs complicates knowledge acquisition and distribution. Students may encounter GenAI materials in their courses and reference books, which undermines trust in educational content and their ability to critically analyze information. The challenge of non-authenticity extends to other media forms, including audio, images, and video. GenAI can create deepfake videos, photorealistic images, and synthesized speech almost identical to human-produced media. Educators must verify the authenticity of student submissions and avoid spreading manipulated or misleading information.

Ditta and Aslam (2024) argue that AI in education raises new risks regarding the authenticity of generated content in AIEPs. GenAI's ability to produce content indistinguishable from human-created material blurs the line between genuine and GenAI information, which is particularly concerning in educational settings where information integrity is critical. Traditional evaluation methods like grading for coherence, writing style, and originality are inadequate as GenAI can mimic human writing styles accurately, raising concerns about academic integrity. Alier et al. (2024) conclude that resolving these non-authenticity risks requires a multifaceted approach.

Educators need knowledge and tools to identify GenAI content and differentiate it from human-created material. Digital literacy training for educators and students about AI technologies' capabilities and limitations would be beneficial. Educational institutions should develop clear policies and guidelines regarding GenAI content use while promoting ethical standards for content creation and acknowledgement. Technological solutions like digital signatures or watermarking can embed metadata in GenAI content, providing a verifiable record of authenticity. By implementing these measures, educators can maintain the integrity of educational content and empower students to navigate GenAI content confidently.

Ethical Risks

The ethical risks of algorithmic bias in AIEPs are a significant challenge for responsible AI integration in education. As AI influences personalized learning suggestions, student assessment, and academic performance evaluation, there is a potential risk of extending biases present in the training data and worsening educational inequalities. Donlon and Tiernan (2023) describe algorithmic bias as discriminatory behavior by AI algorithms towards specific groups, such as those defined by gender, race, or socioeconomic status. Historical stereotypes in training data can be unintentionally intensified by AI, leading to unfair treatment of minority students.

Addressing algorithmic bias requires efforts in algorithm design, data collection, and model evaluation to ensure fairness, transparency, and accountability in AI-driven decisions in AIEPs. Kayyali (2024) warns that unresolved biases could redefine educational paradigms. To mitigate these risks, Ditta and Aslam (2024) suggest developers adopt mechanisms for addressing errors, biases, and unintended outcomes. Promoting diversity and inclusivity in dataset collection through data augmentation, diverse sampling, and bias mitigation algorithms is crucial. Malik and Aslam (May 2024) call for collaboration between policymakers and educators to develop ethical guidelines, accountability mechanisms, and regulatory frameworks to govern the responsible use of AIEPs and reduce algorithmic bias.

Research Framework

Drawing on the TAM and SDT, the research framework in Figure 1 guides future studies. It examines the efficacy benefits of AIEPs and how the associated risks impact users' sense of relatedness, autonomy, and competence in using AIEPs, their perceived usefulness, and their continued use of these systems.

Figure 1. Research framework

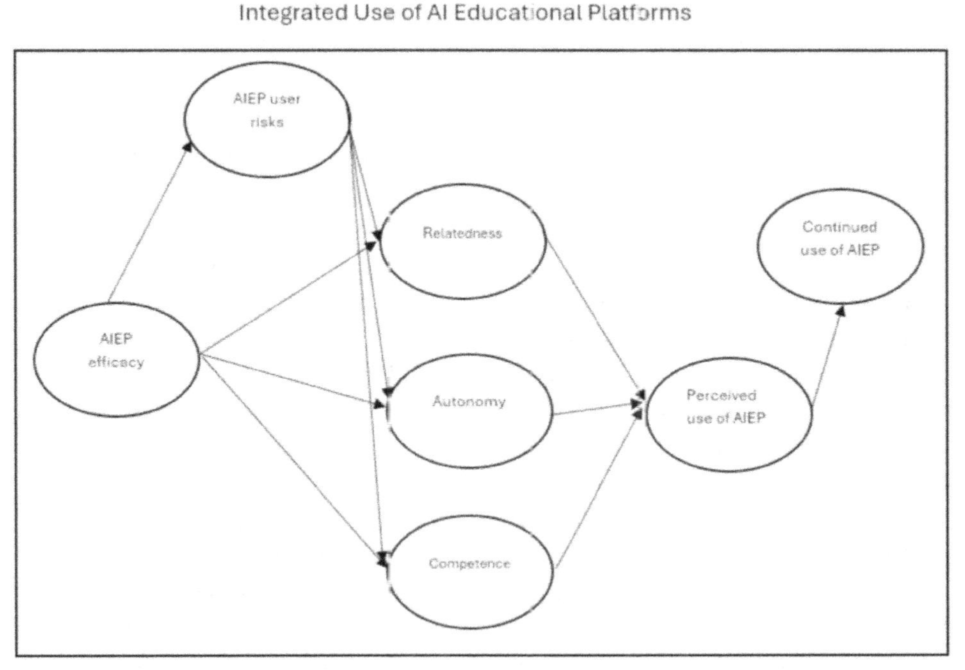

CONCLUSION, LIMITATIONS AND SUGGESTIONS FOR FUTURE RESEARCH

In the modern technological era, AI integration into education is increasingly common, holding great potential to transform traditional teaching methods. AIEPs offer adaptive, personalized, and innovative learning experiences, supporting educators with content creation, student assessment, and academic support. Unlike conventional educational technologies, AIEPs can independently generate new content, simulating human-like thinking, creativity, and adaptability, thus catering to diverse student needs and learning styles. This enhances student learning experiences and reduces the workload for educators and school administrators. AIEPs can improve efficiency and effectiveness in handling academic and non-academic matters through data mining of students' preferences, performance patterns, and feedback. They can adapt instructional strategies in real-time, promoting interactive learning experiences beyond conventional classroom boundaries. Chatbots and virtual assistants in AIEPs provide guidance, instant feedback, and foster self-paced learning and problem-solving skills.

Despite these benefits, integrating AIEPs presents risks. Data security and privacy are major concerns, as the collection and analysis of large amounts of confidential student data raise legal and ethical issues. Robust data protection protocols are critical to mitigate misuse and unauthorized access. Non-authentic risks erode trust in educational content, making it harder to distinguish between original student work and GenAI content, compromising academic integrity. Ethical concerns about algorithmic fairness and biases also pose significant risks, potentially aggravating existing biases and inequalities in student assessment and scoring. To ensure successful AIEP integration, comprehensive training and professional development programs for educators are essential. Educators must be equipped with the knowledge, resources, and skills to leverage AIEP technologies effectively. Balancing human-centric pedagogy and technological innovation is crucial to align AI integration with educational values and aims.

This chapter formulates a research framework (Figure 1) underpinned by TAM and SDT, guiding future researchers in gathering empirical evidence on AIEP integration. It examines AIEP efficacy and risks, considering how these factors influence user relatedness, autonomy, and competence. The findings will shed light on how motivation impacts the perceived and continued use of AIEPs. However, this chapter's limitations include studying AIEPs within a single institution and not addressing content sharing across devices or collaboration with other institutions. Future research should explore these aspects and consider longitudinal structural equation modeling (SEM) designs to assess causality and comparative studies across different countries. This book chapter discusses AI's implications in education, including ethical considerations, the role of educators alongside AI, and future possibilities for enhancing learning outcomes. It serves as a resource for educators, policymakers, and AIEP developers, offering insights into the evolving educational landscape in the AI era.

REFERENCES

Alier, M., García-Peñalvo, F., & Camba, J. D. (2024). Generative Artificial Intelligence in Education: From Deceptive to Disruptive. *International Journal of Interactive Multimedia and Artificial Intelligence*, 5, 5–14. DOI: 10.9781/ijimai.2024.02.011

Almaiah, M. A., & Almulhem, A. (2018). A conceptual framework for determining the success factors of e-learning system implementation using Delphi technique. *Journal of Theoretical and Applied Information Technology*, 96(17), 5962–5976.

Bailey, J. (2023). AI in Education: The leap into a new era of machine intelligence carries risks and challenges, but also plenty of promise. *Education Next*, 23(4), 29–36.

Bisen, I. E., Arslan, E. A., Yildirim, K., & Yildirim, Y. (2021). Artificial intelligence and machine learning in higher education. In *Machine learning approaches for improvising modern learning systems* (pp. 1–17). IGI Global. DOI: 10.4018/978-1-7998-5009-0.ch001

CB Information Services, Inc. (2024). *Compare Studiosity to Competitors*.https://www.cbinsights.com/company/studiosity

Chen, K. C., & Jang, S. J. (2010). Motivation in online learning: Testing a model of self-determination theory. *Computers in Human Behavior*, 26(4), 741–752. DOI: 10.1016/j.chb.2010.01.011

Cheon, J., Lee, S., Crooks, S. M., & Song, J. (2012). An investigation of mobile learning readiness in higher education based on the theory of planned behavior. *Computers & Education*, 59(3), 1054–1064. DOI: 10.1016/j.compedu.2012.04.015

Chheang, V., Sharmin, S., Márquez-Hernández, R., Patel, M., Rajasekaran, D., Caulfield, G., & Barmaki, R. L. (2024, January). Towards anatomy education with generative AI-based virtual assistants in immersive virtual reality environments. In *2024 IEEE International Conference on Artificial Intelligence and eXtended and Virtual Reality (AIxVR)* (pp. 21-30). IEEE. DOI: 10.1109/AIxVR59861.2024.00011

Chiu, T. K., Moorhouse, B. L., Chai, C. S., & Ismailov, M. (2023). Teacher support and student motivation to learn with Artificial Intelligence (AI) based chatbot. *Interactive Learning Environments*, 1–17. DOI: 10.1080/10494820.2023.2172044

Cho, H. T., & Yang, J. S. (2018) How perceptions of organizational politics influence self-determined motivation: The mediating role of work mood. *Asia Pacific Management Review*, 23(1), 60–69. DOI: 10.1016/j.apmrv.2017.05.003

Dahal, N., Manandhar, N. K., Luitel, L., Luitel, B. C., Pant, B. P., & Shrestha, I. M. (2022). ICT tools for remote teaching and learning mathematics: A proposal for autonomy and engagements. *Online Submission*, 2(1), 289–296. DOI: 10.25082/AMLER.2022.01.013

Diacopoulos, M. M., & Crompton, H. (2020). A systematic review of mobile learning in social studies. *Computers & Education*, 154, 103911. Advance online publication. DOI: 10.1016/j.compedu.2020.103911

Ditta, A., & Aslam, M. U. (2024). *Education in the AI Age: Navigating Challenges of Generative AI Integration*. https://www.researchgate.net/publication/380364982

Donlon, E., & Tiernan, P. (2023). Chatbots and Citations: An experiment in academic writing with Generative AI. *Irish Journal of Technology Enhanced Learning*, 7(2), 75–87. DOI: 10.22554/ijtel.v7i2.125

Evans, P. (2015). Self-determination theory: An approach to motivation in music education. *Musicae Scientiae*, 19(1), 65–83. DOI: 10.1177/1029864914568044

G2.com Inc. (2024). *Compare Top 10 ServiceMax Alternatives & Competitors*. https://www.g2.com/products/ptc-servicemax/competitors/alternatives

Gaur, A. S., Sharan, H. O., & Kumar, R. (2024). AI in Education: Ethical Challenges and Opportunities. *The Ethical Frontier of AI and Data Analysis*, IGI Global, 39-54.

Government Technology Agency of Singapore. (February 23, 2023). *Tech and education: How automation and AI are powering learning in Singapore*. https://www.tech.gov.sg/media/technews/tech-and-education-how-automation-and-ai-is-powering-learning-in-singapore/

Grawemeyer, B., Mavrikis, M., Holmes, W., & Gutierrez-Santos, S. (2015). Adapting feedback types according to students' affective states. In *Artificial Intelligence in Education: 17th International Conference, AIED 2015, Madrid, Spain, June 22-26, 2015*. [Springer International Publishing.]. *Proceedings*, 17, 586–590.

Hagger, M. S., & Protogerou, C. (2020). Self-determination theory and autonomy support to change healthcare behavior. *The Wiley handbook of healthcare treatment engagement: Theory, research, and clinical practice*, 141-158.

Hamilton, I., & Swanston, B. (June 6, 2024). *Artificial Intelligence In Education: Teachers' Opinions On AI In The Classroom*. Forbes Media LLC. https://www.forbes.com/advisor/education/it-and-tech/artificial-intelligence-in-school/#:~:text=AI's%20Influence%20on%20Education,5%20cited%20a%20negative%20effect

Herring, M. C., Koehler, M. J., & Mishra, P. (Eds.). (2016). *Handbook of technological pedagogical content knowledge (TPACK) for educators* (Vol. 3, pp. 189–200). Routledge. DOI: 10.4324/9781315771328

Hill, P. W., & Barber, M. (2014). *Preparing for a renaissance in assessment*. Pearson.

Hmoud, M., Swaity, H., Hamad, N., Karram, O., & Daher, W. (2024). Higher education students' task motivation in the generative artificial intelligence context: The case of chatgpt. *Information (Basel)*, 15(1), 33. DOI: 10.3390/info15010033

Holmes, W., Anastopoulou, S., Schaumburg, H., & Mavrikis, M. (2018). *Technology-enhanced personalised learning: Untangling the evidence*. http://www.studie-personalisiertes-lernen.de/en/

Huang, Y. C., Backman, S. J., Backman, K. F., McGuire, F. A., & Moore, D. (2019). An investigation of motivation and experience in virtual learning environments: A self-determination theory. *Education and Information Technologies*, 24(1), 591–611. DOI: 10.1007/s10639-018-9784-5

Ifinedo, P. (2017). Examining students' intention to continue using blogs for learning: Perspectives from technology acceptance, motivational, and social-cognitive frameworks. *Computers in Human Behavior*, 72, 189–199. DOI: 10.1016/j.chb.2016.12.049

Ilić, M. P., Păun, D., Popović Šević, N., Hadžić, A., & Jianu, A. (2021). Needs and performance analysis for changes in higher education and implementation of artificial intelligence, machine learning, and extended reality. *Education Sciences*, 11(10), 568. Advance online publication. DOI: 10.3390/educsci11100568

Joo, J., & Sang, Y. (2013). Exploring Koreans' smartphone usage: An integrated model of the technology acceptance model and uses and gratifications theory. *Computers in Human Behavior*, 29(6), 2512–2518. DOI: 10.1016/j.chb.2013.06.002

Jurayev, T. N. (2023). The use of mobile learning applications in higher education institutes. *Advances in Mobile Learning Educational Research*, 3(1), 610–620. DOI: 10.25082/AMLER.2023.01.010

Kayyali, M. (2024). Future possibilities and challenges of AI in education. In *Transforming education with generative AI: Prompt engineering and synthetic content creation* (pp. 118–137). IGI Global. DOI: 10.4018/979-8-3693-1351-0.ch006

Kim, G. M., & Lee, S. J. (2016). Korean Students' Intentions to Use Mobile-Assisted Language Learning: Applying the Technology Acceptance Model. *International Journal of Contents*, 12(3), 47–53. Advance online publication. DOI: 10.5392/IJoC.2016.12.3.047

Kim, J., Merrill, K., Xu, K., & Sellnow, D. D. (2020). My teacher is a machine: Understanding students' perceptions of AI teaching assistants in online education. *International Journal of Human-Computer Interaction*, 36(20), 1902–1911. DOI: 10.1080/10447318.2020.1801227

Kot, S. O., & Nykyporets, S. S. (2024). *Utilization of artificial intelligence in enhancing English language proficiency in tertiary education. Science and Education in the Third Millennium: Information Technology*. Education, Law, Psychology, Social Sphere, Management.

LearnDash Collaborator. (2018, November 14). *4 Ways Machine Learning Can Improve Online Education*. https://www.learndash.com/4-ways-machine-learning-can-improve-online-education/

Li, C., He, L., & Wong, I. A. (2021). Determinants predicting undergraduates' intention to adopt e-learning for studying english in chinese higher education context: A structural equation modelling approach. *Education and Information Technologies*, 26(4), 4221–4239. DOI: 10.1007/s10639-021-10462-x

Liang, J. K., Eccarius, T., & Lu, C. C. (2019). Investigating factors that affect the intention to use shared parking: A case study of Taipei City. *Transportation Research Part A, Policy and Practice*, 130, 799–812. DOI: 10.1016/j.tra.2019.10.006

Luckin, R., & Holmes, W. (2016). *Intelligence unleashed: An argument for AI in education*. Pearson.

Madi, J., Al Khasawneh, M., & Dandis, A. O. (2024). Visiting and revisiting destinations: Impact of augmented reality, content quality, perceived ease of use, perceived value and usefulness on E-WOM. *International Journal of Quality & Reliability Management*, 41(6), 1550–1571. DOI: 10.1108/IJQRM-10-2023-0314

Malik, A., & Aslam, M. U. (May 2024). *Reimagining Teaching: Exploring Challenges of Generative AI Integration in Education.* https://www.researchgate.net/publication/380365121

Melas, C. D., Zampetakis, L. A., Dimopoulou, A., & Moustakis, V. (2011). Modeling the acceptance of clinical information systems among hospital medical staff: An extended TAM model. *Journal of Biomedical Informatics*, 44(4), 553–564. DOI: 10.1016/j.jbi.2011.01.009 PMID: 21292029

Merhi, M. I., & Meisami, A. (2024). Boosting Students' Engagement with Web-Based Assessment Platforms: A Self-Determination Theory Perspective. *AIS Transactions on Human-Computer Interaction*, 16(2), 216–236. DOI: 10.17705/1thci.00205

Miller, J., & Khera, O. (2010). Digital library adoption and the technology acceptance model: A cross-country analysis. *The Electronic Journal on Information Systems in Developing Countries*, 40(1), 1–19. DOI: 10.1002/j.1681-4835.2010.tb00288.x

Murphy, R. F. (2019). *Artificial Intelligence Applications to Support K-12 Teachers and Teaching: A Review of Promising Applications, Opportunities, and Challenges. Perspective*. RAND Corporation.

Neffati, O. S., Setiawan, R., Jayanthi, P., Vanithamani, S., Sharma, D. K., Regin, R., & Sengan, S. (2021). An educational tool for enhanced mobile e-Learning for technical higher education using mobile devices for augmented reality. *Microprocessors and Microsystems*, 83, 104030. Advance online publication. DOI: 10.1016/j.micpro.2021.104030

Nuha, M. F. A. U., Muklason, A., & Agustiawan, Y. (2024). Enhancing Administrative Efficiency in Pondok Pesantren: Exploring the Acceptance of E-Santren App System for Administrative Tasks. *Procedia Computer Science*, 234, 795–804. DOI: 10.1016/j.procs.2024.03.096

O'bannon, B. W., & Thomas, K. (2014). Teacher perceptions of using mobile phones in the classroom: Age matters! *Computers & Education*, 74, 15–25. DOI: 10.1016/j.compedu.2014.01.006

Obaid, A. J., Bhushan, B., & Rajest, S. S. (Eds.). (2023). *Advanced applications of generative AI and natural language processing models*. IGI Global. DOI: 10.4018/979-8-3693-0502-7

Ozturk, A. B., Bilgihan, A., Nusair, K., & Okumus, F. (2016). What keeps the mobile hotel booking users loyal? Investigating the roles of self-efficacy, compatibility, perceived ease of use, and perceived convenience. *International Journal of Information Management*, 36(6), 1350–1359. DOI: 10.1016/j.ijinfomgt.2016.04.005

Park, E. S., & Park, M. S. (2020). Factors of the technology acceptance model for construction IT. *Applied Sciences (Basel, Switzerland)*, 10(22), 8299. DOI: 10.3390/app10228299

Proton, A. G. (2024). *What is GDPR, the EU's new data protection law?*https://gdpr.eu/what-is-gdpr/

Purwanto, E., Deviny, J., & Mutahar, A. M. (2020). The mediating role of trust in the relationship between corporate image, security, word of mouth and loyalty in M-banking using among the millennial generation in Indonesia. *Management & Marketing*, 15(2), 255–274. DOI: 10.2478/mmcks-2020-0016

Rabaa'i, A. A. (2016). Extending the technology acceptance model (TAM) to assess students' behavioural intentions to adopt an e-learning system: The case of moodle as a learning tool. *Journal of emerging trends in engineering and applied sciences, 7*(1), 13-30.

Rafique, H., Almagrabi, A. O., Shamim, A., Anwar, F., & Bashir, A. K. (2020). Investigating the acceptance of mobile library applications with an extended technology acceptance model (TAM). *Computers & Education*, 145, 103732. Advance online publication. DOI: 10.1016/j.compedu.2019.103732

Reddy, E. V., Reddy, P., Sharma, B., Reddy, K., & Khan, M. G. (2023). Readiness and perception of pacific students to mobile phones for higher education. *Technology. Knowledge and Learning*, 28(3), 1113–1132. DOI: 10.1007/s10758-022-09595-w

Rogers, R. (2017). The motivational pull of video game feedback, rules, and social interaction: Another self-determination theory approach. *Computers in Human Behavior*, 73, 446–450. DOI: 10.1016/j.chb.2017.03.048

Rosli, M. S., Saleh, N. S., Md. Ali, A., & Abu Bakar, S. (2022). Self-determination theory and online learning in university: Advancements, future direction and research gaps. *Sustainability*, 14(21). Advance online publication. DOI: 10.3390/su142114655

Saleh, S. S., Nat, M., & Aqel, M. (2022). Sustainable adoption of e-learning from the TAM perspective. *Sustainability (Basel)*, 14(6), 3690. Advance online publication. DOI: 10.3390/su14063690

Salloum, S. A. (2024). AI Perils in Education: Exploring Ethical Concerns. *Artificial Intelligence in Education: The Power and Dangers of ChatGPT in the Classroom*, 669-675.

Saxena, A. K., García, V., Amin, M. R., Salazar, J. M. R., & Dey, S. (2023). Structure, Objectives, and Operational Framework for Ethical Integration of Artificial Intelligence in Educational. *Sage Science Review of Educational Technology, 6*(1), 88-100. https://journals.sagescience.org/index.php/ssret/article/view/139

6sense. (2024). *Top Competitors and Alternatives of pymetrics*. https://6sense.com/tech/pre-employment-assessment/pymetrics-market-share

ServiceMax. (n.d.). *Artificial Intelligence Scheduling*. https://www.servicemax.com/field-service-manual/artificial-intelligence-scheduling

Sharma, D. M., Ramana, K. V., Jothilakshmi, R., Verma, R., Maheswari, B. U., & Boopathi, S. (2024). Integrating Generative AI Into K-12 Curriculums and Pedagogies in India: Opportunities and Challenges. *Facilitating Global Collaboration and Knowledge Sharing in Higher Education With Generative AI*, IGI Global, 133-161.

Slimi, Z., & Carballido, B. V. (2023). Navigating the Ethical Challenges of Artificial Intelligence in Higher Education: An Analysis of Seven Global AI Ethics Policies. *TEM Journal, 12*(2).

Stupnisky, R. H., BrckaLorenz, A., Yuhas, B., & Guay, F. (2018). Faculty members' motivation for teaching and best practices: Testing a model based on self-determination theory across institution types. *Contemporary Educational Psychology*, 53, 15–26. DOI: 10.1016/j.cedpsych.2018.01.004

Šumak, B., Heričko, M., Pušnik, M., & Polančič, G. (2011). Factors affecting acceptance and use of Moodle: An empirical study based on TAM. *Informatica (Vilnius)*, 35(1), 91–100.

Sun, H., Li, W., & Shen, B. (2017). Learning in physical education: A self-determination theory perspective. *Journal of Teaching in Physical Education*, 36(3), 277–291. DOI: 10.1123/jtpe.2017-0067

Swiecki, Z., Khosravi, H., Chen, G., Martinez-Maldonado, R., Lodge, J. M., Milligan, S., Selwyn, N., & Gašević, D. (2022). Assessment in the age of artificial intelligence. *Computers and Education: Artificial Intelligence*, 3, 100075. Advance online publication. DOI: 10.1016/j.caeai.2022.100075

Tao, D., Fu, P., Wang, Y., Zhang, T., & Qu, X. (2022). Key characteristics in designing massive open online courses (MOOCs) for user acceptance: An application of the extended technology acceptance model. *Interactive Learning Environments*, 30(5), 882–895. DOI: 10.1080/10494820.2019.1695214

Thomas. (2020, August 17). *Natural language processing is changing these 5 industries.* https://fastdatascience.com/natural-language-processing-is-changing-these-5-industries/

Toprak-Yıldız, T. E. (2024). Natural Language Processing Applications in Language Assessment: The Use of Automated Speech Scoring. In *Fostering Foreign Language Teaching and Learning Environments With Contemporary Technologies* (pp. 216-234). IGI Global.

True Interaction. (n.d.). *AI and the Classroom: Machine Learning in Education.* True. https:/www.trueinteraction.com/ai-and-the-classroom-machine-learning-in-education/

TrustRadius. (2013-2024). *SchooLinks Competitors and Alternatives.* https://www.trustradius.com/products/schoolinks/competitors

UBTech Robotics Pte. Ltd. (2012-2023). *AI Lab Solution.* https://www.ubtrobot.com/aiEducation/solutions/aiLabsInSchools?gad_source=1&gclid=Cj0KCQjwtZK1BhDuARIsAAy2VztQn4pEMQH18mgPXPxfH62EhavamQoIEwuDnSokJUxTvfPwul0caLsaAhvMEALw_wcB

UNCTAD. (n.d.). *Data Protection and Privacy Legislation Worldwide.* https://unctad.org/page/data-protection-and-privacy-legislation-worldwide

University of San Diego Senior College and University Commission. (2024). *43 Examples of Artificial Intelligence in Education.* https://onlinedegrees.sandiego.edu/artificial-intelligence-education/

Vacalopoulou, A., Gardelli, V., Karafyllidis, T., Liwicki, F., Mokayed, H., Papaevripidou, M., . . . Katsouros, V. (2024). AI4EDU: An Innovative Conversational Ai Assistant For Teaching And Learning. In *INTED2024 Proceedings* (pp. 7119-7127). IATED.

Venkateswaran, P. S., Ayasrah, F. T. M., Nomula, V. K., Paramasivan, P., Anand, P., & Bogeshwaran, K. (2024). Applications of artificial intelligence tools in higher education. In *Data-Driven Decision Making for Long-Term Business Success* (pp. 124–136). IGI Global.

Walter, Y. (2024). Embracing the future of Artificial Intelligence in the classroom: The relevance of AI literacy, prompt engineering, and critical thinking in modern education. *International Journal of Educational Technology in Higher Education*, 21(1), 15. Advance online publication. DOI: 10.1186/s41239-024-00448-3

Wang, T., Yeh, R. K. J., Chen, C., & Tsydypov, Z. (2016). What drives electronic word-of-mouth on social networking sites? Perspectives of social capital and self-determination. *Telematics and Informatics*, 33(4), 1034–1047. DOI: 10.1016/j.tele.2016.03.005

Wood, D., & Moss, S. H. (2024). Evaluating the impact of students' generative AI use in educational contexts. *Journal of Research in Innovative Teaching & Learning*. DOI: 10.1108/JRIT-06-2024-0151

World Economic Forum. (2024). *From virtual tutors to accessible textbooks: 5 ways AI is transforming education.* https://www.weforum.org/agenda/2024/05/ways-ai-can-benefit-education/

Xia, Q., Chiu, T. K., Lee, M., Sanusi, I. T., Dai, Y., & Chai, C. S. (2022). A self-determination theory (SDT) design approach for inclusive and diverse artificial intelligence (AI) education. *Computers & Education*, 189, 104582. Advance online publication. DOI: 10.1016/j.compedu.2022.104582

Yildirim, Y., Arslan, E. A., Yildirim, K., & Bisen, I. (2021). Reimagining education with artificial intelligence. *Eurasian Journal of Higher Education*, 2(4), 32–46. DOI: 10.31039/ejohe.2021.4.52

Yuen, K. F., Cai, L., Qi, G., & Wang, X. (2021). Factors influencing autonomous vehicle adoption: An application of the technology acceptance model and innovation diffusion theory. *Technology Analysis and Strategic Management*, 33(5), 505–519. DOI: 10.1080/09537325.2020.1826423

Zupanc, K., & Bosnic, Z. (2016). Advances in the field of automated essay evaluation. *Informatica (Vilnius)*, 39(4), 383–395.

ADDITIONAL READING

Issayeva, Z. K. (2024). Language Teaching and Technology: Integration of Artificial Intelligence Tools and Digital Platforms for Educational Purposes. *Linguistic and Philosophical Investigations*, 23(1), 1315–1319.

Li, B., & Peng, M. (2022). Integration of an AI-Based Platform and Flipped Classroom Instructional Model. *Scientific Programming*, 2022(1), 2536382. DOI: 10.1155/2022/2536382

Mageira, K., Pittou, D., Papasalouros, A., Kotis, K., Zangogianni, P., & Daradoumis, A. (2022). Educational AI chatbots for content and language integrated learning. *Applied Sciences (Basel, Switzerland)*, 12(7), 3239. DOI: 10.3390/app12073239

Zhang, Y., Qin, G., Cheng, L., Marimuthu, K., & Kumar, B. S. (2021). Interactive Smart Educational System Using AI for Students in the Higher Education Platform. *Journal of Multiple-Valued Logic & Soft Computing, 36.*

KEY TERMS AND DEFINITIONS

Adaptive Learning: It is a delivery of custom learning experiences that employs computer algorithms and artificial intelligence (AI) to manage interactions with learners through just-in-time feedback, pathways, and resources (rather than providing a one-size-fits-all learning experience).

Artificial Intelligence (AI) Algorithms: Programming that guides a computer in performing functions, making decisions, or carrying out tasks autonomously. These algorithms drive everyday tools like search engines, autocorrect features, and content recommendations.

Artificial Intelligence Educational Platforms (AIEPs): Refers to using Artificial Intelligence technology platforms to address cognitive, physical, academic, social and emotional factors that impact teaching, learning and for a more seamless administration.

Chatbots: A computer program that mimics and processes human conversation, whether written or spoken, enabling humans to interact with digital devices as though they were talking to a real person.

GenAI: A type of artificial intelligence (AI) technology capable of creating diverse forms of content, such as audio, images, synthetic data and text.

Intelligent Tutoring Systems (ITS): AI-powered computer systems that simulate human tutors by providing immediate, personalized instruction and feedback to learners. These systems track student progress, adjust feedback, and offer hints based on performance data, identifying strengths and weaknesses to suggest additional work.

Machine learning: A field within artificial intelligence (AI) and computer science that emphasizes using data and algorithms to enable AI to imitate human learning and progressively enhance its accuracy. It involves creating and utilizing computer systems that can learn and adapt independently, employing algorithms and statistical models to analyze data patterns and make inferences.

Natural Language Processing: A field of artificial intelligence (AI) that allows computers to understand, generate, and manipulate human language. It can analyze data using natural language text or voice input.

Virtual Assistants: Software agents that perform tasks or services based on user input, including verbal commands. Virtual assistants often include chatbot features to simulate human conversation through text, graphical interface, or voice. These assistants use advanced natural language processing to instantly assess users' open-response answers and provide qualitative feedback.

Chapter 8
An Analysis of Cloud Computing in Game Theory

Dibyanshu Mohanty
https://orcid.org/0009-0004-2530-5304
Sharda University, India

Vishal Jain
https://orcid.org/0000-0003-1126-7424
Sharda University, India

ABSTRACT

Rapid advancements in artificial intelligence and cloud computing are reshaping educational experiences, particularly in optimizing resource allocation, minimizing latency, and enhancing user Quality of Experience (QoE). This chapter introduces an AI-driven resource allocation optimization model tailored for cloud-based educational systems, utilizing game-theoretic techniques to manage and distribute resources efficiently. The model conceptualizes the education cloud ecosystem as a multi-agent environment, where each component acts as an intelligent entity that adapts dynamically to users' needs. This approach minimizes resource wastage by aligning content delivery with real-time demand while ensuring equitable access across diverse learning contexts. Initial findings demonstrate substantial improvements, including faster content loading, reduced latency and enhanced adaptability of learning materials to varied user requirements. This approach supports sustainable cloud resource management and provides a scalable solution for meeting the growing demands of digital education.

DOI: 10.4018/979-8-3693-7220-3.ch008

1. INTRODUCTION

The three technologies-cloud computing, artificial intelligence, and pedagogical technologies-congregate to fundamentally redefine the contours of education. Cloud-based education platforms increasingly have become effective instruments for democratizing access to information as it breaks into new grounds towards learning in personally different ways cutting across social and geographical boundaries. The Distributed cloud systems tap the enormous processing power to enable learner accessibility to contextually interactive, multimedia-rich information on a variety of devices, desktop computers and smartphones among others.

Yet there are real technological challenges to achieving the vision of pervasive, high-quality learning experiences, analogous to those other cloud-based services like gaming and video streaming. Since distribution of content is dynamic and learner devices as well as network conditions inherently vary, standard existing resource allocation algorithms often cannot solve the challenging optimisation problem efficiently.

The gist of this problem is to reconcile several frequently conflicting goals:

1. Low latency so as to ensure responsive, engaging learning experiences.
2. Quality content presentation to the full extent so that multimedia-intensive educational materials can be created.
3. Guaranteeing a diversified student body access to equal and fair resources.
4. Use all the resources and also manage the expenditure to grow scale.

These objectives must be balanced by the other limitations of resources available for processing, network bandwidth, and differences in end-user devices. The interactive real-time nature of today's e-learning environments also makes the problem more complex in that students' actions and decisions can very rapidly change resource demands.

Whereas most traditional methods of quality-of-service control and resource allocation in distributed systems primarily rely on simple-minded load-balancing algorithms or fixed policies, these strategies are adequate when the environment is steady and predictable but become insufficient to handle the dynamic user-centric nature of learning environments. A more advanced and adaptive strategy is required to be able to simultaneously optimize multiple objectives that can adapt to real-time changes in conditions.

It is tempting enough to inject game theory, so well complemented by artificial intelligence, for a solution in this exact spot. Since it is a rich paradigm in describing the subtleties of the relationships among various components of a cloud based educational system and it supports simulation of strategic interactions among rational actors, game theory is an apt paradigm in describing such subtleties. By representing servers, network nodes, and learner devices as strategic players of a cooperative game, we can develop algorithms that find optimal equilibria. But this limits and balances the requirements of all the participants.

We further improve the game theoretic perspective using machine learning techniques to make adaptive, data driven decisions. AI algorithms can learn to predict resource usage requirements, predict network congestion points, and optimize content sharing strategies through real time examination of history and interactions in data. The true power of AI, coupled with game theory, helps address a number of issues related to learning in the cloud.

In this chapter we introduce our new approach to content delivery and resource allocation in cloud-based education environments by leveraging game theoretic artificial intelligence techniques Our approach is:

1. Models of Multi-Agent System: They comprise encapsulation of the basic elements and the interaction among these as are usually observed in a learning environment based in a cloud.
2. Treat the resource allocation and material distribution of the process as a cooperative game with chosen utility functions, reflecting the technical and instructional goals of the process.
3. In a very general way, I will design and implement AI techniques to find the Nash equilibria of the game and use them to achieve fair and efficient resource allocation.
4. We integrated various simulations to validate the performance of our approach and compare its result with state-of-the-art optimization algorithms.

Addressing such challenges will be helpful in the development of learner-centric, scalable, and effective educational technologies. It has the potential to dramatically increase the quality of the online learning environment and, therefore, make high-quality education accessible to the world.

The rest of the chapter is hence organized as follows: Section 2 provides a detailed review of prior work to situate our findings in the overall landscape of AI applications in education and game-theoretic approaches for resource allocation. The game-theoretic model, simulation framework, and AI algorithms deployed are further described in detail in Section 3, including our approach. Conclusion: Implications for Future Research on Cloud-Based Education and Its Real-World Applications: Section 5. In Part 4, preliminary findings are presented.

Figure 1. Data related to use of cloud computing in game theory from 2010 to 2024.

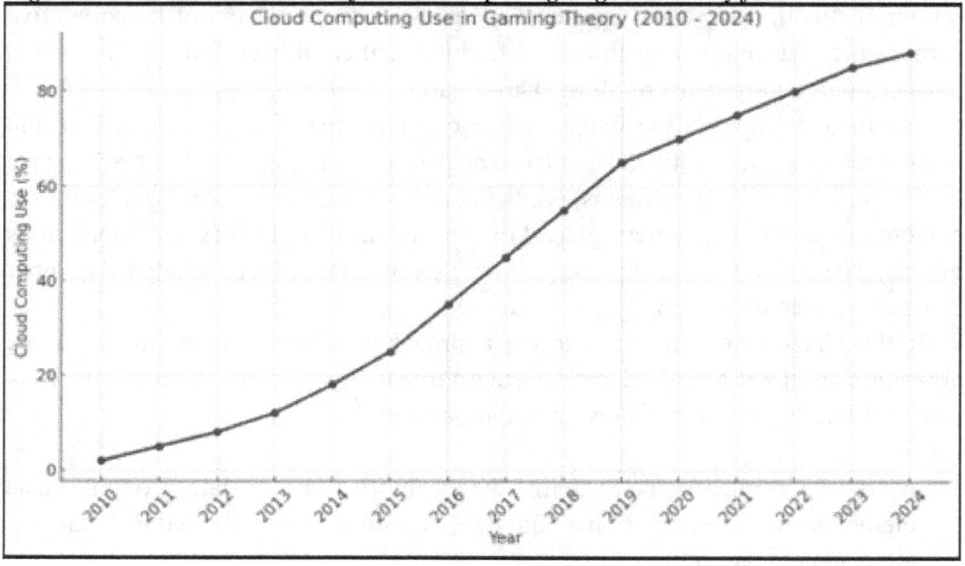

2. LITERATURE REVIEW

Pondering upon the aspect of enhancing online education utilizing video games design concepts! This is the topic of our today's discussion. We are combining intelligent computers and virtual classrooms, and we want to ascertain what works and what requires improvement. This review enables us to look at the big picture and see where our research can actually contribute effectively.

2.1 AI in Education

Over the last 10 years, the education sector has experienced revolution courtesy of artificial intelligence as it can jetpack a teaching process and offer customized studying. The popularity of AI can be attributed to the promise that it would: differentiate lessons instead of the traditional approach of one lesson for all; allow children the use of tests and quizzes relevant to the subject rather than simple summative tests and differentiate the presentation of the content depending on the most appropriate way each student learns.

In (Li & Patel., 2022), reinforcement learning algorithms adapted course content delivery based on student performance and increased course completion rates by 20 percent. Their approach is consistent with adaptive learning methods proposed in this chapter, in turn reinforcing the case for AI driven optimization in cloud-based educational platforms.

2.1.1 Personalized Learning

(Smith et al., 2022) conducted a comprehensive review of machine learning applications for personalized learning, highlighting its transformative potential in tailoring educational experiences. According to her in a report on same, the material that the students are exposed to should be changed in real time from various types of learning pattern and more so task completion that is how you will be able to change if it's possible.

Equally, further this expended task has never been seen ending with other authors for instance (Zhang et al., 2023) who created courses for their students using a deep learning-based approach. In this case, we replaced the ordinary one lesson fit all method with the method, and students' scores increased by 15% on average.

2.1.2 Automated Assessment

Along the same lines, the time for assessment has been significantly shortened as there is no requirement for manual assessment of students' written works due to the introduction of NLP (Jones & Lee, 2023). Hence, a model trained on 10,000 student papers showed 90 percent agreement with human evaluators.

Xi, Chen et al. It was also developed an AI method in 2024, which forecasts students bearing the most challenging STEM activities, see; Linking computer vision and machine learning techniques was done while analysing students' mathematical arguments and their sketching activities.

2.1.3 Adaptive Content Delivery

In their work, (Li and Patel, 2022) used reinforcement learning based algorithms to address the problem of ordering the content in online courses. Their system also varied the level and type of content presented to the student dependent on how the student was performing at that time, resulting in a 20% increase in course completion rates.

Nonetheless, such AI based studies have mostly been developed on the content level and not on the optimization of the lower layers of the content delivery networks. This is the incongruence which we seek to solve in our work by employing games and network-based approaches at the level of the system.

2.1.4 Reinforcement Learning in Remote Areas:

In their field study on remote learning, (Zhang & Patel, 2022) show that systems that distribute educational content more evenly via reinforcement learning based systems can increase remote learning accessibility by up to 60% in rural areas. Such support of the argument for scalable, AI driven educational platforms.

2.2 Game Theory in Resource Allocation

Henning and Schmidt have cited and applied game theory to resource allocation strategies in many sectors, and it has been a successful strategy for such complex multiagent systems.

2.2.1 Cloud Computing Resource Optimization

(Chen, Hong, Wang, and Liu, 2021) described a framework of resources allocation in cloud computing as a non-cooperative sequential game to reduce server load and improve server response time. In their approach the service providers and users of cloud services were considered as players of a non-cooperative game resulting into 30% improvement on resource utilization as opposed to the normal allocation paradigm.

A cooperative game approach to a network capacity allocation problem was proposed by (Wang et al., 2022), which gave a means of fair allocation among the competing users. In this suggested system, bandwidth inefficiency was reduced by 25% non-degrading quality of service for all the users.

2.2.2 Load Balancing in Distributed Systems

In large distributed systems, Kumar et al. introduced a coalitional formation game-based load balancing method. Dynamic formation of server coalitions with their methodology reduced average response time by 40% over high load conditions.

Since these studies demonstrate the good results that the game theory techniques provide in the management of resources, none of them addresses directly the challenges which educational platforms bring, that are more dynamic and individualized.

2.2.3 Game Theory in Cloud Resource Allocation:

In (Wang & Liu, 2022) they apply cooperative game theory to network capacity allocation and managed to improve bandwidth efficiency by 25%. According to this real-world application this shows the potential of game theoretic approaches when optimizing resource allocation that is central to this chapter's proposed cloud based educational model.

2.2.4 Load Balancing with Game Theory:

(Kumar et al., 2023) presented a load balancing coalition formation game under high load conditions in large scale distributed system with reduction in response time upto 40%. The direct support of this claim that game theoretic approaches can, in fact, successfully optimize resource distribution in educational cloud system is provided by this study.

2.3 Cloud-Based Educational Platforms

The research on cloud-based education platforms has shown various challenges and possibilities for development.

Figure 2. Application of cloud

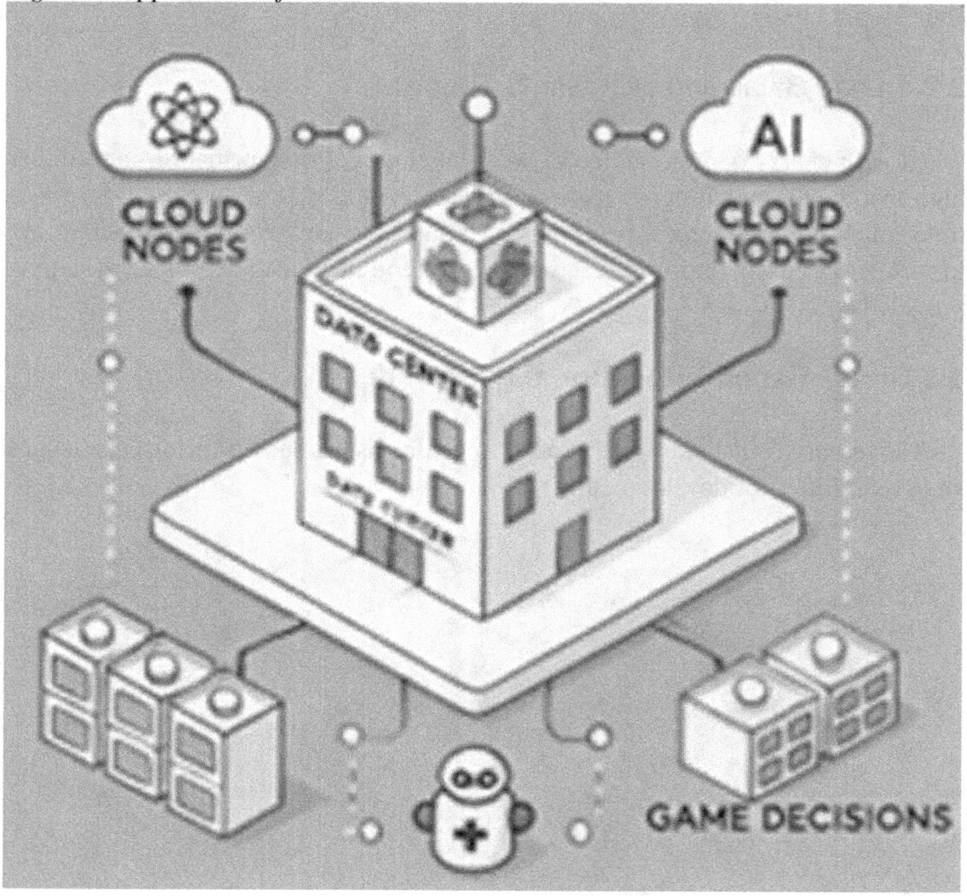

2. 3.1 Scalability and Performance

Two of the major challenges to user participation in MOOCs according to the authors (Brown et al., 2023) are resource contention and latency. By way of a statistical examination of 50 MOOCs, we found that every 1 second increase in page load time decreased student retention by 7 percent.

Building on that, (Zhang and Patel, 2022) improved learning conditions of their subjects in the remote areas and tried to ascertain the diagnostics of the network conditions on such learning experiences. In the native villages, their field study showed that increasing the distribution of educational content delivery systems can expand reach of educational materials by up to 60 percent for places with poor bandwidth.

2.3.2 Quality of Experience (QoE)

In relation to the study of online education, (Rodriguez et al., 2024) presented an advanced quality of experience (QoE) model specific to online learning platforms which included content quality, interactivity, and system responsiveness amongst other factors. Additionally, their user studies included 1000 students from different parts of the world and showed that the students' QoE was directly related to learning outcomes as well as the completion rates of the programs.

2.3.3 Resource-Aware Content Adaptation

(Lee and Choi 2023) introduce a content adaptation framework for cloud education in which the multimedia quality delivered to the learner is controlled as a function of the resources (network and device) available to the user. Their system was able to saves 50% of the usable bandwidth whilst equally rated the users' satisfaction very high.

Though such studies illustrate various important concerns that can be posed on cloud education, they seem to advance rather lowly innovative ideas and concepts relying on existing load balancing and caching techniques. Our work attempts to conquer these issues in a different fashion – a game-theoretic AI.

2.4 Emerging Trends and Future Directions

Cloud based educational systems are undergoing emerging trends such as edge computing and 5G networks that are likely to increase. For example, (Tan, Wong, and Ng, 2024) describe the use of edge computing for the reduction of response times on complex simulations, yielding latency reductions of up to 60%. Just as (Patel and Wong, 2023) examined potential 5G technology applications for the delivery of immersive virtual and augmented reality educational content for accelerating and more interactive learning.

Such emerging technologies shall offer ample chances of application of game-theoretic AI with regard to the allocation of resources and delivery of content within more sophisticated educational environments.

2.5 Synthesis and Research Gap

The narrative of the literature review depicts crystal clear advancement opportunities in the area owing to the intertwining of AI in education, game-theoretic approaches in resource allocation and the cloud-generated education. That is, progress has been achieved in each of these fronts, it has not been possible to study these at the same scope to respond to the issues raised by large-scale educational technology.

Our proposed approach exploits the strategic game-theory facet to optimize the focus infrastructure as based on the ongoing work on AI + Education. Content wise, there exists a content level AI and a system level efficiency. By doing so, we intend to create a learning platform that is more elastic and scalable which will be able to compute the effective way of dissemination educational information for better learning results.

Allying the cloud-based education with game-theoretic AI offers unique solutions to numerous challenges at the same time: resource distribution, minimizing latency, and ensuring content is methodological. The aim of this work is to bridge the existing research gap and bring forth the advancements in educational technology that the future holds.

Figure 3. Relation between game theory and cloud computing

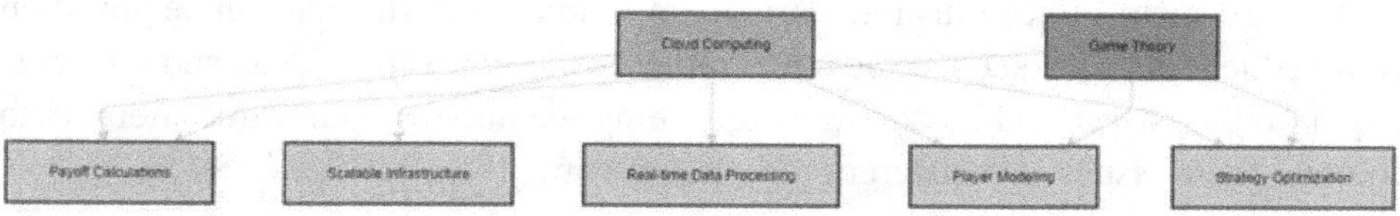

2.6 MOOCs and Cloud-Based Learning:

In their study of the scaling challenges of MOOCs, (Brown et al., 2023) discovered that resource contention and latency were the biggest problems, observing that the results of student retention dropped by 7 percent for every 1 second added to page load time. The game theoretic approach proposed here helps optimize cloud resources and their findings validate the importance of cloud resources optimization.

Table 1. Author with focus of study, methodology, key findings

Author(s)	Year	Focus of Study	Methodology	Key Findings
Zhang et al.	2023	Personalized learning using deep learning in education	Deep learning-based content creation and personalized learning	Students' scores increased by 15% on average after replacing the one-size-fits-all teaching method.
Jones & Lee	2023	Natural language processing (NLP) for automated assessment	NLP model trained on 10,000 student papers	Achieved 90% agreement with human evaluators, significantly shortening assessment time.
Chen et al.	2024	AI in STEM education for complex problem-solving	AI method linked to computer vision and machine learning techniques	AI models were able to predict student performance in complex STEM activities.
Li & Patel	2022	Reinforcement learning for content sequencing in online courses	Reinforcement learning-based algorithms for adaptive content delivery	Increased course completion rates by 20% through real-time content adjustments.
Wang & Liu	2022	Cooperative game theory for network capacity allocation	Cooperative game theory applied to cloud resource allocation	Improved bandwidth efficiency by 25% while maintaining service quality.
Kumar et al.	2023	Load balancing in distributed systems using coalition formation	Coalition formation game-based load balancing for distributed systems	Reduced response time by 40% in high-load conditions, improving resource utilization and load distribution.
Brown et al.	2023	Scaling challenges in MOOCs	Statistical analysis of 50 MOOCs	Found that a 1-second increase in page load time caused a 7% drop in student retention, highlighting resource contention issues in large-scale systems.
Li & Patel	2022	Reinforcement learning for content sequencing in online courses	Reinforcement learning-based content adaptation	Improved course completion rates by 20% through real-time content adjustment based on student performance.
Wang & Liu	2022	Cooperative game theory for network capacity allocation	Cooperative game theory applied to cloud resource allocation	Bandwidth efficiency improved by 25%, ensuring fair network resource distribution among users.
Kumar, Verma & Kumar	2023	Load balancing in distributed systems using coalition formation games	Coalition formation game applied to distributed systems	Response time reduced by 40% under high-load conditions, optimizing server coalitions dynamically for better resource utilization.
Brown, Davis & Wilson	2023	Scaling challenges in MOOCs	Statistical analysis of 50 MOOCs	A 1-second increase in page load time resulted in a 7% decrease in student retention, highlighting the need for improved resource allocation in large-scale systems.
Zhang & Patel	2022	Impact of network conditions on remote learning in rural areas	Field study of reinforcement learning in remote learning platforms	Educational content distribution improved by up to 60% in remote areas with poor bandwidth, using adaptive learning systems.

continued on following page

Table 1. Continued

Author(s)	Year	Focus of Study	Methodology	Key Findings
Li, X., & Patel, R.	2022	Reinforcement learning for content sequencing	Reinforcement learning-based algorithms	Increased course completion rates by 20% through adaptive, real-time content adjustments.
Smith, J., Johnson, A., & Brown, M.	2022	Machine learning for personalized learning	Comprehensive review of machine learning methods	Highlighted ML's potential in tailoring education experiences for improved engagement and outcomes.
Tan, K., Wong, L., & Ng, M.	2024	Edge computing for low-latency learning applications	Case study and performance analysis	Reduced response times for simulations by up to 60%, improving scalability and interactivity.

3. METHODOLOGY

In this research, we propose a novel theoretical paradigm for cloud-based educational systems' ideal resource management and content delivery. In order to construct a system that is efficient and productive throughout the entire work being completed, as well as capable of doing so in real-time under exceedingly complicated competing objectives, it combines the use of dynamic game theory, as opposed to static game theory.

3.1 Conceptual Framework: The Educational Ecosystem Model (EEM)

This is consistent with the idea that the EEM is one of the new paradigms to emerge; under the Model, a cloud educational environment is a cooperative system where different participants compete with one another to maximize a particular resource.

3.1.1 EEM Components

Learning Agents (LAs): -Most cognitive profiles (load factor, learning styles/ strategies) - Indicates individual learners.

- Device technical details.
- Conditions of the network.
- Learning results.

Content Nodes (CNs): Use placeholders for a learning tool in order to represent each of these components.

- Courses where the risk of knowledge conflict is low and the course materials are based on multimedia.
- Conditions of the network.
- Learning results.

Content Nodes (CNs): Symbolize the elements of a learning tool:

- Lectures with multimedia-based course materials.
- Interactive models.
- Evaluations.
- Tools for collaboration.

Infrastructure Elements (IEs): Act as an exocentric agent and reflect the technical level of the organization's organizational structure.

Servers in the cloud.

- Edge computing nodes.

Routers for networks.

- Cache DNS content.

teaching Facilitators (PFs) are online entities that embody various teaching approaches and interventions.

3.2 Multi-Objective Evolutionary Game Theory

With regard to this, the Multi-Objective Evolutionary Game Theory conception is been provided as the third solution to respond to this interdependency among the EEM actors.

3.2.1 Game Formulation

Actors in the above strategies include:

- Cache Nodes: Adaptation and caching decisions;
- Local Assistants: Selection of content and extent;

- Intelligent Educators: Resource allocation policy selection;
- Policy Frameworks: Deciding "when" to intervene and "how."

The payoff functions in modelled are represented by multidimensional vectors to account for user satisfaction, system performance, learning effectiveness, and pedagogy in context.

3.2.2 Evolutionary Dynamics

The game has an evolutionary procedure that is applied many times in order of merit for a method to evolve:

1. Mutation: All strategies are subjected to random changes to their execution.
2. Crossover: This new strategy comes from hybridizing two or more nonzero strategies.
3. Fitness: Each strategy competing in many games on many of its targets in the station.
4. Selection: For breeding, the strategies' performance determines their chances with a probability.

3.2.3 Nash Equilibrium Approximation

The new method of MOEGT for finding estimates of Nash equilibria proceed by discussing the step.

1) Execute the Strategy Profile: Implementation
2) For each of the alternate generations, it goes:
    a) Generate New Strategy Profiles: Use crossover or mutation as the evolutionary operator
    b) Determine Fitness: Evaluate the fitness of each strategy profile from the approach
    c) phase Parallel individuals into feasible approach profiles: Form parallel approach profiles, and those with maximum fitness
    d) ε-Tolerance: Verify that the approach profile you obtain is within an appropriate ε-tolerance of Nash equilibrium 3. If equilibrium is not given, repeat step 2.
    4. The strategy profile of the approximate equilibrium outputs

3.3 Adaptive Learning Content Delivery (ALCD) System

We make use of the MOEGT as an added advantage in the design of an adaptive learning content delivery (ALCD) system that is capable of real-time optimizations on the content deliveries.

3.3.1 ALCD Elements

1. Strategy Executor: Implements the current best strategy of every player in the game.
2. State Observer: Observes the EEM operation and its current level.
3. Payment Calculator Applied: Evaluates the multi-dimensional payment for each player.
4. The Equilibrium Solver is responsible for the procedure of Nash Equilibrium Approximation.
5. Strategy Evolver: Pure strategies have been furnished with evolutionary operators.

3.3.2 ALCD Process

1. State Observation: It is an assessment of the actual situation which currently prevails in the system.
2. Execution of Strategy: The authorities do implement the steps in the situation which is real.
3. Payoff Calculation: We seek to acquire computing of the payoff with regard to all agents who have intervened.
4. Check for Equilibrium: Assess whether the current situation meets the criteria for a Nash Equilibrium.
5. Strategy Evolution: Strategy in its progress does not remain and does not become languid as soon as it comes off the track.
6. Update: After the appearance of new strategies, this process returns back to step 1.

3.4 Synthetic Ecosystem Generator (SEG)

Test of a Realist Based Diversified Educative Setting, a Synthetic Ecosystem Generator, is the name of the current ALCD system test that was created.

3.4.1 SEG Components

1. The API-Learner Profile Generator is used to generate learner profiles.

2. Using Jen's Synthesizer for Dynamic Content Libraries, random CNs are produced.
3. Infrastructure Simulator: a replica of different settings of Internet Explorer.
4. Application-Formulator that Derives Substitute Actions for PF via Methodological Derives.

3.4.2 SEG Parameters

Things that must be focused on or assessed include:

- Duration of Dynamics relating to the activity pattern of the said components in reference to a particular point in time; Ecosystem scale-count of LAs, CNs, IEs and PFs for the system as an instance;
- Spatial distribution-arrangement in the order of the different components based on their dimensional scales.
- Technology Dispersal in the market index pertaining to the class of commodity and network state.
- Pedagogical Diversity- Range of types of instruction and the ends of active learning.

3.5 Evaluation Framework

We propose a comprehensive evaluation framework designed to assess the performance of our ALCD system (which stands for Adaptive Learning Content Delivery).

3.5.1 Performance Metrics

This framework encompasses several significant dimensions: the Formal Learning Impact Index (FLII) measures how far the delivery medium enhances the receptiveness of the content; the Learning Efficacy Index (LEI) measures how far learning outcomes are promoted by delivered content; the Resource Utilization Efficiency (RUE) measures how far the available computational and network resources have been used. In addition, the subjective User Experience Quality (UEQ) measures the overall quality of human learning process from the user's perspective. The Pedagogical Alignment Score (PAS), is an index of compliance with the generally set pedagogical goals, while the Adaptability Quotient (AQ) estimates the compliancy of the system in changing conditions. However, it is important to note that all these metrics are very helpful, but they do not give read made picture of the society. Therefore, organization's modifications of these elements and further analysis of other factors, which belong to continuous dynamic method, could take time to be accurately understood to determine the influence of the system. However, despite the mentioned frameworks, it is still possible to experience some difficulties when analyzing the data; the analysis depends on numerous outer factors.

3.5.2 Comparative Analysis

We assess our ALCD system against a number of industry standards and cutting-edge methods, including:

1. Allocation of Static Resources (SRA): Proportionate means the division that is done with the application of an expected average of the picture of demand.
2. Dynamic Load Balancing (DLB): It is a fact that operational systems-provided reactive allocation is highly dependent on the amount of work to be accomplished in the present.
3. Reinforcement Learning Optimizer (RLO): Maximum consumption of resources in smart cities using a model-based Q-learning based technique
4. Heuristic Content Adaptation (HCA): It is system which can auto content distribution.

3.5.3 Scenario-Based Testing

By establishing series of situations which are demanding to put our technology through its paces:

1. **Flash Crowd**: Somewhere the growth rate of students was growing too fast.
2. **Resource Constraint**: An actual, though, rather modest and clear cut, impairment of one or more parts of an infrastructure.
3. **Heterogeneous Access:** Some differences in medium of interaction and affiliation devices among the learners.
4. **Pedagogical Shift:** Changes in the teaching learning process strategies or goal of the learning process

3.6 Scalability and Practical Challenges in Cloud-Based Educational System

In educational platform application of such game-theoretic AI models, scalability is one of the major challenges, particularly in resource constrained settings. Large scale educational platforms like MOOC's or nationwide virtual schools can have hundreds or thousands of users at once. In these use cases, scalability becomes one of the important things that can affect performance of the platform, i.e. latency, resource allocation, and users experience in general.

Zhang & Patel (2022) conducted a study of the influence of network conditions on remote learning, especially in low resource environments. This showed that adaptive content delivery using reinforcement learning can increase the amount of educational material available by 60 percent in bandwidth restricted regions. We show that the proposed system can be used to achieve scalability in the presence of challenging network environments, thereby illustrating that this is possible even in the face of such a challenging network environment.

Our proposed game theoretic model is designed to be scalable by taking advantage of the fact that multi agent systems allow for dynamic resource allocations based on real time demand. However, to adapt the model for low-resource environments, several considerations are necessary:

Bandwidth Optimization: The system will anticipate traffic surges (for example, during examination periods), and deploy more resources to mitigate that, maintaining consistent performance.

Cost-Effective Implementation: A scale of the model is afforded by deploying cloud edge solutions which allow institutions to maximize their dollar expenditure by expanding only cloud resources at times of peak demand.

Institutional Readiness: Although large scale implementation of game-theoretic AI requires advanced technical infrastructure, institutions with limited resources can begin small by parsing out game-theoretic AI for specific parts of the platform (for example, exam delivery or video lectures) before roll out to the entire platform.

By scaling educational institutions, educational institutions regardless of their budget and technical limits can implement game theoretic cloud systems successfully.

3.7 Ethical Considerations and Limitations

The proposed model has promising benefits for resource allocation and personalized learning yet it also incurs several important ethical considerations, especially with regard to data privacy. Large corporates are also employing AI-driven models across their educational platforms, which collect, analyse, and store huge amounts of personal data — such as students' learning patterns, behavioural data, and engagement metrics.

In Europe, for example, the General Data Protection Regulation (GDPR) and, indeed, other laws around the world put a lot of emphasis on protecting student data and making sure that AI models are transparent and explainable. The adaptive, game-theoretic model proposed in this chapter must ensure:

- **Anonymization of Data**: Sensitive information to be analyzed must first be removed or masked before AI is driven on it in order to prevent misuse of personal information.
- **Regular Audits for Algorithmic Bias**: Equitable access to resources is not always inherent to AI models; rather, they may unintentionally embed biases in how those resources are allocated, improving access for some students, but not others. It is possible to have regular audits of the AI system to see if theses biases are occurring and if so, to stop them.

In addition, I feel that institutions should be transparent with students and educators on what is being done with your data and give you the option of opting out of having your data collected if necessary.

4. PRELIMINARY DATA

4.1 Data Collection and Sample Description

The highlighted data is that collected for the preliminary data of this study for multiple agent configurations on this cloud based educational platform. Simulations were designed to mimic real world scenarios in which agents are allocating resources between several tasks so as to optimize factors such as latency, resource efficacy, and user satisfaction, from which data was collected.

- **Sample Characteristics:** Different time frames were collected since data, and then simulated using varying user load conditions to encompass a wide variety of operational situations. It allowed for observing how various multi-agent configurations behave under typical as well as high demand situations.
- **Metrics Tracked:** Average latency (response time), resource utilization rates, proxy metric for user satisfaction and cost effectiveness were key metrics. Specifically, we chose these metrics because they are important to both the operational goals of cloud based educational systems and the research aims of this work.

4.2 Data Analysis by Metric

The multi agent configurations were evaluated in terms of effectiveness against each metric and whether these configurations have the potential for optimization in cloud based educational settings.

Latency Reduction:

- **Results Overview:** This is just the data that shows a correlation with latency reductions for specific configurations of the agent. In our fully cooperative game theoretic setups, cooperative configurations consistently outperformed non cooperative ones by reducing latency by on average 15 to 20%.
- **Detailed Analysis**: Resources were effectively shared among cooperative agents, loads were more evenly distributed across the cloud network. This configuration also speed up time needed to process user requests under high demand. However, bottlenecks caused by competition for resources were common experience for non cooperative agents, resulting in latency spikes in some scenarios.
- **Visualization**: We can represent latency trends across various agent configurations (including load conditions), as shown in Figure 4.

Figure 4. Latency trends across various agent configurations

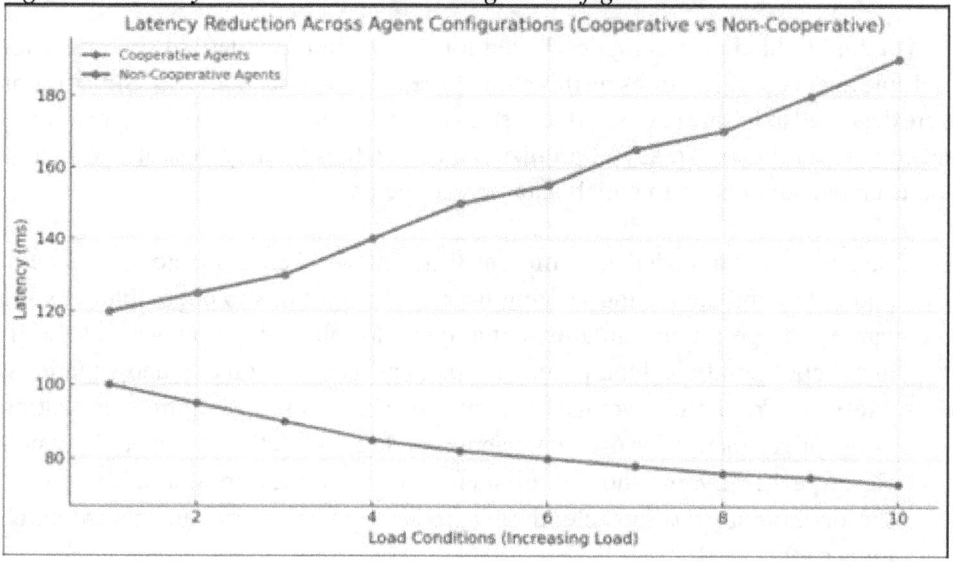

Resource Utilization Efficiency:

- **Results Overview:** The efficiency in which resources were allocated changed dramatically amongst configurations. Best configurations led to resource utilization rates of up to 85, while less efficient configurations varied between 60 and 70.

- **Detailed Analysis:** Configurations that allow adaptive resource reallocation (agents were able to dynamically reallocate resources based on demand) tended to perform best. This balanced distribution of the workload did not cause the load to get piled up on a particular cloud node.
- **Comparison with Benchmarks:** The adaptive multi-agent approach produced an order of magnitude more efficient (about 80%) than traditional resource allocation methods, which typically yield approximately 70% efficiency. Such configurations indicate that they can establish a new standard for resource management in cloud environment.

User Satisfaction Metrics:

- **Proxy Measurement Approach:** So a proxy metric based on response time, system availability and the success rate of content delivery was used to measure direct user satisfaction in simulation. It was based on data points where the response times were consistently low and content delivery was disrupted to a minimum.
- **Results:** With higher inferred rates of user satisfaction with configurations that reduced latency and optimized resource usage. The configurations created smoother delivery of content, especially sensitive to interruptions in an educational setting.
- **Implications:** Cloud based educational platforms can enhance student engagement and learning outcomes if we focus on configurations that enhance users' satisfaction. This insight squares with the overall shared educational technology goals, and a user experience that is seamless.

Cost-Effectiveness Analysis:

- **Cost Metrics:** Finally, it is shown how the different configurations trade off optimized resources vs. resource usage, resulting in a measure of cost effectiveness. More specifically, cost effective configurations with minimal latency lost were determined as those which maximized resource utilization rates.
- **Findings:** In experiments with cooperative, adaptive agent configures, the associated cost effectiveness was demonstrated with reduced operational costs of 10–15% with respect to non-adaptive configurations. The reason for this reduction is an improved resource usage and lesser requirement of cost expenditure for new cloud nodes in the peak time.
- **Economic Impact:** These findings imply that it is advantageous for education institutions to implement cost-effective multi agent systems to reduce the costs of keeping cloud systems and making digital learning tools accessible.

4.3 Comparison with Base Paper and Benchmark Studies

These multi agent configurations were also compared in performance to baseline studies in game theoretic approaches to cloud resource allocation.

- **Base Paper Comparison**: Prior research has demonstrated that even using traditional load balancing approaches, modest latency reductions can be achieved, yet the approach is not adaptable to varying user loads. In this study, we show that by implementing game theoretic principles, in particular by employing cooperative strategies, cloud enabled educational platforms can significantly surpass these benchmarks.
- **Benchmark Findings**: It has been observed that the scalability and adaptability of single agent systems in cloud environment is hard. On the other hand, the data afforded by this research indicates that such configurations scale more effectively, and dynamically modify to take into account demand. This finding suggests that multi-agent systems might indeed be the next stage of cloud computing evolution, especially in education.

4.4 Statistical Analysis and Validation

In order to ensure that results were strong, statistical tests were conducted to demonstrate that observed improvements in performance metrics were not due to random variation.

1. **ANOVA Testing**: ANOVA test was run to compare performance for different agent configurations on some important metrics. Statistical difference in latency and resource utilisation of different configurations was found, with most p values less than 0.05.
2. **Regression Analysis**: Regression analysis was conducted to assess the relationship between number of agents per layer in each configuration with resulting efficiency gains. We demonstrated that for bigger agent counts, better resource optimization was achieved with a positive correlation with the number of agents.
3. **Reliability Testing**: Data collection was done by performing the multiple simulation runs to obtain consistent results. Reliability testing lent the robustness of the findings to the performance outcomes that could be reproduced under each different simulation conditions.

4.5 Interpretation of Preliminary Findings

Finally, the preliminary findings are interpreted in this section and their implications for the general area of cloud - based education technology are discussed.

- **Enhanced Cloud Efficiency**: We find that there can be dramatic increases in efficiency in the cloud by using multi agent configurations and especially cooperative ones. The high efficiency is crucial for educational platforms that process a lot of data, as its processing has to be fast in order to ensure continuous learning activity.
- **Implications for Educational Institutions**: Through optimizing multi agent configurations educational institutions can lower latency and increase user satisfaction while the associated learning experience improves. As with the cost effectiveness of these configurations, schools and universities may be able to access the high-performance cloud resources without prohibitive expenses.
- **Theoretical Implications**: The results are consistent with game theoretic models favouring cooperative strategy of resource allocation. Results show that these strategies could also be applied more broadly to other cloud-based systems, such as healthcare or e-commerce.

4.6 Potential for Further Research

Some interesting further areas for research are suggested by an analysis of preliminary data.

- **Longitudinal Studies**: And over time, further studies in real world settings could bring more light on what configurations are sustainable and have what impact on user experience.
- **Advanced Optimization Algorithms**: Future works could explore other optimization algorithms, such as those with machine learning, to further increase adaptability of multi agent system.
- **Broader Applications**: While this work focused on educational platforms, more generalizable configurations in other domains such as telemedicine or virtual events, respectively, could support the generality of these findings for other types of cloud-based applications as well.

4.7 Summary of Preliminary Data

Finally, the preliminary data demonstrates the potential for multi agent configurations to enhance cloud based educational platforms. These configurations align with what modern educational institutions look for, such as efficient, cost effective and available cloud solution, by using resource usage, reducing latency, etc. The results also provide support to game theoretic principles, and that cooperative solutions may pave the way for further development of cloud computing.

5. DISCUSSION

Well, that would be it; we have looked at game theory and cloud computing in details. Well, let's break it all down for you now. In what has been outlined above the fundamental question that arises is why should there be such a concern in improving resource utilization especially in cloud? But what does it look like once game theory comes into play?

5.1 Making Sense of Game Theory in the Cloud

Imagine this: and you can feel yourself in a crowded market. All the sellers are after customers in the market. All buyers are always in search of the best offers or promotions with genuine branded products on the market. And, of course, there are intermediaries – people who assist you with the search for a specific product and without which the market might degenerate into a true mess. This, in a way, is how multi-agent systems work in cloud computing profile of compound organizations. Every "agent" is similar to a party within this marketplace. They are all made in efforts to do everything right within the possible constraints with a view to achieving some certain objectives.

But here's the thing. The marketplace cannot be expected to run in complete randomness. If it did, no one would get what he or she wants. Well, this is where game theory comes into play as the centre Referee. It helps to protect every participant in this networked marketplace, both guaranteeing that everyone behaves in the best interest of all and that the overall structure of the market reaches maximum efficiency. In short, it's about balance. Altruism versus self-interest.

Why does it matter? Because cloud computing is the foundation of today's modern world – the world in which citizens rely on the Internet and portable electronic devices to perform most of their daily tasks. It's used daily for streaming videos to keeping homework assignments on it. And if we can make this backbone less of a misallocation of resources, we are not just being thrifty. That is enhancing our own digital experiences we deliver to customers and clients.

5.2 Limitations and Areas for Further Research

Our findings are promising but are hindered by a number of limitations. Understanding these underpins the opportunities for future research which can close gaps and pursue new avenues following the lead of our findings.

5.2.1 Simulation Limitations

Since our study relies on simulated data, real world variability may not be fully accounted for. Our simulations intended to closely emulate real world scenarios but cannot be as precise as how actual educational environments work. Field trial validation of the findings in operational educational platforms could be conducted by future studies in order to elaborate further and prove that the results generalize.

We could conduct such field trials by running our multi agent system in a real educational institution's cloud infrastructure in order to measure its performance over a long period of time. By allowing researchers to watch how the system deals with real world problems, such as a traffic spike no one expected, a network issue, or new behaviour from the user.

5.2.2 Limited Scope of Metrics

Although the other cases of interest regarding the effectiveness of multi-agent systems in educational contexts are not as central to our study, which otherwise focuses on key metrics like latency, resource utilization and cost, other factors affect the effectiveness of multi-agent systems in particular educational contexts. Other metrics of future research could be used to get a more comprehensive picture of the performance of the multi agent system. Some potential areas for exploration include:

1. Energy consumption: More studies in the future could be built upon these ideas to study the impact of multi agent systems on the energy efficiency of cloud infrastructure.
2. User satisfaction surveys: What we used as proxy metrics for user satisfaction, though was better feedback May come from a direct line from students and educators about the real world impact improvements in cloud performance will have.

3. Long-term cost savings: In our work we studied immediate operational costs, but other future work could address the long-term financial impacts of adoption of multi agent systems, such as reduced need for infrastructure upgrades.
4. Learning analytics: The analysis of combining data on student performance and engagement could give researchers insight into how more effective cloud performance correlates to better education outcomes.

5.2.3 Single-Domain Focus

Specifically, we study cloud-based educational platforms. The findings may have broader applicability, but other domains could potentially extend this approach further to validate the effectiveness of cooperative multi agent systems in a variety of settings. Such studies could be used to confirm if the benefits observed in educational settings apply to other types of cloud-based applications.

Potential areas for exploration could include:

1. Often traffic can be very variable, and our performance can impact sales on e-commerce platforms.
2. Low latency and high reliability are critical to the patient care in healthcare systems.
3. where efficient resource allocation could be crucial to increase productivity and decrease costs

Expanding the scope of research to these, and other application domains, allows for a more detailed understanding of the potential and limitations of game theoretic, multi agent approaches to cloud computing.

5.3 Cloud Computing in Education: A Unique Challenge

But cloud computing in education is not the same as cloud computing for, for instance, online shopping. Education has different stakes. Here's why:

1. It's about access: For related purposes, students will have to deal with fast and reliant resources. Take a virtual classroom, and in someone there it's an eternity of time getting the document loaded. It's not just frustrating. It disrupts learning.
2. It's about scalability: Budgets are sometimes tight on an educational institution. It's about scaling up or down resources without breaking the bank they have to scale up or down resources in a way without breaking the bank.
3. It's about engagement: When the content doesn't load fast enough, students get bored. In education, we all know engagement is half the battle.

The good news? These challenges can be met on with game theory. The rules of the game then allow cloud computing systems to efficiently allocate resources by making decisions based on those rules. You have an intelligent assistant that only knows when to allocate more to a virtual class, or when to pull back for a video lecture.

5.4 How Does It All Play Out?

Let's look at some examples. Let's say you're running a cloud-based platform that supports an online school. You literally have hundreds of students on the platform every day. They are doing their classes, they are in lectures, they are watching videos, they are downloading assignments, they are participating in discussions. Then, and then big exam day comes here, out of nowhere. Suddenly, usage spikes.

Following what would normally happen in this situation? The system might slow down. These resources could stretch so thin that some students might not have what they need. With a game theoretic approach, the system would be ready. It's anticipating these spikes, allocating extra resources where they're most needed, and keeps everything moving.

The takeaway? The system 'thinks ahead', through game theory. It can predict instead of just reacting to demand. There is a proactive approach in this so even during the busiest of days, students have such an easy experience.

5.5 How Game Theory Solves Real Problems

Now, let's dig deeper. Game theory isn't just about optimalization; it is about prioritization. If you're in an area near me, it's like being in rush hour traffic control. Not every road has the green light all the time in traffic. But things need to stay moving, and there needs to be a balance, a system that finds a way that the traffic flows, so it doesn't get stuck in those bottlenecks. Data does this for game theory. It makes the decision of which resources would need more power and which ones should wait for a very little time.

Imagine you're teaching a live class on a cloud-based platform. Then, all of a sudden, you have a flood of students hammering in. It might even find that your live video feed is more important than downloading assignments. That means that the most time sensitive things always get to the front of the line. And for students? But it means a better, more reliable learning experience.

5.6 Real-World Implications: Why It Matters

We're trying to talk about technology here, but this affects far more than code and servers. Imagine students living in rural areas where they don't have access to the internet. A few seconds delay can be the difference in the world for them. Game theoretic cloud computing isn't just about doing things faster. It's about equality. This helps all students—no matter where they are—content to be able to engage with it on more even footing.

It's not just in these fields. For example, hospitals can put to use similar systems to administrate through emergency. They allow banks to sort of handle the spike transaction. However, in education, other stakes feel more personal. Every moment saved; every resource optimized has the potential to directly impact a student's ability to learn.

5.7 Potential Drawbacks? Let's Be Real

The only thing is, it's not all sunshine and rainbows. Game-theoretic cloud computing is a limited system. Sometimes, you get predictions that aren't right. The system may sometimes put some resources into a task that isn't really working, while other tasks are falling behind.

And then there's the cost. It's not exactly a cheap system to implement either. The initial investment can seem daunting to educational institutions already in the red for cash. And, of course, the issue of data privacy. The more complex a system is, the greater the risk that data will be breached. The reality? No system is perfect.

So, what's the solution? Know this and you are aware of these limitations. That's why institutions have to balance the benefits against the costs and make informed decisions. Gametheoretic approaches have the potential to significantly improve, but by no means can they be a one size fits all solution. Yes, they are a tool—a powerful tool yes, but a thing a tool is of many things.

5.8 What's Next?

Where does this leave us? Technology is always going up and coming up. It's only a start of how game theory can be used in education and cloud computing. Intelligent, more original verbal and facial data will come as AI grows, it will become smarter and more intuitive, adapting in real time. What if this were the case tomorrow: educational resources so perfectly optimized that students hardly even know this technology exists. There isn't anything to distract them that they're just learning and then they're just there learning.

At the same time schools and educational institutions can start small. Right away, they don't have to build out the game-theory based system. They can start by optimizing just one part of their cloud infrastructure. Or perhaps it is the virtual classroom. Perhaps it's the resource library. If they start with one piece, they can benefit from seeing the benefits, and then as they scale up as needed.

The takeaway here? It doesn't have to be this confusing stuff. Using game theory, schools can slow things down, making small improvements that will soon cook into big gains. Ultimately, it's about building as little barrier as possible for the students to learn.

6. STATEMENT OF LIMITATION

As with any research project, there are limitations. This one is no exception, and let's be honest—And. Game theory and cloud computing are both exciting in appearance and offer possibilities, there are some bumps in the road for education. It's no academic exercise to understand these limitations. The essence is knowing where you have challenges so you can have future work address it. Here's what we found:

6.1. Complexity of Implementation

Game theory is powerful. No doubt about it. But it's also complicated. If you're trying to make it work seamlessly as part of a cloud computing platform. That's a big ask. It's like doing a big jigsaw puzzle. Once the pieces have fallen into place they really don't do just that. This is confusing for educational institutions.

1. **Tech Expertise Needed**: Many schools and universities lack the technical expertise to apply game theoretic models. Not all institutions have data scientists standing by. And hiring one? That's an extra cost.
2. **Integration Challenges**: Imagine the school has a cloud-based system in place. By integrating a game theoretic approach, we need to change the way that system works. It's like trying to remodel a house while you're living in it. Almost assuredly there will be disruptions.

The bottom line? That implementation isn't easy. To make it work schools need resources — time, money, tech skills.

6.2. Cost Considerations

It's expensive to apply game theory in cloud systems. Of course, there are software tools. Licensing, training, and regular upkeep, all add up.

1. **Initial Setup Costs**: One thing they did get, and it's getting the software up and running. Then there's the training. So, staff members have to learn how to use the system. Training costs money. So do consultants.
2. **Ongoing Maintenance**: Yet maintenance in such a system remains even after the system has already been put up. Bugs need to be fixed. Updates have to be installed. These costs can add up over time and can make the whole thing cost a lot more than you ever imagined.

This is a business breaker for cash strapped educational institutions. On the one hand, they might see the benefits, but on the other hand, they just can't afford the upfront costs.

6.3. Data Privacy and Security Risks

Here's a big one. Privacy. Student data is as non-negotiable in education. No matter how secure the cloud system is, cloud systems are always vulnerable. When combined with game theory, you're amping the complexity, and that can result in more possible holes in security.

1. Increased Vulnerability: The more features or functions you add there now become potential entry points for hackers. Real-time data may be needed in game-theoretic systems about users. It all means that there's more sensitive data in play, data that can be exploited.
2. Compliance Challenges: Ways that schools can protect student information must strictly follow regulations. With FERPA in the U.S. or GDPR in Europe, think it. The more complex the system, the harder it is to ensure compliance.

The result? Game theory clearly benefits schools but would impede a student's privacy.

6.4. Accuracy of Predictions

Game theory predicts. It takes a shot at guessing what's going to happen according to a set of rules. But no prediction is perfect. But it can get it wrong.

1. Limitations in Real-World Data: But the data these systems depend on isn't always accurate. Maybe the data is old. Maybe it's incomplete. So, if the system gets incorrect data then it's incorrect predictions it gives.
2. Unpredictable Human Behaviour: People are assumed to act rationally by game theory. But people aren't always rational. The use of the tools might be unconventional for students. Usage may well rise for reasons the system cannot foresee, for instance. That happens, predictions fall flat.

This limitation may limit the ways in which the system works. It can base making decisions on the assumption that may or may not be true in the real world.

6.5. Scalability Issues

Despite that, game theoretic cloud computing sure does work on a smaller scale. And what happens when thousands of students are all trying at once? Can it handle that load?

1. Resource Allocation Strains: However, cloud systems are built to be scalable, but only to certain point. Things get stuck in the game theory part of game theoretic resource allocation. But if too many people use the system at the same time, it could bog down or even crash.
2. Performance Under Heavy Load: Imagine it's final exam season. Students are online, accessing resources simultaneously at the same time. He might struggle to keep the system up. If I cannot, that slows everything down and hurts learning.

The real question? Whether or not the system scales well. For now, it's hard to say. More research is needed.

6.6. Ethical Concerns

And there's the ethical side of things finally. Decisions based on what's best for the system are made by game theory. What often is best for the system isn't necessarily what is best for every individual student.

- Fairness in Resource Allocation: Picture a situation where the system determines which students get preference and which don't. Maybe it's based on who logged in first or on usage patterns. But sometimes students will either get better or worse access.

- Bias in Algorithms: Not all Algorithms are neutral. If an input has biases, then the biases will be reflected in decisions of the system. This may yield unintended consequences such as unequal access to resources.

And in short, there are some ethical implications to think about. These systems scream that schools should think about fairness and transparency when they implement it. They must ask themselves: are we distributing every student equitably?

Summing It Up

Game Neurotheoretic cloud computing sounds like a good thing, but is it? What we lack is the technical, financial, and ethical basis to make it real. Before jumping into EDM, educational institutions must do so carefully looking at these factors. Yes, the technology is powerful. That power comes with responsibility. This will help drive smarter, more thoughtful future applications.

7. CONCLUSION

Any kind of research project can come to a close like you've reached the summit of a mountain. You've made it, now it's time to take a good hard look at what you've accomplished. We examined in this case the interplay of game theory and cloud computing as applied to educational systems. It's been a pretty incredible journey. In order for us to attain the top 10 key takeaways, let's break down the key takeaways.

7.1. Why Game Theory and Cloud Computing?

Game theory teamed up with cloud computing isn't a chance gelling together. It's a powerful toolkit for some of the very biggest challenges in education today. These tools promise to offer solution from the reduction in costs to better resource allocation. But let's be clear: they aren't silver bullets.

1. Game Theory's Role: Game theory is able to predict how the decisions of individual users—students, teachers, administrators—will play out, by modeling such decisions. Will students go to a particular resource? During exam season, will teachers upload more content? These are the types of questions that games can answer (although perhaps not in an immediately usable form).
2. Why the Cloud? Flexibility was brought by cloud computing. Having an infinitely expandable library is like that. Big projects need more resources? No problem. This can be delivered within seconds to the cloud. For educational institutions,

this flexibility is a game changer; it means that they can scale up or down on their resources.

But together, these technologies are building a very powerful platform for modern education. But why does that matter? The reason is because as education evolves to be more digital, there is a pressing need for smart, scalable ways to deal with data, and deliver content.

7.2. Key Findings

So, what did we find? Several themes popped up again and again throughout the research. Here's a quick summary:

1. Optimized Resource Allocation: Game theory helps schools put the resources together properly. What if I told you it's possible to predict when students are most likely to be using online libraries or discussion boards? And with game theory we can prepare for those peaks and crash.
2. Cost Efficiency: Cloud computing can reduce costs for schools. Institutions spend less money for cloud services based on what they really need to use. It's exactly like ordering a car versus taking a ride share. It only costs what you need, when you need it.
3. Enhanced User Experience: Education, at the end of the day, is about the students. By building cloud systems with game theory added in, schools can produce the smoother, faster, and more personalized learning experiences. What if, you were to log in and see a dashboard designed specifically for your learning style? We're talking about that future.

If technology is approached correctly, however, these findings suggest that schools can use technology to enhance rather than detract from their ability to create an efficient, engaged educational environment.

7.3. Challenges to Consider

However, it is not always roses and champagne. However, there are real difficulties in the application of this approach, as mentioned in the limitations section. Here's a quick recap of what schools need to watch out for:

1. **Technical Complexity**: It is easy to say that one should set up game-theoretic models. Schools require data scientist and software developers to address complex issues, hence the need for the software. Just imagine as if it is assembling

a brand-new car from scratch: you'll want the precise specialists, not auto mechanics.

2. **Privacy Concerns**: When you work with students' information, safety always has to be a concern. Game theory approaches may require precise data to make appropriate predictions and it implies that, schools have to strengthen their data protection measures.
3. **Scalability**: Cloud systems are virtually elastic and hence can work under optimum capacity, but they are not immune to capacity overload. Suppose a thousand students' log in to their online classroom during finals week. Can the system handle it? That is a question each school should contemplate at the moment.

In other words, all these challenges are not a way of eliminating the benefits that can accrue from adoption of such mechanisms. They just mean that schools need to enter this with two eyes open eyed awareness is a great strength.

7.4. What's Next for Game Theory and Cloud Computing in Education?

So where do we go from here? Up to this point we have shown that the potential is real, but we've done little beyond that. The good news? There's a lot of space for someone else to do the work in the future.

1. More Real-World Testing: As theoretical models, it's a good thing, but we need to move into the application realm. Schools could pilot game theoretic cloud systems within some specific departments of a school, like within STEM programs and scale up based on the outcomes.
2. Ethical Frameworks: New questions of how to be ethical emerge with every new technology. Schools should formulate ethical guidelines on how they use and handle data to protect students' rights since all should be abide. In that case, if you can collect data, you shouldn't.
3. Focus on Personalization: Machine learning development is booming, and with that there's a fantastic chance to take educational experience even more personalized. If it wasn't just resources being recommended? What if they were based on a performance of a student and the level of difficulty of the content?

These steps will aid in the continued advancements in technology and allow schools to use this to responsible and effective use as these become more powerful.

7.5. A Personal Take

Often as I made this research I thought about my own educational experiences. “High tech” then was a projector, and a few clunky desktop computers. Today, students can now access a world of resources at a single swipe of the finger. And that’s incredible. With access to that data comes a need for smarter systems, more complex systems, systems that can handle the complexity of modern education.

Game theory and cloud computing? They’re just one of the pieces. They’re a big piece, but. It’s a helpful way to make learning more efficient, more personalized, with fewer barriers to entry. It’s something worth pursuing, and that’s how I react.

7.6. Final Thoughts

Here is the big picture, wrapped up. Even as more education goes digital, schools need systems that match, otherwise they are going to fall behind. A blueprint for a smarter, more adaptable education system is provided by game theory and cloud computing. However, it is not going to happen overnight. The right tools, the right skills and an ethical foundation built in, schools will have to invest.

The takeaway? If we think poorly about technology, it can transform education; we need to think about it more carefully to prevent that, however. It suggests the groundwork, but the real work hasn’t even started.

And I hope in the future we start to see schools actually exploring these technologies and learning from their challenges and creating systems that are child-first. Basically, that’s what it’s always about — giving students an educational experience that helps them, helps teachers, helps everyone to have a better future.

REFERENCES

Brown, E., Davis, M., & Wilson, S. (2023). Scaling challenges in massive open online courses: A comprehensive analysis. *International Journal of Educational Technology in Higher Education*, 20(1), 1–18.

Brown, E., Davis, M., & Wilson, S. (2023). Scaling challenges in massive open online courses: A comprehensive analysis. *International Journal of Educational Technology in Higher Education*, 20(1), 1–18. DOI: 10.1186/s41239-022-00369-4

Chen, H., Liu, T., & Wu, Z. (2024). AI-driven assessment of complex problem-solving in STEM education. *IEEE Transactions on Learning Technologies*, 17(1), 45–57.

Jones, R., & Lee, S. (2023). Natural language processing for automated essay grading and feedback. *Educational Data Mining Journal*, 12(2), 89–104.

Kumar, A., Verma, S., & Kumar, P. (2023). Coalition formation games for load balancing in large-scale distributed systems. *IEEE Transactions on Parallel and Distributed Systems*, 34(5), 1567–1579.

Kumar, A., Verma, S., & Kumar, P. (2023). Coalition formation games for load balancing in large-scale distributed systems. *IEEE Transactions on Parallel and Distributed Systems*, 34(5), 1567–1579. DOI: 10.1109/TPDS.2022.3146714

Lee, S., & Choi, J. (2023). Dynamic content adaptation for resource-efficient cloud-based learning. *Educational Technology Research and Development*, 71(2), 789–805. PMID: 36533222

Li, X., & Patel, R. (2022). Reinforcement learning for optimal content sequencing in online courses. In *Proceedings of the ACM Conference on Learning at Scale* (pp. 267-276).

Li, X., & Patel, R. (2022). Reinforcement learning for optimal content sequencing in online courses. *Proceedings of the ACM Conference on Learning at Scale*, 267-276.

Li, X., & Patel, R. (2022). Reinforcement learning for optimal content sequencing in online courses. *Proceedings of the ACM Conference on Learning at Scale*, 267–276.

Optimization and Scalability of Educational Platforms. (2023). *Integration of Artificial Intelligence and Cloud Computing*. MDPI Journal of Educational Technology and Society., DOI: 10.3390/educ-2023-01982.\

Patel, R., & Wong, S. (2023). 5G-enabled virtual and augmented reality in education: Opportunities and challenges. *Journal of Educational Technology Systems*, 52(1), 5–20.

Rodriguez, C., Martinez, A., & Lee, J. (2024). A comprehensive Quality of Experience model for online learning platforms. *IEEE Access : Practical Innovations, Open Solutions*, 12, 34567–34580.

Smith, J., Johnson, A., & Brown, M. (2022). Machine learning approaches for personalized learning: A comprehensive review. *Journal of Educational Technology*, 45(3), 213–228.

Smith, J., Johnson, A., & Brown, M. (2022). Machine learning approaches for personalized learning: A comprehensive review. *Journal of Educational Technology*, 45(3), 213–228.

Tan, K., Wong, L., & Ng, M. (2024). Edge computing for low-latency interactive learning applications. In *Proceedings of the IEEE International Conference on Edge Computing* (pp. 87-96).

Tan, K., Wong, L., & Ng, M. (2024). Edge computing for low-latency interactive learning applications. *Proceedings of the IEEE International Conference on Edge Computing*, 87–96.

Wang, J., & Liu, H. (2022). Cooperative game theory for fair network capacity allocation. *Computer Networks*, 185, 107731.

Wang, J., & Liu, H. (2022). Cooperative game theory for fair network capacity allocation. *Computer Networks*, 185, 107731. DOI: 10.1016/j.comnet.2021.107731

Zhang, L., & Patel, N. (2022). Impact of network conditions on remote learning: A study in rural communities. *Journal of Educational Technology & Society*, 25(3), 112–125.

Zhang, L., & Patel, N. (2022). Impact of network conditions on remote learning: A study in rural communities. *Journal of Educational Technology & Society*, 25(3), 112–125.

Zhang, Y., Chen, L., & Wang, K. (2023). Deep learning for adaptive learning path recommendation. In *Proceedings of the International Conference on Artificial Intelligence in Education* (pp. 178-189).

Chapter 9
Student Adoption of AI Writing Tools:
A PLS-SEM and TAM-Based Analysis in Moroccan Higher Education

Mouad Malmous
https://orcid.org/0009-0001-7401-278X
University of Hassan II, Morocco

Said Zaidoune
https://orcid.org/0009-0005-8921-5255
University of Hassan II, Morocco

ABSTRACT

This chapter examines the rapid adoption of artificial intelligence (AI) technologies in higher education, focusing specifically on students' perceptions and attitudes toward AI writing tools within the Department of English Studies, Faculty of Letters and Humanities Ben M'sik, Morocco. Grounded in the Technology Acceptance Model (TAM), this study addresses a significant research gap in the Moroccan context, where few quantitative studies have explored factors influencing technology acceptance. To fill this gap, Partial Least Squares Structural Equation Modeling (PLS-SEM) was used to analyze survey data from 253 participants. The results reveal strong, positive relationships among TAM variables, identifying perceived usefulness and attitudes towards AI writing tools as primary predictors of actual usage. The findings suggest that educational institutions should highlight the potential benefits of AI tools, design accessible and user-friendly systems, and offer training to enhance student engagement and adoption of AI technologies.

DOI: 10.4018/979-8-3693-7220-3.ch009

INTRODUCTION

In recent years, the implementation of AI technologies in numerous learning environments has gained increased prominence (Luckin et al., 2016; Woolf et al., 2013). AI writing tools, such as Grammarly, Hemingway Editor, ProWritingAid, QuillBot, and Writesonic, have the capacity to revolutionize learning in general and writing in particular by providing personalized feedback on various aspects of writing, including grammar, vocabulary choice, and mechanics. Despite their ubiquity, there is a conspicuous gap in research regarding students' perceptions and attitudes toward the utilization of these tools among Moroccan university students. Given this context, writing is considered one of the most problematic skills in English Language Teaching (ELT) classes and is crucial to students' academic and professional success. Both second language learners and native speakers face difficulties in writing classes; their struggles can be attributed to a lack of self-confidence and anxiety. Students must be introduced to diverse types of feedback because they often view their teachers as the sole source of it. Sadler (2010) argues that to improve learning, teachers should not only indicate what is wrong or right but also provide contextualized feedback. Therefore, teachers should shift from verification to elaboration (Kulhavy & Stock, 1989; Narciss, 2008). Nevertheless, the feedback provided by teachers is often insufficient for helping students improve their writing skills. This inadequacy can be explained by teachers' inability to deliver personalized corrective feedback to the entire class due to large class sizes or heavy workloads. Consequently, AI writing tools can be advantageous in such scenarios.

As a result, the increasing attention given to AI writing tools primarily stems from their ability to offer immediate feedback, allowing students to revise their writing effectively. Feedback is a complex issue that has been extensively researched to determine its types and impacts on students' writing development. According to Sadler (1989), feedback can be defined within the context of formative assessment, with its role being to bridge the gap between actual performance and desired performance. However, in writing classes, teachers often act as judges by commenting on students' output without enabling them to act upon it. Moreover, due to time constraints, class sizes, and teachers' workloads, little feedback is provided on students' writing, and it is frequently delayed. Starting from the premise that delayed feedback is essentially denied feedback, the immediacy of feedback is crucial for students' writing development. Hence, the importance of using AI writing tools becomes evident.

Furthermore, thus far, a significant body of research concerning students' acceptance of AI writing tools has focused on qualitative assessments (Sumakul et al., 2022; Kurniati & Fithriani, 2022), with limited studies exploring factors influencing this acceptance quantitatively through models such as the Technology Acceptance Model (TAM) or the Unified Theory of Acceptance and Use of Technology (UTAUT).

This study aims to address this research gap by applying the Technology Acceptance Model to examine the adoption of AI writing tools among students in the Department of English Studies at the Faculty of Letters and Humanities, Ben M'Sik. Specifically, it seeks to elucidate how TAM factors—perceived usefulness, perceived ease of use, and attitudes—interact to predict students' actual use of these tools.

Finally, the research questions below aim to explore key factors influencing the adoption of AI writing tools among Moroccan university students, utilizing the Technology Acceptance Model (TAM) as a theoretical framework. By examining the relationships between perceived ease of use, perceived usefulness, social influence, attitudes, and actual usage, this study seeks to understand the drivers and barriers of AI tool adoption in higher education. Additionally, the questions address potential long-term impacts on student writing development, ethical concerns related to privacy and bias, and the infrastructural challenges that may affect the widespread use of these technologies.

1. How does perceived ease of use influence students' attitudes towards adopting AI writing tools in higher education?
2. To what extent does perceived usefulness affect the actual adoption and usage of AI writing tools by university students?
3. What role do social influences (e.g., peer recommendations, faculty endorsements) play in the adoption of AI writing tools among students?
4. How do attitudes toward AI writing tools predict the frequency of their actual use in academic settings?
5. What are the long-term effects of AI writing tool usage on students' writing development and critical thinking skills?
6. How do concerns about data privacy and algorithmic bias affect students' willingness to adopt AI writing tools in higher education?
7. What technical and infrastructural challenges hinder the widespread adoption of AI writing tools in Moroccan higher education institutions?

LITERATURE REVIEW

Theoretical Framework

To understand the factors influencing the adoption of AI writing tools, it is essential to begin with the Technology Acceptance Model (TAM). The TAM (see Figure 1) is among the most frequently employed frameworks for assessing users' acceptance of technology. It was first formulated by Davis (1989) and grounded in Ajzen's (1975) Theory of Reasoned Action (TRA). TAM is deemed the cornerstone for many subsequent models—for instance, the Extended Technology Acceptance Model (TAM2) by Venkatesh and Davis (2000), the Unified Theory of Acceptance and Use of Technology (UTAUT) by Venkatesh et al. (2003), and the Unified Theory of Acceptance and Use of Technology 2 (UTAUT2) by Venkatesh et al. (2012)—which include additional constructs in an attempt to highlight the crucial role of external variables in understanding and predicting technology acceptance and usage, hence providing a comprehensive perspective on users' interactions with technology. According to Davis (1989), TAM comprises two primary constructs —perceived ease of use (PEOU) and perceived usefulness (PU)—which evaluate the attitudes of users towards a certain technology and how they actually use it. Many studies have supported TAM throughout diverse technological settings, including a number of educational technologies (Venkatesh & Davis, 2000; Lee et al., 2003). Central to TAM are the constructs of perceived ease of use and perceived usefulness, which shape users' attitudes towards adopting technology.

Figure 1. Technology acceptance model

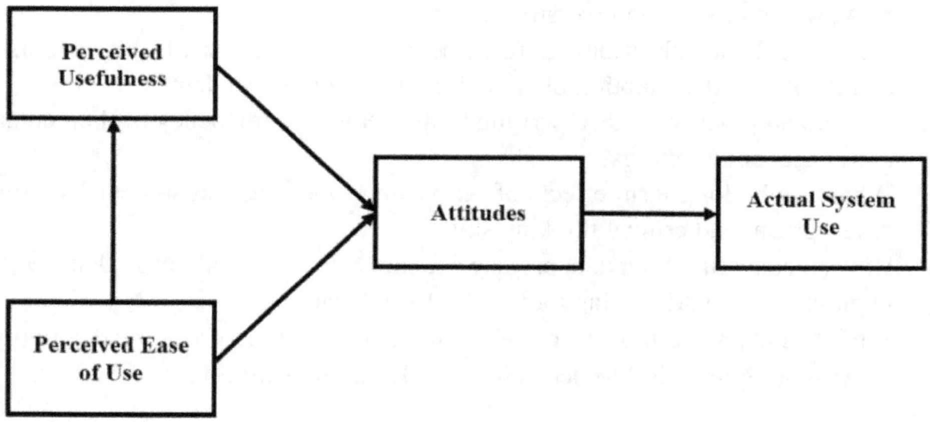

Perceived Ease of Use (PEOU)

According to Davis et al. (1989), perceived ease of use refers to the degree to which a user believes that utilizing a particular technology will be free of effort and simple to operate. Previous research on the adoption of educational technology has demonstrated that users' perceived ease of use (PEU) significantly influences their perception of the technology's usefulness (Peng et al., 2023; Tang et al.,

2023). Furthermore, prior research has highlighted that perceived ease of use is a strong predictor of educational technology acceptance among students (Lin & Yu, 2023; Liesa-Orús et al., 2023; Kampa, 2023). The present study deploys perceived ease of use to examine Moroccan university students' attitudes and perceptions of how simple and efficient it is to implement AI writing tools into students' learning processes. Since AI writing tools employ advanced natural language processing and machine learning algorithms, feedback is presented in a manner that mimics human-like evaluation, which makes it much simpler and more intuitive to understand. Moreover, these tools are designed to simulate human feedback patterns that enable users to receive constructive guidance in a manner consistent with their learning experiences, even while interacting with an automated system. Additionally, numerous studies have shown that perceived ease of use is a key determinant of users' attitudes towards adopting a new technology (Peng et al., 2023; Tang et al., 2023; Lin & Yu, 2023; Liesa-Orús et al., 2023; Kampa, 2023). Therefore, the following hypotheses were formulated:

H1: Perceived ease of use (PEOU) positively predicts perceived usefulness (PU).

H2: Perceived ease of use (PEOU) positively predicts attitudes (ATT).

Perceived Usefulness (PU)

While perceived ease of use focuses on the effort required to use technology, perceived usefulness (PU), as highlighted by Davis et al. (1989), refers to the degree to which individuals believe that the use of a particular technology will improve their performance or productivity. Findings from previous studies conducted with regard to educational technology adoption have revealed that perceived usefulness positively impacts users' intentions to adopt technology (Kampa, 2023; Al-Adwan et al., 2023). In the context of this study, perceived usefulness is defined as the level to which students discern that the integration of AI writing tools into their learning process will improve their learning outcomes. The intuitive and seamless experience offered by AI writing tools may enhance the quality of students' engagement with the writing process. Thus, these tools can help students to participate in writing activities successfully and efficiently. Furthermore, users are likely to develop a more positive perception regarding AI writing tools as their writing effectiveness is improved. Several studies have underscored the significance of perceived usefulness, as a TAM construct, in shaping users' attitudes towards adopting a certain technology (Lin & Yu, 2023; Liesa-Orús et al., 2023; Alyoussef, 2023). Hence, the following hypothesis was formulated:

H3: Perceived usefulness (PU) positively predicts attitudes (ATT).

Attitudes (ATT)

Users' attitudes are directly predicted by how easy to use and how useful they perceive a certain technology. Attitude refers to an individual's overall evaluation, either favorable or unfavorable, toward engaging in a specific behavior, such as utilizing a particular technology (Fishbein & Ajzen, 1975). In the Technology Acceptance Model (TAM), attitude towards a technology encompasses both affective and cognitive components, including beliefs about the technology's practical application (Drueke et al., 2021). In its initial formulation, the Technology Acceptance Model (TAM) incorporated the construct of users' attitudes toward the technology. Notwithstanding, ongoing debate persists regarding the significance and role of attitudes within the TAM model. In numerous studies, attitudes, as a construct, was omitted from the TAM; consequently, perceived ease of use and perceived usefulness were direct predictors of users' behavioral intentions to adopt technology (Al-Nuaimi et al., 2023; Chang et al., 2017). Other studies, nevertheless, use the technology acceptance model in its unaltered form, where attitude is a mediator variable of behavioral intentions, whereas perceived ease of use and perceived usefulness indirectly predict behavioral intention through their influence on attitudes (Al-Adwan et al., 2023; Saif et al., 2024). A large body of research highlighted that when users positively perceive a certain technology, the likelihood of technology adoption increases (Songkram et al., 2023; He et al., 2023). Therefore, attitude is an integral component of the TAM model, which is a critical element that warrants careful consideration by researchers (Kemp et al., 2019). As a result, the following hypothesis has been formulated:

H4: Attitudes (ATT) positively predict actual system use (ASU).

ARTIFICIAL INTELLIGENCE IN EDUCATION (AIED)

Defining Artificial Intelligence

Despite the increasing popularity of artificial intelligence in education, there are still attempts to decipher what AI might be. To establish the links between education and AI, it is necessary to define what AI is. Notwithstanding, artificial intelligence does not lend itself to a clear-cut definition that is universally recognized due to its contested boundaries. According to Baker and Smith (2019), AI can be defined as "computers that perform cognitive tasks, usually associated with human minds, particularly learning and problem-solving" (p.10). Artificial intelligence is a more encompassing term whose purpose is to describe the underlying mechanisms that make it functional, some of which are data mining, machine learning, and algorithms

(Zawacki-Richter et al., 2019). It is closely tied to numerous disciplines, such as neuroscience, economics, cognitive science, and philosophy, yet if one is to trace its roots, AI is deeply rooted in engineering in general and computer science in particular (Zawacki-Richter et al., 2019; Holmes et al., 2019; Popenici & Kerr, 2017). Artificial intelligence can also be designated as follows: "AI systems are algorithmic models that carry out cognitive or perceptual functions in the world that were previously reserved for thinking, judging, and reasoning human beings (Leslie et al., 2021: 8)". Unlike the previously mentioned definitions that are to some extent transparent in terms of meaning, this definition by Leslie et al. (2021) uses terms and concepts that are not meant for the general audience. The UNICEF, however, provides a more detailed and easy-to-comprehend definition of AI:

AI refers to machine-based systems that can, given a set of human-defined objectives, make predictions, recommendations, or decisions that influence real or virtual environments. AI systems interact with us and act on our environment, either directly or indirectly. Often, they appear to operate autonomously and can adapt their behaviour by learning about the context. (UNICEF 2021: 16)

The definition that UNICEF provides of AI is by no means perfect, yet it offers a valuable insight into what AI is and how it operates. This definition alludes to the capacity of AI systems to function autonomously; however, it emphasizes the significant role that humans play at all stages to influence the outcome via human instructions and guidance.

AI in Education

AIED is a multidisciplinary field of inquiry that combines different disciplines such as education, computer science, and psychology. It encourages thorough study and the development of interactive and adaptable environments of learning for different audiences and across all fields of study. AIED is regarded as a powerful tool for enabling advanced paradigms of pedagogy, technological advancements, and scholarly research in education breakthroughs that are considered unattainable in traditional classroom settings, such as the integration of machine learning (ML), computer assisted language learning (CALL), and artificial neural networks (ANN) in different learning scenarios—be they formal, informal, or non-formal (Holmes et al., 2019). AIED empowers collaborative computer-mediated learning, asynchronous language acquisition that happens intermittently, as well as cost-effective personalized learning via an algorithm-based navigation system, which is supported through the application of automated assessment systems, facial recognition technology, and advanced analytical techniques (Nye, 2015; Akgun & Greenhow, 2021). Consequently, there is a growing body of evidence supporting the crucial functions of AI in education. According to Hwang et al. (2020), AI in education "fosters a transformation of knowledge, cognition, and culture" (p.1). Nevertheless, the integration of AI in education has been quite problematic due to ethical justification and considerations. Despite recent efforts to develop ethical instructions for AIED, the lack of a worldwide agreement and standard rules for AIED remains a concern.

Factors Affecting Students' Technology Adoption

The integration of advanced technologies in higher education has gained considerable attention in recent years, in terms of understanding the factors that influence students' adoption of these technologies. Various theoretical models, notably the Technology Acceptance Model (TAM), have been widely used to examine key constructs such as perceived ease of use (PEOU), perceived usefulness (PU), and students' attitudes toward technology. This section provides a comprehensive review of the literature on factors affecting students' technology adoption, drawing on recent studies that focus on artificial intelligence (AI), chatbots, and digital learning tools in educational contexts.

Perceived Usefulness and Ease of Use

Perceived usefulness (PU) and perceived ease of use (PEOU) are central constructs in the TAM framework, both of which have been shown to significantly influence students' intentions to adopt new technologies. Almahri et al. 2020) applied structural equation modeling to investigate the adoption of chatbots in UK universities, finding that PEOU plays a critical role in shaping students' acceptance of these AI tools. Their results indicated that students are more likely to use chatbots if they find them easy to interact with and if they believe these tools can improve their learning outcomes. Similarly, Liu et al. (2020) highlighted the role of PEOU in the adoption of AI writing tools. Their study revealed that ease of use was a key predictor of technology acceptance, as students were more inclined to use AI tools when the interface was user-friendly and required minimal effort. The authors further noted that ease of use directly impacts perceived usefulness, meaning that if a student finds a tool easy to operate, they are more likely to perceive it as beneficial for their academic tasks. Chocarro et al. (2021) explored the acceptance of AI in higher education, focusing on the relationship between ease of use, usefulness, and students' overall acceptance of AI-driven learning platforms. Their findings align with previous research, showing that both PU and PEOU significantly influence students' behavioral intentions. However, they also emphasized that the ease of use has a more substantial effect on students' initial acceptance, while perceived usefulness tends to play a more important role in sustained use.

Attitudes Towards Technology

In addition to PEOU and PU, attitudes toward technology are a critical factor in determining students' adoption behaviors. Al-Abdullatif (2023) examined students' perceptions of chatbots in learning environments, integrating TAM with the value-based adoption model to assess the broader attitudinal aspects of technology adoption. The study found that positive attitudes towards chatbots, shaped by factors such as usefulness and ease of use, were instrumental in predicting students' acceptance. Furthermore, students who perceived chatbots as enhancing the quality of learning interactions were more likely to adopt them. Kemp et al. (2019) developed a taxonomy of factors that influence attitudes towards educational technologies, emphasizing the importance of student-centric designs that enhance engagement and satisfaction. Their study identified key attitudinal drivers, including perceived relevance to academic success, peer influence, and previous experiences with similar technologies. The authors argued that positive attitudes are essential for fostering long-term adoption and technology integration within academic settings. Furthermore, Liesa-Orús et al. (2023) used structural equation modeling to examine the relationship between attitudes, ease of use, and usefulness among older university students. They found that students' attitudes towards digital tools, including e-learning platforms, were shaped not only by perceived ease of use but also by their self-efficacy and confidence in using these technologies. The study underscored the importance of addressing students' confidence levels and ensuring that they feel competent in using digital tools to foster positive attitudes and higher adoption rates.

Social Influence and Peer Interaction

Social influence and peer interaction also play a significant role in the adoption of educational technologies. Al-Adwan et al. (2023) extended TAM to predict students' intentions to use metaverse-based learning platforms, finding that social influence, including recommendations from peers and instructors, had a considerable impact on students' technology adoption behaviors. Their results indicated that students were more likely to use new platforms when they observed positive experiences among their peers or when the technology was endorsed by authoritative figures in their academic environment.

Social interaction also emerged as a crucial factor in a study by Chen et al. (2020), which focused on students' use of chatbots for learning Chinese. The authors reported that students who engaged in collaborative learning through chatbot interactions demonstrated higher acceptance levels compared to those who used the chatbot individually. This finding suggests that peer interaction and collaborative experiences can enhance students' motivation to adopt new technologies, as shared experiences help to reduce the perceived risks associated with novel tools. Similarly, Saif et al. (2024) validated the TAM framework in the context of ChatGPT adoption in education, noting that social influence played a pivotal role in students' decision to use the AI-powered tool. They found that students were more inclined to adopt ChatGPT when they perceived that their peers were using it successfully, highlighting the importance of social learning and collective experiences in driving technology adoption.

Trust and Risk Perception

Trust in technology is another critical factor that influences students' adoption behaviors. Choung, David, and Ross (2023) explored the role of trust in the acceptance of AI technologies, demonstrating that students' willingness to adopt AI tools was closely linked to their level of trust in the system's reliability and accuracy. The study revealed that students who trusted AI to deliver consistent and accurate outputs were more likely to adopt these technologies, while those who perceived AI as unreliable or risky were hesitant to engage with it. Drueke et al. (2021) evaluated the impact of forced distance learning during the COVID-19 pandemic, using TAM to assess students' acceptance of digital learning platforms. They found that trust in the platform's security and data privacy was a significant predictor of students' acceptance in a remote learning context where students relied heavily on digital tools for their educational activities. Their findings suggested that universities need to ensure transparency and security to build trust and facilitate the adoption of digital platforms. Kelly, Kaye, and Oviedo-Trespalacios (2023) conducted a systematic review of factors contributing to the acceptance of AI, concluding that trust and risk perception are central to technology adoption. Their review identified a range of factors that influence trust, including the transparency of AI systems, the perceived competence of the technology, and the ethical implications of AI use. The authors argued that addressing these factors is essential for promoting trust and, consequently, higher rates of adoption among students.

Institutional Support and Training

Institutional support and the availability of training resources have been widely recognized as influential factors in technology adoption. Mohd Rahim et al. (2022) examined the role of institutional support in the adoption of AI-based chatbots in higher education, employing a hybrid PLS-SEM-neural network model to analyze the relationship between institutional factors and adoption behaviors. Their findings indicated that students who received adequate support and training from their institutions were more likely to adopt AI chatbots, as they felt more confident and prepared to use the technology. Al Darayseh (2023) also emphasized the importance of institutional support in the adoption of AI writing tools, noting that students who had access to training and technical assistance reported higher levels of acceptance. The study highlighted the need for universities to provide continuous support and resources to ensure that students are comfortable using new technologies in cases where the technology is complex or unfamiliar. Lin and Yu (2023) extended TAM to examine students' use of digital academic reading tools, finding that institutional support played a critical role in facilitating technology adoption. Their results showed that students who received training and guidance from their institutions were more likely to perceive the tools as useful and easy to use, which in turn influenced their behavioral intentions to adopt the technology. The authors argued that providing comprehensive training programs is essential for overcoming initial resistance and fostering long-term adoption of educational technologies.

Motivation and Perceived Value

Students' motivation and perceived value of the technology are important factors that drive adoption. Al-Abdullatif (2023) incorporated the value-based adoption model into TAM to explore students' motivations for using chatbots in learning environments. The study revealed that students were more likely to adopt chatbots if they perceived the technology as adding value to their learning experience, such as enhancing engagement, providing instant feedback, and improving academic performance. Al-Abdullatif further noted that students who valued the flexibility and efficiency offered by chatbots were more motivated to integrate the technology into their daily academic routines. Kemp, Palmer, and Strelan (2019) also identified motivation as a key determinant of students' attitudes towards technology adoption. Their study found that students who perceived educational technologies as directly contributing to their academic success were more motivated to use these tools, while those who viewed the technology as irrelevant or burdensome were less likely to adopt it. The authors stressed the importance of designing technologies that align with students' academic goals and providing clear demonstrations of how technology can enhance learning outcomes.

Challenges and Opportunities in AI Integration for Non-Western Educational Systems

Beyond theoretical models, practical studies on AI writing tools in educational settings further highlight the relevance of these frameworks. The integration of artificial intelligence (AI) in educational systems has emerged as a significant area of research within non-Western contexts, where socio-economic and cultural factors play critical roles in shaping the adoption process. As educational institutions increasingly explore the potential of AI technologies to enhance teaching and learning outcomes, understanding the challenges, ethical considerations, and long-term impacts associated with these innovations is essential. The existing literature reveals a diverse array of experiences and perspectives on AI adoption across various regions, reflecting a landscape that is both promising and fraught with obstacles. Studies conducted in regions such as Africa and the Middle East underscore the necessity of addressing infrastructural deficits and ethical dilemmas while leveraging the opportunities that AI presents for improving educational practices (Oubibi et al., 2022; Kiemde & Kora, 2020; Shwedeh et al., 2024). This literature review aims to synthesize findings from key studies in the field, critically examining the implications of AI integration in educational contexts and highlighting the need for a nuanced understanding of its diverse applications and effects.

AI Adoption in Non-Western Countries

A pivotal study by Oubibi et al. (2022) explores the challenges and opportunities for AI adoption in Morocco. Utilizing a qualitative approach, the authors conducted interviews with educators and policymakers, uncovering significant barriers such as inadequate infrastructure, limited access to data, and a lack of political commitment to AI initiatives. This study effectively highlights the contextual challenges faced in North Africa, as similar findings have emerged in other studies indicating the pervasive issues of infrastructure and policy support across various regions in Africa (Arakpogun et al., 2021; Kiemde & Kora, 2020). However, while the study contributes valuable insights into the unique socio-political and economic contexts of Morocco, its findings may not be universally applicable across all regions, underscoring the need for further research that captures the diversity of experiences within the continent.

In a literature review, Kiemde and Kora (2020) synthesize existing research on the development of AI in Africa, revealing critical obstacles, including insufficient technical expertise and investment in AI research. While this review provides a broad overview of the landscape, it relies heavily on secondary data, which may obscure recent developments and nuanced realities within individual countries. As evidenced by Umezuruike and Ngugi (2020), who conducted qualitative analyses of case studies focusing on the challenges of big data adoption in Sub-Saharan Africa, the educational landscape is significantly affected by socio-economic disparities that limit access to AI technologies. Both studies collectively highlight the importance of addressing these challenges to foster an environment conducive to effective AI integration in educational systems.

Arakpogun et al. (2021) adopt a mixed-methods approach that combines qualitative interviews and quantitative surveys with educational and business leaders across Africa. Their research reveals that while AI holds transformative potential for enhancing educational outcomes and driving economic growth, significant infrastructural deficits and policy gaps continue to impede effective integration. This mixed methods approach enriches the findings by providing both qualitative and quantitative perspectives; however, the diversity of respondents may introduce variability that complicates generalizations. In a similar vein, Shwedeh et al. (2024) conduct a case study analysis in the UAE, examining the adoption of AI tools in higher education. Their research identifies a strong alignment between AI adoption and sustainability goals while also emphasizing a critical need for professional development to facilitate effective use of AI tools among educators. This finding resonates with Khlaif et al. (2024), who noted that university teachers in the Middle East express optimism about AI's potential for student assessment yet highlight their concerns about preparedness and training. Although these studies showcase progressive stances towards AI integration in regions like the UAE, the variability in infrastructural readiness and educational philosophies in other non-Western contexts necessitates a careful examination of each region's unique circumstances.

Technological Integration and Infrastructure

The inclusion of AI chatbots in higher education requires strong technical infrastructure and a user-oriented design approach. Sandu and Gide (2019) emphasize the significance of implementing AI technologies to support active learning. They further posit that AI chatbots could provide personalized and timely responses to student queries, thus reducing the workload of academic staff and enhancing institutional resource efficiency. The integration is required for an educational frame supporting enhancement in education and active learning. Effective chatbot design, according to Rejón-Guardia and Vich-I-Martorell (2020), facilitates smooth administrative workflows and improves student interactions. Their study highlights the necessity for user-centered designs and iterative improvements based on student feedback to ensure successful integration. By prioritizing user needs and preferences, educational institutions can develop intuitive chatbots that enhance efficiency in educational processes. Mohd Rahim et al. (2022) also probes the factors leading to chatbot acceptance through a hybrid PLS-SEM and neural network research method. Their research shows perceived usefulness and perceived ease of use as key determinants in chatbots' adoption. Their findings agree with those of Keong (2022) and Pillai et al. (2023), who identify ease of use as a substantial determinant of user acceptance. To successfully integrate technology, educational institutions should develop systems that are reliable and user-friendly. Malik et al. (2021) also stresses the significance of convenience and performance improvements in encouraging chatbot use among students. This way, user convenience could open more avenues for students' engagement and usage of the chatbots provided by these institutions. Hence, institutions should focus on user-friendly design and strong infrastructure for a better implementation of AI chatbots.

User Experience and Engagement

User experience is a crucial factor in adopting and making AI chatbots effective in education. For instance, Malik et al. (2021) mention convenience and improved performance as the chief drivers of student adoption. Their study reveals that chatbots should provide practical benefits designed with user convenience to make engagement possible. Such learning tools make educational institutions more supportive of the learning experience. The results from the studies undertaken by Chen et al. (2020) and Belda-Medina and Calvo-Ferrer (2022) in the domain of AI tools for language learning revealed that better learning outcomes could be achieved through the application of an interactive and attractive chatbot interface. Their study suggests that learners using chatbots were far better in vocabulary and conversational fluency, respectively; hence, chatbots could be particularly effective in presenting additional learning practice of the target language. Therefore, chatbots can offer a smart and adaptable learning experience based on each learner's requirements, which could accommodate for the needs of each student during the learning process.

Neo (2022), and Kumar and Silva (2020) also underscore the importance of trustworthiness and accuracy in cultivating positive user experiences. There is a need to boost user trust and acceptance by ensuring the accuracy of responses from the chatbot. This further suggests that improvement in these aspects will help boost user experience, and user trust will encourage more use of chatbot technologies in learning institutions. The issue of trust in relation to chatbot acceptance is also examined by Almahri et al. (2020). Their research findings imply that perceived ease of use, utility, and trust served as substantial determinants of chatbots' adoption. They also suggest that user trust can only be achieved once users are exposed to chatbots' practical benefits in education and granted user-friendly systems with chatbot technology, where adequate support would be provided in real-time to create a pleasant learning experience. Institutions are encouraged to allocate resources towards creating reliable and user-friendly chatbot systems that provide live support to assure a satisfying user experience.

Educational Outcomes and Performance

AI chatbots have the potential to greatly enhance educational outcomes by providing immediate assistance and personalized feedback. According to Malik et al. (2021) and Pillai et al. (2023), chatbots can improve students' academic performance by offering practical benefits and convenience. Their research emphasizes the importance of chatbots' practicality and ease of use in enhancing student engagement. Belda-Medina and Calvo-Ferrer (2022) and Chen et al. (2020) assert that AI tools can enhance vocabulary and conversational fluency, underscoring their ability to provide valuable supplementary language practice. By employing a hybrid PLS-SEM and neural network approach, Mohd Rahim et al. (2022) further stresses the role of chatbots in improving educational outcomes as well as highlight the importance of effective and trusted chatbot systems. They suggest that investing in reliable AI tools can enhance student engagement and satisfaction. In the same vein, Neo (2022) and Slepankova (2021) argue that addressing various stakeholder concerns—which primarily revolve around trust, transparency, and sustainability—is critical for building user confidence. By addressing user concerns, educational institutions can build trust and guarantee successful integration of chatbot technology.

Long-Term Impact of AI Writing Tools on Students' Writing Development

A growing body of research investigates the long-term impacts of AI writing tools on students' writing development. Marzuki et al. (2023) employs a qualitative approach to explore the perspectives of EFL teachers regarding AI tools, revealing that while improvements in students' writing structure were noted, concerns about over-reliance on AI potentially stunting critical thinking and independent writing skills were also prevalent. This critical observation underscores the need for further longitudinal studies that assess the sustained effects of AI on student development over time, which aligns with the findings of Gayed et al. (2022), who conducted an experimental study evaluating the impact of an AI writing assistant on English language learners. Their results suggest enhanced grammatical accuracy and fluency; however, the authors caution against potential dependency on AI for writing tasks, highlighting the delicate balance between leveraging technology and fostering student independence.

Nazari et al. (2021) utilize a randomized controlled trial to assess the effectiveness of AI-powered digital writing assistants in higher education, concluding that while these tools enhance technical writing skills, they do not necessarily foster deeper engagement in the writing process. This finding underscores the critical importance of instructor involvement in the integration of AI technologies, a theme echoed in

Wu's (2024) examination of AI tools like ChatGPT in EAP classrooms. Wu's research indicates significant improvements in writing performance but warns of the risks of dependence on AI feedback. This dual focus on benefits and potential pitfalls contributes to a richer discussion of AI's role in educational contexts, yet the limited scope within a specific academic environment may constrain broader applicability.

Lee (2020) presents a longitudinal study tracking writing development among EFL students using automated writing evaluation. The findings indicate positive effects on writing mechanics, revealing that sustained development requires instructor involvement beyond automated feedback. While the longitudinal nature of the study offers valuable insights into the temporal dynamics of AI adoption, the specific population examined may not represent the diverse experiences of all EFL learners. Thus, a more comprehensive understanding of the long-term impact of AI writing tools would benefit from studies that encompass a wider array of educational contexts and demographic groups.

Ethical Concerns Surrounding AI in Education

The ethical implications of AI integration in education are paramount to understanding its adoption and effectiveness. Salloum (2024) provides a conceptual analysis of ethical frameworks, identifying key challenges such as student privacy and data security. While the study effectively underscores the necessity of ethical guidelines, its lack of empirical data limits the applicability of its findings in practical scenarios. This gap emphasizes the urgent need for further research that incorporates real-world applications of ethical principles in educational contexts. Nguyen et al. (2023), in their qualitative study involving focus groups of educators and students, propose ethical principles for AI use in education, emphasizing transparency, accountability, and inclusivity. These principles align with the ethical considerations presented by Han et al. (2023), who conducted qualitative interviews with educators to explore the ethical and pedagogical impacts of AI in education, revealing that AI can inadvertently reinforce biases, necessitating a critical examination of AI systems' design and implementation. While these studies provide a foundational understanding of ethical concerns, the focus group format employed by Nguyen et al. (2023) may restrict the diversity of perspectives represented, potentially overlooking critical voices in the conversation surrounding ethical AI use. The growing concern regarding the ethical implications of AI adoption is further compounded by the challenges of ensuring equitable access to AI technologies. As Slimi and Carballido (2023) discuss in their analysis of global AI ethics policies, the lack of inclusive frameworks can exacerbate existing inequalities in education, a point echoed by Córdova and Vicari (2022), who highlight practical ethical issues that arise in the context of AI integration in learning environments. Collectively, these studies emphasize the need for robust ethical guidelines that account for the diverse socio-cultural landscapes in which AI technologies are deployed.

Challenges and Recommendations

In spite of the promises of chatbots in tertiary education, several challenges—which can obstruct the adoption of such technology—emerge. According to Sandu and Gide (2019), the main predictors for a successful implementation are user acceptance, technical infrastructure, and ongoing support. Therefore, by making these predictors a priority through investing in user-friendly and reliable chatbots that provide support, user trust can be built. Similarly, Neo (2022) and Slepankova (2021) shed light on the significance of addressing accuracy and reliability concerns in promoting user trust. As indicated by Ragheb et al. (2022) and Almahri et al. (2020), social influence is a strong determinant of students' attitudes toward the use of chatbots. Their studies collectively suggest that adequate training and support are decisive factors in promoting the practical benefits of chatbots and creating an engaging learning environment. Keong (2022) and Kumar and Silva (2020) call for more research on the long-term effects of chatbots on educational outcomes and their application across various learning contexts. By prioritizing the development of reliable and easy-to-use systems with assured support, institutions can positively influence user trust and promote the widespread adoption of chatbot technologies. The journey toward AI adoption in non-Western educational contexts is marked by a complex interplay of challenges and opportunities that demand careful navigation. While AI technologies hold the potential to transform educational experiences and outcomes, significant barriers related to infrastructure, ethical considerations, and pedagogical practices must be addressed to ensure equitable access and effective integration. The reviewed literature emphasizes the importance of tailoring AI strategies to specific regional needs and contexts, advocating for a collaborative approach that engages educators, policymakers, and technologists alike in the pursuit of sustainable educational innovations (Arakpogun et al., 2021; Khlaif et al., 2024; Salloum, 2024). As the landscape of AI in education continues to evolve, ongoing research will be crucial in informing best practices and guiding the responsible implementation of these technologies in diverse educational settings.

METHODOLOGY

Research Design

The present study adopts a quantitative research design aimed at investigating the acceptance of AI-powered writing tools among students at the Faculty of Letters and Humanities, Ben M'Sik. This research seeks to empirically assess the relationships among key constructs of the Technology Acceptance Model (TAM), including attitudes toward AI writing tools, perceived usefulness, and perceived ease of use. The primary objective is to analyze how these constructs interact to predict students' behavioral intentions and actual use of AI writing tools in their academic practices. By employing TAM as the theoretical framework, the study aims to provide an understanding of the factors that influence student acceptance of emerging technologies in educational contexts. Additionally, the quantitative approach enables the collection of objective data that can be used to identify statistically significant trends, which contributes to the broader discourse on technology integration in higher education.

Sampling and Data Collection

A total of 253 students from the Department of English Studies at the Faculty of Letters and Humanities, Ben M'Sik participated in this study. The recruitment of participants was done through convenience sampling. Data was collected until data saturation was achieved. The data were collected using an online survey questionnaire that was distributed via Google Forms. The survey contained five parts. The first part dealt with demographic data such as gender, study level, and stream. The other four sections contained questions that measured user perceptions regarding ease of use, perceived usefulness, attitude towards AI writing tools, and actual system use. Items were assessed using a five-point Likert scale, with responses ranging from strongly disagree to strongly agree for each statement.

Data Analysis

To analyze the data garnered from the online survey, Partial Least Squares Structural Equation Modelling (PLS-SEM) was utilized. Research findings show that PLS-SEM is suitable for such kinds of investigations as it can account for complexity within models where there are multiple constructs and a relatively small sample size (Hair et al. 2018). The evaluation involved testing the measurement model (reliability and validity) and the structural model (theoretical relationships between constructs). The evaluation process using PLS-SEM was twofold. Initially, the assessment of the measurement model was performed to examine the reliability and validity of the variables. The reliability was assessed through Cronbach's alpha, composite reliability (rho_a), and composite reliability (rho_c); whereas average variance extracted (AVE), The Fornell-Larcker criterion, and Heterotrait-Monotrait (HTMT) ratio were deployed to examine the validity of the constructs. The assessment of the structural model was carried out to assess the theoretical associations between the different constructs. To this end, path coefficients of the TAM variables—attitudes, perceived ease of use, perceived usefulness, and acceptance of AI writing tools—were calculated to determine the strength and significance of the relationships among these constructs.

RESULTS

Demographic Data

Table 1 showcases the demographic characteristics of the participants. A total of 253 students from the Department of English studies at the Faculty of Letters and Humanities Ben M'sik responded to the online form, of which 130 male (51,4%) and 123 females (48,6%), which suggests a balanced gender distribution. Most of the respondents were undergraduate students enrolled in both Applied Linguistics (65,4%) and American Culture Studies (20,2%) streams. As for graduate students, 23 (9,5%) participants enrolled in the Moroccan American Studies MA program, whereas 12 (4,9%) participants enrolled in the Applied Linguistics for Language Teaching MA program. Most respondents (80,2%) had previous experience with AI writing tools, which shows that most of the participants are acquainted with such tools.

Table 1. Demographic data

Demographic Data	Frequency	Percentage
	Gender	
Female	123	48,6%
Male	130	51,4%
	Educational Level	
S1	90	34,2%
S3	60	22,8%
S5	68	25,9%
S1 (MA)	33	12,5%
S3 (MA)	12	4,6%

continued on following page

Table 1. Continued

Demographic Data	Frequency	Percentage
	Stream	
American Culture Studies	49	20,2%
Applied Linguistics	159	65,4%
Applied Linguistics for Language Teaching (MA)	12	4,9%
Moroccan American Studies (MA)	23	9,5%
	Previous Experience with AI Writing Tools	
Yes	203	80,2%
No	50	19,8%

Measurement Model Evaluation

The initial phase in assessing the measurement model was to determine its construct validity, which means the extent to which the items measure the intended construct (Hair et al., 2019). Table 2 displays the indicator loadings. The indicator loadings values were greater than the suggested value of 0.7 (Hair et al., 2010), suggesting a moderate to high level of loading. Afterwards, the Cronbach's alpha coefficient (α) and composite reliability (CR) of each construct were computed to assess the internal consistency reliability. All constructs' composite reliability values exceeded the threshold of 0.7, ranging from 0.89 to 0.93, and all the Cronbach's alpha values were between 0.87 and 0.90, indicating a good to high level of reliability. Subsequently, the convergent validity was examined via computing the Average Variance Extracted (AVE) of all variables. The AVE values ranged from 0.6 to 0.73, exceeding the 0.5 recommended value (Hair et al., 2019; Fornell & Larcker, 1981). The AVE values, therefore, suggest that each variable explains more than 50% of variance among its items.

Table 2. Reliability analysis

	Cronbach's alpha	Composite reliability (rho_a)	Composite reliability (rho_c)	Average variance extracted (AVE)
Actual System Use	0.902	0.920	0.927	0.717
Attitude	0.905	0.921	0.930	0.730
Perceived Ease of Use	0.868	0.903	0.905	0.659
Perceived Usefulness	0.872	0.892	0.908	0.666

The last stage in evaluating the measurement model of this study was computing the discriminant validity values, which determine how a construct is distinct from other constructs and do not measure the same concepts (Hair et al., 2019). It is measured via computing both the Fornell-Larcker criterion and Heterotrait-Monotrait (HTMT) ratio. The diagonal elements in Table 3 represent the square root of the average variance extracted (AVE) for each variable, which must be greater than the correlations with other variables. The results indicate that all constructs satisfy theFornell-Larcker criterion hence discriminant validity is satisfactory (Henseler et al., 2015). Our findings suggest that the measurement model satisfy the requirements for both convergent and discriminant validity, thereby supporting the reliability and validity of all constructs utilized in the present paper. These HTMT values were also less than the recommended threshold of 0.85, as illustrated in Table 4, thus confirming discriminant validity of the model of this study.

Table 3. Fornell-Larcker criterion

	Actual System Use	Attitudes	Perceived Ease of Use	Perceived Usefulness
Actual System Use	**0.847**			
Attitudes	0.786	**0.854**		
Perceived Ease of Use	0.744	0.745	**0.812**	
Perceived Usefulness	0.800	0.841	0.658	**0.816**

Table 4. Heterotrait-Monotrait ratio (HTMT)

	Heterotrait-monotrait ratio (HTMT)
Attitudes <-> Actual System Use	0.836
Perceived Ease of Use <-> Actual System Use	0.826
Perceived Ease of Use <-> Attitudes	0.798
Perceived Usefulness <-> Actual System Use	0.841
Perceived Usefulness <-> Attitudes	0.848
Perceived Usefulness <-> Perceived Ease of Use	0.723

Structural Model Evaluation

Once the reliability and validity of the model were confirmed, we moved to assess the structural model. To this end, the size of standardized path coefficients (β), t-values (t), and significance levels (p-values) for each hypothesis were calculated (see Table. 5) as suggested by Hair et al. (2019). The findings of testing the hypotheses indicate that perceived ease of use ($\beta = 0.658$, $t = 14.376$, $p < 0.001$) has a significant positive impact on perceived usefulness, thus supporting hypothesis H1. Similarly, perceived ease of use ($\beta = 0.337$, $t = 6.842$, $p < 0.001$) significantly influences attitudes, supporting hypothesis H2. Perceived usefulness ($\beta = 0.620$, $t = 12.716$, $p < 0.001$) also has a significant positive influence on attitudes, confirming hypothesis H3. Moreover, attitudes ($\beta = 0.786$, $t = 24.653$, $p < 0.001$) have a significant, positive affect on actual system use, which confirms hypothesis H4. The high t-values and low p-values for all these hypotheses indicate strong statistical significance at the 0.1% level. These results suggest that perceived ease of use and perceived usefulness are critical predictors of attitudes toward AI writing tools (see Figure 2), which in turn significantly influence actual system use. Therefore, the data confirmed all four hypotheses (H1, H2, H3, and H4), which demonstrates that the relationships within the structural model are statistically significant, and the model has substantial explanatory power for understanding the factors influencing actual system use.

Table 5. Results of the hypothesis testing

Hypothesis	**Path Coefficient (β)**	**t-value**	**p-value**	**Supported**
H1: Perceived Ease of Use → Perceived Usefulness	0.658	14.376	< 0.001	Yes
H2: Perceived Ease of Use → Attitudes	0.337	6.842	< 0.001	Yes
H3: Perceived Usefulness→ Attitudes	0.620	12.716	< 0.001	Yes
H4: Attitudes → Actual System Use	0.786	24.653	< 0.001	Yes

Figure 2. Standardized path coefficient results

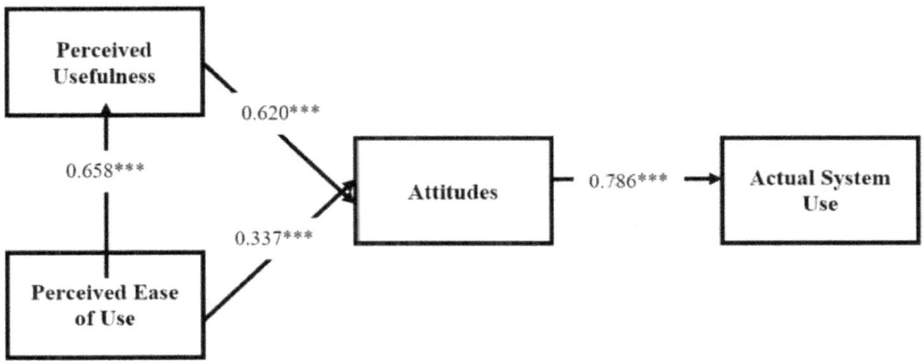

Given that this study sought to assess students' acceptance of AI writing tools, the analysis revealed a high predictive power for the dependent variables: Perceived Usefulness, Attitudes, and Actual System Use (as shown in Table 6). The analysis revealed strong predictive capabilities for the dependent constructs: Perceived Usefulness, Attitudes, and Actual System Use.

According to Hair et al. (2023), the Q^2 values demonstrate the predictive power of the model in regard to the constructs out-of-samples. The higher the Q^2 values, the more accurate outcomes prediction when applied to new data. Q^2 values greater than 0.35 are considered significant, as recommended by Hair et al. (2023). In the present research, all Q^2 values exceeded the recommended threshold of 0.35—Perceived Usefulness (0.499), Attitudes (0.630), and Actual System Use (0.605)—which highlights the robust predictive relevance of the model and therefore its high accuracy in predicting students' acceptance of AI writing tools.

As indicated by Shmueli and Koppius (2011), the high values of the coefficient of determination (R^2), which measures the model's explanatory power, affirm the model's reliability in explaining the variance within the TAM constructs. R^2 values are between 0 and 1, with higher values implying a greater explanatory power. R^2 values of 0.75, 0.50, and 0.25 can be deemed significant, medium, and weak, respectively (Henseler et al., 2009; Hair et al., 2011). In the case of our model, R^2 values for Perceived Ease of Use (0.433), Perceived Usefulness (0.678), and Actual System Use (0.617) underscore moderate to substantial explanatory power. These findings highlight the crucial roles of perceived ease of use (PEOU) and usefulness (PU) in shaping attitudes (ATT) in turn influence actual system use (ASU).

Table 6. R-squared and Q- squared values

Construct	R-squared	Q-squared
Perceived Usefulness	0.433	0.678
Attitudes	0.678	0.617
Actual System Use	0.617	0.605

Pearson correlation was carried out in Smart PLS to assess the relationship between Perceived Usefulnes, Actual System Use, Attitudes, and Perceived Ease of Use. Table 7 below provides a summary of the results.

The results revealed that a strong positive relationship exists among all constructs. For instance, a significant positive correlation was observed between Actual System Use and Attitudes ($r = .79$, $p < .01$), which indicates that students who frequently use AI writing tools tend to have more positive attitudes towards them. The findings also show that Actual System Use was significantly related to both Perceived Ease of Use ($r = .74$, $p < .01$) and Perceived Usefulness ($r = .80$, $p < .01$). This suggests that students who perceive AI writing tools as easy to use and useful exhibit a greater tendency to adopt and utilize them.

Attitudes were strongly correlated with Perceived Ease of Use ($r = .75$, $p < .01$) and Perceived Usefulness ($r = .84$, $p < .01$), which underscores that students who have positive attitudes towards AI writing tools also find them easy to use and beneficial. Furthermore, Perceived Ease of Use demonstrated a significant positive association with Perceived Usefulness ($r = .66$, $p < .01$), which indicates that if students consider AI writing tools easy to use, they also tend to find them practical.

Table 7. Correlation coefficients among the TAM variables

	Actual System Use	Attitudes	Perceived Ease of Use	Perceived Usefulness
Actual System Use	1.000	0.786**	0.744**	0.800**
Attitudes	0.786**	1.000	0.745**	0.841**
Perceived Ease of Use	0.744**	0.745**	1.000	0.658**
Perceived Usefulness	0.800**	0.841**	0.658**	1.000

**. Correlation is significant at the 0.01 level (2-tailed).

DISCUSSION AND IMPLICATIONS

The pivotal role that artificial intelligence plays in redefining the educational landscape necessitates a profound comprehension of users' acceptance and willingness to use and incorporate AI into their teaching and learning. To this end, the TAM was deployed in this study to attain this understanding. To our knowledge, the present study is the first attempt to investigate the main factors influencing AI writing tools acceptance amongst Moroccan university students. The present study, therefore, expands upon the established literature on AI writing tools' adoption and offers numerous recommendations for various stakeholders and different educational settings for a better implementation of these tools' in Moroccan universities. This section is devoted to the outcomes of this study and their implications. The results are grouped and interpreted in conformity with the connections amongst the variables introduced by the research model.

Perceived Ease of Use and Perceived Usefulness

As stated by Davis (1989), the most influential factor in improving users' perceptions and attitudes towards the adoption and integration of emerging technologies is perceived ease of use (PEOU). The results indicate that perceived ease of use is a strong predictor of perceived usefulness (H1). These findings align with the results of prior research, which collectively associate the ease of use with enhanced perceived utility (Choung et al., 2023; Davis, 1989; Dignum, 2020). This entails that when students are dealing with user-friendly AI writing tools, they perceive them as being useful. Hence, the usefulness of these tools depends heavily on the simplicity and intuitive design of these tools. Instructors and AI writing tools' designers should prioritize the simplicity of navigation, the reduction of technical complexities, and the necessity of little to no prior training and knowledge when dealing with such tools. These measures not only help with the initial adoption of educational technologies but also promote sustained engagement and effective learning outcomes. By making the user experience smoother, educational practitioners can encourage greater acceptance and integration of technological tools, thereby enhancing the educational value that learners perceive.

Perceived Ease of Use and Attitudes

Within the realm of artificial intelligence, a large body of research underscores the key function of perceived ease of use in forecasting students' attitudes (Chocarro et al., 2021; Malik et al., 2021; Neo, 2022; Aslam et al., 2022; Belda-Medina & Calvo-Ferrer, 2022; Kumar & Silva, 2020; Almahri et al., 2020). The results garnered from the present study demonstrate perceived ease of use has a strong influence on attitudes (H2), which contradicts previous studies assessing students' acceptance of AI writing tools (Al-Abdullatif, 2023; Chen et al., 2020). These results are congruent with previous research findings by (Chocarro et al., 2021; Davis, 1989; Lee et al., 2009; Marangunić & Granić, 2015; Park, 2009; Venkatesh & Davis, 2000), which ascertained that perceived ease of use was a key predictor of customers' acceptance of new technologies. The findings imply that as students perceive AI writing tools as easy to use, their attitudes towards utilizing these tools become more positive. Thus, designing and developing AI writing tools that are user-friendly is of paramount importance in encouraging students to adopt and accept these tools. In order to effectuate this ease of use, developers should design AI writing tools that are easy to operate by means of designing simple interfaces. Furthermore, students should be equipped to apply these tools effectively across different devices to ensure accessibility for most students.

Perceived Usefulness and Attitudes

Like perceived ease of use, perceived usefulness has a strong, direct effect on users' attitudes towards utilizing a novel technology (Davis, 1989). The results of this research show that students' attitudes were influenced by how useful they perceive AI writing tools (H3). These outcomes are compatible with previous studies (Liu et al., 2020; Chen et al., 2020; Al Darayseh, 2023; Almahri et al., 2020; Ragheb et al., 2022; Aslam et al., 2022). The results imply that there is a strong connection between students' attitudes towards accepting AI-powered writing tools and the evaluation of these tools' utility for their academic performance. Therefore, instructors need to highlight the possible benefits of incorporating these tools into students' learning process, such as providing real-time and personalized feedback, tracking students' progress and development in different areas and at various stages of the writing process, and highlighting areas for improvement. Furthermore, students should be trained on how to effectively deploy AI writing tools in their writing assignments. To this end, effective training sessions on how to use educational technologies for academic purposes, clear articulation of the tangible advantages of these tools', and the presentation of case studies that prove these tools beneficial can all foster more positive attitudes towards their implementation. This positive disposition is crucial in sustaining the use and integration of AI writing tools into numerous educational practices, which in turn can lead to more positive learning outcomes.

Attitudes and Actual System Use

The results of this research suggest that students' actual system use of AI writing tools is impacted in a positive and strong manner by students' attitudes (H4). These results further suggest the positive relationship between students' attitudes and their adoption of AI tools observed in earlier studies (Okonkwo & Ade-Ibijola, 2021; Al Darayseh, 2023; Kelly et al., 2022; Belda-Medina & Calvo-Ferrer, 2022; Chatterjee & Bhattacharjee, 2020) The results yielded from this research highlight the significance of the attitudes in determining their actual acceptance of AI writing tools; when students' have positive behaviors towards AI writing tools, they tend to accept and adopt these tools. This has serious pedagogic implications for the development and support of educational technologies. The institutional and strategic impetus should therefore be directed towards developing and maintaining positive learner attitudes through the adoption of strategies that offer continuous support, which solicit and act on user perceptions, and allow a learning community with a supportive culture of using technology. Positive reinforcement, successful use case recognition, peer support networks—these measures all serve to develop students' willingness to use AI writing tools. If attitudes towards educational technologies are shaped positively, higher actual use of such a system can be expected from students, thus optimizing the use of such technologies for enhanced educational outcomes.

Ethical Dimensions and Cognitive Implications of AI in Education

The ethical dimension of AI adoption in educational contexts regarding privacy concerns and algorithmic biases warrants considerable attention. Many institutions are exploring the implementation of AI writing tools, yet the current discourse lacks comprehensive strategies for safeguarding student data. Oubibi et al. (2022) highlight that while AI technologies promise enhanced educational outcomes, they also pose significant risks to student privacy in regions like North Africa where regulatory frameworks may be underdeveloped. Furthermore, the design of AI systems can inadvertently perpetuate biases in feedback and evaluation processes, thereby affecting students' learning experiences and outcomes (Kiemde & Kora, 2020; Shwedeh et al., 2024). The lack of rigorous ethical guidelines and frameworks raises questions about the potential for discrimination in educational assessments, which could disproportionately affect marginalized groups. This highlights the urgent need for educational institutions to not only adopt AI technologies but also to critically evaluate the ethical implications associated with their use, ensuring that AI integration aligns with principles of equity and justice in education.

Moreover, the cognitive implications of AI use in education are profound and require thoughtful examination. The potential for over-reliance on automated feedback mechanisms may hinder the development of students' critical thinking skills over time. Research indicates that while AI tools can provide immediate support and enhance writing skills, they may also lead students to depend heavily on these technologies, ultimately stunting their ability to engage in reflective and independent thinking (Marzuki et al., 2023; Gayed et al., 2022). Institutions must consider how the integration of AI impacts not only academic performance but also cognitive development and long-term learning outcomes. As Khlaif et al. (2024) suggest, educators should balance the use of AI tools with pedagogical practices that promote critical engagement and self-efficacy. By fostering an educational environment that encourages the responsible use of AI while simultaneously nurturing essential cognitive skills, educators can better prepare students for the complexities of an AI-enhanced world.

Challenges and Opportunities in Personalizing Education with AI Tools

As AI continues to shape personalized learning, it offers educators the potential to tailor educational experiences to individual student needs. However, the future of AI integration in education is contingent upon addressing key barriers such as the resistance of educators, which stems from both intrinsic and extrinsic factors. Teachers often cite concerns regarding technical complexity, inadequate infrastructure, and the potential ethical dilemmas of AI-driven personalization, such as bias and privacy issues (Choi et al., 2023; Halaweh, 2023; Sabzalieva & Valentini, 2023). AI tools, while powerful, cannot achieve their full potential in personalized learning unless educators are confident and prepared to incorporate them into their practices. Future developments in AI must address these challenges by investing in teacher training, providing continuous technical support, and ensuring that institutions have the necessary infrastructure to support AI integration (Mehdaoui, 2024; Hamlaoui, 2021; Konaklı & Akdeniz, 2022).

Additionally, while AI presents many advantages, its integration into educational institutions has been slow, especially in regions with insufficient resources. In many cases, a lack of internet access, outdated technologies, and large class sizes hinder the seamless adoption of AI tools, exacerbating resistance from educators (Ertmer, 1999; Mercader & Gairín, 2020; Mehdaoui, 2024). For AI to be successfully adopted on a wide scale, there must be concerted efforts to overcome these barriers, especially in developing regions. Without addressing the fundamental issues of accessibility and support, AI integration risks deepening educational inequalities rather than promoting the personalized learning it promises (Marks et al., 2020; Stüber, 2018; Hamlaoui, 2021).

The Integration of AI with Emerging Educational Technologies: A Forward-Looking Perspective

Recent advancements in AI integration with emerging educational technologies such as the Metaverse, virtual reality (VR), augmented reality (AR), and mixed reality (MR) provide a glimpse into the future of education. These technologies, when combined with AI, offer students immersive and interactive learning environments that enhance engagement and understanding. The convergence of AI with AR/VR allows for the creation of personalized, data-driven experiences where learners can interact with content in ways previously unimaginable. AI can tailor these immersive environments based on individual student progress, ensuring more effective learning outcomes (Zawish et al., 2024; Morin et al., 2022). This integration not only changes how content is delivered but also how students and educators engage with the material, shifting towards a more collaborative and interactive pedagogical approach (Khan et al., 2022; Mozumder et al., 2022).

However, challenges remain in scaling these technologies in regions with limited access to advanced infrastructure. Despite the potential of AI and XR technologies, their adoption has been uneven due to technical, financial, and pedagogical barriers. Educators may face difficulties integrating these tools effectively due to insufficient training and the lack of supporting infrastructure in educational institutions. The cost of AR/VR headsets and the high demands of computing power pose significant obstacles, especially in developing countries. Moreover, the immersive nature of these technologies may require a shift in traditional teaching methods, necessitating a reconsideration of the role of the teacher in this AI-driven landscape (Rinaldi et al., 2020; Khan et al., 2022). For AI and immersive technologies to truly revolutionize education, institutions must invest in infrastructure and professional development to equip educators with the tools and knowledge needed to utilize these systems effectively (Ghafoor et al., 2020; Siriwardhana et al., 2021).

Looking ahead, the integration of AI with educational technologies like the Metaverse is poised to evolve further as 6G networks and edge computing become more prevalent. These technologies will reduce latency and improve real-time interactions, making the delivery of high-quality, immersive learning experiences more feasible. AI's role in automating feedback, personalizing content, and managing complex learning environments will become more sophisticated as these systems learn from vast amounts of student data and interactions. However, to ensure equitable access to these emerging tools, future research and policy must focus on addressing digital divides and ensuring that educators worldwide are prepared to integrate these cutting-edge technologies into their classrooms (Zawish et al., 2024; Mozumder et al., 2022).

Balancing AI's Technical Utility with Pedagogical Concerns in Critical Thinking Development

The integration of Artificial Intelligence (AI) in education, in relation to fostering critical thinking, presents a multifaceted landscape that requires more than just a focus on its perceived ease of use and usefulness. While studies acknowledge AI's capacity to enhance critical thinking by providing real-time feedback and adaptive learning experiences, the pedagogical and cognitive challenges remain underexplored. For instance, AI tools like chatbots or automated essay scoring systems may enhance efficiency, but they also risk creating a reliance on machine-generated feedback. This can lead to passive learning behaviors, where students might prioritize surface-level corrections over deep analytical engagement (Darwin et al., 2024; Marzuki et al., 2023; Hapsari & Wu, 2022). Therefore, while AI can aid in the development of critical thinking, educators must ensure that its use promotes, rather than hinders, active inquiry and independent problem-solving.

Critical thinking thrives on a foundation of skepticism, inquiry, and contextual analysis, areas where human oversight remains crucial. As noted by studies like Muthmainnah et al. (2022), AI enhances students' trust and self-confidence by providing rapid feedback. However, the same studies caution that without pedagogical strategies to foster deeper reflection, AI's role may become counterproductive. For example, students might default to accepting AI feedback without questioning the underlying assumptions or exploring alternative perspectives, thus inhibiting the development of higher-order thinking skills (Muthmainnah et al., 2022; Ray, 2023). Moreover, AI tools are often designed with one-size-fits-all algorithms, which may not account for individual learning nuances, further limiting the potential for personalized cognitive growth (Hapsari & Wu, 2022; Marzuki et al., 2023).

A balanced approach to AI integration requires a critical analysis of potential drawbacks, such as the cognitive offloading effect. When students rely heavily on AI-generated outputs for decision-making or problem-solving, their ability to engage in self-directed learning diminishes. The findings of Darwin et al. (2024) and others stress the importance of designing AI tools that stimulate curiosity and critical inquiry rather than merely facilitating rote learning or basic comprehension. AI should be viewed as an adjunct to, rather than a replacement for, human cognitive effort in education (Darwin et al., 2024; Hapsari & Wu, 2022). Thus, future pedagogical models must prioritize fostering independent learning skills to ensure that students remain active participants in the learning processes.

CONCLUSIONS, LIMITATIONS, AND FUTURE RESEARCH

The adoption of AI writing tools in higher education is a multifaceted phenomenon when considering the academic context of Moroccan universities, as examined in this study. The rapid development of artificial intelligence (AI) technologies has prompted significant changes in educational environments, with tools such as Grammarly and ProWritingAid offering valuable feedback to improve students' writing. This study aimed to investigate the perceptions, attitudes, and actual use of AI-powered writing tools among students in the Department of English Studies at the Faculty of Letters and Humanities Ben M'Sik, using the Technology Acceptance Model (TAM) to understand the underlying factors driving this adoption.

The key constructs of TAM—perceived ease of use (PEOU), perceived usefulness (PU), and attitudes—were central to the analysis, and the findings revealed strong interrelations among these constructs, affirming the model's applicability in this context. Perceived ease of use was shown to have a significant impact on students' perceptions of the usefulness of AI writing tools. As Davis (1989) posited, users are more likely to adopt a technology if they find it simple and straightforward to use. In this study, students indicated that the ease with which they could operate AI writing tools played a crucial role in determining whether they perceived the tools as useful for their academic writing tasks. The relationship between perceived ease of use and perceived usefulness supports findings from prior studies, which highlight that simplicity in design and ease of integration into academic work are critical for positive technology acceptance (Chocarro et al., 2021; Liu et al., 2020). The intuitive nature of AI tools—through features such as real-time feedback, grammar correction, and vocabulary enhancement—significantly reduced students' cognitive load, allowing them to focus more on improving their writing skills. This ease of use translated into an increased perception of the value these tools bring to academic work, which in turn influenced attitudes toward their adoption.

Furthermore, perceived usefulness was found to be a strong predictor of students' attitudes toward AI tools. The study demonstrated that students who believed AI writing tools could improve their academic performance and writing quality were more likely to hold positive attitudes toward their use. This finding aligns with existing literature on educational technology adoption, where perceived usefulness consistently emerges as a key factor influencing user attitudes and intentions to use new technologies (Al-Adwan et al., 2023; Lee et al., 2009). In the context of AI writing tools, the ability to receive immediate, personalized feedback on writing tasks was seen as a major benefit, addressing long-standing challenges in writing instruction, such as the limited availability of individualized feedback due to teacher workload (Narciss, 2008). Attitudes toward AI tools were also found to be a significant predictor of actual system use. Students who expressed positive attitudes were more likely to integrate these tools into their daily academic activities, underscoring the central role that attitudes play in the adoption process, as suggested by the Technology Acceptance Model (Venkatesh & Davis, 2000). This finding suggests that fostering positive attitudes among students is crucial for increasing the actual use of AI writing tools. The positive feedback loops between attitude and use demonstrate that once students recognize the practical benefits of these tools, they are more inclined to continue using them, leading to sustained engagement with AI technology in academic writing.

However, while the benefits of AI writing tools are evident, the study also uncovered concerns regarding the potential over-reliance on these technologies. Students expressed fears that heavy dependence on AI-generated feedback might hinder their development of independent critical thinking and writing skills. This issue, also identified in prior research, suggests that while AI tools can provide significant support, they should be used as a supplement to traditional instruction rather than a replacement (Marzuki et al., 2023). Over-reliance on AI tools could lead to a form of cognitive offloading, where students rely on automated feedback instead of engaging deeply with the writing process. Therefore, educators must strike a balance by incorporating AI tools into the curriculum in ways that encourage critical reflection and independent problem-solving. Additionally, the immediacy of AI feedback addresses a major limitation in traditional feedback mechanisms, where delays in receiving instructor feedback often undermine the effectiveness of writing instruction (Sadler, 1989). AI tools provide real-time corrections and suggestions, which students can act upon immediately, thereby promoting active learning. This feature was particularly valued by students, who noted that the rapid feedback cycle helped them identify and correct mistakes more efficiently than traditional methods would allow.

Beyond improving writing skills, AI writing tools also foster a sense of autonomy and self-regulation among students. The ability to receive personalized feedback without having to wait for instructor input empowered students to take control of their learning process, which is a critical element in fostering lifelong learning habits. As educational environments increasingly emphasize self-directed learning, AI tools offer a practical solution for enabling students to engage with material at their own pace and improve their academic performance autonomously (Al-Abdullatif, 2023; Liesa-Orús et al., 2023). Despite these benefits, the study acknowledges that the adoption of AI tools is contingent on the availability of adequate technical infrastructure and institutional support. Many students reported that their use of AI tools was hindered by limited access to reliable internet connections and up-to-date devices, a challenge that is especially pertinent in regions with infrastructural deficits (Oubibi et al., 2022). The success of AI integration in education thus depends not only on student attitudes and perceptions but also on the provision of necessary resources and technical support from educational institutions. As such, institutions must invest in infrastructure development and provide continuous technical assistance to ensure equitable access to AI technologies.

This study contributes valuable insights into the adoption of AI writing tools among Moroccan university students, but it is not without limitations. The study's restricted sample size, drawn exclusively from a single department within the Faculty of Letters and Humanities, Ben M'Sik, limits the broader applicability of its findings to other educational contexts. While the research provides valuable insights into AI writing tool adoption in this specific setting, it does not capture the experiences of students from different academic disciplines, institutions, or regions across Morocco. The homogeneity of the sample could mean that important factors influencing technology adoption, such as disciplinary differences, institutional resources, or regional disparities, are not adequately reflected in the results. This limitation affects the generalizability of the study's conclusions and reduces its ability to offer insights applicable to a more diverse student population. To enhance the representativeness of future studies, expanding the sample to include students from a variety of academic backgrounds, institutions, and regions would provide a more comprehensive understanding of AI tool adoption in higher education. Additionally, such diversity would enable researchers to better account for contextual variations that may influence student attitudes, behaviors, and the overall adoption process.

The reliance on self-reported data is another limitation of the study. While survey data provides useful insights into students' perceptions and attitudes, self-reporting is inherently subjective and may introduce response bias (Hair et al., 2019). Students may have over- or under-reported their use of AI tools due to social desirability or misunderstandings of the survey questions. Incorporating objective measures, such as tracking actual usage data from AI platforms, could provide a more accurate assessment of student behavior. Furthermore, the study employed a cross-sectional design, which captures data at a single point in time. While this design offers a snapshot of students' attitudes and behaviors, it does not account for changes over time. Longitudinal research is needed to explore how students' perceptions and usage of AI tools evolve as they become more familiar with the technology or as new AI features are introduced Another limitation lies in the exclusive focus on the Technology Acceptance Model (TAM). While TAM is a robust model for explaining technology adoption, it does not account for other relevant factors, such as social influence, facilitating conditions, or individual differences in technology proficiency. Future research could benefit from integrating other models, such as the Unified Theory of Acceptance and Use of Technology (UTAUT), to capture a more holistic understanding of the factors driving AI adoption (Venkatesh et al., 2012).

To address the limitations of the present study, several directions for future research are recommended. First, expanding the sample to include students from different academic disciplines, institutions, and regions is essential to capture a more representative understanding of AI tool adoption in higher education. Future qualitative research should focus on exploring how AI writing tools are adopted across different academic disciplines and institutions in order to examine how cultural, social, and infrastructural factors influence this process. Longitudinal studies involving interviews and focus groups can provide insights into how students' attitudes and skills, particularly in critical thinking and writing, evolve with continued AI use. Investigating the role of social influence, such as peer and faculty endorsements, can uncover strategies for encouraging wider adoption. Additionally, qualitative studies should address the ethical concerns related to data privacy, algorithmic fairness, and bias, ensuring AI tools promote equity and trust in educational settings. Finally, exploring the integration of AI with immersive technologies like virtual reality can offer a deeper understanding of personalized, interactive learning experiences.

Future research should also explore the impact of social influence and peer interactions on AI tool adoption. As noted in other studies, social influence plays a significant role in shaping students' technology adoption behaviors (Al-Adwan et al., 2023). Understanding how peer recommendations or instructor endorsements influence students' decisions to adopt AI tools could provide insights into how to encourage wider adoption. Additionally, there is a need for more research on the long-term impact of AI writing tools on students' writing development. While this study focused on the initial adoption of AI tools, it remains unclear whether continued use of these tools leads to sustained improvements in writing skills. Longitudinal studies could investigate whether AI tools help students develop not only technical writing skills but also higher-order thinking skills, such as critical analysis and creativity.

The ethical implications of AI tool adoption also warrant further investigation. As AI becomes more prevalent in education, issues related to data privacy, algorithmic fairness, and the potential for bias must be carefully considered (Leslie et al., 2021). Future research should examine how AI tools can be designed to ensure transparency, equity, and fairness in educational assessments. This is especially important as AI systems increasingly influence decisions related to student performance and progression. Addressing these ethical concerns will be critical for promoting trust in AI technologies among students and educators alike (Nguyen et al., 2023). Finally, future research should explore how AI writing tools can be integrated with other emerging technologies, such as virtual reality (VR), augmented reality (AR), and mixed reality (MR), to create more immersive and interactive learning experiences. As Zawish et al. (2024) suggest, the combination of AI with these technologies has the potential to revolutionize education by offering personalized, data-driven experiences that adapt to individual student needs. Such integration, however, presents practical challenges, particularly in regions with limited technological infrastructure. Future studies should investigate the feasibility of combining AI with immersive technologies in diverse educational settings, particularly in developing countries where access to cutting-edge technology may be limited.

REFERENCES

Al-Abdullatif, A. M. (2023). Modeling Students' perceptions of chatbots in learning: Integrating technology acceptance with the value-based adoption model. *Education Sciences,* 13(11), 1151https://doi.org/DOI: 10.3390/educsci13111151

Al-Adwan, A. S., Li, N., Al-Adwan, A., Abbasi, G. A., Albelbisi, N. A., & Habibi, A. (2023). Extending the technology acceptance model (TAM) to Predict University Students' intentions to use metaverse-based learning platforms. *Education and Information Technologies*, 28(11), 15381–15413. DOI: 10.1007/s10639-023-11816-3 PMID: 37361794

Al Darayseh, A. (2023). Factors influencing the adoption of AI writing tools in higher education. *Computers & Education*, 175, 104368. DOI: 10.1016/j.compedu.2021.104368

Al-Nuaimi, M. N., Al Sawafi, O. S., Malik, S. I., Al-Emran, M., & Selim, Y. F. (2023). Evaluating the actual use of learning management systems during the covid-19 pandemic: An integrated theoretical model. *Interactive Learning Environments*, 31(10), 6905–6930. DOI: 10.1080/10494820.2022.2055577

Almahri, F. A. J., Bell, D., & Merhi, M. (2020). Understanding student acceptance and use of chatbots in the United Kingdom universities: a structural equation modelling approach. *In 2020 6th International Conference on Information Management (ICIM)* (pp. 284-288). IEEE. https://doi.org/DOI: 10.1109/ICIM49319.2020.244712

Alyoussef, I. Y. (2023). The impact of massive open online courses (MOOCs) on knowledge management using integrated innovation diffusion theory and the technology acceptance model. *Education Sciences*, 13(6), 531. DOI: 10.3390/educsci13060531

Arakpogun, E. O., Elsahn, Z., Olan, F., & Elsahn, F. (2021). Artificial intelligence in Africa: Challenges and opportunities. *The Fourth Industrial Revolution: Implementation of Artificial Intelligence for Growing Business Success*, 375–388. https://doi.org/DOI: 10.1007/978-3-030-62796-6_22

Aslam, W.; Ahmed Siddiqui, D.; Arif, I.; Farhat, K. Chatbots in the Frontline: Drivers of Acceptance. *Kybernetes2022*. ahead-of-print. https://doi.org/DOI: 10.1108/K-11-2021-1119

Baker, T., & Smith, L. (2019). Educ-AI-tion rebooted? Exploring the future of artificial intelligence in schools and colleges. *Retrieved from Nesta Foundation website*: https://media.nesta.org.uk/documents/Future_of_AI_and_education_v5_WEB.pdf

Belda-Medina, J., & Calvo-Ferrer, J. R. (2022). Using chatbots as AI conversational partners in language learning. *Applied Sciences (Basel, Switzerland)*, 12(17), 8427. DOI: 10.3390/app12178427

Chang, C. T., Hajiyev, J., & Su, C. R. (2017). Examining the students' behavioral intention to use e-learning in Azerbaijan? The general extended technology acceptance model for e-learning approach. *Computers & Education*, 111, 128–143. DOI: 10.1016/j.compedu.2017.04.010

Chatterjee, S., & Bhattacharjee, K. K. (2020). Adoption of artificial intelligence in higher education: A quantitative analysis using structural equation modelling. *Education and Information Technologies*, 25(5), 3443–3463. DOI: 10.1007/s10639-020-10159-7

Chen, H. L., Vicki Widarso, G., & Sutrisno, H. (2020). A chatbot for learning Chinese: Learning achievement and technology acceptance. *Journal of Educational Computing Research*, 58(6), 1161–1189. DOI: 10.1177/0735633120929622

Chocarro, R., Cortinas, M., & Villanueva, M. L. (2021). Understanding AI acceptance in higher education: The role of ease of use and usefulness. *Journal of Computer Assisted Learning*, 37(5), 1461–1473. DOI: 10.1111/jcal.12563

Choi, S., Jang, Y., & Kim, H. (2023). Influence of pedagogical beliefs and perceived trust on teachers' acceptance of educational artificial intelligence tools. *International Journal of Human-Computer Interaction*, 39(4), 910–922. DOI: 10.1080/10447318.2022.2049145

Choung, H., David, P., & Ross, A. (2023). Trust in AI and its role in the acceptance of AI technologies. *International Journal of Human-Computer Interaction*, 39(9), 1727–1739. DOI: 10.1080/10447318.2022.2050543

Córdova, P. R., & Vicari, R. M. (2022, August). Practical ethical issues for artificial intelligence in education. In *International Conference on Technology and Innovation in Learning, Teaching and Education* (pp. 437–445). Cham: Springer Nature Switzerland. https://doi.org/DOI: 10.1007/978-3-031-22918-3_34

Darwin, D., Rusdin, D., Mukminatien, N., Suryati, N., Laksmi, E. D., & Marzuki, . (2024). Critical thinking in the AI era: An exploration of EFL students' perceptions, benefits, and limitations. *Cogent Education*, 11(1), 2290342. DOI: 10.1080/2331186X.2023.2290342

Davis, F. D. (1989). Perceived usefulness, perceived ease of use, and user acceptance of information technology. *Management Information Systems Quarterly*, 13(3), 319–340. DOI: 10.2307/249008

Dignum, V. (2019). *Responsible artificial intelligence: how to develop and use AI in a responsible way* (Vol. 2156). Springer., DOI: 10.1007/978-3-030-30371-6

Drueke, B., Mainz, V., Lemos, M., Wirtz, M. A., & Boecker, M. (2021). An evaluation of forced distance learning and teaching under pandemic conditions using the technology acceptance model. *Frontiers in Psychology*, 12, 701347. DOI: 10.3389/fpsyg.2021.701347 PMID: 34751220

Ertmer, P. A. (1999). Addressing first-and second-order barriers to change: Strategies for technology integration. *Educational Technology Research and Development*, 47(4), 47–61. DOI: 10.1007/BF02299597

Fishbein, M., & Ajzen, I. (1977). Belief, attitude, intention, and behavior: An introduction to theory and research.

Gayed, J. M., Carlon, M. K. J., Oriola, A. M., & Cross, J. S. (2022). Exploring an AI-based writing assistant's impact on English language learners. *Computers and Education: Artificial Intelligence*, 3, 100055. DOI: 10.1016/j.caeai.2022.100055

Hair, J. F., Risher, J. J., Sarstedt, M., & Ringle, C. M. (2019). When to use and how to report the results of PLS-SEM. *European Business Review*, 31(1), 2–24. DOI: 10.1108/EBR-11-2018-0203

Hair, J. F., Sarstedt, M., Ringle, C. M., & Gudergan, S. P. (2018). *Advanced Issues in Partial Least Squares Structural Equations Modeling (PLS-SEM)*. Sage., DOI: 10.3926/oss.37

Halaweh, M. (2023). ChatGPT in education: Strategies for responsible implementation. *Contemporary Educational Technology*, 15(2), ep421. Advance online publication. DOI: 10.30935/cedtech/13036

Hamlaoui, S. (2021). Teachers' resistance to educational change and innovations in the Middle East and North Africa: A case study of Tunisian universities. In Ouaissa, R., Pannewick, F., & Strohmaier, A. (Eds.), *Re-Configurations* (pp. 171–184). Springer VS., DOI: 10.1007/978-3-658-31160-5_11

Han, B., Nawaz, S., Buchanan, G., & McKay, D. (2023, June). Ethical and pedagogical impacts of AI in education. In *International Conference on Artificial Intelligence in Education* (pp. 667–673). Cham: Springer Nature Switzerland. https://doi.org/ DOI: 10.1007/978-3-031-36272-9_54

He, S., Jiang, S., Zhu, R., & Hu, X. (2023). The influence of educational and emotional support on e-learning acceptance: An integration of social support theory and TAM. *Education and Information Technologies*, 28(9), 11145–11165. DOI: 10.1007/s10639-023-11648-1 PMID: 36818430

Henseler, J., Ringle, C. M., & Sarstedt, M. (2015). A new criterion for assessing discriminant validity in variance-based structural equation modeling. *Journal of the Academy of Marketing Science*, 43(1), 115–135. DOI: 10.1007/s11747-014-0403-8

Holmes, W., Bialik, M., & Fadel, C. (2019). *Artificial Intelligence in Education: Promises and Implications for Teaching and Learning*. Center for Curriculum Redesign. https://www.curriculumredesign.org/our-work/artificial-intelligence-in-education/

Hwang, G. J., Xie, H., Wah, B. W., & Gašević, D. (2020). Vision, challenges, roles and research issues of Artificial Intelligence in Education. *Computers and Education: Artificial Intelligence*, 1, 100001. Advance online publication. DOI: 10.1016/j.caeai.2020.100001

Kampa, R. K. (2023). Combining technology readiness and acceptance model for investigating the acceptance of m-learning in higher education in India. *Asian Association of Open Universities Journal*, 18(2), 105–120. DOI: 10.1108/AAOUJ-10-2022-0149

Kelly, S., Kaye, S. A., & Oviedo-Trespalacios, O. (2023). What factors contribute to the acceptance of artificial intelligence? A systematic review. *Telematics and Informatics*, 77, 101925. DOI: 10.1016/j.tele.2022.101925

Kemp, A., Palmer, E., & Strelan, P. (2019). A taxonomy of factors affecting attitudes towards educational technologies for use with technology acceptance models. *British Journal of Educational Technology*, 50(5), 2394–2413. DOI: 10.1111/bjet.12833

Keong, W. E. Y. (2022). Factors Influencing Adoption Intention Towards Chatbots as a Learning Tool. In The International Conference in Education (ICE), *Proceedings*; Faculty of Social Sciences and Humanities, UTM: Johor Bahru, Malaysia (pp. 96-99).

KIEMDE., S. M. A., & KORA, A. D. (2020, December). The challenges facing the development of AI in Africa. In *2020 IEEE International Conference on Advent Trends in Multidisciplinary Research and Innovation (ICATMRI)* (pp. 1–6). IEEE. https://doi.org/DOI: 10.1109/ICATMRI51801.2020.9398454

Konaklı, T., & Akdeniz, R. K. (2022). The emergence, reasons and results of resistance to change in teachers. *International Journal on Lifelong Education and Leadership*, 8(1), 1–19. DOI: 10.25233/ijlel.1107137

Kulhavy, R. W. (1977). Feedback in written instruction. *Review of Educational Research*, 47(2), 211–232. DOI: 10.3102/00346543047002211

Kumar, A., & Silva, E. (2020). AI in education: Enhancing learning experiences through technology. *British Journal of Educational Technology*, 51(4), 1111–1130. DOI: 10.1111/bjet.12946

Lee, Y. J. (2020). The long-term effect of automated writing evaluation feedback on writing development. *English Teaching*, 75(1), 67–92. DOI: 10.15858/engtea.75.1.202003.67

Leslie, D., Burr, C., Aitken, M., Cowls, J., Katell, M., & Briggs, M. (2021). Artificial intelligence, human rights, democracy, and the rule of law: a primer. arXiv preprint arXiv:2104.04147.

Liesa-Orús, M., Latorre-Cosculluela, C., Sierra-Sánchez, V., & Vázquez-Toledo, S. (2023). Links between ease of use, perceived usefulness and attitudes towards technology in older people in university: A structural equation modelling approach. *Education and Information Technologies*, 28(3), 2419–2436. DOI: 10.1007/s10639-022-11292-1 PMID: 35996745

Lin, Y., & Yu, Z. (2023). Extending Technology Acceptance Model to higher-education students' use of digital academic reading tools on computers. *International Journal of Educational Technology in Higher Education*, 20(1), 34. DOI: 10.1186/s41239-023-00403-8

Liu, Z.. (2020). The role of perceived ease of use in the acceptance of AI writing tools among students. *Computers & Education*, 158, 103983. DOI: 10.1016/j.compedu.2020.103983

Luckin, R., Holmes, W., Griffiths, M., & Forcier, L. B. "Intelligence unleashed." *An argument for AI in Education 18* (2016). https://www.pearson.com/corporate/about-pearson/what-we-do/innovation/smarter-digital-tools/intelligence-unleashed.html

Malik, R., Shrama, A., Trivedi, S., & Mishra, R. (2021). Adoption of chatbots for learning among university students: Role of perceived convenience and enhanced performance. [iJET]. *International Journal of Emerging Technologies in Learning*, 16(18), 200–212. Retrieved August 10, 2024, from https://www.learntechlib.org/p/220124/. DOI: 10.3991/ijet.v16i18.24315

Marangunić, N., & Granić, A. (2015). Technology acceptance model: A literature review from 1986 to 2013. *Universal Access in the Information Society*, 14(1), 81–95. DOI: 10.1007/s10209-014-0348-1

Marks, A., & AL-Ali, M. (2020). Digital transformation in higher education: A framework for maturity assessment. [IJACSA]. *International Journal of Advanced Computer Science and Applications*, 11(12), 504–513. DOI: 10.14569/IJACSA.2020.0111261

Marzuki, W., Widiati, U., Rusdin, D., Darwin, , & Indrawati, I. (2023). The impact of AI writing tools on the content and organization of students' writing: EFL teachers' perspective. *Cogent Education*, 10(2), 2236469. DOI: 10.1080/2331186X.2023.2236469

Mehdaoui, A. (2024). Unveiling barriers and challenges of AI technology integration in education: Assessing teachers' perceptions, readiness, and anticipated resistance. *Futurity Education*, 4(4), 95–108. DOI: 10.57125/FED.2024.12.25.06

Mercader, C., & Gairín, J. (2020). University teachers' perception of barriers to the use of digital technologies: The importance of the academic discipline. *International Journal of Educational Technology in Higher Education*, 17(4), 1–14. DOI: 10.1186/s41239-020-0182-x

Mohd Rahim, N. I., & Iahad, A., N., Yusof, A. F., & A. Al-Sharafi, M. (. (2022). AI-based chatbots adoption model for higher-education institutions: A hybrid PLS-SEM-neural network modelling approach. *Sustainability*, 14(19), 12726. DOI: 10.3390/su141912726

Narciss, S. (2008). Feedback strategies for interactive learning tasks. *Handbook of research on educational communications and technology/Erlbaum.*

Neo, M. (2022). THE MERLIN PROJECT: MALAYSIAN STUDENTS'ACCEPTANCE OF AN AI CHATBOT IN THEIR LEARNING PROCESS. *Turkish Online Journal of Distance Education*, 23(3), 31–48. DOI: 10.17718/tojde.1137122

Nye, B. D. (2015). Intelligent tutoring systems by and for the developing world: A review of trends and approaches for educational technology in a global context. *International Journal of Artificial Intelligence in Education*, 25(2), 177–203. DOI: 10.1007/s40593-014-0028-6

Okonkwo, C. W., & Ade-Ibijola, A. O. (2021). Chatbots applications in education: A systematic review. *Computers & Education: Artificial Intelligence*, 2, 100033. DOI: 10.1016/j.caeai.2021.100033

Oubibi, M., Zhou, Y., Oubibi, A., Fute, A., & Saleem, A. (2022). The challenges and opportunities for developing the use of data and artificial intelligence (AI) in North Africa: Case of Morocco. In *International Conference on Digital Technologies and Applications* (pp. 80–90). Cham: Springer International Publishing. https://doi.org/ DOI: 10.1007/978-3-031-02447-4_9

Park, S. Y. (2009). An analysis of the technology acceptance model in understanding university students' behavioral intention to use e-learning. *Journal of Educational Technology & Society*, 12(3), 150–162. https://www.jstor.org/stable/jeductechsoci.12.3.150

Peng, M. Y. P., Xu, Y., & Xu, C. (2023). Enhancing students' English language learning via M-learning: Integrating technology acceptance model and SOR model. *Heliyon*, 9(2), e13302. Advance online publication. DOI: 10.1016/j.heliyon.2023.e13302 PMID: 36755609

Pillai, S., Malik, M., & Mohd Rahim, N. (2023). AI in education: Challenges and opportunities for chatbot technology. *Journal of Computer Assisted Learning*, 39(2), 319–335. DOI: 10.1111/jcal.12776

Popenici, S. A. D., & Kerr, S. (2017). Exploring the impact of artificial intelligence on teaching and learning in higher education. *Research and Practice in Technology Enhanced Learning*, 12(1), 22. DOI: 10.1186/s41039-017-0062-8 PMID: 30595727

Ragheb, M. A., Tantawi, P., Farouk, N., & Hatata, A. (2022). Investigating the acceptance of applying chat-bot (Artificial intelligence) technology among higher education students in Egypt. *International Journal of Higher Education Management*, 8(2). Advance online publication. DOI: 10.24052/IJHEM/V08N02/ART-1

Rejón-Guardia, F., & Vich-I-Martorell, G. A. (2020). Design and acceptance of chatbots for information automation in university classrooms. *In EDULEARN20 Proceedings* (pp. 2452-2462). IATED https://doi.org/DOI: 10.21125/edulearn.2020.0757

Sabzalieva, E., & Valentini, A. (2023). *ChatGPT and artificial intelligence in higher education: Quick start guide*. UNESCO., https://www.iesalc.unesco.org/wp-content/uploads/2023/04/ChatGPT-and-Artificial-Intelligence-in-higher-education-Quick-Start-guide_EN_FINAL.pdf

Sadler, D. R. (1989). Formative assessment and the design of instructional systems. *Instructional Science*, 18(2), 119–144. DOI: 10.1007/BF00117714

Sadler, D. R. (2014). Beyond feedback: Developing student capability in complex appraisal. In *Approaches to assessment that enhance learning in higher education* (pp. 45–60). Routledge., DOI: 10.1080/02602930903541015

Saif, N., Khan, S. U., Shaheen, I., ALotaibi, F. A., Alnfiai, M. M., & Arif, M. (2024). Chat-GPT; validating Technology Acceptance Model (TAM) in education sector via ubiquitous learning mechanism. *Computers in Human Behavior*, 154, 108097. DOI: 10.1016/j.chb.2023.108097

Salloum, S. A. (2024). AI perils in education: Exploring ethical concerns. In *Artificial Intelligence in Education: The Power and Dangers of ChatGPT in the Classroom* (pp. 669–675). Springer Nature Switzerland., DOI: 10.1007/978-3-031-52280-2_43

Sandu, N., & Gide, E. (2019, September). Adoption of AI-Chatbots to enhance student learning experience in higher education in India. In *2019 18th international conference on information technology based higher education and training (ITHET)* (pp. 1-5). IEEE.

Shmueli, G., & Koppius, O. R. (2011). Predictive analytics in information systems research. *Management Information Systems Quarterly*, 35(3), 553–572. DOI: 10.2307/23042796

Shwedeh, F., Salloum, S. A., Aburayya, A., Fatin, B., Elbadawi, M. A., Al Ghurabli, Z., & Al Dabbagh, T. (2024). AI adoption and educational sustainability in higher education in the UAE. In *Artificial Intelligence in Education: The Power and Dangers of ChatGPT in the Classroom* (pp. 201–229). Springer Nature Switzerland., DOI: 10.1007/978-3-031-52280-2_14

Slepankova, T. (2021). The long-term effects of AI chatbots in education. *British Journal of Educational Technology*, 52(5), 1602–1617. DOI: 10.1111/bjet.13098

Slimi, Z., & Carballido, B. V. (2023). Navigating the ethical challenges of artificial intelligence in higher education: An analysis of seven global AI ethics policies. *TEM Journal, 12*(2). https://doi.org/DOI: 10.18421/TEM122-02

Songkram, N., Chootongchai, S., Osuwan, H., Chuppunnarat, Y., & Songkram, N. (2023). Students' adoption towards behavioral intention of digital learning platform. *Education and Information Technologies*, 28(9), 11655–11677. DOI: 10.1007/s10639-023-11637-4 PMID: 36846495

Stüber, J. (2018). Barriers of digital technologies in higher education: A teachers' perspective from a Swedish University. [Unpublished master's thesis]. Linnaeus University. https://www.diva-portal.org/smash/get/diva2:1201871/FULLTEXT01.pdf

Sumakul, D. T. Y., Hamied, F. A., & Sukyadi, D. (2022, February). Students' perceptions of the use of AI in a writing class. *In 67th TEFLIN International Virtual Conference & the 9th ICOELT 2021* (TEFLIN ICOELT 2021) (pp. 52-57). Atlantis Press. https://doi.org/DOI: 10.2991/assehr.k.220201.009

Tang, X., Zainal, S. R. B. M., & Li, Q. (2023). Multimedia use and its impact on the effectiveness of educators: A technology acceptance model perspective. *Humanities & Social Sciences Communications*, 10(1), 1–11. DOI: 10.1057/s41599-023-02458-4

Umezuruike, C., & Ngugi, H. N. (2020). Imminent challenges of adoption of big data in educational systems in Sub-Saharan Africa nations. *International Journal of Recent Technology and Engineering*, 8(5), 4544–4550. DOI: 10.35940/ijrte.E6885.018520

Venkatesh, V., & Davis, F. D. (2000). A theoretical extension of the technology acceptance model: Four longitudinal field studies. *Management Science*, 46(2), 186–204. DOI: 10.1287/mnsc.46.2.186.11926

Venkatesh, V., Morris, M. G., Davis, G. B., & Davis, F. D. (2003). User acceptance of information technology: Toward a unified view. *Management Information Systems Quarterly*, 27(3), 425–478. DOI: 10.2307/30036540

Venkatesh, V., Thong, J. Y. L., & Xu, X. (2012). Consumer acceptance and use of information technology: Extending the unified theory of acceptance and use of technology. *Management Information Systems Quarterly*, 36(1), 157–178. DOI: 10.2307/41410412

Woolf, B. P., Lane, H. C., Chaudhri, V. K., & Kolodner, J. L. (2013). AI grand challenges for education. *AI Magazine*, 34(4), 6684. DOI: 10.1609/aimag.v34i4.2490

Zawacki-Richter, O., Marín, V. I., Bond, M., & Gouverneur, F. (2019). Systematic review of research on artificial intelligence applications in higher education–where are the educators? *International Journal of Educational Technology in Higher Education*, 16(1), 1–27. DOI: 10.1186/s41239-019-0171-0

ADDITIONAL READING

Abdaljaleel, M., Barakat, M., Alsanafi, M., Salim, N. A., Abazid, H., Malaeb, D., Mohammed, A. H., Hassan, B. A. R., Wayyes, A. M., Farhan, S. S., Khatib, S. E., Rahal, M., Sahban, A., Abdelaziz, D. H., Mansour, N. O., AlZayer, R., Khalil, R., Fekih-Romdhane, F., Hallit, R., & Sallam, M. (2024). A multinational study on the factors influencing university students' attitudes and usage of ChatGPT. *Scientific Reports*, 14(1), 1983. DOI: 10.1038/s41598-024-52549-8 PMID: 38263214

Supriyanto, E., Setiawan, A., Chamsudin, A., Yuliana, I., & Wantoro, J. (2024, June). Exploring Student Perceptions and Acceptance of ChatGPT in Enhanced AI-Assisted Learning. In *2024 International Conference on Smart Computing, IoT and Machine Learning (SIML)* (pp. 291-296). IEEE.

Tram, N. H. M., & Tran-Thanh, V. (2024). The Role of Supportive Environments in Shaping EFL Teachers' Adoption of ChatGPT. In *Innovations in Technologies for Language Teaching and Learning* (pp. 55–78). Springer Nature Switzerland. DOI: 10.1007/978-3-031-63447-5_4

Velli, K., & Zafiropoulos, K. (2024). Factors That Affect the Acceptance of Educational AI Tools by Greek Teachers—A Structural Equation Modelling Study. *European Journal of Investigation in Health, Psychology and Education*, 14(9), 2560–2579. DOI: 10.3390/ejihpe14090169 PMID: 39329837

KEY TERMS AND DEFINITIONS

Artificial Intelligence (AI): A field of technology focused on creating systems capable of performing tasks that typically require human intelligence, such as learning, reasoning, and problem-solving.

Educational Technology: The application of digital tools and techniques to enhance learning, teaching, and assessment within educational contexts.

Partial Least Squares (PLS-SEM): A variance-based SEM method used for analyzing relationships in complex models, especially in cases of smaller sample sizes.

Perceived Ease of Use: The degree to which a user believes that a particular technology will be easy to operate and free from effort.

Perceived Usefulness: The extent to which a person believes that using a specific technology will enhance their performance or productivity.

Social Influence: The impact of peers, instructors, or societal factors on an individual's decision to adopt a new technology.

Structural Equation Modeling (SEM): A statistical technique that allows researchers to examine complex relationships among multiple variables, often used in technology adoption studies.

Student Engagement: The level of interest, motivation, and active participation demonstrated by students in their educational activities.

Technology Acceptance Model (TAM): A theoretical framework used to understand and predict individuals' acceptance and usage of new technologies, based on perceived usefulness and ease of use.

Writing Tools: Digital applications, often powered by AI, that assist users in improving writing quality by providing feedback on grammar, style, and clarity.

Chapter 10
Multimodal Classification of the Arabic Alphabet:
An Artificial Intelligence Approach for Handwriting, Sign Language, and Braille

Sarra Rouabhi
Laboratoire de Codage et Sécurité d'Information (LACOSI), Département d'Electronique, Faculté de Génie Electrique, Université des Sciences et de la Technologie d'Oran Mohamed Boudiaf, Oran, Algeria

Redouane Tlemsani
Laboratoire de Codage et Sécurité d'Information (LACOSI), Département d'Electronique, Faculté de Génie Electrique, Université des Sciences et de la Technologie d'Oran Mohamed Boudiaf, Oran, Algeria

ABSTRACT

This chapter examines the application of artificial intelligence techniques for multimodal classification of the Arabic alphabet across three key domains: handwriting, sign language, and braille. Each modality employs a specialized methodology tailored to its unique requirements. For handwritten Arabic character recognition, a hybrid model combining particle swarm optimization and a support vector classifier achieves a test accuracy of 90.29%. Arabic sign language alphabet classification utilizes MediaPipe for hand landmark detection alongside Inception ResNet v2 for feature extraction, followed by a custom neural network, achieving a test accuracy of 93.77%. Arabic braille character recognition employs EfficientNet B3 for feature extraction with a simple neural network for classification, resulting in a macro-average F1-score of 81.33%. These AI-driven approaches underscore the potential for enhancing Arabic language education and accessibility, offering valuable support

DOI: 10.4018/979-8-3693-7220-3.ch010

for learners with diverse needs and abilities.

INTRODUCTION

The Arabic language, with its rich cultural heritage and complex linguistic features, serves as a vital medium of communication for over 400 million speakers worldwide (Comrie, 2003). Its multifaceted nature, encompassing written script, sign language, and Braille representations, presents both a fascinating linguistic phenomenon and a significant challenge for automated recognition systems (Lorigo, 2006). These diverse modalities of Arabic are not merely forms of expression; they are fundamental tools for education, particularly for learners with varied abilities and needs (El-Sawy, 2017). In the educational sphere, the effective instruction and acquisition of Arabic characters (Marcelli, 2012), sign language gestures (Abdel-Fattah, 2005), and Braille characters (Al-Salman, 2007) are crucial for developing literacy and linguistic proficiency. Traditional teaching methodologies, however, often struggle to accommodate the diverse learning requirements of all students, especially those with visual or auditory impairments. This educational gap presents an opportunity for technological intervention, particularly through the application of Artificial Intelligence (AI).

The integration of AI in Arabic language education holds the potential to revolutionize accessibility and inclusivity. AI-driven systems can offer tailored learning experiences, adapting to individual student needs and learning styles. For instance, AI models can provide real-time feedback on Arabic handwriting, facilitating the mastery of its cursive script (Gocen & Aydemir, 2020). In the realm of Arabic Sign Language, AI can accurately recognize and correct hand gestures, enhancing communication skills. Similarly, for Braille learners, AI can identify errors in dot patterns and offer guidance, supporting visually impaired students in their literacy journey (Chen et al., 2020). Furthermore, AI's capacity to process and analyze extensive datasets enables continuous refinement of educational resources (Balaha & El-Kady, 2023). As these systems learn from user interactions, they become increasingly adept at recognizing the nuances of Arabic in its various forms, leading to more precise and reliable educational tools.

Recent years have witnessed significant advancements in AI-based classification techniques, particularly in deep learning architectures and hybrid models. These developments aim to enhance recognition accuracy, facilitating the creation of effective systems for teaching Arabic characters across written, signed, and Braille modalities. This chapter will examine key methodologies employed in recent literature, focusing on three primary areas:

1. Arabic Alphabet Classification
2. Arabic Sign Language Gesture Detection
3. Braille Arabic Characters Recognition

By exploring these areas, this chapter aims to provide a comprehensive overview of the current state of AI applications in Arabic language education, highlighting innovative approaches and potential future directions in this rapidly evolving field.

MAIN FOCUS OF THE CHAPTER

The primary objective of this chapter is to develop and evaluate robust AI models for classifying the Arabic alphabet across three modalities: written, signed, and Braille. By addressing the unique challenges presented by each modality, this research seeks to demonstrate the effectiveness and versatility of modern AI architectures in processing various forms of linguistic representation. Through this exploration, the aim is to advance the field of multilingual AI applications and contribute to more inclusive and accessible Arabic language education. The application of AI in this context has the potential to empower educators and learners alike, making the process of acquiring language skills more engaging, effective, and equitable. This chapter will demonstrate the efficacy of artificial intelligence in recognizing Arabic features across three modalities through distinct experiments for each:

1. Classification of Handwritten Arabic Characters Using a Hybrid Approach of PSO and SVC
2. Classification of the Arabic Sign Alphabet Using Conv-MediaPipe
3. Classification of the Arabic Braille Alphabet Using CNN

The chapter is structured as follows: It begins with an introduction, followed by detailed descriptions of each experiment. Each section will present the methodology, results, and discussion of findings. The chapter concludes with a comprehensive summary of the research outcomes and their implications for Arabic language education and AI applications.

CLASSIFICATION OF HANDWRITTEN ARABIC CHARACTERS USING A HYBRID APPROACH OF PSO AND SVC

Methodology

This section details the methodology and innovative techniques implemented in our study on classifying handwritten Arabic characters. Our hybrid approach, which combines Particle Swarm Optimization (PSO) and Support Vector Classifier (SVC), is designed to enhance the accuracy and efficiency of automatic Arabic script recognition.

Feature Extraction

Convolutional Neural Networks (CNNs) are widely used for extracting features from images, including handwritten character images (Varshni & Thakral, 2019). CNNs automatically detect hierarchical features such as edges and curves, as well as character shapes in the case of handwriting recognition (Munien & Viriri, 2021). In our approach, we extracted 1,408 features using DenseNet-201 and 1,920 features using EfficientNet-B2 from Arabic handwritten character images. These feature sets were then concatenated to enhance the recognition rate, as shown in Figure 1.

Figure 1. Feature extraction architecture

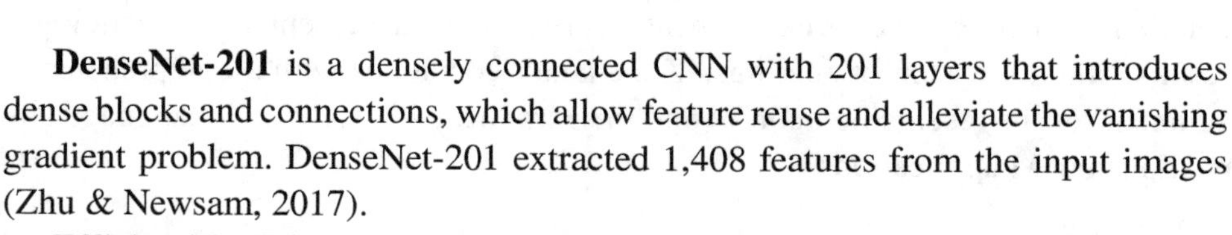

DenseNet-201 is a densely connected CNN with 201 layers that introduces dense blocks and connections, which allow feature reuse and alleviate the vanishing gradient problem. DenseNet-201 extracted 1,408 features from the input images (Zhu & Newsam, 2017).

EfficientNet-B2, part of the EfficientNet family, employs a compound scaling method that uniformly scales the network's width, depth, and resolution. In our experiment, EfficientNet-B2 extracted 1,920 features (Koonce, 2021).

To leverage the strengths of both models, we concatenated their feature representations. This process creates a single, higher-dimensional feature vector combining complementary information from DenseNet-201 and EfficientNet-B2. Mathematically, let f_dense (1,408 dimensions) represent the feature vector from DenseNet-201, and f_eff (1,920 dimensions) represent the feature vector from EfficientNet-B2. The concatenated feature vector, denoted as f_concat, is defined as:

$$f\_concat = [f\_dense, f\_eff] \quad (1)$$

This results in a feature representation of 3,328 dimensions (1,408 + 1,920), capturing a broader range of features from both architectures.

Feature Selection

After concatenating the features, we applied the bio-inspired Particle Swarm Optimization (PSO) algorithm to select the most relevant features. PSO is a population-based optimization algorithm inspired by the social behavior of birds and fish (Krisshna & Deepak, 2014). In feature selection, PSO efficiently searches for an optimal subset of features that maximizes classification performance, such as accuracy.

Classification

The Support Vector Classifier (SVC) is a supervised learning algorithm that constructs a hyperplane or set of hyperplanes in a high-dimensional space to separate different classes (Giacinto & Percisci, 2008). The SVC algorithm selects a hyperplane that maximizes the margin between classes, effectively handling high-dimensional and non-linear data using kernel functions (Lau & Wu, 2003).

In our study, the SVC classifier was employed to recognize handwritten Arabic characters using a subset of features selected through the Particle Swarm Optimization (PSO) process. The PSO-SVC hybrid approach is particularly effective for high-dimensional data, as PSO identifies the most relevant features, while SVC efficiently classifies the data using these optimized features.

We used Radial Basis Function (RBF) kernel in our SVC implementation due to its ability to handle non-linear decision boundaries, which are prevalent in handwritten Arabic character recognition, where variations in writing styles and shapes introduce complexity. The RBF kernel allows SVC to capture intricate patterns in the data, ensuring accurate classification.

Parameter Optimization: The performance of the SVC depends heavily on the choice of hyperparameters, including:

- **C (Regularization parameter)**: Controls the trade-off between achieving a wide margin and correctly classifying training examples. A higher **C** value penalizes misclassified points more, whereas a lower **C** allows for a wider margin but may result in more misclassifications.

- **Gamma (Kernel coefficient)**: Defines how far the influence of a single training example reaches. A lower gamma value results in a broader decision region, while a higher gamma value focuses on nearby points, creating more intricate decision boundaries.

In our experiments, we performed a grid search to optimize the values of C and gamma, ensuring that the SVC model was fine-tuned for the best possible classification performance. The combination of feature selection via PSO and hyperparameter optimization in SVC allowed us to achieve high classification accuracy for handwritten Arabic characters.

Experimental Results

This section presents the results of our experiments. Initially, we combined the features extracted from DenseNet-201 and EfficientNet-B2 and applied PSO to select the most relevant features for the classification task. Finally, we used SVC to classify the Arabic handwritten characters.

The combination of PSO for feature selection and the SVC classifier, as shown in Figure 2, led to improved recognition performance. PSO efficiently explores the feature space, identifying a subset of features that enhance classification accuracy. The selected features were used to train the SVC, which leveraged their discriminative power to make accurate predictions.

Figure 2. Proposed Arabic handwritten character recognition system architecture

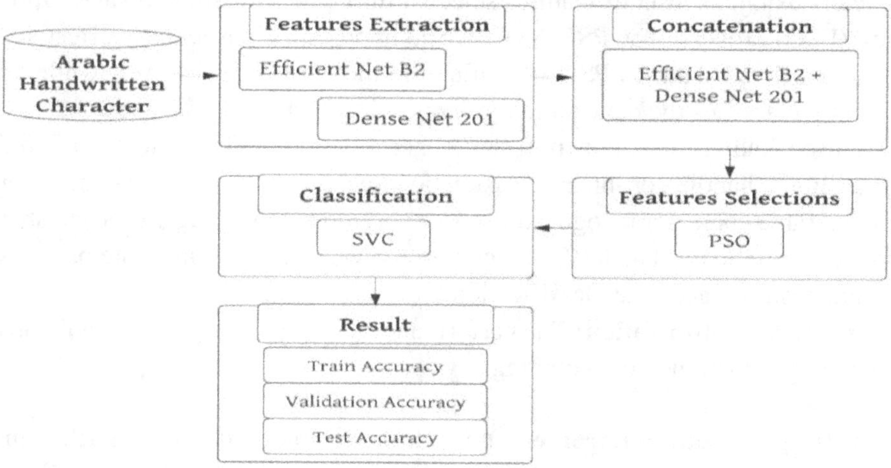

Table 1 summarizes the hyperparameters used for the PSO-SVC hybrid model. Key parameters include the number of particles, iterations, and selected features, along with the test data split and PSO velocity update parameters.

Table 1. The Hyperparameters for PSO-SVC hybridization

Hyperparameter	Description	Value
num-particles	Number of particles in the PSO algorithm	20
num-iterations	Number of iterations for the PSO algorithm	100
num-features	Number of features in the dataset	3328
test-size	Proportion of the dataset used for testing	0.2
random-stat	Random seed for reproducibility	42
inertia-weight	Inertia weight for velocity update	0.9
cognitive-weight	Cognitive weight for velocity update	1.5
social-weight	Social weight for velocity update	1.5

The algorithm referred to in Figure 3 begins with particle initialization, where the positions and velocities of the particles are randomly initialized. Then, for each iteration, the following steps occur:

- **Particle Initialization**: Positions and velocities of particles are initialized randomly.
- **Velocity and Position Update**: Particles update their positions based on personal best and global best positions.
- **Suitability Evaluation**: Each particle's fitness is evaluated.
- **Personal Best Update**: Particles update their personal best if their new position improves fitness.
- **Global Best Update**: The global best position is updated by comparing all particles' suitability.
- **Feature Selection**: Features are selected based on the global best position.
- **SVC Training**: The SVC model is trained using the selected features.
- **Performance Evaluation**: The trained SVC model is evaluated using the test data.
- **Convergence Visualization**: A graph is plotted to visualize the algorithm's convergence.

Figure 3. The flowchart represents the steps of the PSO-SVC algorithm

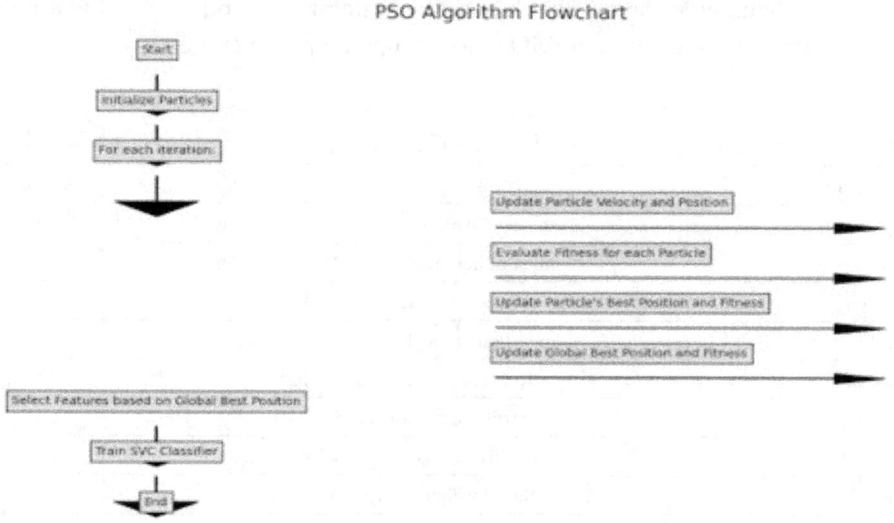

The performance of the system, including test accuracy, precision, recall, and F1-score (Chicco, D, 2021), is summarized in Table 2. The PSO-SVC model achieved a test accuracy of 90.20%, demonstrating its effectiveness in recognizing handwritten Arabic characters.

Table 2. Test results for accuracy, macro, and weighted avg

Metrics	**EfficientNet B2 + DenseNet 201**
	PSO-SVC
Test accuracy	90.20%
Macro avg Precision	90.00%
Macro avg Recall	91.00%
Macro avg F1-score	90.00%
Weighted avg Precision	91.00%
Weighted avg Recall	90.00%
Weighted avg F1-score	90.00%

The results show a high level of accuracy in recognizing handwritten Arabic characters, confirming the efficacy of the PSO-SVC approach. However, there is room for improvement, particularly for characters with lower classification performance. Further refinement of the feature selection and classification techniques could address these issues.

The macro-averaged precision, recall, and F1-score all reached 90.00%, reflecting a balanced performance across all Arabic character classes. These metrics indicate that the system maintains consistent accuracy, regardless of class frequency or complexity, providing a comprehensive evaluation of its ability to classify characters effectively (Rouabhi, 2024).

This limitation, where the accuracy does not exceed 90%, can be attributed to several factors. First, certain Arabic characters have very similar shapes, such as ʿAin ( ) and Ghain ( ), where the only distinguishing feature is the presence of a diacritic (dot). This subtle difference can be challenging for the classifier to detect, especially when the handwriting is less consistent or the quality of the image is suboptimal.

Figure 4. An example of the similarity between the two characters Ain and Ghin, and the difference between the writing of the character Shin

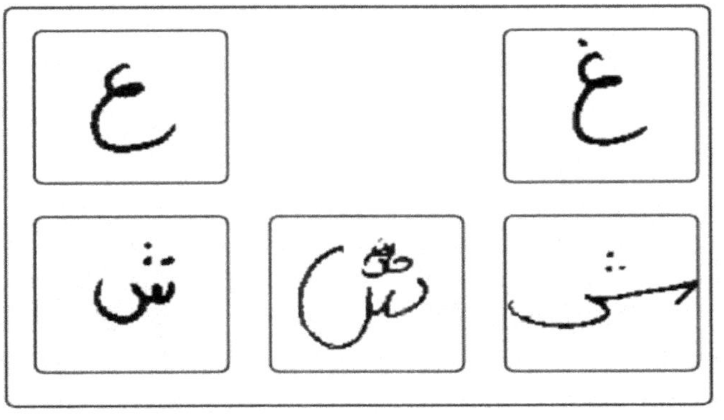

Moreover, the variability in handwriting styles adds another layer of complexity. Different individuals may write the same character in slightly different ways, varying in stroke thickness, slant, or curvature. For example, some may use more cursive, rounded forms, while others may use angular or disjointed writing styles. These variations, as depicted in the figure, make the classification task more difficult, as the algorithm must account for a broader range of patterns for each character class. This variability often leads to slight misclassifications, particularly for characters that share similar structural features.

the convergence of the PSO algorithm, illustrated in Figure 5, shows the improvement in classification accuracy over the iterations. This graph helps assess the algorithm's efficiency and provides insights for fine-tuning the system's parameters.

Figure 5. PSO convergence graph" accuracy as a function of iterations

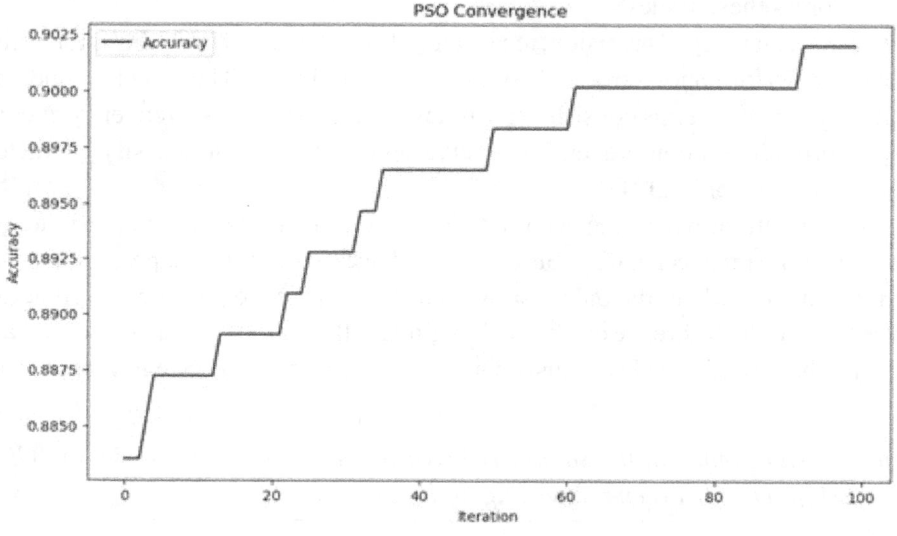

Discussion

The classification of handwritten Arabic characters presents several unique challenges due to the complexity of the script, including variations in writing styles, character shapes, and connectivity between letters. These factors make traditional classification methods less effective, particularly when dealing with large, diverse datasets. The hybrid approach of PSO and SVC is particularly well-suited to address these challenges by optimizing the feature selection process and ensuring robust classification.

By leveraging PSO, a bio-inspired optimization algorithm, the feature space can be efficiently explored to select the most relevant features from a vast pool. PSO's strength lies in its ability to adaptively converge toward the global best solution, making it an excellent choice for complex problems like handwritten character recognition. This ensures that the system is not overwhelmed by irrelevant or redundant features, which often reduce the accuracy of traditional models.

The SVC classifier, with its ability to construct non-linear decision boundaries, complements this by effectively separating complex character classes in high-dimensional feature spaces. When combined, PSO optimizes the input features, while SVC capitalizes on this optimization to deliver higher classification performance. This hybrid approach makes the algorithm highly valuable for intelligent artificial systems designed to recognize complex handwritten scripts like Arabic, where variability and intricacy are significant obstacles.

CLASSIFICATION OF THE ARABIC SIGN ALPHABET USING CONV-MEDIAPIPE

Methodology

This section details the steps used in our study to recognize the signs of the Arabic alphabet. The methodology comprises four main components: dataset selection, pre-processing, feature extraction, and classification.

Dataset

The study utilizes the Arabic Sign Language Alphabet (AASL) RGB dataset, published in 2023 (Al-Barham & Alsharkawi, 2023). This comprehensive dataset consists of 7,857 raw and fully labeled RGB images, covering the entire alphabet of Arabic sign language. The dataset's creation involved over 200 contributors and incorporates various configurations, including variable illumination, backgrounds, angles, sizes, and resolutions. Specialists meticulously examined, verified, and cleaned the collected material to maintain an exceptional level of quality. The AASL dataset is publicly available via Kaggle.

Figure 6. Example of 31 sign Arabic alphabet

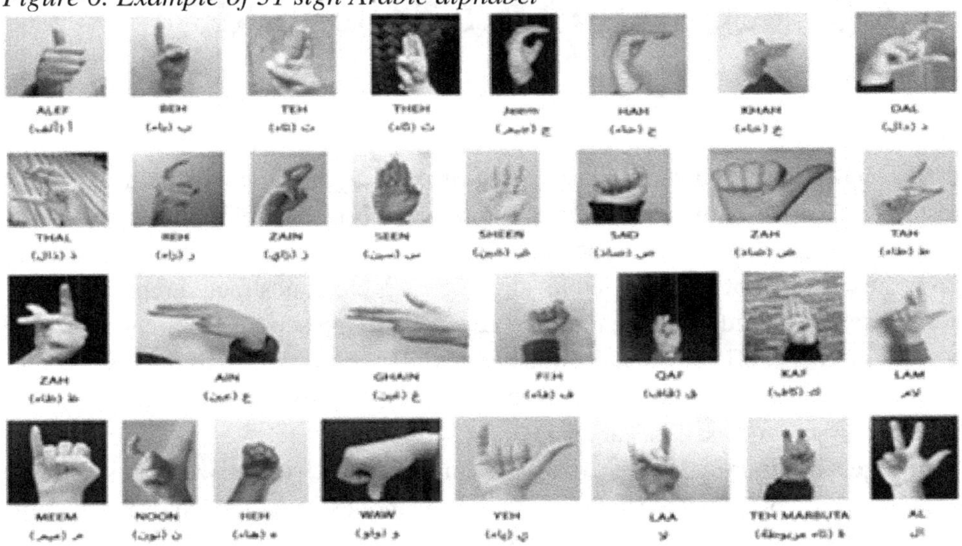

Pre-processing

The pre-processing stage involves two key steps: skeletonization using MediaPipe and image resizing.

Skeletonization using MediaPipe: the MediaPipe library (Zhang & Bazarevsky, 2020) was utilized during the pre-processing stage to extract skeletal hand landmarks. The process involved detecting 21 key hand points against a black background using the MediaPipe tool (Harris & Agoes, 2021). This technique results in enhanced skeletal images that capture the essential structure of hand gestures, as shown in Figure 6. These processed images were stored and subsequently used for training the classification model.

Figure 7. Images of Arabic alphabet signs transformed using MediaPipe

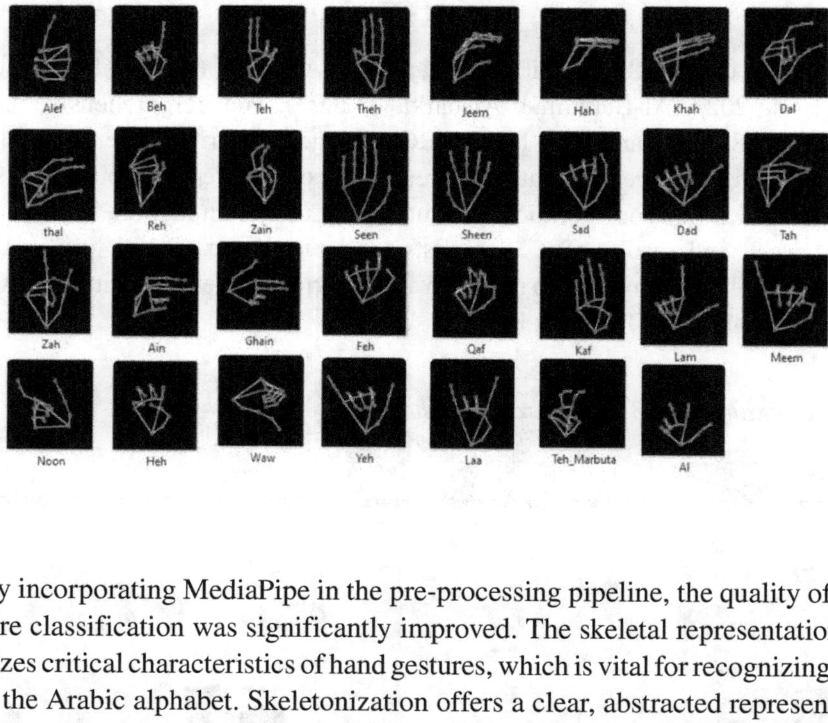

By incorporating MediaPipe in the pre-processing pipeline, the quality of hand gesture classification was significantly improved. The skeletal representation emphasizes critical characteristics of hand gestures, which is vital for recognizing signs from the Arabic alphabet. Skeletonization offers a clear, abstracted representation of the hand pose, reducing the noise and complexity present in raw images, which is particularly beneficial when dealing with similar gestures such as those in Arabic sign language. This step helps the model focus on key structural details, ensuring better accuracy in classification tasks.

Image Resizing: In this step, images from the dataset were resized to a standardized dimension of 224 × 224 pixels, the required input size for the feature extraction model. This resizing operation ensures consistency across all images, regardless of their original dimensions, and facilitates the efficient processing by the neural network. The resizing operation is mathematically represented by the equation:

$$\mathrm{Im}age - resized = resize(original - \mathrm{Im}age, (224,224)) \quad (2)$$

By resizing images uniformly, we ensure that the feature extraction model processes consistent image data, reducing variations that could affect model performance.

Feature Extraction

For the feature extraction phase, the Inception ResNet V2 model (Szegedy & Ioffe, 2017) was selected, as shown in Figure 3, due to its depth and advanced architecture, comprising over 150 layers. This deep architecture allows the model to capture a complex hierarchical representation of the features in Arabic alphabet sign images. Two key components of the model enhance its feature extraction capabilities:

- **Residual Blocks:** These blocks (Shafiq & Gu, 2022) allow the model to bypass layers, mitigating the vanishing gradient problem and enabling more efficient learning in deep networks.
- **Inception Modules:** These modules (Targ, Almeida & Lyman, 2016) apply convolutions at different scales, which helps the model capture a wide range of features at multiple spatial levels.

By utilizing Inception ResNet V2, our goal was to isolate essential features that would improve the classification accuracy of Arabic alphabet signs, identifying even subtle details in complex gestures.

Classification

In the classification phase, a neural network was constructed (Dongare, A. D., Kharde, R. R., & Kachare, A. D. 2012) to process the attributes distilled by Inception ResNet V2. The architecture comprises a normalization layer, followed by two densely connected layers, containing 256 and 128 neurons, respectively. Both layers incorporate L2 and L1 regularizations to mitigate overfitting. The final output is derived from a dense layer using softmax activation, enabling the prediction of the category for each hand gesture (Uzair, M., & Jamil, N. 2020, November). This method leverages the deep features extracted by Inception ResNet V2, ensuring accurate classification of hand gestures while maintaining the model's generalizability through regularization techniques.

Experimental Results

This section reveals the main outcomes of our study, including training and validation accuracy ratios, test accuracy, and evaluative metrics such as macro-average precision, recall, and F1-score. These results are complemented by a diagram showing the number of misclassified images across different categories associated with the Arabic alphabet classification.

For the classification task of Arabic alphabet signs, after preprocessing via MediaPipe and resizing to 224 × 224 pixels, the neural network employs the Inception ResNet V2 model with 'max' pooling. All training parameters are enabled, followed by a batch normalization layer to standardize activations during training, enhancing convergence, as shown in Figure 8. The hidden layers include two dense layers: the first with 256 neurons and the second with 128 neurons, both using L2 and L1 regularization with ReLU activation. The output layer is a dense layer with softmax activation, predicting the probability of each class among the 31 Arabic alphabet signs. The Adamax algorithm, with a learning rate of 0.001, was used to optimize the model over 100 epochs.

Figure 8. Stages in the detection of signs in the Arabic alphabet

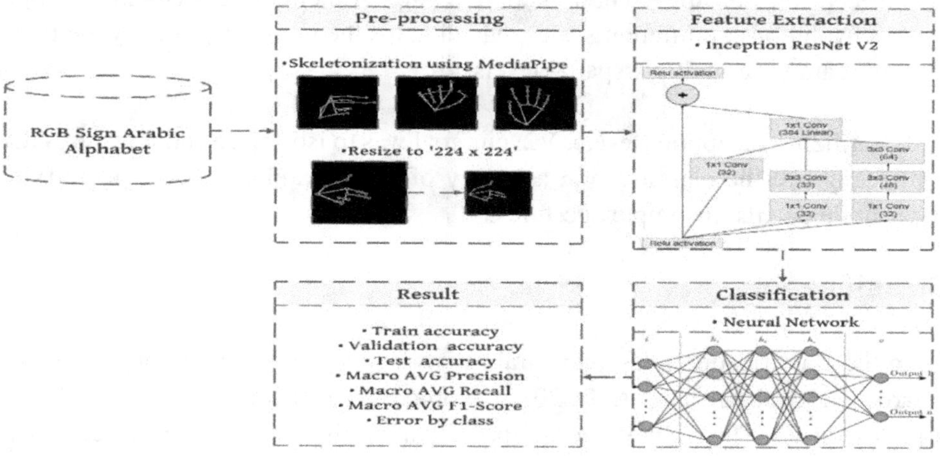

Model Performance: Table 3 presents the performance metrics of the model:

Table 3. Model performance metrics

Train Accuracy (%)	Validation Accuracy (%)	Test Accuracy (%)
99.14	95.83	93.77

The graph in Figure 9 illustrates the progression of training and validation accuracy as well as loss over the training epochs. Notably, the model achieved significant convergence around the 36th epoch, indicating that it can attain optimal results without requiring a large number of epochs.

Figure 9. Graph of 'train/validation' accuracy and loss

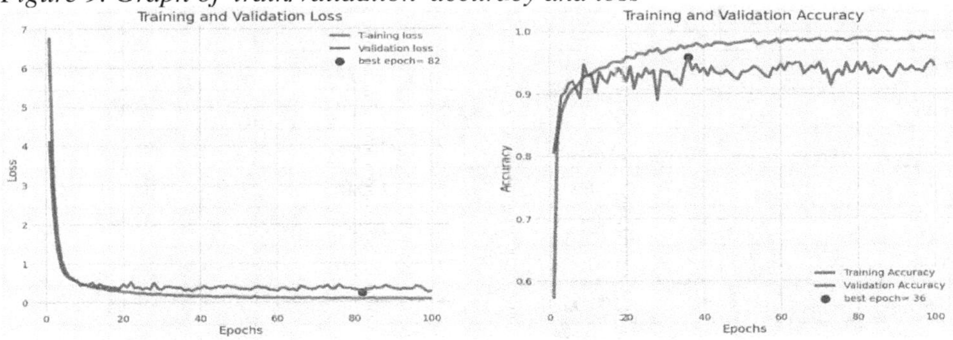

Performance Metrics: Table 4 outlines the classification performance across various Arabic alphabet signs. Precision, recall, and F1-score are provided for each class. While some classes, such as Ain, Al, Alef, and Jeem, achieved perfect metrics, other classes like Beh, Dal, and Qaf exhibited lower scores, suggesting areas for potential improvement.

Table 4. Performance metrics for Arabic alphabet signs classification

Class	Precision (%)	Recall (%)	F1-Score (%)
Ain	100.00	100.00	100.00
Al	100.00	100.00	100.00
Alef	100.00	100.00	100.00
Beh	86.67	100.00	92.86
Dad	85.71	100.00	92.31
Dal	72.73	80.00	76.19
Feh	100.00	80.00	88.89
Ghain	100.00	90.00	94.74
Hah	88.89	100.00	94.12
Heh	85.71	66.67	66.67
Jeem	100.00	100.00	100.00

continued on following page

Table 4. Continued

Class	Precision (%)	Recall (%)	F1-Score (%)
Kaf	92.86	100.00	96.30
Khah	100.00	100.00	100.00
Laam	100.00	100.00	100.00
Meem	100.00	91.67	95.65
Noon	83.33	100.00	90.91
Qaf	77.78	77.78	77.78
Reh	72.73	80.00	76.19
Sad	92.31	100.00	96.00
Seen	100.00	100.00	100.00
Sheen	93.33	100.00	96.55
Tah	100.00	90.00	94.74
Teh	100.00	92.31	96.00
Teh_Marbuta	100.00	100.00	100.00
Thal	100.00	100.00	100.00
Theh	100.00	92.31	96.00
Waw	100.00	100.00	100.00
Yeh	92.86	100.00	96.30
Zah	85.71	60.00	70.59
Zain	100.00	88.89	94.12
Accuracy			93.77
Macro Avg	93.89	93.21	93.27

Macro-averaged precision: This shows the model's overall accuracy in its predictions, averaged across all classes. The 93.89% macro precision indicates that, on average, the model made correct predictions for most classes.

Macro-averaged recall: This reflects how well the model identified instances across all classes. A 93.21% macro recall suggests that, on average, the model successfully identified most signs.

Macro-averaged F1-Score: With an F1-Score of 93.27%, this metric highlights that the model achieves a good balance between precision and recall across most classes.

Implications of Performance Metrics: These metrics illustrate how well the model performs on a per-class basis, highlighting strengths and weaknesses in its classification ability. The near-perfect metrics for some classes (Ain, Jeem, Laam, etc.) suggest that the model has learned these signs very well. However, classes like Dal, Heh, and Zah, with lower precision, recall, and F1-scores, show room for improvement, either through better data augmentation, model tuning, or additional training data.

Analysis of Misclassifications: The misclassification count across different classes provides insight into where the model might need improvement. The graph in Figure 10 illustrates the number of misclassified images per class, with the following highlights:

- Zah: This class had the highest number of misclassified.
- Heh: There were 3 misclassified images.
- Feh, Dal, Qaf, Reh: Each had 2 misclassified images.

Overall, 21 out of 337 images were misclassified, which accounts for about 6.2% of the dataset. This low number of errors demonstrates the model's strong performance, but it also indicates that certain signs like Zah and Heh may require more precise feature extraction or better training examples to reduce misclassifications.

Figure 10. Graph of images misclassified of each class

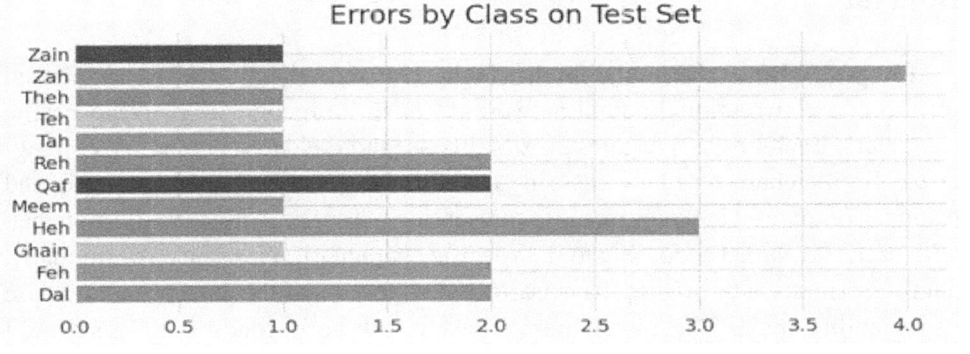

Discussion

In the context of education, precise and reliable performance metrics are essential for developing AI systems that are trusted by educators and students alike. AI-powered educational tools, such as sign language recognition systems, need to demonstrate high accuracy to ensure students with disabilities receive the correct support and learning material. The metrics used here, such as precision, recall, and F1-score, provide a transparent way to measure the system's reliability. By addressing the weaker areas of the model (like Zah and Heh misclassifications), the educational tool can be optimized to better serve its users, enhancing inclusivity, and ensuring accurate communication.

CLASSIFICATION OF THE ARABIC BRAILLE ALPHABET USING CNN

Methodology

In this experiment, we explored the effectiveness of combining the Efficient-Net B3 model with a simple neural network to classify images of Arabic Braille characters. This approach highlights the importance of artificial intelligence (AI) algorithms in the field of education, particularly in supporting individuals with visual impairments. The application of AI in recognizing Braille characters can significantly enhance accessibility, allowing visually impaired students to interact with educational materials more efficiently and independently.

Dataset

The Arabic Braille Character Dataset is a specialized collection of images tailored for training convolutional neural networks (CNNs) in recognizing Arabic Braille characters. Each image measures 50 x 50 pixels, and the dataset contains 99 images per Braille character class, ensuring a well-balanced collection for training and testing. This dataset includes images representing the entire Arabic Braille alphabet, with each file named according to the specific character it represents. Additionally, data augmentation techniques have been applied to expand the dataset and increase its variability, making the model more robust to real-world conditions. This dataset is a critical resource for developing assistive technologies aimed at automating the reading and interpretation of Arabic Braille (Elaraby, N., 2024).

Pre-processing

Data augmentation plays a vital role in preparing image datasets for machine learning tasks like Braille character recognition. By applying techniques such as horizontal flipping, rotation, brightness and contrast adjustments, gamma modification, and random cropping, the dataset becomes more diverse, enhancing the model's ability to generalize to unseen data. These transformations simulate variations in lighting, orientation, and conditions that may occur in real-world scenarios. For example, flipping and rotating the images allows the model to learn to recognize Braille characters from multiple angles, while adjustments in brightness and contrast improve its resilience under varying lighting conditions. Ultimately, this augmentation prevents overfitting, making the model more capable of accurately classifying Braille characters across different scenarios.

Figure 11. Images of braille Arabic characters after augmentation

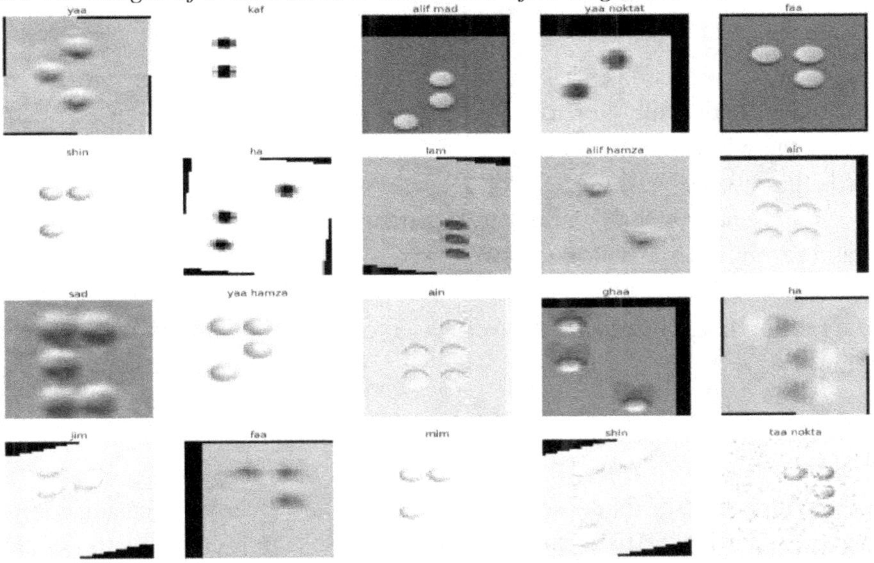

Feature Extraction

EfficientNet B3 was chosen for feature extraction due to its advanced performance and computational efficiency. This convolutional neural network architecture scales depth, width, and resolution in a balanced manner, making it an optimal choice for extracting relevant features from low-resolution images such as those used for Arabic Braille characters (Alhichri, H., 2021).

EfficientNet B3 is particularly well-suited for tasks like Braille recognition because it captures intricate details from low-resolution images without excessive computational overhead. It extracts texture, shape, and structural features from the Braille dots, which are essential for differentiating the characters. Thanks to its compound scaling method, EfficientNet B3 balances network depth (number of layers), width (number of channels per layer), and input resolution, ensuring that the model remains efficient while maintaining high accuracy.

The scaling coefficients for EfficientNet B3, derived from the compound scaling formula, adjust the model's capacity without dramatically increasing computational costs:

$$New\ Size = (\alpha^{d} \cdot \beta^{\omega} \cdot \gamma^{\tau}) \cdot Base\ Size \quad (3)$$

where:

- d is the depth scaling factor,
- w is the width scaling factor,
- r is the resolution scaling factor,
- α, β, γ alpha, beta, and gamma are constants controlling how the depth, width, and resolution are scaled respectively.

The scaling coefficients are derived based on the following compound scaling equation:

$\alpha \cdot \beta^{2} \cdot \gamma^{2} \approx 2$ Eq.4

This ensures that the model scales uniformly without overly increasing computational cost. Specifically, EfficientNet B3 applies these scaling coefficients as follows:

- $\alpha = 1.2$ (depth multiplier),
- $\beta = 1.1$ (width multiplier),
- $\gamma = 1.15$ (resolution multiplier).

By leveraging these scaling factors, EfficientNet B3 improves on the baseline EfficientNet B0, allowing for deeper layers, wider convolutions, and higher resolution input images, thereby enhancing feature extraction for Braille characters.

Classification

Following feature extraction using EfficientNet B3, a simple neural network is used for classification. The base model is set as trainable, allowing its weights to be fine-tuned during training to further optimize the extracted features. A BatchNormalization layer is added to stabilize training and increase efficiency. The network's hidden layer consists of 256 neurons, using L2 and L1 regularization to prevent overfitting. Additionally, a Dropout layer deactivates 40% of the neurons during training, increasing the model's robustness by making it less reliant on specific features. The output layer uses a softmax activation function to classify the Braille characters, as in Figure 12.

The model is compiled using the Adamax optimizer, known for its adaptive learning rate, and the categorical_crossentropy loss function. Performance is evaluated using metrics such as accuracy, F1-score, and Area Under the Curve (AUC), providing a comprehensive view of the model's effectiveness.

Figure 12. Stages in the classification of braille Arabic characters

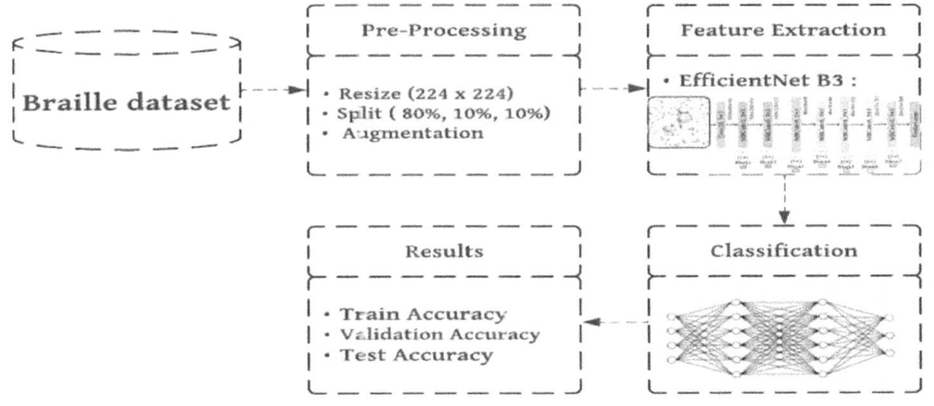

Experimental Results

The experimental results for Arabic Braille alphabet classification using EfficientNet B3 combined with a simple neural network are visualized in Figure 12, which depicts the training and validation performance over multiple epochs in terms of loss, accuracy, and F1 score.

- Training and Validation Loss: The loss curve shows a significant decline in both training and validation loss as the number of epochs increases. This indicates that the model is effectively learning and minimizing the difference between the predicted and actual outputs. The fact that the training and validation loss curves converge suggests that the model is not overfitting and generalizes well to unseen data, maintaining a balance between learning from the training data and applying this knowledge to validation data.
- Training and Validation Accuracy: The accuracy curve shows a steady increase for both training and validation sets, stabilizing near the 30th epoch. The high level of accuracy across both datasets indicates the model's ability

to reliably classify Arabic Braille characters. The close alignment between the training and validation accuracy implies that the model generalizes well and can effectively apply what it has learned during training to new data without overfitting.

- F1 Score: The F1 score is a critical metric because it provides a balanced view of the model's performance, considering both precision and recall. The graph shows that the F1 score for both training and validation data is high and converges over the epochs, demonstrating that the model is not biased toward any specific class and maintains a balance in detecting all classes.

Figure 13. Graph of 'train/validation' accuracy and loss

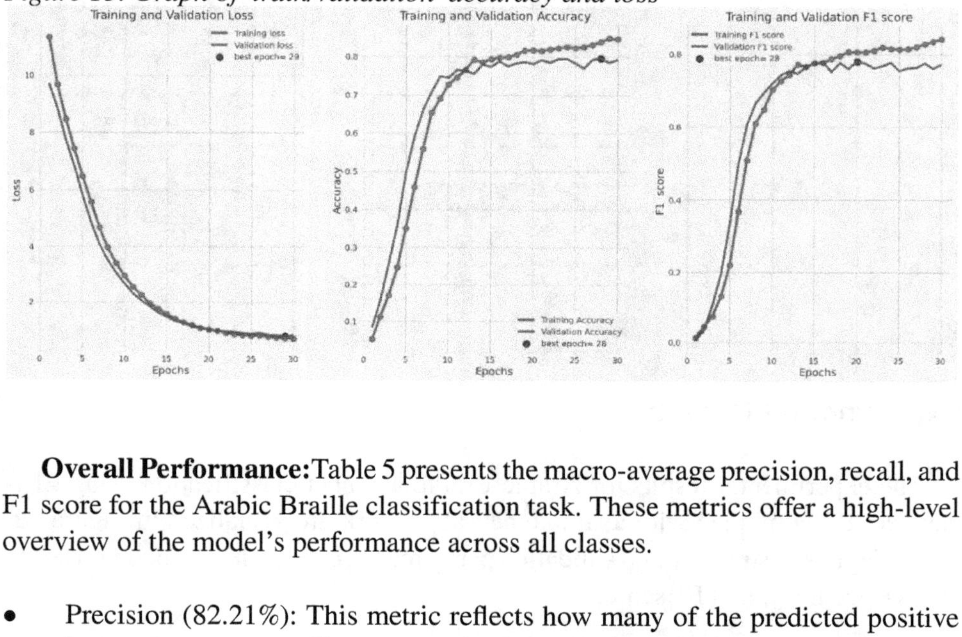

Overall Performance: Table 5 presents the macro-average precision, recall, and F1 score for the Arabic Braille classification task. These metrics offer a high-level overview of the model's performance across all classes.

- Precision (82.21%): This metric reflects how many of the predicted positive instances were actually correct. An average precision of 82.21% indicates that the model is highly effective in identifying the correct Braille characters.
- Recall (81.82%): Recall measures how well the model finds all relevant instances within the dataset. With a recall of 81.82%, the model successfully identifies the majority of the Braille characters, indicating that it is thorough in its predictions.
- F1-Score (81.33%): This score represents the harmonic mean of precision and recall. An F1-score of 81.33% shows a good balance between the two, suggesting that the model can maintain a balanced performance across the various classes of Braille characters.

Table 5. The macro average for Arabic alphabet braille classification.

Metrics	Precision (%)	recall (%)	f1-score (%)
macro avg	82.21	81.82	81.33

Class-wise Performance: Table 6 provides detailed performance metrics for each Arabic Braille character, giving insights into which classes the model performs well on and which may require further improvement.

- High-Performance Classes: Certain characters, such as "alif," "baa," and "dhad," exhibit exceptionally high precision, recall, and F1 scores, reflecting the model's strong ability to recognize these characters accurately. These results suggest that these characters have distinct and easily distinguishable features that the model can detect without confusion.
- Underperforming Classes: Some classes, such as "dad" and "dal," show significantly lower scores, particularly in precision. This underperformance could be due to the visual similarity between certain characters, leading to confusion during classification. Additionally, insufficient representation of these characters in the training data might have impacted the model's ability to generalize well for these specific cases.
- Variable Scores: Certain characters like "yaa hamza" and "waw hamza" show lower performance metrics. These characters might pose unique challenges for the model due to their intricate dot patterns or less frequent appearance in the dataset, making it harder for the model to differentiate between similar-looking classes.

Table 6. Performance metrics for Arabic alphabet braille classification

Class	Precision (%)	recall (%)	f1-score (%)
ain	73.33	100.00	84.62
alif	100.00	100.00	100.00
alif hamza	100.00	100.00	100.00
alif mad	100.00	100.00	100.00
baa	100.00	100.00	100.00
dad	35.71	45.45	40.00
dal	50.00	18.18	26.67
dhad	100.00	100.00	100.00
dhal	100.00	100.00	100.00

continued on following page

Table 6. Continued

Class	Precision (%)	recall (%)	f1-score (%)
faa	50.00	81.82	62.07
gaf	100.00	100.00	100.00
ha	100.00	100.00	100.00
haa	45.45	45.45	45.45
jim	45.45	45.45	45.45
kaf	100.00	100.00	100.00
khaa	100.00	100.00	100.00
lam	100.00	100.00	100.00
mim	100.00	72.73	84.21
noun	22.22	18.18	20.00
raa	100.00	100.00	100.00
sad	100.00	100.00	100.00
shin	78.57	100.00	88.00
sin	100.00	100.00	100.00
taa	50.00	54.55	52.17
taa nokta	100.00	100.00	100.00
thaa	100.00	63.64	77.78
waw	100.00	100.00	100.00
waw hamza	50.00	45.45	47.62
yaa	100.00	100.00	100.00
yaa hamza	30.00	27.27	28.57
yaa noktat	100.00	100.00	100.00

Discussion

The application of AI algorithms like EfficientNet B3 in education has transformative potential, particularly for individuals with disabilities. In this context, the classification of Arabic Braille characters using CNNs exemplifies how AI can revolutionize educational accessibility. By automating the recognition of Braille characters, AI-powered systems can bridge the gap for visually impaired learners, enabling them to access, read, and interact with educational materials more independently. This technological advancement reduces the need for human intervention in Braille transcription, accelerates learning, and provides greater autonomy to students with visual impairments.

High-performing classes indicate that the model can reliably differentiate between Braille characters that have distinct features or are well-represented in the dataset. Low performance for certain classes highlights potential issues with class imbalance or similar feature patterns among characters, which could cause misclassification. Further data augmentation or more advanced feature extraction techniques might help to address these issues.

AI algorithms also ensure that educational systems are inclusive, accommodating diverse needs. As more educational tools adopt AI-powered recognition systems, the possibilities for personalized and accessible learning environments continue to expand. This is particularly important in the era of digital learning, where the ability to tailor resources to individual needs is crucial for equitable education.

CONCLUSION

In conclusion, this research demonstrates that AI has the potential to revolutionize Arabic language education by making it more accessible, personalized, and effective for all learners, regardless of their abilities or preferred learning modalities. As these technologies evolve, they promise to play an increasingly important role in creating more inclusive and equitable educational environments. The three experiments conducted showcase how AI can be effectively applied to classify and recognize different representations of the Arabic alphabet: For handwritten Arabic character recognition, a hybrid approach combining Particle Swarm Optimization (PSO) and Support Vector Classifier (SVC) achieved a test accuracy of 90.20%. This method efficiently selected relevant features and constructed non-linear decision boundaries to handle the complexity of Arabic script. Arabic sign language alphabet classification using a combination of MediaPipe for hand landmark detection and Inception ResNet v2 for feature extraction, followed by a custom neural network, attained a test accuracy of 93.77%. This approach effectively captured the nuances of hand gestures in Arabic sign language. Arabic braille character recognition leveraging EfficientNet B3 for feature extraction and a simple neural network for classification resulted in a macro-average F1-score of 81.33%. This method demonstrated the ability to accurately classify braille characters, though with some variability across different characters. These AI-driven approaches show great promise for creating more inclusive and accessible educational tools for Arabic language learners, particularly those with diverse needs and abilities. By automating the recognition of handwriting, sign language gestures, and braille characters, these systems can provide real-time feedback, personalized learning experiences, and increased independence for learners.

REFERENCES

Abdel-Fattah, M. A. (2005). Arabic sign language: A perspective. *Journal of Deaf Studies and Deaf Education*, 10(2), 212–221. DOI: 10.1093/deafed/eni007 PMID: 15778217

Al-Barham, M., Alsharkawi, A., Al-Yaman, M., Al-Fetyani, M., Elnagar, A., SaAleek, A. A., & Al-Odat, M. (2023). RGB Arabic alphabets sign language dataset. *arXiv preprint arXiv:2301.11932*.

Al-Salman, A., AlOhali, Y., AlKanhal, M., & AlRajih, A. (2007). An arabic optical braille recognition system.

Alhichri, H., Alswayed, A. S., Bazi, Y., Ammour, N., & Alajlan, N. A. (2021). Classification of remote sensing images using EfficientNet-B3 CNN model with attention. *IEEE Access : Practical Innovations, Open Solutions*, 9, 14078–14094. DOI: 10.1109/ACCESS.2021.3051085

Balaha, M. M., El-Kady, S., Balaha, H. M., Salama, M., Emad, E., Hassan, M., & Saafan, M. M. (2023). A vision-based deep learning approach for independent-users Arabic sign language interpretation. *Multimedia Tools and Applications*, 82(5), 6807–6826. DOI: 10.1007/s11042-022-13423-9

Chen, L., Chen, P., & Lin, Z. (2020). Artificial intelligence in education: A review. *IEEE Access : Practical Innovations, Open Solutions*, 8, 75264–75278. DOI: 10.1109/ACCESS.2020.2988510

Chicco, D., Tötsch, N., & Jurman, G. (2021). The Matthews correlation coefficient (MCC) is more reliable than balanced accuracy, bookmaker informedness, and markedness in two-class confusion matrix evaluation. *BioData Mining*, 14(1), 1–22. DOI: 10.1186/s13040-021-00244-z PMID: 33541410

Comrie, B. (Ed.). (2003). *The Major Languages of South Asia, the Middle East and Africa*. Taylor & Francis. DOI: 10.4324/9780203412336

Dongare, A. D., Kharde, R. R., & Kachare, A. D. (2012). Introduction to artificial neural network. [IJEIT]. *International Journal of Engineering and Innovative Technology*, 2(1), 189–194.

El-Sawy, A., Loey, M., & El-Bakry, H. (2017). Arabic handwritten characters recognition using convolutional neural network. *WSEAS Transactions on Computer Research*, 5(1), 11–19.

Elaraby, N., Barakat, S., & Rezk, A. (2024). A generalized ensemble approach based on transfer learning for braille character recognition. *Information Processing & Management*, 61(1), 103545. DOI: 10.1016/j.ipm.2023.103545

Giacinto, G., Perdisci, R., Del Rio, M., & Roli, F. (2008). Intrusion detection in computer networks by a modular ensemble of one-class classifiers. *Information Fusion*, 9(1), 69–82. DOI: 10.1016/j.inffus.2006.10.002

Gocen, A., & Aydemir, F. (2020). Artificial intelligence in education and schools. *Research on Education and Media*, 12(1), 13–21. DOI: 10.2478/rem-2020-0003

Harris, M., & Agoes, A. S. (2021, November). Applying hand gesture recognition for user guide application using MediaPipe. In *2nd International Seminar of Science and Applied Technology (ISSAT 2021)* (pp. 101-108). Atlantis Press.

Koonce, B., & Koonce, B. (2021). EfficientNet. *Convolutional neural networks with swift for Tensorflow: image recognition and dataset categorization*, 109-123. 1913-1920.

Krisshna, N. A., Deepak, V. K., Manikantan, K., & Ramachandran, S. (2014). Face recognition using transform domain feature extraction and PSO-based feature selection. *Applied Soft Computing*, 22, 141–161. DOI: 10.1016/j.asoc.2014.05.007

Lau, K. W., & Wu, Q. H. (2003). Online training of support vector classifier. *Pattern Recognition*, 36(8), 1913–1920. DOI: 10.1016/S0031-3203(03)00038-4

Lorigo, L. M., & Govindaraju, V. (2006). Offline Arabic handwriting recognition: A survey. *IEEE Transactions on Pattern Analysis and Machine Intelligence*, 28(5), 712–724. DOI: 10.1109/TPAMI.2006.102 PMID: 16640258

Marcelli, A., Parziale, A., & Santoro, A. (2012, September). Modeling handwriting style: a preliminary investigation. In *2012 International Conference on Frontiers in Handwriting Recognition* (pp. 411-416). IEEE. DOI: 10.1109/ICFHR.2012.234

Munien, C., & Viriri, S. (2021). Classification of hematoxylin and eosin-stained breast cancer histology microscopy images using transfer learning with EfficientNets. *Computational Intelligence and Neuroscience*, 2021(1), 5580914. DOI: 10.1155/2021/5580914 PMID: 33897774

Rouabhi, S., Azerine, A., Tlemsani, R., Essaid, M., & Idoumghar, L. (2024). Conv-ViT fusion for improved handwritten Arabic character classification. *Signal, Image and Video Processing*, 18(S1), 1–18. DOI: 10.1007/s11760-024-03158-5

Shafiq, M., & Gu, Z. (2022). Deep residual learning for image recognition: A survey. *Applied Sciences (Basel, Switzerland)*, 12(18), 8972. DOI: 10.3390/app12188972

Szegedy, C., Ioffe, S., Vanhoucke, V., & Alemi, A. (2017, February). Inception-v4, inception-resnet and the impact of residual connections on learning. *Proceedings of the AAAI Conference on Artificial Intelligence*, 31(1), •••. DOI: 10.1609/aaai.v31i1.11231

Targ, S., Almeida, D., & Lyman, K. (2016). Resnet in resnet: Generalizing residual architectures. *arXiv preprint arXiv:1603.08029*.

Uzair, M., & Jamil, N. (2020, November). Effects of hidden layers on the efficiency of neural networks. In *2020 IEEE 23rd international multitopic conference (INMIC)* (pp. 1-6). IEEE. DOI: 10.1109/INMIC50486.2020.9318195

Varshni, D., Thakral, K., Agarwal, L., Nijhawan, R., & Mittal, A. (2019, February). Pneumonia detection using CNN based feature extraction. In *2019 IEEE international conference on electrical, computer and communication technologies (ICECCT)* (pp. 1-7). IEEE. DOI: 10.1109/ICECCT.2019.8869364

Zhang, F., Bazarevsky, V., Vakunov, A., Tkachenka, A., Sung, G., Chang, C. L., & Grundmann, M. (2020). Mediapipe hands: On-device real-time hand tracking. *arXiv preprint arXiv:2006.10214*.

Zhu, Y., & Newsam, S. (2017, September). Densenet for dense flow. In *2017 IEEE international conference on image processing (ICIP)* (pp. 790-794). IEEE. DOI: 10.1109/ICIP.2017.8296389

ADDITIONAL READING

Luqman, H., & El-Alfy, E. S. M. (2021). Towards hybrid multimodal manual and non-manual Arabic sign language recognition: MArSL database and pilot study. *Electronics (Basel)*, 10(14), 1739. DOI: 10.3390/electronics10141739

Mahdikhanlou, K., & Ebrahimnezhad, H. (2020). Multimodal 3D American sign language recognition for static alphabet and numbers using hand joints and shape coding. *Multimedia Tools and Applications*, 79(31), 22235–22259. DOI: 10.1007/s11042-020-08982-8

Saleem, S. I., Abdulazeez, A. M., & Orman, Z. (2021). A new segmentation framework for arabic handwritten text using machine learning techniques. *Computers, Materials & Continua*, 68(2), 2727–2754. DOI: 10.32604/cmc.2021.016447

Zerdoumi, S., Jhanjhi, N. Z., Habeeb, R. A. A., & Hashem, I. A. T. (2023). A deep learning based approach for extracting Arabic handwriting: Applied calligraphy and old cursive. *PeerJ. Computer Science*, 9, e1465. DOI: 10.7717/peerj-cs.1465 PMID: 38192476

KEY TERMS AND DEFINITIONS

Artificial Intelligence (AI): A branch of computer science focused on creating systems that can perform tasks that typically require human intelligence, such as visual perception, speech recognition, and decision-making.

Braille Recognition: The use of technology to automatically identify and interpret Braille characters, enabling accessibility for visually impaired users.

Data Processing: The collection, manipulation, and analysis of data to extract useful information, often used in machine learning and artificial intelligence applications.

Deep Learning: A subset of machine learning involving neural networks with multiple layers, used to model complex patterns in large amounts of data.

Handwritten Character Recognition: A technology that uses image processing and AI to interpret and digitize handwritten characters, facilitating digital archiving and analysis.

Inception ResNet V2: A deep neural network architecture that combines residual connections with inception modules, enhancing feature extraction and classification accuracy.

MediaPipe: An open-source framework for building multimodal perception pipelines, commonly used for real-time hand landmark detection in sign language recognition.

Multimodal Classification: The process of classifying data across multiple forms or modes, such as text, images, and gestures, often used in applications like language recognition.

Particle Swarm Optimization (PSO): A bio-inspired optimization algorithm based on the social behaviors of birds and fish, often used for feature selection in machine learning.

Support Vector Classifier (SVC): A supervised learning algorithm that identifies the optimal hyperplane to classify data points, widely used in high-dimensional data classification tasks.

Chapter 11
Generative Artificial Intelligence and the 4C Learning Skills for the 21st Century

Pınar Mıhcı Türker
https://orcid.org/0000-0002-2382-3806
Aksaray University, Turkey

Mücahit Öztürk
Aksaray University, Turkey

ABSTRACT

This chapter explores the relationship between generative artificial intelligence (AI) and the 21st-century 4C learning skills: critical thinking, creativity, collaboration, and communication. This chapter provides an overview of the core characteristics of these skills and examines research on how generative AI influences their development. Generative AI presents significant opportunities to foster 4C learning skills by stimulating students' thought processes, encouraging critical perspectives on problems, and enabling innovative solutions. Additionally, generative AI-supported platforms can enhance student communication and facilitate collaborative work. While generative AI offers transformative potential, a balanced and cautious approach is recommended to ensure it best serves students' educational interests.

DOI: 10.4018/979-8-3693-7220-3.ch011

INTRODUCTION

Artificial intelligence, which has been on the agenda since 1943, is the ability of a computer or computer-controlled robot to have human-like characteristics such as reasoning, exploring and learning from experience, and performing complex tasks (Britannica, 2024). Artificial intelligence will lead to significant changes in many areas, such as health, agriculture, production, transportation, security, and energy, with its ability to perform some tasks instead of humans (Martinez et al., 2019). Artificial intelligence, which emerged from Alan Turing's question "Can machines think?" can today perform many activities such as customer service, language translations, e-mail filters, online recommendation systems, chatbots, fraud detection, and creating music playlists. Historically, many technologies such as machine learning, neural networks, deep learning, big data, and natural language processing have been included in the artificial intelligence ecosystem. While traditional artificial intelligence initially had the ability to make predictions, solve problems, and analyze using data, today, with technological developments (Page vd., 2018), it has transformed into a technology that can learn from data sets and produce its own content or data, such as text, sound, and images (Cooper & Tang, 2024). When OpenAI released ChatGPT in 2022, a new phase was reached, and artificial intelligence became a technology that talks to users, guides them, and produces content in line with the demands. Generative artificial intelligence enables the development of personalized learning resources and methods, as well as the simulation of scenarios that enhance students' learning (Shi et al., 2024). Artificial intelligence is a tool used in the infrastructure of learning management systems, in the evaluation of students, and in performance monitoring (Mao et al., 2024).

Generative artificial intelligence offers various opportunities for teachers and students. Platforms like ChatGPT that use generative artificial intelligence can provide academic support to students and guide them in preparing their assignments by generating real-time responses. Using generative artificial intelligence tools, teachers can design dynamic and interactive learning environments and deliver experiences that can enhance collaborative and creative learning (Bansal et al., 2024). Chatbots can contribute to the development of communication and critical thinking skills by providing real-time and guiding answers to students' questions and enabling the exchange of ideas (Ruiz-Rojas et al., 2024; Yan et al., 2024). Many qualities, such as critical thinking, problem solving, communication, and creative thinking, fall within the scope of 21st century skills. Critical thinking, creativity, collaboration, and communication, referred to as the 21st century 4C skills, are the competence areas required for students to participate in the workforce and integrate into the modern world (OECD, 2018). Educational institutions should integrate 4C skills into their curriculum and teaching practices to ensure that students meet the expectations of the sectors (Herlinawati et al., 2024). Appropriate pedagogical approaches and technologies should be used in this process (Fitriati et al., 2023). Collaboration with generative artificial intelligence, today's rapidly developing technology, can contribute to the development of students' 4C skills (Ivcevic & Grandinetti, 2024). In addition to the positive contributions of generative artificial intelligence to the learning process of students, it also has risky aspects in terms of ethical rules and assessment methods (Mateus et al., 2024).

Generative artificial intelligence is rapidly transforming education and many other fields, with the opportunities and potential risks it offers. This section provides information about the features, areas of use, and tools used in generative artificial intelligence and discusses its benefits and limitations in the teaching process. In the following sections, its impact on developing the 21st century 4C skills, which are considered an important competence area for students today, is evaluated.

GENERATİVE ARTİFİCİAL INTELLİGENCE

Generative artificial intelligence is one of the fastest and most transformative technological tools to emerge in recent years. It is envisaged that generative artificial intelligence tools will produce content instead of humans in many areas such as art, literature, software, etc. (Abbott & Rothman 2022). Generative artificial intelligence is used in many sectors. Traditional search engines list Web pages that contain the information the user wants. Users have to go through these pages one by one to reach the information they are looking for, which causes a waste of time. Chatbots such as ChatGPT, Gemini, and Microsoft Copilot can produce detailed answers to questions from users. These tools provide feedback in the context desired by the user, in everyday or academic language, and according to the level of the target audience. With these features, generative artificial intelligence tools allow users to access information within the framework they want without wasting time. Using the ChatGPT infrastructure, tools such as Canva, SiderAI, and Midjourney can create impressive images and videos in line with the demands and descriptions from users. The Canva magic tool can design visuals that we can use as presentations or social media posts within the framework of commands from the user. In addition, the artificial intelligence tool in Canva can edit photos and make them more impressive, convert the texts we enter into a more eye-catching format, and create videos. Sider provides chat, reading, writing, image, and video editing services. The platform can summarize the content of text files, convert images to text, enhance image files, and remove text and background. Users can perform many activities, such as converting text to images and videos and summarizing videos.

Translation platforms such as Deepl, QuillBot, etc. prepare more effective texts for writers and researchers by checking grammar, fluency, and expression errors. DeepL provides text or file-based translation, customer service in different languages, professional communication solutions, and text enhancement. QuillBot has features such as text summarization, plagiarism detection, an artificial intelligence detector, and citation generation, in addition to translation and fluency checking. Tools such as Gamma, Beautiful.AI, etc. design original presentations using text, images, and graphics on topics determined by users. Gamma allows you to create presentations, documents, and Web sites in many languages without requiring any technical knowledge. You can quickly and easily create interactive galleries, graphics, diagrams, and tables, edit these contents, and make them mobile compatible. Beautiful.ai enables you to prepare presentations with impressive visuals for many sectors, such as marketing, sales, and education. Anyword is a platform used in the marketing sector, allowing texts to be created for advertisements on social media, e-mail, and Web sites. ElevenLabs provides individuals, institutions, or content producers with the opportunity to create realistic voices that resemble human voices in various languages and accents. It can be used to create audiobooks, explanatory videos, or podcasts. WIX is a platform that helps design and edit websites for many sectors, whether individual or corporate. It is enough to provide information about the site you want to set up to the artificial intelligence assistant. The website created by the productive artificial intelligence can be personalized and edited. Runway allows you to create and edit creative designs, unique visuals, and videos. Shortwave performs AI-powered email searches. It allows the user to ask questions in their inbox, allowing them to delete old conversations and unnecessary emails. Suno can create high-quality songs with various instruments, vocals, and sound effects based on commands. Tools such as SurveyMonkey, Quizizz, Kahoot!, etc. use artificial intelligence to create online surveys, exams, and feedback within the framework determined by the users. SurveyMonkey helps users create online surveys, feedback, and evaluation forms that include a wide range of question types and are easily customizable, using many survey templates powered by artificial intelligence. The forms you create can be shared with users by embedding them in a Web site as a WEB link, email or iframe. With the advanced reporting module, the collected data can be quickly analyzed and interpreted. SurveyMonkey is actively used in many sectors, such as education, health, marketing, and public and financial services. Quizizz is an online assessment tool that offers students the opportunity to learn while having fun and evaluate themselves interactively through gamification. In addition to online exams, it provides interactive videos, flashcards that can strengthen memory, and passages that facilitate understanding with artificial intelligence. Kahoot! is a platform that offers students the opportunity to learn and test themselves by playing games. Interactive activities that include many different types of questions and slides can be designed with artificial intelligence, and students' data can be analyzed.

Platforms such as Eightify and TubeOnAI are applications that summarize YouTube videos and reduce users' time loss. Eightify is a useful Chrome extension used to learn the important points of Youtube videos before watching them. It can show the output of its summaries in many languages. TubeOnAI is an AI-powered tool that summarizes Youtube, podcast, and WEB content. It can be used as a browser extension or an Android and iOS application. Generative artificial intelligence has contributed to advances that encourage innovation and facilitate processes in many areas, paving the way for the development of potential applications in the field of education (Shahzad et al., 2024). Table 1 shows commonly used generative artificial intelligence tools.

Table 1. Generative artificial intelligence tools

Tools	Purpose of Use
ChatGPT	Chatbot
Microsoft Copilot	
Google Gemini	
Midjourney	Image Generator
Sider	
Micoroft Creat	
Canva	
Sider	
Dall-e	
Adobe Firefly	
Pictory	Video Generator
Synthesys	
DeepBrain	
HeyGen	
Google Translate	Translate
DeepL	
Quillbot	
Taia	

continued on following page

Table 1. Continued

Tools	Purpose of Use
Gamma	Slides Generator
Beautiful.ai	
Tome	
Simplified	
Prezi	
Anyword	Text Generator
Copy Shark	
Wordtune	
Scalenut	
Jasper	
Lovo.ai	Audio Generator
Murf	
Synthesis	
Eightify	Video Summarizer
TubeOnAI	
Notta	
Wix	WEB Site Generator
Framer	
Jimdo	
SurveyMonkey	Online Survey and Quiz Generator
Quizizz	
Kahoot!	
Socrative	

GENERATİVE ARTİFİCİAL INTELLİGENCE İN EDUCATİON

The powerful capabilities of generative artificial intelligence, such as natural language processing and the ability to produce meaningful content including text, images, music, and video, have affected the education-teaching process, and its potential benefits and possible risks have begun to be discussed by researchers. Generative artificial intelligence can provide students with a learning experience that is at their level, act as a teaching assistant for teachers (Hsu & Ching, 2023), and offer remarkable opportunities for personalized learning and innovative teaching methods (Cooper &Tang, 2024). Researchers have begun to examine the impact of generative artificial intelligence in different fields such as medicine (Heng et al., 2023), engineering (Qadir, 2023), arts (Carceller, 2024), communication (Pavlik, 2023), and language education (Law, 2024).

Shi et al. (2024) evaluated the effect of situational interactive teaching facilitated by generative artificial intelligence on learning outcomes and flow experiences. The data of the study was collected from survey and test questions to examine students' cognitive levels, learning effectiveness, flow experiences, and subjective evaluations throughout the teaching process. The results showed that situational interactive teaching facilitated by generative artificial intelligence significantly improved students' cognitive, affective, and psychomotor skills compared to traditional methods. It was suggested that generative artificial intelligence can be effectively applied in law education and should be encouraged for the teaching process. Hsu and Ching (2023) investigated the potential use of generative artificial intelligence tools such as ChatGPT in education and suggested that these tools could help both teachers and students. It can provide support to teachers in designing and evaluating the teaching process and making suggestions for improving the process. It can provide students with personalized learning opportunities and improve their creative thinking, reading, and writing skills. Researchers expressed reservations about the confidentiality and integrity of data and ethical issues that may arise in the use of generative artificial intelligence. Shahzad et al. (2024) investigated the awareness, acceptance, and adoption of ChatGPT developed by OpenAI in higher education institutions in China. Quantitative data collected from university students was analyzed by structural equation modeling. The results of the study showed that ChatGPT awareness significantly affected ChatGPT adoption intention. Perceived ease of use, usefulness, and intelligence significantly mediated the relationship between ChatGPT awareness and ChatGPT adoption intention. In addition, perceived trust significantly moderated the relationship between ChatGPT awareness and perceived ease of use, usefulness, and intelligence. Going forward, the researchers suggested that students should consider safe use in the evaluation process of generative artificial intelligence to develop their critical thinking and creativity, and that guidelines and instructions should be clearly specified.

Koh et al. (2024) examined word clouds that can serve as a scaffold for students' reflection, critical thinking, and content learning. Traditional, semantic, and generative artificial intelligence were used in the creation of word clouds, and users were evaluated. The study, conducted on two different groups of Chinese and English learners, revealed that generative artificial intelligence provided accurate, creative, and accessible word clouds for students and encouraged students to discuss and generate ideas with each other. Cox (2023) reviewed recent academic articles in English, Chinese, and Japanese to identify ethical challenges that may arise in the use of ChatGPT. The study, which examined studies on the use of ChatGPT in higher education, revealed that empirical research on the use of generative artificial intelligence in education is at an early stage and that these studies mostly address issues of ethics, academic integrity, evaluation, and data privacy. The researcher stated that considering the rapid development and proliferation of generative artificial intelligence, there is a need for more empirical studies to develop ethical policies for educators' use. Maphoto et al. (2024) examined the effect of generative artificial intelligence on the development of academic writing skills in their study with university students participating in the distance education process. The perceptions of the faculty and students regarding the artificial intelligence-supported module integrated into the learning management system were evaluated. The findings of the study demonstrated the potential of generative artificial intelligence on the development of academic writing skills.

Additionally, the importance of developing user-friendly interfaces and preparing user guides and instructions was emphasized. Yu and Guo (2023) presented an overview of the current status, problems, and future of generative artificial intelligence, stating that there are problems in terms of openness, privacy, reliability, and fairness. Researchers have proposed developing explainable and fair algorithms for generative artificial intelligence, upgrading encryption technology, establishing relevant laws and regulations to protect data, and improving the quality and quantity of datasets. Opportunities for personalized and intelligent teaching and collaborative learning have been seen. Kelly et al. (2023) investigated the views of Australian university students on generative artificial intelligence by collecting data through a survey. In general, it was observed that students had low levels of knowledge, experience, and confidence in using generative artificial intelligence tools. The results varied according to students' age, program of study, and nationality. As students' experience increased, their confidence in using generative artificial intelligence tools increased. It was revealed that some students were confident in using generative artificial intelligence tools even though they had never used them. The results of the study showed the potential for using generative artificial intelligence tools for educational purposes and the need for students to interact more with these tools. Xia et al. (2023) investigated how generative artificial intelligence can transform assessment methods in higher education.

For this purpose, 32 research articles on generative artificial intelligence and student assessment were examined through document analysis. It was seen that most of the articles were written in the recent past, and the results showed that assessment methods should be changed to take responsibility for students' learning and improve their integrity. The research suggested that for the successful transformation of assessment in higher education, teacher professional development activities should be provided for assessment, artificial intelligence, and digital literacy, teachers' beliefs about human and artificial intelligence assessment should be strengthened;

and teachers should be innovative to ensure the transformation in assessment. Mao et al. (2024) examined the potential opportunities and challenges for the use of generative artificial intelligence in education and student assessment. The results of the study showed that it has become imperative to teach students how to use generative artificial intelligence ethically. In addition, an artificial intelligence literacy consisting of application, originality, and accountability should be developed to prepare students for the future. It was emphasized that new methods and designs are needed in generative artificial intelligence supported assessment and the importance of developing teachers' artificial intelligence literacy and competence.

Mateus et al. (2024) investigated the opinions of university faculty members on the use of generative artificial intelligence in communication education. The opinions of 22 faculty members working in communication faculties in Mexico, Peru, and Spain were obtained. Faculty members viewed generative artificial intelligence as both an ally and a competitor as a tool with varying effects. Providing support for students to use generative artificial intelligence tools, establishing ethical protocols, and reviewing evaluation methods are among the issues that faculty members consider important. Ward et al. (2024) examined how universities can improve teaching and learning with generative artificial intelligence. The researchers believe that generative artificial intelligence offers an opportunity for universities to make long-needed structural changes. It has been seen that time and resources are needed for faculty members to learn how to use generative artificial intelligence effectively and to transfer it to the teaching process in an ethical and critical manner. Universities should work on developing artificial intelligence assistants and adaptive learning systems to help faculty members with limited time to improve their teaching processes. It has been recommended that attention be paid to inclusiveness, transparency, privacy, and security issues and that necessary measures be taken.

Cantaş et al. (2024) investigated the effect of university students' artificial intelligence anxiety on 21st century skills and lifelong learning. It was observed that teacher candidates had a moderate level of artificial intelligence anxiety; their perception of having 21st century skills was strong, and they were aware of the importance of lifelong learning. Positive relationships emerged between the use of artificial intelligence-supported tools, 21st century skills, and lifelong learning. Habib et al. (2024) aimed to examine the effect of generative artificial intelligence on students' creative thinking and to provide information on how teachers can use generative artificial intelligence in classroom teaching. In the study conducted with a mixed method in a creative thinking course, the effect of ChatGPT on students' creative thinking was evaluated within the framework of the flexibility, fluency, and originality of the data produced. The results of the study showed that generative artificial intelligence supports creative thinking. The researchers emphasized the importance of creative thinking for the learning process and emphasized the developmental effect of students in struggling with difficulties and producing solutions to problems. It was stated that generative artificial intelligence tools may have negative effects in terms of self-confidence in the learning process and that caution should be exercised in this regard. In their literature review examining the potential of artificial intelligence to affect critical thinking skills through collaborative learning with peers, Baskoro et al. (2023) concluded that generative artificial intelligence tools have the ability to develop higher-level thinking skills such as critical thinking, but teachers need to be under regular supervision and problems may arise in terms of honesty.

Rojas et al. (2024) studied the perceptions of university students regarding the impact of generative artificial intelligence tools such as Canva, ChatPDF, and you.com on critical thinking and collaborative learning. It was observed that the vast majority of university students were familiar with generative artificial intelligence tools, and a significant portion of them used these tools. Canva, ChatPDF, and you.com were popular generative artificial intelligence tools among students. Students believed that generative artificial intelligence tools could improve critical thinking and collaborative work. Although students were familiar with generative artificial intelligence tools, it was revealed that academic and technical support should be provided for the use of these tools. Dai et al. (2024) evaluated the problems encountered in professional communication education in the intercultural context and the potential of artificial intelligence to solve some of these problems. Generative artificial intelligence can provide an immersive learning experience that surpasses traditional language education in terms of different cultures. However, there are limitations in terms of bias, emotional intelligence, and natural tooth processing.

These limitations can be reduced with strategic measures such as data set organization, continuous improvement, and human feedback. Generative artificial intelligence can provide a dynamic learning environment in terms of developing communication skills. It has been stated that more comprehensive studies are needed to better understand the impact of generative artificial intelligence in learning environments and to reduce possible biases. Barana et al. (2023) evaluated the supportive role of ChatGPT in solving mathematical problems and its effect on students' problem solving and critical thinking from the perspective of faculty members and students. Students were asked to solve the given mathematical problems and compare their solutions with ChatGPT. During this process, faculty members also observed the students. As a result of the research, it was revealed that generative artificial intelligence could contribute to the development of students' problem-solving strategies and critical thinking. The need for strong control mechanisms in the use of generative artificial intelligence tools in the teaching process has been emphasized. Lu et al. (2024) examined the impact of generative AI-supported instruction on pre-service teachers' professional self-efficacy and higher-order thinking skills. In the study conducted with a quasi-experimental design, it was observed that the experimental group that received generative artificial intelligence-supported teaching skills training had significantly better self-efficacy and higher-order thinking skills compared to traditional methods. The opportunities and possible risks of using generative artificial intelligence in the teaching process are a phenomenon that has been expressed together in early research.

GENERATIVE ARTIFICIAL INTELLIGENCE IN EDUCATION: OPPORTUNITIES AND CHALLENGES

Early-stage research on the use of generative artificial intelligence in education has highlighted several opportunities and potential problems. AlAli and Wardat (2024) examined the opportunities and barriers that arise with the integration of generative artificial intelligence into the educational environment. For this purpose, the opinions of educators, policymakers, students, and technologists were taken. Generative artificial intelligence has the potential to enrich the learning experience, adapt instruction to students' learning style, provide real-time feedback, and encourage creativity. However, it is necessary to determine the ethical framework to ensure the correct and safe use of generative artificial intelligence for educational purposes. There are also areas that may cause problems, such as the confidentiality of personal data, transparency, accountability, and the accuracy and lack of bias in the content produced. Fuller and Barnes (2024) assessed student and faculty perceptions of the integration of generative artificial intelligence into graduate education. Students expressed the benefits of generative artificial intelligence in terms of time savings and academic support, but they worried that relying on ChatGPT to prepare assignments could diminish the value of a university education and could impact the development of problem-solving and leadership skills. Faculties mentioned the advantages of generative artificial intelligence, such as providing different perspectives and support for the teaching process. On the other hand, the potential to hinder the development of teamwork, problem solving, and leadership skills has been expressed. The researchers suggested that to reduce the potential negative impacts of generative artificial intelligence, teachers and students should work together to develop strategies and establish clear ethical guidelines.

Islam and Islam (2024) investigated the potential opportunities and challenges of ChatGPT in academia through a literature review. The results showed that ChatGPT has opportunities and challenges for research, education, personal skills development, and social aspects. In terms of research, there are opportunities to study with additional resources, facilitate data analysis and interpretation, and enhance creativity and innovation. In terms of education, there are positive effects such as cooperative and personalized learning, evaluation, improving performance, and taking responsibility. However, there are problems such as providing accurate and reliable information, insufficient support, misunderstanding the content, technical problems, adapting to the new model, privacy, and ethical concerns. Preiksaitis and Rose (2023) evaluated the potential opportunities and limitations of generative artificial intelligence in medical education through a literature review. The findings demonstrated several potential applications of generative artificial intelligence, such as self-directed learning, generating simulation scenarios, and authoring assistance. However, issues such as honesty, accuracy of data, and possible negative effects on learning were also raised. Capraro et al. (2024) examined the impact of generative artificial intelligence on socioeconomic inequality in work, education, and health. Generative artificial intelligence can increase workplace productivity and create new jobs, but these benefits are unevenly spread. In the field of education, it can provide personalized learning experiences for students but also widen the digital divide. It can improve diagnosis and access to healthcare, but it can also deepen existing inequalities. Researchers have drawn attention to the many positive features of generative artificial intelligence that make life easier, as well as its potential to further increase socioeconomic disadvantages.

Algorithms used to develop artificial intelligence technologies can also pose significant risks (Martin, 2019), and one of these risks is algorithmic bias. Algorithmic bias is the process by which algorithms used to automate or assist in decision-making about people violate norms of justice and equality, producing discriminatory results that negatively affect certain individuals or groups in the workplace or society. This means providing certain individuals or groups with greater advantages or disadvantages than others (Kordzadeh & Ghasemaghaei, 2022). The harms that may arise from algorithmic biases are stated in two ways. The first of these is the withholding of opportunities or resources from certain groups or the unfair distribution of a good among groups. Another harm occurs in the form of a systematic negative representation of a group or the lack of a positive representation (Baker & Hawn, 2022). Algorithmic biases cause important ethical concerns that cause individuals to make wrong decisions and be misled. Various mathematical strategies are proposed in computer science studies to address these ethical concerns (Favaretto et al., 2019). Algorithmic biases also have negative effects on people's thinking skills and cause individuals to make wrong decisions.

Another ethical concern regarding artificial intelligence is over-reliance on artificial intelligence. Over-reliance on AI occurs when users accept recommendations generated by artificial intelligence without question. This often occurs when individuals have difficulty assessing the reliability of AI or how much trust to place in its recommendations (Passi & Vorvoreanu, 2022). Over-reliance on artificial intelligence without critical evaluation brings many risks. Because artificial intelligence suggestions contain biases or errors (Buçinca et al., 2021). For example, artificial intelligence systems used to predict crime are criticized for perpetuating biases against certain demographic groups (Mikalef et al., 2023). However, over-reliance on artificial intelligence can negatively affect students' critical and analytical thinking abilities by making them less able to independently analyze information, construct logical arguments, and make well-reasoned decisions (Koos & Wachsmann, 2023). Ready-made answers produced by artificial intelligence can negatively affect the development of students' cognitive skills by preventing them from conducting comprehensive research and critically evaluating sources (Santiago et al., 2023). There is a significant gap in the literature regarding the long-term effects of over-reliance on artificial intelligence systems in terms of basic cognitive skills such as decision-making, critical thinking, and analytical thinking (Zhai et al., 2024).

To mitigate the risks that may arise from over-reliance on artificial intelligence, educational strategies should emphasize the importance of questioning artificial intelligence-generated content, comparing it to human-generated insights, and understanding artificial intelligence's limitations. To get students to use artificial intelligence tools in a more nuanced and critical way, Dergaa et al. (2023) suggest that they think about the biases that are built into artificial intelligence outputs and do activities that require them to evaluate and combine information from different sources. Measures to be taken to ensure balanced use by reducing over-reliance on AI can be listed as follows:

- Learning about artificial intelligence models will help users develop appropriate levels of trust in artificial intelligence (Yin et al. 2019).
- Ensuring that users see both correct and incorrect predictions will help them develop appropriate impressions (Passi & Vorvoreanu, 2022).
- Over time, users become complacent about artificial intelligence systems and spend less effort evaluating artificial intelligence recommendations.

The following cognitive forcing strategies can be used that can be effective in shifting users from a fast and automatic thought process to a slow and careful thought process (Buçinca et al., 2021):

- Asking a person to make a decision before seeing the AI's suggestion may help them make the right decisions, as people have made better decisions when they saw the AI's suggestion after making an unaided decision.
- Changing the response time of the AI system will allow them to think about the task and predict their own decision-making processes and the AI's decision-making processes (Park et al., 2019)

- Systems can be improved by alerting users when they accept a risky proposition. It is important to help people think about their own decision-making processes (Passi, & Vorvoreanu, 2022).

The application of the above-mentioned strategies in both learning environments and daily life is considered important in terms of demonstrating a balanced approach to artificial intelligence technologies. The use of generative artificial intelligence in learning and teaching processes seems positive despite some limitations and risks for teachers and students. The potential of many of the generative artificial intelligence tools currently being developed to develop students' 21st century skills such as critical thinking, creative thinking, collaboration, and communication has been demonstrated in relatively few theoretical and applied studies.

21ST CENTURY 4C LEARNING SKILLS

Among the basic competencies of the 21st century, 4C skills are of great importance for preparing students for increasingly complex living and working environments. Although many experts do not agree on the exact definition of 21st century skills (Van Laar et al., 2017), 4C skills have been defined as important competencies in this sense (Silber-Varod et al., 2019). 4C skills consist of critical thinking, creativity, communication, and collaboration and are considered among the basic skills that every individual should have today (Marwa et al., 2023). Developing these four basic skills also means nurturing the abilities required for social development in the future (Ye and Xu, 2023). Because the ability to communicate and cooperate is necessary for students to be a part of the community. In addition, there will be various problems in social life that students will need to criticize and expect a suitable solution to solve the problem. Solutions will be designed and implemented by people who can think creatively and critically. Creative individuals will be able to produce creative and original ideas (Kembara et al., 2019). In this context, it is important to examine each skill in its own context.

Critical thinking, one of the basic thinking skills of 21st century education (Facione, 2023), is an evaluative mental process in which information is analyzed inductively and deductively (Nainggolan et al., 2019). Critical thinking skills are not only related to individuals' recall of information but are also very important in learning environments as they enable individuals to understand the presented material more deeply (Dwyer et al., 2012; Halpern, 2003). Critical thinking begins with simple experiences such as observing a difference, encountering a puzzling question or problem, and questioning someone's statement, and progresses to more complex experiences such as applying higher-order thinking skills such as reasoning, questioning, and evaluating alternative explanations (Spector & Ma, 2019). Critical thinking is essential both academically and for evaluating information, solving problems, and making informed decisions (Quinn et al., 2020; Shanta & Wells, 2022). Critical thinking also draws on other skills such as communication, information literacy, and the ability to examine, analyze, interpret, and evaluate evidence (Scott, 2015).

Creativity is another component of the 4C skills. Students with creative skills have the ability to successfully use idea generation techniques; these individuals generate new and valuable ideas, develop creative ideas, and can analyze their own ideas thoroughly, and these individuals have a wide range of qualities such as being able to evaluate ideas and maximize their potential (P21, 2015; Trilling & Fadel, 2009). Creativity is the ability to find new ways to solve problems. It refers to innovative ways of dealing with situations based on imagination and thought (Kumar & Kukreja, 2024). Creativity can be defined as a way of thinking that uses various techniques to generate new ideas and useful concepts; outlines, develops, analyzes, and evaluates the original idea to achieve maximum results (NEA, 2010). Creativity is trying new approaches, innovations, and inventions to be successful in a subject. Creative thinking includes sub-skills such as creating diverse, valuable, and new ideas, working creatively with other individuals, and being able to implement innovations (Chiruguru, 2020). Creative thinking allows students to think outside the box without adhering to rules. Through creative thinking, students can come up with alternative solutions to a problem from various perspectives (Brata et al., 2023).

Another skill expected from individuals in the 21st century is collaboration skills. Collaboration is an activity that involves multiple people interacting both individually and in groups according to learning goals (Kurniawan, 2021). Collaboration is about working together to achieve a goal and the talent, expertise, and intelligence demonstrated in this process. Collaboration includes sub-skills such as working effectively and respectfully with diverse teams, being flexible and helpful to achieve a common goal, assuming shared responsibility, and valuing the contribution of each team member (Chiruguru, 2020). Utilizing collaboration in the learning process allows students to bring together their knowledge, skills, and experiences to better understand and learn from each other. The two main characteristics of collaboration in the learning process are that students are grouped and gain knowledge through social interaction with their peers (Ramadevi et al., 2023). In this process, students need to be taught and practiced specific skills such as brainstorming and role-playing (Sharma and Wang, 2019), as well as communication skills such as active listening, asking questions, and restating strategies, so that they can collaborate successfully (Haq et al., 2021).

Like other 4C skills, communication skills have been ranked as the highest priority skills to be acquired by both students and teachers by 2030 (OECD 2019). Teaching students to communicate effectively and efficiently is a major challenge facing all pedagogical institutions (Morreale et al., 2017). Strong communication skills include the ability to express thoughts clearly and persuasively, both orally and in writing, to articulate ideas, to convey instructions, to be coherent, and to motivate others through speaking (NEA, 2010). This skill has sub-skills such as language skills, understanding the context and reading the audience to ensure that the message is conveyed correctly (Tigas and Santoso, 2021), expressing thoughts and ideas effectively using oral, written, and non-verbal communication skills, effective listening, and communicating effectively across languages and cultures (Chiruguru, 2020). Through communication, students can communicate ideas, messages, understandings, and income to educators, peers, groups, or the entire class (Purnawirawan et al., 2019). When communication skills are combined with collaboration skills, the student has practical communication skills, both oral and written, which means the development of teamwork skills and the ability to communicate effectively across groups (Susanti and Arista, 2019).

To equip students with skills for the future, 4C skills need to be integrated into classrooms, schools, and districts across the country (Erdoğan, 2019). Artificial intelligence, which has the potential to revolutionize educational environments by personalizing learning experiences and providing real-time assessments (Alam, 2022; Kamalov et al., 2023), can adapt teaching content to suit the unique needs and learning styles of each student, making education more engaging and productive (Darwin et al., 2023). In this context, artificial intelligence holds promise for the development of important thinking skills such as 4C skills (Spector and Ma, 2019). For example, using AI technology to support critical thinking (Zhu, 2015), implementing a virtual environment to build and assess higher-level questioning skills (Ketelhut et al., 2010), and enhancing computational thinking through robotics (Angeli and Valanides, 2019) are among the promising applications of AI used to support the development of the human mind.

21ST CENTURY 4C LEARNING SKILLS AND GENERATIVE ARTIFICIAL INTELLIGENCE

Extensive research has been published on the effects of artificial intelligence tools on thinking skills in education. However, there is a lack of consistency in the findings of these studies. While some studies show that artificial intelligence tools have a positive effect, other studies examining the effect on the same higher-order thinking skill report either no significant effect or a negative effect (Ilgun Dibek et al., 2024). Despite these contradictions, it is possible to say that artificial intelligence provides contextual learning in which students must be active; it is a way to take students to the next level in social change that requires them to be innovative and creative (Oktradiksa et al., 2021). Many researchers have used artificial intelligence in their studies and have suggested that the application of artificial intelligence in education has the potential to improve the quality of educational management, enhance education, and support learning outcomes (Chen et al., 2020). It has also been observed that the integration of artificial intelligence and thinking skills into education can help develop critical thinking, problem solving, and technology skills (Huang & Qiao, 2022; Lin & Chen, 2020).

Critical Thinking and Generative Artificial Intelligence

Artificial intelligence is increasingly seen as a powerful tool to increase critical thinking skills in educational environments (Darwin et al., 2023). Because in the current era, personalized learning is using artificial intelligence to help students perform at a higher level by making adjustments according to their differences. This is seen as an indication that artificial intelligence should be used in the future to improve human intelligence and adapt to individual differences (Spector and Ma, 2019). Artificial Intelligence -powered tools provide students with interactive learning experiences and challenge them to apply their knowledge to real-world problems. In this way, they enable students to develop skills such as analysis, synthesis, and evaluation (Almeida & Simoes, 2019). In addition, artificial Intelligence -powered natural language processing tools facilitate meaningful discussions between students and virtual assistants or chatbots by encouraging critical thinking through contextually relevant responses (Barsoun et al., 2022; Cotton et al., 2023; Goda et al., 2014; Hapsari & Wu, 2022). Ruiz-Rojas et al. (2024) emphasize that generative artificial intelligence tools can promote critical thinking skills:

- ChatGPT is a natural language processing tool that can produce consistent and contextual responses to user queries. ChatGPT has been used as a virtual moderator in online discussions, providing students with different perspectives and encouraging critical discussion (Pavlik, 2023).
- Canva, on the other hand, is an online platform that enables collaborative creation of visual resources such as mind maps, presentations, and graphics. Canva has been used for group projects where students can work together to visualize concepts and educational strategies. This tool promotes teamwork and creativity, which are necessary for developing collaborative and critical thinking skills (Ruiz-Rojas et al., 2024).

- Chat PDF is a tool that allows students to interact with PDF documents through natural conversations. This tool facilitates the exploration and analysis of complex documents, allowing students to ask questions and receive contextual responses (Yu et al., 2023). This can have positive effects on students' critical thinking skills.

It is also possible to come across variable results regarding the effects of artificial intelligence on critical thinking skills. Because Aymen and Zakarya (2014) state that students' use of artificial intelligence has both positive and negative results on critical thinking skills. In cases where students have the necessary critical thinking skills, using artificial intelligence broadens their perspectives and can further improve this by encountering new situations where they can apply their analytical skills. On the other hand, the result is negative for students who do not have sufficient critical thinking skills, because artificial intelligence only makes them more dependent in this case and makes them less critical thinkers as it greatly impairs their ability to evaluate and analyze the information presented to them. Although the benefits of artificial intelligence in developing critical thinking skills are clear, there are also important limitations that should be noted. One of the primary concerns is that generative artificial intelligence systems limit a person's ability to develop different perspectives (Darwin et al., 2023). It is thought that algorithmic biases that occur in social media and other environments can unintentionally narrow the range of analytical results and thus limit the scope of critical analysis (Sasahara et al., 2021). This limitation is due to the lack of personalization of artificial intelligence algorithms. It is also emphasized that the inherent limitations of artificial intelligence in understanding nuances such as emotional subtleties can lead to incomplete or erroneous analyses (Heimerl et al., 2022). These limitations require a balanced approach that includes human control to ensure both reliability and objectivity; in this way, it will be possible to avoid situations that may negatively affect critical thinking (Zhai vd., 2024).

Creativity and Generative Artificial Intelligence

Creativity is a fundamental 21st-century skill taught globally in educational systems. Similarly, artificial intelligence significantly impacts many areas, such as education (Marrone et al., 2022). Generative artificial intelligence-based teaching systems can create teaching situations that encourage students' interest in learning and innovative awareness, stimulate students' imagination and creativity, and are conducive to open-mindedness that is not limited by the limitations of traditional thinking (Li et al., 2024). Indeed, studies have shown that generative artificial intelligence-supported tools such as ChatGPT are effective in developing students' creative thinking and critical thinking skills (Yılmaz and Karaoğlan Yılmaz, 2023). Additionally, research has suggested that artificial intelligence technologies play a supporting role in developing creativity-related skills such as curiosity, perseverance, persistence, and mindfulness (Belpaeme et al., 2018; Gordon et al., 2015). Generative artificial intelligence-supported tools offer many advantages to unleash students' creative thinking potential (Mhlanga, 2023; Sallam, 2023):

- Generative artificial intelligence powered tools offer new ideas and perspectives that teachers and students can integrate into their work. They have the capacity to generate diverse and original responses to questions and challenges, thus helping teachers and students nurture their creative potential.
- Generative artificial intelligence powered tools can facilitate interactive learning and dialogue, encouraging the development of creative thinking. Users can ask questions, receive unpredictable answers, and stimulate their thinking through interactions with the model.
- Generative artificial intelligence powered tools can be customized to meet students' individual needs, enabling personalized support and guidance in developing their creative skills.
- Through Generative artificial intelligence powered tools, students can experiment with various ideas and concepts, test them in practice, and receive feedback. This allows them to develop their creative thinking and explore innovative approaches to teaching.

As can be seen, artificial intelligence-powered education focuses on encouraging students' creative thinking, discovering their potential, and developing students' lifelong learning qualities (Liv d., 2024), providing students with many advantages that can help them develop their creative thinking skills. On the other hand, research advocates a cautious approach to integrating artificial intelligence into creative education. While some studies show that various artificial intelligence tools make significant contributions to the development of creativity (Diamond, 2013; Rudolph et al., 2023), others make negative statements about the use of artificial intelligence, arguing that over-reliance on content generated by Chatbots and ChatGPTs may overshadow creativity skills in students (Kcoli, 2023). The capacity of artificial intelligence to generate “new” ideas is a controversial issue because its knowledge is based on pre-existing data, raising ethical issues related to intellectual property and plagiarism (Habib et al., 2024).

Collaboration and Generative Artificial Intelligence

In today's fast-paced work environment, collaboration is essential for success. However, coordinating efforts across teams can be challenging (Ruiz-Rojas et al., 2024). This is where generative artificial intelligence tools come into play (Michel-Villarreal et al., 2023). These innovative tools leverage generative artificial intelligence algorithms to facilitate collaboration and streamline workflow processes. Studies have shown that generative artificial intelligence tools can facilitate effective communication and encourage collaboration, which can lead to better learning outcomes (Ruiz-Rojas et al., 2024). Generative artificial intelligence supported instruction is conducive to developing students' practical skills, team problem-solving skills, and collaborative skills, which is conducive to students' overall development (Li et al., 2024). Generative artificial intelligence can help collaboration in the following ways (Luckin & Holmes, 2016):

- Adaptive group formation uses artificial intelligence techniques and information about individual participants to create the most appropriate group for a specific collaborative task. The goal is to design a group of students with similar cognitive levels and similar interests, or to create a group where participants bring different but complementary knowledge and skills.
- Artificial intelligence-based expert support provides interactive support to collaborating students. Expert support can be used to train systems to recognize when students have trouble understanding the concepts they share with each other or to provide targeted support at the right time. It also has the ability to show students (and their teachers) how well an individual contributes to group work. This is a difficult activity to isolate and evaluate.
- Intelligent virtual agents included in the collaborative process can be an expert participant participating in online student interaction, a virtual peer, or someone the participants can teach themselves. For example, the artificial student may have intentional misunderstandings or provide alternative perspectives to stimulate productive discussion or thought.
- With a large number of students working in multiple collaborative groups, it may be impossible for one person to understand the sheer volume of data that participants generate in their discussions. The intelligent moderator uses artificial intelligence techniques such as machine learning and shallow text processing to analyze and summarize discussions, allowing a human instructor to guide students toward productive collaboration. For example, the system can provide alerts to inform human instructors about important events that may require their intervention or support (such as students straying from the topic or repeating misunderstandings).

While the integration of artificial intelligence into collaborative learning is transformative, it also presents its own challenges. Educators must be equipped to effectively incorporate artificial intelligence tools into their teaching methodologies, and students need guidance to navigate artificial intelligence - enabled learning environments.

Communication and Generative Artificial Intelligence

Communication is an important factor for student success (Ford and Riley, 2003). Generative artificial intelligence is increasingly being used as a promising tool, especially in improving students' communication skills. Generative artificial intelligence offers many potentials for personalized, interactive, and adaptive learning experiences that cater to students' individual needs and preferences (Rusmiyanto et al., 2023). Opportunities for the impact of artificial intelligence on communication can be summarized as follows:

- Students who want to improve their communication skills can interact with artificial intelligence-based tools. These tools can simulate communication processes, provide language correction, and provide vocabulary and grammar help. They can also engage students in dialogue, enable them to express their thoughts and ideas effectively, and improve their communication skills (Michel-Villarreal et al., 2023).
- Generative artificial intelligence can provide personalized learning experiences by tailoring educational content to students' individual needs. This personalization can increase engagement and effectiveness because students receive customized support that matches their skill level and learning style (Agrawal et al., 2024).
- Generative artificial intelligence-powered chatbots and virtual assistants can instantly assess communication skills such as speech patterns and language use, providing rapid feedback and practice (Zhou, 2024).
- The ability of artificial intelligence platforms to provide education to a large number of users simultaneously and to provide high-quality communication education to diverse and geographically dispersed audiences is important for communication education of educational institutions and individuals (Agrawal et al., 2024).
- Generative artificial intelligence platforms can enable students and artificial intelligence virtual characters to engage in natural conversational interactions, simulate various application scenarios for education, and develop students' oral communication and English application skills (Zhou, 2024).

Although generative artificial intelligence systems have been positively recognized for improving the quantity and quality of communication, providing just-in-time, personalized support in large-scale environments, and improving the sense of connection, it is a fact that they bring with them a number of concerns. The first of these concerns is stated as surveillance. Accordingly, although artificial intelligence can strengthen the communication bond, students are uncomfortable with the measurement of their unconscious behaviors, such as eye tracking or facial expression analysis. Another uncomfortable situation is responsibility. Although students believe that artificial intelligence systems will increase the quantity and quality of instructional communication, they are concerned that artificial intelligence may provide unreliable answers and negatively affect their grades (Seo et al., 2021). Another concern is that artificial intelligence will lead to a decrease in human interaction. Effective communication training often relies on interpersonal interactions that artificial intelligence systems cannot fully replicate. The lack of human interaction can limit the development of nuanced communication skills and emotional intelligence (Agrawal et al., 2024). The ease with which generative artificial intelligence tools provide rapid answers may deter students from engaging in comprehensive research and generating insights (Zhai, 2024).

CONCLUSION

The opportunities and possible concerns offered by generative artificial intelligence in education are expressed; the effects of these technologies on 4C skills are included. Based on the results obtained, it can be said that artificial intelligence has led to significant changes in the field of education as well as in many other fields today and will continue to do so in the future. For this reason, it is necessary to reconsider the environments, methods, and each element addressed within the scope of education at every point where educational environments and generative artificial intelligence intersect with education. 4C skills are skills that are very important and valuable in both business and social life in today's world. The development of 4C skills in learning environments has been emphasized in many studies. It is an undeniable fact that generative artificial intelligence can help teachers in this sense and ease the burden of teachers. Artificial intelligence offers students personalized learning opportunities, activates critical thinking skills with the help of discussion environments, and improves their creativity by providing them with different perspectives. In this process, it can strengthen both the collaboration process and students' communication skills. However, it is important to focus on the limitations and concerns brought by generative artificial intelligence and to take measures against these concerns. It is seen that there are still significant gaps in the literature and practice in this sense. In summary, the implications of this section for teachers and education stakeholders are as follows:

- In order to transfer artificial intelligence technologies to the classroom environment, appropriate strategies need to be created, the infrastructure needs to be organized, and teachers need to be informed about this issue.
- Teachers should inform students about the possible risks of artificial intelligence technologies (algorithmic biases, overconfidence, etc.). In addition, training should be provided on strategies that students can use to demonstrate a balanced approach to the use of artificial intelligence tools.
- The ethical side of artificial intelligence technology, which covers different aspects of education, is still a controversial issue. Supervision and regulation need to be carried out, and different mechanisms need to be put into effect in this regard.

In addition, more studies need to be conducted in the literature to determine the effects of generative artificial intelligence technologies on 4C skills. Thus, clear results can be achieved by minimizing differences of opinion.

REFERENCES

Abbott, R., & Rothman, E. (2023). Disrupting creativity: Copyright law in the age of generative artificial intelligence. *Fla. L. Rev., 75*.

Agrawal, L., Lanjewar, P., Deshpande, S., Jawarkar, P., Gaur, V., & Dive, A. (2024). The Impact of AI on Communication Skills Training Opportunities and Challenges. *Nanotechnology Perceptions*, •••, 1167–1173.

AlAli, R., & Wardat, Y. (2024). Opportunities and Challenges of Integrating Generative Artificial Intelligence in Education. *International Journal of Religion*, 5(7), 784–793. DOI: 10.61707/8y29gv34

Alam, A. (2022). Employing adaptive learning and intelligent tutoring robots for virtual classrooms and smart campuses: Reforming education in the age of artificial intelligence. *Advanced Computing and Intelligent Technologies: Proceedings of ICACIT 2022*. Singapore: Springer Nature. https://doi.org/DOI: 10.1007/978-981-19-2980-9_32

Almeida, F., & Simoes, J. (2019). The role of serious games, gamification, and industry 4.0 tools in the education 4.0 paradigm. *Contemporary Educational Technology*, 10(2), 120–136. DOI: 10.30935/cet.554469

Angeli, C., & Valanides, N. (2020). Developing young children's computational thinking with educational robotics: An interaction effect between gender and scaffolding strategy. *Computers in Human Behavior*, 105, 105954. DOI: 10.1016/j.chb.2019.03.018

Aymen, D. I. F., & Zakarya, B. (2024). *The Influence of Artificial Intelligence on Students' Critical Thinking* (Doctoral dissertation), University center of Abdalhafid Boussouf-MILA.

Baker, R. S., & Hawn, A. (2022). Algorithmic bias in education. *International Journal of Artificial Intelligence in Education*, 32(4), 1–41. DOI: 10.1007/s40593-021-00285-9

Bansal, G., Mitchell, A., & Li, D. (2024). A Panel Report on Higher Education in the Age of AI from the Perspective of Academic Leaders in the Midwest US. *Communications of the Association for Information Systems*, 54(1), 360–375. DOI: 10.17705/1CAIS.05413

Barana, A., Marchisio, M., & Roman, F. (2023). Fostering Problem Solving and Critical Thinking in Mathematics through Generative Artificial Intelligence. *20th International Conference on Cognition and Exploratory Learning in Digital Age (CELDA 2023).*

Barsoun, S. S., Elnagar, M. S., & Awad, B. M. (2022). The effectiveness of using a cognitive style-based Chatbot in developing science concepts and critical thinking skills among preparatory school pupils. *European Scientific Journal*, 18(2), 52. DOI: 10.19044/esj.2022.v18n22p52

Baskoro, G., Mariza, I., & Sutapa, I. N. (2023). Innovation to Improve Critical Thinking Skills in the Generation Z using Peeragogy as a Learning Approach and Artificial Intelligence (AI) as a Tool. *Jurnal Teknik Industri: Jurnal Keilmuan dan Aplikasi Teknik Industri, 25*(2), 121-130.

Belpaeme, T., James, K., Aditi, R., Brian, S., & Fumihide, T. (2018). Social robots for education: A review. *Science Robotics*, 3(21), 1–9. DOI: 10.1126/scirobotics.aat5954 PMID: 33141719

Brata, D. P. N., Utomo, E. S., & Farhan, A. (2023). Developing Students' 4C Skills (Communication, Collaboration, Creativity, Critical Thinking): Psychomotor Assessment Techniques in Visionary Schools. *QALAMUNA: Jurnal Pendidikan, Sosial, dan Agama, 15*(2), 1127-1138. https://doi.org/. DOI: 10.37680/qalamuna.v15i2.3900

Britannica (2024). Çevrimiçi ansiklopedi. 10 Haziran 2024 tarihinde https://www.britannica.com/technology/artificial-intelligence adresinden alınmıştır.

Buçinca, Z., Malaya, M. B., & Gajos, K. Z. (2021). To trust or to think: cognitive forcing functions can reduce overreliance on AI in AI-assisted decision-making. *Proceedings of the ACM on Human-computer Interaction, 5*(CSCW1), 1-21. https://doi.org/DOI: 10.1145/3449287

Cantas, Ç., Soyer, C., & Batur, Ö. (2024). Examination of Undergraduate Students' Artificial Intelligence Anxiety, Multidimensional 21st Century Skills, and Lifelong Learning Levels in Terms of Various Variables. *Turkish Online Journal of Educational Technology-TOJET*, 23(3), 29–53.

Capraro, V., Lentsch, A., Acemoglu, D., Akgun, S., Akhmedova, A., Bilancini, E., Bonnefon, J.-F., Brañas-Garza, P., Butera, L., Douglas, K. M., Everett, J. A. C., Gigerenzer, G., Greenhow, C., Hashimoto, D. A., Holt-Lunstad, J., Jetten, J., Johnson, S., Kunz, W. H., Longoni, C., & Viale, R. (2024). The impact of generative artificial intelligence on socioeconomic inequalities and policy making. *PNAS Nexus*, 3(6), pgae191. DOI: 10.1093/pnasnexus/pgae191 PMID: 38864006

Carceller, A. T. (2024). The ARTificial Revolution: Challenges for Redefining Art Education in the Paradigm of Generative Artificial Intelligence. *Digital Education Review*, 45(45), 84–90. DOI: 10.1344/der.2024.45.84-90

Chen, S. Y., Lai, Y. H., & Lin, Y. S. (2020). Research on head-mounted virtual reality and computational thinking experiments to improve the learning effect of AIoT maker course: Case of earthquake relief scenes. *Frontiers in Psychology*, 11, 1164. DOI: 10.3389/fpsyg.2020.01164 PMID: 32581963

Chiruguru, S. B. (2020). The essential skills of 21st century classroom (4Cs). *Project: The role of 4Cs (Critical Thinking, Creative Thinking, Collaboration and Communication) in the 21st Century Classroom.*

Cooper, G., & Tang, K. S. (2024). Pixels and Pedagogy: Examining Science Education Imagery by Generative Artificial Intelligence. *Journal of Science Education and Technology*, 33(4), 1–13. DOI: 10.1007/s10956-024-10104-0

Cotton, D. R. E., Cotton, P. A., & Shipway, J. R. (2024). Chatting and cheating: Ensuring academic integrity in the era of ChatGPT. *Innovations in Education and Teaching International*, 61(2), 228–239. DOI: 10.1080/14703297.2023.2190148

Cox, G. M. (2024). Artificial Intelligence and the Aims of Education: Makers, Managers, or Inforgs? *Studies in Philosophy and Education*, 43(1), 15–30. DOI: 10.1007/s11217-023-09907-2

Darwin, R. D., Mukminatien, N., Suryati, N., & Laksmi, E. D. (2023). Critical thinking in the AI era: An exploration of EFL students' perceptions, benefits, and limitations. *Cogent Education*, 11(1), 2290342. Advance online publication. DOI: 10.1080/2331186X.2023.2290342

Dergaa, I., Chamari, K., Zmijewski, P., & Saad, H. B. (2023). From human writing to artificial intelligence generated text: Examining the prospects and potential threats of chatgpt in academic writing. *Biology of Sport, 40*(2), 615–622. https://doi.org/. 2023.125623DOI: 10.5114/biolsport

Diamond, A. (2013). Executive functions. *Annual Review of Psychology*, 64(1), 135–168. DOI: 10.1146/annurev-psych-113011-143750 PMID: 23020641

Dwyer, C. P., Hogan, M. J., & Stewart, I. (2012). An evaluation of argument mapping as a method of enhancing critical thinking performance in e-learning environments. *Metacognition and Learning*, 7(3), 219–244. DOI: 10.1007/s11409-012-9092-1

Erdoğan, V. (2019). Integrating 4C skills of 21st century into 4 language skills in EFL classes. *International Journal of Education and Research*, 7(11), 113–124.

Facione, P. A. (2023). "Critical Thinking: What It Is and Why It Counts", Insight Assessment., https://insightassessment.com/iaresource/critical-thinking-what-it-is-and-why-it-counts/

Favaretto, M., De Clercq, E., & Elger, B. S. (2019). Big Data and discrimination: Perils, promises and solutions. A systematic review. *Journal of Big Data*, 6(1), 12. DOI: 10.1186/s40537-019-0177-4

Fitriati, F., Rosli, R., Iksan, Z., & Hidayat, A. (2024). Exploring challenges in preparing prospective teachers for teaching 4C skills in mathematics classroom: A school-university partnership perspectives. *Cogent Education*, 11(1), 2286812. DOI: 10.1080/2331186X.2023.2286812

Ford, J. D., & Riley, L. A. (2003). Integrating communication and engineering education: A look at curricula, courses, and support systems. *Journal of Engineering Education*, 92(4), 325–328. DOI: 10.1002/j.2168-9830.2003.tb00776.x

Fuller, M., & Barnes, N. (2024). The impact of ChatGPT on teaching and learning in higher education: Exploring the dual perspectives of participants who were students and teachers. *New Directions for Higher Education*, 2024(207), 31–46.

Goda, Y., Yamada, M., Matsukawa, H., Hata, K., & Yasunami, S. (2014). Conversation with a chatbot before an online EFL group discussion and the effects on critical thinking. *Journal of Information Systems Education*, 13(1), 1–7. DOI: 10.12937/ejsise.13.1

Goplani, V. (2024). The Emergent Role of Artificial Intelligence (AI) in Fostering Collaborative Learning Experiences. https://integranxt.com/blog/the-emergent-role-of-artificial-intelligence-ai-in-fostering-collaborative-learning-experiences/

Gordon, G., Cynthia, B., & Susan, E. (2015, March 2–5). Can children catch curiosity from a social robot? [Paper presentation]. *Tenth Annual ACM/IEEE International Conference on Human-Robot Interaction*, Portland, OR, USA.

Habib, S., Vogel, T., Anli, X., & Thorne, E. (2024). How does generative artificial intelligence impact student creativity?. *Journal of Creativity, 34*(1), 100072. https://doi.org/. 2023.100072. DOI: 10.1016/j.yjoc

Halpern, D. F. (2003). *Thought and knowledge: An introduction to critical thinking* (4th ed.). Laurence Erlbaum Associates.

Hapsari, I. P., & Wu, T. T. (2022). AI Chatbots learning model in English speaking skill: Alleviating speaking anxiety, boosting enjoyment, and fostering critical thinking. *International Conference on Innovative Technologies and Learning*, Portugal https://doi.org/DOI: 10.1007/978-3-031-15273-3_49

Haq, I. U., Anwar, A., Rehman, I. U., Asif, W., Sobnath, D., Sherazi, H. H. R., & Nasralla, M. M. (2021). Dynamic group formation with intelligent tutor collaborative learning: A novel approach for next generation collaboration. *IEEE Access : Practical Innovations, Open Solutions*, 9, 143406–143422. DOI: 10.1109/ACCESS.2021.3120557

Heimerl, A., Weitz, K., Baur, T., & André, E. (2022). Unraveling ML models of emotion with NOVA: Multi-level explainable AI for non-experts. *IEEE Transactions on Affective Computing*, 13(3), 1155–1167. DOI: 10.1109/TAFFC.2020.3043603

Heng, A., Abidin, A. Z. Z., Ng, C. J., Cheong, M. L., & Tamil, A. M. (2023). ChatGPT and clinical practice guidelines just a tap away. *The Medical Journal of Malaysia*, 78(1), 7. PMID: 36715184

Herlinawati, H., Marwa, M., Ismail, N., Liza, L. O., & Situmorang, D. D. B. (2024). The integration of 21st century skills in the curriculum of education. *Heliyon*, 10(15), e35148. DOI: 10.1016/j.heliyon.2024.e35148 PMID: 39170322

Hsu, Y. C., & Ching, Y. H. (2023). Generative artificial intelligence in education, part one: The dynamic frontier. *TechTrends*, 67(4), 603–607. DOI: 10.1007/s11528-023-00863-9

Hu, X., Liu, Y., Huang, J., & Mu, S. (2022). The Effects of Different Patterns of Group Collaborative Learning on Fourth-Grade Students' Creative Thinking in a Digital Artificial Intelligence Course. *Sustainability (Basel)*, 14(19), 12674. DOI: 10.3390/su141912674

Huang, X., & Qiao, C. (2022). Enhancing computational thinking skills through artificial intelligence education at a STEAM high school. *Science & Education*, 33(2), 383–403. DOI: 10.1007/s11191-022-00392-6

Ilgun Dibek, M., Sahin Kursad, M., & Erdogan, T. (2024). Influence of artificial intelligence tools on higher order thinking skills: A meta-analysis. *Interactive Learning Environments*, •••, 1–23. DOI: 10.1080/10494820.2024.2402028

Islam, I., & Islam, M. N. (2024). Exploring the opportunities and challenges of ChatGPT in academia. *Discover Education*, 3(1), 31. DOI: 10.1007/s44217-024-00114-w

Ivcevic, Z., & Grandinetti, M. (2024). Artificial intelligence as a tool for creativity. *Journal of Creativity*, 34(2), 100079. DOI: 10.1016/j.yjoc.2024.100079

Kamalov, F., Calonge, D. S., & Gurrib, I. (2023). New era of Artificial intelligence in education: Towards a sustainable multifaceted revolution. *Sustainability (Basel)*, 15(16), 1–27. DOI: 10.3390/su151612451

Kelly, A., Sullivan, M., & Strampel, K. (2023). Generative artificial intelligence: University student awareness, experience, and confidence in use across disciplines. *Journal of University Teaching & Learning Practice*, 20(6), 12. DOI: 10.53761/1.20.6.12

Kembara, M. D., Rozak, R. W. A., & Hadian, V. A. (2019, Mart). Based lectures to improve students' 4C (communication, collaboration, critical thinking, and creativity) skills. *International Symposium on Social Sciences, Education, and Humanities (ISSEH 2018).* Atlantis Press. DOI: 10.2991/isseh-18.2019.6

Ketelhut, D. J., Nelson, B. C., Clarke, J., & Dede, C. (2010). A multi-user virtual environment for building and assessing higher order inquiry skills in science. *British Journal of Educational Technology*, 41(1), 56–68. DOI: 10.1111/j.1467-8535.2009.01036.x

Koh, E., Zhang, L., Lee, A. V. Y., & Wang, H. (2024). Revolutionizing word clouds for teaching and learning with generative artificial intelligence: Cases from China and Singapore. *IEEE Transactions on Learning Technologies*, 17, 1416–1427. DOI: 10.1109/TLT.2024.3385009

Kooli, C. (2023). Chatbots in education and research: A critical examination of ethical implications and solutions. *Sustainability (Basel)*, 15(7), 5614. DOI: 10.3390/su15075614

Koos, S., & Wachsmann, S. (2023). Navigating the impact of ChatGPT/GPT4 on legal academic examinations: Challenges, opportunities and recommendations. *Media Iuris*, 6(2), 255–270. DOI: 10.20473/mi.v6i2.45270

Kordzadeh, N., & Ghasemaghaei, M. (2022). Algorithmic bias: Review, synthesis, and future research directions. *European Journal of Information Systems*, 31(3), 388–409. DOI: 10.1080/0960085X.2021.1927212

Kurniawan, T. T. (2021). Development of 4C-Based Hots Assessment To Improve Critical Thinking Skills in Grade 6 Students of Kudus Elementary School. [Pendidikan Dan Pengajaran]. *JURNAL PAJAR*, 5(3), 675–683. DOI: 10.33578/pjr.v5i3.8319

Law, L. (2024). Application of generative artificial intelligence (GenAI) in language teaching and learning: A scoping literature review. *Computers and Education Open*, 6, 100174. DOI: 10.1016/j.caeo.2024.100174

Li, X., Wang, S., Li, J., & Li, Z. (2024). A Study of Artificial Intelligence-Assisted Teaching on the Cultivation of Students' Creative Ability. *Applied Mathematics and Nonlinear Sciences*, 9(1), 1–18. DOI: 10.2478/amns.2023.2.01283

Lin, P. H., & Chen, S. Y. (2020). Design and evaluation of a deep learning recommendation based augmented reality system for teaching programming and computational thinking. *IEEE Access : Practical Innovations, Open Solutions*, 8, 45689–45699. DOI: 10.1109/ACCESS.2020.2977679

Luckin, R., & Holmes, W. (2016). Intelligence unleashed: An argument for AI in education. https://discovery.ucl.ac.uk/id/eprint/1475756/

Mao, J., Chen, B., & Liu, J. C. (2024). Generative artificial intelligence in education and its implications for assessment. *TechTrends*, 68(1), 58–66. DOI: 10.1007/s11528-023-00911-4

Maphoto, K. B., Sevnarayan, K., Mohale, N. E., Suliman, Z., Ntsopi, T. J., & Mokoena, D. (2024). Advancing students' academic excellence in distance education: Exploring the potential of generative AI integration to improve academic writing skills. *Open Praxis*, 16(2), 142–159. DOI: 10.55982/openpraxis.16.2.649

Marrone, R., Taddeo, V., & Hill, G. (2022). Creativity and artificial intelligence—A student perspective. *Journal of Intelligence*, 10(3), 65. DOI: 10.3390/jintelligence10030065 PMID: 36135606

Martin, K. (2019). Designing ethical algorithms. *MIS Quarterly Executive*, 18(5), 2. https://aisel.aisnet.org/misqe/vol18/iss2/5/

Martinez, D., Malyska, N., Streilein, B., Caceres, R., Campbell, W., Dagli, C., Gadepally, V., Greenfeld, K., Hall, R., King, A., Lippmann, R., Miller, B., Reynolds, D., Richardson, F., Sahin, C., Tran, A., Trepagnier, P., & Zipkin, J. (2019). *Artifcial intelligence: Short history, present developments, and future outlook*. Massachusetts Institute of Technology.

Mateus, J. C., Cappello, G., Lugo, N., & Guerrero-Pico, M. (2024). Communication Educators Facing the Arrival of Generative Artificial Intelligence: Exploration in Mexico, Peru, and Spain. *Digital Education Review*, (45), 106–114. DOI: 10.1344/der.2024.45.106-114

Michel-Villarreal, R., Vilalta-Perdomo, E., Salinas-Navarro, D. E., Thierry-Aguilera, R., & Gerardou, F. S. (2023). Challenges and opportunities of generative AI for higher education as explained by ChatGPT. *Education Sciences*, 13(9), 856. DOI: 10.3390/educsci13090856

Mikalef, P., Lemmer, K., Schaefer, C., Ylinen, M., Fjørtoft, S. O., Torvatn, H. Y., Gupta, M., & Niehaves, B. (2023). Examining how AI capabilities can foster organizational performance in public organizations. *Government Information Quarterly*, 40(2), 101797. DOI: 10.1016/j.giq.2022.101797

Mishra, P., & Mehta, R. (2017). Educators What We Get Wrong About 21st-Century Learning: Results of a Survey. *Journal of Digital Learning in Teacher Education*, 33(1), 6–19. DOI: 10.1080/21532974.2016.1242392

Morreale, Sherwyn P., Joseph M. Valenzano, and Janessa A. Bauer. (2017). Why Communication Education Is Important: A Third Study on the Centrality of the Discipline's Content and Pedagogy. *Communication Education* 66: 402–22. https://doi.org/. 1265136. DOI: 10.1080/03634523.2016

Nainggolan, O. T. P., Salim, D., Prasetiyo, A., & Marthien, V. A. (2020,). Integrating the Framework of 21st Century Learning (4C) into Creative Music Learning. *1st International Conference on Interdisciplinary Arts and Humanities.*https://doi.org/ DOI: 10.5220/0008562602340239

NEA. (2010). Preparing 21st Century Students for a Global Society: An Educator's Guide to 'The Four Cs'. Washington DC, National Education Association. www .nea.org/ tools/52217. Htm

OECD. (2018). Collaborative problem-solving. In The encyclopedia of social network analysis and mining, Vol. V. https://doi.org/DOI: 10.1007/978-1-4939-7131-2_100128

OECD. (2019). Future of Education and Skills 2030: A Series of Concept Notes. Paris: OECD Learning Compass. https://www.oecd.org/education/2030-project/teaching-and-learning/learning /learningcompass-2030/OECD_Learning_Compass_2030_Concept_Note_ Series.pdf

Oktradiksa, A., Bhakti, C. P., Kurniawan, S. J., & Rahman, F. A. (2021, Ekim). Utilization artificial intelligence to improve creativity skills in society 5.0. *Journal of Physics: Conference Series*. IOP Publishing.

Page, J., Bain, M., & Mukhlish, F. (2018). The risks of low level narrow artifcial intelligence. In 2018 IEEE international conference on intelligence and safety for robotics (ISR) (pp. 1-6). IEEE.

Park, J. S., Barber, R., Kirlik, A , & Karahalios, K. (2019). A slow algorithm improves users' assessments of the algorithm's accuracy. *Proceedings of the ACM on Human-Computer Interaction, 3*(CSCW), 1-15. DOI: 10.1145/3359204

Partnership for 21st Century Learning (P21). (2015). P21 framework definitions. http://www.p21.org/our-work/p21-framework

Passi, S., & Vorvoreanu, M. (2022). Overreliance on AI literature review. *Microsoft Research*. https://www.microsoft.com/en-us/research/uploads/prod/2022/06/Aether-Overreliance-on-AI-Review-Final-6.21.22.pdf

Pavlik, J. V. (2023). Collaborating with ChatGPT: Considering the implications of generative artificial intelligence for journalism and media education. *Journalism & mass communication educator, 78*(1), 84-93. https://doi.org/. DOI: 10.1177/10776958221149577

Preiksaitis, C., & Rose, C. (2023). Opportunities, challenges, and future directions of generative artificial intelligence in medical education: Scoping review. *JMIR Medical Education*, 9, e48785. DOI: 10.2196/48785 PMID: 37862079

Purnawirawan, O., Sudana, I. M., & Harlanu, M. (2019). Assessment of 4C softskills characteristics in learning productive graphic design subject for vocational. *Journal of Vocational Career Education*, 53-60.

Qadir, J. (2023). Engineering education in the era of ChatGPT: Promise and pitfalls of generative AI for education. In *2023 IEEE Global Engineering Education Conference (EDUCON)* (pp. 1-9). IEEE. DOI: 10.1109/EDUCON54358.2023.10125121

Quinn, S., Hogan, M., Dwyer, C., Finn, P., & Fogarty, E. (2020). Development and validation of the student-educator negotiated critical thinking dispositions scale (SENCTDS). *Thinking Skills and Creativity*, 38(4), 100710–100717. DOI: 10.1016/j.tsc.2020.100710

Ramadevi, J., Sushama, C., Balaji, K., Talasila, V., Sindhwani, N., & Mukti, . (2023). AI enabled value-oriented collaborative learning: Centre for innovative education. *The Journal of High Technology Management Research*, 34(2), 100478. DOI: 10.1016/j.hitech.2023.100478

Rudolph, J., Tan, S., & Tan, S. (2023). ChatGPT: Bullshit spewer or the end of traditional assessments in higher education? *Journal of Applied Learning and Teaching*, 6(1), 342–363. DOI: 10.37074/jalt.2023.6.1.9

Ruiz-Rojas, L. I., Salvador-Ullauri, L., & Acosta-Vargas, P. (2024). Collaborative working and critical thinking: Adoption of generative artificial intelligence tools in higher education. *Sustainability (Basel)*, 16(13), 5367. DOI: 10.3390/su16135367

Rusmiyanto, R., Huriati, N., Fitriani, N., Tyas, N. K., Rofi'i, A., & Sari, M. N. (2023). The role of artificial intelligence (AI) in developing English language learner's communication skills. *Journal of Education*, 6(1), 750–757.

Santiago, C. S.Jr, Embang, S. I., Conlu, M. T. N., Acanto, R. B., Lausa, S. M., Ambojia, K. W. P., Laput, E. Y , Aperocho, M. D. B., Malabag, B. A., & Balilo, B. B.Jr. (2023). Utilization of writing assistance tools in research in selected higher learning institutions in the philippines: A text mining analysis. *International Journal of Learning. Teaching and Educational Research*, 22(11), 259–284. DOI: 10.26803/ijlter.22.11.14

Sasahara, K., Chen, W., Peng, H., Ciampaglia, G. L., Flammini, A., & Menczer, F. (2021). Social influence and unfollowing accelerate the emergence of echo chambers. *Journal of Computational Social Science*, 4(1), 381–402. DOI: 10.1007/s42001-020-00084-7

Luna Scott, C. (2015). The futures of learning 2: What kind of learning for the 21st century?.

Seo, K., Tang, J., Roll, I., Fels, S., & Yoon, D. (2021). The impact of artificial intelligence on learner–instructor interaction in online learning. *International Journal of Educational Technology in Higher Education*, 18(54), 54. Advance online publication. DOI: 10.1186/s41239-021-00292-9 PMID: 34778540

Shahzad, M. F., Xu, S., & Javed, I. (2024). ChatGPT awareness, acceptance, and adoption in higher education: The role of trust as a cornerstone. *International Journal of Educational Technology in Higher Education*, 21(1), 46. DOI: 10.1186/s41239-024-00478-x

Shanta, S., & Wells, J. G. (2022). T/E design based learning: Assessing student critical thinking and problem solving abilities. *International Journal of Technology and Design Education*, 32(1), 267–285. DOI: 10.1007/s10798-020-09608-8

Sharma, S. K., & Wang, X. (2019). Collaborative distributed Q-learning for RACH congestion minimization in cellular IoT networks. *IEEE Communications Letters*, 23(4), 600–603. DOI: 10.1109/LCOMM.2019.2896929

Shi, S. J., Li, J. W., & Zhang, R. (2024). A study on the impact of Generative Artificial Intelligence supported Situational Interactive Teaching on students' 'flow' experience and learning effectiveness—A case study of legal education in China. *Asia Pacific Journal of Education*, 44(1), 112–138. DOI: 10.1080/02188791.2024.2305161

Spector, J. M., & Ma, S. (2019). Inquiry and critical thinking skills for the next generation: From artificial intelligence back to human intelligence. *Smart Learning Environments*, 6(1), 1–11. DOI: 10.1186/s40561-019-0088-z

Susanti, E., & Arista, A. (2019). Analisa tingkat pengetahuan guru terhadap kompetensi 4C. *Seminar Nasional Ilmu Sosial dan Teknologi (SNISTEK)*, 2, 73-78.

Susilo, S. (2015). Curriculum of EFL Teacher Education and Indonesian Qualification Framework: A Blip of the Future Direction. The dynamics of the journal. *Science*, 15(1), 11–24.

Tigas Tri Kurniawan, Santoso, S. U. (2021). Developing 4c - based hots assessment to improve students' critical thinking skills at grade vi elementary schools in kudus districts. *Jurnal PAJAR. 5*, 675-683. https://doi.org/ DOI: 10.33578/pjr.v5i3.8319

Trilling, B., & Fadel, C. (2009). *21st Century Skills: Learning for Life in Our Times*. John Wiley & Sons.

Voogt, J., & Roblin, N. P. (2012). A comparative analysis of international frameworks for 21st century competences: Implications for national curriculum policies. *Journal of Curriculum Studies*, 44(3), 299–321. DOI: 10.1080/00220272.2012.668938

Ward, D., Loshbaugh, H. G., Gibbs, A. L., Henkel, T., Siering, G., Williamson, J., & Kayser, M. (2024). How Universities Can Move Forward With Generative AI in Teaching and Learning. *Change*, 56(1), 47–54. DOI: 10.1080/00091383.2024.2297635

Xia, Q., Weng, X., Ouyang, F., Lin, T. J., & Chiu, T. K. (2024). A scoping review on how generative artificial intelligence transforms assessment in higher education. *International Journal of Educational Technology in Higher Education*, 21(1), 40. DOI: 10.1186/s41239-024-00468-z

Yan, W., Nakajima, T., & Sawada, R. (2024). Benefits and Challenges of Collaboration between Students and Conversational Generative Artificial Intelligence in Programming Learning: An Empirical Case Study. *Education Sciences*, 14(4), 433. DOI: 10.3390/educsci14040433

Ye, P., & Xu, X. (2023). A case study of interdisciplinary thematic learning curriculum to cultivate "4C skills". *Frontiers in Psychology*, 14, 1080811. DOI: 10.3389/fpsyg.2023.1080811 PMID: 36960001

Yilmaz, R., & Yilmaz, F. G. K. (2023). The effect of generative artificial intelligence (AI)-based tool use on students' computational thinking skills, programming self-efficacy and motivation. *Computers and Education: Artificial Intelligence*, 4, 100147. DOI: 10.1016/j.caeai.2023.100147

Yu, H., & Guo, Y. (2023, June). Generative artificial intelligence empowers educational reform: Current status, issues, and prospects. [). Frontiers Media SA.]. *Frontiers in Education*, 8, 1183162. DOI: 10.3389/feduc.2023.1183162

Yu, P., Mulli, J., Syed, Z. A. S., & Umme, L. (Eds.). (2023). *Facilitating Global Collaboration and Knowledge Sharing in Higher Education with Generative AI*. IGI Global, ABD.

Zhai, C., Wibowo, S., & Li, L. D. (2024). The effects of over-reliance on AI dialogue systems on students' cognitive abilities: A systematic review. *Smart Learning Environments*, 11(1), 28. DOI: 10.1186/s40561-024-00316-7

Zhou, P. (2024). Real time feedback and E-learning intelligent entertainment experience in computer English communication based on deep learning. *Entertainment Computing*, 100752, 100752. Advance online publication. DOI: 10.1016/j.entcom.2024.100752

Zhu, X. (2015, March). Machine teaching: An inverse problem to machine learning and an approach toward optimal education. In *Proceedings of the AAAI conference on artificial intelligence*. DOI: 10.1609/aaai.v29i1.9761

ADDITIONAL READING

Bakhshandeh, B. (2024). *The Impact of the Current 4Cs Skills Gap in Organizations: Using Emotional Intelligence to Develop Competencies*. CRC Press. DOI: 10.4324/9781003462316

Celik, I., Gedrimiene, E., Siklander, S., & Muukkonen, H. (2024). The affordances of artificial intelligence-based tools for supporting 21st-century skills: A systematic review of empirical research in higher education. *Australasian Journal of Educational Technology*, 40(3), 19–38. DOI: 10.14742/ajet.9069

Guerra, E. (2024). The contribution of critical thinking to STEM disciplines at the time of generative intelligence. *STEM Education*, 4(1), 71–81. DOI: 10.3934/steme.2024005

Houssaini, M. S., Aboutajeddine, A., Toughrai, I., & Ibrahimi, A. (2024). Development of a design course for medical curriculum: Using design thinking as an instructional design method empowered by constructive alignment and generative AI. *Thinking Skills and Creativity*, 52, 101491. DOI: 10.1016/j.tsc.2024.101491

KEY TERMS AND DEFINITIONS

4C Learning Skills: The essential competencies of critical thinking, creativity, collaboration, and communication required for success in the 21st century.

Algorithmic Bias: An unintended bias in AI algorithms that can lead to unfair or unbalanced outcomes, often due to imbalanced training data or biased design.

Artificial Intelligence (AI): The capability of machines to perform tasks that typically require human intelligence, such as learning, problem-solving, and adapting to new information.

Collaborative Learning: An educational approach where students work together to solve problems or complete tasks, often enhanced by AI tools that facilitate communication and teamwork.

Critical Thinking: The ability to objectively analyze information and evaluate evidence before forming a conclusion, crucial in AI-supported learning environments.

Generative AI: A type of artificial intelligence that can create new content, such as text, images, or audio, based on the data it has been trained on.

Natural Language Processing (NLP): An AI capability that allows machines to understand, interpret, and respond to human language, used in tools like chatbots and virtual assistants in education.

Personalized Learning: Tailoring educational content to meet the unique needs and learning styles of individual students, often facilitated by AI-driven analytics.

Self-Regulated Learning: A learning process where students take control of their own learning pace and goals, which can be supported by AI-driven feedback and tools.

Virtual Assistant: An AI-powered tool that provides real-time support and guidance to students, helping them with information retrieval and learning tasks.

Chapter 12
Transforming Hybrid Service-Learning With Generative AI: The LivePBL Ada-Rob Communication Skills Design Approach

Ying Liu
London School of Science and Technology, UK

Joy Cyprian Dsouza
London School of Science and Technology, UK

Yuanyuan Li
Capital Normal University, China

Ting Zhao
Beijing Youth and Politics Vocational College, China

ABSTRACT

This chapter introduces the Ada-Rob Skill Communication Design Approach, an innovative framework leveraging generative AI to address communication challenges in service-learning environments. As traditional pedagogies struggle to engage effectively with the social, professional, and civic complexities of real-world applications, the Ada-Rob approach enhances communication through two key components: 'Ada,' which supports adaptive and personalized learning, and 'Rob,' which emphasizes role-based, structured interactions. In this framework, "skill communication" refers to expertise-specific interactions enabled by structured

DOI: 10.4018/979-8-3693-7220-3.ch012

collaboration, while "communication skill" encompasses general communicative abilities. The Ada-Rob approach provides a flexible, scalable solution that uses generative AI to foster dynamic and collaborative learning experiences, balancing structured communication with individualized learning pathways.

INTRODUCTION

In recent years, research and development in Generative AI (Gen AI) have rapidly advanced, especially in its applications for education (Hwang & Chen, 2023). Gen AI represents a new type of AI technology, including models like the series of OpenAI's ChatGPT (Generative Pre-trained Transformer) (OpenAI, 2023), capable of generating novel content, ideas, or solutions with user-interactive natural language interfaces. Unlike traditional AI, these tools are empowered through large language models (LLMs). They interact with users in a more intuitive manner, yet require minimal coding effort to develop applications, making them more widely accessible and adaptable in applicational contexts. In education, Gen AI is seemingly emerging as a highly disruptive tool (Păvăloaia & Necula, 2023). UNESCO mandate calls for a human-centred approach to AI with an AI competency framework for students (UNESCO, 2024a) and teachers (UNESCO, 2024b). As UNESCO (2024c) reported, personalised tutoring systems leverage Gen AI to provide individualised instruction that adapts to students' learning paces and styles. Content creation tools use Gen AI to generate customised learning materials, potentially saving educators time. Automated feedback platforms use Gen AI to provide instant assignment feedback, seemingly enhancing learning speed but risking inaccuracies and over-reliance on computerised assessments.

This chapter is concerned with how to critically explore the potential of Gen AI through design for "service-learning". Service-learning began in the early 20th century with John Dewey's idea of learning through real-world experiences (Jacoby, 1996). It is a structured learning experience that involves students engaging in service to meet community-identified needs while connecting these experiences to academic coursework. Today, service-learning even expanded into K-12 education (Schwartz & Meuers, 2024), emphasising civic engagement and critical thinking, e.g.:

- Addressing global issues, e.g., blending academic learning with professional and community services,
- Fostering empathy and leadership, and
- Enhancing learning through active involvement in service activities, such as pre-service teachers in schools or social workers in rural communities.

However, as to be argued, the full potential of service-learning is often unscalable (Rodríguez-Zurita et al., 2024) because of many remaining critical issues.

One of such issues concerns developing countries. Developing countries face barriers (Verger et al., 2014) that hinder effective communication (Buff et al., 2015; Carr et al., 2021; Corbett & Kendall, 1998) in developing service-learning. The context of communication has made it increasingly necessary to explore how technology and intentional design can leverage the context to improve communication effectiveness. Particularly in the post-era of the COVID-19 pandemic responding to global challenges, the evolving landscape of service-learning demands innovative hybrid communication approaches (Alstete et al., 2023) that link academic curriculums with real-world community engagement. Another central argument in this chapter is that service-learning still needs a methodology for human-centric communication. This is also due to the lack of intelligent methods of effectively connecting

- Academic knowledge with real-world applications, and
- Social learning experiences and collaborative co-learning design for the projects.

This is where Gen AI can play a vital role, acting as an explorer, enabler, facilitator, and more, again, within various communication contexts.

The research being reported in this chapter began in China. It is based on the project called LivePBL (Linking Vocal Education through Project-Based Learning). LivePBL emerged during the COVID-19 emergency. It was a pioneering initiative to connect teachers, parents, and children through service-learning. Initially launched as an online platform for training digital literacy for teachers, families, and children (Wang et al., 2020), LivePBL established and facilitated hybrid learning environments that bridged academic content with community engagement (Liu et al., 2022). This approach was especially critical during the pandemic, allowing pre-service teacher students (Zhou et al., 2023) to continue professional development while directly engaging with local communities. As we transitioned into the post-COVID-19 era, the educational landscape faces the dual challenges of converging classroom-based education and community-based learning with social practices, as well as tackling schools' inequalities while fostering equity in diversity (since local communities are diverse (Hong et al., 2024).

In China, one of the most distinctive challenges in service-learning still is the recent educational reform called the "Double Reduction" policy (Li & He, 2023). The policy aims to shift learning away from "learning for the exam only". The policy sets a reduction in homework and promotes more private tutoring. To achieve this, many critical changes must be made; additional responsibilities must be placed on teachers. Teachers must redesign, plan, and manage lessons during and after school hours. Teachers have a vast academic burden on students. Having been more involved in their children's off-classroom education, teachers must understand what and how to engage more significantly with community-based learning initiatives. To engage with social or civic organisations, it is crucial to enhance communication among schools, educators, students, and parents in social (Poole, 2021; Yan, 2022). It became increasingly evident through our research that, enhancing learning within service contexts required more than just connecting participants. Service-learning needs better and more effective design methods for teachers to understand communication.

Although the research is set in China, to a greater extent, developing countries face similar critical situations. For example, characterised by economic challenges, rapid urbanisation, and resource constraints, developing countries depend on scheduled visits where students travel to communities for specific projects and rely on face-to-face interaction, direct mentorship, and in-person in-field collaboration. Their communication models focus on building relationships through physical presence and observation. Therefore, the learning has severe barriers:

- Difficulty in reaching communities;
- Limited access to expertise;
- Time constraints due to infrequent visits; and
- Language, cultural, and ethical barriers that complicate communication.

These barriers restrict an academic institution's ability to provide consistent, scalable support and mentorship, limiting opportunities for growth and development. By incorporating Gen AI in hybrid communication, these traditional service models can be expanded, ensuring more frequent, accessible, and scalable interactions while still retaining the value of in-person engagements when necessary. In response to the needs identified above, this chapter innovates and establishes a structured design approach named "Ada-Rob Skill Communication," where Ada-Rob signifies "Adaptive" and "Role-Based." The chapter demonstrates how the approach facilitates essential communication by using ChatGPT (a Gen AI tool). Before presenting this design framework, it is necessary to define the disciplinary scope and emphasise the intersections of key research areas that underpin the chapter's contributions.

On Methodology: Structured Design Approach for Service-Learning

In service-learning, "design" is intentionally planning and structuring learning experiences and integrating academic content with community service. Effective design in service-learning incorporates critical elements such as goal setting and reflection; to ensure learning outcomes, the design aligns with educational curriculums (Resch & Schrittesser, 2023). Hence, design in service-learning is not just about the logistics of implementing projects (Bringle & Hatcher, 1999). Here, the focus is on constructing a design approach that guides the stakeholders through cycles of action and reflection, enabling them to have more and better communicative opportunities to develop skills which benefit all.

On Applications: The Use of Soft Gen AI Tools

Gen AI methodologies can be regarded as Hard or Soft. Hard Gen AI (H-Gen-AI) emphasises automation and deterministic outcomes through algorithms and deep learning, suitable for areas like robotics and predictive analytics. In contrast, Soft Gen AI (S-Gen-AI) adopts a human-centred, adaptive approach, incorporating human input to balance AI's capabilities with creativity, ethics, and decision-making. The research being reported in this chapter prioritises S-Gen-AI to enhance communication in hybrid service-learning environments. The Ada-Rob approach aims to enhance Gen AI support rather than replace communication regarding human interaction.

Two Sides of the Same Coin: Adaptive and Role-Based Communication

A long-standing theoretical gap in service-learning is understanding where and how learning occurs (Eyler & Giles, 1999). Yet, service-learning must happen within communication among collaborative stakeholders' teamwork that provides community services (Zainuri & Huda, 2023). "Role-based service" is one side of service-learning communication, focusing on roles that bridge academic learning and community service, including educators, students, mentors, and community partners. The success of skill development relies on role-based collaborative efforts. Conversely, "adaptive learning" personalises learning utilising S-Gen-AI and facilitates contexts for skill exchange among participants, enhancing both learning and service outcomes.

Use Cases for Skill Communication

To demonstrate the potential of the Ada-Rob approach, use cases are designed for skill development. Moreover, it is essential to equip students with 21st-century skills for addressing complex challenges. Sustainable skill development is crucial in a rapidly evolving world. With advancements in technology and experiential learning models, digital engagement offers many opportunities to integrate academic learning with real-world experiences seamlessly. However, in developing countries, hybrid service-learning encounters significant obstacles, as previously noted, which hinder the full potential of this approach. Many schools need more support for service-learning. Cultural resistance and limited awareness among educators can restrict progress (Cornet et al., 2024).

However, despite the obstacles mentioned above, the real barrier lies in pedagogies that are not keeping pace with the local rapid economic and technological advancements. As argued here, the barrier lies in the lack of effective hybrid communication that integrates digital and in-person interactions.

As previously introduced, the Ada-Rob approach emphasises dynamic interaction between participants and learning contexts (Doyle et al., 2024), focusing on "skill communication" rather than traditional "communication skills". More specifically, the chapter will demonstrate how the Ada-Rob approach can be applied to developing essential 21st-century skills:

1. Critical thinking,
2. Problem-solving,
3. Independent learning,
4. Active participation in research, and
5. Reflective practice.

Skill communication involves the processes and methods used to teach, transfer, and adapt skills in educational and training contexts. This makes using a S-Gen-AI tool in communication contexts in effective skill exchange through teaching techniques, demonstrations, and guidance. Unlike generic communication skills (Mohammed & Ozdamli, 2024), which cover general abilities (McNatt, 2020) like speaking and listening, skill communication targets the responsive adaptation of pedagogies to support skill development. Arguably, without effective skill communication, skill development remains restricted, limiting, e.g.,

- The use of S-Gen-AI to foster professional and social engagement during skills conveyed, learned, and applied;
- The use of S-Gen-AI to tailor the necessary processes to enable transferring skills; and therefore,
- The overall skill developmental opportunities for collaboration and stakeholders' relationship-building.

Scalability and Ethics

The Ada-Rob approach must also address Gen AI ethics (Hagendorff, 2024). Gen AI ethics is one of the most complex and concerned areas, shaped by extensively diverse research directions, including ethical frameworks like deontology (rights-based) and utilitarianism (outcome-based). Cultural perspectives on Gen AI vary, with developed countries emphasising individual rights and transparency while developing countries view the ethics with prioritised collectivism. Gen AI ethics in service-learning is foremost domain-sensitive: in healthcare, privacy is critical for patient data; in commerce, transparency in algorithmic decisions may be prioritised over privacy. In education, fairness and bias are vital ethical concerns. To explore a H-Gen-AI design (not S-Gen-AI), ethical issues arise from Value-Sensitive Design and Explainable AI (Sadek et al , 2023), embedding ethics into systems or regulatory efforts, from principles-based to risk-based frameworks. Studies in these areas are out of this chapter's scope.

However, it is necessary to note that, Ada-Rob embodies the principles of the S-Gen-AI, which is inherently based on a "human-in-the-loop" design (Kritikos & Iphofen, 2023). Figure 1 illustrates the Ada-Rob approach. Unlike rigid regulatory frameworks that attempt a one-size-fits-all solution, the Ada-Rob approach views ethical issues as evolving throughout a project's lifecycle. This ensures that decision-making remains grounded in the ethical responsibility of a project design. The moral impact on individual stakeholders and communities is directly collaborated on and monitored during the project design.

The potential of the Ada-Rob approach to leverage Gen AI extends far beyond the use cases designed for China. Traditional service-learning models, which rely on direct communication, reflective journaling, reporting, and scheduled field visits, face significant limitations. The Ada-Rob approach can overcome these barriers by using S-Gen-AI tools to provide continuous, role-based access, bridge communication gaps, blend digital and in-person interactions, and tailor learning experiences to meet diverse needs.

Figure 1. Ada-Rob approach

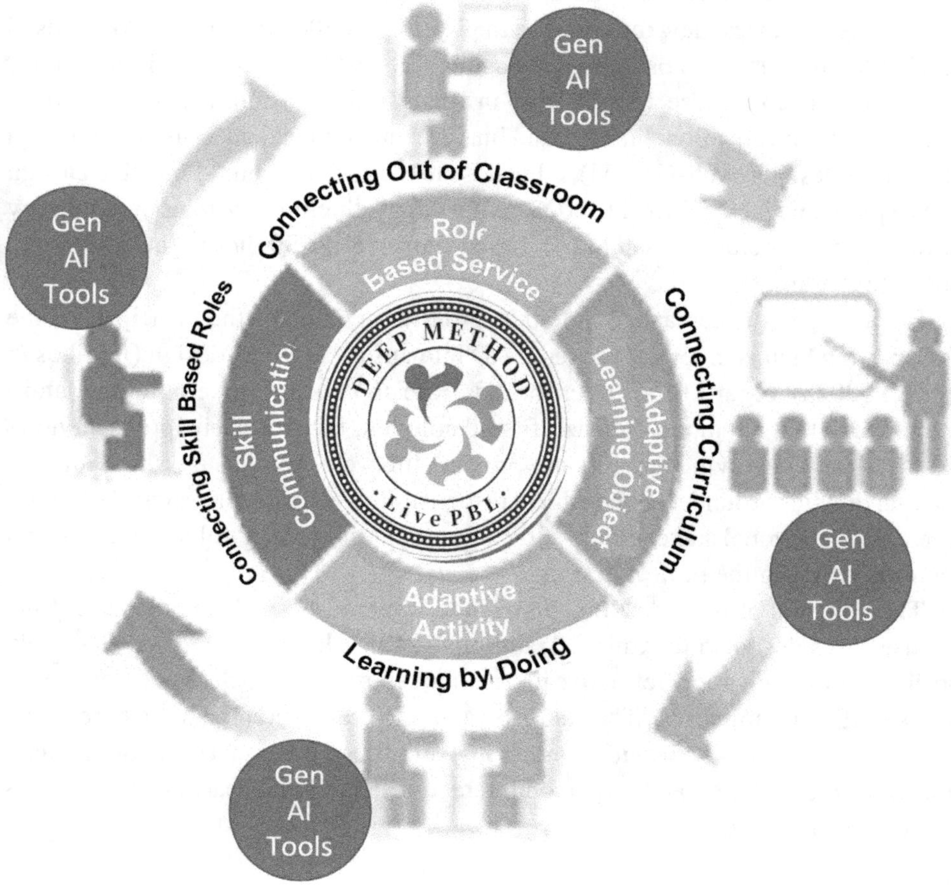

Chapter Structure

The rest of the chapter is organised as follows.

Section 2 reviews the existing literature on integrating S-Gen-AI in service-learning environment. It critiques traditional AI systems for their lack of contextual awareness and personalisation. The section lays the theoretical foundation for the Ada-Rob approach, which is presented as a more adaptive, human-centred methodology that enhances communication, collaboration, and skill development in service-learning settings.

Section 3 outlines the research methodology that the Ada-Rob approach adopts. It details how the design approach integrates role-based and adaptive communication strategies, ensuring that the Gen AI tool can be used dynamically in different communicative contexts, e.g., critical thinking and problem-solving in real-world scenarios.

Section 4 focuses on the practical implementation of the Ada-Rob approach in service-learning contexts. It discusses various use cases where the design approach has been applied, showing how it facilitates effective communication and collaboration between students, educators, and community partners.

Section 5 concludes with the significant implications of this research and development, the limitations and future research.

Figure 2. An illustration of AI history

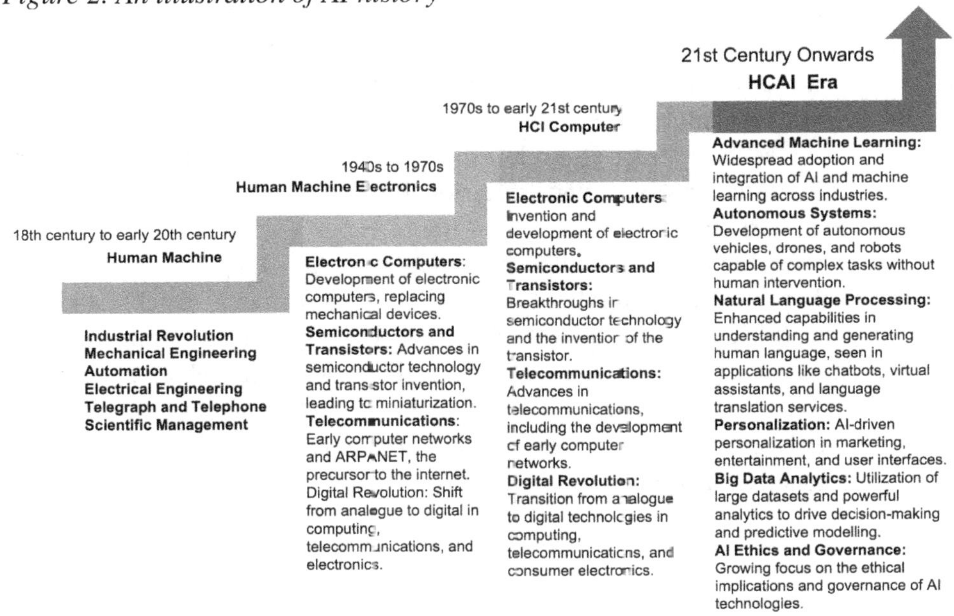

THE LITERATURE FOUNDATION FOR ADA-ROB APPROACH TO USE GEN AI

This section critically synthesises the relevant literature on applying Gen AI in service-learning. It establishes the need for the Ada-Rob approach. It grounds the approach in the appropriate conceptual framework. As Figure 2 illustrates AI history briefly, Gen-AI is a new type of AI technology. Powered by advanced models like ChatGPT, Gen-AI transformed the communication between humans and digital information tools (Sengar et al., 2024) from the following four aspects:

1) Enhanced Interaction and Accessibility. Gen AI enables more accessible communication by allowing users to interact with technology in natural language. This type of communication reduces the need for specialised knowledge to access information. It breaks down barriers by translating complex data into understandable insights, making information accessible to a broader audience. Allowing individuals to design and use technology without technical expertise or sophisticated tools as prerequisites.
2) Personalised and Context-Sensitive Responses. Rather than navigating a predefined interface, Gen AI analyses user inputs, provides relevant suggestions, and offers personalised guidance. This adaptability enhances user experience, making interactions more like conversations with a knowledgeable assistant.
3) Real-Time Feedback and Learning. Gen AI's ability to provide real-time feedback. It can instantly analyse data, generate insights, and suggest next steps, creating a dynamic feedback loop. This real-time interaction is particularly valuable in education, customer service, and professional settings where immediate guidance and adaptive support are crucial.
4) Humanising Technology. By understanding and mimicking human-like communication patterns, Gen AI helps make interactions more relatable and less mechanical. This human-like interface reduces the intimidation factor often associated with advanced technologies, fostering more comfortable and engaging user experiences. It supports emotional and empathetic interactions, which are increasingly important in applications such as mental health, customer service, and personalised learning.

Table 1. Hard gen AI or soft gen AI

Hard Gen AI or Soft Gen AI in Layers of LLMs	
Large Language Models (LLMs) **Input Layer**: Takes in the raw text data. **Embedding Layer**: Converts words into dense vectors that represent their semantic meaning. **Attention Layers**: Multiple transformer layers that apply self-attention mechanisms to capture relationships between words. **Feedforward Layers**: Dense layers that process the output of the attention layers.	
Hard Gen AI	**Soft Gen AI**
Definition: Hard Gen AI refers to AI systems with generalised cognitive abilities akin to human intelligence. They can understand, learn, and apply knowledge across a wide range of tasks. **Goal in LLM Context:** To create a model that not only understands and generates language but can also perform reasoning, problem-solving, and possess self-awareness.	**Definition**: Soft AI, in this context, refers to AI systems specialised in specific tasks, but when combined, they give an impression of general intelligence. They do not possess true general cognitive abilities. **Goal in LLM Context**: To create specialised models that perform exceptionally well in specific tasks and can be integrated to mimic general capabilities.
Coupling LLMs Strategies	
Cognitive Modules: Each cognitive function (e.g., memory, reasoning, perception) can be developed as a loosely coupled module, integrated into the LLM framework. This allows for independent development and optimisation. **Inter-layer Communication**: Loose coupling can be applied between layers to allow flexibility. For instance, the attention mechanism can be decoupled to allow different attention strategies for different tasks. **Scalability**: By loosely coupling the layers, the system can scale different parts independently. For example, the reasoning module can be scaled separately from the language generation module. **Safety and Robustness**: Loose coupling ensures that updates or failures in one module do not cascade through the entire system, enhancing the overall safety and robustness.	**Specialised Modules**: Each layer or set of layers in the LLM can be specialised for a particular task, such as text generation, sentiment analysis, or translation. These modules can be loosely coupled to form a cohesive system. **Independent Upgrades**: Loose coupling allows for individual components (e.g., embedding layers for different languages) to be updated or replaced without affecting the entire model. **Integration of External Tools**: Integrate external tools or APIs. Loose coupling enables seamless integration and interaction with these tools, enhancing functionality without tightly binding the components. **Modularity in Layers**: Layers in an LLM can be designed to be modular. For instance, attention layers can be modified independently to improve performance for specific tasks without altering the feedforward layers.
Summary	
Goal: Achieve general cognitive abilities. **Layers:** Loosely coupled cognitive modules within the LLM framework. **Benefits** Scalability, safety, independent development of cognitive functions.	**Goal**: Perform specialised tasks effectively, creating an illusion of general intelligence. **Layers:** Specialised and modular layers within the LLM. **Benefits:** Flexibility, ease of integration, independent upgrades.

At the application level, Gen AI has diverse design approaches (Hsu et al., 2024; Huang, 2023; Inie et al., 2023; Scharpnick & Monahan, 2023; Zimmerman & Forlizzi, 2014), such as utilising algorithms that identify patterns and information to create new outputs, facilitating tasks like language translation and content generation, or developing tools that expand content creation capabilities across various domains by integrating ICT applications (e.g., desktop, web, mobile apps, and enterprise resource platforms) with user interfaces.

Here, Gen AI design is primarily regarded in two main types: H- and S-Gen-AI. These categories reflect different design orientations in developing Gen AI applications, each with distinct characteristics, strengths, and focus areas. Table 1 illustrates the distinguishing factors between H- and S-Gen-AI. Similar notions exist, such as "Strong or Weak AI" (Liu, 2021) and "Deep or Shallow" AI (Ankita et al., 2023).

Hard Gen AI

Here H-Gen-AI is referred to as being a conventional approach to modelling a full or semi-automation of human intelligence intended to meet deterministic outcomes. It utilises AI techniques to develop models with minimal human input, leveraging technologies such as deep learning, advanced neural networks, and substantial computational resources. H-Gen-AI has been commonly applied in advanced robotics, autonomous systems, predictive analytics, and other applications where high accuracy and reliability are essential.

Recent research also highlights several H-Gen-AI tools in educational contexts, emphasising their potential to create personalised and dynamic learning experiences. Among these, Generative Adversarial Networks (GANs) stand out for their ability to generate realistic simulations, enhancing interactive learning environments (Saxena & Cao, 2005). Reinforcement Learning (RL) is another significant approach (Kaelbling et al., 1996) used to develop intelligent tutoring systems that adapt to students' actions and feedback. While H-Gen-AI applications in education offer substantial advancements in tailoring educational content to individual learners, there are notable limitations in how genuinely educating these experiences are.

One crucial critique is that H-Gen-AI design cannot often incorporate personal contexts into social and collaborative learning, such as the learner's background, prior knowledge, specific learning environment, or emotional state, into their responses to social and community teamwork (Horvath, 2024; Ruiz-Rojas et al., 2024; Yan et al., 2024). The learning they offer is typically limited to adjusting content based on immediate performance data or fundamental user interactions, which can result in a one-size-fits-all approach that fails to engage or address the unique needs of each student deeply.

Another critique is that these H-Gen-AI driven systems should adequately support teachers in designing lesson plans or structuring broader educational strategies (Su & Yang 2023). While they can generate content, answer questions, and offer tutoring, the functionalities are not yet dedicated enough to assist teachers in co-designing lesson plans tailored to available stakeholders' partnerships so as to align with curriculum standards and learning objectives in and out of classrooms. Effective personalisation in education requires integrating broader contextual factors and supporting teachers in design using Gen AI beyond mere content delivery.

Soft Gen AI

S-Gen-AI focuses on human-centred, adaptive, and flexible approaches to modelling (Taylor et al., 2024). It emphasises adaptability to context, blending AI's capabilities with human design creativity. S-Gen-AI is often used in creative industries, personalised learning, collaborative tools, customer service, and any domain where human judgment, ethics, and adaptability are artistically or socially central and complex. S-Gen-AI has also been applied in education and centred on human-centric, adaptive, and flexible modelling approaches (Lim et al., 2023; Nguyen, 2023; Su & Yang 2023). It underpins our design approach, emphasising contextual adaptability and blending AI's strengths with human' teaching and learning.

Bahroun et al. (2023) emphasise the adaptability of S-Gen-AI in personalised education; however, a critical limitation is the lack of deep contextual personalisation. AI systems often fail to incorporate personal factors, such as a student's cultural background, social learning, collaborative learning, specific learning experiences, or emotional states, which are crucial for truly personalised learning. This critique highlights that while Gen AI can tailor content superficially based on performance data, it still fails to address more social and collaborative aspects of human learning needs.

Salvador-Ullauri and Acosta-Vargas (2024) praise S-Gen-AI tools for enhancing collaboration and critical thinking. Still, there are concerns about students becoming overly reliant on AI-driven suggestions during group work. This dependence can undermine the development of independent problem-solving skills and reduce the quality of human-to-human interaction. Moreover, Gen AI tools do not have collaborative settings; therefore, certain types of collaborative problem-solving approaches are limited.

Samala et al. (2024) Discuss the use of S-Gen-AI in decision-making within service learning, similarly to highlighting the role of S-Gen-AI in creative problem-solving. However, their models are designed somewhere between H- and S-Gen-AI, which mostly provide suggestions based on algorithmic logic. This shortcoming also raises questions on the appropriateness of relying on the decisions that require human empathy, contextual understanding, and ethical judgment.

In summary, extensive research shows that diverse design approaches have been applied to Gen AI development. However, navigating the design between H- and S-Gen-AI is essential. Although many S-Gen-AI technologies seem to be powerful (see Table 2 illustrates S-Gen-AI Design Approaches), the implementations of the applications are often fragmented and unscalable because of significantly lacking a clear design orientation.

Table 2. Soft Gen AI design approaches

Soft Gen AI Design Approaches
Soft Generative AI design focuses on human-centred, adaptable, and context-aware systems that integrate AI's computational power with human creativity and intuition. Unlike hard AI approaches, which are more rigid and task-specific, soft AI emphasizes flexibility, user interaction, and real-time adaptability. Below are key design principles and methodologies
Human-centred design is foundational in soft AI, prioritizing the needs, preferences, and contexts of users. In HCD, AI systems are developed through iterative processes that involve constant user feedback, ensuring that the systems evolve to meet human expectations. This approach enables AI to be intuitive, context-aware, and responsive to real-time changes in user behaviour.
Adaptive AI and Context Awareness. Soft AI design often incorporates adaptive algorithms that allow the AI system to adjust its behaviour based on the specific context in which it operates. These systems use real-time data, such as user input or environmental changes, to modify their outputs and processes dynamically.
Co-Design and Participatory Design. Incorporating co-design, where users are active participants in the design process, ensures that AI tools are tailored to specific needs and contexts. This approach helps prevent the disconnect that can occur when AI systems are designed without considering the day-to-day realities of the people who will use them.
Interactive and Iterative Learning. Soft AI systems are typically designed to learn continuously from interactions with users. This iterative learning process allows AI systems to evolve based on both explicit feedback and observed behaviour, making them more responsive and personalized over time.

Diverse Structured Design Orientations

From a philosophical standpoint, "orientation" in design is a multifaceted concept encompassing the cognitive structures that guide the design process. In designing an application of Gen AI in service-learning, orientation involves object-oriented activities (Torvinen, 2017). Design orientation navigates using Gen AI within a pedagogy to connect learners, educators, and other stakeholders, who are crucial not only to use Gen AI to incorporate real-world situations (Stuedahl, 2015) but also to guide real-world scenarios structurally so as to engage service-learning projects.

Design orientation is foundational to how individuals navigate and make sense of their ideas within a complex and ever-changing reality(Wilson, 2008). The following unclear orientations in a Gen AI design approach can lead to confusion and inefficiencies (Zirar et al., 2023):

1) Lack of guiding explicitly structuring learning purposes. Many S-Gen-AI design approaches are not specifically tailored for educational applications, often focusing on generic AI functionalities that are not directly translatable to academic needs. The design and implementation of AI models frequently

prioritise technical capabilities over practical usability in specific domains like education. S-Gen-AI design often aims to be flexible but lacks the instructional elements needed to support teaching and learning processes effectively.

2) Lack of guiding explicitly who the users are. Many design approaches are unclear about whether they are intended for developers to implement computationally or to guide end-users directly. This is crucial because the lack of clarity can result in S-Gen-AI models that are technically advanced but user-unfriendly, particularly for teachers and learners who are not AI experts. This ambiguity creates a disconnect between the potential of these models and their actual usability in and out of classroom settings.
3) Complexity and Cost-Effectiveness Issues. Broader criticisms of S-Gen-AI designs are that they are overly complex and not cost-effective. This argument also extends to the user experience, where teachers may struggle to use Gen AI tools effectively without substantial training or support.
4) Lack of navigating feedback. The automated nature of many AI feedback mechanisms often does not align with pedagogical standards, creating a disconnect between Gen AI generated feedback and actual educational goals. The over-reliance on automation reflects a preference for H-Gen-AI principles, which prioritise efficiency and control, over the adaptive, human-centred approach that S-Gen-AI seeks to embody.
5) Insufficient Human-Gen AI Collaboration. The support for collaboration between human teachers and Gen AI is particularly inadequate. Effective S-Gen-AI design should construct human input.

Service-Learning

With the diverse approaches discussed above, the application domain, i.e., service-learning adds contexts where Gen AI tool is used. This subsection reviews how communication functions within a service-learning environment. It justifies the need for effective communication strategies that bridge academic learning with community engagement.

Service-learning began in the early 20th century with John Dewey's idea of learning through real-world experiences (Jacoby, 1996). It gained momentum in the 1960s during the Civil Rights Movement, linking education with social justice. The term was formalised in the 1980s as universities integrated service with structured learning, and federal support grew in the 1990s through programs like AmeriCorps. By the 2000s, service-learning expanded into K-12 education (Vincent, 2021), emphasising civic engagement and critical thinking. Today, service-learning intertwines academic coursework with community service (Dolgon et al., 2017), aiming to, e.g.:

- Addressing global issues, e.g., blending academic learning with professional and community services,
- Fostering empathy and leadership, and
- Enhancing learning through active involvement in service activities, such as pre-service teachers in schools or social workers in rural communities.

Service-learning lacks support for human-centric communication between

- Academic knowledge and real-world applications;
- Social learning experiences and collaborative co-learning design

These aspects can be better supported by utilising a S-Gen-AI tool as an explorer, enabler, or facilitator.

Service-learning has undergone a significant transformation. The landscape of service-learning is evolving, particularly in response to global challenges like the COVID-19 pandemic. Service-learning demands innovative hybrid approaches that link academic learning with real-world community engagement. This hybrid service-learning has the potential to enrich students' learning experiences by involving them in real-world challenges. Driven by technological advancements, innovative pedagogical models, and a growing emphasis on digital skills, these emerging contexts necessitate exploring how structured design can enhance communication within a hybrid service-learning environment.

Developed countries have seen a remarkable integration of digital technologies into service-learning, enhancing how students' access, engage with, and reflect on their service activities. Platforms such as "GivePulse" and "VolunteerMatch" connect students with service opportunities, streamlining the process and broadening the scope of participation (GivePulse, 2024). Moreover, institutions like Stanford University have developed programs such as Cardinal Service, which emphasise digital engagement and sustainability, preparing students to address complex global challenges in innovative ways (StanfordUniversity, 2023).

Service-learning in developed countries also incorporates cutting-edge pedagogical models, such as project-based learning (Redmond, 2023), virtual service-learning (García-Gutiérrez et al., 2021), and hybrid approaches (Suresh et al., 2022) that blend in-person and online experiences. These models reflect the adaptability and evolving nature of service-learning, allowing it to meet diverse educational needs and expand its impact on students and communities. However, while service-learning thrives in developed contexts, developing countries face significant barriers that impede implementation. One of the most critical challenges is that, in many developing regions, even rural areas, there has been rapid ICT development. However, without an adequate design approach, integrating technology into education remains a distant goal.

Nevertheless, hybrid learning is the most cost-effective and sustainable solution. Without it, financial constraints pose even more substantial difficulties (Masino & Niño-Zarazúa, 2016), where limited funding hampers the establishment and sustainability of service-learning programs; schools and institutions lack the resources to provide training, materials, and support for educators and students. This makes it challenging to incorporate service-learning into the curriculum.

There is another good justification to develop an adequate design approach. Considering cultural and institutional barriers further complicate service-learning (Rodríguez-Zurita et al., 2024), many education systems in developing countries remain rooted in traditional learning methods, with little emphasis on social and experiential learning (Duarte et al., 2023). Service-learning is often viewed as a supplementary activity rather than a core education component. This results in a lack of support and recognition for service-learning. Despite these challenges, service-learning holds significant potential.

Leveraging Gen AI for Skill Communication in Service-Learning

For effective service-learning to take place, the essential human-centred and communicative components must be established, including:

- Effective communication and coordinated activities
- Collaborative partnerships
- Addressing community-identified needs
- Encouraging student engagement and amplifying student voice
- Reflection, which transforms service experiences into meaningful learning opportunities

For these operations, several methodologies help bridge academic content with community service. Table 3 illustrates the fundamental ones. However, meaningful learning experiences are indeed limited without communication. It is no surprise, then, that despite long-standing debates and persistent gaps in theory, the central question remains: Where is the learning in service-learning (Eyler & Giles, 1999)?

The role of communication in service-learning has rapidly emerged as a critical area of research and development due to its profound impact on both educational outcomes and community engagement (Buff et al., 2015; Corbett & Kendall, 1998; Dumlao, 2018; Voorhees, 2016). Communication in service-learning refers to the interaction and exchange of information within service-learning contexts. In theory, effective communication strategies are at the heart of bridging academic knowledge with community engagement. These theories are constructed from diverse orientations, e.g., the role of transdisciplinary communication, communication as a critical inquiry, interpersonal or intercultural competency communication in service-learning.

Nevertheless, the exchanges must be meaningful and impactful enough to enhance learning experiences, foster social responsibility, and address community needs. As introduced previously, the research reported here has taken skill development as the domain. How is communication critical to developing the skills? The term "skill communication" (Dumlao, 2018) is used to distinguish itself from the conventional term "communication skill" (Tucker et al., 1998; Vanoye-García et al., 2024).

Skill communication refers to the processes and methods used to convey, teach, or transfer skills, typically within educational, training, or instructional contexts. It focuses on an environment that facilitates the effective exchange and transfer of skills, such as teaching capacities, demonstrating procedures, or guiding others through tasks. Focusing on skill communication rather than merely basic communication abilities. Gen AI can better support methods and techniques for transferring skills.

Table 3. Service-learning methodologies

Service Learning Methodologies
Direct Service Learning. Direct service learning involves students working directly with individuals or groups in the community. This approach emphasizes personal, face-to-face interaction and real-time problem-solving in social service settings.
Indirect Service Learning. In indirect service learning, students engage in activities that benefit the community, though they do not have direct contact with the beneficiaries. This often involves organizing events or working behind the scenes on broader community projects.
Research-Based Service Learning. In this model, students collaborate with community organizations to conduct research that benefits the community. The goal is to use academic research to inform real-world solutions.
Advocacy Service Learning. Advocacy-based service learning involves students in raising awareness and promoting social change around issues that affect the community. Students work on campaigns, policy advocacy, or public education initiatives.
Reflection-Based Service Learning. Reflection is central to many service-learning methodologies but can also be the focus of the approach itself. Through structured reflective activities such as journaling, discussions, and presentations, students integrate their community service experiences with academic learning.
Experiential Service Learning. Experiential service learning emphasizes applying theoretical knowledge in real-world settings. This approach allows students to explore the practical implications of what they are learning in the classroom.
Problem-Based Service Learning (PBSL). PBSL is a problem-solving oriented approach where students work to address specific problems identified by the community. The goal is to apply academic knowledge to develop solutions that benefit the community.
Critical Service Learning. This approach emphasizes addressing systemic inequalities and injustices. Critical service learning challenges students to engage with the power dynamics and social structures that contribute to community issues.
Community-Based Learning (CBL). CBL integrates academic learning with meaningful community service and engagement. It emphasizes collaborative work between students and community partners, fostering learning through addressing real-world challenges.
Reflective Practice. Reflective practice requires students to critically examine their actions and experiences, connecting them to theoretical learning. This approach is often used in fields such as healthcare, education, and social work.
Participatory Action Research (PAR). PAR involves students working with community members as co-researchers to identify problems and develop actionable solutions. This methodology emphasizes collaboration and empowers communities.
Collaborative Learning. Collaborative learning involves students working together to solve problems or complete projects. This approach emphasizes teamwork, communication, and peer-to-peer learning.
Service-Learning Integrated Curriculum. This model embeds service-learning activities directly into the curriculum, ensuring that students engage with community issues as part of their academic study. Reflection and service activities are often graded components.
Project-Based Learning (PBL). PBL is an inquiry-based learning method where students actively explore real-world problems and challenges through projects. The project culminates in a final presentation or solution that addresses the issue.

Again, skills are conveyed, learned, and applied while facilitating professional and social engagement take place in collaborative settings.

On the other hand, communication skills focus on the generic ability to communicate effectively to convey, receive, and interpret messages effectively in various contexts. It is a generic competency that encompasses a range of abilities, including speaking, listening, writing, nonverbal communication, and interpersonal interaction. At present, developing skills is severely limited without effective skill communication in a learning environment. Consequently, collaborative settings for professional and social engagement provide little opportunities or insufficient support for building relationships with service learning stakeholders.

RESEARCH METHODOLOGY: ADA-ROB SKILL COMMUNICATION DESIGN APPROACH

This section outlines the research methodology used in this chapter, focusing on the research background, the design approach, and the pilot use cases that demonstrate the practical application of the Ada-Rob approach.

Methodological Design Approach

A methodology's primary purpose is to provide a coherent and consistent approach to problem-solving solutions, ensuring that methods are applied systematically to achieve reliable, valid, and replicable results (Angotti et al., 2011). Methodology includes various components (Celio et al., 2011), such as methods, principles, theories, and frameworks. Applying AI to enhance education is not just about technology but a methodological challenge: which AI, for whom and for what? Here, the research positions service-learning as an application domain. The research aligns with the methodological design (Bowie & Cassim, 2016) of S-Gen-AI, emphasising human-centred and adaptable approaches that leverage contextual understanding. Such an approach is essential for effective and practical skill development in hybrid learning environments.

An approach is the overall broad strategy and vision for achieving the objective. It reflects, e.g.,

- What and why to tackle the issues,
- The guiding principles, and
- The general direction of what can be done.

The terms "approach" and "methodology" are closely related and often used alternatively, but they are distinct concepts. Once the approach is established, the methodology details the steps, methods, tools, and techniques needed. For example, an approach like qualitative sets a mindset focused on something that needs to be explored in depth. The methodology then specifies the methods—like interviews or observations—and the reasoning behind these choices. In summary, the approach provides the "why" and the strategic direction, while the methodology delivers the "how," making the strategy actionable. Together, they ensure the work is guided by vision and grounded in practical implementation.

A critical methodological issue in skill development is the mixed design orientation seen commonly. In real-world educational settings, skill acquisition often depends on human intermediaries—educators, trainers, and mentors—who convey and translate expertise. However, current Gen AI designs are orientated towards automating human intelligence, assuming developers can seamlessly implement the models. Such a design orientation overlooks the complexity of human-facilitated learning and creates overly complex models. The reliance on coded automation fails to account for the context-dependent nature of skill development, where the role of a human-centric partnership is crucial. As a result, these Gen AI-driven models, intended to replicate expert processes, often become too rigid and difficult to implement effectively in educational settings. To bridge this gap, our design approach with S-Gen-AI re-centres the design around structural adaptability.

Design is a systematic process of planning and modelling solutions to meet needs, adapting to various contexts like education, engineering, and technology. Its purpose is to create functional, user-required outcomes by applying guiding principles (Tijsma et al., 2020). However, a design approach needs orientation to align with project goals and context, ensuring coherence in the soft nature of Gen AI application. Without orientation, design efforts risk becoming fragmented and ineffective.

Service-learning can be viewed as a design approach. For example, the interest in design approaches is growing to develop communication in education. A good case is the dialogic pedagogical design approach in classroom-based teaching and learning (Koichu et al., 2022). However, service-learning also aims to enhance engagement and effectiveness outside the classroom. Another critical limitation of the dialogic design approach is that it involves a step-by-step structured design through problem identification, planning, development, testing, and evaluation. This approach is too generic to guide teaching and learning in the context of service-learning because the challenge intensifies when using Gen AI.

Ada-Rob Skill Communication Design Approach

As discussed, various existing design approaches, such as design thinking and human-centred design, offer strengths but raise questions about their suitability, particularly for hybrid communication in service-learning. The Ada-Rob design represents a structured approach characterised by openness and adaptability.

One side of service-learning communication is called “role-based service”, which is orientated towards a network of roles working together to facilitate learning, such as educators, students, mentors, trainers, coaches, community partners, and institutional leaders. The success of service-learning critically relies on the collaborative efforts of each who plays a vital role in delivering impactful service that meets educational and community needs.

The other side of service-learning communication is called “adaptive learning,” which is at the heart of personalising the learning experience by dynamically adjusting the content, pace, and approach based on the individual needs in the evolving context of the service environment. Adaptive learning leverages learning insights, real-time feedback, and flexible instructional methods to create a learning experience tailored to each student's abilities, interests, and progress.

The Ada-Rob approach differentiates itself from other design methodologies. The ultimate goal is to utilise Gen AI to construct communication that fosters skill development. To achieve this, it promotes meaningful and impactful connections among stakeholders so as to enable adaptive and context-sensitive knowledge exchanges. Key components to incorporate into the templates include 'role-based service'. Such a service sets contexts where learning takes place among academic and collaborative efforts among including educators, students, and mentors. It emphasises 'adaptive learning,' which tailors the learning experience using learning insights and flexible instructional strategies. Figure 3 illustrates the Ada-Rob use case framework to incorporate Ada-Rob components into templates.

Figure 3. Ada-Rob use case framework

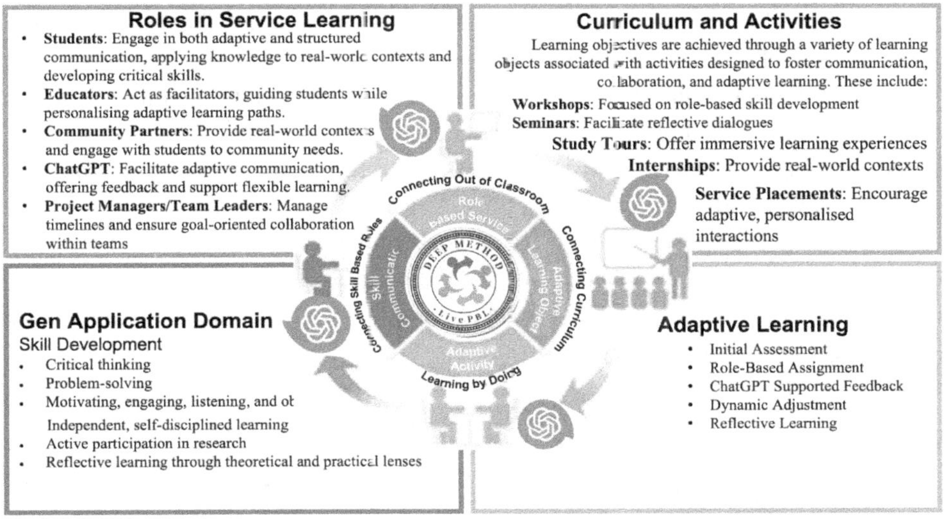

Research Setting

The LivePBL (Live Project-Based Learning) research setting explores innovative service-learning approaches across academic institutions and community settings, emphasising hybrid teaching methods and cross-cultural collaboration (Liu et al., 2022; Wang et al., 2020; Zhang et al., 2022; Zhou et al., 2023). This research was conducted in partnership with multiple institutions, including the Music College at Capital Normal University in Beijing, China, and Dibyabhumi College in Nepal, which served as a support school. The research also involved engagement with a social community in Dalian, China, a key family community partner. Participants included university music students from Capital Normal University and Social Work Development students from Dibyabhumi College based in Nepal. This setting provided a diverse and dynamic context for piloting the Ada-Rob approach, fostering a unique blend of academic and community-based learning experiences in designing the Gen AI use cases. The research was structured in two phases, each reflecting distinct approaches to digital and AI-assisted service-learning aimed at enhancing educational outcomes in skill communication.

The first phase of the LivePBL research was conducted during the COVID-19 pandemic, focusing on hybrid digital service-learning to respond to the unprecedented challenges of maintaining education continuity. This phase combined online and in-person elements to facilitate project-based learning in a hybrid environment. Academic institutions included the Music College at Capital Normal University and Dibyabhumi College, where students participated in collaborative digital projects despite the restrictions posed by the pandemic. The hybrid format utilised digital platforms and tools to support communication, collaboration, and learning engagement, enabling students to continue their educational journeys in a safe and adaptable manner. The focus was on integrating digital literacy within the service-learning projects, allowing students to engage with real-world problems while developing critical skills.

Building on the experiences of the first phase, the second phase introduced Gen AI to assist in service-learning. The use cases of ChatGPT were designed to support students in skill development. This phase involved the same academic partners and expanded the hybrid model by incorporating Gen AI to assist with personalised learning.

USE CASES OF ADA-ROB SKILL COMMUNICATION

This section presented the use cases, illustrating how the Ada-Rob approach creates an interactive and personalised educational experience that engages students, families, and educators, hence moving beyond traditional instruction outside of the classroom. As outlined the objectives of the specific use cases designed are to leverage Ada-Rob with ChatGPT to target critical 21st-century skills:

1) Critical thinking
2) Problem-solving
3) Motivating, engaging, listening, and observing
4) Active participation in research
5) Reflective learning through theoretical and practical lenses

Appendix 1 provides detailed use case templates demonstrating its application in the context of the five skill sets.

User Scenario on Family Digital Literacy – Video Creation on Kindness

In LivePBL hybrid service-learning environment, children and parents were tasked with designing a three-minute video promoting the concept of "kindness," integrating digital literacy skills with creative expression. This task was introduced during a session that combined in-person and online elements, setting the stage for an interactive, reflective learning experience. ChatGPT played a role in guiding stakeholders through this creative process, acting as a supportive tool that facilitated, e.g., critical thinking and collaboration. Appendix 2 illustrates the use cases of the Ada-Rob approach.

What and How ChatGPT Was Used

During the hybrid session, teachers explained the task, emphasising the key elements of video design, such as message clarity, visual storytelling, and audience impact. ChatGPT was used to generate prompts and provide ongoing guidance, helping students and their parents brainstorm and structure their video concepts. For example, ChatGPT offered suggestions like, "What are three key messages you want your video on kindness to convey?" and "How can you use visuals, music, or text to enhance your message?" ChatGPT also served as a real-time feedback tool during the video planning phase. When students shared their initial ideas, the AI provided tailored feedback, prompting them to think critically about their creative choices. It had asked, "How does your video start? Does it immediately capture the viewer's attention? What visuals will you use to represent kindness?" These prompts helped students refine their ideas, making their video content more impactful and engaging.

Role of Teaching Assistants and Observations

Pre-service teaching students were engaged as teaching assistants, observing the hybrid session and later conducting online follow-up sessions with parents and children. ChatGPT supported these assistants by generating reflective questions to guide the students during the video creation. Questions like, "Why did you choose this scene to represent kindness? How could you improve it to make the message clearer?" helped students critically evaluate their work, enhancing their ability to make purposeful and thoughtful design decisions.

Critical Skills Developed

Teacher students learned to evaluate their understanding of who teaching assistants are and what teaching assistants do. Students were asked to analyse and discuss the effectiveness of their communication and adapt their designs based on feedback from ChatGPT. They were motivated to think about how their video choices could best communicate the theme of kindness.

Students learned how children's designing a video is different and how they need to find other solutions to support children and parents, such as how to visually represent abstract concepts or how to engage the audience emotionally within a limited timeframe. By working with their parents and engaging with teaching assistants, students learned to collaborate effectively, gaining insights into video editing tools and digital storytelling techniques.

Stakeholders, including students, parents, and teaching assistants, were asked to maintain learning journals, documenting their creative journey, challenges faced, and lessons learned. ChatGPT facilitated this process by generating reflective prompts: "What did you learn about conveying messages through visuals? How can you apply this skill in other areas of your life?" By integrating ChatGPT with the human guidance of Ada-Rob Skill Communication to the environment of teaching assistants, the Ada-Rob design bridged the gap between digital literacy and real-world application, making the learning process more meaningful and relevant.

Problem-Solving: Interactive Workshops in Action

In hands-on presentation workshops certified by CPD, teacher students were challenged to apply their understanding of teaching assistants and adapt their support methods when guiding children and their parents through the creation of a kindness-themed video. ChatGPT played a role in these sessions, providing feedback and helping students adjust their guidance to suit the children's needs. For instance, when students initially struggled with explaining abstract concepts like kindness to young children, ChatGPT generated various suggestions such as, "How might you represent kindness through simple everyday actions that children understand? What, When and How have you shared with or helped a friend?"

ChatGPT's feedback encouraged teacher students to think critically about visual storytelling, as it would prompt questions like, "How can you use colours and music to enhance the emotional tone of your video?" These prompts not only enhanced problem-solving but also pushed them to adapt their methods based on the audience. These, namely, children, required different approaches from those typically used with older learners.

Students learned through experience how working with children's cognitive levels and emotional engagement differs from adult learners. They found themselves seeking solutions on how to simplify complex ideas, represent abstract concepts visually. Teaching assistants, with support from ChatGPT, provided additional guidance, giving feedback on script revisions, visual choices, and overall message clarity.

As part of this process, the stakeholders, including students, parents, and teaching assistants, maintained learning journals to document their creative journey. ChatGPT contributed by generating reflective prompts, such as, "What did you learn about adjusting your message for younger audiences? How could this skill benefit you in future teaching scenarios?"

By integrating ChatGPT through the Ada-Rob approach, this scenario bridged the gap between digital literacy and practical application, making the learning process more relevant and personalised. This reflection not only enhanced their digital skills but also built a foundation for future teaching and mentoring roles.

Motivating, Engaging, Listening, and Observing: Storytelling with a Digital Presentation

Students were tasked with creating digital presentations that told a story about their personal experiences with kindness. ChatGPT played the role of a co-creator, sparking creativity and guiding students through the process of crafting narratives. For example, when a student struggled to start, ChatGPT might prompt, "Think of a time when you showed kindness—how did you feel, and how could you represent that moment visually using images, sounds, or text?"

The storytelling sessions encouraged students to think deeply about how they could translate abstract concepts like kindness into a digital format. Students were prompted by ChatGPT with questions such as, "How would you use colour and music to highlight the emotional impact of your story?" These inquiries led students to engage with multimedia elements, improving their observational skills and helping them better understand how visual and auditory choices can enhance narrative depth.

Teaching assistants observed the students' initial attempts to design their digital stories and provided real-time feedback using ChatGPT as a support tool. When students presented their draft videos, teaching assistants asked, "What elements of your story do you think are the most engaging, and how could you refine them?" ChatGPT would then offer suggestions based on the student's responses, motivating them with prompts like, "How could you make your audience feel the kindness you experienced by adding background music or visuals?". This session not only enhanced students' digital literacy but also developed their observational skills.

Independent and Self-Disciplined Learning

In this self-paced learning scenario, each stakeholder—students, parents, and teaching assistants—was assigned a specific role and given autonomy to manage their tasks (i.e., creating a segment of their kindness video). ChatGPT can assist individuals through their learning journeys. For example, students were asked to set goals for each session by responding to ChatGPT prompts such as, "What specific task do you want to complete today?" This interactive engagement fostered self-discipline, transforming independent learning from a solitary activity into a guided experience that builds confidence and organisational skills.

ChatGPT also prompted them with questions like, "What part of your video needs the most work today—audio, visuals, or script? Set a realistic goal for this session and explain how you will achieve it." Student received personalised feedback based on their responses. If a student struggled to complete the video script, ChatGPT would provide guidance such as, "Focus on finishing the introduction to your video today and outline the remaining sections for tomorrow. What key points will you emphasise in your opening scene?"

Parents, as stakeholders, were also involved in managing their roles in assisting their children's projects. ChatGPT supported parents by offering task-related guidance like, "How can you help your child balance their creative ideas with time management? Set a goal together for today's work." This enabled parents to contribute meaningfully to their child's progress while learning essential organisational techniques.

Teaching assistants (TA), assigned to monitor students' progress and provide support, used ChatGPT to track each learner's progress. The AI system prompted TAs with questions like, "Which students are behind on their tasks? How can you offer targeted feedback to help them catch up?" This kept teaching assistants engaged in monitoring and adjusting support for each student.

Through the Ada-Rob co-design, each stakeholder had an active role in managing their learning goals. ChatGPT's adaptive prompts ensured tasks were completed efficiently while encouraging students, parents, and teaching assistants to reflect on their progress. This method not only enhanced time management and self-discipline for students but also strengthened the role of parents and teaching assistants in guiding the learning process.

Actively Participating in Research

In a classroom transformed into an Ada-Rob hub of hybrid communities, students engage in analysing non-formal learning sources they have explored throughout their project. Students shift through various materials, such as websites, articles, and interview notes, working collaboratively to understand how non-formal data contributes to their broader study.

ChatGPT plays a role in this process, prompting students with inquiries that challenge their analytical thinking. For example, ChatGPT might ask, "What patterns are emerging from the non-formal data you've collected, and how do these findings influence the direction of your learning?" As another example, students were asked to research how acts of kindness are represented in online communities and non-formal sources, such as blogs, forums, and social media posts. After gathering data, they turned to ChatGPT to support the analysis of these varied sources. ChatGPT guided students with questions like, "What are the common themes across different online communities in how kindness is defined or displayed?" This allowed students to draw connections between the diverse perspectives they encountered, helping them identify overarching themes in their research.

Teaching assistants played supportive roles by observing how students responded to ChatGPT's prompts and guiding them in synthesising information into coherent findings. For example, when students struggled to conclude their data, ChatGPT prompted, "What might explain the differences in how kindness is represented in a social media post versus a blog article?" This encouraged students to think critically about the context and audience of their sources, deepening their understanding of informal research.

ChatGPT offers feedback as students move through the information analysis and presentation stages. Students were empowered to generate new learning experiences by critically engaging with their data and reflecting on how non-formal sources contributed to their understanding of kindness. Through this active engagement in research, students gained confidence in their ability to conduct research.

Reflecting on Learning Experiences: Connecting Theory with Practice

Students who had completed a digital literacy project on kindness were prompted to reflect on their experiences with the technical aspects of creating a kindness-themed video. After the project presentation, professors and mentors facilitated a reflective session in which ChatGPT prompted students with questions like, "How did the digital tools you used to shape how you felt and expressed kindness? What challenges did you face in aligning your message with the visual and audio elements?"

During the reflection, ChatGPT encouraged students to connect their classroom learning to real-world applications. For example, if a student had struggled to design a script that conveyed the message of kindness, ChatGPT might prompt, "How did your theoretical knowledge of narrative structure help you overcome obstacles in crafting your video's message?" This allowed students to not only reflect on their learning outcomes but also understand how theoretical concepts such as narrative building, visual symbolism, and audience engagement played into their project.

When students expressed that they found it challenging to apply digital storytelling concepts in practice, ChatGPT might generate follow-up questions like, "What would you do differently next time to ensure your digital tools enhance rather than obscure your message?" This fostered deeper critical thinking and encouraged students to plan improvements for future projects actively. Using ChatGPT's adaptive reflection prompts, students internalised their learning in a structured way. They emerged from these reflective sessions with not only a firmer grasp of digital literacy but also a clearer sense of how to apply those skills in social contexts.

CONCLUSION

This chapter explored the intersection of S-Gen-AI and service-learning through the Ada-Rob approach. To establish skill communication. The Ada-Rob approach focused on how S-Gen-AI tools, such as ChatGPT, can improve communication, collaboration, and skill development among stakeholders. By connecting academic with practical community engagement, the Ada-Rob approach and its use case design in LivePBL provide valuable insights into the strengths, limitations, and future research directions of this design approach.

Summary

This chapter argued that,

1) Current limitations in service-learning include a lack of human-centric communication design approach.
2) The challenge is how to connect academic knowledge with real-world applications effectively.
3) The current Gen AI design approaches lack the systematic, dynamic communication and social interactions necessary in service-learning, making it difficult to scale Gen AI's full potential.
4) The Ada-Rob approach introduces a structured, adaptive framework that combines role-based communication and personalised learning. This approach uses Soft Gen AI tools to facilitate adaptive dialogue and collaborative learning tailored to various stakeholders.

The chapter contributes:

1) A new design approach (Ada-Rob) that addresses critical gaps in communication and coordination in service-learning environments.
2) Practical applications and use cases demonstrating how Gen AI can enhance communication in hybrid learning environments, improve critical thinking, and promote coherent and consistent engagement with real-world community projects.
3) A detailed analysis of the potential of Gen AI to transform service-learning by supporting context-sensitive, collaborative learning experiences, positioning Soft Gen AI as a supporter rather than a replacement for human interaction.

Limitations

Despite its strengths, the Ada-Rob approach presents limitations. One challenge lies in defining clear metrics for communicative success. While its flexibility is a strength, well-established criteria are needed to evaluate effectiveness in participant engagement, skill development, and community impact. Another area of focus is balancing structure and flexibility. The system's adaptive elements should not overshadow the need for a structured learning experience, and maintaining this balance is critical for ensuring that learning objectives are met. Integrating Ada-Rob with existing service-learning frameworks can be complex, as it may require alignment with established methods. Finally, implementing Ada-Rob will likely need adequate training.

Future Research Implications

Ethics of Soft-Gen-AI: in Human-Tamed Life Cycle vs. on One-Size-Fits-All Frameworks

Although the Ada-Rob approach offers an innovative and significant methodological approach, how does the Ada-Rob approach advance the design thinking on the ethical aspects of using Gen AI? The potential of the Ada-Rob approach embodies the core principles of the S-Gen-AI framework, which is inherently based on a "human-in-the-loop" design. Unlike rigid regulatory frameworks that often attempt a one-size-fits-all solution, the Ada-Rob approach views ethical issues as elements that evolve throughout the lifecycle of a project. This ensures that decision-making remains grounded in a project ethical responsibility, especially when monitoring and collaborating on projects that directly impact communities. By leveraging role-based learning, the Ada-Rob approach allows individuals to access only the information and tools specific to their responsibilities. This creates a structured and secure flow of knowledge while maintaining the integrity of ethical practices. Furthermore, the model emphasises the importance of individual agency and control over information sharing. For example, workshop conversations and interactions can be used but remain private unless individuals choose to release the information. This fosters transparency and accountability, reinforcing ethical collaboration. Moreover, the adaptive nature of the system allows it to evolve alongside its users, tailoring learning experiences to both individual needs in contextual demands. Throughout this process, ethical standards are continually upheld, ensuring that the approach is not only flexible and responsive but also aligned with standards of responsibility and accountability in diverse environments.

Layered and Flexible Scalability

On Openness and Role Based in Adaptive Learning. One of its standout implications on learning methodologies is its role-based openness and adaptiveness. How does this enhance flexible communication that is designed to be scalable to various educational and community settings? In developing countries, this openness and adaptability are crucial in service-learning, where needs and contexts can change quickly in line with the rapid PESTLE change (political, economic, social, technological, legal and environmental). The hybrid communication approach needs to merge role-based service with adaptive learning.

On Co-designed Service Collaboration. How can Ada-Rob potentially enhance service-learning outcomes in terms of both the efficiency and effectiveness of the learning? Co-designed collaboration is a central element in the learning process, as it highlights the roles of educators, students, mentors, and community partners in a cooperative communication network. A sense of shared responsibility fosters mutual support among participant stakeholders, contributing to a more connected and impactful service-learning experience.

On Integrating Traditional and Ada-Rob Communication Models. How can the Ada-Rob approach further lay the foundation for scaling the applications in developing countries, where socio-economic, cultural, and technological barriers in communication often fail to the progress of service-learning? Common traditional models include

1. Direct Communication,
2. Reflective Journaling and Reporting, and
3. Scheduled Field Visits.

Traditional service-learning often depends on scheduled visits where students travel to communities for specific projects. Following traditional communication between educational institutions, students, and community partners, developing countries rely on face-to-face interaction, direct mentorship, and in-person in-field collaboration. These models focus on building relationships through physical presence, observation, and hands-on work within communities.

The potential of the Ada-Rob approach to use Gen AI is not just reflected by the use cases designed for China. Skill communication can address the barriers to service learning in developing countries by integrating S-Gen-AI tools and hybrid pedagogies, advancing

1. Ongoing access to expertise, overcoming time, location, and stakeholders' resource constraints.

2. Frequent digital interactions supplementing infrequent visits to hard-to-reach communities.
3. Adapting pedagogies to bridge cultural gaps through skill development.
4. Blending in-person and digital engagement that ensures fostering collaboration through professional relationships; and
5. Tailoring learning to individual and contextual needs across diverse environments.

APPENDIX II

INCORPORATES ADA-ROB COMPONENTS INTO SPECIFIC USE CASES WITH CHATGPT

Figure 4. Use case 1

Hard Gen AI or Soft Gen AI in Layers of LLMs

Large Language Models (LLMs)

Input Layer: Takes in the raw text data.
Embedding Layer: Converts words into dense vectors that represent their semantic meaning.
Attention Layers: Multiple transformer layers that apply self-attention mechanisms to capture relationships between words.
Feedforward Layers: Dense layers that process the output of the attention layers.

Hard Gen AI	Soft Gen AI
Definition: Hard Gen AI refers to AI systems with generalised cognitive abilities akin to human intelligence. They can understand, learn, and apply knowledge across a wide range of tasks. **Goal in LLM Context:** To create a model that not only understands and generates language but can also perform reasoning, problem-solving, and possess self-awareness.	**Definition**: Soft AI, in this context, refers to AI systems specialised in specific tasks, but when combined, they give an impression of general intelligence. They do not possess true general cognitive abilities. **Goal in LLM Context**: To create specialised models that perform exceptionally well in specific tasks and can be integrated to mimic general capabilities.

Coupling LLMs Strategies

Cognitive Modules: Each cognitive function (e.g., memory, reasoning, perception) can be developed as a loosely coupled module, integrated into the LLM framework. This allows for independent development and optimisation. **Inter-layer Communication**: Loose coupling can be applied between layers to allow flexibility. For instance, the attention mechanism can be decoupled to allow different attention strategies for different tasks. **Scalability**: By loosely coupling the layers, the system can scale different parts independently. For example, the reasoning module can be scaled separately from the language generation module. **Safety and Robustness**: Loose coupling ensures that updates or failures in one module do not cascade through the entire system, enhancing the overall safety and robustness.	**Specialised Modules**: Each layer or set of layers in the LLM can be specialised for a particular task, such as text generation, sentiment analysis, or translation. These modules can be loosely coupled to form a cohesive system. **Independent Upgrades**: Loose coupling allows for individual components (e.g., embedding layers for different languages) to be updated or replaced without affecting the entire model. **Integration of External Tools**: Integrate external tools or APIs. Loose coupling enables seamless integration and interaction with these tools, enhancing functionality without tightly binding the components. **Modularity in Layers**: Layers in an LLM can be designed to be modular. For instance, attention layers can be modified independently to improve performance for specific tasks without altering the feedforward layers.

Summary

Goal: Achieve general cognitive abilities. **Layers:** Loosely coupled cognitive modules within the LLM framework. **Benefits** Scalability, safety, independent development of cognitive functions.	**Goal:** Perform specialised tasks effectively, creating an illusion of general intelligence. **Layers:** Specialised and modular layers within the LLM. **Benefits:** Flexibility, ease of integration, independent upgrades.

Figure 5. Use case 2

Soft Gen AI Design Approaches
Soft Generative AI design focuses on human-centred, adaptable, and context-aware systems that integrate AI's computational power with human creativity and intuition. Unlike hard AI approaches, which are more rigid and task-specific, soft AI emphasizes flexibility, user interaction, and real-time adaptability. Below are key design principles and methodologies
Human-centred design is foundational in soft AI, prioritizing the needs, preferences, and contexts of users. In HCD, AI systems are developed through iterative processes that involve constant user feedback, ensuring that the systems evolve to meet human expectations. This approach enables AI to be intuitive, context-aware, and responsive to real-time changes in user behaviour.
Adaptive AI and Context Awareness. Soft AI design often incorporates adaptive algorithms that allow the AI system to adjust its behaviour based on the specific context in which it operates. These systems use real-time data, such as user input or environmental changes, to modify their outputs and processes dynamically.
Co-Design and Participatory Design. Incorporating co-design, where users are active participants in the design process, ensures that AI tools are tailored to specific needs and contexts. This approach helps prevent the disconnect that can occur when AI systems are designed without considering the day-to-day realities of the people who will use them.
Interactive and Iterative Learning. Soft AI systems are typically designed to learn continuously from interactions with users. This iterative learning process allows AI systems to evolve based on both explicit feedback and observed behaviour, making them more responsive and personalized over time.

Figure 6. Use case 3

Service Learning Methodologies
Direct Service Learning. Direct service learning involves students working directly with individuals or groups in the community. This approach emphasizes personal, face-to-face interaction and real-time problem-solving in social service settings.
Indirect Service Learning. In indirect service learning, students engage in activities that benefit the community, though they do not have direct contact with the beneficiaries. This often involves organizing events or working behind the scenes on broader community projects.
Research-Based Service Learning. In this model, students collaborate with community organizations to conduct research that benefits the community. The goal is to use academic research to inform real-world solutions.
Advocacy Service Learning. Advocacy-based service learning involves students in raising awareness and promoting social change around issues that affect the community. Students work on campaigns, policy advocacy, or public education initiatives.
Reflection-Based Service Learning. Reflection is central to many service-learning methodologies but can also be the focus of the approach itself. Through structured reflective activities such as journaling, discussions, and presentations, students integrate their community service experiences with academic learning.
Experiential Service Learning. Experiential service learning emphasizes applying theoretical knowledge in real-world settings. This approach allows students to explore the practical implications of what they are learning in the classroom.
Problem-Based Service Learning (PBSL). PBSL is a problem-solving oriented approach where students work to address specific problems identified by the community. The goal is to apply academic knowledge to develop solutions that benefit the community.
Critical Service Learning. This approach emphasizes addressing systemic inequalities and injustices. Critical service learning challenges students to engage with the power dynamics and social structures that contribute to community issues.
Community-Based Learning (CBL). CBL integrates academic learning with meaningful community service and engagement. It emphasizes collaborative work between students and community partners, fostering learning through addressing real-world challenges.
Reflective Practice. Reflective practice requires students to critically examine their actions and experiences, connecting them to theoretical learning. This approach is often used in fields such as healthcare, education, and social work.
Participatory Action Research (PAR). PAR involves students working with community members as co-researchers to identify problems and develop actionable solutions. This methodology emphasizes collaboration and empowers communities.
Collaborative Learning. Collaborative learning involves students working together to solve problems or complete projects. This approach emphasizes teamwork, communication, and peer-to-peer learning.
Service-Learning Integrated Curriculum. This model embeds service-learning activities directly into the curriculum, ensuring that students engage with community issues as part of their academic study. Reflection and service activities are often graded components.
Project-Based Learning (PBL). PBL is an inquiry-based learning method where students actively explore real-world problems and challenges through projects. The project culminates in a final presentation or solution that addresses the issue.

REFERENCES

Alstete, J. W., Flavian, H., & Petrova, K. (2023). Guest editorial: Hybrid, blended and mixed-mode learning quality: more lessons learned in the COVID pandemic and beyond. *Quality Assurance in Education*, 31(1), 1–3. DOI: 10.1108/QAE-02-2023-205

Angotti, T., Doble, C., & Horrigan, P. (2011). *Service-Learning in Design and Planning: Educating at the Boundaries*. NYU Press., DOI: 10.2307/j.ctt21pxmfs

Ankita, M., M., Sharma, I., & Kumar, A. (2023). Comparative Analysis of Shallow Learning and Deep Learning. 2023 International Conference on Next Generation Electronics (NEleX) DOI: 10.1109/NEleX59773.2023.10421385

Bahroun, Z., Anane, C., Ahmed, V., & Zacca, A. (2023). Transforming Education: A Comprehensive Review of Generative Artificial Intelligence in Educational Settings through Bibliometric and Content Analysis. *Sustainability (Basel)*, 15(17), 12983. DOI: 10.3390/su151712983

Bowie, A., & Cassim, F. (2016). Linking classroom and community: A theoretical alignment of service learning and a human-centered design methodology in contemporary communication design education. *Education as Change*, 20(1). Advance online publication. DOI: 10.17159/1947-9417/2016/556

Bringle, R. G., & Hatcher, J. A. (1999). Reflection in Service Learning: Making Meaning or Experience. *Evaluation/Reflection, 23*, 179-185. https://digitalcommons.unomaha.edu/slceeval/23

Buff, S. M., Jenkins, K., Kern, D., Worrall, C., Howell, D., Martin, K., Brown, D., White, A., & Blue, A. (2015). Interprofessional service-learning in a community setting: Findings from a pilot study. *Journal of Interprofessional Care*, 29(2), 159–161. DOI: 10.3109/13561820.2014.934956 PMID: 25003549

Carr, J. M., Santos-Rogers, K., & Kanyongo, G. (2021). Improving student and faculty communication: The impact of texting and electronic feedback on building relationships and the perception of care. *Research in Learning Technology*, 29. Advance online publication. DOI: 10.25304/rlt.v29.2463

Celio, C. I., Durlak, J., & Dymnicki, A. (2011). A Meta-Analysis of the Impact of Service-Learning on Students. *Journal of Experiential Education*, 34(2), 164–181. DOI: 10.1177/105382591103400205

Corbett, J. B., & Kendall, A. R. (1998). Evaluating Service Learning in the Communication Discipline. *Journalism & Mass Communication Educator*, 53(4), 66–76. DOI: 10.1177/107769589805300406

Cornet, P., Jones, A., Lee, M., & Williams, K. (2024). Service learning in schools: Challenges and opportunities. *Journal of Educational Development*, 15(2), 112–130.

Dolgon, C., Mitchell, T. D., & Eatman, T. K. (Eds.). (2017). *The Cambridge Handbook of Service Learning and Community Engagement*. Cambridge University Press., DOI: 10.1017/9781316650011

Doyle, J., Chiari, S., Pearl, P., Ellis, K., Völler, S., Shaw, C., & Hezel, B. (2024). Transforming young adults' climate learning and actions through a co-created climate communication retreat. *Environmental Education Research*, •••, 1–19. DOI: 10.1080/13504622.2024.2348693

Duarte, J., Morais, M., & Pereira, R. (2023). Hybrid Learning Environments: A Pathway to Inclusive Higher Education. *Journal of Educational Technology & Society*, 26(2), 75–88.

Dumlao, R. (2018). *A Guide to Collaborative Communication for Service-Learning and Community Engagement Partners*. Routledge.

Eyler, J., & Giles, D. E. (1999). *Where's the Learning in Service-Learning?* Jossey-Bass.

García-Gutiérrez, J., Ruiz-Corbella, M., & Manjarrés Riesco, Á. (2021). Virtual Service-Learning in Higher Education. A Theoretical Framework for Enhancing its Development. *Frontiers in Education*, 5, 630804. Advance online publication. DOI: 10.3389/feduc.2020.630804

GivePulse. (2024). The Rising Value of Volunteerism: GivePulse for Maximizing Impact. https://learn.givepulse.com

Hagendorff, T. (2024). Mapping the Ethics of Generative AI: A Comprehensive Scoping Review. *Arxiv*. https://doi.org//arXiv.2402.08323DOI: 10.48550

Hong, L., Wan, Y.-y., Yang, W., Gong, Z., Hu, X.-y., & Ma, G. (2024). Two decades of academic service-learning in Chinese higher education: A review of research literature. *Applied Research in Quality of Life*, 19(5), 2171–2212. Advance online publication. DOI: 10.1007/s11482-024-10318-9

Horvath, J. C. (2024). [*Critical Problems Gen AI Poses for Learning*. https://hbsp.harvard.edu/inspiring-minds/the-limits-of-gen-ai-educators-in-higher-ed]. *Artificial Intelligence*, 3, •••.

Hsu, H.-P., Mak, J., Werner, J., White-Taylor, J., Geiselhofer, M., Gorman, A., & Torrejon Capurro, C. (2024). Preliminary Study on Pre-Service Teachers' Applications and Perceptions of Generative Artificial Intelligence for Lesson Planning. *Journal of Technology and Teacher Education*, 32(3), 409–437.

Huang, Y. (2023). *The Future of Generative AI: How GenAI Would Change Human-Computer Co-creation in the Next 10 to 15 Years* CHI PLAY Companion '23: Companion Proceedings of the Annual Symposium on Computer-Human Interaction in Play.

Hwang, G. J., & Chen, N. S. (2023). Exploring the potential of generative artificial intelligence in education: Applications, challenges, and future research directions. *Journal of Educational Technology & Society*, 26(2).

Inie, N., Falk, J., & Tanimoto, S. (2023). Designing Participatory AI: Creative Professionals' Worries and Expectations about Generative AI *CHI Conference on Human Factors in Computing Systems*, Association for Computing Machinery, New York, NY, USA. DOI: 10.1145/3544549.3585657

Jacoby, B. (1996). *Service-Learning in Higher Education: Concepts and Practices*. Jossey-Bass.

Kaelbling, L. P., Littman, M. L., & Moore, A. W. (1996). Reinforcement Learning A Survey. *Journal of Artificial Intelligence Research*, 4, 237–285. https://www.cs.cmu.edu/~tom/10701_sp11/slides/Kaelbling.pdf. DOI: 10.1613/jair.301

Koichu, B., Schwarz, B. B., Heyd-Metzuyanim, E., Tabach, M., & Yarden, A. (2022). Design practices and principles for promoting dialogic argumentation via interdisciplinarity. *Learning, Culture and Social Interaction*, 37, 100657. https://doi.org/https://doi.org/10.1016/j.lcsi.2022.100657. DOI: 10.1016/j.lcsi.2022.100657

Kritikos, M., & Iphofen, R. (2023). A Human in the Loop Approach/Human Oversight. In Iphofen, R. (Ed.), *Ethical AI Surveillance in the Workplace* (Vol. 10, pp. 67–68). Emerald Publishing Limited., DOI: 10.1108/S2398-601820230000010028

Li, J., & He, Y. (2023). Unpacking "Double Reduction" Policy in China: Ideas, Values, and Practices. *Beijing International Review of Education*, 5(3), 337–341. DOI: 10.1163/25902539-05030009

Lim, W. M., Gunasekara, A., Pallant, J. L., Pallant, J. I., & Pechenkina, E. (2023). Generative AI and the future of education: Ragnarök or reformation? A paradoxical perspective from management educators. *International Journal of Management Education*, 21(2), 100790. https://doi.org/https://doi.org/10.1016/j.ijme.2023.100790. DOI: 10.1016/j.ijme.2023.100790

Liu, B. (2021). "Weak AI" is Likely to Never Become "Strong AI", So What is its Greatest Value for us? *Arxiv*. https://arxiv.org/pdf/2103.15294

Liu, Y., Li, Y., Yang, S., Ren, T., Li, H., Hogg, A., Shah, P., Li, J., Zhang, Y., & Chhetri, A. (2022). A hybrid and non-formal music education connecting China's local family communities and cultures with Nepal. [IJI]. *International Journal for Infonomics*, 15(1), 2088–2093. Advance online publication. DOI: 10.20533/iji.1742.4712.2022.0218

Masino, S., & Niño-Zarazúa, M. (2016). What works to improve the quality of student learning in developing countries? *International Journal of Educational Development*, 48, 53–65. https://doi.org/https://doi.org/10.1016/j.ijedudev.2015.11.012. DOI: 10.1016/j.ijedudev.2015.11.012

McNatt, B. (2020). Service-learning: An experiment to increase interpersonal communication confidence and competence. *Education + Training*, 62(2), 129–144. DOI: 10.1108/ET-02-2019-0039

Mohammed, F. S., & Ozdamli, F. (2024). A Systematic Literature Review of Soft Skills in Information Technology Education. *Behavioral Sciences (Basel, Switzerland)*, 14(10), 894. DOI: 10.3390/bs14100894 PMID: 39457766

Nguyen, N. D. (2023). Exploring the role of AI in education. *London Journal of Social Sciences*, (6), 84–95. DOI: 10.31039/ljss.2023.6.108

Open, A. I. (2023). ChatGPT: Optimizing Language Models for Dialogue Available at. https://openai.com/blog/chatgpt

Păvăloaia, V.-D., & Necula, S.-C. (2023). Artificial Intelligence as a Disruptive Technology—A Systematic Literature Review. *Electronics (Basel)*, 12(5), 1102. DOI: 10.3390/electronics12051102

Poole, A. H. (2021). *Promoting Diversity, Equity, and Inclusion in Library and Information Science through Community-Based Learning. Diversity, Divergence.* Dialogue.

Redmond, A. R. (2023). Combining Project-Based Learning and Service-Learning in Teaching Global Issues. In Butcher, C., Bhasin, T., Gordon, E., & Hallward, M. C. (Eds.), *The Palgrave Handbook of Teaching and Research in Political Science* (pp. 231–243). Springer International Publishing., DOI: 10.1007/978-3-031-42887-6_20

Resch, K., & Schrittesser, I. (2023). Using the Service-Learning approach to bridge the gap between theory and practice in teacher education. *International Journal of Inclusive Education*, 27(10), 1118–1132. DOI: 10.1080/13603116.2021.1882053

Rodríguez-Zurita, D., Jaya-Montalvo, M., Moreira-Arboleda, J., Raya-Diez, E., & Carrión-Mero, P. (2024). Sustainable development through service learning and community engagement in higher education: a systematic literature review. *International Journal of Sustainability in Higher Education, ahead-of-print*(ahead-of-print). https://doi.org/DOI: 10.1108/IJSHE-10-2023-0461

Ruiz-Rojas, L. I., Salvador-Ullauri, L., & Acosta-Vargas, P. (2024). Collaborative Working and Critical Thinking: Adoption of Generative Artificial Intelligence Tools in Higher Education. *Sustainability (Basel)*, 16(13), 5367. DOI: 10.3390/su16135367

Sadek, M., Markauskaite, L., Rousell, D., & Collin, P. (2023). Guidelines for Integrating Value Sensitive Design in Responsible AI Toolkits. *Arxiv*. https://doi.org//arXiv.2403.00145DOI: 10.48550

Salvador-Ullauri, L., & Acosta-Vargas, P. (2024). Collaborative Working and Critical Thinking: Adoption of Generative Artificial Intelligence Tools in Higher Education. *Sustainability (Basel)*, 16(3), 5367. Advance online publication. DOI: 10.3390/su16135367

Samala, A. D., Rawas, S., Wang, T., Reed, J. M., Kim, J., Howard, N.-J., & Ertz, M. (2024). Unveiling the landscape of generative artificial intelligence in education: A comprehensive taxonomy of applications, challenges, and future prospects. *Education and Information Technologies*. Advance online publication. DOI: 10.1007/s10639-024-12936-0

Saxena, D., & Cao, J. (2005). Generative Adversarial Networks (GANs): Challenges, Solutions, and Future Directions. *Arxiv*. https://arxiv.org/vc/arxiv/papers/2005/2005.00065v1.pdf

Scharpnick, M., & Monahan, A. (2023). *Building the Future of UX in a World of Generative AI*. https://media-publications.bcg.com/Building-the-Future-of-UX-in-a-World-of-Generative-AI.pdf

Schwartz, A., & Meuers, A. (2024). Service-Learning: Empowering students to practice their civic character. https://www.character.org/service-learning

Sengar, S. S., Hasan, A. B., Kumar, S., & Carroll, F. (2024). Generative artificial intelligence: A systematic review and applications. *Multimedia Tools and Applications*. Advance online publication. DOI: 10.1007/s11042-024-20016-1

StanfordUniversity. (2023). Cardinal Service: Engaging Students in Public Service. https://cardinalservice.stanford.edu

Stuedahl, D. (2015). Future Orientation in Design, Participation and Learning no. 26, 2015, pp. DOI: . *Interaction Design and Architecture(s) Journal - IxD&A, 26*, 13.DOI: 10.55612/s-5002-026-009

Su, J., & Yang, W. (2023). Unlocking the Power of ChatGPT: A Framework for Applying Generative AI in Education. *ECNU Review of Education*, 6(3), 355–366. DOI: 10.1177/20965311231168423

Suresh, A., Wighton, N. M., Sorensen, T. E., Palladino, T. C., & Pinto-Powell, R. C. (2022). A hybrid educational approach to service learning: Impact on student attitudes and readiness in working with medically underserved communities. *Medical Education Online*, 27(1), 2122106. Advance online publication. DOI: 10.1080/10872981.2022.2122106 PMID: 36120928

Taylor, R. R., O'Dell, B., & Murphy, J. W. (2024). Human-centric AI: Philosophical and community-centric considerations. *AI & Society*, 39(5), 2417–2424. DOI: 10.1007/s00146-023-01694-1

Tijsma, G., Hilverda, F., Scheffelaar, A., Alders, S., Schoonmade, L., Blignaut, N., & Zweekhorst, M. (2020). Becoming productive 21 century citizens: A systematic review uncovering design principles for integrating community service learning into higher education courses. *Educational Research*, 62(4), 390–413. DOI: 10.1080/00131881.2020.1836987

Torvinen, L. T. (2017). *The concept of orientation in teachers' thinking and practices in business education*. Institute of Education, University of London.

Tucker, M. L., McCarthy, A. M., Hoxmeier, J. A., & Lenk, M. M. (1998). Community Service Learning Increases Communication Skills Across the Business Curriculum. *Business Communication Quarterly*, 61(2), 88–99. DOI: 10.1177/108056999806100211

UNESCO. (2024a). AI competency framework for students. https://www.unesco.org/en/articles/ai-competency-framework-students

UNESCO. (2024b). AI competency framework for teachers. https://unesdoc.unesco.org/ark:/48223/pf0000391104

UNESCO. (2024c). Guidance for Generative AI in Education and Research. https://unesdoc.unesco.org/ark:/48223/pf0000386693

Vanoye-García, A. Y., Menchaca-Torre, H. L., & López-Navarro, G. M. (2024). From Classroom to Community: Building Sustainability Competencies Through Service Learning in the Public Sector. 2024 IEEE Global Engineering Education Conference (EDUCON), Verger, A., Edwards Jr, D. B., & Altinyelken, H. K. (2014). Learning from all? The World Bank, aid agencies and the construction of hegemony in education for development. *Comparative Education*, 50(4), 381–399. DOI: 10.1080/03050068.2014.918713

Vincent, C. S. (2021). Critically Engaged Civic Learning: A Comprehensive Restructuring of Service-Learning Approaches. *Michigan Journal of Community Service Learning*, 27(2). Advance online publication. DOI: 10.3998/mjcsloa.3239521.0027.205

Voorhees, E. (2016). The Service-Learning Scholar Model: Maximizing Impact by Improving Communication and Student Voice in Service Learning. *Undergraduate Journal of Service Learning & Community-Based Research*, 5, 1–13. DOI: 10.56421/ujslcbr.v5i0.239

Wang, Y., Liu, X., Zhang, Y., Sang, X., & Wang, M. (2020). The first model of family education on the delivery of bilingual British NCC digital literacy qualifications in Dalian, China — Engaging and motivating children. *Proceedings of the International Conference on Education in Mathematics, Science and Technology (ICEMST)*, Istanbul, Turkey, 21-24 March.

Wilson, T. D. (2008). Activity theory in information seeking. *Annual Review of Information Science & Technology*, 42(1), 43. DOI: 10.1002/aris.2008.1440420111

Yan, W.-X., Nakajima, T., & Sawada, R. (2024). Benefits and Challenges of Collaboration between Students and Conversational Generative Artificial Intelligence in Programming Learning: An Empirical Case Study. *Education Sciences*, 14(4), 433. DOI: 10.3390/educsci14040433

Yan, Z. (2022). *Implementing a 21st century competency-based curriculum through lesson study: Teacher learning about cross-curricular and online pedagogy*. Routledge. https://orcid.org/0000-0001-9305-884X

Zainuri, A., & Huda, M. (2023). Empowering Cooperative Teamwork for Community Service Sustainability: Insights from Service Learning. *Sustainability (Basel)*, 15(5), 4551. DOI: 10.3390/su15054551

Zhang, L., Ren, T., Xie, Y., Tian, Z., Tang, T., & Li, Y. (2022). Student Choirs and Virtual Social Practices by LivePBL: Linking Vocal Education with Project Based Learning. *Literacy Information and Computer Education Journal*, 13(1), 3860–3666. DOI: 10.20533/licej.2040.2589.2022.0482

Zhou, Y., Ren, T., Chen, N., Li, J., Lu, K., Li, Y., Acharya, A., Shah, P., Hogg, A., & Liu, Y. (2023). Student virtual social practices between China and Nepal. *International Journal of Technology and Inclusive Education*, 12(1), 1802–1807. https://infonomics-society.org/wp-content/uploads/Student-Virtual-Social-Practices-between-China-and-Nepal.pdf. DOI: 10.20533/ijtie.2047.0533.2023.0223

Zimmerman, J., & Forlizzi, J. (2014). *Research Through Design in HCI.* Springer., DOI: 10.1007/978-1-4939-0378-8_8

Zirar, A., Ali, S. I., & Islam, N. (2023). Worker and workplace Artificial Intelligence (AI) coexistence: Emerging themes and research agenda. *Technovation*, 124, 102747. DOI: 10.1016/j.technovation.2023.102747

ADDITIONAL READING

Dubay, C. M., & Richards, M. B. (2024). Leveraging Artificial Intelligence In Project-Based Service Learning To Advance Sustainable Development: A Pedagogical Approach For Marketing Education. *Marketing Education Review*, 34(4), 1–17. DOI: 10.1080/10528008.2024.2411975

Evenstein Sigalov, S., Cohen, A., & Nachmias, R. (2024). Transforming higher education: A decade of integrating wikipedia and wikidata for literacy enhancement and social impact. *Journal of Computers in Education*, 1-43.

Macías-Gómez-Estern, B., & Lalueza, J. L. (2024). Navigating I-positionings in higher education Service Learning as hybrid scenarios: A case study. *Learning, Culture and Social Interaction*, 45, 100805. DOI: 10.1016/j.lcsi.2024.100805

Mei, C. W., Konar, R., & Kumar, J. (2024). The Role of AI Chatbots in Transforming Guest Engagement and Marketing in Hospitality. In *Integrating AI-Driven Technologies Into Service Marketing* (pp. 595–620). IGI Global. DOI: 10.4018/979-8-3693-7122-0.ch029

KEY TERMS AND DEFINITIONS

21st-Century Skills: A set of skills considered essential for success in the modern world, including critical thinking, creativity, collaboration, and communication.

Adaptive Learning: A learning approach that tailors content and pacing based on the individual needs and progress of the learner, promoting a personalized education experience.

Artificial Intelligence (AI): A branch of computer science focused on creating systems capable of performing tasks that typically require human intelligence, such as decision-making and problem-solving.

Blended Learning: A method of education that combines traditional face-to-face classroom experiences with online learning to offer a flexible approach to teaching.

Collaborative Learning: A learning approach where students work together to solve problems, complete tasks, or develop projects, promoting teamwork and knowledge sharing.

Generative AI (Gen AI): A type of artificial intelligence that can create new content, including text, images, and sounds, based on the data it was trained on, often using models like ChatGPT.

Personalized Learning: An educational method that seeks to customize learning experiences to meet individual student needs, interests, and goals, often utilizing AI tools to adjust content.

Role-Based Interaction: A communication approach in educational settings where each participant assumes a specific role, such as mentor or learner, to enhance structured and meaningful exchanges.

Service-Learning: An educational strategy that integrates community service with academic learning, allowing students to apply their knowledge in real-world contexts while fostering civic responsibility.

Skill Communication: A targeted form of communication focused on conveying specific skills through structured collaboration, distinct from general communication skills.

APPENDIX I: INCORPORATES ADA-ROB COMPONENTS INTO TEMPLATES WITH CHATGPT

Table 4.

The Ada-Rob design approach is a structured methodology that emphasises openness and adaptability in hybrid communication within service-learning environments. Unlike other design methodologies, such as design thinking or human-centred design, Ada-Rob focuses on integrating academic learning with community service through diverse roles and adaptive learning strategies.	
Key Components of Ada-Rob Approach	**Role-Based Service:** This component facilitates the collaborative efforts of various roles—including educators, students, mentors, trainers, coaches, community partners, and institutional leaders—to bridge academic learning with community service. The success of service learning relies on the coordination and communication among these roles to deliver impactful services that meet both educational and community needs. **Adaptive Learning:** Adaptive learning personalizes the learning experience by dynamically adjusting content, pace, and instructional methods based on individual needs. It leverages data-driven insights, real-time feedback, and flexible instructional strategies to tailor the learning experience to each participant's abilities, interests, and progress within the evolving context of the service environment.

Prompt Template 1: Enhancing Collaboration Among Service-Learning Stakeholders

Objective	Target Skill(s)	Instructions	Expected Outcomes
To strengthen collaborative skills among service-learning stakeholders by addressing a shared community issue through role-based contributions.	Collaboration, communication, problem-solving	**Step 1:** Identify a community-based issue that is relevant to the goals of the service-learning project. **Step 2:** Assign roles to key stakeholders, such as educators (guidance), students (research or fieldwork), mentors (advice), and community partners (local insights). **Step 3:** Each stakeholder uses ChatGPT to generate insights, guidance, or resources based on their role and expertise. **Step 4:** Hold joint sessions to share individual contributions, refine solutions, and discuss the interdependence of each role. **Step 5:** Reflect as a group on how the collaboration among diverse stakeholders enhanced problem-solving.	Stronger collaborative efforts, where each stakeholder recognizes their role in addressing community needs, fostering an understanding of how service learning relies on the contributions of educators, students, mentors, and community partners.

Prompt Template 2: Customising Learning Pathways for Different Stakeholders Using Adaptive Learning

Objective	Target Skill(s)	Instructions	Expected Outcomes
To create personalized, adaptive learning experiences for each service learning stakeholder group using AI-driven tools.	Adaptive learning, individualized instruction, engagement.	**Step 1:** Conduct a needs assessment for each stakeholder group (e.g., educators may need pedagogical strategies, students may need research guidance, mentors may need leadership development). **Step 2:** Use ChatGPT to provide tailored content and learning pathways for each group. **Step 3:** Stakeholders engage in personalized activities, receiving real-time feedback to adjust their learning approach. **Step 4:** Use adaptive tools to track progress and make modifications as needed based on real-time feedback. **Step 5:** Encourage each stakeholder to reflect on how the adaptive learning process has influenced their contributions to the service project.	Enhanced engagement and skill development as each stakeholder experiences a personalized journey that supports their unique role within the service-learning ecosystem

Prompt Template 3: Reflective Stakeholder Learning through Theory and Practice Integration

Objective	Target Skill(s)	Instructions	Expected Outcomes
To develop reflective skills by encouraging each stakeholder in the service-learning environment to integrate theoretical knowledge with practical application.	Reflection, theory-to-practice integration, stakeholder collaboration	**Step 1:** Each stakeholder (educator, student, mentor, community partner) selects a theoretical framework relevant to their role (e.g., educators focus on pedagogical theory, students on research methods, mentors on leadership, community partners on sustainability practices). **Step 2:** Apply the theory in a practical setting, documenting the process and outcomes. **Step 3:** Use ChatGPT to generate reflective prompts tailored to each stakeholder's role, asking them to compare theoretical expectations with practical results. **Step 4:** Stakeholders share their reflections in a collaborative session, identifying where theory helped or needed adjustment in practice. **Step 5:** Use insights from the reflection to refine future practices within the service-learning context.	Each stakeholder deepens their understanding of how theoretical knowledge can be practically applied in real-world service learning, fostering a reflective, adaptive learning environment.

Chapter 13
The Future of AI in Education:
Predictions and Emerging Trends

Mustafa Kayyali
https://orcid.org/0000-0003-3300-262X
HE Higher Education Ranking, Syria

ABSTRACT

This chapter explores the expanding role of artificial intelligence (AI) in education, focusing on future projections and emerging trends shaping the next generation of learning. AI has already transformed educational landscapes, fostering personalized learning experiences, adaptive technologies, and automated administrative processes. This chapter examines upcoming AI-driven innovations poised to enhance educational outcomes further. Key trends, including intelligent tutoring systems, AI-powered assessments, and data-driven learning analytics, are analyzed for their potential impact. The chapter also addresses the ethical and practical challenges posed by AI in education, such as algorithmic bias and privacy concerns. By understanding these evolving dynamics, educators and policymakers can better prepare for a future where AI contributes positively to global learning environments.

INTRODUCTION

Artificial Intelligence (AI) is no longer a distant futuristic concept but a transformative force that has invaded practically every facet of our lives, including education (Ford, 2021). The application of AI in education signifies a fundamental paradigm change, as it challenges established methods of teaching and learning, making room for more efficient, personalized, and data-driven approaches. From K-12 education to

DOI: 10.4018/979-8-3693-7220-3.ch013

higher education and beyond, AI technologies are transforming how students learn, how professors teach, and how educational institutions manage their operations.

Historically, education systems have been built around a one-size-fits-all approach, with a uniform curriculum, pacing, and evaluation methods that appeal to the average student (Tenon & Epler, 2021). This method typically overlooks the particular requirements, abilities, and learning styles of individual individuals. AI, with its potential to transform this model by providing tailored learning experiences that adapt to the specific needs of each student (Kolluru et al, 2018). AI-powered systems may analyze students' progress in real-time, identify areas where they need improvement, and give customized learning resources to help them achieve. This shift toward individualized learning is not just a fad but a fundamental upheaval in how education is offered and consumed. One of the most important consequences of AI in education is the emergence of adaptive learning systems (Kabudi et al, 2021). These systems employ algorithms to analyze data on student performance and automatically alter the content, pace, and difficulty of classes to match each learner's level. This technology enables students to move at their own pace, giving greater flexibility and autonomy in the learning process (Kayyali, 2021). By finding patterns in how students learn, AI can anticipate issues before they happen, giving early interventions and support that can prevent learning gaps from developing. This is especially critical in large classrooms where professors may struggle to provide individualized attention to every student.

In addition to increasing student learning, AI has also shown to be a valuable tool for instructors and educational administrators. AI can automate administrative activities such as grading, scheduling, and attendance tracking, freeing up time for educators to focus on more meaningful interactions with students (Srinivasa et al, 2022). Intelligent tutoring systems (ITS) give extra support, acting as virtual assistants that help professors construct lesson plans, analyze student work, and even provide feedback on hard activities such as essays (Nguyen et al, 2023). These systems not only increase the efficiency of the classroom but also allow for more creative and innovative teaching approaches. Professors can employ AI-generated insights to adapt their lessons, making them more interesting and relevant to each student's learning experience. The incorporation of AI into education is not without its hurdles (Alam, 2021). The fast development of AI technology has raised fundamental considerations concerning the ethical implications of their usage in education. Issues such as data privacy, algorithmic prejudice, and the possibility of AI to replace human professors have spurred concerns among educators, legislators, and technologists. Ensuring that AI systems are built and implemented in ways that meet ethical norms and protect students' rights is a vital consideration as we move forward. Furthermore, there is a rising concern that dependence on AI could exacerbate the digital divide, as access to AI-driven educational technologies may be limited in under-resourced colleges or regions.

Despite these obstacles, the potential benefits of AI in education are too enormous to ignore (Pedro et al, 2019a). AI has the power to level the playing field, enabling equal opportunity for students from all backgrounds to attend high-quality education. By making education more individualized, inclusive, and efficient, AI might play a crucial role in tackling some of the most urgent concerns in education today, such as achievement gaps, teacher shortages, and student disengagement. As we move into the future, it becomes increasingly evident that AI will continue to play a crucial role in the growth of education. Emerging trends like AI-driven exams, intelligent content production, and virtual learning environments are just the beginning of what is conceivable (Kaswan et al, 2024). In the future years, we may anticipate AI to not only enhance existing educational methods but to fundamentally rethink what it means to learn, teach, and lead in an AI-enhanced society. This chapter will investigate these developing trends in-depth, offering insights into the ways AI is likely to affect the future of education and highlighting the significant problems and opportunities that lie ahead. By studying both the current applications and future possibilities of AI in education, we want to provide a complete picture of how this technology will continue to revolutionize the educational landscape.

HISTORICAL CONTEXT: HOW AI HAS SHAPED EDUCATION

AI has been quietly impacting education for decades, long before its transformative potential became a prominent topic of conversation (Pedro et al, 2019b). The origins of AI in education may be traced back to the 1960s when early studies on computer-assisted instruction began to emerge (McCalla, 2023). Though the technology was basic by today's standards, it represented the beginning of a journey that would eventually integrate AI into educational procedures. Over the past half-century, AI has progressed from simple tools and learning aids to extremely sophisticated systems that are altering the way students learn and professors teach (Kannan & Munday, 2018). Understanding how AI has influenced education historically provides significant insights into its current and future applications.

In its early phases, AI's role in education was essentially exploratory (Khosravi et al, 2022). In the 1960s and 1970s, educational academics began examining how computers could enhance learning in specific subject areas, particularly mathematics and logic (Guzdial & du Boulay, 2019). These early trials gave rise to some of the first intelligent tutoring systems (ITS), such as PLATO (Programmed Logic for Automatic Teaching Operations), a system developed at the University of Illinois (Cope & Kalantzis, 2023). PLATO was a pioneering project that utilized computer terminals to offer instructional information, providing students with immediate feedback on their responses (Jones & Latzko-Toth, 2017). While restricted in breadth and reach, PLATO revealed the promise of technology to promote tailored learning, an idea that would continue to expand with AI. The 1980s saw a surge in the creation of AI-driven educational technologies, particularly when developments in computing power made it possible to design more sophisticated learning environments (Ng et al, 2023). During this period, researchers began working on building AI systems that could mimic human tutoring. These technologies, known as intelligent tutoring systems (ITS), attempt to deliver tailored education by adapting to the learner's speed, knowledge level, and specific needs. ITS systems might evaluate student behavior, provide real-time feedback, and even suggest alternative learning methodologies when a student struggles with a concept (Holstein et al, 2017). The idea was to establish a virtual tutor that could deliver the kind of targeted help generally only accessible in one-on-one teacher-student interactions.

By the 1990s, AI was gaining popularity as a promising tool for increasing the quality and accessibility of education (Chassignol et al, 2018). Educational institutions began to understand the value of AI in enhancing traditional teaching techniques (Chen et al, 2020). One of the most important advances during this period was the expanding use of AI to enhance remote learning (Alam, 2021). As the internet grew more widely accessible, online learning platforms started utilizing AI to distribute instructional information to a bigger audience. AI-powered solutions could automate grading, create interactive learning experiences, and even monitor student interest and involvement in real time (Rekha et al, 2024). This was a huge advance toward individualized, scalable education.

During the early 2000s, AI in education evolved from experimental systems to practical applications with observable impacts (Aberšek, 2019). Learning management systems (LMS) and online educational platforms began employing AI to enhance the learning experience on a broader scale. These systems may offer customized learning routes depending on individual student performance, letting students focus on areas where they require the most improvement. Automated grading systems for assignments and examinations also become increasingly popular, allowing professors to focus on more complicated responsibilities such as curriculum creation and one-on-one student interaction (Monat & Gannon, 2018). AI's involvement in education was no longer only about experimentation—it was becoming a fundamental part of the educational infrastructure. As AI technology improved, its powers went beyond tutoring and administrative help (Khare et al, 2018). The 2010s ushered in a new era for AI in education, as big data analytics, machine learning, and natural language processing (NLP) began to fuel more complex applications. AI-driven platforms such as Coursera, edX, and Khan Academy began employing machine learning algorithms to personalize educational content at a massive scale (Marwan, 2020).

These platforms evaluated data from millions of users to find trends in learning behavior and propose content that corresponded with individual needs. This level of customization made it possible for students around the world to obtain high-quality education tailored to their unique strengths and shortcomings, breaking down obstacles to learning that had previously seemed insurmountable.

One of the most important advances during this period was the advent of adaptive learning systems, which represent one of the most profound ways AI has influenced education thus far (Kabudi et al, 2021). These systems can analyze a student's progress in real time and change the content and tempo of classes accordingly. For example, an adaptive learning platform may provide more tasks on a topic a student is struggling with or rush through topics they have already learned. This kind of individualized attention, made possible by AI, offers a more dynamic and adaptable learning experience than traditional educational approaches, where all students are expected to advance at the same speed. AI has also played a vital role in streamlining administrative processes in education, lowering the burden on professors and educational institutions (Ahmad et al, 2022). Automated grading methods have advanced in accuracy, now capable of analyzing not only multiple-choice tests but also more complicated tasks such as essays. AI systems may analyze grammar, coherence, and even the quality of arguments given in student essays, delivering both comments and scores. For professors, this means more time can be allocated to student interaction, curriculum creation, and creative teaching approaches, rather than being weighed down by time-consuming duties like grading. AI has expanded access to education by breaking down linguistic barriers. Through natural language processing and machine translation, AI-powered platforms like Duolingo and Google Translate have enabled students from non-English-speaking backgrounds to access instructional materials in their native language (Bowden et al, 2024). AI-powered chatbots and virtual assistants have also increased student support services, answering frequently asked questions, assisting with course choices, and even conducting tutoring on demand. These AI-driven technologies have allowed educational institutions to provide more personalized, responsive services at a fraction of the expense of human labor.

The COVID-19 pandemic further boosted the implementation of AI in education (Pantelimon, 2021). As universities and colleges globally transitioned to remote learning, the need for AI-powered solutions expanded tremendously. AI tools helped facilitate virtual classrooms, automate administrative duties, and provide tailored learning experiences in a time when in-person instruction was severely constrained. The pandemic underlined the significance of scalable, adaptive education systems, pushing AI to the center of the discourse about the future of learning. In looking at the historical context, it's apparent that AI's journey in education has been one of slow progression, moving from experimental systems in the 1960s to fully integrated tools that serve both students and educators today (Pham & Sampson, 2022).

Each decade has brought significant developments in technology, as AI has gotten increasingly sophisticated in its ability to analyze data, tailor learning experiences, and increase the efficiency of educational systems. What previously appeared like science fiction is now a reality, with AI playing a vital role in how education is provided worldwide (Cox, 2021). As AI continues to advance, its impact on education will undoubtedly deepen. The historical history of AI in education not only illustrates its promise to enhance teaching and learning but also reminds us of the necessity to approach new technologies intelligently (Seldon et al, 2020). The lessons learned from decades of AI research and implementation give a blueprint for navigating the problems that lie ahead. By building on the foundation developed over the past half-century, educators, technologists, and politicians can work together to create an educational system that uses the full potential of AI to support student success and fair access to learning opportunities.

CURRENT APPLICATIONS OF AI IN THE CLASSROOM

The classroom of today appears substantially different from what it did a few decades ago, partly due to the integration of new technologies (Varier et al, 2017). Among these, Artificial Intelligence (AI) is playing an increasingly major role in influencing modern educational methods. From increasing student learning experiences to aiding instructors in managing their classrooms, AI has woven itself into the fabric of education in once inconceivable ways. AI technologies have evolved past the experimental stage and are now widely applied in classrooms across the globe, with real-world applications that are improving the quality of education, increasing student engagement, and enabling individualized learning experiences (Alam, 2023).

One of the most transformational applications of AI in the classroom is its capacity to deliver individualized learning (Jaiswal & Arun, 2021). Traditionally, classrooms have followed a one-size-fits-all model, where a single curriculum is meant to fulfill the needs of a whole group of students (Bondie et al, 2019). This strategy often leaves some students struggling to keep up while others may remain unchallenged, as it does not account for the various learning speeds and demands of individual learners. AI has transformed this dynamic by introducing adaptive learning platforms that adjust instructional content to each student's individual needs (Gligorea et al, 2023). These technologies analyze student performance data in real time, highlighting areas where students thrive or need further guidance. Based on this information, AI-driven systems can give tailored learning routes, delivering resources that are more relevant to a student's current understanding of a subject.

This not only promotes learning results but also raises student motivation, as they can engage with information at a speed that fits them. AI-powered tutoring systems are another key application in the classroom (Rizvi, 2023). These intelligent tutoring systems (ITS) can replicate one-on-one interactions with students, providing customized instruction in disciplines ranging from mathematics to languages. Unlike human tutors, AI tutors are available 24/7, making it easy for students to obtain support whenever they need it (Chiu et al, 2023). These systems can break down complex topics into simpler, digestible bits, delivering explanations and examples until a student fully grasps the material. AI tutors can also provide quick feedback, allowing students to remedy mistakes and reinforce learning as they proceed (Alam, 2023b). This sort of individualized attention was previously only available to students who could afford private tutoring, but AI is democratizing access to these resources, bringing high-quality, tailored learning support to classrooms globally. AI also plays a big role in automating administrative duties that normally demand considerable amounts of professors' time (Acemoglu & Restrepo, 2018). Tasks like grading papers, maintaining timetables, and even tracking student attendance can be automated using AI technologies, freeing up professors to focus more on instruction and student engagement. Automated grading, in particular, has become a key tool for managing big classrooms where judging student work may be exceedingly time-consuming (Messer et al, 2024). AI systems are now capable of grading not only objective assessments like multiple-choice questions but also more complicated assignments like essays. These systems may analyze grammar, coherence, and even the quality of an argument, delivering both grades and comments. While AI-driven grading systems are not without their flaws, they greatly reduce the administrative burden on professors, allowing them to commit more time to meaningful classroom interactions.

In addition to grading, AI technologies are also being utilized to evaluate student data to provide deeper insights into classroom dynamics (Dimitriadou & Lanitis, 2023). AI can track how students interact with instructional content, how engaged they are throughout courses, and even how well they comprehend the material. By gathering and analyzing this data, AI systems can provide professors with actionable insights that assist them in identifying students who may be struggling or falling behind. This data-driven approach to education allows professors to act early, offering extra support to students who need it most. Moreover, AI can help professors develop more successful lesson plans by showing them what works and what doesn't, based on real-time feedback from student performance data. These insights allow educators to make educated judgments on curriculum adjustments, leading to more effective teaching practices. AI has also found a role in classroom administration, where it supports maintaining a disciplined and productive learning environment. For instance, AI systems can analyze student behavior during virtual or in-person sessions, recognizing trends that signal a lack of engagement or disruptive behavior. Some AI tools can even utilize facial recognition and emotion-detection technology to determine how attentive or interested students are during a class, providing professors with rapid feedback on the effectiveness of their teaching methods. While the use of such tools raises ethical concerns surrounding privacy, their potential to improve classroom management and promote student engagement is obvious.

Virtual learning environments have become another key application of AI in education, notably in the wake of the COVID-19 pandemic, which drove many institutions to convert to online learning (Kayyali, 2020). AI technology has proved essential in establishing interactive, engaging, and accessible virtual classrooms. These environments are designed to imitate the experience of an in-person class, allowing students to participate in discussions, ask questions, and communicate with their peers in real-time. AI-powered platforms can also monitor student progress during virtual lessons, providing comments and recommendations to both students and professors. Furthermore, AI can encourage peer-to-peer learning in these contexts by pairing students who are struggling with particular ideas with those who have mastered them, building a collaborative and supportive learning community.

One of the more future applications of AI in the classroom is the deployment of virtual teaching assistants (Chen et al, 2023). These AI-driven assistants can help professors handle classroom responsibilities, such as answering frequently asked questions, giving reminders about assignments, or even conducting small group tutoring sessions. Virtual teaching assistants are especially beneficial in large classrooms, when a teacher may not have the capacity to address every student's question or concern during a lesson (Kim et al, 2020). By doing basic duties and offering extra education, virtual assistants allow professors to focus on more complicated parts of teaching, such as leading conversations or devising new lesson plans. AI's influence on language learning has also been substantial (Pokrivcakova, 2019). Language-learning programs like Duolingo employ AI to tailor the learning experience, customizing lessons based on how quickly students are improving and which areas they find problematic (Sandor & Sándor, 2023). AI-powered language tutors can engage students in discussions, delivering real-time corrections on grammar, pronunciation, and sentence structure. By delivering rapid feedback and the flexibility to practice language skills at any time, these AI technologies have become an invaluable resource for students learning new languages. In addition, AI-driven translation technologies allow students to access learning materials in many languages, breaking down language barriers and enabling more inclusiveness in the classroom.

Incorporating AI into colleges has also been beneficial in aiding students with disabilities (Kharbat et al, 2021). AI solutions, such as speech recognition software and text-to-speech programs, allow students with visual, auditory, or learning challenges to engage more completely in classroom activities. For instance, AI-powered software can transcribe lectures for students who are deaf or hard of hearing, or turn text into voice for individuals with dyslexia (Zdravkova, 2022). These technologies have considerably expanded the inclusivity of education, guaranteeing that all students, regardless of their ability, have the opportunity to study and achieve in the classroom. AI has the potential to alter how professors and students approach education, but its impact is not confined to what happens within the classroom (Schiff, 2021). The incorporation of AI is also influencing educational policy and curriculum design at a broader level. Educational institutions are employing AI to evaluate huge volumes of data to make informed decisions about resource allocation, curriculum creation, and policy revisions. This data-driven strategy enables colleges and universities to respond to the growing requirements of students and educators, ensuring that educational systems stay agile and responsive to the problems of the future.

AI's current uses in the classroom are numerous and varied, increasing both the learning experience for students and the teaching experience for educators. From personalized learning platforms and intelligent tutoring systems to AI-driven administrative tools and virtual teaching assistants, AI is altering how education is delivered. While there are still problems and ethical concerns that need to be addressed, the promise of AI to improve educational outcomes and make learning more accessible is obvious. As AI technology continues to improve, its applications in the classroom will likely become even more crucial to the future of education.

PREDICTIONS FOR AI IN EDUCATION: WHAT'S NEXT?

As AI continues to improve, its potential to change the educational landscape grows tremendously (Seldon et al, 2020). The current applications of AI in education are certainly astounding, but the future promises far bigger possibilities. From inventing new techniques of learning to altering educational systems, AI is set to cause dramatic changes in how students learn and how professors teach. Predicting the future of AI in education includes envisioning more personalized, efficient, and inclusive educational systems that harness AI's potential to build dynamic learning environments tailored to the needs of every individual (Kayyali, 2024). One of the most anticipated breakthroughs is the emergence of adaptive learning platforms. Shortly, these algorithms are projected to become increasingly more complex, expanding beyond basic content customization. Instead of merely altering the pace or difficulty level of lessons, AI-driven systems will be able to anticipate the demands of learners based on predictive data. These technologies will collect and analyze large amounts of data from many sources—student interactions, performance history, and even social behavior—to give a completely tailored learning experience. For example, an

AI system might identify that a student tends to struggle more during the morning hours and propose altering their learning schedule to the afternoon when they are more interested and focused. Over time, AI could comprehend not only academic preferences but also emotional states, enabling a more holistic learning experience that is responsive to the cognitive and emotional demands of each student.

AI's predictive power also extends to educational outcomes (Pedro et al, 2019c). In the future, AI systems will likely be able to predict a student's academic success with a high degree of accuracy based on real-time data. This prediction power could enable earlier intervention techniques for students in danger of falling behind. Instead of waiting until a kid fails an exam or shows indications of disengagement, instructors and colleges officials might use AI insights to detect at-risk students before they reach a crisis point. These preventive interventions might be designed for each kid, potentially incorporating tailored tutoring programs, mentorship opportunities, or improvements to their learning environment. As a result, educational institutions will be able to minimize dropout rates, boost graduation rates, and ensure that all students receive the support they need to succeed (Johnson & Stage, 2018). One interesting forecast is the potential for AI to assist lifelong learning. In the future, AI won't just be utilized in colleges but will accompany individuals throughout their lives, promoting ongoing learning and skill development. As the world of work becomes increasingly mechanized and technology-driven, the demand for reskilling and upskilling will only grow.

AI will help bridge this gap by creating tailored learning routes that change with an individual's career (Bukartaite & Hooper, 2023). For instance, an AI platform might monitor a person's employment performance and offer courses, certificates, or micro-credentials to help them stay competitive in the job market. This kind of dynamic, ongoing education will ensure that learners can adjust to changes in the workforce, keep current skills, and achieve long-term career success. The idea of education being confined to a set moment in a person's life, such as university or college, will diminish as AI enables education to become a lifetime companion (Seldon et al, 2020). The role of AI in the classroom is also projected to evolve beyond what we see now. As AI systems grow more clever, they will take on progressively more complex educational roles, potentially acting as co-professors or mentors. Rather than simply aiding professors with administrative responsibilities or delivering feedback on assignments, future AI systems could help build entire curriculums, altering the material dynamically based on real-time input. In other circumstances, AI might even be able to facilitate group conversations or guide project-based learning, giving students individualized support while professors focus on managing the broader educational experience. These powerful AI teaching technologies could ensure that each student gets the attention they need, even in huge classrooms, making education more egalitarian and inclusive.

One important development we may foresee is the integration of AI with emotional and social learning (Jones et al, 2019). While present AI tools are mostly focused on academic success, future systems will likely contain a deeper understanding of students' emotional and social well-being. These systems could track indications like engagement, motivation, and emotional responses to various learning scenarios, delivering insights into how students are feeling and whether they need further emotional support. For example, an AI system might observe that a student who was previously engaged is getting increasingly frustrated with their studies, causing the system to modify the difficulty level or warn the teacher that the student may need help. AI might also enhance social connections among students by offering group projects based on matching personalities and developing teamwork, collaboration, and interpersonal skills, which are crucial for success in the real world.

Another potential trend in AI and education is the advent of immersive learning environments (Jayadurga & Rathika, 2023). Virtual reality (VR) and augmented reality (AR) are already starting to penetrate colleges, but as AI advances, these technologies will become even more engaging and intelligent. Imagine a world where AI-powered VR settings allow students to witness historical events firsthand or conduct virtual science experiments with real-time feedback from an AI teacher (Chitra, 2019). These immersive learning experiences could make education more engaging and hands-on, especially for disciplines that are difficult to teach through standard techniques. AI-enhanced VR and AR settings could potentially benefit students with diverse learning styles, providing them with alternate approaches to absorbing hard subjects. This might drastically enhance student engagement, making learning more pleasurable and productive.

A more controversial forecast is the rise of fully automated, AI-driven colleges (Saaida, 2023). While it's doubtful that AI will completely replace human professors shortly, there is a rising chance that specific educational environments will be entirely administered by AI. In remote or underserved places where competent professors are uncommon, AI systems could provide high-quality education to students who might otherwise have restricted access to learning opportunities. These AI classrooms might be outfitted with adaptive learning systems, virtual tutors, and AI-driven administrative tools, guaranteeing that students obtain a thorough education even in the absence of human professors. While this poses ethical problems about the role of professors and the nature of education, it also presents an opportunity to close educational gaps and bring learning to areas that have historically been left behind.

Ethical considerations around AI in education are another area that will undoubtedly emerge as the technology becomes more powerful (Stahl, 2021). Future talks will need to address concerns such as data privacy, bias in AI algorithms, and the role of AI in measuring student achievement. As AI systems become more incorporated into education, ensuring that these systems are fair, transparent, and ethical will be paramount. Policymakers, educators, and technologists will need to work together to design legislation and guidelines that protect students' rights while yet allowing AI to enhance the educational experience (Holmes et al, 2022). Additionally, educators will need to be trained not only in how to use AI technologies but also in how to critically analyze them to ensure they are serving the best interests of students.

In the coming years, AI could also revolutionize how educational institutions work at an administrative level (Pedro et al, 2019d). AI may be used to streamline college timetables, manage resources more efficiently, and even predict trends in enrollment or student needs. For example, AI systems could examine demographic data to anticipate variations in student populations, allowing institutions to prepare for future changes in demand for certain courses or programs. AI-driven analytics could also assist colleges optimize resource allocation, ensuring that cash, technology, and people are directed where they are most needed. This level of operational efficiency could make educational institutions more responsive to the changing requirements of their students, providing a more flexible and adaptive educational system. The future of AI in education holds immense potential to alter every element of learning and teaching. As AI continues to improve, we may expect increasingly personalized, immersive, and efficient educational experiences that respond to the particular requirements of students and the broader difficulties facing educational systems. While there are still many unknowns about how AI will ultimately affect education, the forecasts for its future use imply that we are on the edge of a revolution that will redefine what it means to learn, teach, and succeed in the 21st century. The key will be ensuring that AI is applied in ways that are ethical, egalitarian, and focused on boosting human potential. If done well, AI might be the driving force behind a more inclusive, innovative, and effective global education system.

EMERGING TRENDS IN AI-DRIVEN LEARNING TOOLS

The landscape of education has been radically revolutionized by AI-driven learning technologies, and this transformation continues to evolve at a rapid pace (Ozer et al, 2024). As AI technology improves, we are witnessing the introduction of novel learning technologies that are redefining how students gain knowledge, how professors connect with learners, and how education systems adapt to the requirements of an increasingly diverse student body. These rising trends suggest a future where learning is more individualized, dynamic, and engaging, unleashing new opportunities for both students and educators. One of the most significant trends in AI-driven learning tools is the rise of intelligent tutoring systems (ITS) (Ivanović et al, 2022). These systems, backed by complex algorithms, are designed to give one-on-one tutoring sessions that replicate the direction a human tutor may offer. Unlike traditional classroom situations where professors must cater to an entire group of students with various requirements, intelligent tutoring systems focus on individual learners, delivering individualized feedback and instruction based on their performance. These systems have gotten increasingly complex, leveraging data analytics to analyze a student's progress, identify their strengths and shortcomings, and deliver tailored interventions to improve learning results. The versatility of these AI-powered instructors allows students to learn at their own pace and gives them individualized help, leading to greater retention and understanding of challenging subjects.

Another significant trend in AI-driven learning tools is the integration of AI with augmented reality (AR) and virtual reality (VR) to build immersive learning environments (Gandedkar et al, 2021). These technologies provide students with dynamic, hands-on experiences that can be difficult to attain in traditional classroom settings. For example, students can utilize VR to take virtual field trips to historical locations, investigate the human body at a microscopic level, or recreate real-world experiments in physics and chemistry. AI adds another layer of intricacy to these experiences by customizing the information in real time to a student's performance or preferences. This form of immersive learning engages students in ways that standard textbooks and lectures cannot, making it particularly beneficial for courses that need visualization and active engagement. AI is also driving the development of new collaborative learning technologies (Wise et al, 2021). Traditional education frequently requires a substantial amount of individual work, yet many future occupations require strong cooperation and collaboration abilities. AI-driven platforms are emerging that facilitate group projects by matching students with complementary strengths, evaluating their interactions, and delivering real-time feedback on cooperation dynamics. For instance, an AI tool might recognize if one student is dominating the conversation in a collaborative project, and offer strategies to better balance participation. These technologies build a more equitable and effective collaborative experience, ensuring that all students are engaged and contributing to the group's success. Furthermore, they teach crucial soft skills such as communication, problem-solving, and leadership, which are essential for success in both academia and the industry.

Another rising trend is the use of AI in formative and summative evaluations (Hooda et al, 2022). AI-driven assessment systems are becoming increasingly accurate in measuring student performance, not only by analyzing test responses but also by evaluating more sophisticated elements like critical thinking, creativity, and problem-solving ability. These technologies may analyze student work swiftly and efficiently, delivering rapid feedback that helps students learn from their mistakes in real-time. Additionally, AI can assess long-term growth and discover patterns in student behavior, revealing insights that professors might miss (Chen, 2023). For example, AI might notice that a student is persistently struggling with a particular type of question across various topics, allowing the teacher to intervene with tailored instruction. AI-driven exams are thus contributing to a more data-informed approach to education, helping professors make better decisions about how to educate their students. A particularly intriguing trend is the emergence of natural language processing (NLP) tools that can help language acquisition. NLP technology enables AI systems to perceive, interpret, and synthesize human language, making it an invaluable tool for teaching languages. AI-powered language learning apps and platforms, like Duolingo and Babbel, are growing more complex, giving individualized courses that adjust to a learner's skill level (Singha et al, 2024). These systems may now provide real-time feedback on speech, grammar, and sentence structure, allowing learners to enhance their language skills with minimum human interaction. Additionally, AI-powered chatbots can imitate discussions with native speakers, allowing learners the option to practice their abilities in a low-pressure environment. This form of dynamic, real-time feedback accelerates the language learning process and makes it more accessible to learners throughout the world.

AI-driven learning tools are also increasing their reach by addressing the requirements of students with disabilities (Rai et al, 2024). Accessibility is a rising concern in the development of educational technologies, and AI is playing a crucial role in making learning more inclusive. For example, AI-powered transcription services may transform oral lectures into text in real-time, aiding students who are deaf or hard of hearing. Similarly, AI systems that offer text-to-speech capabilities can help students with visual impairments or dyslexia access written content. Furthermore, AI-driven learning platforms can provide individualized help to students with cognitive challenges, giving adapted lessons or alternate learning formats that cater to their specific needs (Strielkowski et al, 2024). These tools are breaking down barriers to education and ensuring that all students have the opportunity to achieve, regardless of their physical or cognitive limitations. A trend that is gaining popularity is the use of AI for emotional and behavioral analytics. By evaluating students' facial expressions, voice tones, and interest levels, AI can acquire insights into their emotional states and learning practices. This information can be important for professors, allowing them to determine when students are struggling, disengaged, or experiencing stress. For example, if an AI system detects that a student's attention is waning during a certain sort of lecture, it can offer other learning materials or activities that might re-engage the learner. These insights assist build a more responsive and supportive learning environment, one that respects the emotional and psychological sides of learning, not simply the intellectual.

A trend that is expected to shape the future of AI-driven learning systems is the concept of lifelong learning (Saaida, 2023). As the pace of technological change accelerates, the skills necessary in the employment market are increasing swiftly.

AI-driven learning technologies are increasingly being created not just for traditional K-12 or higher education environments, but for continuous learning throughout one's life. These platforms can assist professionals upskill and reskill by giving tailored learning pathways that adapt to their job goals and performance. For example, AI-powered platforms might recommend certain courses or certifications depending on an individual's employment performance and the current demands of the labor market. By making education more flexible and accessible, AI is helping to build a culture of lifelong learning that is important for staying competitive in today's fast-changing world. The growing trends in AI-driven learning technologies indicate a fundamental transformation in how education is delivered and experienced. These tools are making learning more personalized, engaging, and accessible, while also providing professors with the data and insights they need to better serve their students. As AI continues to improve, we should expect even more innovative learning technologies that push the boundaries of what is possible in education, generating new opportunities for students and educators alike. The important problem moving forward will be ensuring that these technologies are applied in ways that are ethical, egalitarian, and focused on augmenting human learning experiences rather than replacing them.

ETHICAL CONCERNS IN AI-DRIVEN PERSONALIZED LEARNING

The incorporation of AI in education offers substantial prospects for innovation, especially via individualized learning (Pedro et al, 2019). Nevertheless, these improvements bring out numerous ethical considerations that must not be overlooked. AI systems possess the capacity to influence both the educational experience and the social-emotional growth of pupils, frequently without the direct oversight or comprehension of the individuals these technologies aim to assist. Confronting these ethical dilemmas is crucial to guaranteeing that AI improves education equitably, inclusively, and responsibly, while preventing any accidental harm to students, educators, or society as a whole

Data Privacy and Student Autonomy

A primary ethical challenge about AI in tailored learning is data privacy (Murdoch, 2021). Artificial intelligence systems rely significantly on extensive datasets to customize educational experiences for individual learners (Colchester et al, 2017). These datasets frequently encompass not only academic records but also behavioral patterns, personal preferences, and, in certain instances, physiological data such as eye-tracking and emotional responses. While this information can be essential for tailoring schooling, it also represents a huge breach of privacy. Students and their families may lack a comprehensive understanding of the scope of data collection and its utilization, hence prompting questions around consent and autonomy. The data collected from pupils must be managed with the utmost care to prevent misuse. For instance, personal data could be sold to third-party companies or repurposed for non-educational applications, such as targeted advertising or recruitment by enterprises. Without stringent data protection standards, student data can become subject to breaches, theft, or other forms of exploitation. This creates a contradiction between the benefits of individualized learning and the necessity to preserve students' privacy rights. The way AI systems function can impede student autonomy. While AI-driven platforms provide students more flexibility over their learning pace and style, they frequently do so within a framework that is tightly prescribed by algorithms (Ejjami, 2024). This can hinder a student's ability to make independent choices and may lead to an over-reliance on AI advice. In this way, AI could unintentionally limit a student's capacity for self-directed learning, since they may start to trust machine ideas more than their own judgment.

Bias and Inequality

Bias is another key ethical concern that occurs when AI is employed in education (Akgun & Greenhow, 2022). AI systems are just as neutral as the data they are educated on, and educational datasets often reflect existing societal disparities. For example, students from underrepresented racial or socio-economic backgrounds may perform differently in academic contexts due to structural disadvantages. If these inequalities are not appropriately accounted for in AI algorithms, the system could reinforce existing biases, disproportionately penalize previously underrepresented groups. One real-world example of this comes from a college admissions algorithm that was discovered to favor applicants from affluent families, as the data used to train the algorithm overrepresented privileged individuals (Akchurin & Chouhy, 2024). Such biases might also show in grading systems, where AI might rate students' work not based on its worth, but according to patterns in the data that reflect pre-existing inequities. This risks establishing a loop where kids from disadvantaged families receive lower grades, fewer chances, and less support, further entrenching the disparity between them and their classmates. To prevent prejudice, developers of AI systems must emphasize the construction of varied and representative datasets. They must also ensure that these systems are regularly inspected and updated to adjust for any new biases. Moreover, educators must be trained to understand and resist these prejudices, ensuring that AI is used as a tool for fairness and inclusiveness rather than an instrument of greater discrimination.

Transparency and Accountability

Transparency is vital when it comes to the ethical deployment of AI in personalized learning (van der Vorst & Jelicic, 2019). Students, parents, and educators need to understand how AI systems work, what data is being collected, and how choices are made. Unfortunately, many AI systems operate as "black boxes," meaning that the decision-making process is hidden from consumers. This lack of transparency can present serious concerns, especially when AI systems are used to make key decisions such as grades, course placements, or interventions in a student's learning path. For instance, if a student is recognized by an AI system as being at risk of falling behind, it is crucial to understand why the system made that judgment. Was it based on the student's achievement in a particular topic, their engagement levels, or a mix of factors?

Without explicit explanations, students and educators may be kept in the dark, unable to debate or rectify erroneous AI judgments. This can lead to a lack of trust in AI systems and possibly worsen existing injustices if AI actions are not adequately evaluated. Accountability is directly connected to openness. Who is accountable when an AI system makes a mistake? Should the blame go on the developers who designed the technology, the instructors who administered it, or the institution that oversees its use? Clear lines of responsibility are vital to ensuring that AI technologies are used ethically and responsibly. Educational institutions must have tools in place to allow students to debate AI-driven decisions and must be prepared to act when AI systems make errors (George, 2023). Additionally, AI developers must be held accountable for ensuring that their systems are trustworthy, fair, and transparent.

Human Element in Education

One of the most serious ethical problems regarding AI in personalized learning is the potential erosion of the human element in education (Costa, 2023). While AI can offer efficiency, data-driven insights, and personalized support, it cannot replace the emotional and social components of human teaching. Education is not simply about teaching knowledge; it is also about cultivating critical thinking, creativity, empathy, and resilience. These traits are best nurtured through meaningful interactions between students and professors, something that AI, at least in its current state, cannot fully imitate. There is a risk that as AI gets more incorporated into education, it could lead to a depersonalization of learning, where students are treated as data points rather than individuals with unique needs, emotions, and goals (Filgueiras, 2023). This could be particularly devastating for students who require emotional assistance, such as those suffering with mental health concerns or severe life circumstances. In these circumstances, the presence of a kind and attentive instructor can make all the difference in a student's capacity to succeed. To avoid this problem, AI should be considered as a tool that enhances, rather than replaces, human teachers. Educators must continue to play a major role in the learning process, employing AI to enhance their teaching but not to reduce their personal relationship with pupils. AI should be utilized to automate tedious chores and deliver insights that help teachers better understand their pupils, freeing up time for more meaningful interactions that stimulate emotional and intellectual growth.

Ethical considerations surrounding AI-driven tailored learning are complicated (Tariq, 2024). Issues like data protection, bias, openness, accountability, and the human factor all need to be carefully explored as AI becomes more integrated into education. These challenges are not insurmountable, but they demand thinking and proactive approaches from educators, developers, policymakers, and institutions alike. By addressing these ethical challenges head-on, we can ensure that AI acts as a force for good in education, increasing learning experiences without compromising the principles of fairness, inclusivity, and human dignity.

AI AND THE DIGITAL DIVIDE: BRIDGING OR WIDENING THE GAP?

The digital divide refers to the gap between persons and groups having access to contemporary information and communication technology and those without (Van Dijk, 2017). AI-driven individualized learning has the ability to both bridge and deepen this difference, particularly when it comes to impoverished pupils who lack resources. On the one hand, AI can democratize access to education by giving individualized learning experiences to students who may not have access to high-quality teachers or educational materials. On the other side, if not applied appropriately, AI could worsen existing inequities by further marginalizing students who lack access to the technology, infrastructure, or digital literacy necessary to benefit from these systems. Understanding how AI may either bridge or deepen the digital divide demands a closer look at the factors driving technology access, infrastructure, and educational results. It also demands a careful approach to policy, design, and execution to ensure that the most vulnerable children are not left behind in the rush to deploy AI technologies in education.

The Potential of AI to Bridge the Digital Divide

AI has the potential to change education by providing individualized learning experiences that adjust to each student's needs (Chen et al, 2020). This could be particularly advantageous for pupils in under-resourced regions, where educational possibilities are generally limited. In locations where there is a shortage of trained teachers, AI can assist bridge the gap by allowing pupils access to high-quality, tailored teaching that they may not otherwise receive. AI-driven platforms may provide real-time feedback, monitor student progress, and adapt learning courses based on a student's strengths and limitations, helping to level the playing field amongst students from diverse socio-economic backgrounds. AI can help democratize access to educational content. In many poor communities, textbooks and other learning resources are either old or inaccessible (Weishart, 2020). AI platforms can offer digital versions of textbooks, video lessons, and interactive exercises, making high-quality content accessible to anybody with an internet connection. In this approach, AI might potentially bridge the digital divide by providing students from underprivileged backgrounds with access to resources that were previously out of reach. Language difficulties can also be solved with AI. In multicultural or multilingual settings, where educational materials may only be available in dominant languages, AI-powered translation technologies can enable students to learn in their home tongue. This fosters inclusiveness and removes barriers to learning for children who may otherwise struggle to keep up in classrooms where instruction is not in their first language. AI might also support instructors in under-resourced schools, helping them manage big class numbers and providing them with insights into individual student performance (Kasun, 2024). By automating typical administrative duties, AI frees up teachers' time, allowing them to focus on more meaningful interactions with their students. This kind of support can be revolutionary in schools where teachers are stretched thin, allowing them skills to manage their workload more effectively and ensuring that no student falls between the cracks.

The Risk of AI Widening the Digital Divide

Despite these potential benefits, there is a major risk that AI could increase the digital gap, especially if access to the technology remains uneven. For AI to have a good impact on individualized learning, students must have access to gadgets, dependable internet, and digital literacy abilities (Alakrash & Abdul Razak, 2021). In many underprivileged communities, particularly in rural or economically deprived metropolitan regions, these resources are not readily available. In locations with inadequate internet connectivity or a lack of digital devices, kids are unlikely to benefit from AI-driven educational tools, no matter how smart or successful those tools could be. This creates a two-tiered system where kids with access to technology receive better, individualized instruction, while others without it continue to rely on traditional, and often worse, learning techniques. This mismatch can worsen existing educational disparities, as pupils who lack access to AI technology fall further behind their peers. The application of AI in education can be costly, and schools in underfunded locations may not be able to finance the necessary infrastructure. AI-driven systems require significant investment in hardware, software, and ongoing maintenance, as well as teacher training to guarantee that educators know how to use these technologies effectively (Kim, 2024). Without substantial financial support, schools serving impoverished pupils may struggle to integrate AI into their classrooms, further entrenching the digital divide. The difficulty of digital literacy also plays a crucial role in the growing of the digital divide. Many poor pupils, as well as their families and teachers, lack the digital literacy skills essential to utilize AI-based platforms efficiently. Even if the technology is available, students may not know how to use it in a way that optimizes its instructional value. This digital illiteracy can inhibit students from fully benefiting from AI-driven tailored learning, leaving them at a disadvantage compared to their more tech-savvy peers.

Structural Inequality and AI

Another concern is that AI systems could inadvertently exacerbate existing disparities due to the way they are developed and trained (Capraro et al, 2024). AI algorithms are only as good as the data they are trained on, and if this data is biased or incomplete, the systems can produce biased outcomes. For example, if an AI system is trained on data that over-represents wealthier students, it may be more likely to favor learning patterns and behaviors that are typical within this group, while failing to detect the skills and needs of kids from poor backgrounds. AI systems generally rely on criteria such as engagement, involvement, and academic performance to assess pupils. However, students from poor backgrounds may experience external barriers, such as lack of access to quiet study places or financial obligations, that impair their ability to interact with AI-driven learning tools. If AI systems do not account for these issues, they could wrongly classify these students as less capable or less engaged, reinforcing damaging stereotypes and further marginalizing them in the educational process. To address these concerns, developers of AI systems must be cognizant of the ways in which their algorithms can perpetuate structural inequalities. This necessitates broadening the datasets used to train AI, ensuring that these systems are built to recognize and accommodate the different circumstances and obstacles faced by impoverished kids. Moreover, schools and governments must work together to ensure that AI systems are implemented in a way that promotes equity, rather than exacerbates inequality.

Policy Solutions and Collaborative Efforts

Closing the digital divide in the context of AI-driven personalized learning will require a coordinated effort from governments, educational institutions, tech businesses, and civil society organizations (George, 2024). Public policy has a key role to play in ensuring that all students, regardless of their socio-economic level, have access to the technology and resources necessary to benefit from AI. Investment in infrastructure is a vital component of this effort. Governments must prioritize the provision of high-speed internet access to underserved areas, particularly in rural regions where connectivity remains a key obstacle to the use of AI-driven educational tools. Additionally, funding must be committed to guarantee that schools in low-income neighborhoods can offer kids with access to equipment such as laptops or tablets, which are vital for engaging with AI platforms. Teacher training is also crucial. AI cannot be properly integrated into education without skilled instructors who know how to use these tools in ways that boost learning (Chen et al, 2020). Professional development programs that focus on digital literacy and the pedagogical application of AI can empower teachers to harness technology in ways that help all students, particularly those from impoverished backgrounds. Collaboration between IT businesses and educational institutions can also assist bridge the digital divide. Many IT businesses have the resources and experience to develop AI-driven learning platforms that are accessible and inexpensive for schools in poor locations. By engaging with educators and policymakers, these companies can help design solutions that address the needs of impoverished students and guarantee that AI is used to promote equity in education.

AI-driven personalized learning has the ability to either bridge or worsen the digital divide, depending on how it is deployed. While AI can give poor kids with access to high-quality, tailored learning experiences, the hazards of deepening inequality are enormous. Addressing these difficulties will need intelligent policy, inclusive design, and major investment in infrastructure and digital literacy. By prioritizing equity in the development and deployment of AI in education, we can ensure that all students have the opportunity to benefit from the revolutionary potential of these technologies, regardless of their background or circumstances.

THE FUTURE OF PERSONALIZED LEARNING THROUGH AI

The future of personalized learning through AI holds the possibility of fundamentally altering education by personalizing the learning experience to fit the individual requirements, preferences, and talents of each student (Zohuri & Mossavar-Rahmani, 2024). As AI technology continues to progress, personalized learning is moving from a broad educational idea into a practical, data-driven approach to education, where every student may engage with content that is customized for them in real-time. This transformation can narrow learning gaps, boost student engagement, and empower individuals to take control of their education in ways that were previously imagined.

At the basis of AI-driven personalized learning is the concept of adaptive learning (Rane et al, 2023). Adaptive learning systems use algorithms to assess enormous amounts of student data—from academic achievement and behavior to learning styles and preferences—and adapt the curriculum and teaching techniques accordingly. These systems continuously capture data on each student's development, highlighting areas where they thrive and regions where they struggle. Based on this data, the system can adjust the content, the pace of instruction, and even the format in which the material is presented. This ensures that no student is left behind or feels unchallenged, as the learning environment changes to meet them where they are in their educational journey. In traditional classroom settings, professors are sometimes forced to teach to the "middle," meaning that they have to plan their lessons to suit the average level of student comprehension (Lang, 2021). This technique unavoidably leaves some students distracted, either because the content is either challenging or too easy. AI, however, provides a more customized approach. With the power of individualized learning, each student receives the exact degree of help they need. For example, if a student is struggling with a particular math idea, an AI-driven learning platform can deliver more practice problems or interactive courses that target their specific area of trouble. Conversely, if a student exhibits mastery of a concept, the system can expedite them to more difficult content, ensuring they are always challenged and interested. This ongoing tweaking of the learning process increases the potential for every learner to achieve.

One of the most significant consequences of individualized learning through AI is its ability to create increased student autonomy (Maghsudi et al, 2021). Personalized learning systems allow students to take an active role in their education by offering them more control over how and when they learn. AI-powered learning platforms generally contain features that allow students to set their own goals, track their progress, and choose which learning activities to engage with next (Yu et al, 2017). This self-directed method not only promotes motivation but also teaches vital skills like time management, critical thinking, and self-assessment. As students become more involved in their learning processes, they create a sense of ownership over their education, which can lead to increased academic performance and a lifetime love of learning. AI-driven individualized learning is also making education more accessible by addressing the different requirements of students. In any particular classroom, students can have a wide range of learning preferences, cultural backgrounds, and cognitive capacities. AI can level the playing field by providing customized learning experiences that address these disparities. For instance, students with learning difficulties, such as dyslexia or ADHD, can benefit from AI tools that offer alternate learning formats, such as audio versions of textbooks or visual aids (Barua et al, 2022). Similarly, students who are English language learners can employ AI-driven translation and language support technologies to help them understand and participate in course content. By adjusting to the demands of individual learners, AI-driven personalized learning systems ensure that all students have equitable access to high-quality education.

Another area where individualized learning using AI shows significant potential is in the development of emotional intelligence and social skills (Velagaleti et al, 2024). While personalized learning has generally focused on academic outcomes, the future will undoubtedly see AI systems that also track and support students' social-emotional development. By evaluating data from student interactions, facial expressions, and engagement levels, AI systems can offer insights into a student's emotional condition and provide treatments to increase well-being. For example, if a student is frequently distracted or frustrated, the system can suggest exercises geared to build resilience or enhance focus. This holistic approach to individualized learning understands that academic performance is intimately related to emotional and social well-being and tries to help both in tandem. In higher education and professional learning, the future of individualized learning with AI has even more possibilities. As AI becomes more integrated into university curriculums and corporate training programs, learners will have access to increasingly sophisticated technologies that offer tailored learning routes (Renz & Hilbig, 2020). These tools will not only assess academic performance but also examine a learner's career objectives, hobbies, and industry demands. For example, an AI system may recommend certain courses, internships, or skill development opportunities depending on a student's chosen career path or a professional's performance in the workplace. This kind of tailored career advising can assist bridge the gap between university and employment, ensuring that learners are prepared with the skills they need to succeed in the modern workforce.

Moreover, individualized learning with AI is not restricted to formal education situations (Sajja et al, 2024). Lifelong learning is becoming increasingly crucial in today's quickly changing world, where technology breakthroughs are transforming sectors and job markets. AI-powered personalized learning platforms are evolving to address the needs of lifelong learners, enabling flexible, on-demand education that can be adapted to an individual's schedule and goals. These platforms will continue to increase in scope, offering learners access to a large choice of courses, certificates, and learning experiences that can be customized to their specific interests and professional objectives. As a result, the borders between formal education and continual learning will blur, making education a lifelong undertaking that adapts to each individual's needs. One of the most interesting advancements in personalized learning through AI is the potential for AI to anticipate and prevent student dropouts. By analyzing large volumes of student data, AI can uncover trends that imply a student is at risk of falling behind or dropping out. These systems can then intervene early by offering additional support, such as tutoring, counseling, or focused learning materials, to help the student stay on course. Early intervention is vital in minimizing disengagement and dropout, and AI systems can play a critical role in ensuring that every student has the support they need to succeed.

However, like with all technological improvements, the emergence of personalized learning through AI comes with problems. Data privacy and ethical considerations are at the center of conversations concerning AI in education. Personalized learning systems rely largely on the collecting and analysis of student data, which raises problems regarding how this data is utilized, who has access to it, and how it is safeguarded (Regan & Jesse, 2019). Educators, legislators, and AI developers must work together to design systems that emphasize data security and respect ethical norms in the use of AI for personalized learning. Additionally, it is crucial to ensure that the benefits of AI-driven individualized learning are accessible to all students, regardless of financial background or geographic location. The future of individualized learning with AI is both hopeful and complicated (Luan, 2020). As AI continues to grow, it will alter the way students learn by giving more tailored, adaptable, and interesting educational experiences. By addressing the specific needs of each learner, AI-driven personalized learning systems can eliminate achievement disparities, boost student engagement, and prepare individuals for success in an increasingly dynamic environment. However, to fully achieve this promise, it is important to overcome the obstacles of data protection, accessibility, and equity, ensuring that personalized learning through AI stays an impluse for positive change in education.

CHALLENGES AND ETHICAL CONSIDERATIONS IN AI EDUCATION

The integration of AI in education brings great prospects for individualized learning, efficiency, and innovation (Chen, 2020). With these opportunities come enormous problems and ethical considerations that need to be properly investigated and handled. As AI becomes increasingly ingrained in educational systems worldwide, educators, politicians, developers, and institutions must manage these obstacles to guarantee that AI serves students without compromising ethical standards or educational values. The deployment of AI in education is not only a technological issue but one that overlaps with major ethical dilemmas about privacy, fairness, bias, accountability, and the greater purpose of education.

One of the most significant difficulties related to AI in education is the issue of data privacy and security (Luan et al, 2020). AI-driven systems, particularly those involved in personalized learning, rely largely on the collection and processing of vast volumes of student data. This covers not only academic performance data but also behavioral information, personal preferences, and even biometric data in some situations. While this data is vital for generating individualized learning experiences, it also offers substantial privacy threats (Dishon, 2017). If incorrectly managed, sensitive information could be revealed, exploited, or hacked, leading to serious harm to students and their families. Ensuring the privacy and security of student data must be a major focus for developers and organizations (Force, 2017). This entails developing robust data protection rules, encryption mechanisms, and compliance with privacy standards like the General Data Protection Regulation (GDPR) or the Family Educational Rights and Privacy Act (FERPA).

Another ethical challenge in AI education is the possibility of bias in AI algorithms (Slimi & Carballido, 2023). AI systems are only as good as the data they are trained on. If the data utilized to train these systems is biased or incomplete, the resulting algorithms may perpetuate existing inequities and preconceptions. For example, if an AI-driven assessment tool is trained on data that largely represents students from rich backgrounds, it may fail to effectively assess or help students from marginalized or underrepresented areas. This can result in unfair outcomes, where particular groups of students are disproportionately penalized by AI-based decisions. To overcome this, AI developers must prioritize the inclusion of diverse and representative datasets while training their models. Additionally, continual monitoring and auditing of AI systems are important to uncover and minimize biases that may occur over time. The question of fairness extends beyond algorithmic bias and into wider concerns about parity in access to AI-powered educational tools. AI can increase learning results for all students, but there is a risk that it could expand the gap between students who have access to cutting-edge technology and those who do not. In many regions of the world, colleges and students lack the resources to install advanced AI systems, such as high-speed internet, current gadgets, and technical support. This digital divide disproportionately impacts students from low-income households, rural locations, and developing countries. If access to AI-enhanced education remains unequal, it could aggravate educational inequities rather than address them (Holstein & Doroudi, 2021). Policymakers and educational institutions must work together to guarantee that AI tools are accessible to all students, regardless of their socioeconomic level or geographical location, and that they are not left behind in the shifting educational landscape. Another problem arises in the subject of accountability and transparency in AI-driven decision-making (Cheong,

2024). As AI systems take on more prominent roles in assessing students, offering learning courses, and even making predictions about academic success, it becomes essential to establish clear lines of accountability. Who is accountable when an AI system makes an inaccurate or damaging decision?

For example, if an AI tool wrongly identifies a student as underperforming or places them in a lower-level class based on faulty data, how should such errors be addressed, and who bears the responsibility?

Ensuring transparency in how AI systems operate is vital for retaining trust in these technologies (Felzmann et al, 2019). Educational institutions must provide comprehensive explanations of how AI systems make choices, what data is used, and what measures are in place to address errors or inaccuracies. Students, parents, and educators should have a clear knowledge of the role AI plays in the educational process and the capacity to contest or appeal choices made by AI systems.

The impact of AI on the function of instructors and the educational experience also creates ethical problems (Akgun & Greenhow, 2022). While AI can enhance teaching by automating administrative work, delivering individualized feedback, and generating data-driven insights, it should not replace the human parts of education that are vital to student growth. Education is not just about the transmission of knowledge but also about promoting critical thinking, creativity, emotional intelligence, and social skills—qualities that are best cultivated through human interaction. Over-reliance on AI could lead to a depersonalization of education, where students are treated as data points rather than individuals with unique needs and aspirations (George, 2023). It is crucial to strike a balance between harnessing AI for efficiency and keeping the irreplaceable human ties between professors and students. Educators must stay integral to the learning process, employing AI as a tool to enhance their teaching rather than a replacement for their knowledge and judgment. The ethical concerns of AI in education also extend to the broader philosophical questions concerning the purpose of education. As AI technologies progressively affect the learning experience, there is a risk that education could become overly focused on measurable outcomes and data-driven efficiency, sidelining crucial components of holistic development (Saltman, 2020). For example, AI can value abilities and information that are easily quantifiable, such as test results, over more abstract traits like critical thinking, empathy, and creativity. This could lead to an education system that favors performance measurements over the growth of well-rounded, reflective persons. Educators, politicians, and AI developers must engage in critical discussions about the role of AI in influencing the future of education and ensuring that it aligns with the broader aims of fostering human growth, citizenship, and lifelong learning.

The application of AI in education raises concerns regarding the ethical development and deployment of AI technology (Nguyen et al, 2023). The AI business is fast-moving, and not all engineers or firms prioritize ethical considerations in the push to innovate. It is vital to establish ethical rules and regulatory frameworks that ensure AI technologies used in education comply with concepts of justice, transparency, accountability, and inclusivity. Collaborations between governments, educational institutions, and AI developers are crucial to designing rules that respect students' rights while supporting innovation in the sector. Furthermore, educators and institutions need to encourage digital literacy among students, teaching them how to engage critically with AI technologies, understand their limitations, and utilize them responsibly in their learning journeys. While AI has enormous promise for changing education, it also brings a complex array of problems and ethical implications that cannot be disregarded (Stahl, 2021). Ensuring data privacy, eliminating algorithmic bias, encouraging equal access, maintaining accountability, and keeping the human parts of education are all significant concerns that must be addressed as AI becomes more incorporated into the learning process. As we move forward, it is crucial to approach AI in education with caution, ensuring that technology developments are guided by ethical principles and a dedication to supporting inclusive, meaningful, and fair learning experiences for all students.

CONCLUSION

As we progress further into the 21st century, the role of artificial intelligence (AI) in education is poised to become even more critical, presenting tremendous prospects for improving teaching and learning at all levels. The investigation of AI's existing applications and its future possibilities reveals a fast-shifting educational landscape, one where technology plays an increasingly essential role. From personalized learning and adaptive systems to AI-powered examinations and intelligent tutoring, AI is altering how education is given, accessed, and experienced by both students and educators. However, the road ahead is not without its hurdles. The future of AI in education rests on how well we can combine the benefits of these developing technologies with the ethical, social, and logistical concerns that follow their adoption.

One of the most intriguing parts of AI's introduction into education is its ability to make learning more individualized and accessible. The traditional paradigm of education, with its standardized curricula and teaching methods, has long struggled to satisfy the particular requirements of various learners. AI offers a solution by providing tailored learning experiences that can change in real time to a student's abilities, preferences, and progress. This kind of customization has the potential to drastically improve learning results, particularly for students who may have been left behind by more conventional educational institutions. As AI continues to evolve, we may expect increasingly more complex systems that offer deeper insights into student learning, creating opportunities for more tailored interventions and support. AI's impact extends beyond the classroom, bringing major benefits to professors and educational administrators. By automating time-consuming chores such as grading, scheduling, and administrative duties, AI frees up important time for educators to focus on more meaningful, high-impact activities like student engagement and instructional design. Intelligent tutoring systems and AI-powered lesson planning tools enable professors to develop more effective and innovative curricula, while AI-generated analytics provide real-time feedback on student performance. As AI becomes more integrated into educational operations, the job of the teacher will develop, transitioning from an information dispenser to a facilitator of tailored learning experiences, a mentor, and a guide who aids students in navigating their unique learning paths.

Despite its promise, the widespread implementation of AI in education brings serious ethical and practical challenges that must be carefully explored. One of the most important concerns is the issue of data privacy. AI systems generally require vast amounts of data to work efficiently, prompting questions about how student information is collected, stored, and used. Ensuring the privacy of students' data must be a major focus as AI technologies continue to be researched and applied. Similarly, concerns concerning algorithmic bias and fairness in AI-driven decision-making processes must be addressed. If AI systems are educated on biased data, they risk perpetuating inequities in education rather than eradicating them. Policy-makers, educators, and technologists must work together to design AI systems that are transparent, fair, and accountable, ensuring that they serve the best interests of all students.

Another difficulty facing AI's inclusion in education is the possibility of greater inequality. While AI has the potential to democratize education by delivering tailored learning opportunities to all students, access to these technologies is not yet universal. In under-resourced collges and localities, students may not have the same possibilities to benefit from AI-driven learning tools as their peers in affluent ones. Bridging this digital divide will be vital to ensure that AI's benefits are equitably dispersed across the global education landscape. Governments and educational institutions must prioritize investments in infrastructure, teacher training, and digital literacy initiatives to ensure that AI technology can be effectively adopted in all educational settings, regardless of socioeconomic level.

As AI continues to transform education, it is vital to consider the potential consequences on the role of professors and educational professionals. While AI can enhance the efficiency and effectiveness of teaching, there is a rising concern that it could lead to the dehumanization of education, replacing human interaction with automated processes. This concern underlines the need to carefully explore how AI can enhance, rather than replace, the job of professors. Professors add a human element to education that AI cannot replicate: empathy, emotional intelligence, and the capacity to inspire and motivate students. The future of education will likely be a hybrid approach, where AI supports professors in delivering individualized and data-driven training, but the human touch remains at the heart of the learning experience. Ensuring that educators are equipped with the skills and training to effectively integrate AI into their teaching will be vital to the success of AI in education.

Looking ahead, the future of AI in education is packed with potential. Emerging developments like AI-driven content creation, immersive virtual learning environments, and intelligent feedback systems promise to further change how students learn and how instructors teach. These technologies have the potential to make education more engaging, interactive, and personalized to individual requirements, ultimately leading to greater educational outcomes and a more dynamic learning experience. However, attaining this vision will require a united effort from educators, engineers, and policymakers to solve the obstacles connected with AI's application. As we continue to investigate the possibilities of AI in education, it is vital to remain conscious of the broader societal ramifications. AI is not a cure for all of education's difficulties, and its success will rely on how wisely and ethically it is integrated into existing institutions. Ensuring that AI technologies are developed to support, rather than undermine, the aims of equity, inclusion, and quality education for all must be a guiding concept moving ahead. The future of AI in education is both exciting and complicated. The potential for AI to alter education is huge, enabling new ways to tailor learning, enhance teaching, and improve educational results. Yet, this transition will not come without its hurdles. The successful integration of AI into education will entail resolving fundamental challenges linked to ethics, equity, and the shifting role of professors. As we pass this new era of AI-driven education, it is crucial to keep focused on the ultimate goal: developing learning environments that empower students, assist educators, and enable equal access to high-quality education for everyone. By doing so, we can harness the power of AI to create a brighter, more inclusive future for education.

REFERENCES

Aberšek, B. (2019). *The impact of innovative ICT education and AI on the pedagogical paradigm*. Cambridge Scholars Publishing.

Acemoglu, D., & Restrepo, P. (2018). Artificial intelligence, automation, and work. In *The economics of artificial intelligence: An agenda* (pp. 197–236). University of Chicago Press.

Ahmad, S. F., Alam, M. M., Rahmat, M. K., Mubarik, M. S., & Hyder, S. I. (2022). Academic and administrative role of artificial intelligence in education. *Sustainability (Basel)*, 14(3), 1101. DOI: 10.3390/su14031101

Akchurin, M., & Chouhy, G. (2024). Designing Better Access to Education? Unified Enrollment, School Choice, and the Limits of Algorithmic Fairness in New Orleans School Admissions. *Qualitative Sociology*, 47(2), 1–43. DOI: 10.1007/s11133-024-09565-x

Akgun, S., & Greenhow, C. (2022). Artificial intelligence in education: Addressing ethical challenges in K-12 settings. *AI and Ethics*, 2(3), 431–440. DOI: 10.1007/s43681-021-00096-7 PMID: 34790956

Alakrash, H. M., & Abdul Razak, N. (2021). Technology-based language learning: Investigation of digital technology and digital literacy. *Sustainability (Basel)*, 13(21), 12304. DOI: 10.3390/su132112304

Alam, A. (2021, November). Possibilities and apprehensions in the landscape of artificial intelligence in education. In *2021 International Conference on Computational Intelligence and Computing Applications (ICCICA)* (pp. 1-8). IEEE. DOI: 10.1109/ICCICA52458.2021.9697272

Alam, A. (2023). Harnessing the Power of AI to Create Intelligent Tutoring Systems for Enhanced Classroom Experience and Improved Learning Outcomes. In *Intelligent Communication Technologies and Virtual Mobile Networks* (pp. 571–591). Springer Nature Singapore. DOI: 10.1007/978-981-99-1767-9_42

Alam, A. (2023, June). Intelligence unleashed: An argument for AI-enabled learning ecologies with real world examples of today and a peek into the future. In AIP Conference Proceedings (Vol. 2717, No. 1). AIP Publishing.

Barua, P. D., Vicnesh, J., Gururajan, R., Oh, S. L., Palmer, E., Azizan, M. M., Kadri, N. A., & Acharya, U. R. (2022). Artificial intelligence enabled personalised assistive tools to enhance education of children with neurodevelopmental disorders—A review. *International Journal of Environmental Research and Public Health*, 19(3), 1192. DOI: 10.3390/ijerph19031192 PMID: 35162220

Bondie, R. S., Dahnke, C., & Zusho, A. (2019). How does changing "one-size-fits-all" to differentiated instruction affect teaching? *Review of Research in Education*, 43(1), 336–362. DOI: 10.3102/0091732X18821130

Bowden, J., Abdelzaher, E., & Essam, B. A. (2024). Translanguaging and Mobility in Higher Education Institutions: Challenges and Strategies. In War, Mobility, Displacement and Their Impact on Higher Education (Vol. 55, pp. 11-32). Emerald Publishing Limited.

Bukartaite, R., & Hooper, D. (2023). Automation, artificial intelligence and future skills needs: An Irish perspective. *European Journal of Training and Development*, 47(10), 163–185. DOI: 10.1108/EJTD-03-2023-0045

Capraro, V., Lentsch, A., Acemoglu, D., Akgun, S., Akhmedova, A., Bilancini, E., Bonnefon, J.-F., Brañas-Garza, P., Butera, L., Douglas, K. M., Everett, J. A. C., Gigerenzer, G., Greenhow, C., Hashimoto, D. A., Holt-Lunstad, J., Jetten, J., Johnson, S., Kunz, W. H., Longoni, C., & Viale, R. (2024). The impact of generative artificial intelligence on socioeconomic inequalities and policy making. *PNAS Nexus*, 3(6), pgae191. DOI: 10.1093/pnasnexus/pgae191 PMID: 38864006

Chassignol, M., Khoroshavin, A., Klimova, A., & Bilyatdinova, A. (2018). Artificial Intelligence trends in education: A narrative overview. *Procedia Computer Science*, 136, 16–24. DOI: 10.1016/j.procs.2018.08.233

Chen, L., Chen, P., & Lin, Z. (2020). Artificial intelligence in education: A review. *IEEE Access : Practical Innovations, Open Solutions*, 8, 75264–75278. DOI: 10.1109/ACCESS.2020.2988510

Chen, Y., Jensen, S., Albert, L. J., Gupta, S., & Lee, T. (2023). Artificial intelligence (AI) student assistants in the classroom: Designing chatbots to support student success. *Information Systems Frontiers*, 25(1), 161–182. DOI: 10.1007/s10796-022-10291-4

Cheong, B. C. (2024). Transparency and accountability in AI systems: Safeguarding wellbeing in the age of algorithmic decision-making. *Frontiers in Human Dynamics*, 6, 1421273. DOI: 10.3389/fhumd.2024.1421273

Chitra, L. (2019). *Artificial intelligence meets augmented reality*. BPB Publications.

Chiu, T. K., Moorhouse, B. L., Chai, C. S., & Ismailov, M. (2023). Teacher support and student motivation to learn with Artificial Intelligence (AI) based chatbot. *Interactive Learning Environments*, •••, 1–17. DOI: 10.1080/10494820.2023.2172044

Colchester, K., Hagras, H., Alghazzawi, D., & Aldabbagh, G. (2017). A survey of artificial intelligence techniques employed for adaptive educational systems within e-learning platforms. *Journal of Artificial Intelligence and Soft Computing Research*, 7(1), 47–64. DOI: 10.1515/jaiscr-2017-0004

Cope, B., & Kalantzis, M. (2023). A little history of e-learning: Finding new ways to learn in the PLATO computer education system, 1959–1976. *History of Education*, 52(6), 905–936. DOI: 10.1080/0046760X.2022.2141353

Costa, S. (2023). Artificial intelligence in education: Challenges and opportunities in learning.

Cox, A. M. (2021). Exploring the impact of Artificial Intelligence and robots on higher education through literature-based design fictions. *International Journal of Educational Technology in Higher Education*, 18(1), 3. DOI: 10.1186/s41239-020-00237-8

Dimitriadou, E., & Lanitis, A. (2023). A critical evaluation, challenges, and future perspectives of using artificial intelligence and emerging technologies in smart classrooms. *Smart Learning Environments*, 10(1), 12. DOI: 10.1186/s40561-023-00231-3

Dishon, G. (2017). New data, old tensions: Big data, personalized learning, and the challenges of progressive education. *Theory and Research in Education*, 15(3), 272–289. DOI: 10.1177/1477878517735233

Ejjami, R. (2024). The future of learning: AI-based curriculum development. *Int J Multidiscip Res*, 6(4).

Felzmann, H., Villaronga, E. F., Lutz, C., & Tamò-Larrieux, A. (2019). Transparency you can trust: Transparency requirements for artificial intelligence between legal norms and contextual concerns. *Big Data & Society*, 6(1), 2053951719860542. DOI: 10.1177/2053951719860542

Filgueiras, F. (2023). Artificial intelligence and education governance. *Education, Citizenship and Social Justice*, •••, 17461979231160674.

Force, J. T. (2017). Risk Management Framework for Information Systems and Organizations: A System Life Cycle Approach for Security and Privacy (Discussion Draft) (No. NIST Special Publication (SP) 800-37 Rev. 2 (Draft)). National Institute of Standards and Technology.

Ford, M. (2021). Rule of the robots: How artificial intelligence will transform everything. Hachette UK.

Gandedkar, N. H., Wong, M. T., & Darendeliler, M. A. (2021, June). Role of virtual reality (VR), augmented reality (AR) and artificial intelligence (AI) in tertiary education and research of orthodontics: An insight. [). WB Saunders.]. *Seminars in Orthodontics*, 27(2), 69–77. DOI: 10.1053/j.sodo.2021.05.003

George, A. S. (2023). Preparing students for an AI-driven world: Rethinking curriculum and pedagogy in the age of artificial intelligence. *Partners Universal Innovative Research Publication*, 1(2), 112–136.

George, A. S. (2023). The Potential of Generative AI to Reform Graduate Education. *Partners Universal International Research Journal*, 2(4), 36–50.

George, A. S. (2024). Bridging the Digital Divide: Understanding the Human Impacts of Digital Transformation.

Gligorea, I., Cioca, M., Oancea, R., Gorski, A. T., Gorski, H., & Tudorache, P. (2023). Adaptive learning using artificial intelligence in e-learning: A literature review. *Education Sciences*, 13(12), 1216. DOI: 10.3390/educsci13121216

Guzdial, M., & du Boulay, B. (2019). The history of computing. The Cambridge handbook of computing education research, 11.

Holmes, W., Persson, J., Chounta, I. A., Wasson, B., & Dimitrova, V. (2022). *Artificial intelligence and education: A critical view through the lens of human rights, democracy and the rule of law*. Council of Europe.

Holstein, K., & Doroudi, S. (2021). Equity and artificial intelligence in education: will" aied" amplify or alleviate inequities in education? arXiv preprint arXiv:2104.12920.

Holstein, K., McLaren, B. M., & Aleven, V. (2017, March). Intelligent tutors as teachers' aides: exploring teacher needs for real-time analytics in blended classrooms. In Proceedings of the seventh international learning analytics & knowledge conference (pp. 257-266).

Hooda, M., Rana, C., Dahiya, O., Rizwan, A., & Hossain, M. S. (2022). Artificial intelligence for assessment and feedback to enhance student success in higher education. *Mathematical Problems in Engineering*, 2022(1), 5215722. DOI: 10.1155/2022/5215722

Ivanović, M., Klašnja-Milićević, A., Paprzycki, M., Ganzha, M., Bădică, C., Bădică, A., & Jain, L. C. (2022). *Current trends in AI-based educational processes—an overview. Handbook on Intelligent Techniques in the Educational Process* (Vol. 1). Recent Advances and Case Studies.

Jaiswal, A., & Arun, C. J. (2021). Potential of Artificial Intelligence for transformation of the education system in India. *International Journal of Education and Development Using Information and Communication Technology*, 17(1), 142–158.

Jayadurga, D. R., & Rathika, M. S. (2023). *Significance and Impact of Artificial Intelligence and Immersive Technologies in the field of Education. International Journal of Recent Technology and Engineering*. IJRTE.

Johnson, S. R., & Stage, F. K. (2018). Academic engagement and student success: Do high-impact practices mean higher graduation rates? *The Journal of Higher Education*, 89(5), 753–781. DOI: 10.1080/00221546.2018.1441107

Jones, S., & Latzko-Toth, G. (2017). Out from the PLATO cave: Uncovering the pre-Internet history of social computing. *Internet Histories*, 1(1-2), 60–69. DOI: 10.1080/24701475.2017.1307544

Jones, S. M., McGarrah, M. W., & Kahn, J. (2019). Social and emotional learning: A principled science of human development in context. *Educational Psychologist*, 54(3), 129–143. DOI: 10.1080/00461520.2019.1625776

Kabudi, T., Pappas, I., & Olsen, D. H. (2021). AI-enabled adaptive learning systems: A systematic mapping of the literature. *Computers and Education: Artificial Intelligence*, 2, 100017. DOI: 10.1016/j.caeai.2021.100017

Kannan, J., & Munday, P. (2018). New trends in second language learning and teaching through the lens of ICT, networked learning, and artificial intelligence.

Kasun, G. S., Liao, Y. C., Margulieux, L. E., & Woodall, M. (2024, June). Unexpected outcomes from an AI education course among education faculty: Toward making AI accessible with marginalized youth in urban Mexico. [). Frontiers Media SA.]. *Frontiers in Education*, 9, 1368604. DOI: 10.3389/feduc.2024.1368604

Kaswan, K. S., Dhatterwal, J. S., & Ojha, R. P. (2024). AI in personalized learning. In *Advances in Technological Innovations in Higher Education* (pp. 103–117). CRC Press. DOI: 10.1201/9781003376699-9

Kayyali, M. (2020). Post COVID-19: New era for higher education systems. *International Journal of Applied Science and Engineering*, 8(2), 131–145. DOI: 10.30954/2322-0465.2.2020.6

Kayyali, M. (2021). Positive Impact of High Technology on Higher Education.

Kayyali, M. (2024). Future possibilities and challenges of AI in education. In *Transforming education with generative AI: Prompt engineering and synthetic content creation* (pp. 118–137). IGI Global. DOI: 10.4018/979-8-3693-1351-0.ch006

Kharbat, F. F., Alshawabkeh, A., & Woolsey, M. L. (2021). Identifying gaps in using artificial intelligence to support students with intellectual disabilities from education and health perspectives. *Aslib Journal of Information Management*, 73(1), 101–128. DOI: 10.1108/AJIM-02-2020-0054

Khare, K., Stewart, B., & Khare, A. (2018). Artificial intelligence and the student experience: An institutional perspective. The International Academic Forum (IAFOR).

Khosravi, H., Shum, S. B., Chen, G., Conati, C., Tsai, Y. S., Kay, J., & Gašević, D. (2022). Explainable artificial intelligence in education. *Computers and Education: Artificial Intelligence*, 3, 100074.

Kim, J. (2024). Leading teachers' perspective on teacher-AI collaboration in education. *Education and Information Technologies*, 29(7), 8693–8724. DOI: 10.1007/s10639-023-12109-5

Kim, J., Merrill, K., Xu, K., & Sellnow, D. D. (2020). My teacher is a machine: Understanding students' perceptions of AI teaching assistants in online education. *International Journal of Human-Computer Interaction*, 36(20), 1902–1911. DOI: 10.1080/10447318.2020.1801227

Kolluru, V., Mungara, S., & Chintakunta, A. N. (2018). Adaptive learning systems: Harnessing AI for customized educational experiences. [IJCSITY]. *International Journal of Computer Science and Information Technologies*, 6(1), 2. DOI: 10.5121/ijcsity.2018.6302

Lang, J. M. (2021). *Small teaching: Everyday lessons from the science of learning*. John Wiley & Sons.

Luan, H., Geczy, P., Lai, H., Gobert, J., Yang, S. J., Ogata, H., Baltes, J., Guerra, R., Li, P., & Tsai, C. C. (2020). Challenges and future directions of big data and artificial intelligence in education. *Frontiers in Psychology*, 11, 580820. DOI: 10.3389/fpsyg.2020.580820 PMID: 33192896

Maghsudi, S., Lan, A., Xu, J., & van Der Schaar, M. (2021). Personalized education in the artificial intelligence era: What to expect next. *IEEE Signal Processing Magazine*, 38(3), 37–50. DOI: 10.1109/MSP.2021.3055032

Marwan, A. (2020). Impact of artificial intelligence on education for employment:(learning and employability Framework).

McCalla, G. (2023). The history of artificial intelligence in education–the first quarter century. In *Handbook of artificial intelligence in education* (pp. 10–29). Edward Elgar Publishing. DOI: 10.4337/9781800375413.00010

Messer, M., Brown, N. C., Kölling, M., & Shi, M. (2024). Automated grading and feedback tools for programming education: A systematic review. *ACM Transactions on Computing Education*, 24(1), 1–43. DOI: 10.1145/3636515

Monat, J. P., & Gannon, T. F. (2018). Two professors' experience with competency-based education. *The Journal of Competency-Based Education*, 3(2), e01061. DOI: 10.1002/cbe2.1061

Murdoch, B. (2021). Privacy and artificial intelligence: Challenges for protecting health information in a new era. *BMC Medical Ethics*, 22(1), 1–5. DOI: 10.1186/s12910-021-00687-3 PMID: 34525993

Ng, D. T. K., Lee, M., Tan, R. J. Y., Hu, X., Downie, J. S., & Chu, S. K. W. (2023). A review of AI teaching and learning from 2000 to 2020. *Education and Information Technologies*, 28(7), 8445–8501. DOI: 10.1007/s10639-022-11491-w

Nguyen, A., Ngo, H. N., Hong, Y., Dang, B., & Nguyen, B. P. T. (2023). Ethical principles for artificial intelligence in education. *Education and Information Technologies*, 28(4), 4221–4241. DOI: 10.1007/s10639-022-11316-w PMID: 36254344

Nguyen, T. T., Thuan, H. T., & Nguyen, M. T. (2023). Artificial Intelligent (AI) in teaching and learning: A comprehensive review. ISTES BOOKS, 140-161.

Ozer, M., Kose, Y., Kucukkaya, G., Mukasheva, A., & Ciris, K. (2024). Adapting to the AI Disruption: Reshaping the IT Landscape and Educational Paradigms. arXiv preprint arXiv:2409.10541.

Pantelimon, F. V., Bologa, R., Toma, A., & Posedaru, B. S. (2021). The evolution of AI-driven educational systems during the COVID-19 pandemic. *Sustainability (Basel)*, 13(23), 13501. DOI: 10.3390/su132313501

Pedro, F., Subosa, M., Rivas, A., & Valverde, P. (2019). Artificial intelligence in education: Challenges and opportunities for sustainable development.

Pham, S. T., & Sampson, P. M. (2022). The development of artificial intelligence in education: A review in context. *Journal of Computer Assisted Learning*, 38(5), 1408–1421. DOI: 10.1111/jcal.12687

Pokrivcakova, S. (2019). Preparing teachers for the application of AI-powered technologies in foreign language education. *Journal of Language and Cultural Education*, 7(3), 135–153. DOI: 10.2478/jolace-2019-0025

Rai, H. L., Saluja, N., & Pimplapure, A. (2024). Ethical and Social Impact of AI Driven Analysis for Students with Learning Disabilities Processes. *Journal of Electrical Systems*, 20(7s), 2704–2715.

Rane, N., Choudhary, S., & Rane, J. (2023). Education 4.0 and 5.0: Integrating artificial intelligence (AI) for personalized and adaptive learning. Available at *SSRN* 4638365. DOI: 10.2139/ssrn.4638365

Regan, P. M., & Jesse, J. (2019). Ethical challenges of edtech, big data and personalized learning: Twenty-first century student sorting and tracking. *Ethics and Information Technology*, 21(3), 167–179. DOI: 10.1007/s10676-018-9492-2

Rekha, K., Gopal, K., Satheeskumar, D., Anand, U. A., Doss, D. S. S., & Elayaperumal, S. (2024, May). Ai-Powered Personalized Learning System Design: Student Engagement and Performance Tracking System. In 2024 4th International Conference on Advance Computing and Innovative Technologies in Engineering (ICACITE) (pp. 1125-1130). IEEE.

Renz, A., & Hilbig, R. (2020). Prerequisites for artificial intelligence in further education: Identification of drivers, barriers, and business models of educational technology companies. *International Journal of Educational Technology in Higher Education*, 17(1), 14. DOI: 10.1186/s41239-020-00193-3

Rızvı, M. (2023). Investigating AI-Powered Tutoring Systems that Adapt to Individual Student Needs, Providing Personalized Guidance and Assessments. *The Eurasia Proceedings of Educational and Social Sciences*, 31, 67–73. DOI: 10.55549/epess.1381518

Saaida, M. B. (2023). AI-Driven transformations in higher education: Opportunities and challenges. *International Journal of Educational Research and Studies*, 5(1), 29–36.

Sajja, R., Sermet, Y., Cikmaz, M., Cwiertny, D., & Demir, I. (2024). Artificial intelligence-enabled intelligent assistant for personalized and adaptive learning in higher education. *Information (Basel)*, 15(10), 596. DOI: 10.3390/info15100596

Saltman, K. J. (2022). *The alienation of fact: Digital educational privatization, AI, and the false promise of bodies and numbers*. MIT Press. DOI: 10.7551/mitpress/14387.001.0001

Sandor, C., & Sándor, C. (2023). The role of innovative technologies in learning a foreign language.

Schiff, D. (2021). Out of the laboratory and into the classroom: The future of artificial intelligence in education. *AI & Society*, 36(1), 331–348. DOI: 10.1007/s00146-020-01033-8 PMID: 32836908

Seldon, A., Abidoye, O., & Metcalf, T. (2020). *The Fourth Education Revolution Reconsidered: Will Artificial Intelligence Enrich Or Diminish Humanity?* Legend Press Ltd.

Singha, S., Singha, R., & Jasmine, E. (2024). Enhancing Language Teaching Materials Through Artificial Intelligence: Opportunities and Challenges. AI in Language Teaching, Learning, and Assessment, 22-42.

Slimi, Z., & Carballido, B. V. (2023). Navigating the Ethical Challenges of Artificial Intelligence in Higher Education: An Analysis of Seven Global AI Ethics Policies. TEM Journal, 12(2).

Srinivasa, K. G., Kurni, M., & Saritha, K. (2022). Harnessing the Power of AI to Education. In *Learning, teaching, and assessment methods for contemporary learners: pedagogy for the digital generation* (pp. 311–342). Springer Nature Singapore. DOI: 10.1007/978-981-19-6734-4_13

Stahl, B. C. (2021). *Artificial intelligence for a better future: an ecosystem perspective on the ethics of AI and emerging digital technologies*. Springer Nature. DOI: 10.1007/978-3-030-69978-9

Strielkowski, W., Grebennikova, V., Lisovskiy, A., Rakhimova, G., & Vasileva, T. (2024). AI-driven adaptive learning for sustainable educational transformation. *Sustainable Development (Bradford)*, sd.3221. DOI: 10.1002/sd.3221

Tariq, M. U. (Ed.). (2024). *AI-Driven Learning and Engagement in Higher Education*. IGI Global. DOI: 10.4018/979-8-3693-4074-5

Tenon, S. R., & Epler, P. (Eds.). (2020). *Evaluation of principles and best practices in personalized learning*. IGI Global. DOI: 10.4018/978-1-7998-4237-8

van der Vorst, T., & Jelicic, N. (2019). Artificial Intelligence in Education: Can AI bring the full potential of personalized learning to education?.

Van Dijk, J. A. G. M. (2017). Digital divide: Impact of access. The international encyclopedia of media effects, 1, 1-11.

Varier, D., Dumke, E. K., Abrams, L. M., Conklin, S. B., Barnes, J. S., & Hoover, N. R. (2017). Potential of one-to-one technologies in the classroom: Teachers and students weigh in. *Educational Technology Research and Development*, 65(4), 967–992. DOI: 10.1007/s11423-017-9509-2

Velagaleti, S. B., Choukaier, D., Nuthakki, R., Lamba, V., Sharma, V., & Rahul, S.Sesha Bhargavi Velagaleti. (2024). Empathetic Algorithms: The Role of AI in Understanding and Enhancing Human Emotional Intelligence. *Journal of Electrical Systems*, 20(3s), 2051–2060. DOI: 10.52783/jes.1806

Weishart, J. E. (2020). Democratizing education rights. *Wm. & Mary Bill Rts. J.*, 29, 1.

Wise, A. F., Knight, S., & Shum, S. B. (2021). Collaborative learning analytics. International handbook of computer-supported collaborative learning, 425-443. DOI: 10.1007/978-3-030-65291-3_23

Yu, H., Miao, C., Leung, C., & White, T. J. (2017). Towards AI-powered personalization in MOOC learning. npj Science of Learning, 2(1), 15.

Zdravkova, K. (2022). The potential of artificial intelligence for assistive technology in education. In Handbook on Intelligent Techniques in the Educational Process: Vol 1 Recent Advances and Case Studies (pp. 61-85). Cham: Springer International Publishing. DOI: 10.1007/978-3-031-04662-9_4

Zohuri, B., & Mossavar-Rahmani, F. (2024). Revolutionizing education: The dynamic synergy of personalized learning and artificial intelligence. *International Journal of Advanced Engineering and Management Research*, 9(1), 143–153. DOI: 10.51505/ijaemr.2024.9111

ADDITIONAL READING

Grassini, S. (2023). Shaping the future of education: Exploring the potential and consequences of AI and ChatGPT in educational settings. *Education Sciences*, 13(7), 692. DOI: 10.3390/educsci13070692

Schiff, D. (2021). Out of the laboratory and into the classroom: The future of artificial intelligence in education. *AI & Society*, 36(1), 331–348. DOI: 10.1007/s00146-020-01033-8 PMID: 32836908

Selwyn, N. (2022). The future of AI and education: Some cautionary notes. *European Journal of Education*, 57(4), 620–631. DOI: 10.1111/ejed.12532

Williamson, B., & Eynon, R. (2020). Historical threads, missing links, and future directions in AI in education. *Learning, Media and Technology*, 45(3), 223–235. DOI: 10.1080/17439884.2020.1798995

Zhang, K., & Aslan, A. B. (2021). AI technologies for education: Recent research & future directions. *Computers and Education: Artificial Intelligence*, 2, 100025. DOI: 10.1016/j.caeai.2021.100025

KEY TERMS AND DEFINITIONS

Adaptive Learning: An educational approach that uses AI to customize learning experiences based on individual student needs, allowing each learner to progress at their own pace.

Algorithmic Bias: A systematic error in AI systems that can lead to unfair treatment of certain groups, often due to biases present in the data used to train the algorithms.

Artificial Intelligence (AI): The simulation of human intelligence processes by machines, especially computer systems, which is widely used in education to enhance personalized learning and automate administrative tasks.

Data-Driven Learning Analytics: The analysis of large datasets to assess student performance, engagement, and progress, enabling educators to make informed decisions on improving educational outcomes.

Ethical AI: The practice of developing and using AI technologies in ways that respect privacy, promote fairness, and mitigate biases, ensuring AI applications in education are equitable and responsible.

Intelligent Tutoring Systems (ITS): AI-based systems designed to provide personalized instruction to students by mimicking the guidance of a human tutor.

Learning Management Systems (LMS): Software applications that facilitate the administration, documentation, tracking, reporting, and delivery of educational courses or training programs.

Natural Language Processing (NLP): A branch of AI that enables computers to understand, interpret, and respond to human language, often used in educational tools for tasks like grading and language learning.

Personalized Learning: An educational method in which AI tailors instruction, resources, and assessments to fit the individual learning needs and preferences of each student.

Virtual Learning Environments (VLE): Online platforms where students and educators interact, often enhanced by AI to provide adaptive content, collaborative tools, and real-time feedback.

Chapter 14
Artificial Intelligence in Education:
Emerging Trends, Ethical Considerations, and Future Directions

Houda Boumediene
University of Laghouat, Algeria

Mustapha Bouakkaz
https://orcid.org/0000-0003-0338-2069
University of Laghouat, Algeria

ABSTRACT

This concluding chapter synthesizes the integration of Artificial Intelligence (AI) in education, underscoring its transformative potential across learning, teaching, and administrative domains. The authors examine pivotal AI applications, such as personalized learning, automated assessment, and enhanced classroom management, emphasizing how these innovations boost student engagement and learning outcomes. Alongside these advancements, the chapter critically addresses ethical challenges associated with AI in education, including algorithmic bias, data privacy issues, and the risk of reducing human interaction. The chapter illustrates AI's practical applications and effectiveness through case studies and examples, such as AI-driven tools like DreamBox and Georgia State University's student success platform. To support the ethical use of AI, the authors highlight the need for strategies to mitigate biases, ensure diverse and representative datasets, and uphold stringent data privacy standards.

DOI: 10.4018/979-8-3693-7220-3.ch014

INTRODUCTION

Artificial intelligence in education is one of the newest trends that will revolutionize the way students learn, instructors teach, and institutions function more quickly than ever. With an immense capacity for data analysis and prediction of outcomes, besides adaptability to the needs of each learner, AI reworks traditional educational models for personalization and efficiency, and wider access (Fiok et al.,2022). AI-driven technologies, such as adaptive learning systems, automated assessment tools, and intelligent classroom management, are going to disrupt the education sector in their effort to solve some of the most critical challenges within the industry. The only challenge is that where there's immense opportunity, there's far more complex ethical deliberation that must be addressed if AI is ever going to benefit all universal education stakeholders (Al-Mansoori & Salem, 2023).

According to Zhang & Aslan (2021), the most promising contribution AI can make in education is personalized learning. Contrary to traditional models of teaching, where teaching is one-size-fits-all, AI enables students to proceed at their own pace by adjusting the speed and content of learning to the needs and capabilities of students. Innovation enhances student participation and performance but raises a number of concerns related mainly to fairness in algorithmic biases and recommendations for educational decision-making. Meanwhile, the growing involvement of AI in accelerating assessment processes, performing administrative chores, and even managing classrooms will further ease the workload; this, too, could be felt as dependence solely on AI would reduce human contact, which is a vital component of learning.

This chapter, therefore, focuses on major applications of AI in education, identifies the emerging trends, and examines some of the ethical dilemmas associated with its use. The aim was to explore trends, ethical considerations, and future directions that AI in education has taken and can take, while recommendations for responsible integration are provided. In the light of this, therefore, this paper will attempt to outline the full exposition of the current impact of AI on education with discussions on issues like data privacy, algorithm bias, and loss of human touch in learning for making considerations toward harnessing these technologies in an ethical manner for future development. Going forward, as AI continues to evolve, thoughtfulness in design and collaboration by all stakeholders involved will be important-a design and collaboration based on ethical grounds-so that AI enhances rather than undermines the education process.

This research seeks to answer the following research questions:

1. What are the most common uses of AI in education, and how do they affect learning outcomes, teaching practices, and administrative procedures?

2. What are the emerging trends in AI that shape the future of education, and what might their benefits and limitations be?
3. What are the ethical dilemmas that might occur in the use of AI in educational settings related to data privacy, algorithmic bias, and human elements in learning?
4. How do educational institutions make responsible integrations of AI technologies, addressing ethical concerns while protecting all stakeholders' interests?
5. What are some recommendations that can be made to ensure AI is applied ethically and effectively in education, given the current challenges and future potential?

These questions will be useful in providing a holistic framework for understanding the opportunities and challenges posed by AI in education, thereby informing future research and policy development.

LITERATURE REVIEW

AI-Powered Personalized Learning

Tang and Su (2024) claimed that AI-driven personalized learning systems create a radical departure from traditional one-size-fits-all models of education. It analyzes data on students' performance, habits, and preferences for the personalization of educational content, pace, and feedback. By integrating AI algorithms, there is more potential for personalized learning platforms to adapt the needs of every learner and provide a tailor-made educational experience best suited for optimizing learning outcomes. Such AI-powered, adaptive learning systems parse real-time data about a student's understanding of the material and oblige dynamically with lesson plans that are responsive to fill knowledge gaps. AI-driven systems of personalized learning can work out the exact rate at which a student learns any content put up and can provide adaptive instructions accordingly. In those cases, when the learner demonstrates poor mastery of some topic, the AI system would recommend additional exercises or an explanation in another form until the concept is fully internalized. When a student performs well, then the system moves him/her to the next level of difficulty in order not to let him/her get bored and disengage. It is tailored according to each student's personal capabilities and tempo of learning, which increases the effectiveness and appeal of learning manifold. Some AI-powered platforms had already given their fillip to personalized learning (Kamalov, et al.,2023) and among them, the most renowned ones are: DreamBox, Knewton, Smart Sparrow.

- *DreamBox*: This is an adaptive learning of mathematics whereby AI continuously changes the difficulty regarding how students are answering some math questions. The platform gives teachers differentiated instructions to guide students along individualized learning paths that build upon strengths and address weaknesses. It's designed to support both in-class and remote learning.
- *Knewton*: Through its adaptive learning technology, Knewton continuously monitors students' performance and personalizes digital educational content for them. Virtual, AI-driven platform hosting a system in support of creating a learning profile for every learner by including targeted instruction about knowledge gaps while concepts are mastered.
- *Smart Sparrow*: It is an adaptive e-learning solution that covers real-time personalized feedback to be provided to the students. This intelligent tutoring system responds to a student's individual learning behavior and adapts to instructional content in ways that help improve student engagement in retaining knowledge. Of late, it has highly been utilized in allowing the instructors to build customized adaptive lessons.

Buckingham and Luckin (2019) stated that AI-powered personalized learning systems already show their clear, positive impact on both student engagement and learning outcomes. This is because the AI tools decrease frustration that is generally created by lessons when they turn out to be too hard or too easy by adjusting content to the needs of the learner. When students learn at their own pace, they can generally remain interested and become motivated; this pays off in the form of better overall academic performance. Further, increased student engagement reduces dropout rates, improving learning retention. Adaptive learning platforms have incentivized students toward greater student autonomy with more confidence in their learning process, since instantaneous feedback and support of students are personalized. These bridges are learning gaps, which traditional methods sometimes are not able to handle. Besides this, AI-driven personalized learning urges an approach to be taken towards education that is centered around students, and hence allows different individual routes for their learning path, which again caters to different cognitive styles. This is likely to be particularly effective in the case of students with special learning needs or those students who need extra help in obtaining academic success.

While personalized learning systems bring about enormous benefits, they also raise enormous challenges in respect of algorithmic bias. An AI algorithm is only as good as the quality and diversity of data on which it trains. If the data are sourced through limited sources, representative of restricted cultural, socio-economic, and demographic sections, then the AI itself might end up developing biased pathways of learning (Fiok et al.,2022). It may also further in equally affect students from underrepresented groups due to the inequalities of their learning experiences. For example, an AI-based learning platform may be trained on data from one socio-economic or cultural demographic. Therefore, it might not satisfy the needs of students from any other diverse backgrounds. Recommendations may not suit the style or need for learning that a student may have and hence may keep them at a disadvantage (Buckingham & Luckin, 2019):

- *Mitigation Strategies*: The only way developers and educators can address algorithmic bias is by making use of several major strategies that include rearing the AI systems on diverse datasets, reflecting huge variations of learners from various cultural, socio-economic, and educational backgrounds. Hence, recommendations offered by AI are representative and nondiscriminatory, inclusive of learning pathways.
- *Ongoing Monitoring and Evaluation*: Any AI system should be continuously monitored for bias detection and correction. Monitoring system performance through different student groups will show the developers where biased outcomes occur, thus they may be fixed before significant burdens on students are placed.
- *Algorithm Design Transparency*: In other words, developers and instructors are to collaborate in opening the internal mechanism of algorithms. When educators comprehend how the AI system constructs personalized recommendations, they will be ready to ensure coherence in learning pathways with ethical principles and equity (Al-Mansoori & Salem,2023).

Automated Assessment Tools

One of the most critical applications of AI in education is automated assessment (Mouta et al.,2024) which provides a suite of technologies to make the process of grading student work easier and more efficient. AI-driven grading tools like GradeScope and Edmentum are leading suppliers of educational technology, harnessing the power of NLP and machine learning to assess students' submissions such as essays, quizzes, and exams. These systems analyze grammar, the structure of content, coherence, and strength of arguments in students' work using algorithms that—up to a point—mimic human judgment.

- *GradeScope:* This is a popular web-based platform designed by a designated team at UC Berkeley, used to grade assignments and exams automatically. With GradeScope, teachers can grade faster because it scans the handwritten submissions and auto-categorizes the answers, therefore, saving time with consistent results. Also, the detailed feedback on the work can be shared with the students.

- *Edmentum*: An education software solution providing a suite of AI-driven tools, inclusive of auto-grading. Edmentum's platform is designed to deliver immediate feedback and adaptive learning pathways based on student performance. This system is frequently utilized to manage online courses, assessments, and other learning management duties. These platforms work not only to make grading more efficient, but they also seek to offer feedback more opportune and accurate to the students, which plays a very integral role in continuous learning and improvement.

Most importantly, Zhang & Aslan (2021) claimed that automated assessment offers several key advantages compared to traditional manual grading methods:

- *Speed*: One of the most significant advantages with any AI-based grading system is their speed. What would be a matter of several hours or even days for a human grader becomes merely minutes or even seconds for an AI system. This is quite helpful in large classes or MOOCs where it would be unrealistic to grade a thousand-plus assignments by hand.
- *Precision*: AI-based grading systems can uphold one standard of grading, hence reducing human error and subjectivism. This system grades all the work using the same criterion, so fairness and objectivity in the grades are guaranteed. Sometimes, human graders could be inconsistent because a single graduator may grade multiple voluminous works over time, but with an AI, there is no room for this disparity.
- *Timely Feedback*: Evidence of AI-based tooling shows that it provides instant feedback to students, thereby helping them in assessing areas where improvement is required. In most cases, because of this lateness, feedback is always divorced from learning in traditional settings. Automated systems bridge this gap by facilitating learners with prompt, actionable insights into their performance.

Despite the many benefits of automated assessment systems, there are several notable limitations (Fiok et al.,2022):

- *Creativity*: AI is not quite effective at correctly evaluating creative work. For instance, about essays, although AI serves to grade grammatical and syntactical structure, it often misses out on creativity or originality of a student's argument or writing style. This becomes all the more problematic in areas of literature, art, or humanities, where, often enough, creativity is one of the core elements of evaluation.

- *Context*: AI-based grading systems lack in analyzing the context or any implicit meaning inherent in the student response. For instance, while an AI system may excel in grading multiple-choice questions or formula-type answers, it might misinterpret more complex responses that are contextually predisposed to require understanding subtle themes or cultural nuances.
- *Subtle work*: difficult for an AI system to score, work relies on subtle and cross-disciplinary thinking. For instance, work that integrates historical, philosophical, and literary analysis may be a daunting task for the AI system to score effectively because, in most cases, it lacks deep domain knowledge and flexibility in thinking while making such decisions. The latter in turn bring an increasingly hybrid approach in which human graders come together with AI-based systems: for example, AI carries out the more formulaic or objective tasks, such as multiple-choice questions and factual responses, while human educators go through and grade the most complex, creative, and context-sensitive assignments (Al-Mansoori &Salem,2023).

Classroom Management and Administrative AI Tools

Kamalov et al., (2023) explained that AI also has a transformative role in classroom management and administrative tasks by allowing educators and institutions to focus their efforts much more on instruction and less on routine, repetitive activities. Automating school administration for tracking attendance and student scheduling, communication, is where AI plays an important role in workflow streamlining, easing burdens, and enhancing efficiencies overall. These can help in attending to queries by students of a routine nature, such as class schedules, deadlines, and frequently asked questions on campus resources. These indeed function within a very short span of time, saving human staff the ability to deal with higher-level problems. Similarly, student enrollment, distribution of assignments, and tracking of performance are all possible in an AI system. On the other hand, AI tools can dig deep into administrative data sets in order to find correlations, which can lead to predictions about future trends. This could include such things as forecasting student enrollment numbers, expectations for the numbers of students requiring certain courses, and even identifying students likely to drop out. AI serves a given educational institution by availing data-driven insights to make active decisions and interventions that would aid student performance and resource allocation. This is in tandem with the study undertaken by Haddock et al. (2022).

One of the most outstanding examples where AI serves educational administration relates to how Georgia State University uses predictive analytics to keep students on track toward graduation. The university developed an AI-powered system that tracked a range of metrics on student performance and engagement. It digs deep into data ranging from course grades to attendance, even to something apparently unrelated like financial aid status, to make its predictions of which students are likely to fail or drop out. This early identification enables an institution of higher learning to identify students who may be at risk and, through specific targeted interventions such as tutoring or counseling, or in some instances financial aid, to increase their retention rate. Current performance tracking in the AI system forecasts future academic difficulties; therefore, enabling educators to timely assist students before they get behind. This proactive approach has resulted in noticeable enhancements in the retention and graduation rate for the students (Kamalov, et al., 2023).

Despite the growing reliance on AI to automate various educational processes, the role of educators remains critical to ensuring the effective integration of these tools. They should master integrating AI technologies into learning environments while remaining at the center to develop and promote critical thinking, creativity, and emotional support. Educators, on the other hand, have to provide an interpretation of the insights from the data produced by AI and apply them to make the realization of personalized instruction a right fitted to the needs of every student. This is especially important in professional development, which will ensure that educators develop the competencies to work with the AI systems and stand a better chance of deploying the technologies to improve student engagement and outcome.

Secondly, educators will also play a very important role in providing a human touch to balance AI-driven automation. With AI automating most administrative and routine instructional tasks, educators must emphasize personalized instruction, mentorship, and development of emotional intelligence. AI integration in schools should support teachers, enabling them to spend more time going deeper and on a personal level with students, while education remains a collaborative process done among human beings. This way alone can educators guarantee that AI enhances learning without lessening the important human factor in teaching.

While AI tools introduce several benefits both administratively and in classroom management, there is indeed a concern that human interaction might be lost in academic institutions. In a situation where AI mechanisms take over even more administrative tasks, even instructional roles, the personal touch between students and educators might get lost. Human interaction in education is necessary for the emotional intelligence, cooperation, and empathy-skills that no AI will be able to mimic. In those instances when students interact with institutions of education mainly through AI systems and not with human instructors or any other staff, they may become alienated or disconnected from the institution itself. This is most vital in sensitive areas such as counseling or mentorship, where the human touch acts essentially in the support of students' emotional and mental well-being. There does, of course, exist a balancing act in weighing these risks for the fine balance between AI-driven automation and human interaction. AI shall support and not replace human educators and administrators so as to retain personal, emotional, and social contact within education. This could be facilitated through blended learning models in which AI performs routine tasks while educators can focus on mentorship, personalized instruction, and emotional support.

Related Works

AI has been the focus of considerable research in education regarding its benefits and ethical implications. One of the main foci in this regard is in personalized learning, in which research into adaptive learning systems like DreamBox and Knewton has promised much. These types of AI-based learning systems modify content in real-time based on the progress and further learning needs of each learner (Senthil, 2015). With these platforms offering pathways that are personalized, this would add further potential to increase engagement and move toward better learning outcomes. However, Bender et al. (2021) pointed out the possible algorithmic bias and said that if AI systems are trained on non-diverse datasets, they will most likely be prejudicially disadvantaged against underrepresented groups. It is this very risk that necessitates data representative of the diverse populations they are purposed to serve.

The advantages of AI have been evident in terms of automated assessment: "Platforms like Grade Scope and Edmentum already use AI to grade student work, which provides much quicker, more timely feedback than traditional methods of grading" (Haddock et al., 2022). These kinds of tools can greatly reduce the time it takes to grade and free the educators to spend more time on instruction. However, the deficiency of these AI-powered assessment systems becomes apparent about creative or subtle work. While human assessors can accurately grade assignments that often require subjective interpretation, AI may fail. Therefore, what is needed is a balanced approach between AI and human assessment.

AI is equally helpful in managing classrooms optimally due to its administrative role. For example, studies show that AI-powered tools could automate routine tasks and thereby save educators time for teaching and engaging with students more (Ronald et al., 2018). Predictive analytics at Georgia State University help in singling out those who are likely to fail so targeted interventions may be provided for them. It will help educators in taking proactive steps by analyzing the pattern of student data to improve student outcomes and reduce dropout rates.

However, even with such benefits, the usage of AI in educational settings raises ethical concerns. Haddock et al., (2022) discussed some of the other associated risks: privacy violations and the ethical dilemmas developing from vast data collection practices. Since most AI systems depend on a lot of information from students for efficiently carrying out tasks, the chances of misuse or breach of data increase at a tremendous rate. Nguyen and Nadi (2022) have also highlighted that clearer guidelines and policies on the use of AI in educational settings are required to protect the privacy of students and ensure ethical practices. The previous studies provide a good overview of how AI may transform education but also point to a number of ethical and practical challenges. For every benefit from AI-driven innovation in educational settings, measures must be provided that minimize risks while complying with ethical standards to ensure responsible deployment.

EMERGING TRENDS IN AI FOR EDUCATION

AI in Experiential and Lifelong Learning

The other emerging trend of AI in education is that this is its place in experiential and lifelong learning. The AI-enabled technologies are creating an immersive learning environment with the help of virtual and augmented reality that enables practical learning experiences. In fact, these technologies have allowed learners to engage in real-world scenarios, (Mouta et al.,2024) that had hitherto not been possible in conventional classroom settings.

AI-Powered VR and AR for Immersive Learning: AI-powered VR and AR systems will break learning barriers in medical studies, engineering, and scientific disciplines by allowing students to experience various complex processes and environments virtually. For example, some of the leading medical applications include virtual surgery and other procedure simulations that can be conducted without risk using VR-enabled simulations. AI helps in generating realistic dynamic scenarios where students can make decisions and get real-time feedback. This pragmatic approach will enhance the students' clinical skills and confidence before they see actual patients. For example, virtual dissections or surgeries let students study human anatomy in great depth. These are the kinds of immersive learning experiences that would be very challenging to replicate in a live classroom setting.

In engineering studies, AI-enabled VR/AR lets students learn about complex machinery and systems without the need for physical access. Virtual models of complex machines, students interact with inner work and can even try changes in their design. Such an immersive technique of learning gives a better understanding of the theoretical concepts by trying to apply them in realistic simulation. In the case of engineering students, they can virtually take apart and put together engines, test the prototype of a design, and also simulate industrial processes to help them in better learning in the classrooms. In fields like that, VR and AR come in and offer students an experiential learning environment whereby they get hands-on practical experience that adds to their theoretical knowledge. Besides that, immersive technologies also afford the learner an opportunity to make mistakes and learn from them in a safe environment, which enhances problem-solving and builds confidence (Mouta et al.,2024)

Apart from reimagining formal education, AI plays an important role in lifelong learning in that it assists professionals in continuous skill development processes where the demands within the industry are fast changing. In today's world, the industries that pertain to technology, finances, and healthcare keep on changing with each passing day. Hence, workers have to go along with the emerging knowledge, tools, and methodologies. AI-driven platforms are helping professionals pursue customized learning with interactive, updated content relevant to their career aspirations and learning requirements. In artificial intelligence learning platforms like Coursera and Udemy, course suggestions for customers come based on learning history and customer preferences.

Additionally, various Learning Platforms use AI in tracking learner progress, identifying skill gaps, and suggesting relevant courses or modules that could help learners achieve specific career objectives. AI-driven platforms provide real-time feedback, adaptive learning material to ensure professionals are growing in skills continuously and effectively relevant to their personal and professional development. The added advantage of AI is that, through the big data sets, it can analyze and predict trends emerging from these industries and inform them of recommendations for skills that will likely also be in demand shortly. This will, therefore, help the professional to remain relevant and competitive against the shifting sands of industry changes. AI empowers education to become more accessible and inclusive, offering students with disabilities personalized learning opportunities, and will fundamentally change experiential and lifelong learning through immersive technologies such as VR and AR. As AI continues to evolve, its role in making education more adaptive, more accessible, and more effective will grow increasingly central to the way we learn and develop throughout our lives.

AI for Inclusive Education

Probably the most promising trend in AI for education pertains to the issue of inclusion-especially for students with disabilities. Already, AI-powered tools are starting to be game-changers in the way this group of learners interacts with course content, students with physical impairments, cognitive impairments, and sensory impairments. This further helps educators, in turn supported by AI technologies, to create an increasingly inclusive educational environment that caters to such students who usually struggle to access learning resources. It is a shift to inclusivity that reveals AI's potential to contribute to reducing learning barriers and widening participation in all levels of education.

AI for Accessibility Tools

The emerging technologies, such as Microsoft's Immersive Reader and Google's Live Transcribe, are just a few examples of AI-powered learning enhancement tools for people with disabilities. Such tools facilitate the interaction of students with content through active engagement, while educators also can communicate more effectively with learners of a wide range.

- Immersive Reader: This tool is designed to help students with reading disabilities by using AI to make text more readable using font sizes, spacing, and color contrast. It also provides speech-to-text capability in cases where some students with visual impairments or dyslexia can understand the content more audibly than conventionally. The tool minimizes distraction and increases engagement by personalizing the content to meet needs. Furthermore, real-time translation features promote linguistic diversity among learners and make content more accessible to students for whom that language might not be their first.
- Live Transcribe is an AI-powered application that transcribes spoken language in real-time into text. This makes it invaluable for students who have hearing disabilities. Live Transcribe can provide captions for these students in the class, whether in classroom discussions, lectures, or conversations. In learning environments which would normally tend to present them with high levels of obstacles, this feature by Live Transcribe enables such students to keep pace and respond.

AI's Greater Role in Encouraging Inclusivity and Accessibility

Beyond these tools, AI can help with greater inclusion because it personalizes the content and navigation of educational resources to meet the diverse learning styles, preferences, cognitive needs, and linguistic backgrounds of individual students. Such flexibility, in turn, allows all students to actively engage in learning, whether they have a language barrier or some kind of attention deficit. For example, AI now provides real-time translation so students without the primary instructional language can participate in classroom discussions and learn from content that would otherwise be inaccessible. Similarly, AI-powered speech recognition software helps students unable to use their hands physically by facilitating voice-activated commands on learning platforms to independently navigate educational content.

Personalization and Equity in Learning

AI further supports inclusive education by offering the possibility for personalized learning trajectories for each student. With the use of systems influenced by AI, one can allow real-time adjustments in the adaptation of content based on a student's progress and the offering of supplementary material or additional exercises when necessary-that is, the highest level of personalization-so students with different abilities or learning needs are guaranteed appropriate accommodation toward their success. For instance, with AI technology, the learning disabilities that students have need not be a burden since content provided would be in many forms: visual, auditory, and kinesthetic, which applies to their specific way of learning. In addition to this, the role of AI in promoting inclusivity extends to an institutional level. Schools can employ AI systems to analyze the performance data of students and develop personalized learning pathways to meet the diverse needs of their student populations. In this way, AI helps ensure that every student receives the resources and support they need to succeed, encouraging equity in opportunity throughout their schooling experience.

Diversifying Inclusivity through AI

AI furthers inclusivity in several dimensions, including improving access. It lets educational institutions offer learning experiences adapted to students with disabilities, as well as students with different cultural, linguistic, and cognitive diversities. In such a way, each learner has an equal opportunity to be successful irrespective of his or her abilities and challenges. Removing participation barriers and guaranteeing adaptive and personalized learning experiences, AI has proved to help in building more equitable and inclusive educational settings for all learners.

ETHICAL CONSIDERATIONS: DATA PRIVACY AND ALGORITHMIC BIAS

The word "*ethics*" comes from the Greek ethos, which means "*way of living*." Ethics relates to the study of the reasons behind our moral judgments and how humans treat each other and nature. Ethical principles are based on notions of right and wrong, good and bad, just and unjust. On a more general level, ethics critically reflects on the behavior of humans and human interaction in such a way that it aims for, but is never fully able to achieve, fairness and justice.

In ethics, fairness means being treated as everyone else and being treated with no undue special treatment or consideration. It is a principle based upon moral judgment—how people decide what is morally correct or incorrect. The term *moral* is derived from the Latin *mores*, which means "customs" or "habits." Morality often has to do with right actions and behavior, with the moral of any story usually intended to teach right behavior. When applied objectively, morals denote a course of conduct deemed right or proper by the individual's conscience or by society at large, often in relation to good character and worthy ideals regarding human behavior. For its part, immoral describes actions or behavior that are wrong or unethical, including but not limited to common crimes like theft or lying.

Ethics, basically speaking, involves basic questions of how individuals and society should act. It gives a guideline to moral judgment and making ethical decisions. Ethics is not static; it is dynamic; it evolves with societies and cultures. It forms an important guide for human behavior as societies become increasingly complex to help individuals and communities define what is equitable, just, and morally right. The ethical issues related to AI in education become critical, since the application of AI technologies increasingly affects students, educators, and institutions. The sections below show the key ethical challenges for the AI-based educational systems concerning data privacy and security, algorithmic bias, and balance between AI automation and human interaction. With AI systems deeply embedded in education, significant ethical challenges have emerged in the protection of data, fairness of algorithms, and over-dependency on technology. A very important point is to ensure responsible and ethical AI applications in educational contexts to avoid unintended consequences that could undermine the benefits it offers. Three such critical ethical issues will be discussed herein: data privacy and security, algorithmic bias, and balancing AI with human interaction (Buckingham & Luckin, 2019).

Data Privacy and Security

According to Tang & Su, (2024), the system gathers huge volumes of data on students, ranging from personal information and academic performance to even learning behavior and sometimes social interaction. The foregoing information is subsequently utilized to devise personalized learning experiences aimed at predicting student success while improving overall efficiencies in education. Yet, it is this sensitive volume that gives rise to serious concerns regarding data privacy and security. The student information, if not well secured, is bound to be breached, misused, or exploited by malicious actors. Beyond conventional risks of compromised data, many AI systems require continuous collection of information, which involves the problem of not being able to keep sensitive information secure beyond a certain period. Potential identity theft, unauthorized access, and exploitation for commercial or other non-academic purposes are some of the threats and consequences regarding improper data management activities. Moreover, many learning institutions may not be able to acquire the expertise or resources to implement good cybersecurity measures to protect such data (Coeckelbergh,2020).

Besides, the storage of student information for long-term purposes also poses another challenge. As AI systems continue to gather and process data on students, the institution has to identify for how long this data should be retained and how securely it shall be maintained. Unsuitable methods of storing data can result in failure to address privacy issues in the future, especially when data is retained without identified rules or policies regarding the time such data needs to be deleted. Therefore, it is necessary that AI systems utilizing such information are transparent in collecting, storing, and using the data of students. In this respect, both the school administration and AI developers must ensure that all stakeholders-students, parents, and educators-are fully informed about what kind of data is collected, the reason for collecting it, or what its use will be later. This way, it instills trust and ensures that students and their parents make wiser decisions regarding their rights to privacy.

It also must be mindful of data protection through various laws, importantly *the General Data Protection Regulation.* Probably the most comprehensive recent legislation in data protection for any regional market, the GDPR lays high standards regarding the collection, storage, and processing of personal data in the European Union. The GDPR significantly affects educational institutions in that explicit consent by students or guardians regarding data collection is foremost, storage must be secure, and means must be provided to access, correct, or erase personal information. This would mean that educational institutions also have to implement similar ethical policies in safeguarding their data from AI systems around the world, so that the information of students is safe and within the bounds of legality. This would include encryption, anonymization techniques, and security methods of storing data. Besides this, developers of AI technologies should give importance to collecting only a bare minimum amount of information about students for the proper operation of the system (Tang & Su,2024).

Algorithmic Bias

Risks of Biased AI Systems One of the most controversial ethical issues related to AI in education concerns algorithmic bias of AI. Algorithms are merely as good as the data they get trained on. If algorithms are designed, and actually even trained on biased and unrepresentative data, then the AI system might itself encourage and further worsen inequities in education. For instance, AI, which was originally and primarily trained on data from one culture, socio-economic background, or geographic region, fails to make an accurate assessment of other students' abilities or learning needs. Bias in algorithms can be manifested through unfair learning outcomes, recommendations of inappropriate learning material, misclassification of performance by students, or disproportionate disadvantage to under-represented and marginalized groups of students. For example, an AI system, which was trained on historical data of the educational gap between rich and poor, would continue to exacerbate such inequalities by allocating less challenging content to students from poorer families and more advanced learning opportunities to the privileged class (Kamalov et al., 2023). This might further stretch the inequalities and result in more marginalization of poor learners.

In real life, biased AI use has come in the form of an algorithm in the UK, which predicted student grades during the COVID-19 pandemic in lieu of the cancelled in-person exams. The algorithm sharply downgraded students from disadvantaged schools, exacerbating inequality. On the other hand, several AI systems have been designed to handle diverse and representative data-such as the predictive analytics system at Georgia State University-and have gone on to support students across different demographics by recognizing those at risk way in advance and supporting improved retention rates. Another problem is relying too much on past data to predict student performance. Most AI systems project forward from past trends. For example, if this information is biased, reflecting disparities in systemic achievement for certain demographic groups, then the AI system could encode such biases, further depriving these groups of equitable learning opportunities. Such an AI system, trained on data reflecting lower achievement levels among minority students, for instance, may continue recommending lower-level content and hence deny the chance to these students to be academically challenged.

All these risks can be mitigated only if AI systems in education are appropriately trained with diverse and representative data. The application of the data during training should make sure it represents a wide array of students, from different cultural, ethnic, socio-economic, and geographic backgrounds. That way, fairness will be maintained across all populations of students. Second, regular auditing of AI systems using algorithms for bias detection should be done to weed out any potential biases. Continuous feedback loops from educators will also help in identifying errors or biases that might arise and thus allow continuous improvements.

Furthermore, ethics of AI design need to be directed at considerations that ensure equity, transparency, and accountability. Diverse nature development teams, made up of individuals from different walks of life, can help identify sources of potential bias during the design stage. Such collaborative efforts may avoid reinforcing existing inequities through multiple points of view informing the creation process.

Another significant problem tagged along with AI in education is data privacy. AI systems require unlimited volumes of student data for personalization of learning experiences, prediction of performance, automation of routine administrative tasks, etc. In fact, collecting, storing, and utilizing this information contributes to serious privacy concerns. Personal details related to students' academic performance, behavioral data, and even sensitive information like health conditions may be misused if proper safeguards are not provided. For instance, in 2020, a serious data breach occurred in the online proctoring service ProctorU and affected the personal data of more than 440,000 students. The incidents being discussed show that educational contexts may face important levels of AI application and can be disclosed to sensitive data disclosure. Therefore, academic institutions, along with AI developers, should focus on strict data protection through encryption, anonymization, and adherence to regulations such as GDPR or FERPA in the United States. It also calls for institutions to be transparent in terms of what data they are collecting from students and parents, how the data is used, and who has access to such data. Consent should always be obtained before collecting personal data, with an option to opt out without affecting the students' educational experience. Neglecting these may result in erosion of trust in AI systems and hence may impede their implementation effectively within educational settings.

OVER-RELIANCE ON AI

While AI is increasingly being applied in grading, content delivery, and classroom management, there is an emerging concern about overdependence on the AI system at the expense of human interaction. AI can efficiently manage many tasks; however, it lacks the emotional quotient, emotional intelligence, and creativity so important in holistic education. As developing critical thinking, creativity, and emotional growth are features hard for AI systems to promote, human educators play a very important role in the students' character development. For instance, AI systems tend to optimize for easily measurable outputs, including test scores and academic achievement. While these are important measures, they are not likely to reflect the depth of educational objectives, such as social-emotional competencies development, ethical reasoning, and creative problem-solving. On the other hand, human teachers engage students in open-ended discussions, challenge assumptions, and elicit deep reflective thinking-qualities associated with intellectual development that AI cannot replicate.

In addition, teachers are in a better position to note various emotional or social problems that students may be experiencing and, if possible, guide and counsel them or provide mentorship. AI is incapable of fully comprehending the intricacies of human behavior and, therefore, cannot replace the relational dimension of teaching that gives rise to a person's personal and social development. While AI can, for example, afford personalized learning based on academic data, it cannot by any means provide emotional support, encouragement, or motivation that students often need from their educator. The solution may be found in the blended learning models in which AI supports and supplements but does not replace human educators. Instructors could devote their energies to those more complex, sophisticated elements of teaching that help students develop the kind of critical thinking, creativity, and emotional maturity made possible by AI handling routine tasks like grading or administrative work. This means, in short, AI can support efficiency without sacrificing the vital human dimensions of teaching so essential for deeper learning and student development. In short, while AI has revolutionary potential in education, there must be consideration about data privacy, algorithmic bias, and the overuse of AI. Well-designed systems of AI, based on considerations of equity, transparency, and privacy, can help teachers offer more inclusive and customized learning experiences. Yet, educators must remain at the heart of the process of learning to ensure that AI amplifies and does not replace important human elements in this process. With this balance, AI has the potential to duly enhance educationally desired outcomes equitably for all learners.

Limitation of AI in Developing Creativity, Emotional Intelligence, and Critical Thinking

AI has increasingly found application in many sectors; therefore, it is only normal that it finds its way into education. AI plays a transformative role in automating tasks, personalizing learning, and making administrative processes efficient. While AI holds great potential to streamline processes in education, it faces enormous limitations in fostering creativity, emotional intelligence, and critical thinking-skills innately human. Thus, this portrays the many limitations of AI, which, if not tamed, will promote AI from being a tool to enhance human education to completely replacing it.

One of the critical limitations in AI is that it has not been able to enable creativity. While an AI system may process large amounts of data, identify patterns, and create material based on algorithms, it is inherently restricted when considering creative imagination. Most processes of creativity involve making illogical connections, playing with abstract thoughts, and thinking outside the box of defined knowledge-all areas that are hard for AI to work with.

While AI can create music, art, and even written content, such output is usually derivative, resting heavily on previously inputted data and patterns. For instance, AI-generated artwork or writing, while impressive in some cases, lacks the same spontaneity and innovation as that provided by human creativity. Where human creativity works best is in situations involving brainstorming, open-ended problem-solving, and cross-disciplinary thinking-those activities when individuals pull from personal experiences, emotions, and intuition. AI alone cannot go beyond what it has been trained for and, therefore, genuinely cannot innovate beyond what is at hand. Thus, since AI can enable creativity in terms of providing the tools or suggesting ideas, it cannot replace this uniquely human capacity for creativity born of experience, emotion, and abstract thought.

Another limitation of AI, which is very critical, is its inability to provide emotional intelligence. Emotional intelligence refers to the ability to identify, explain, and react to one's emotions and those of others. It forms a basis for relationships, empathy, and understanding of social dynamics-skills of vital importance in schools where personal interaction and emotional support are crucial for student success. Whereas AI systems can recognize sentiment in text or detect facial expressions, they don't understand or experience emotions themselves. A good example: AI might identify a student's frustration based on facial cues or tone of voice but cannot provide the type of empathetic response that a human teacher can. It also needs some degree of emotional intelligence in recognizing, not just feelings, but understanding where the client is coming from and often responding with support, encouragement, or guidance. Clearly, this deeper level of emotional matching, as claimed in mentoring, counseling, and personal development, is beyond the capability of present technologies in AI. Within the learning environment, emotional intelligence plays an important role in helping to create a relationship-based learning atmosphere. While guiding students with a set academic curriculum, it helps the student deal with his or her personal problems. No AI, no matter how progressive, can provide the level of human interaction required to nurture these deeper dimensions of human emotion. Even though AI itself may be of great service in personalized academic support, second to none are human educators in facilitating the emotional development and well-being of students.

One of the limitations AI faces in fostering critical thinking involves analyzing, evaluating, and synthesizing information; it questions assumptions, considers multiple perspectives. While AI is excellent in data processing and giving insights from such data, it cannot engage in reflective thinking nor question-based assumptions. Critical thinking involves the ability to reason beyond established rules or data. Human educators push students to interrogate evidence, consider alternative perspectives, and reflect thoughtfully-a skill set AI cannot replicate. To use one example, while AI can lead content delivery or assess students on specified parameters that have been set, it cannot engage students in the deeper reflective processes involved in testing arguments, considering ethical consequences, or comprehending richness in real-world problems. This places human teachers in a unique position to facilitate processes in students that involve the instillation of intellectual curiosity, the encouragement of debate, and the enhancement of analytical thinking-skills inherently hard to quantify and, therefore, hard for AI systems to teach or assess. Although AI systems can certainly support critical thinking by providing access to information and data-driven insights to learners, they cannot replace teachers in challenging students to think deeply and critically.

It is best, therefore, to regard AI as augmentation, rather than replacement, of human teaching to overcome these limitations. Grading, data analysis, and content delivery are the routine tasks which could be given to AI, freeing up the teacher to attend to more complex and subtle tasks in education such as the development of creativity, emotional intelligence, and critical thinking. By integrating AI, educators are thus able to offer balanced learning environments in which students benefit from personalized, data-driven insight but also engage in deeper, reflective learning. Blended learning models, in which AI supports and supplements human educators, not replace them, prevent over-reliance on AI in education. AI can handle administrative tasks and deliver customized academic support, freeing teachers to develop those non-quantifiable skills so important for personal and intellectual growth. This lets AI drive efficiency and personalization without sacrificing those human dimensions of education that spur creativity, emotional intelligence, and critical thinking.

AI FOR LIFELONG LEARNING AND EXPERIENTIAL EDUCATION

With industries continuing to grow and change, both in relation to new technological development and changing economic demands, the requirement for lifelong learning is more important than ever. In that respect, professionals in all fields have to continuously update their existing skills in order to remain relevant in their respective fields. AI has the potential to really transform how lifelong learning works by offering personalized learning pathways and immediate feedback, enabling professionals to approach educational pursuits in a way that reflects their needs and aspirations within their career. *AI has the Potential to Support Customised Learning Pathways (Mouta et al.,2024) and Real-Time Feedback for Professionals* by *AI-driven platforms* which can push personalized learning to very granular levels of each learner's specific skills, knowledge gaps, and professional objectives. While most models still assume a one-size-fits-all approach, adaptive learning pathways, powered by AI, adjust in real-time as progress in learning is made. This is much more relevant in a scenario where business professionals can hardly find the time to learn and focus on what matters most to them. Furthermore, *Learning Paths Personalization*, in fact, AI algorithms can assess a learner's past knowledge and experiences, and even preferences, to suggest an individualized curriculum that would serve their needs best. For example, a data science professional may smoothly progress to advanced topics in machine learning right after mastering the basics of statistics, while a total beginner in this sphere will be routed from the foundational content. AI personalizes learning to the individual learner so that they are not confronted with complicated topics before being ready, nor bored with content already mastered.

Flexibility makes lifelong learning more efficient and effective. Moreover, *Real-Time Feedback,* perhaps one of the most valuable benefits of AI in education is its ability to provide immediate, real-time feedback to the learner. It, in turn, helps the professionals correct their mistakes, understand complex ideas, and improve in the process of learning. For instance, an AI-powered platform will analyze the performance of a marketing professional on some mock project provided through AI and give suggestions regarding how one can fine-tune the strategies or missing points in the analysis. Such instant feedback allows learners to make immediate adjustments and speeds up the process of learning and knowledge retention (Mouta et al.,2024). Also, AI-powered systems can track learners' performance and regulate learning speed. If a learner performs below average in a certain concept, the system can offer extra content or alternative explanations to address the gap. On the other hand, if the learner is performing above expectation, the platform introduces more complex content in order for him/her to be constantly enrolled and challenged.

AI has already struck some serious chords in lifelong learning through platforms like *Coursera, LinkedIn Learning, and Udacity* using artificial intelligence in recommending courses in line with a user's career goals, interest, and past learning behavior. These platforms tout a wide variety of learning experiences in technical skills such as coding and engineering to leadership and management training. With every advancement in AI, these platforms will continue to be curated, allowing professionals to have skill sets that could be highly specialized. As such, it is expected that the requirement for lifelong learning will increasingly intensify in industries fully transformed by forces of automation, AI, and other technologies at the bleeding edge. It is here that AI may be summoned to realize a lasting solution in personalized lifetimes of learning adjusted to changing industry trends and technologies (Selwyn, 2021). It is for these reasons that lifelong learning influenced by AI is foreseen to bring about considerable changes within the following spheres:

- *Technology and IT*: With the rapid growth of industries in artificial intelligence, machine learning, cybersecurity, and blockchain, the need for updating the skill sets of tech professionals has grown incredibly. AI-enabled learning platforms will facilitate this by carving out personalized learning pathways focused on the latest tools, languages, and frameworks. For example, AI recommendations might include taking new courses in emerging programming languages or machine learning algorithms, considering current industry demands and the accumulated experience a professional has built up over time.

- *Healthcare*: AI-driven systems could also power seamless continuing education for healthcare professionals. With continuous evolution in the knowledge base and practices of medicine, this may include personalized learning recommendations based on a physician's specialty, thus keeping them on par with the latest in research, treatment protocols, and guidelines. Examples include AI-driven platforms that give surgeons virtual opportunities to practice new surgical techniques or, in some instances, even provide real-time feedback during virtual dissections. AI will also contribute to keeping doctors ahead in the trends related to patient care, diagnosis, and emerging options for treatment, since AI can analyze massive amounts of data.
- *Finance and Business*: Even finance is getting quite changed by the interventions of AI, Fintech, and data analytics. AI-powered learning platforms in finance can hence help the professionals by offering tailored courses on topics like blockchain, financial modeling, and algorithmic trading. These would be able to track market trends and modify the learning material accordingly in real time, therefore letting professionals at any point in time learn about the updated tools and practices. AI can also be used by business professionals in leadership, management, and strategic decision-making training through realistic simulations and giving a practical feel for how to run organizations in the digital age (Buckingham & Luckin, 2019).
- *Manufacturing and Engineering*: Increased automation and smart manufacturing technologies require professionals in these sectors to be in a continuous cycle of learning new skills related to robotics, AI integration, and digital manufacturing processes. AI-powered platforms can provide engineers and technicians with personalized learning experiences to stay relevant. For instance, it could provide bespoke training on how to use machine learning in order to enhance production lines or how to build AI-driven systems for application in industry. Even more to this, such platforms can make simulations available that allow professionals to, for example, practice their knowledge in virtual environments without requiring physical resources.

Several key developments might be expected in how AI will support lifelong learning as industries continue to evolve (Selwyn, 2021). First, AI systems will increasingly analyze market trends and industry developments in real time and immediately adjust learning content to reflect such changes. For example, professionals will have access to dynamic learning resources that are up-to-date and always relevant to their fields.

- *AI-Driven Mentorship*: Other than personalized learning, AI can provide more advanced forms of mentorship. AI-driven systems can easily play the role of a virtual career mentor and can be utilized for providing personalized advice regarding career development or suggesting emerging skills or gap in skills.
- *Cross-Industry Competency Building*: AI-driven learning platforms will support cross-disciplinary skills due to the convergence of industries and the rise of new interdisciplinary fields like biotech and fintech. Such systems will suggest learning trajectories that combine insights from multiple fields and help professionals navigate increasingly complicated and changing career landscapes (Selwyn, 2021).

BRIDGING THE DIGITAL DIVIDE

Given that AI-driven education is going to rise, one of the most fundamental challenges facing educators today is how to ensure all students from different walks of life will access these advanced technologies. Indeed, one of the major obstacles to deploying AI in a fair manner is something normally known as the digital divide-the gap between those with and without access to up-to-date technology. This divide can only be bridged through strategic investments in technological infrastructure. The way a targeted approach can ensure that AI-powered learning becomes available to students of all sets is by investing in technological infrastructure (Coeckelbergh,2020).

Taken in a broader perspective, the first-order business of closing the digital divide involves the building of robust technological infrastructure locally, nationally, and globally (Mouta et al.,2024) . For many students, especially those from low-income or rural areas, internet access, devices, and other required technology are quite problematic and insufficient to support AI-driven learning. In communities where access to such tools is unreliable, students may fall even further behind their peers, deepening existing educational inequalities.

Government, education, and private sectors should address the following priority concerns in order to bridge this gap:

- *Broadband Internet Access*: High above all, high-speed internet access needs to be facilitated in order to access AI-based learning platforms, digital classrooms, and online resources. Investment in the expansion of affordable and reliable internet infrastructure in underserved areas is paramount so that all walks of students across different socio-economic backgrounds may avail themselves of AI-driven education.

- *Digital Devices and Tools*: In the case of AI-enhanced educations, students need digital devices for learning. Such digital devices may include laptops, tablets, or smartphones. Schools or governments can work in collaboration with technology companies to ensure that students who cannot afford devices are supported at subsidized rates. Some initiatives on subsidies for such devices or providing them free for low-income students would reduce barriers to access.
- *Teacher Training and Support*: The investment in the training of teachers is equally crucial because, without it, teachers would not be able to host AI tools in their classrooms. Unless properly trained and supported, teachers in under-resourced schools may fail to tap into the full power of AI technologies, leading to increased digital gaps. Professional development programs should be provided to assure educators of the knowledge and abilities necessary for effective functioning in a learning environment driven by AI.
- *Renewable Energy Solutions*: Lack of or limited access to electricity in far-flung or under-served areas of the country has served as a potential cause for arresting the application of digital technology in education. Investments in renewable energy solutions, such as solar power, can provide the infrastructure that will support AI-powered learning even in the most energetic access-poor regions.
- *Equity of Access to AI-driven Education along Socioeconomic Groups*: In addition to infrastructure investments, discussed above, policies and programs that target specific challenges for each group will be necessary for equality in access to AI-driven education. While AI has the potential to democratize education by providing an experience of personalized learning at scale, without deliberate efforts at making such technologies accessible for all, the benefits of AI can indeed remain concentrated in the better-off communities. Following are strategies that can enable this equity in access:
- *Public-Private Partnerships*: Collaboration between governments, NGOs, and private technology companies can raise much-needed resources for the underfunding of schools and institutions. Such collaborations can pave the way for funding programs to distribute devices, expand internet access, and build AI-powered learning curricula fitting for underserved groups. *Localized Content and Languages*, AI-driven education tools should be developed in a manner to support any language and cultural context. For example, an AI-driven platform should be designed with multilingual capability, with its content reflecting the cultural diversity of users, thus making them accessible to students from non-English speaking regions or with different cultural norms. In addition to *Subsidized Artificial Intelligence-based Platforms* which would become easily accessible to students falling into low-income categories.

Given the opportunity by way of access to quality education content at minimal or no cost, students from marginalized categories would be availed of opportunities extended as well as to those coming from wealthier categories.

- *Community- and School-Based Access Programs*: Community centers or school-based facilities with computers and internet access could be established as places where students can access AI learning at home, while schools and communities provide different levels of mentorship and support to ensure students from underserved areas take maximum advantage of AI-enhanced education (Buckingham & Luckin, 2019).

This was brought home with the COVID-19 pandemic, with schools of all levels making the shift to online learning. In large parts of the country and the world, the digital divide led to lost learning because many students from low-income or rural backgrounds had a lack of technological resources to participate in the remote learning process. Equitable access to AI-driven education is therefore a development priority of today's world and for the future at our doorstep-as part of this recovery. It is the job of governments, schools, and technology companies to make sure that AI technologies reach the student masses and not only a privileged few in affluent or urban areas; otherwise, this may further widen existing inequities and leave several million students behind who cannot afford to participate in AI-enhanced learning (Kamalov, et al.,2023)

FUTURE DIRECTIONS: ETHICAL AI DEVELOPMENT IN EDUCATION

With AI playing an increasingly important role in education, further development of AI technologies in the future will need to be informed by ethics that ensure AI technologies serve students, educators, institutions, and society at large (Zhang & Aslan, 2021) . Probably the most important development of the future related to AI in education lies in establishing ethical frameworks that guide the design, implementation, and use of AI systems. These frameworks should therefore be instilled with equity, transparency, and accountability, and be inclusive if AI is to make a positive contribution to the learning experience without perpetuating existing biases or inequities.

A process for the creation of ethical AI frameworks involves the development of clear guidelines which answer the major ethical challenges proposed by AI technologies, such as data privacy, algorithmic bias, and over-reliance on automation. The ideal framework (Tang & Su,2024) should, where possible, rest on the following principles:

- *Fairness and Equity*: AI systems should be designed to treat all students equitably, offering personalized learning opportunities without reinforcing stereotypes or discriminatory practices. This will involve training AI on diverse datasets and continuous auditing of systems to detect and mitigate bias.
- *Transparency*: The use of AI systems in education should be transparent. Educators, students, and parents have to be made aware of how these AI systems make decisions and why certain recommendations are pointed out to them where personal data is being used. This helps build confidence and ensures that AI serves responsibly.
- *Data Privacy and Security*: Ethical AI frameworks will need to put in place stern rules concerning the collection, storage, and usage of students' data. The data minimization strategies should be put in place to reduce the amount of personal information collected, and where possible, anonymize the data. Moreover, it is of importance that compliance with set regulations, such as the GDPR, be observed in efforts toward ensuring the protection of students' privacy.
- *Human-Centered Approach*: AI has to supplement the role of human educators, not replace it. Ethics mechanisms need to be developed to ensure that AI technologies are used only to enhance learning but without compromising critical human elements in education, such as empathy, emotional support, and interpersonal communication.

Successful framing of ethical AI requires collaboration between educators, policymakers, and AI developers (Nguyen et al., 2023) ; each of them brings a different perspective and is distinctly important in the molding of how AI should be applied in educational settings. T*eachers and administrators* work closely with students and thoroughly understand the dynamics of the classroom. Their input in this case is invaluable as it ensures that the design of AI systems will respond to real needs for both students and educators alike. Also, *Educators* can point out where AI could support personalized learning and engagement, and administrative tasks. Most importantly, *Decision-makers*, Governments and education establishments are striving to include more AI use in these sectors. With this, policymakers are expected to introduce legislation and policies that will help in the ethical development of AI while at the same time protecting students' rights. This includes the development of laws addressing aspects like data privacy, reduction of bias, and responsible use of AI technologies. Policies should also work toward encouraging AI literacy inclusion in the curriculum to prepare students for the future where AI will be omnipresent.

CONCLUSION

AI will disrupt education by making learning more personalized, effective, and inclusive. Adaptive learning systems, automated assessment tools, and AI-powered classroom management are strong in their potential for crafting an educational experience that can meet the needs of individual learners, thus improving performance, enhancing engagement, and reducing dropout rates. Additionally, AI in immersive learning environments, such as VR and AR, leverages the benefits of experiential learning for students. Furthermore, AI allows professionals to continue lifelong learning with a tailored path. Equally important, AI has the potential to redress historical inequities in education: improving the accessibility and relevance of learning for students with disabilities and providing high-quality, scalable education resources via digital platforms. Despite this huge promise, integration into education also carries a number of ethical considerations. These range from data privacy and security to algorithmic bias, and even overuse of AI in ways that would reduce human interaction-a critical element in emotional and social learning. The addressing of such concerns is cardinal in ensuring that AI makes the education resource richer without perpetuating current inequalities or inventing new forms of discrimination.

These challenges necessitate the development of ethical frameworks that would ensure AI systems are nondiscriminatory, transparent, and accountable. It is such frameworks that need to guide the development and deployment of AI technologies in education toward ensuring that all students, irrespective of their background, benefit from AI-enhanced learning. AI systems should be free from bias and have robust security measures to protect sensitive information about students. While AI has immense potential to magnify education greatly, it should support and not replace human teachers. Teachers cannot be replaced by machines because they provide something which machines cannot: enhanced critical thinking, creativity, and emotional intelligence in students. This balance of AI innovation and equity in education could only be developed with the collaboration of educators, policymakers, AI developers, and all other stakeholders involved in it. Educators should commit to lifelong learning as they get equipped in using various AI tools while maintaining their important and irreplaceable place in the learning process. Professional development programs in the education system will have to be provided so educators could master AI tools and understand how to effectively integrate AI with more traditional teaching methods to create a more enriching and interactive learning environment. This is one of the major risks of AI in education, implying that not all students from various cultural, socio-economic, and geographical backgrounds will enjoy equal opportunities for learning. The more representative and varied datasets that AI is trained on, the lesser the perpetuation of biases. It should therefore be under constant auditing for bias detection with the aim of ensuring that those errors are corrected for giving all students fair and personalized learning and not just the privileged few.

Furthermore, the inception of AI has highlighted many key concerns regarding information security and privacy. Since AI platforms amass immense levels of data about students, it has become quite critical for institutions to monitor its safety closely. Institutions should implement strict security measures such as encryption and anonymization to prevent leakage and misuse. Schools and AI developers are supposed to follow the laws like GDPR strictly to ensure protection standards about data privacy. This, in turn, builds trust between the students, parents, and institutions regarding how these data are collected and used. AI technologies should extend the capabilities of human educators, not replace them, in such a way that teachers are able to provide more personalized and effective instruction while retaining the human elements so vital for deep learning. True reform in education through AI means that every student is entitled to it, irrespective of their socio-economic background or geographical location. So, students from underserved locations do lack the much-required technological infrastructure due to the digital divide that has been a cause for great concern. There is a dire need for investment by governments and educational institutions on the creation of expanded broadband, affordable digital devices, and community-based learning centers in order to ensure that all students are privileges with AI-powered learning.

Life-long learning is gaining tremendous importance as industries evolve rapidly due to changes in technology. AI will enable continuous education through customized learning paths in relation to specific professional requirements. Public-private partnerships would be of high importance in keeping AI-driven learning platforms reasonably priced and accessible, ensuring that professionals can stay competitive in a job market that constantly evolves. Finally, there is a need to embed AI literacy into the curriculum. Students have to be aware of not only how AI tools are used but, importantly, how AI works and what the ethical considerations are. These understandings will place our next generations in a vantage position whereby they will be more capable of critically engaging with AI technologies and making contributions in driving the creation of ethical AI systems. But balancing this against a commitment to best ethical practices, equity, and human interaction will guarantee that AI enhances rather than undermines the foundation of human elements in education.

REFERENCES

Al-Mansoori, S., & Salem, M. B. (2023). The role of artificial intelligence and machine learning in shaping the future of cybersecurity: Trends, applications, and ethical considerations. *International Journal of Stochastic Analysis*, 8(9), 1–16.

Bender, S. M. (2022). Algorithmic Elections. *Michigan Law Review*, 121(121.3), 489. DOI: 10.36644/mlr.121.3.algorithmic

Boumediene, H., Bavaharji, M., & Berrahal, F. K. (2018). The effect of using Twitter on improving EFL students' writing: A case study. *International Journal of Humanities and Social Science Invention*, 7(5), 26–32.

Buckingham Shum, S., & Luckin, R. (2019). Learning analytics and AI: Politics, pedagogy and practices. *British Journal of Educational Technology*, 50(6), 2785–2793. DOI: 10.1111/bjet.12880

Chen, L., Chen, P., & Lin, Z. (2020). Artificial intelligence in education: A review. *IEEE Access : Practical Innovations, Open Solutions*, 8, 75264–75278. DOI: 10.1109/ACCESS.2020.2988510

Coeckelbergh, M. (2020). *AI ethics*. MIT Press. DOI: 10.7551/mitpress/12549.001.0001

Dimitriadou, E., & Lanitis, A. (2023). A critical evaluation, challenges, and future perspectives of using artificial intelligence and emerging technologies in smart classrooms. *Smart Learning Environments*, 10(1), 12. DOI: 10.1186/s40561-023-00231-3

Fiok, K., Farahani, F. V., Karwowski, W., & Ahram, T. (2022). Explainable artificial intelligence for education and training. *The Journal of Defense Modeling and Simulation*, 19(2), 133–144. DOI: 10.1177/15485129211028651

Gocen, A., & Aydemir, F. (2020). Artificial intelligence in education and schools. *Research on Education and Media*, 12(1), 13–21. DOI: 10.2478/rem-2020-0003

Haddock, A., Ward, N., Yu, R., & O'Dea, N. (2022). Positive effects of digital technology use by adolescents: A scoping review of the literature. *International Journal of Environmental Research and Public Health*, 19(21), 14009. DOI: 10.3390/ijerph192114009 PMID: 36360887

Holmes, W., Bialik, M., & Fadel, C. (2019). Artificial intelligence in education: Promises and implications for teaching and learning. Center for Curriculum Redesign. https://curriculumredesign.org/wp-content/uploads/AI-in-Education-CCR-2019.pdf

Hwang, G. J., Xie, H., Wah, B. W., & Gašević, D. (2020). Vision, challenges, roles and research issues of Artificial Intelligence in Education. *Computers and Education: Artificial Intelligence*, 1, 100001. DOI: 10.1016/j.caeai.2020.100001

Kamalov, F., Santandreu Calonge, D., & Gurrib, I. (2023). New era of artificial intelligence in education: Towards a sustainable multifaceted revolution. *Sustainability (Basel)*, 15(16), 12451. DOI: 10.3390/su151612451

Luckin, R., Holmes, W., Griffiths, M., & Forcier, L. B. (2016). Intelligence unleashed: An argument for AI in education. Pearson Education. https://www.pearson.com/content/dam/one-dot-com/one-dot-com/global/Files/about-pearson/innovation/open-ideas/Intelligence_Unleashed_Pearson.pdf

Mouta, A., Torrecilla-Sánchez, E. M., & Pinto-Llorente, A. M. (2024). Design of a future scenarios toolkit for an ethical implementation of artificial intelligence in education. *Education and Information Technologies*, 29(9), 10473–10498. DOI: 10.1007/s10639-023-12229-y

Nguyen, A., Ngo, H. N., Hong, Y., Dang, B., & Nguyen, B. P. T. (2023). Ethical principles for artificial intelligence in education. *Education and Information Technologies*, 28(4), 4221–4241. DOI: 10.1007/s10639-022-11316-w PMID: 36254344

Ouyang, F., & Jiao, P. (2021). Artificial intelligence in education: The three paradigms. *Computers and Education: Artificial Intelligence*, 2, 100020. DOI: 10.1016/j.caeai.2021.100020

Prasad, A., Kumar, A. S., Sharma, P., Irawati, I. D., Chandrashekar, D. V., Musirin, I. B., & Abdullah, H. M. A. (2023). Artificial Intelligence in Computer Science: An Overview of Current Trends and Future Directions. *Advances in Artificial and Human Intelligence in the Modern Era*, 43-60.

Ronald, R. (2018). 'Generation rent'and intergenerational relations in the era of housing financialisation. *Critical Housing Analysis*, 5(2), 14–26. DOI: 10.13060/23362839.2018.5.2.439

Selwyn, N. (2021). *Should robots replace teachers? AI and the future of education*. Polity Press.

Tang, L., & Su, Y. S. (2024). Ethical Implications and Principles of Using Artificial Intelligence Models in the Classroom: A Systematic Literature Review.

Van der Aalst, W. M. (2016). *Data science in action: Principles and ethics of big data*. Springer., DOI: 10.1007/978-3-662-49851-4_1

Williamson, B. (2020). *Big data in education: The digital future of learning, policy, and practice*. Sage Publications.

Zhang, K., & Aslan, A. B. (2021). AI technologies for education: Recent research & future directions. *Computers and Education: Artificial Intelligence*, 2, 100025. DOI: 10.1016/j.caeai.2021.100025

Zhang, K., & Aslan, I. (2021). Ethical issues in AI-powered education systems: A comparative review. *Journal of Educational Technology & Society*, 24(4), 79–91. https://www.j-ets.net/ETS/journals/24_4/6.pdf

Zhou, X., Xu, S., & Chen, C. (2022). AI-driven adaptive learning systems and their impact on student engagement. *Journal of Artificial Intelligence in Education*, 32(2), 289–312. DOI: 10.1007/s40593-022-00265-1

ADDITIONAL READING

Beck, J., Stern, M., & Haugsjaa, E. (1996). Applications of AI in Education. *XRDS: Crossroads. The ACM Magazine for Students*, 3(1), 11–15.

Chiu, T. K., Xia, Q., Zhou, X., Chai, C. S., & Cheng, M. (2023). Systematic literature review on opportunities, challenges, and future research recommendations of artificial intelligence in education. *Computers and Education: Artificial Intelligence*, 4, 100118. DOI: 10.1016/j.caeai.2022.100118

Kaviyaraj, R., & Uma, M. (2021, March). A survey on future of augmented reality with AI in education. In *2021 International Conference on Artificial Intelligence and Smart Systems (ICAIS)* (pp. 47-52). IEEE. DOI: 10.1109/ICAIS50930.2021.9395838

Su, J., & Zhong, Y. (2022). Artificial Intelligence (AI) in early childhood education: Curriculum design and future directions. *Computers and Education: Artificial Intelligence*, 3, 100072. DOI: 10.1016/j.caeai.2022.100072

Wu, Y. (2023). Integrating generative AI in education: How ChatGPT brings challenges for future learning and teaching. *Journal of Advanced Research in Education*, 2(4), 6–10. DOI: 10.56397/JARE.2023.07.02

KEY TERMS AND DEFINITIONS

Algorithmic Bias: The tendency of AI algorithms to produce biased results due to non-diverse training data, which can lead to unfair outcomes for certain groups in educational settings.

Artificial Intelligence (AI): A field of computer science that enables machines to simulate human intelligence, including problem-solving, learning, and decision-making processes in education.

Automated Assessment: The use of AI to evaluate student work, such as quizzes and assignments, providing fast and consistent feedback to enhance the learning process.

Classroom Management: The application of AI tools to help educators organize and streamline classroom activities, such as attendance tracking, student engagement monitoring, and resource management.

Data Privacy: The protection of personal information gathered from students in AI systems, ensuring that data is securely stored and only used for its intended educational purposes.

Ethical Considerations: Moral principles guiding the responsible use of AI in education, including concerns about data privacy, algorithmic bias, and the human role in teaching.

Intelligent Tutoring Systems: AI-powered platforms that provide personalized guidance and feedback to students, adapting to their individual learning needs and paces.

Personalized Learning: An educational approach supported by AI to tailor learning experiences to the individual needs, strengths, and progress of each student.

Predictive Analytics: The use of AI to analyze past student data to forecast future academic performance, enabling early interventions for students at risk of falling behind.

Virtual and Augmented Reality (VR/AR): Technologies enhanced by AI to create immersive learning environments, enabling experiential learning that simulates real-world scenarios.

Chapter 15

Identifying the Applications of Artificial Intelligence in Educational Entrepreneurship Development: A Qualitative Research Based on Thematic Analysis

Mahnaz Zolfaghari
https://orcid.org/0000-0002-8558-8530
Indiana University, Bloomington, USA

Aidin Salamzadeh
https://orcid.org/0000-0001-6808-1327
CIICESI, ESTG, Polytechnic of Porto, Portugal

Omid Afsharpour
https://orcid.org/0009-0003-7781-968X
Iowa State University, USA

ABSTRACT

In the rapidly evolving fields of education, entrepreneurship, and artificial intelligence, understanding the applications of AI in educational entrepreneurship is essential. This chapter adopts an applied research approach, using qualitative methods such

DOI: 10.4018/979-8-3693-7220-3.ch015

as a systematic literature review and semi-structured interviews with 14 experts from education, entrepreneurship, and AI. Through thematic analysis, 1830 initial themes were distilled into 42 first-level themes, categorized into 20 second-level themes, and ultimately consolidated into three overarching themes. These global themes reveal AI's impact on enhancing learning productivity, streamlining instructional methods, and advancing educational administration and leadership. The findings underscore AI's transformative potential in educational entrepreneurship, providing a comprehensive framework highlighting AI's diverse contributions to the education system.

INTRODUCTION

In today's rapidly evolving technological landscape, artificial intelligence (AI) has become a transformative force across various fields, including education. The COVID-19 pandemic further highlighted the importance of digital infrastructure in education as remote learning became the norm worldwide. This shift has created opportunities for educational entrepreneurship, as each deficiency in the system presents a potential area for innovation. The advancement of AI in education offers educators unique opportunities to create novel teaching and learning environments that have yet to be fully explored. The Dartmouth research project in 1955 defined artificial intelligence as machines capable of exhibiting behavior that is as intelligent as humans (McCarthy et al., 1955). In the context of this research, artificial intelligence is conceptualized as a system's ability to comprehensively analyze and interpret data, learn from that data, and utilize acquired knowledge to adapt and achieve specific goals in a flexible manner (Kaplan and Haenlein, 2018).

Artificial intelligence in education (AIED) refers to the use of AI technologies to enhance educational processes and outcomes. AI-driven tools and applications can facilitate personalized learning, automate administrative tasks, and provide data-driven insights to improve teaching strategies and student performance (Luckin & Holmes, 2016). The integration of AI in education can transform traditional pedagogical approaches, making the learning-teaching process more adaptive, engaging, and efficient (Bond et al., 2020). For instance, AI-powered learning platforms can customize educational content to meet individual student needs, thus promoting a more personalized learning experience (Verma et al., 2021). This aligns with the philosophies of educational visionaries like Montessori, where education is tailored to individual needs, and the focus is on creating a dynamic teaching-learning system rather than adhering to bureaucratic structures.

Educational entrepreneurship refers to entrepreneurial activities within the educational domain. It involves creating new value through innovative educational products, processes, or services (Musoke & Badru, 2018; Hess, 2007). There is a need to study the connection between Education and entrepreneurship, which has the potential to drive educational entrepreneurship by providing tools and technologies that can address the complex challenges faced by educational systems. Also, educational entrepreneurship requires a shift and transformation in the prevailing values within the university environment (Yadolahi et al., 2014).

Purpose and Importance of the Research

This study, conducted in 2022, aims to explore the specific applications of AI in educational entrepreneurship development, particularly within the primary to secondary education domain. By examining the innovative uses of AI within this context, the research seeks to identify key trends, challenges, and opportunities that can inform future educational practices and policies. By conducting a systematic literature review and qualitative interviews with experts in AI, education, and entrepreneurship, this study seeks to identify and validate the potential domains where AI can be effectively implemented to foster educational entrepreneurship. The importance of this research lies in its potential to provide a comprehensive model of AI applications in educational entrepreneurship. As educational systems worldwide face unprecedented challenges (Bozkurt & Sharma, 2021), such as the need for personalized learning and the integration of technology in teaching (Baker, 2019), Understanding how AI can be incorporated into the education system through the lens of educational entrepreneurship is crucial. This research can offer valuable insights for educators, policymakers, and entrepreneurs, guiding future innovations in the education sector. Moreover, the findings of this research can contribute to a deeper understanding of how AI can be leveraged to create more effective, equitable, and inclusive educational environments. By highlighting successful AI applications and identifying best practices, this study can help educational institutions and entrepreneurs navigate the complexities of digital transformation and harness the power of AI to improve educational outcomes.

LITERATURE REVIEW

Applications of Artificial Intelligence in Education

The application of artificial intelligence in education (AIED) has garnered significant attention due to its potential to transform teaching and learning processes. This literature review highlights recent advancements and implications of AI in education, drawing from studies indexed in Scopus, Web of Science, and Google Scholar. Artificial intelligence (AI) has shown great potential for various aspects of the education system, as highlighted by Chen (2020). It can be applied in managerial processes, content creation, and educational planning, as well as in facilitating the learning processes that students engage in. The field of AI in Education (AIED) encompasses three key domains: pedagogical model, content model, and learner model, as defined by Luckin and Holmes (2016). Khare, Stewart, and Khare (2018) emphasized the significance of AI in enhancing the student experience and operational efficiency within educational institutions. Their study discusses how AI contributes to personalized learning experiences, administrative tasks automation, and adaptive learning platforms. Additionally, Tuomi (2018) discusses the impact of AI on learning, teaching, and education policies, highlighting that AI can transform educational practices. Dai and Ke (2022) explore the educational applications of AI in simulation-based learning. Their systematic mapping review indicates that AI-driven simulations can offer immersive learning experiences, allowing students to engage in practical scenarios that enhance their understanding and skills (Dai & Ke, 2022).

Furthermore, UNESCO (2019) addresses the challenges and opportunities of AI in education for sustainable development. The report underscores the potential of AI to bridge educational gaps, promote inclusive education, and enhance learning outcomes globally, while also cautioning against the ethical and equity issues that need to be addressed to ensure fair access to AI technologies in education. Nawaz, Gomes, and Saldeen (2020) discuss AI applications in educational administration, particularly during the COVID-19 pandemic. They highlight how AI technologies were leveraged to maintain educational continuity, manage library resources, and support remote learning during the crisis (Nawaz, Gomes, & Saldeen, 2020). Crompton and Burke (2023) review the state of AI in higher education, highlighting how AI tools facilitate the teaching-learning process through assessment/evaluation, predicting, AI assistant, Intelligent Tutoring System (ITS), and managing student learning. Moreover, Perrotta and Selwyn (2019) explore the relational understanding of AI in education by deep learning. Luo (2019) investigates the changes in educational management in the era of AI, highlighting how AI-driven tools and systems can streamline administrative processes, enhance decision-making, and improve the efficiency of educational institutions.

Taneri (2020) discusses the role of AI in higher education, focusing on its potential to provide customized teaching and learning experiences. Malik, Tayal, and Vij (2018) analyze the role of AI in education and teaching, highlighting its ability to transform traditional teaching methods. They explore how AI can support teachers by automating administrative tasks, providing intelligent tutoring systems, and offering data-driven insights to enhance educational strategies. Hwang, Xie, Wah, and Gasevic (2020) provide a comprehensive overview of the vision, challenges, roles, and research issues of AI in education. Their article emphasizes the importance of understanding the various roles AIED can play, including intelligent tutee, intelligent learning tool and policy-making advisor. In special education, Drigas and Ioannidou (2012) examine how AI can cater to students with special needs. Their review indicates that AI applications, such as speech recognition and personalized learning platforms, can significantly improve accessibility and individualized support for students with disabilities (Drigas & Ioannidou, 2012). Chen, Xie, Zou, and Hwang (2020) address the application and theory gaps during the rise of AI in education. They provide a great contribution of the existing knowledge of AI applications in educational settings and the theoretical frameworks guiding these applications.

Furthermore, Baker (2000) discusses the roles of models in AI and education research, providing a prospective view on how different AI models can be utilized in educational research to enhance learning outcomes and streamline educational processes. Schiff (2021) takes AI out of the laboratory and into the classroom, discussing the probable applications of AI in education considering the different roles that AI can play in the teach-learning process. Finally, Holmes, Bialik and Fadel (2019) discuss the promises and implications of AI in education. Their work highlights the potential of AI to transform teaching and learning by providing AI in learning experiences, automating administrative tasks, and offering real-time feedback and support to both teachers and students. AI technologies not only enhance instructional methodologies and administrative efficiency but also promote inclusive education by addressing the needs of diverse learners. As educational systems continue to evolve, the integration of AI offers promising avenues for innovation and improvement in teaching and learning practices (Felix & Webb, 2024).

Educational Entrepreneurship

The field of entrepreneurship has seen substantial growth in the education domains as it intersects with the need for innovative approaches to teaching and learning (Hoppe et al., 2017). This literature review synthesizes recent findings from Scopus, Web of Science, and Google Scholar to highlight key themes and developments in educational entrepreneurship. Entrepreneurship is generally perceived as a driver of sustainable development and growth (OECD/EU, 2019). While Research relating to the impact of primary and secondary school engagement with entrepreneurship is very limited, due to the complex, varied, and constantly evolving nature of entrepreneurship (Wasim et al., 2023; Valenciano et al., 2019; Hess, 2007), educational entrepreneurship can be described as the creation of new value in the educational context (Smith & Peterson, 2006). This new value generated by educational entrepreneurship can manifest in various aspects of the education system, including the processes involved, the inputs utilized, the outputs produced, and the overall educational outcomes (Ahanchian & Ghorooneh, 2019; Man,2010; Musoke & Badru,

2018) It involves the integration of resources to introduce innovative educational products and services (Lacatus & Staiculescu, 2016).

In essence, educational entrepreneurship entails managing the supply and demand of innovative educational offerings, thereby generating value within the educational domain (Ahanchian & Ghorooneh, 2019; Man,2010; Musoke & Badru, 2018). Adopting a systematic approach to the education system (Hoy & Miskel, 2013), educational entrepreneurship is viewed as a means of creating new value and fostering innovation across three dimensions: inputs, processes, and outputs (Man,2010). This implies that educational entrepreneurship encompasses the development and enhancement of educational resources, the implementation of innovative teaching and learning methods, and the attainment of improved educational outcomes (Ahanchian & Ghorooneh, 2019; Man,2010; Musoke & Badru, 2018). Innovation and entrepreneurship expand beyond the typical boundaries of business and economics programs in higher education (Kayyali, 2023). Digital transformations and the utilization of AI have propelled schools towards autonomy, decentralization, and customization (Lacatus and Staiculescu, 2016; Hess, 2007).

Educational entrepreneurs use instructional programs to establish connections across various institutional areas (Kindel & Stevens, 2021; Yusof et al., 2010; Lackéus, 2015). Also, Smith and Peterson (2006) mention that educational entrepreneurs as social entrepreneurs in education are highly focused on outcomes. These encompass individuals who design alternative training or assistance initiatives for educators and administrators, alongside innovation of products and services that aid educators and administrators in their instructional, administrative, and managerial roles (Smith & Peterson, 2006). Nanni (2021) explores educational entrepreneurship within an intensive English as a Foreign Language (EFL) program in Thailand. This case study reveals how educational technology and project-based learning (PBL) contribute to innovation and enhanced learning outcomes. Kindel and Stevens (2021) further examine the nuances of educational entrepreneurship, distinguishing it from broader entrepreneurial efforts. Kindel emphasizes the unique challenges and opportunities within educational contexts, such as the need for customized solutions tailored to specific educational environments and student needs. These studies collectively highlight the transformative potential of integrating entrepreneurship into educational frameworks.

METHODOLOGY

Data Collection Method

This study adopts a qualitative research method. To extract and analyze the relationship between the themes derived from the interviews, an interpretive paradigm, systematic literature review, semi-structured interviews, and thematic analysis have been employed. Thematic analysis is a foundational qualitative method used to identify, analyze, and report patterns within qualitative data in this study (Braun & Clarke, 2006; Nowell et al., 2017; Maguire & Delahunt, 2017).

Systematic Literature Review

To address the research questions, a systematic literature review was conducted focusing on the application of artificial intelligence in educational entrepreneurship. This review aimed to comprehensively understand the existing literature and explore the proposed models, leading to a comprehensive understanding of the research area. The systematic literature review employed in this study was both independent and applied in nature. Additionally, the review followed a descriptive approach through textual narrative synthesis (Xiao & Watson, 2017) to provide a thorough analysis of the collected data. A descriptive systematic literature review aims to provide a comprehensive report on the existing literature rather than focusing on developing it further. In a textual narrative synthesis, relevant research articles are collected in an organized and objective manner, and based on selected keywords, the identified research is examined in relation to the main research topic. Through this synthesis, relevant articles are identified and screened based on their ability to provide information that addresses the research questions. An effective systematic literature review typically involves three primary stages: 1) planning for the review, 2) conducting the review, and 3) reporting the review (Kitchenham & Charters, 2007; Brereton et al., 2007). Relevant literature was identified using databases such as Scopus, Google Scholar, and Web of Science, ensuring a comprehensive coverage of relevant sources. In the planning stage of the systematic literature review, the researcher recognizes the need for conducting the specific research, formulates the research questions, and designs the research methodology. The next step involves reviewing the available resources to identify relevant and notable sources. The researcher then extracts, analyses, and synthesizes the information gathered from these sources. Finally, in the reporting stage, the researcher publishes the final findings of the systematic review.

Table 1. Reporting the findings of the systematic literature review

Relevant Articles		
Web of Science: 55	**Scopus: 78**	**Total: 133**
In the initial step, the articles were filtered based on being journal or conference articles, the data range was customized between 2000 to 2024, and the language was restricted to English.		
First scanning: reviewing the abstracts		
Web of Science: 31	Scopus: 34	Total: 65
After scanning and reviewing the abstracts, irrelevant articles that couldn't answer the research questions or had unrelated topics were eliminated.		
Appraisal of the quality of articles: reviewing the passage		
Web of Science: 18	Scopus: 26	Total: 44

Following an appraisal of the quality of articles and reviewing the entire passages, those that were highly relevant and fit within the research framework were selected. Articles that were found in both databases were considered only once.

Result: 44 articles

Figure 1. Clustering of keywords based on their relevance to the research topic, visualized using VOSviewer with data from Scopus titles, keywords and abstracts

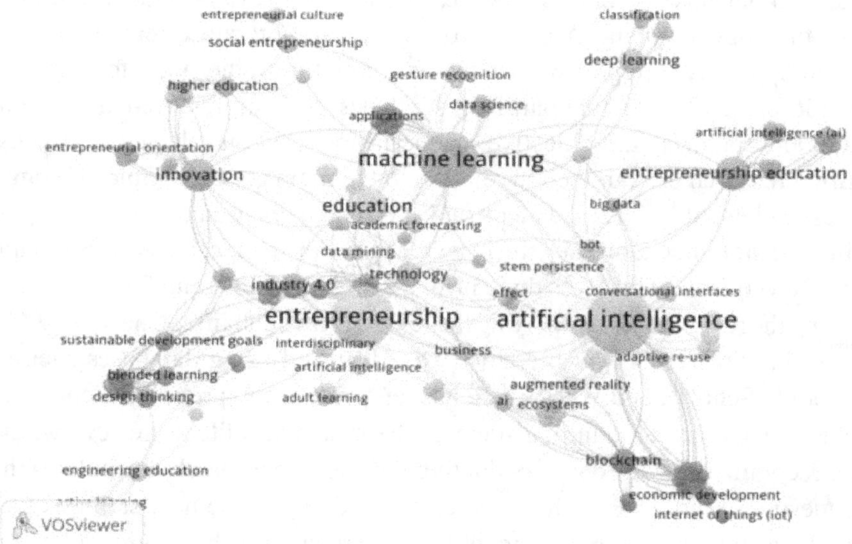

Identify the Research Questions

Identifying the appropriate research questions is crucial for the successful completion of a systematic literature review (Kitchenham & Charters, 2007). The accuracy of identifying research questions determines the inclusion of relevant sources in the review (Xiao & Watson, 2017). Therefore, this research aims to address the following key questions:

- What are the specific applications of artificial intelligence in the development of educational entrepreneurship?
- How can the applications of artificial intelligence in educational entrepreneurship development be classified?

Prototype of the Conceptual Framework Extracted from the Systematic Literature Review

By analyzing the literature review findings, key concepts, themes, and relationships among variables are identified and organized into a conceptual framework. This framework provides a visual representation of the interconnections and theoretical underpinnings of the research topic. By exploring the intersection of artificial intelligence in educational domains and educational entrepreneurship, this research seeks to uncover how the applications of AI can contribute to the creation of new educational value and foster innovation in the inputs, processes, and outputs of the education system. The aim is to identify the potential of AI in transforming educational entrepreneurship and its impact on the overall educational landscape. Considering all related research, this research's focus is on exploring the applications of artificial intelligence in three main domains within the education sector: educational administration, instruction, and learning. These axes are used in the first framework to investigate how AI can contribute to enhancing and optimizing these areas, leading to improved educational outcomes and experiences through the lens of educational entrepreneurship.

Figure 2. Prototype of the conceptual framework of the applications of artificial intelligence in educational entrepreneurship development

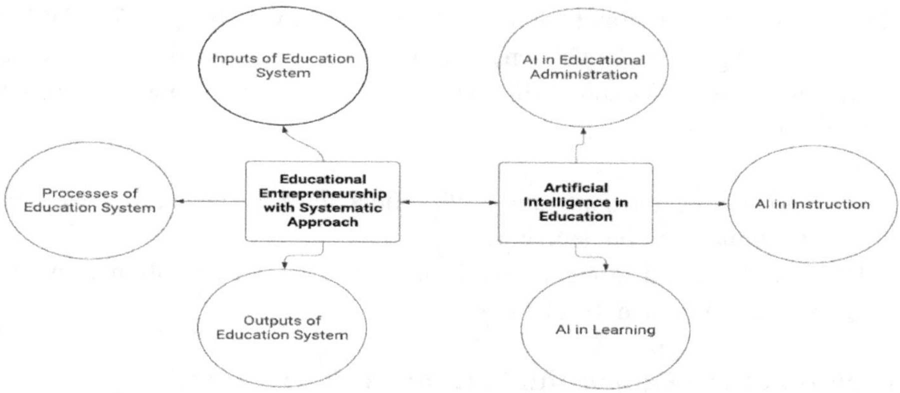

Semi-structured Interview

A semi-structured interview is a form of verbal communication where the interviewer seeks to gather information and insights related to the research questions (Longhurst, 2009; Bazargan, 2022). In this research, a semi-structured interview protocol has been developed to address the main research questions (Campbell et al., 2013). The protocol includes the following steps:

1-Identifying research questions, 2-Participant selection, 3-Conducting the interviews and recording, 4-Analyzing the interviews. The interviews will continue until data saturation is reached. Data saturation occurs when the researcher starts to encounter repetitive information and no new insights or themes emerge from the interviews (Faulkner and Trotter, 2017). At this point, it can be inferred that sufficient data has been gathered to address the research questions comprehensively.

Research Participants

The selection of participants for the interviews in this research is a critical step in ensuring that valuable insights and expertise are obtained (Longhurst, 2009). The participants are purposefully selected based on their relevance and expertise in the fields of artificial intelligence, education, and entrepreneurship (Palinkas et al., 2013). By including scientific and administrative specialists, as well as elites in these domains, the research aims to gather diverse perspectives and in-depth knowledge (Longhurst, 2009; Creswell, 2007). The selection of participants who possess a deep understanding of the subject matter will contribute to the richness and validity of the interview data. Scientific specialists can provide insights into the technical aspects of artificial intelligence, while administrative specialists can offer perspectives on the implementation and management of educational entrepreneurship initiatives. Elites in the field bring extensive experience and expertise, providing valuable insights and innovative ideas (Gentles et al., 2015) (Etikan et al., 2016).

The following criteria have been applied to determine an appropriate sample (Tong et al., 2007; Creswell, 2007):

- Involvement in related research and authorship: Participants should have engaged in research activities relevant to the topic and ideally have authored or co-authored scholarly publications in the field.
- Related administrative experiences: Participants should possess a minimum of three years of relevant administrative experience, which can provide valuable insights and perspectives related to the research topic.
- Specialization in the research area: Participants should have a specialized background or major directly related to the subject matter of the research, indicating their expertise in the field.

These criteria ensure that the selected participants possess the necessary knowledge, experience, and expertise to contribute meaningfully to the research and address the research questions effectively. In **Appendix 1**, detailed information about the research participants is provided.

DATA ANALYSIS METHOD

Thematic Analysis

Thematic analysis is a methodology employed to identify, analyze, and report patterns that emerge from qualitative data. It involves systematically examining the contextual data and transforming diverse and distributed data into meaningful and descriptive insights (Braun & Clarke, 2006).

What the Theme is and how to Recognize It

Themes can be understood as a manifestation of prominent information that is directly relevant to the research questions, allowing for the exploration of latent patterns and uncovering underlying meanings and concepts (Braun & Clarke, 2006). Themes serve as patterns that help to interpret the phenomenon under study and organize the observations made (Research Prospect, 2023). They represent distinctive and recurring features within the data that convey specific perceptions and experiences related to the research questions (Braun & Clarke, 2006, Nowell et al., 2017; Christou, 2022). According to Strauss and Corbin1990, a theme can be seen as a form of concept classification. Concepts refer to labels assigned to events or phenomena, while features are attributes associated with a theme, and dimensions represent the range to which these features are attributed (Bazargan, 2022). Identifying themes is a critical aspect of finding the relationships between components of this qualitative research and lies at the core of the research process (Braun & Clarke, 2006; Nowell et al., 2017; Christou, 2022). The recognition of themes can be influenced by common sense, the researcher's values and experiences, as well as any inherent biases. A theme analysis is a qualitative approach, there is no fixed rule regarding the amount of data required to establish a theme. Instead, the determination of a theme depends on the extent to which it addresses the research questions rather than meeting specific quantitative criteria (Braun & Clarke, 2006). In theme analysis, various scholars may adopt different classifications to identify themes. Some researchers classify themes based on hierarchy, while others focus on the essence of the concept (Braun & Clarke, 2006; Nowell et al., 2017).

For the purposes of this research, the thematic network method proposed by Attride-Stirling (Attride-Stirling, 2001) has been employed to classify themes. In the initial step of the analysis, basic themes (equivalent to open codes in the systematic grounded theory method) are extracted from the data. Subsequently, second organizing themes and global themes are identified to develop the final model for the research. This approach allows for a systematic and structured analysis of the data, ensuring that key themes and patterns are identified and organized in a coherent manner (Attride-Stirling, 2001; Braun & Clarke, 2006).

Thematic Analysis; Step by Step

The analysis process comprised four key steps (Braun & Clarke, 2006; Nowell et al., 2017; Attride-Stirling, 2001).

1. Extracting Raw Themes: Each interview was meticulously examined, sentence by sentence, resulting in 1830 raw basic themes.
2. Organizing Themes: Themes from each interview were compiled into a table to facilitate comparison and identify commonalities and differences.
3. Categorizing Themes: The basic themes were reviewed and categorized into 42 organizing themes focused on AI applications in educational entrepreneurship.

4. Constructing an Analytic Network: An analytic network was created to visualize relationships among organizing themes and global themes were identified to capture overarching patterns and insights.

Rigor of Research Methodology

Validity

Validity is defined as the extent to which a concept is accurately measured in a quantitative study (Heale & Twycross, 2015). Several measures including a systematic literature review, semi-structured interviews with purposeful sampling, reaching data saturation in the data collection process, and a multi-step process of thematic analysis were taken to ensure content and construct validity in this study.

Reliability

Reliability is the agreement between two efforts to measure the same trait through maximally similar methods. Validity is represented in the agreement between two attempts to measure the same trait through maximally different methods, as a matter of fact, Reliability refers to the reproducibility of the measurements (Heale & Twycross, 2015; Hammersley, 1987).

In this study, besides the above strategies employed for validity, 2 other strategies have been employed to ensure stability and equivalence of reliability:

- Member Checking: After transcribing and analyzing the findings, the data were shared with the respondents to gauge their reactions to the analyses. Furthermore, once the data were analyzed by one researcher, they were reviewed by two other researchers to ensure consistency and accuracy (Sanjari et al., 2014).
- Peer review: To calculate reliability, the percentage agreement method was utilized. In this approach, the data were coded by two coders at different times. The codes derived from the interviews were then compared across the two different times and perspectives to determine the degree of agreement (O'Connor & Joffe, 2020; Guttman, 1945). This process involved selecting a few interviews randomly, coding them at two different times, and labeling similar codes as agreement and dissimilar codes as disagreement. The frequency of agreement and disagreement was then used in a formula to calculate the reliability of coding over the two times and perspectives.

In this study, three interviews were randomly selected and coded by two researchers over a three-day interval. A total of 701 key concepts (basic themes) were extracted, with 246 concepts showing agreement between the coders. The calculated reliability in this test-retest was 70%, which, being above 60%, confirms the reliability of the coding process (O'Connor & Joffe, 2020; Campbell et al., 2013, Sürücü & Maslakçı, 2020; Lombard et al., 2004).

Table 2. Calculating percent of the agreement

Percent of the Agreement (Reliability): 2×246 × 100 = 70.1 701

FINDINGS

What are the Applications of Artificial Intelligence in Educational Entrepreneurship Development?

The findings of the research indicate that there are various applications of artificial intelligence in the development of educational entrepreneurship. Based on the analysis of 14 interviews with participants from the fields of artificial intelligence, entrepreneurship, and education, 42 first organizing themes were identified, which are reported in **Appendix 2**. For more exact details about the process of extracting themes from the interviews, some parts of the answers are provided in **Appendix 3**.

How the Applications of Artificial Intelligence in Educational Entrepreneurship Development Can be Classified?

Based on the systematic literature review and the prior explanation, the applications of artificial intelligence in educational domains were categorized into three dimensions: administrative tasks, instruction, and learning. Additionally, educational entrepreneurship can be defined as the pursuit of innovative value creation within the education system, utilizing artificial intelligence as a tool. Through the interview process with the elites in the field, the model of applications of artificial intelligence in educational entrepreneurship development was enriched and enhanced. The expertise and experiences shared by the interviewees provided valuable input that contributed to the comprehensive understanding of how artificial intelligence can be applied effectively in the context of educational entrepreneurship. As a result, the applications of artificial intelligence in educational entrepreneurship development were incorporated into three primary axes: enhancing the productivity of the learning process, enhancing productivity and organizing the processes and the methods of instruction, and enhancing productivity in educational administration and leadership affairs.

Table 3. Extracting the global themes from the first and second organizing themes

The applications of artificial intelligence in educational entrepreneurship development		
First organizing themes	**Second organizing themes**	**Global themes**
2-Time management of teaching-learning activities/10-Increasing accuracy in the processes of teaching-learning/12- Identifying student-teacher behaviors encountering an educational stimulus/15- Enhancing the quality of teaching-learning processes	Improvement of the quality of learning	Enhancing the productivity of the learning process
7-Optimizing and organizing the learning process/16-Upgrading the productivity of the teaching-learning processes	Optimizing and organizing learning processes	
1-Facilitating cooperative learning	Facilitating cooperative learning	
35-Facilitating and promoting the quality of learning of disabled people	Facilitating disabled individuals' learning	
3-Organizing the process of educational content creation/6- Identifying students' favorite course topics	Organizing the process of educational content creation	enhancing productivity and organizing the processes and methods of instruction enhancing productivity and organizing the processes and methods of instruction
12-Identifying student-teacher behaviors encountering an educational stimulus/15-Enhancing the quality of teaching-learning processes/16-Upgrading the productivity of the teaching-learning processes/35-Facilitating and promoting the quality of learning of disabled people	Augmenting the productivity of the teaching process	

continued on following page

Table 3. Continued

The applications of artificial intelligence in educational entrepreneurship development		
First organizing themes	**Second organizing themes**	**Global themes**
4-Organizing giving feedback/ 9-Facilitating doing homework/20- Augmenting the productivity of selecting a proper educational approach in order to educational improvement/ 37-Identifying the reason for educational problems	Organizing giving feedback	
11-Optimizing and organizing the process of appraisal and evaluation/25-Decreasing the judgment and bias in the process of educational evaluation/26-Prevention of exam cheating	Optimizing and organizing educational evaluation	
21-Artificial intelligence as an educational assistant at the teachers' level/38-Designing intelligent robots as an educational assistant	Creating intelligent robots as education system assistants	
13-Improvement and enhancing the quality of decision-making in educational administration	Optimizing and improving the quality of the decision-making process in educational management	Enhancing the productivity of educational administration and leadership Enhancing the productivity of educational administration and leadership
22-Enhancing the productivity of performing administrative tasks and educational services/30-Developing AI-based applications in pervasive platforms	Optimizing and increasing the quality of operational processes and executing the education system's services	
5-Enhancing the quality of educational planning and curriculum/31-Transforming the curriculum and establishing an interdisciplinary curriculum	Transforming the curriculum and establishing an interdisciplinary and intradisciplinary curriculum	
28-Increasing the productivity of school and class management/30- Developing AI-based applications in pervasive platforms/34-Implementing augmented reality and virtual reality related to AI techniques to achieve educational objectives	Increasing the efficiency and productivity of educational tasks	
17-Organizing and enhancing the productivity of collecting educational data/18-Organizing and enhancing the productivity of advanced search processes/41-Making educational profiles to facilitate performance and personality appraisal	Organizing and enhancing the productivity of the educational data collection process	

continued on following page

Table 3. Continued

The applications of artificial intelligence in educational entrepreneurship development		
First organizing themes	**Second organizing themes**	**Global themes**
19-Increasing the productivity in analyzing and modelling and classification of educational data (extracted from teaching-learning processes)/34- Implementing augmented reality and virtual reality related to AI techniques to achieve educational objectives/41-Making educational profiles to facilitate performance and personality appraisal	Increasing the productivity of analyzing and modelling and classification educational data	
24- Augmenting the productivity of financial management of educational budget and expenditures	Augmenting the productivity of financial management of educational budget and expenditures	
14- Optimizing the process of training needs assessment	Optimizing the process of educational needs assessment	
42- Optimizing the process of educational counselling	Optimizing the process of educational counselling	
36- Augmenting the quality and organizing the process of both students' and employees' performance measurement/40-Enhancing the efficiency in professional progress for students and teachers	Enhancing the efficiency in professional progress for students and teachers	
27- Boosting the accuracy and validity of educational supervision	Boosting the accuracy and validity of educational supervision	

DISCUSSION

Enhancing the Productivity of the Learning Process

The concept of learning, as defined by most resources, involves a change in behavior resulting from experience (Houwer et al., 2013). It is the effect of experience on behavior. On the other hand, productivity is defined as the ratio of input (resources or services) to output (resources or services) (Tangen, 2002). Tangen emphasizes that productivity is central to efficiency and effectiveness, as well as improving performance, enhancing quality, and expediting tasks. "Learning outside of the classroom has also been made possible because of technology. Students are no longer limited to face-to-face learning since technological advancements have made it possible for students to choose whether they want to attend class either face-to-face or online or both" (Delgado et al., 2015). "Virtual learning programs have evolved and matured so that today many are interactive, incorporate video and other media, promote collaborative and shared workspaces, and can be accessed on smartphones and other devices" (Gross et al., 2015).

Artificial intelligence aids students' collaboration learning and distance learning education (Ogunode et al., 2024). According to the U.S. Department of Education, Office of Educational Technology (2023), AI may improve a technology's ability to meet students where they are, build on their strengths, and grow their knowledge and skills. The organizing themes within the global theme of "Enhancing the productivity of the learning process" encompass various aspects that contribute to maximizing the effectiveness, quality, and efficiency of learning (Tangen, 2005; Holmes et al., 2019; Crompton & Burke, 2023). These include focusing on improving the quality of learning experiences (Xianhua, 2019; Khosravi et al., 2023), optimizing and organizing learning processes, facilitating cooperative learning, and providing support and resources to enable individuals with disabilities to participate in the learning process (Drigas & Ioannidou, 2012).

Enhancing Productivity and Organizing the Processes and Methods of Instruction

The global theme of "Enhancing productivity and organizing the processes and methods of instruction" is derived from organizing themes that include organizing the process of educational content creation, augmenting the productivity of the teaching process, organizing giving feedback, optimizing, and organizing educational evaluation, and creating intelligent robots as education system assistants. To extract this global theme, the researchers utilized the general teaching model proposed by Robert Glaser in 1962. The general teaching model serves as a comprehensive framework for designing, implementing, evaluating, and improving education across different educational levels (Miles & Robinson, 1969). This model comprises four major components: instructional objectives, entry behavior, instructional procedure, and performance assessment (Biswas and Paul, 2019). According to the U.S. Department of Education (2023), AI models and AI-enabled systems may have potential to strengthen formative assessments.

By focusing on these organizing themes, the overall aim is to enhance the productivity of instruction while also organizing the various processes and methods involved in teaching (Malik et al., 2018; Tangen, 2005). This entails streamlining the creation of educational content, improving the efficiency of teaching practices (Khosravi et al., 2023), establishing effective feedback mechanisms, optimizing evaluation methods (Felix & Webb, 2024; Crompton & Burke, 2023), and exploring the potential of intelligent robots as valuable resources in the education system (Holmes et al., 2019). These efforts contribute to creating a structured and productive instructional environment that fosters effective teaching and learning experiences (Verma et al., 2021).

Enhancing the Productivity of Educational Administration and Leadership

The global theme of "Enhancing the productivity of educational administration and leadership" is derived from various organizing themes that encompass different aspects of educational management and leadership. The concept of management is often defined based on its duties or functions, as outlined by Henri Fayol in 1949. Fayol identified five key functions of management: planning, organizing, commanding, coordinating, and controlling. The concept of management overlaps with that of leadership, a notion of great contemporary interest in most countries in the developed world (Bush, 2007; Igbokwe, 2023, Akbar et al., 2024). Educational leaders, including school administrators, teachers, and other staff members, play a crucial role in changing various factors within the school (Hoy & Miskel, 2013), such as curriculum content, teaching methods, assessment strategies, and cultural norms, to enhance academic progress (Igbokwe, 2023). As the educational landscape undergoes profound shifts propelled by technological advancements, societal changes, and global challenges, the imperative for effective leadership becomes increasingly conspicuous (Akbar et al., 2024).

In this scope, we assume the educational entrepreneurs as transformational leaders as they have a great contribution to promoting educational innovation and restructuring the education systems by creating a vision for the future, building a culture of collaboration, and empowering others to become leaders themselves (Ye et al., 2024). According to Ogunode et al. (2024), artificial intelligence significantly contributes to the successful implementation of educational administration and planning programs. The theme of enhancing the productivity of educational leadership involves effectively and efficiently performing the duties of an educational leader in relation to staff and students to facilitate the achievement of educational goals (Luo, 2019). Drawing inspiration from Fayol's management functions model, this theme encompasses various topics, including optimizing decision-making processes in educational management, improving operational processes and the delivery of education services (Almaghrabi,2024), transforming the curriculum to establish intradisciplinary approaches (Baker, 2000), increasing the efficiency and productivity of educational tasks, organizing and enhancing the productivity of data collection processes (Khosravi et al., 2023), analyzing and modeling educational data, managing financial aspects of the educational budget and expenditures, assessing educational needs, providing effective educational counseling, enhancing professional development opportunities for students and teachers, and ensuring accurate and valid educational supervision. By addressing these organizing themes, educational leaders can work towards enhancing their productivity and effectiveness in managing and leading educational institutions (Igbokwe, 2023).

CONCLUSION

This study examined the application of AI in educational entrepreneurship development using a qualitative approach. Initially, a systematic literature review was conducted to define the research questions and delineate the scope of the study. Following this, semi-structured interviews were employed to gather insights from experts on the research questions. Finally, thematic analysis was utilized to identify the main components that address the research questions. The thematic analysis yielded three overarching global themes: enhancing the productivity of the learning process, optimizing, and organizing instructional processes and methods, and advancing the productivity of educational administration and leadership. Each of these themes includes specific subsets, as outlined in Table 3. It is important to note that the aim of this study is to identify potential applications of AI that have the capacity to transform the educational system through the lens of educational entrepreneurship. By understanding best practices for AI implementation, educators and administrators can maximize these benefits, fostering innovation and scalability while addressing unique institutional needs.

LIMITATIONS

One of the significant limitations of this research was the difficulty in accessing experts in the field of artificial intelligence. However, the use of platforms such as LinkedIn helped increase participant responses for collaboration. Another limitation was the scarcity of the literature on educational entrepreneurship. Additionally, due to the novelty of the research topic, the researcher had to provide interviewees with a comprehensive overview of the potential for transformation in the education sector through artificial intelligence at the beginning of each interview. Furthermore, this study was limited to 14 interviewees within a single country and cultural context, which may influence the variability of results, as is often the case with qualitative research. Additionally, aspects such as the cultural and ethical perspectives on AI usage, along with considerations for providing necessary infrastructure, were not explored in depth, as the primary focus of this research was on identifying AI applications within educational settings. These limitations highlight the need for future studies that can broaden the scope across diverse contexts and examine the structural and ethical dimensions of AI integration in education.

RECOMMENDATIONS

This study explored various educational domains and methods for implementing AI applications. It is recommended that researchers conduct a deeper investigation into each of the themes identified in this research, namely enhancing productivity in learning, improving the quality of instruction, and increasing efficiency in educational administration and leadership. Additionally, to validate the final conceptual model, researchers can develop and distribute questionnaires within the target community for each theme. This approach could yield more precise models for the application of AI in educational entrepreneurship. Also, Future research should consider the ethical implications of AI in education, including data privacy, algorithmic bias, and the potential for exacerbating educational inequalities, particularly in under-resourced regions. Addressing these issues is essential for fostering responsible and equitable AI use in education. Additionally, more comprehensive case studies of AI implementations across diverse regions and educational settings could provide valuable insights into best practices and scalable solutions that ensure fair access and minimize disparities in the application of artificial intelligence within educational contexts.

Figure 3. The final model of the applications of artificial intelligence in educational entrepreneurship development

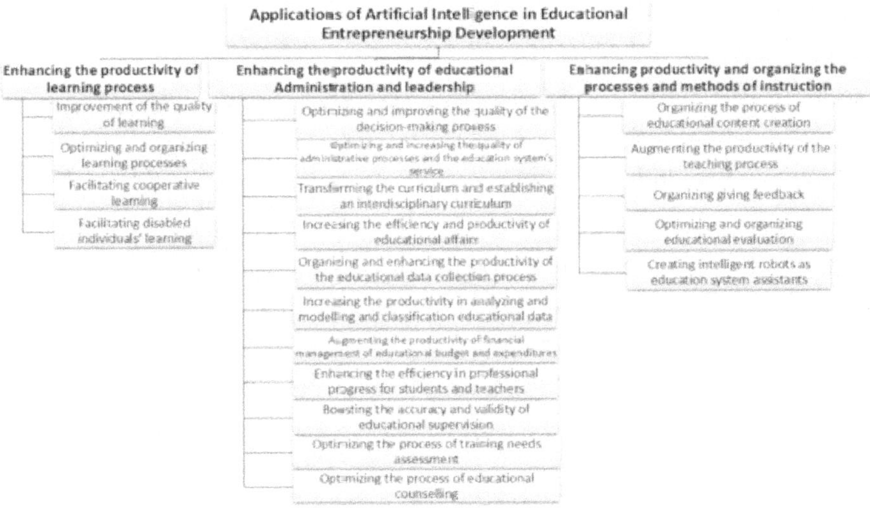

REFERENCES

Ahanchian, M. R., & Ghorooneh, D. (2019). *Educational entrepreneurship*. SAMT Publisher.

Akbar, S., & Pranajaya, S. A. Nurkadarwati, Hoesny, R., & Mutmainnah, I. (2024). Leadership dynamics in the era of educational transformation: Integrating the concept of adaptable leadership in sustainable educational administration. *International Journal of Teaching and Learning (INJOTEL), 2*(1), 223–235. Retrieved from http://injotel.org/index.php/12/article/view/61

Almaghrabi, H., Soh, B., & Li, A. (2024). Using ML to predict user satisfaction with ICT technology for educational institution administration. *Information (Basel)*, 15(4), 218. DOI: 10.3390/info15040218

Attride-Stirling, J. (2001). Thematic networks: An analytic tool for qualitative research. *Qualitative Research*, 1(3), 385–405. DOI: 10.1177/146879410100100307

Baker, M. J. (2000). The roles of models in artificial intelligence and education research: A prospective view. *International Journal of Artificial Intelligence in Education, 11*, 122–143. Retrieved from https://telearn.hal.science/hal-00190395/document

Baker, R. S. (2019). Challenges for the future of educational data mining: The Baker learning analytics prizes. *Journal of Educational Data Mining*, 11(1), 1–17. https://www.researchgate.net/publication/335517632_Challenges_for_the_Future_of_Educational_Data_Mining_The_Baker_Learning_Analytics_Prizes

Bazargan, A. (2022). *An introduction to qualitative and mixed methods research*. Didar Publisher.

Biswas, R., & Paul, A. (2019). Effectiveness of basic teaching model (BTM) of teaching education at higher secondary level. [JETIR]. *Journal of Emerging Technologies and Innovative Research*, 6(3). https://www.jetir.org/papers/JETIR1903K33.pdf

Bond, M., Khosravi, H., De Laat, M., Bergdahl, N., Negrea, V., Oxley, E., Pham, P., Chong, S. W., & Siemens, G. (2024). A meta systematic review of artificial intelligence in higher education: A call for increased ethics, collaboration, and rigor. *International Journal of Educational Technology in Higher Education*, 21(4), 4. Advance online publication. DOI: 10.1186/s41239-023-00436-z

Bozkurt, A., & Sharma, R. C. (2021). Emergency remote teaching in a time of global crisis due to Coronavirus pandemic. *Asian Journal of Distance Education*, 15(1), 1–6. https://www.researchgate.net/publication/341043562_Emergency_remote_teaching_in_a_time_of_global_crisis_due_to_CoronaVirus_pandemic

Braun, V., & Clarke, V. (2006). Using thematic analysis in psychology. *Qualitative Research in Psychology*, 3(2), 77–101. DOI: 10.1191/1478088706qp063oa

Brereton, P., Kitchenham, B. A., Budgen, D., Turner, M., & Khalil, M. (2007). Lessons from applying the systematic literature review process within the software engineering domain. *Journal of Systems and Software*, 80(4), 571–583. DOI: 10.1016/j.jss.2006.07.009

Bush, T. (2007). Educational leadership and management: Theory, policy, and practice. *South African Journal of Education*, 27(3), 391–406. https://files.eric.ed.gov/fulltext/EJ1150205.pdf

Campbell, J. L., Quincy, C., Osserman, J., & Pedersen, O. K. (2013). Coding in-depth semistructured interviews: Problems of unitization and intercoder reliability and agreement. *Sociological Methods & Research*, 42(3), 294–320. DOI: 10.1177/0049124113500475

Chen, L., Chen, P., & Lin, Z. (2020). Artificial intelligence in education: A review. *IEEE Access : Practical Innovations, Open Solutions*, 8, 75264–75278. DOI: 10.1109/ACCESS.2020.2988510

Chen, X., Xie, H., Zou, D., & Hwang, G.-J. (2020). Application and theory gaps during the rise of artificial intelligence in education. *Computers and Education: Artificial Intelligence*, 1, 100002. DOI: 10.1016/j.caeai.2020.100002

Christou, P. A. (2022). How to use thematic analysis in qualitative research. *Journal of Qualitative Research in Tourism*. Retrieved from https://www.researchgate.net/publication/369146265_How_to_use_Thematic_Analysis_in_Qualitative_Research

Creswell, J. W. (2007). *Qualitative inquiry and research design: Choosing among five approaches* (2nd ed.). SAGE Publications.

Crompton, H., & Burke, D. (2023). Artificial intelligence in higher education: The state of the field. *International Journal of Educational Technology in Higher Education*, 20(1), 22. https://educationaltechnologyjournal.springeropen.com/articles/10.1186/s41239-023-00392-8. DOI: 10.1186/s41239-023-00392-8

Dai, C. P., & Ke, F. (2022). Educational applications of artificial intelligence in simulation-based learning: A systematic mapping review. *Computers and Education: Artificial Intelligence, 3*, 100087. Retrieved from https://www.sciencedirect.com/science/article/pii/S2666920X2200042X

Delgado, A. J., Wardlow, L., McKnight, K., & O'Malley, K. (2015). Educational technology: A review of the integration resources and effectiveness of technology in K-12 classrooms. *Journal of Information Technology Education*, 14, 397–416. https://www.jite.org/documents/Vol14/JITEv14ResearchP397-416Delgado1829.pdf. DOI: 10.28945/2298

Drigas, A. S., & Ioannidou, R. E. (2012). Artificial intelligence in special education: A decade review. *International Journal of Engineering Education*, 28(6), 1366–1372. https://www.researchgate.net/publication/249656322_Artificial_intelligence_in_special_education_A_decade_review

Etikan, I., Musa, S. A., & Alkassim, R. S. (2016). Comparison of convenience sampling and purposive sampling. *American Journal of Theoretical and Applied Statistics*, 5(1), 1–4. https://www.researchgate.net/publication/304339244_Comparison_of_Convenience_Sampling_and_Purposive_Sampling. DOI: 10.11648/j.ajtas.20160501.11

Faulkner, S. L., & Trotter, S. P. (2017). Data saturation. In *The International Encyclopedia of Communication Research Methods*. John Wiley & Sons., DOI: 10.1002/9781118901731.iecrm0060

Felix, J., & Webb, L. (2024, January 23). *Use of artificial intelligence in education delivery and assessment.* The Parliamentary Office of Science and Technology (POST). Retrieved from https://researchbriefings.files.parliament.uk/documents/POST-PN-0712/POST-PN-0712.pdf

Gentles, S. J., Charles, C., Ploeg, J., & McKibbon, K. (2015). Sampling in qualitative research: Insights from an overview of the methods literature. *The Qualitative Report*, 20(11), 1772–1789. https://nsuworks.nova.edu/tqr/vol20/iss11/5. DOI: 10.46743/2160-3715/2015.2373

Gross, B., & Jochim, A. (Eds.). (2015). *Uncovering the productivity promise of rural education. The SEA of the Future* (Vol. 4). Building State Capacity & Productivity Center at Edvance Research, Inc., Retrieved from https://compcenternetwork.org/sites/default/files/archive/SEAF_Vol4_ProdPromiseOfRuralEdu.pdf#page=29

Guttman, L. (1945). A basis for analyzing test-retest reliability. *Psychometrika*, 10(4), 255–282. DOI: 10.1007/BF02288892 PMID: 21007983

Hammersley, M. (1987). Some notes on the terms ‘validity’ and ‘reliability’. *British Educational Research Journal*, 13(1), 73–81. DOI: 10.1080/0141192870130107

Heale, R., & Twycross, A. (2015). Validity and reliability in quantitative studies. *Evidence-Based Nursing*, 18(3), 66–67. DOI: 10.1136/eb-2015-102129 PMID: 25979629

Fayol, H. (1949). *General and Industrial Management Sir Isaac Pitman & Sons* (Storrs, C., Trans.).

Hess, F. M. (2007). The case for educational entrepreneurship: Hard truths about risk, reform, and reinvention. *Phi Delta Kappan*, 89(1), 21–30. https://www.aei.org/wp-content/uploads/2011/10/20070913_PDKEntrepreneurship.pdf. DOI: 10.1177/003172170708900105

Holmes, W., Bialik, M., & Fadel, C. (2019). *Artificial intelligence in education: Promises and implications for teaching and learning*. Center for Curriculum Redesign. Retrieved from https://www.researchgate.net/publication/332180327_Artificial_Intelligence_in_Education_Promise_and_Implications_for_Teaching_and_Learning

Hoppe, M., Westerberg, M., & Leffler, E. (2017). Educational approaches to entrepreneurship in higher education – A view from the Swedish horizon. *Education + Training*, 59(7/8), 751–765. DOI: 10.1108/ET-12-2016-0177

Houwer, J., Barnes-Holmes, D., & Moors, A. (2013). What is learning? On the nature and merits of a functional definition of learning. *Psychonomic Bulletin & Review*, 20(4), 631–642. DOI: 10.3758/s13423-013-0386-3 PMID: 23359420

Hoy, W., & Miskel, C. G. (2013). *Educational administration: Theory, research, and practice* (9th ed.). McGraw-Hill Higher Education.

Hwang, G.-J., Xie, H., Wah, B. W., & Gasevic, D. (2020). Vision, challenges, roles and research issues of artificial intelligence in education. *Computers and Education: Artificial Intelligence*, 1, 100001. DOI: 10.1016/j.caeai.2020.100001

Igbokwe, I. C. (2023). Application of artificial intelligence (AI) in educational management. *International Journal of Scientific and Research Publications*, 13(3), 300. https://www.ijsrp.org/research-paper-0323.php?rp=P13512782. DOI: 10.29322/IJSRP.13.03.2023.p13536

Kaplan, A., & Haenlein, M. (2018). Siri Siri in my hand: Who’s the fairest in the land? On the interpretations, illustrations, and implications of artificial intelligence. *Business Horizons*, 62(1), 15–25. DOI: 10.1016/j.bushor.2018.08.004

Kayyali, M. (2023). Promoting entrepreneurship and innovation in higher education. *International Journal of Innovation and Entrepreneurship*, 2(1), 1–26. https://www.researchgate.net/publication/373923500_Promoting_Entrepreneurship_and_Innovation_in_Higher_Education

Khare, K., Stewart, B., & Khare, A. (2018). Artificial intelligence and the student experience: An institutional perspective. *IAFOR Journal of Education, 6*(3), 99–116. Retrieved from https://www.researchgate.net/publication/329366517_Artificial_Intelligence_and_the_Student_Experience_An_Institutional_Perspective

Khosravi, H., Sadiq, S., & Amer-Yahia, S. (2023). Data management of AI-powered education technologies: Challenges and opportunities. *Learning Letters*, 1, 2. Advance online publication. DOI: 10.59453/XLUD7002

Kindel, A. T., & Stevens, M. L. (2021). What is educational entrepreneurship? Strategic action, temporality, and the expansion of US higher education. *Theory and Society*, 50(3), 577–605. DOI: 10.1007/s11186-021-09443-3

Kitchenham, B., & Charters, S. (2007). *Guidelines for performing systematic literature reviews in software engineering* (Version 2.3). EBSE Technical Report, School of Computer Science and Mathematics, Keele University, and Department of Computer Science, University of Durham. Retrieved from https://www.researchgate.net/publication/302924724_Guidelines_for_performing_Systematic_Literature_Reviews_in_Software_Engineering

Lacatus, M. L., & Staiculescu, M. (2016). Entrepreneurship in education. *International Conference Knowledge-Based Organization, 22*(2). https://doi.org/DOI: 10.1515/kbo-2016-0075

Lackéus, M. (2015). *Entrepreneurship in education: What, why, when, how*. OECD Publishing., Retrieved from https://www.oecd.org/cfe/leed/BGP_Entrepreneurship-in-Education.pdf

Lombard, M., Snyder-Duch, J., & Campanella Bracken, C. (2005). *Practical resources for assessing and reporting intercoder reliability in content analysis research projects.* Retrieved from https://www.researchgate.net/publication/242785900_Practical_Resources_for_Assessing_and_Reporting_Intercoder_Reliability_in_Content_Analysis_Research_Projects

Longhurst, R. (2009). Interviews: In-depth, semi-structured. In *International encyclopedia of human geography* (pp. 580–584). https://doi.org/DOI: 10.1016/B978-008044910-4.00458-2

Luckin, R., & Holmes, W. (2016). *Intelligence unleashed: An argument for AI in education*. Pearson.https://www.researchgate.net/publication/299561597_Intelligence_Unleashed_An_argument_for_AI_in_Education

Luo, S. (2019). Research on the change of educational management in the era of artificial intelligence. In *Proceedings of the 2019 12th International Conference on Intelligent Computation Technology and Automation (ICICTA)*. https://doi.org/ DOI: 10.1109/ICICTA49267.2019.00101

Maguire, M., & Delahunt, B. (2017). Doing a thematic analysis: A practical, step-by-step guide for learning and teaching scholars. *All Ireland Journal of Teaching and Learning in Higher Education (AISHE-J), 9*(3). Retrieved from https://ojs.aishe.org/index.php/aishe-j/article/view/335

Malik, G., Tayal, D. K., & Vij, S. (2018). An analysis of the role of artificial intelligence in education and teaching. In P. K. Sa, S. Sahni, B. B. Gupta, & S. P. Singh (Eds.), *Recent findings in intelligent computing techniques* (Advances in Intelligent Systems and Computing, Vol. 707, pp. 421–429). Springer Nature. https://doi.org/ DOI: 10.1007/978-981-10-8639-7_42

Man, T. W. Y. (2010). *Clarifying the domain of educational entrepreneurship: Implications for studying leadership, innovation and change*. The Hong Kong Institute of Education. Retrieved fromhttps://www.eduhk.hk/apclc/roundtable2010/paper/Clarifying%20Educational%20Entrepreneurship-Thomas%20Wing%20Yan%20MAN.pdf

McCarthy, J., Minsky, M. L., Rochester, N., & Shannon, C. E. (1955). *A proposal for the Dartmouth summer research project on artificial intelligence*. Stanford University. Retrieved from http://www-formal.stanford.edu/jmc/history/dartmouth/dartmouth.html

Miles, D. T., & Robinson, R. E. (1969). *General planning framework for general teaching model*. Retrieved from https://www.homeofbob.com/pedagogy/plan/generalTeachingModel.html#:~:text=A%20general%20teaching%20model%20is,any%20length%20of%20instructional%20time

Musoke, G. G., & Badru, M. (2018). Educational entrepreneurship (EE): Delineating and highlighting its domain, importance, and feasibility in Uganda's context. [Edu-Learn]. *Journal of Education and Learning*, 12(1), 126–136. https://www.researchgate.net/publication/324236127_Educational_Entrepreneurship_EE_Delineating_and_Highlighting_Its_Domain_Importance_and_Feasibility_in_Uganda's_Context

Nanni, A. (2021). Educational entrepreneurship in an intensive English program in Thailand: A case study. *SAGE Open*, 11(1), 2158244021998694. Advance online publication. DOI: 10.1177/2158244021998694

Nawaz, N., Gomes, A. M., & Saldeen, M. A. (2020). Artificial intelligence (AI) applications for library services and resources in COVID-19 pandemic. *Journal of Critical Reviews*, 7(18), 1951–1955. https://www.researchgate.net/publication/342865777_Artificial_intelligence_AI_applications_for_library_services_and_resources_in_COVID-19_pandemic

Nowell, L. S., Norris, J. M., White, D. E., & Moules, N. J. (2017). Thematic analysis: Striving to meet the trustworthiness criteria. *International Journal of Qualitative Methods*, 16(1), 1609406917733847. Advance online publication. DOI: 10.1177/1609406917733847

O'Connor, C., & Joffe, H. (2020). Intercoder reliability in qualitative research: Debates and practical guidelines. *International Journal of Qualitative Methods*, 19, 1–13. DOI: 10.1177/1609406919899220

OECD/EU. (2019). Supporting entrepreneurship and innovation in higher education in Austria. OECD Skills Studies. OECD Publishing, Paris. https://doi.org/DOI: 10.1787/1c45127b-en

Ogunode, N. J., Idoko, G., & ThankGod, P. (2024). Artificial intelligence and implementation of educational administration and planning programme in Nigerian tertiary institutions. *International Journal of Academic Integrity and Curriculum Development, 1*(1), 41–47. Retrieved from https://academicajournal.com/IJAICD/article/view/13

Palinkas, L. A., Horwitz, S. M., Green, C. A., Wisdom, J. P., Duan, N., & Hoagwood, K. (2013). Purposeful sampling for qualitative data collection and analysis in mixed method implementation research. *Administration and Policy in Mental Health*, 42(5), 533–544. DOI: 10.1007/s10488-013-0528-y PMID: 24193818

Perrotta, C., & Selwyn, N. (2019). Deep learning goes to school: Toward a relational understanding of AI in education. *Learning, Media and Technology*, 45(3), 251–264. DOI: 10.1080/17439884.2020.1686017

Research Prospect. (2023). *Thematic analysis – A guide with examples.* Retrieved from https://www.researchprospect.com/thematic-analysis/

Sanjari, M., Bahramnezhad, F., Khoshnavay Fomani, F., Shoghi, M., & Cheraghi, M. A. (2014). Ethical challenges of researchers in qualitative studies: The necessity to develop a specific guideline. *Journal of Medical Ethics and History of Medicine.* Retrieved from https://www.researchgate.net/publication/269712541_Ethical_challenges_of_researchers_in_qualitaive_studies_The_necessiy_to_develop_a_specific_guideline

Schiff, D. (2021). Out of the laboratory and into the classroom: The future of artificial intelligence in education. *AI & Society*, 36(1), 331–348. DOI: 10.1007/s00146-020-01033-8 PMID: 32836908

Schiff, D., Smith, K., & Peterson, J. L. (2006). What is educational entrepreneurship? In F. M. Hess (Ed.), *Educational entrepreneurship: Realities, challenges, possibilities*. Harvard Education Press. Retrieved from http://www.social-capital.net/docs/What_is_Educational_Entrepreneurship.pdf

Strauss, A., & Corbin, J. M. (1990). *Basics of qualitative research: Grounded theory procedures and techniques*. SAGE Publications, Inc.

Sürücü, L., & Maslakçı, A. (2020). Validity and reliability in quantitative research. *Business & Management Studies: An International Journal, 8*(3), 2694–2726. Retrieved from https://www.researchgate.net/publication/344379869_Validity_and_Reliability_in_Quantitative_Research

Taneri, G. U. (2020). *Artificial intelligence & higher education: Towards customized teaching and learning and skills for an AI world of work.* University of California, Berkeley, Center for Studies in Higher Education. Retrieved from https://eric.ed.gov/?id=ED606654

Tangen, S. (2002). Understanding the concept of productivity. In *Proceedings of the 7th Asia Pacific Industrial Engineering and Management Systems Conference (APIEMS2002), Taipei.* Retrieved from https://www.academia.edu/35502335/Understanding_the_concept_of_productivity?bulkDownload=thisPaper-topRelated-sameAuthor-citingThis-citedByThis-secondOrderCitations&from=cover_page

Tangen, S. (2005). Demystifying productivity and performance. *International Journal of Productivity and Performance Management*, 54(1), 34–46. DOI: 10.1108/17410400510571437

Tong, A., Sainsbury, P., & Craig, J. (2007). Consolidated criteria for reporting qualitative research (COREQ): A 32-item checklist for interviews and focus groups. *International Journal for Quality in Health Care : Journal of the International Society for Quality in Health Care*, 19(6), 349–357. DOI: 10.1093/intqhc/mzm042 PMID: 17872937

Tuomi, I. (2020). The use of artificial intelligence (AI) in education. *Research for CULT Committee*. Retrieved from https://www.europarl.europa.eu/RegData/etudes/BRIE/2020/629222/IPOL_BRI(2020)629222_EN.pdf

United Nations Educational, Scientific and Cultural Organization. (2019). *Artificial intelligence in education: Challenges and opportunities for sustainable development*. Paris, France: UNESCO. Retrieved from https://unesdoc.unesco.org/ark:/48223/pf0000366994

U.S. Department of Education, Office of Educational Technology. (2023). *Artificial intelligence and the future of teaching and learning: Insights and recommendations*. Washington, DC: U.S. Department of Education. Retrieved from https://www2.ed.gov/documents/ai-report/ai-report.pdf

Valenciano, J. de P., Uribe-Toril, J., & Ruiz-Real, J. L. (2019). Entrepreneurship and education in the 21st century: Analysis and trends in research. *Journal of Entrepreneurship Education*, 22(4). https://www.researchgate.net/publication/334825222_Entrepreneurship_and_Education_in_the_21st_Century_Analysis_and_Trends_in_Research

Verma, A., Kumar, Y., & Kohli, R. (2021). Study of AI techniques in quality educations: Challenges and recent progress. *SN Computer Science*, 2(238), 238. Advance online publication. DOI: 10.1007/s42979-021-00635-3

Wasim, J., Youssef, M. H., Christodoulou, I., & Reinhardt, R. (2023). The path to entrepreneurship: The role of social networks in driving entrepreneurial learning and education. *Journal of Management Education*, 48(3), 459–493. DOI: 10.1177/10525629231219235

Xianhua, L. (2019). Research on the effect of artificial intelligence technology on English learning efficiency. In *Proceedings of the 12th International Conference on Intelligent Computation Technology and Automation (ICICTA)*. https://doi.org/ DOI: 10.1109/ICICTA49267.2019.00123

Xiao, Y., & Watson, M. (2017). Guidance on conducting a systematic literature review. *Journal of Planning Education and Research*, 37(1), 1–20. DOI: 10.1177/0739456X17723971

Yadolahi Farsi, J., Modarresi, M., Motavaseli, M., & Salamzadeh, A. (2014). Institutional factors affecting academic entrepreneurship: The case of University of Tehran. *Economic Analysis*, 47(1–2), 139–159. https://core.ac.uk/download/pdf/33812235.pdf

Ye, Y., Wang, J., & Weerasawainon, A. (2024). Enhancing the transformation leadership skill and capacities of educational leaders at all levels, from teachers to administrators. *Educational Administration: Theory and Practice, 30*(5), 6177–6181. Retrieved from https://kuey.net/index.php/kuey/article/view/3915

Yusof, M., Abdul-Samad, Z., Hassan, F., Darus, Z. M., Mohammad, M. F., & Zaharim, A. (2010). Academic entrepreneurship and innovation in higher education: An integrated framework for Malaysian universities. *Advanced Educational Technologies.* Retrieved from https://www.researchgate.net/publication/228410765_Academic_Entrepreneurship_and_Innovation_in_Higher_Education_An_Integrated_Framework_for_Malaysian_Universities

ADDITIONAL READING

Alqahtani, M. (2023). Artificial intelligence and entrepreneurship education: A paradigm in Qatari higher education institutions after COVID-19 pandemic. *International Journal of Data and Network Science*, 7(2), 695–706. DOI: 10.5267/j.ijdns.2023.3.002

Bell, R., & Bell, H. (2023). Entrepreneurship education in the era of generative artificial intelligence. *Entrepreneurship Education*, 6(3), 229–244. DOI: 10.1007/s41959-023-00099-x

Giuggioli, G., & Pellegrini, M. M. (2023). Artificial intelligence as an enabler for entrepreneurs: A systematic literature review and an agenda for future research. *International Journal of Entrepreneurial Behaviour & Research*, 29(4), 816–837. DOI: 10.1108/IJEBR-05-2021-0426

Renz, A., & Hilbig, R. (2020). Prerequisites for artificial intelligence in further education: Identification of drivers, barriers, and business models of educational technology companies. *International Journal of Educational Technology in Higher Education*, 17(1), 14. DOI: 10.1186/s41239-020-00193-3

Voronov, V. V., Menshikov, V. V., & Ruza, O. P. (2023). Artificial intelligence: A catalyst for entrepreneurship education in the Baltics. *Baltic Region*, 15(3), 45–65. DOI: 10.5922/2079-8555-2023-3-3

KEY TERMS AND DEFINITIONS

Artificial Intelligence (AI): The development of computer systems that can perform tasks typically requiring human intelligence, such as learning, reasoning, and problem-solving.

Educational Administration: The management and organization of educational institutions, involving strategic planning, resource allocation, and decision-making.

Educational Entrepreneurship: The pursuit of innovative practices, products, and services in education to create new value and enhance educational outcomes.

Instructional Methods: Techniques and strategies used by educators to facilitate learning, including lectures, discussions, and AI-assisted tools.

Learning Productivity: The efficiency and effectiveness of the learning process, often enhanced through AI tools that support personalized and adaptive learning experiences.

Qualitative Research: A research method focused on exploring concepts and understanding experiences through non-numerical data, such as interviews and thematic analysis.

Systematic Literature Review: A structured approach to reviewing and synthesizing research literature on a specific topic, ensuring comprehensive and unbiased findings.

Thematic Analysis: A method for identifying, analyzing, and reporting patterns or themes within qualitative data, used to interpret underlying meanings.

Transformative Potential: The capability of AI to significantly change and improve educational practices, from administrative efficiency to personalized learning.

Virtual Learning Environments: Online platforms that provide educational resources, tools, and interactions, often enhanced by AI for an interactive and customized experience.

APPENDIX I

Table 4. Research participants information

Row	Last Degree	Work Experience	University of Last Degree
1	Masters in AI	Image Processing Engineer at Farazpardazan Company- Teaching in AI Group	K. N. Toosi University of Technology
2	PhD in AI	Data Scientist at Fanap Company	Shahrood University of Technology
3	PhD in Software Engineering	Lecturer at Amirkabir University of Technology	Amirkabir University of Technology
4	PhD Candidate in AI and Robotics	Teaching and Research Assistant in AI Group	University of Tehran
5	PhD in Mechanical Engineering (Robotics)	Associate Professor in AI and Robotics Group, University of Tehran	Laval University, Canada
6	PhD Candidate in AI and Robotics	Teaching and Research Assistant in AI Group	University of Tehran
7	PhD Candidate in AI and Robotics	Teaching and Research Assistant in AI Group	University of Tehran
8	PhD in Electrical Engineering	Assistant Professor in AI and Robotics Group, Iran University of Science and Technology	Sharif University of Technology
9	PhD in Entrepreneurship	Lecturer at University of Tehran	University of Tehran
10	PhD Candidate in Economy of Higher Education	Teaching and Research Assistant in Educational Management Group	University of Tehran
11	PhD in Entrepreneurship	Assistant Professor in Business Management Group	University of Tehran
12	PhD in Image Processing	Assistant Professor in AI and Robotics Group, K. N. Toosi University of Technology	Australian National University
13	PhD Candidate in Economy of Higher Education	Teaching and Research Assistant in Educational Management Group	University of Tehran
14	PhD in Educational Management and Planning	Assistant Professor in Educational Management Group, Allameh Tabataba'i University	International University of India

APPENDIX II

Table 5. Extracting first organizing themes

	Interviewees' code		First Organizing Themes
1	1/4/6/7/8/9/10	17	Facilitating cooperative learning
2	1/4/7/10	11	Time management of teaching-learning activities
3	1/2/3/4/6/8/7/10/12	86	Organizing the process of educational content creation
4	1/3/4/6/5/7/8/10/12	26	Organizing giving feedback
5	1/6/8/10/13/14	28	Enhancing the quality of educational planning and curriculum
6	1/2/3/4/6/7/12	29	Identifying students' favorite course topics
7	1/2/3/4/5/6/7/8/9/10/11/12/13/14	149	Optimizing and organizing the learning process
8	1/2/3/4/5/6/7/8/9/10/12/13/14	93	Organizing the processes and methods of instruction
9	1/6/3/7/10	8	Facilitating doing homework
10	4/7/10/13	15	Increasing accuracy in the processes of teaching-learning
11	1/2/4/5/6/7/8/10/12/13/14	113	Optimizing and organizing the process of appraisal and evaluation
12	1/2/4/6/7/9/10/12/13	68	Identifying student-teacher behaviors encountering an educational stimulus
13	1/2/6/11/12/13/14	31	Improvement and enhancing the quality of decision-making in educational administration
14	1/2/3/4/5/6/7/10/11/12/13/14	38	Optimizing the process of training needs assessment
15	1/4/7/3/10/12	12	Enhancing the quality of teaching-learning processes
16	1/3/4/5/6/7/10/8/13	37	Upgrading the productivity of the teaching-learning processes
17	1/4/5/6/8/14	37	Organizing and enhancing the productivity of collecting educational data
18	1/3/4/6/7/8/12/13	32	Organizing and enhancing the productivity of advanced search processes
19	1/2/4/5/6/7/8/10/12/13	164	Increasing the productivity in analyzing and modelling and classification of educational data (extracted from teaching-learning processes)
20	1/2/3/6/7/13	15	Augmenting the productivity of selecting a proper educational approach in order to educational improvement
21	1/2/5/7/10/13/14	32	Artificial intelligence as an educational assistant at the teachers' level
22	4/6/7/8/10/9/12/11/12/13/14	51	Enhancing the productivity of performing administrative tasks and educational services
23	1/4/10/13/14	21	Transforming the traditional definition of a teacher
24	10/11/12/13/14	31	Augmenting the productivity of financial management of educational budget and expenditures
25	4/6/8/10/13/14	27	Decreasing the judgment and bias in the process of educational evaluation
26	10/12/13	19	Prevention of exam cheating
27	10/12	12	Boosting the accuracy and validity of educational supervision
28	9/10/13/14	16	Increasing the productivity of school and class management
29	5/9/10/11/12/13/14	80	Achieving educational purposes systematically
30	3/4/6/7/8/9/10/11/12/13/14	74	Developing AI-based applications in pervasive platforms
31	7/8/10/13	20	Transforming the curriculum and establishing an interdisciplinary curriculum

continued on following page

Table 5. Continued

	Interviewees' code		First Organizing Themes
32	4/9/10/14	6	Transforming the traditional students' role
33	5/10/13/14	25	Establishing the necessity for revising the traditional
34	6/7/10/12	22	Implementing augmented reality and virtual reality related to AI techniques to achieve educational objectives
35	12	15	Facilitating and promoting the quality of learning of disabled people
36	3/4/5/6/7/10/14	28	Augmenting the quality and organizing the process of both students' and employees' performance measurement
37	2/3/4/5/6/7/10/12/13	23	Identifying the reason for educational problems
38	4/5/10/12	16	Designing intelligent robots as an educational assistant
39	9/10/11/12/13/14	33	Providing AI-based platforms for building smart schools
40	1/10/13/14	30	Enhancing the efficiency in professional progress for students and teachers
41	6/10	14	Making educational profiles to facilitate performance and personality appraisal
42	1/6/13	7	Optimizing the process of educational counselling

APPENDIX III

Optimizing and Organizing the Learning Process

This theme is extracted from interviews numbered 1 through 14, with a frequency of 149 mentions.

Interviewee 1:

"The next topic is producing suitable content for personalized learning. We can design appropriate content based on the parameters we want to measure and the content available on the web relevant to the topic. For instance, if someone wants to learn a language, what level of content and in what manner should be provided to them to achieve the best learning outcome? In other words, the content should neither be so difficult that we understand nothing nor so easy that we learn nothing. For example, someone who is learning programming can be given suggestions based on the projects they have posted on their GitHub, indicating that the next step in their learning could be advanced Python. This can be achieved through web analysis and reinforcement learning."

Interviewee 1 on optimizing:

"Reinforcement learning reaches the optimal point in action through trial and error. For example, it might raise the classroom temperature once to see how much the students' performance is affected. Thus, using reinforcement learning techniques, any criterion can be evaluated, whether it is the level of student engagement in the teaching process, educational assessment, or environmental temperature. These evaluations can then be used to optimize educational actions, resulting in the maximization of the desired parameters. For instance, the time students spend collaborating and engaging, or the rate of finding suitable jobs after education."

Interviewee 4:

"In the context of personalized learning, artificial intelligence can identify students' interests from early elementary levels. Transformers have significant applications in this area. For example, a research project by DeepMind, a subsidiary of Google, introduced an AI system called Gato. This system uses a neural network to perform 604 different tasks. Traditionally, neural networks were designed for single tasks.

Gato can receive various types of inputs, such as text, audio, and images, process them through transformers for tokenization, and then generate appropriate outputs."

Interviewee 8:

"One of the areas where artificial intelligence can optimize education is personalized learning. Additionally, by using computer vision applications and employing a camera, the interactive learning process can be monitored. Another topic that is always discussed in education is the issue of fair assessment."

Interviewee 3:

"In general, we can enhance both soft skills, such as team leadership or teamwork, and the ability to learn through artificial intelligence. For example, using a combination of computer vision and machine learning methods, we can improve a student's handwriting. Alternatively, a student could take a photo of an integral, input it into the machine, and the machine would help solve the problem."

Optimizing and Organizing the Process of Appraisal and Evaluation

This theme is extracted from interviews 1, 2, 4, 5, 6, 7, 8, 10, 12, 13, and 14, with a frequency of 113 mentions.

Interviewee 6:

"In the field of proofreading, they faced a heavy load of assignments, and this caused many problems in teaching physics and programming, such as tracking completed exercises. In such situations, text mining comes in handy for processing texts. For example, students' exam papers can be uploaded into a system, and in such circumstances, using an OCR (Optical Character Recognition), the photo or scan of the exam papers is converted into text. This tool converts the photo to writing; when there are writings on the image, it converts those writings into a Word file."

Interviewee 7:

"For routine educational tasks, we can consider the use of artificial intelligence more extensively. Tasks like grading exam papers, providing feedback, and processes where we have good data available that has been collected uniformly. Therefore, we can train a machine on such data, allowing it to learn and produce convergent results."

Interviewee 4:

"Surveys are usually subject to bias, whereas analyzing teaching quality based on an AI system is much more accurate. For instance, based on the videos available of a teacher's lessons, we can determine the teacher's rating in teaching. This includes evaluating how much the teacher uses active teaching methods. An AI system can also determine the optimal time for providing feedback. For example, if a student is very upset, today may not be the best time to ask them questions."

Interviewee 5:

"Artificial intelligence can have positive applications as long as it serves the teacher. It can be useful in designing questions or grading answer sheets. For instance, deep learning methods can be used in question design. In other words, a combination of deep learning and GAN (Generative Adversarial Networks) methods can open up new possibilities for creating new questions that are not significantly different from the old ones."

Enhancing the Productivity of Performing Administrative Tasks and Educational Services

This theme is extracted from interviews 4, 6, 7, 8, 9, 10, 11, 12, 13, and 14, with 51 mentions.

Interviewee 4:

"In the future, the role of teachers and professors will be completely transformed. For example, when reading an unclear article, an artificial intelligence system can be embedded to provide supplementary information to the learner, allowing the learner to better understand the content. Additionally, the speed of article writing will increase, thereby accelerating the pace of scientific progress."

Interviewee 13:

"One aspect that strengthens your work is examining the applications of artificial intelligence in schools with a detailed perspective, while also considering AI from a systematic and multi-level viewpoint in the education system. By adopting a systemic approach, both at the micro level for teachers and classrooms and at the macro level for administrators and policymakers, these elements can interact to achieve an optimal integration of AI. These applications at three levels aim to fulfill the main educational goals of equity, quality education, and achieving deep learning among students."

Interviewee 14:

"One of the main areas that artificial intelligence can revolutionize is the curriculum. There has always been a challenge in education regarding how long traditional teaching methods should continue. Questions arise about how many hours per week should be dedicated to sciences, or at what grade level computer literacy should begin. For instance, currently, only high school students have technology and computer courses, which are not present at the elementary level. This raises the question of whether, with the advent of the Fourth Industrial Revolution, the curriculum should be revised based on digital transformation. Such a profound change in the curriculum would also necessitate changes in the recruitment of creative teachers and the budget allocated to teachers. All these factors, approached systematically, would impact student learning."

Interviewee 10:

"The development of AI-based education also leads to the creation of smart campuses and educational centers, such as digital libraries or intelligent administrative systems. For example, when you enter a library, it recognizes you without needing a card, and immediately guides you to your desired book in the best possible way by knowing its title."

Compilation of References

Abbott, R., & Rothman, E. (2023). Disrupting creativity: Copyright law in the age of generative artificial intelligence. *Fla. L. Rev., 75*.

Abdel-Fattah, M. A. (2005). Arabic sign language: A perspective. *Journal of Deaf Studies and Deaf Education*, 10(2), 212–221. DOI: 10.1093/deafed/eni007 PMID: 15778217

Aberšek, B. (2019). *The impact of innovative ICT education and AI on the pedagogical paradigm*. Cambridge Scholars Publishing.

Acemoglu, D., & Restrepo, P. (2018). Artificial intelligence, automation, and work. In *The economics of artificial intelligence: An agenda* (pp. 197–236). University of Chicago Press.

Afzaal, M., Zia, A., Nouri, J., & Fors, U. (2024). Informative feedback and explainable AI-based recommendations to support students' self-regulation. *Technology. Knowledge and Learning*, 29(1), 331–354. DOI: 10.1007/s10758-023-09650-0

Agarwal, B., & Lahoti, Y. (2022). Harnessing Artificial Intelligence in higher education: Perspective and practices among educators. *NeuroQuantology : An Interdisciplinary Journal of Neuroscience and Quantum Physics*, 20(13), 4340–4351. DOI: 10.48047/nq.2022.20.13.NQ88529

Aggarwal, D. (2023). Integration of innovative technological developments and AI with education for an adaptive learning pedagogy. *China Petroleum Processing and Petrochemical Technology*, 23(2), 709–714. https://zgsyjgysyhgjs.cn/index.php/reric/article/pdf/02-709.pdf

Aghaziarati, A., Nejatifar, S., & Abedi, A. (2023). Artificial Intelligence in Education: Investigating Teacher Attitudes. *AI and Tech in Behavioral and Social Sciences*, 1(1), 35–42. DOI: 10.61838/kman.aitech.1.1.6

Agrawal, L., Lanjewar, P., Deshpande, S., Jawarkar, P., Gaur, V., & Dive, A. (2024). The Impact of AI on Communication Skills Training Opportunities and Challenges. *Nanotechnology Perceptions*, •••, 1167–1173.

Ahanchian, M. R., & Ghorooneh, D. (2019). *Educational entrepreneurship*. SAMT Publisher.

Ahmad, S. F., Alam, M. M., Rahmat, Mohd. K., Mubarik, M. S., & Hyder, S. I. (2022). Academic and Administrative Role of Artificial Intelligence in Education. Sustainability, 14(3), 1101. MDPI AG. Retrieved from http://dx.doi.org/]DOI: 10.3390/su14031101

Ahmad, K., Iqbal, W., El-Hassan, A., Qadir, J., Benhaddou, D., Ayyash, M., & Al-Fuqaha, A. (2023). Data-driven artificial intelligence in education: A comprehensive review. *IEEE Transactions on Learning Technologies.*

AI for T&L in Education. AI and assessment design. (2024) https://libraryguides.vu.edu.au/c.php?g=966085&p=7019124

Aithal, P. S., & Aithal, S. (2019). Analysis of higher education in Indian National Education Policy Proposal 2019 and its implementation challenges. [IJAEML]. *International Journal of Applied Engineering and Management Letters*, 3(2), 1–35. DOI: 10.47992/IJAEML.2581.7000.0039

Akavova, A., Temirkhanova, Z., & Lorsanova, Z. (2023). Adaptive learning and artificial intelligence in the educational space. E3S Web of Conferences, Akgun, S., & Greenhow, C. (2022). Artificial intelligence in education: Addressing ethical challenges in K-12 settings. *AI and Ethics*, 2(3), 431–440.

Akbar, S., & Pranajaya, S. A. Nurkadarwati, Hoesny, R., & Mutmainnah, I. (2024). Leadership dynamics in the era of educational transformation: Integrating the concept of adaptable leadership in sustainable educational administration. *International Journal of Teaching and Learning (INJOTEL), 2*(1), 223–235. Retrieved from http://injotel.org/index.php/12/article/view/61

Akchurin, M., & Chouhy, G. (2024). Designing Better Access to Education? Unified Enrollment, School Choice, and the Limits of Algorithmic Fairness in New Orleans School Admissions. *Qualitative Sociology*, 47(2), 1–43. DOI: 10.1007/s11133-024-09565-x

Akgun, S., & Greenhow, C. (2022). Artificial intelligence in education: Addressing ethical challenges in K-12 settings. *AI and Ethics*, 2(3), 431–440. DOI: 10.1007/s43681-021-00096-7 PMID: 34790956

Akinrinola, O., Okoye, C. C., Ofodile, O. C., & Ugochukwu, C. E. (2024). Navigating and reviewing ethical dilemmas in AI development: Strategies for transparency, fairness, and accountability. *GSC Advanced Research and Reviews, 18*(3), 050-058. DOI: DOI: 10.30574/gscarr.2024.18.3.0088

Akinwalere, S. N., & Ivanov, V. (2022). Artificial intelligence in higher education: Challenges and opportunities. *Border Crossing*, 12(1), 1–15. DOI: 10.33182/bc.v12i1.2015

Akyuz, Y. (2020). Effects of intelligent tutoring systems (ITS) on personalized learning (PL). *Creative Education*, 11(06), 953–978. DOI: 10.4236/ce.2020.116069

Al Darayseh, A. (2023). Factors influencing the adoption of AI writing tools in higher education. *Computers & Education*, 175, 104368. DOI: 10.1016/j.compedu.2021.104368

Al-Abdullatif, A. M. (2023). Modeling Students' perceptions of chatbots in learning: Integrating technology acceptance with the value-based adoption model. *Education Sciences,* 13(11), 1151https://doi.org/DOI: 10.3390/educsci13111151

Al-Adwan, A. S., Li, N., Al-Adwan, A., Abbasi, G. A., Albelbisi, N. A., & Habibi, A. (2023). Extending the technology acceptance model (TAM) to Predict University Students' intentions to use metaverse-based learning platforms. *Education and Information Technologies*, 28(11), 15381–15413. DOI: 10.1007/s10639-023-11816-3 PMID: 37361794

Alakrash, H. M., & Abdul Razak, N. (2021). Technology-based language learning: Investigation of digital technology and digital literacy. *Sustainability (Basel)*, 13(21), 12304. DOI: 10.3390/su132112304

AlAli, R., & Wardat, Y. (2024). Opportunities and Challenges of Integrating Generative Artificial Intelligence in Education. *International Journal of Religion*, 5(7), 784–793. DOI: 10.61707/8y29gv34

Alam, A. (2022). Employing adaptive learning and intelligent tutoring robots for virtual classrooms and smart campuses: Reforming education in the age of artificial intelligence. *Advanced Computing and Intelligent Technologies: Proceedings of ICACIT 2022*. Singapore: Springer Nature. https://doi.org/DOI: 10.1007/978-981-19-2980-9_32

Alam, A. (2023, June). Intelligence unleashed: An argument for AI-enabled learning ecologies with real world examples of today and a peek into the future. In AIP Conference Proceedings (Vol. 2717, No. 1). AIP Publishing.

Alam, A. (2021, November). Possibilities and apprehensions in the landscape of artificial intelligence in education. In *2021 International Conference on Computational Intelligence and Computing Applications (ICCICA)* (pp. 1-8). IEEE. DOI: 10.1109/ICCICA52458.2021.9697272

Alam, A. (2023). Harnessing the Power of AI to Create Intelligent Tutoring Systems for Enhanced Classroom Experience and Improved Learning Outcomes. In Rajakumar, G., Du, K. L., & Rocha, Á. (Eds.), *Intelligent Communication Technologies and Virtual Mobile Networks* (pp. 571–591). Springer Nature Singapore., DOI: 10.1007/978-981-99-1767-9_42

Al-Barham, M., Alsharkawi, A., Al-Yaman, M., Al-Fetyani, M., Elnagar, A., SaAleek, A. A., & Al-Odat, M. (2023). RGB Arabic alphabets sign language dataset. *arXiv preprint arXiv:2301.11932*.

Alenezi, A. (2023). Teacher perspectives on AI-driven gamification: Impact on student motivation, engagement, and learning outcomes. *Information Technologies and Learning Tools*, 97(5), 138–148. DOI: 10.33407/itlt.v97i5.5437

Alhichri, H., Alswayed, A. S., Bazi, Y., Ammour, N., & Alajlan, N. A. (2021). Classification of remote sensing images using EfficientNet-B3 CNN model with attention. *IEEE Access : Practical Innovations, Open Solutions*, 9, 14078–14094. DOI: 10.1109/ACCESS.2021.3051085

Alier, M., García-Peñalvo, F., & Camba, J. D. (2024). Generative Artificial Intelligence in Education: From Deceptive to Disruptive. *International Journal of Interactive Multimedia and Artificial Intelligence*, 5, 5–14. DOI: 10.9781/ijimai.2024.02.011

Ali, O., Murray, P. A., Momin, M., Dwivedi, Y. K., & Malik, T. (2024). The effects of artificial intelligence applications in educational settings: Challenges and strategies. *Technological Forecasting and Social Change*, 199, 123076. DOI: 10.1016/j.techfore.2023.123076

Almaghrabi, H., Soh, B., & Li, A. (2024). Using ML to predict user satisfaction with ICT technology for educational institution administration. *Information (Basel)*, 15(4), 218. DOI: 10.3390/info15040218

Almahri, F. A. J., Bell, D., & Merhi, M. (2020). Understanding student acceptance and use of chatbots in the United Kingdom universities: a structural equation modelling approach. *In 2020 6th International Conference on Information Management (ICIM)* (pp. 284-288). IEEE. https://doi.org/DOI: 10.1109/ICIM49319.2020.244712

Almaiah, M. A., & Almulhem, A. (2018). A conceptual framework for determining the success factors of e-learning system implementation using Delphi technique. *Journal of Theoretical and Applied Information Technology*, 96(17), 5962–5976.

Al-Mansoori, S., & Salem, M. B. (2023). The role of artificial intelligence and machine learning in shaping the future of cybersecurity: Trends, applications, and ethical considerations. *International Journal of Stochastic Analysis*, 8(9), 1–16.

Almeida, F., & Simoes, J. (2019). The role of serious games, gamification, and industry 4.0 tools in the education 4.0 paradigm. *Contemporary Educational Technology*, 10(2), 120–136. DOI: 10.30935/cet.554469

Almusaed, A., Almssad, A., Yitmen, I., & Homod, R. Z. (2023). Enhancing student engagement: Harnessing "AIED"'s power in hybrid education—A review analysis. *Education Sciences*, 13(7), 632. DOI: 10.3390/educsci13070632

Al-Nuaimi, M. N., Al Sawafi, O. S., Malik, S. I., Al-Emran, M., & Selim, Y. F. (2023). Evaluating the actual use of learning management systems during the covid-19 pandemic: An integrated theoretical model. *Interactive Learning Environments*, 31(10), 6905–6930. DOI: 10.1080/10494820.2022.2055577

Alqahtani, T., Badreldin, H. A., Alrashed, M., Alshaya, A. I., Alghamdi, S. S., bin Saleh, K., Alowais, S. A., Alshaya, O. A., Rahman, I., Al Yami, M. S., & Albekairy, A. M. (2023). The emergent role of artificial intelligence, natural learning processing, and large language models in higher education and research. *Research in Social & Administrative Pharmacy*, 19(8), 1236–1242. DOI: 10.1016/j.sapharm.2023.05.016 PMID: 37321925

Al-Salman, A., AlOhali, Y., AlKanhal, M., & AlRajih, A. (2007). An arabic optical braille recognition system.

Alstete, J. W., Flavian, H., & Petrova, K. (2023). Guest editorial: Hybrid, blended and mixed-mode learning quality: more lessons learned in the COVID pandemic and beyond. *Quality Assurance in Education*, 31(1), 1–3. DOI: 10.1108/QAE-02-2023-205

Alyoussef, I. Y. (2023). The impact of massive open online courses (MOOCs) on knowledge management using integrated innovation diffusion theory and the technology acceptance model. *Education Sciences*, 13(6), 531. DOI: 10.3390/educsci13060531

Amisha., Malik, P., &Pathania, M., &Rathaur, V. K. (2019). Overview of artificial intelligence in medicine. *Journal of family medicine and primary care, 8*(7), 2328-2331. .DOI: 10.4103/jfmpc.jfmpc_440_19

Angeli, C., & Valanides, N. (2020). Developing young children's computational thinking with educational robotics: An interaction effect between gender and scaffolding strategy. *Computers in Human Behavior*, 105, 105954. DOI: 10.1016/j.chb.2019.03.018

Angotti, T., Doble, C., & Horrigan, P. (2011). *Service-Learning in Design and Planning: Educating at the Boundaries*. NYU Press., DOI: 10.2307/j.ctt21pxmfs

Ankita, M., M., Sharma, I., & Kumar, A. (2023). Comparative Analysis of Shallow Learning and Deep Learning. 2023 International Conference on Next Generation Electronics (NEleX) DOI: 10.1109/NEleX59773.2023.10421385

Annus, N. (2023). Weigh the pros and cons of using Artificial Intelligence in education. *International journal of science, engineering and technology, 11*(3), 2-5.

Anwar, A., Haq, I. U., Mian, I. A., Shah, F., Alroobaea, R., Hussain, S., & Umar, F. (2022). Applying Real-Time Dynamic Scaffolding Techniques during Tutoring Sessions Using Intelligent Tutoring Systems. *Mobile Information Systems*, 2022(1), 6006467. DOI: 10.1155/2022/6006467

Arakpogun, E. O., Elsahn, Z., Olan, F., & Elsahn, F. (2021). Artificial intelligence in Africa: Challenges and opportunities. *The Fourth Industrial Revolution: Implementation of Artificial Intelligence for Growing Business Success*, 375–388. https://doi.org/DOI: 10.1007/978-3-030-62796-6_22

Arshed, N., Ahmad, W., & Hanif, U. (2022). A spatial, temporal exploration of factors motivating academia-industry collaboration. *Journal of the Knowledge Economy*, 13(1), 521–540. DOI: 10.1007/s13132-021-00729-6

Aslam, W.; Ahmed Siddiqui, D.; Arif, I.; Farhat, K. Chatbots in the Frontline: Drivers of Acceptance. *Kybernetes2022*. ahead-of-print. https://doi.org/DOI: 10.1108/K-11-2021-1119

Attride-Stirling, J. (2001). Thematic networks: An analytic tool for qualitative research. *Qualitative Research*, 1(3), 385–405. DOI: 10.1177/146879410100100307

Australian Human Rights Commission. (2023) "Utilising ethical AI in the Australian education System", Submission to the Standing Committee on Employment, Education and Training. Available at https://humanrights.gov.au/sites/default/files/inquiry_into_the_use_of_generative_artificial_intelligence_in_the_australian_education_system_14_july_2023_0.pdf

Aymen, D. I. F., & Zakarya, B. (2024). *The Influence of Artificial Intelligence on Students' Critical Thinking* (Doctoral dissertation), University center of Abdalhafid Boussouf-MILA.

Baah-Boateng, W. (2013). Human Capital Development: The Case of Education as a Vehicle for Africa's Economic Transformation.

Bahroun, Z., Anane, C., Ahmed, V., & Zacca, A. (2023). Transforming Education: A Comprehensive Review of Generative Artificial Intelligence in Educational Settings through Bibliometric and Content Analysis. *Sustainability (Basel)*, 15(17), 12983. DOI: 10.3390/su151712983

Baidya, M., & C, A. K. (2024). Artificial Intelligence in education: Understanding benefits, limitations, and prospects for the future. *International journal for multi-disciplinary research, 6*(2), 1-9.

Bailey, J. (2023). AI in Education: The leap into a new era of machine intelligence carries risks and challenges, but also plenty of promise. *Education Next*, 23(4), 29–36.

Baker, M. J. (2000). The roles of models in artificial intelligence and education research: A prospective view. *International Journal of Artificial Intelligence in Education, 11*, 122–143. Retrieved from https://telearn.hal.science/hal-00190395/document

Baker, T., & Smith, L. (2019). Educ-AI-tion rebooted? Exploring the future of artificial intelligence in schools and colleges. *Retrieved from Nesta Foundation website*: https://media.nesta.org.uk/documents/Future_of_AI_and_education_v5_WEB.pdf

Baker, R. S. (2019). Challenges for the future of educational data mining: The Baker learning analytics prizes. *Journal of Educational Data Mining*, 11(1), 1–17. https://www.researchgate.net/publication/335517632_Challenges_for_the_Future_of_Educational_Data_Mining_The_Baker_Learning_Analytics_Prizes

Baker, R. S., & Hawn, A. (2022). Algorithmic bias in education. *International Journal of Artificial Intelligence in Education*, 32(4), 1–41. DOI: 10.1007/s40593-021-00285-9

Balaha, M. M., El-Kady, S., Balaha, H. M., Salama, M., Emad, E., Hassan, M., & Saafan, M. M. (2023). A vision-based deep learning approach for independent-users Arabic sign language interpretation. *Multimedia Tools and Applications*, 82(5), 6807–6826. DOI: 10.1007/s11042-022-13423-9

Balasubramaniam, N., Kauppinen, M., Rannisto, A., Hiekkanen, K., & Kujala, S. (2023). Transparency and explainability of AI systems: From ethical guidelines to requirements. *Information and Software Technology*, 159, 107197. DOI: 10.1016/j.infsof.2023.107197

Bansal, G., Mitchell, A., & Li, D. (2024). A Panel Report on Higher Education in the Age of AI from the Perspective of Academic Leaders in the Midwest US. *Communications of the Association for Information Systems*, 54(1), 360–375. DOI: 10.17705/1CAIS.05413

Barana, A., Marchisio, M., & Roman, F. (2023). Fostering Problem Solving and Critical Thinking in Mathematics through Generative Artificial Intelligence. *20th International Conference on Cognition and Exploratory Learning in Digital Age (CELDA 2023).*

Barsoun, S. S., Elnagar, M. S., & Awad, B. M. (2022). The effectiveness of using a cognitive style-based Chatbot in developing science concepts and critical thinking skills among preparatory school pupils. *European Scientific Journal*, 18(2), 52. DOI: 10.19044/esj.2022.v18n22p52

Barua, P. D., Vicnesh, J., Gururajan, R., Oh, S. L., Palmer, E., Azizan, M. M., Kadri, N. A., & Acharya, U. R. (2022). Artificial intelligence enabled personalised assistive tools to enhance education of children with neurodevelopmental disorders—A review. *International Journal of Environmental Research and Public Health*, 19(3), 1192. DOI: 10.3390/ijerph19031192 PMID: 35162220

Baskoro, G., Mariza, I., & Sutapa, I. N. (2023). Innovation to Improve Critical Thinking Skills in the Generation Z using Peeragogy as a Learning Approach and Artificial Intelligence (AI) as a Tool. *Jurnal Teknik Industri: Jurnal Keilmuan dan Aplikasi Teknik Industri, 25*(2), 121-130.

Bates, T., Cobo, C., Mariño, O., & Wheeler, S. (2020). Can artificial intelligence transform higher education? *International Journal of Educational Technology in Higher Education*, 17(1), 1–12. DOI: 10.1186/s41239-020-00218-x

Bazargan, A. (2022). *An introduction to qualitative and mixed methods research.* Didar Publisher.

Bearman, M., Ryan, J., & Ajjawi, R. (2023). Discourses of artificial intelligence in higher education: A critical literature review. *Higher Education*, 86(2), 369–385. DOI: 10.1007/s10734-022-00937-2

Belda-Medina, J., & Calvo-Ferrer, J. R. (2022). Using chatbots as AI conversational partners in language learning. *Applied Sciences (Basel, Switzerland)*, 12(17), 8427. DOI: 10.3390/app12178427

Belpaeme, T., James, K., Aditi, R., Brian, S., & Fumihide, T. (2018). Social robots for education: A review. *Science Robotics*, 3(21), 1–9. DOI: 10.1126/scirobotics.aat5954 PMID: 33141719

Bender, S. M. (2022). Algorithmic Elections. *Michigan Law Review*, 121(121.3), 489. DOI: 10.36644/mlr.121.3.algorithmic

Bennani, S., Maalel, A., & Ben Ghezala, H. (2022). Adaptive gamification in E-learning: A literature review and future challenges. *Computer Applications in Engineering Education*, 30(2), 628–642. DOI: 10.1002/cae.22477

Bisen, I. E., Arslan, E. A., Yildirim, K., & Yildirim, Y. (2021). Artificial intelligence and machine learning in higher education. In *Machine learning approaches for improvising modern learning systems* (pp. 1–17). IGI Global. DOI: 10.4018/978-1-7998-5009-0.ch001

Biswas, R., & Paul, A. (2019). Effectiveness of basic teaching model (BTM) of teaching education at higher secondary level. [JETIR]. *Journal of Emerging Technologies and Innovative Research*, 6(3). https://www.jetir.org/papers/JETIR1903K33.pdf

Blodgett, S. L., & Madaio, M. (2021). Risks of AI foundation models in education. *arXiv preprint arXiv:2110.10024.*

Boden, A. M. (2018). *Artificial intelligence: A very short introduction.* Oxford University Press. DOI: 10.1093/actrade/9780199602919.001.0001

Bombardelli, O. (2020). Inclusive education and its implementation: International practices. *Education and Self Development*, 15(3), 37–46. DOI: 10.26907/esd15.3.03

Bondie, R. S., Dahnke, C., & Zusho, A. (2019). How does changing "one-size-fits-all" to differentiated instruction affect teaching? *Review of Research in Education*, 43(1), 336–362. DOI: 10.3102/0091732X18821130

Bond, M., Khosravi, H., De Laat, M., Bergdahl, N., Negrea, V., Oxley, E., Pham, P., Chong, S. W., & Siemens, G. (2024). A meta systematic review of artificial intelligence in higher education: A call for increased ethics, collaboration, and rigor. *International Journal of Educational Technology in Higher Education*, 21(4), 4. Advance online publication. DOI: 10.1186/s41239-023-00436-z

Bostrom, N. (2016). *Superintelligence: Paths, Dangers, Strategies.* Oxford University Press.

Boumediene, H., Bavaharji, M., & Berrahal, F. K. (2018). The effect of using Twitter on improving EFL students' writing: A case study. *International Journal of Humanities and Social Science Invention*, 7(5), 26–32.

Bourke, R. (2018). Self-assessment to incite learning in higher education: Developing ontological awareness. *Assessment & Evaluation in Higher Education*, 43(5), 827–839. DOI: 10.1080/02602938.2017.1411881

Bowden, J., Abdelzaher, E., & Essam, B. A. (2024). Translanguaging and Mobility in Higher Education Institutions: Challenges and Strategies. In War, Mobility, Displacement and Their Impact on Higher Education (Vol. 55, pp. 11-32). Emerald Publishing Limited.

Bowie, A., & Cassim, F. (2016). Linking classroom and community: A theoretical alignment of service learning and a human-centered design methodology in contemporary communication design education. *Education as Change*, 20(1). Advance online publication. DOI: 10.17159/1947-9417/2016/556

Bozkurt, A., Karadeniz, A., Baneres, D., Guerrero-Roldán, A. E., & Rodríguez, M. E. (2021). Artificial intelligence and reflections from educational landscape: A review of AI Studies in half a century. *Sustainability (Basel)*, 13(2), 800. DOI: 10.3390/su13020800

Bozkurt, A., & Sharma, R. C. (2021). Emergency remote teaching in a time of global crisis due to Coronavirus pandemic. *Asian Journal of Distance Education*, 15(1), 1–6. https://www.researchgate.net/publication/341043562_Emergency_remote_teaching_in_a_time_of_global_crisis_due_to_CoronaVirus_pandemic

Brata, D. P. N., Utomo, E. S., & Farhan, A. (2023). Developing Students' 4C Skills (Communication, Collaboration, Creativity, Critical Thinking): Psychomotor Assessment Techniques in Visionary Schools. *QALAMUNA: Jurnal Pendidikan, Sosial, dan Agama, 15*(2), 1127-1138. https://doi.org/. DOI: 10.37680/qalamuna.v15i2.3900

Braun, V., & Clarke, V. (2006). Using thematic analysis in psychology. *Qualitative Research in Psychology*, 3(2), 77–101. DOI: 10.1191/1478088706qp063oa

Brereton, P., Kitchenham, B. A., Budgen, D., Turner, M., & Khalil, M. (2007). Lessons from applying the systematic literature review process within the software engineering domain. *Journal of Systems and Software*, 80(4), 571–583. DOI: 10.1016/j.jss.2006.07.009

Bringle, R. G., & Hatcher, J. A. (1999). Reflection in Service Learning: Making Meaning or Experience. *Evaluation/Reflection, 23*, 179-185. https://digitalcommons.unomaha.edu/slceeval/23

Britannica (2024). Çevrimiçi ansiklopedi. 10 Haziran 2024 tarihinde https://www.britannica.com/technology/artificial-intelligence adresinden alınmıştır.

Britton, B., & Vallis, C. (2023). *Digital facelift: Emerging tools and typologies for educational media.* ASCILITE Publications. DOI: 10.14742/apubs.2023.552

Broussard, M. (2019). *Artificial Unintelligence: How computers misunderstand the world.* The Mit Press.

Brown, E., Davis, M., & Wilson, S. (2023). Scaling challenges in massive open online courses: A comprehensive analysis. *International Journal of Educational Technology in Higher Education*, 20(1), 1–18.

Buçinca, Z., Malaya, M. B., & Gajos, K. Z. (2021). To trust or to think: cognitive forcing functions can reduce overreliance on AI in AI-assisted decision-making. *Proceedings of the ACM on Human-computer Interaction, 5*(CSCW1), 1-21. https://doi.org/DOI: 10.1145/3449287

Buckingham Shum, S., & Luckin, R. (2019). Learning analytics and AI: Politics, pedagogy and practices. *British Journal of Educational Technology*, 50(6), 2785–2793. DOI: 10.1111/bjet.12880

Buff, S. M., Jenkins, K., Kern, D., Worrall, C., Howell, D., Martin, K., Brown, D., White, A., & Blue, A. (2015). Interprofessional service-learning in a community setting: Findings from a pilot study. *Journal of Interprofessional Care*, 29(2), 159–161. DOI: 10.3109/13561820.2014.934956 PMID: 25003549

Bukartaite, R., & Hooper, D. (2023). Automation, artificial intelligence and future skills needs: An Irish perspective. *European Journal of Training and Development*, 47(10), 163–185. DOI: 10.1108/EJTD-03-2023-0045

Bulathwela, S., Pérez-Ortiz, M., Holloway, C., & Shawe-Taylor, J. (2021). Could AI democratise education? Socio-technical imaginaries of an edtech revolution. *arXiv preprint arXiv:2112.02034*.

Bush, T. (2007). Educational leadership and management: Theory, policy, and practice. *South African Journal of Education*, 27(3), 391–406. https://files.eric.ed.gov/fulltext/EJ1150205.pdf

Butow, P., & Hoque, E. (2020). Using artificial intelligence to analyse and teach communication in healthcare. *The Breast*, 50, 49–55. DOI: 10.1016/j.breast.2020.01.008 PMID: 32007704

Campbell, J. L., Quincy, C., Osserman, J., & Pedersen, O. K. (2013). Coding in-depth semistructured interviews: Problems of unitization and intercoder reliability and agreement. *Sociological Methods & Research*, 42(3), 294–320. DOI: 10.1177/0049124113500475

Cantas, Ç., Soyer, C., & Batur, Ö. (2024). Examination of Undergraduate Students' Artificial Intelligence Anxiety, Multidimensional 21st Century Skills, and Lifelong Learning Levels in Terms of Various Variables. *Turkish Online Journal of Educational Technology-TOJET*, 23(3), 29–53.

Capraro, V., Lentsch, A., Acemoglu, D., Akgun, S., Akhmedova, A., Bilancini, E., Bonnefon, J.-F., Brañas-Garza, P., Butera, L., Douglas, K. M., Everett, J. A. C., Gigerenzer, G., Greenhow, C., Hashimoto, D. A., Holt-Lunstad, J., Jetten, J., Johnson, S., Kunz, W. H., Longoni, C., & Viale, R. (2024). The impact of generative artificial intelligence on socioeconomic inequalities and policy making. *PNAS Nexus*, 3(6), pgae191. DOI: 10.1093/pnasnexus/pgae191 PMID: 38864006

Carceller, A. T. (2024). The ARTificial Revolution: Challenges for Redefining Art Education in the Paradigm of Generative Artificial Intelligence. *Digital Education Review*, 45(45), 84–90. DOI: 10.1344/der.2024.45.84-90

Carlos, R.-C. (2023). Artificial Intelligence and Education. *South Florida Journal of Development*, 4(2), 641–655. DOI: 10.46932/sfjdv4n2-001

Carr, J. M., Santos-Rogers, K., & Kanyongo, G. (2021). Improving student and faculty communication: The impact of texting and electronic feedback on building relationships and the perception of care. *Research in Learning Technology*, 29. Advance online publication. DOI: 10.25304/rlt.v29.2463

Catlin, D., & Blamires, M. (2019). Designing robots for special needs education. Technology, knowledge and learning, 24(2), 291-313.

CB Information Services, Inc. (2024). *Compare Studiosity to Competitors.*https://www.cbinsights.com/company/studiosity

Çela, E., Potluri, R. M., & Vajjhala, N. R. (2025). A Comprehensive Meta-Analysis of IoT Integration for Data-Driven Decision Making in Education. In Thandekkattu, S., & Vajjhala, N. (Eds.), *Designing Sustainable Internet of Things Solutions for Smart Industries* (pp. 27–50). IGI Global., DOI: 10.4018/979-8-3693-5498-8.ch002

Celio, C. I., Durlak, J., & Dymnicki, A. (2011). A Meta-Analysis of the Impact of Service-Learning on Students. *Journal of Experiential Education*, 34(2), 164–181. DOI: 10.1177/105382591103400205

Chaika, O. (2023). The role of artificial intelligence in higher education. *Молодь і ринок*, (6/214), 69-74. DOI: DOI: 10.24919/2308-4634.2023.287898

Chan, C. K. Y., & Luo, J. (2020). Towards an inclusive student partnership: Rethinking mentors' disposition and holistic competency development in near-peer mentoring. *Teaching in Higher Education*, •••, 1–18.

Chang, H. S., Fu, M. C., Hu, J., & Marcus, S. I. (2016). Google DeepMind'sAlpha-Go: operations research's unheralded role in the path-breaking achievement. *Or/Ms Today, 43*(5), 24-30.

Chang, C. T., Hajiyev, J., & Su, C. R. (2017). Examining the students' behavioral intention to use e-learning in Azerbaijan? The general extended technology acceptance model for e-learning approach. *Computers & Education*, 111, 128–143. DOI: 10.1016/j.compedu.2017.04.010

Chan, K. S., & Zary, N. (2019). Applications and challenges of implementing artificial intelligence in medical education: Integrative review. *JMIR Medical Education*, 5(1), e13930. DOI: 10.2196/13930 PMID: 31199295

Channa, F. R., Sarhandi, P. S. A., Bugti, F., & Pathan, H. (2021). Harnessing Artificial Intelligence in Education for Preparing Learners for the 21st Century. *Elementary Education Online, 20*(5), 3186–3192. Retrieved from https://ilkogretim-online.org/index.php/pub/article/view/5747

Chan, Y. K. C., & Hu, W. (2023). Students' voices on generative AI: Perceptions, benefits, and challenges in higher education. *International Journal of Educational Technology in Higher Education*, 20(1), 43. DOI: 10.1186/s41239-023-00411-8

Charmet, F., Tanuwidjaja, H. C., Ayoubi, S., Gimenez, P.-F., Han, Y., Jmila, H., Blanc, G., Takahashi, T., & Zhang, Z. (2022). Explainable artificial intelligence for cybersecurity: A literature survey. *Annales des Télécommunications*, 77(11), 789–812. DOI: 10.1007/s12243-022-00926-7

Chassignol, M., Khoroshavin, A., Klimova, A., & Bilyatdinova, A. (2018). Artificial Intelligence trends in education: A narrative overview. *Procedia Computer Science*, 136, 16–24. DOI: 10.1016/j.procs.2018.08.233

Chatterjee, S., & Bhattacharjee, K. K. (2020). Adoption of artificial intelligence in higher education: A quantitative analysis using structural equation modelling. *Education and Information Technologies*, 25(5), 3443–3463. DOI: 10.1007/s10639-020-10159-7

Chembe, C., Nasilele, N. B., & Msendo, R. (2023). The Fuss about Artificial Intelligence in Education Sector: Shculd we Worry? *Zambia ICT Journal*, 7(2), 30–35. DOI: 10.33260/zictjournal.v7i2.269

Chen, H. L., Vicki Widarso, G., & Sutrisno, H. (2020). A chatbot for learning Chinese: Learning achievement and technology acceptance. *Journal of Educational Computing Research*, 58(6), 1161–1189. DOI: 10.1177/0735633120929622

Chen, H., Liu, T., & Wu, Z. (2024). AI-driven assessment of complex problem-solving in STEM education. *IEEE Transactions on Learning Technologies*, 17(1), 45–57.

Chen, K. C., & Jang, S. J. (2010). Motivation in online learning: Testing a model of self-determination theory. *Computers in Human Behavior*, 26(4), 741–752. DOI: 10.1016/j.chb.2010.01.011

Chen, L., Chen, P., & Lin, Z. (2020). Artificial intelligence in education: A review. *IEEE Access : Practical Innovations, Open Solutions*, 8, 75264–75278. DOI: 10.1109/ACCESS.2020.2988510

Chen, S. Y., Lai, Y. H., & Lin, Y. S. (2020). Research on head-mounted virtual reality and computational thinking experiments to improve the learning effect of AIoT maker course: Case of earthquake relief scenes. *Frontiers in Psychology*, 11, 1164. DOI: 10.3389/fpsyg.2020.01164 PMID: 32581963

Chen, X., Xie, H., Zou, D., & Hwang, G.-J. (2020). Application and theory gaps during the rise of artificial intelligence in education. *Computers and Education: Artificial Intelligence*, 1, 100002. DOI: 10.1016/j.caeai.2020.100002

Chen, Y., Jensen, S., Albert, L. J., Gupta, S., & Lee, T. (2023). Artificial intelligence (AI) student assistants in the classroom: Designing chatbots to support student success. *Information Systems Frontiers*, 25(1), 161–182. DOI: 10.1007/s10796-022-10291-4

Cheong, B. C. (2024). Transparency and accountability in AI systems: Safeguarding wellbeing in the age of algorithmic decision-making. *Frontiers in Human Dynamics*, 6, 1421273. DOI: 10.3389/fhumd.2024.1421273

Cheon, J., Lee, S., Crooks, S. M., & Song, J. (2012). An investigation of mobile learning readiness in higher education based on the theory of planned behavior. *Computers & Education*, 59(3), 1054–1064. DOI: 10.1016/j.compedu.2012.04.015

Cheung, G. W., Cooper-Thomas, H. D., Lau, R. S., & Wang, L. C. (2023). Reporting reliability, convergent and discriminant validity with structural equation modeling: A review and best-practice recommendations. *Asia Pacific Journal of Management*, •••, 1–39. DOI: 10.1007/s10490-023-09871-y

Chheang, V., Sharmin, S., Márquez-Hernández, R., Patel, M., Rajasekaran, D., Caulfield, G., & Barmaki, R. L. (2024, January). Towards anatomy education with generative AI-based virtual assistants in immersive virtual reality environments. In *2024 IEEE International Conference on Artificial Intelligence and eXtended and Virtual Reality (AIxVR)* (pp. 21-30). IEEE. DOI: 10.1109/AIxVR59861.2024.00011

Chicco, D., Tötsch, N., & Jurman, G. (2021). The Matthews correlation coefficient (MCC) is more reliable than balanced accuracy, bookmaker informedness, and markedness in two-class confusion matrix evaluation. *BioData Mining*, 14(1), 1–22. DOI: 10.1186/s13040-021-00244-z PMID: 33541410

Chiruguru, S. B. (2020). The essential skills of 21st century classroom (4Cs). *Project: The role of 4Cs (Critical Thinking, Creative Thinking, Collaboration and Communication) in the 21st Century Classroom.*

Chitra, L. (2019). *Artificial intelligence meets augmented reality*. BPB Publications.

Chiu, T. K., Moorhouse, B. L., Chai, C. S., & Ismailov, M. (2023). Teacher support and student motivation to learn with Artificial Intelligence (AI) based chatbot. *Interactive Learning Environments*, 1–17. DOI: 10.1080/10494820.2023.2172044

Chocarro, R., Cortinas, M., & Villanueva, M. L. (2021). Understanding AI acceptance in higher education: The role of ease of use and usefulness. *Journal of Computer Assisted Learning*, 37(5), 1461–1473. DOI: 10.1111/jcal.12563

Cho, H. T., & Yang, J. S. (2018). How perceptions of organizational politics influence self-determined motivation: The mediating role of work mood. *Asia Pacific Management Review*, 23(1), 60–69. DOI: 10.1016/j.apmrv.2017.05.003

Choi, S., Jang, Y., & Kim, H. (2023). Influence of pedagogical beliefs and perceived trust on teachers' acceptance of educational artificial intelligence tools. *International Journal of Human-Computer Interaction*, 39(4), 910–922. DOI: 10.1080/10447318.2022.2049145

Choung, H., David, P., & Ross, A. (2023). Trust in AI and its role in the acceptance of AI technologies. *International Journal of Human-Computer Interaction*, 39(9), 1727–1739. DOI: 10.1080/10447318.2022.2050543

Christou, P. A. (2022). How to use thematic analysis in qualitative research. *Journal of Qualitative Research in Tourism*. Retrieved from https://www.researchgate.net/publication/369146265_How_to_use_Thematic_Analysis_in_Qualitative_Research

Coeckelbergh, M. (2020). *AI ethics*. MIT Press. DOI: 10.7551/mitpress/12549.001.0001

Colchester, K., Hagras, H., Alghazzawi, D., & Aldabbagh, G. (2017). A survey of artificial intelligence techniques employed for adaptive educational systems within e-learning platforms. *Journal of Artificial Intelligence and Soft Computing Research*, 7(1), 47–64. DOI: 10.1515/jaiscr-2017-0004

Comrie, B. (Ed.). (2003). *The Major Languages of South Asia, the Middle East and Africa*. Taylor & Francis. DOI: 10.4324/9780203412336

Cooper, G., & Tang, K. S. (2024). Pixels and Pedagogy: Examining Science Education Imagery by Generative Artificial Intelligence. *Journal of Science Education and Technology*, 33(4), 1–13. DOI: 10.1007/s10956-024-10104-0

Cope, B., & Kalantzis, M. (2023). A little history of e-learning: Finding new ways to learn in the PLATO computer education system, 1959–1976. *History of Education*, 52(6), 905–936. DOI: 10.1080/0046760X.2022.2141353

Corbett, J. B., & Kendall, A. R. (1998). Evaluating Service Learning in the Communication Discipline. *Journalism & Mass Communication Educator*, 53(4), 66–76. DOI: 10.1177/107769589805300406

Córdova, P. R., & Vicari, R. M. (2022, August). Practical ethical issues for artificial intelligence in education. In *International Conference on Technology and Innovation in Learning, Teaching and Education* (pp. 437–445). Cham: Springer Nature Switzerland. https://doi.org/DOI: 10.1007/978-3-031-22918-3_34

Cornet, P., Jones, A., Lee, M., & Williams, K. (2024). Service learning in schools: Challenges and opportunities. *Journal of Educational Development*, 15(2), 112–130.

Costa, S. (2023). Artificial intelligence in education: Challenges and opportunities in learning.

Cotton, D. R. E., Cotton, P. A., & Shipway, J. R. (2024). Chatting and cheating: Ensuring academic integrity in the era of ChatGPT. *Innovations in Education and Teaching International*, 61(2), 228–239. DOI: 10.1080/14703297.2023.2190148

Cox, A. M. (2021). Exploring the impact of Artificial Intelligence and robots on higher education through literature-based design fictions. *International Journal of Educational Technology in Higher Education*, 18(1), 3. DOI: 10.1186/s41239-020-00237-8

Cox, G. M. (2024). Artificial Intelligence and the Aims of Education: Makers, Managers, or Inforgs? *Studies in Philosophy and Education*, 43(1), 15–30. DOI: 10.1007/s11217-023-09907-2

Creswell, J. W. (2007). *Qualitative inquiry and research design: Choosing among five approaches* (2nd ed.). SAGE Publications.

Crompton, H., & Burke, D. (2023). Artificial intelligence in higher education: The state of the field. *International Journal of Educational Technology in Higher Education*, 20(1), 22. https://educationaltechnologyjournal.springeropen.com/articles/10.1186/s41239-023-00392-8. DOI: 10.1186/s41239-023-00392-8

Crompton, H., & Song, D. (2021). The potential of Artificial Intelligence in higher education. *Revista Virtual Universidad CatólicadelNorte*, 1-4(62), 1–4. Advance online publication. DOI: 10.35575/rvucn.n62a1

Dahal, N., Manandhar, N. K., Luitel, L., Luitel, B. C., Pant, B. P., & Shrestha, I. M. (2022). ICT tools for remote teaching and learning mathematics: A proposal for autonomy and engagements. *Online Submission*, 2(1), 289–296. DOI: 10.25082/AMLER.2022.01.013

Dai, C. P., & Ke, F. (2022). Educational applications of artificial intelligence in simulation-based learning: A systematic mapping review. *Computers and Education: Artificial Intelligence, 3*, 100087. Retrieved from https://www.sciencedirect.com/science/article/pii/S2666920X2200042X

Damiano, A. D., Lauria, E. J. M., Sarmiento, C., & Zhao, N. (2024). Early perceptions of teaching and learning using generative AI in higher education. *Journal of Educational Technology Systems*, 52(3), 346–375. DOI: 10.1177/00472395241233290

Darwin, D., Rusdin, D., Mukminatien, N., Suryati, N., Laksmi, E. D., & Marzuki, . (2024). Critical thinking in the AI era: An exploration of EFL students' perceptions, benefits, and limitations. *Cogent Education*, 11(1), 2290342. DOI: 10.1080/2331186X.2023.2290342

Davenport, T. H., & Ronanki, R. (2018). Artificial intelligence for the real world. *Harvard Business Review*, 96(1), 108–116.

Davies, H. C., Eynon, R., & Salveson, C. (2021). The mobilisation of AI in education: A Bourdieusean field analysis. *Sociology*, 55(3), 539–560. DOI: 10.1177/0038038520967888

Davis, F. D. (1989). Perceived usefulness, perceived ease of use, and user acceptance of information technology. *Management Information Systems Quarterly*, 13(3), 319–340. DOI: 10.2307/249008

De la Vall, R. R. F., & Araya, F. G. (2023). Exploring the benefits and challenges of AI-language learning tools. *International Journal of Social Sciences and Humanities Invention*, 10(01), 7569–7576. DOI: 10.18535/ijsshi/v10i01.02

Deeva, G., Bogdanova, D., Serral, E., Snoeck, M., & De Weerdt, J. (2021). A review of automated feedback systems for learners: Classification framework, challenges and opportunities. *Computers & Education*, 162, 104094. DOI: 10.1016/j.compedu.2020.104094

Delgado, A. J., Wardlow, L., McKnight, K., & O'Malley, K. (2015). Educational technology: A review of the integration resources and effectiveness of technology in K-12 classrooms. *Journal of Information Technology Education*, 14, 397–416. https://www.jite.org/documents/Vol14/JITEv14ResearchP397-416Delgado1829.pdf. DOI: 10.28945/2298

Dergaa, I., Chamari, K., Zmijewski, P., & Saad, H. B. (2023). From human writing to artificial intelligence generated text: Examining the prospects and potential threats of chatgpt in academic writing. *Biology of Sport, 40*(2), 615–622. https://doi.org/. 2023.125623DOI: 10.5114/biolsport

Diacopoulos, M. M., & Crompton, H. (2020). A systematic review of mobile learning in social studies. *Computers & Education*, 154, 103911. Advance online publication. DOI: 10.1016/j.compedu.2020.103911

Diamond, A. (2013). Executive functions. *Annual Review of Psychology*, 64(1), 135–168. DOI: 10.1146/annurev-psych-113011-143750 PMID: 23020641

Díaz-Rodríguez, N., Del Ser, J., Coeckelbergh, M., de Prado, M. L., Herrera-Viedma, E., & Herrera, F. (2023). Connecting the dots in trustworthy Artificial Intelligence: From AI principles, ethics, and key requirements to responsible AI systems and regulation. *Information Fusion*, 99, 101896. DOI: 10.1016/j.inffus.2023.101896

Dignum, V. (2019). *Responsible artificial intelligence: how to develop and use AI in a responsible way* (Vol. 2156). Springer., DOI: 10.1007/978-3-030-30371-6

Dillenbourg, P. (2016). The evolution of research on digital education. *International Journal of Artificial Intelligence in Education*, 26(2), 544–560. DOI: 10.1007/s40593-016-0106-z

Dimitriadou, E., & Lanitis, A. (2023). A critical evaluation, challenges, and future perspectives of using artificial intelligence and emerging technologies in smart classrooms. *Smart Learning Environments*, 10(1), 12. DOI: 10.1186/s40561-023-00231-3

Dishon, G. (2017). New data, old tensions: Big data, personalized learning, and the challenges of progressive education. *Theory and Research in Education*, 15(3), 272–289. DOI: 10.1177/1477878517735233

Ditta, A., & Aslam, M. U. (2024). *Education in the AI Age: Navigating Challenges of Generative AI Integration*. https://www.researchgate.net/publication/380364982

Dolgon, C., Mitchell, T. D., & Eatman, T. K. (Eds.). (2017). *The Cambridge Handbook of Service Learning and Community Engagement*. Cambridge University Press., DOI: 10.1017/9781316650011

Dongare, A. D., Kharde, R. R., & Kachare, A. D. (2012). Introduction to artificial neural network. [IJEIT]. *International Journal of Engineering and Innovative Technology*, 2(1), 189–194.

Donlon, E., & Tiernan, P. (2023). Chatbots and Citations: An experiment in academic writing with Generative AI. *Irish Journal of Technology Enhanced Learning*, 7(2), 75–87. DOI: 10.22554/ijtel.v7i2.125

Doyle, J., Chiari, S., Pearl, P., Ellis, K., Völler, S., Shaw, C., & Hezel, B. (2024). Transforming young adults' climate learning and actions through a co-created climate communication retreat. *Environmental Education Research*, •••, 1–19. DOI: 10.1080/13504622.2024.2348693

Drigas, A. S., & Ioannidou, R. E. (2012). Artificial intelligence in special education: A decade review. *International Journal of Engineering Education*, 28(6), 1366–1372. https://www.researchgate.net/publication/249656322_Artificial_intelligence_in_special_education_A_decade_review

Drueke, B., Mainz, V., Lemos, M., Wirtz, M. A., & Boecker, M. (2021). An evaluation of forced distance learning and teaching under pandemic conditions using the technology acceptance model. *Frontiers in Psychology*, 12, 701347. DOI: 10.3389/fpsyg.2021.701347 PMID: 34751220

Duarte, J., Morais, M., & Pereira, R. (2023). Hybrid Learning Environments: A Pathway to Inclusive Higher Education. *Journal of Educational Technology & Society*, 26(2), 75–88.

Duggal, N. (2024). Incredible advantages of AI: Notable 23 benefits of AI. Retrieved from-https://www.simplilearn.com/advantages-and-disadvantages-of-artificial-intelligence-article

Du, K. L., & Swamy, M. N. (2013). *Neural networks and statistical learning*. Springer Science & Business Media.

Dumlao, R. (2018). *A Guide to Collaborative Communication for Service-Learning and Community Engagement Partners*. Routledge.

Dwyer, C. P., Hogan, M. J., & Stewart, I. (2012). An evaluation of argument mapping as a method of enhancing critical thinking performance in e-learning environments. *Metacognition and Learning*, 7(3), 219–244. DOI: 10.1007/s11409-012-9092-1

Ejjami, R. (2024). The future of learning: AI-based curriculum development. *Int J Multidiscip Res*, 6(4).

Elaraby, N., Barakat, S., & Rezk, A. (2024). A generalized ensemble approach based on transfer learning for braille character recognition. *Information Processing & Management*, 61(1), 103545. DOI: 10.1016/j.ipm.2023.103545

El-Sabagh, H. A. (2021). Adaptive e-learning environment based on learning styles and its impact on development students' engagement. *International Journal of Educational Technology in Higher Education*, 18(1), 53. DOI: 10.1186/s41239-021-00289-4

El-Sawy, A., Loey, M., & El-Bakry, H. (2017). Arabic handwritten characters recognition using convolutional neural network. *WSEAS Transactions on Computer Research*, 5(1), 11–19.

Erdoğan, V. (2019). Integrating 4C skills of 21st century into 4 language skills in EFL classes. *International Journal of Education and Research*, 7(11), 113–124.

Ertel, W. (2018). *Introduction to artificial intelligence*(2nd ed.). Springer.

Ertmer, P. A. (1999). Addressing first-and second-order barriers to change: Strategies for technology integration. *Educational Technology Research and Development*, 47(4), 47–61. DOI: 10.1007/BF02299597

Etikan, I., Musa, S. A., & Alkassim, R. S. (2016). Comparison of convenience sampling and purposive sampling. *American Journal of Theoretical and Applied Statistics*, 5(1), 1–4. https://www.researchgate.net/publication/304339244_Comparison_of_Convenience_Sampling_and_Purposive_Sampling. DOI: 10.11648/j.ajtas.20160501.11

Evans, P. (2015). Self-determination theory: An approach to motivation in music education. *Musicae Scientiae*, 19(1), 65–83. DOI: 10.1177/1029864914568044

Eyler, J., & Giles, D. E. (1999). *Where's the Learning in Service-Learning?* Jossey-Bass.

Faccia, A., Ridon, M., & Cavaliere, L. P. L. (2024). The AI Application for an Automated Education System. In *Innovation in the University 4.0 System based on Smart Technologies* (pp. 176–199). Chapman and Hall/CRC. DOI: 10.1201/9781003425809-12

Facione, P. A. (2023). "Critical Thinking: What It Is and Why It Counts", Insight Assessment., https://insightassessment.com/iaresource/critical-thinking-what-it-is-and-why-it-counts/

Farahani, M. S., & Ghasemi, G. (2024). Artificial intelligence and inequality: challenges and opportunities. *Qeios, 7*, 1-14. https://radensa.ru/wp-content/uploads/2024/05/Artificial_Intelligence_and_Inequality_Challenges_.pdf

Farrelly, T., & Baker, N. (2023). Generative artificial intelligence: Implications and considerations for higher education practice. *Education Sciences*, 13(11), 1109. DOI: 10.3390/educsci13111109

Faulconer, E., Griffith, J., & Gruss, A. (2021). The impact of positive feedback on student outcomes and perceptions. *Assessment & Evaluation in Higher Education*, 47(2), 1–10.

Faulkner, S. L., & Trotter, S. P. (2017). Data saturation. In *The International Encyclopedia of Communication Research Methods*. John Wiley & Sons., DOI: 10.1002/9781118901731.iecrm0060

Favaretto, M., De Clercq, E., & Elger, B. S. (2019). Big Data and discrimination: Perils, promises and solutions. A systematic review. *Journal of Big Data*, 6(1), 12. DOI: 10.1186/s40537-019-0177-4

Fayol, H. (1949). *General and Industrial Management Sir Isaac Pitman & Sons* (Storrs, C., Trans.).

Felix, J., & Webb, L. (2024, January 23). *Use of artificial intelligence in education delivery and assessment.* The Parliamentary Office of Science and Technology (POST). Retrieved from https://researchbriefings.files.parliament.uk/documents/POST-PN-0712/POST-PN-0712.pdf

Felzmann, H., Villaronga, E. F., Lutz, C., & Tamò-Larrieux, A. (2019). Transparency you can trust: Transparency requirements for artificial intelligence between legal norms and contextual concerns. *Big Data & Society*, 6(1), 2053951719860542. DOI: 10.1177/2053951719860542

Ferrara, E. (2023). Fairness and bias in artificial intelligence: A brief survey of sources, impacts, and mitigation strategies. *Sci*, 6(1), 3. DOI: 10.3390/sci6010003

Filgueiras, F. (2023). Artificial intelligence and education governance. *Education, Citizenship and Social Justice*, •••, 17461979231160674.

Finnie-Ansley, J., Denny, P., Becker, A. B., Luxton-Reilly, A., & Prather, J. (2022). The robots are coming: Exploring the implications of openai codex on introductory programming. In *Proceedings of the 24th Australasian Computing Education Conference*, 10-19.https://doi.org/DOI: 10.1145/3511861.3511863

Fiok, K., Farahani, F. V., Karwowski, W., & Ahram, T. (2022). Explainable artificial intelligence for education and training. *The Journal of Defense Modeling and Simulation*, 19(2), 133–144. DOI: 10.1177/15485129211028651

Fishbein, M., & Ajzen, I. (1977). Belief, attitude, intention, and behavior: An introduction to theory and research.

Fitria, T. N. (2021, December). Artificial intelligence (AI) in education: Using AI tools for teaching and learning process. In *Prosiding Seminar Nasional & Call for Paper STIE AAS* (Vol. 4, No. 1, pp. 134-147).

Fitriati, F., Rosli, R., Iksan, Z., & Hidayat, A. (2024). Exploring challenges in preparing prospective teachers for teaching 4C skills in mathematics classroom: A school-university partnership perspectives. *Cogent Education*, 11(1), 2286812. DOI: 10.1080/2331186X.2023.2286812

Floridi, L., & Chiriatti, M. (2020). GPT-3: Its nature, scope, limits, and consequences. *Minds and Machines*, 30(4), 681–694. DOI: 10.1007/s11023-020-09548-1

Force, J. T. (2017). Risk Management Framework for Information Systems and Organizations: A System Life Cycle Approach for Security and Privacy (Discussion Draft) (No. NIST Special Publication (SP) 800-37 Rev. 2 (Draft)). National Institute of Standards and Technology.

Ford, M. (2021). Rule of the robots: How artificial intelligence will transform everything. Hachette UK.

Ford, J. D., & Riley, L. A. (2003). Integrating communication and engineering education: A look at curricula, courses, and support systems. *Journal of Engineering Education*, 92(4), 325–328. DOI: 10.1002/j.2168-9830.2003.tb00776.x

Fowler, D. S. (2023). AI in Higher Education: Academic Integrity, Harmony of Insights, and Recommendations. *Journal of Ethics in Higher Education*, (3), 127–143. DOI: 10.26034/fr.jehe.2023.4657

Fuller, M., & Barnes, N. (2024). The impact of ChatGPT on teaching and learning in higher education: Exploring the dual perspectives of participants who were students and teachers. *New Directions for Higher Education*, 2024(207), 31–46.

G2.com Inc. (2024). *Compare Top 10 ServiceMax Alternatives & Competitors*. https://www.g2.com/products/ptc-servicemax/competitors/alternatives

Gandedkar, N. H., Wong, M. T., & Darendeliler, M. A. (2021, June). Role of virtual reality (VR), augmented reality (AR) and artificial intelligence (AI) in tertiary education and research of orthodontics: An insight. [). WB Saunders.]. *Seminars in Orthodontics*, 27(2), 69–77. DOI: 10.1053/j.sodo.2021.05.003

García-Peñalvo, F. J., Corell, A., Abella-García, V., & Grande-de-Prado, M. (2021). *"Recommendations for mandatory online assessment in higher education during the COVID-19 pandemic," in Radical Solutions for Education in a Crisis Context*. Springer.

García-Gutiérrez, J., Ruiz-Corbella, M., & Manjarrés Riesco, Á. (2021). Virtual Service-Learning in Higher Education. A Theoretical Framework for Enhancing its Development. *Frontiers in Education*, 5, 630804. Advance online publication. DOI: 10.3389/feduc.2020.630804

Gaur, A. S., Sharan, H. O., & Kumar, R. (2024). AI in Education: Ethical Challenges and Opportunities. *The Ethical Frontier of AI and Data Analysis*, IGI Global, 39-54.

Gayed, J. M., Carlon, M. K. J., Oriola, A. M., & Cross, J. S. (2022). Exploring an AI-based writing assistant's impact on English language learners. *Computers and Education: Artificial Intelligence*, 3, 100055. DOI: 10.1016/j.caeai.2022.100055

Gentles, S. J., Charles, C., Ploeg, J., & McKibbon, K. (2015). Sampling in qualitative research: Insights from an overview of the methods literature. *The Qualitative Report*, 20(11), 1772–1789. https://nsuworks.nova.edu/tqr/vol20/iss11/5. DOI: 10.46743/2160-3715/2015.2373

George, A. S. (2024). Bridging the Digital Divide: Understanding the Human Impacts of Digital Transformation.

George, A. S. (2023). Preparing students for an AI-driven world: Rethinking curriculum and pedagogy in the age of artificial intelligence. *Partners Universal Innovative Research Publication*, 1(2), 112–136.

George, A. S. (2023). The Potential of Generative AI to Reform Graduate Education. *Partners Universal International Research Journal*, 2(4), 36–50.

George, B., & Wooden, O. (2023). Managing the strategic transformation of higher education through artificial intelligence. *Administrative Sciences*, 13(9), 196. DOI: 10.3390/admsci13090196

Giacinto, G., Perdisci, R., Del Rio, M., & Roli, F. (2008). Intrusion detection in computer networks by a modular ensemble of one-class classifiers. *Information Fusion*, 9(1), 69–82. DOI: 10.1016/j.inffus.2006.10.002

Gill, S. S., Xu, M., Patros, P., Wu, H., Kaur, R., Kaur, K., & Buyya, R. (2024). Transformative effects of ChatGPT on modern education: Emerging Era of AI Chatbots. *Internet of Things and Cyber-Physical Systems*, 4, 19–23. DOI: 10.1016/j.iotcps.2023.06.002

Giray, G. (2021). An assessment of student satisfaction with e-learning: An empirical study with computer and software engineering undergraduate students in Turkey under pandemic conditions. *Education and Information Technologies*, 26(6), 1–23. DOI: 10.1007/s10639-021-10454-x PMID: 33686329

GivePulse. (2024). The Rising Value of Volunteerism: GivePulse for Maximizing Impact. https://learn.givepulse.com

Gligorea, I., Cioca, M., Oancea, R., Gorski, A.-T., Gorski, H., & Tudorache, P. (2023). Adaptive learning using artificial intelligence in e-learning: A literature review. *Education Sciences*, 13(12), 1216. DOI: 10.3390/educsci13121216

Gocen, A., & Aydemir, F. (2020). Artificial intelligence in education and schools. *Research on Education and Media*, 12(1), 13–21. DOI: 10.2478/rem-2020-0003

Goda, Y., Yamada, M., Matsukawa, H., Hata, K., & Yasunami, S. (2014). Conversation with a chatbot before an online EFL group discussion and the effects on critical thinking. *Journal of Information Systems Education*, 13(1), 1–7. DOI: 10.12937/ejsise.13.1

Goodman, B., & Flaxman, S. (2017). European Union regulations on algorithmic decision-making and a “right to explanation”. *AI Magazine*, 38(3), 50–57. DOI: 10.1609/aimag.v38i3.2741

Goplani, V. (2024). The Emergent Role of Artificial Intelligence (AI) in Fostering Collaborative Learning Experiences. https://integranxt.com/blog/the-emergent-role-of-artificial-intelligence-ai-in-fostering-collaborative-learning-experiences/

Gordon, G., Cynthia, B., & Susan, E. (2015, March 2–5). Can children catch curiosity from a social robot? [Paper presentation]. *Tenth Annual ACM/IEEE International Conference on Human-Robot Interaction*, Portland, OR, USA.

Government Technology Agency of Singapore. (February 23, 2023). *Tech and education: How automation and AI are powering learning in Singapore*. https://www.tech.gov.sg/media/technews/tech-and-education-how-automation-and-ai-is-powering-learning-in-singapore/

Graf, A. (2023). Exploring the role of personalization in adaptive learning environments. *International Journal Software Engineering and Computer Science (IJSECS), 3*(2), 50-56. https://journal.lembagakita.org/ijsecs/article/view/1200

Grassini, S. (2023). Shaping the future of education: Exploring the potential and consequences of AI and ChatGPT in educational settings. *Education Sciences*, 13(7), 692. DOI: 10.3390/educsci13070692

Grawemeyer, B., Mavrikis, M., Holmes, W., & Gutierrez-Santos, S. (2015). Adapting feedback types according to students' affective states. In *Artificial Intelligence in Education: 17th International Conference, AIED 2015, Madrid, Spain, June 22-26, 2015.* [Springer International Publishing.]. *Proceedings*, 17, 586–590.

Gross, B., & Jochim, A. (Eds.). (2015). *Uncovering the productivity promise of rural education. The SEA of the Future* (Vol. 4). Building State Capacity & Productivity Center at Edvance Research, Inc., Retrieved from https://compcenternetwork.org/sites/default/files/archive/SEAF_Vol4_ProdPromiseOfRuralEdu.pdf#page=29

Gual-Montolio, P., Jaén, I., Martínez-Borba, V., Castilla, D., & Suso-Ribera, C. (2022). Using artificial intelligence to enhance ongoing psychological interventions for emotional problems in real-or close to real-time: A systematic review. *International Journal of Environmental Research and Public Health*, 19(13), 7737. DOI: 10.3390/ijerph19137737 PMID: 35805395

Guenther, P., Guenther, M., Ringle, C. M., Zaefarian, G., & Cartwright, S. (2023). Improving PLS-SEM use for business marketing research. *Industrial Marketing Management*, 111, 127–142. DOI: 10.1016/j.indmarman.2023.03.010

Guttman, L. (1945). A basis for analyzing test-retest reliability. *Psychometrika*, 10(4), 255–282. DOI: 10.1007/BF02288892 PMID: 21007983

Guzdial, M., & du Boulay, B. (2019). The history of computing. The Cambridge handbook of computing education research, 11.

Habib, S., Vogel, T., Anli, X., & Thorne, E. (2024). How does generative artificial intelligence impact student creativity?. *Journal of Creativity, 34*(1), 100072. https://doi.org/. 2023.100072. DOI: 10.1016/j.yjoc

Haddock, A., Ward, N., Yu, R., & O'Dea, N. (2022). Positive effects of digital technology use by adolescents: A scoping review of the literature. *International Journal of Environmental Research and Public Health*, 19(21), 14009. DOI: 10.3390/ijerph192114009 PMID: 36360887

Hage, J., & Verheij, B. (1999).Rechtsinformatica: de stand van zaken in de wetenschap. *A. Oskamp and A. Lodder (reds.), Informatietechnologie voor juristen. Handboek voor de jurist in de 21e eeuw*, Kluwer, 65-92.http://www.metajur.unimaas.nl/~bart/

Hagger, M. S., & Protogerou, C. (2020). Self-determination theory and autonomy support to change healthcare behavior. *The Wiley handbook of healthcare treatment engagement: Theory, research, and clinical practice*, 141-158.

Hair, J. F., Risher, J. J., Sarstedt, M., & Ringle, C. M. (2019). When to use and how to report the results of PLS-SEM. *European Business Review*, 31(1), 2–24. DOI: 10.1108/EBR-11-2018-0203

Hair, J. F., Sarstedt, M., Ringle, C. M., & Gudergan, S. P. (2018). *Advanced Issues in Partial Least Squares Structural Equations Modeling (PLS-SEM)*. Sage., DOI: 10.3926/oss.37

Halaweh, M. (2023). ChatGPT in education: Strategies for responsible implementation. *Contemporary Educational Technology*, 15(2), ep421. Advance online publication. DOI: 10.30935/cedtech/13036

Halpern, D. F. (2003). *Thought and knowledge: An introduction to critical thinking* (4th ed.). Laurence Erlbaum Associates.

Hamet, P., & Tremblay, J. (2017).Artificial intelligence in medicine. *metabolism, 69*, S36-S40.DOI: 10.1016/j.metabol.2017.01.011

Hamilton, I., & Swanston, B. (June 6, 2024). *Artificial Intelligence In Education: Teachers' Opinions On AI In The Classroom*. Forbes Media LLC. https://www.forbes.com/advisor/education/it-and-tech/artificial-intelligence-in-school/#:~:text=AI's%20Influence%20on%20Education,5%20cited%20a%20negative%20effect

Hamlaoui, S. (2021). Teachers' resistance to educational change and innovations in the Middle East and North Africa: A case study of Tunisian universities. In Ouaissa, R., Pannewick, F., & Strohmaier, A. (Eds.), *Re-Configurations* (pp. 171–184). Springer VS., DOI: 10.1007/978-3-658-31160-5_11

Hammersley, M. (1987). Some notes on the terms 'validity' and 'reliability'. *British Educational Research Journal*, 13(1), 73–81. DOI: 10.1080/0141192870130107

Han, B., Nawaz, S., Buchanan, G., & McKay, D. (2023, June). Ethical and pedagogical impacts of AI in education. In *International Conference on Artificial Intelligence in Education* (pp. 667–673). Cham: Springer Nature Switzerland. https://doi.org/DOI: 10.1007/978-3-031-36272-9_54

Han, J., Pei, J., & Kamber, M. (2011). *Data mining: concepts and techniques*. Elsevier.

Hannan, E., & Liu, S. (2023). AI: New source of competitiveness in higher education. *Competitiveness Review*, 33(2), 265–279. DOI: 10.1108/CR-03-2021-0045

Hapsari, I. P., & Wu, T. T. (2022). AI Chatbots learning model in English speaking skill: Alleviating speaking anxiety, boosting enjoyment, and fostering critical thinking. *International Conference on Innovative Technologies and Learning*, Portugal https://doi.org/DOI: 10.1007/978-3-031-15273-3_49

Haq, I. U., Anwar, A., Rehman, I. U., Asif, W., Sobnath, D., Sherazi, H. H. R., & Nasralla, M. M. (2021). Dynamic group formation with intelligent tutor collaborative learning: A novel approach for next generation collaboration. *IEEE Access : Practical Innovations, Open Solutions*, 9, 143406–143422. DOI: 10.1109/ACCESS.2021.3120557

Haque, M. S. (2002). E-governance in India: Its impacts on relations amongcitizens, politicians and public servants. *International Review of Administrative Sciences*, 68(2), 231–250. DOI: 10.1177/0020852302682005

Harris, M., & Agoes, A. S. (2021, November). Applying hand gesture recognition for user guide application using MediaPipe. In *2nd International Seminar of Science and Applied Technology (ISSAT 2021)* (pp. 101-108). Atlantis Press.

Harry, A. (2023). Role of AI in Education. [INJURITY]. *Interdiciplinary Journal and Hummanity*, 2(3), 260–268.

Hassija, V., Chamola, V., Mahapatra, A., Singal, A., Goel, D., Huang, K., & Hussain, A. (2024). Interpreting black-box models: a review on explainable artificial intelligence. *Cognitive Computation, 16*(1), 45-74. https://doi.org/DOI: 10.1007/s12559-023-10179-8

Haykin, S. (2010). *Neural networks and learning machines*. Pearson Education.

Heale, R., & Twycross, A. (2015). Validity and reliability in quantitative studies. *Evidence-Based Nursing*, 18(3), 66–67. DOI: 10.1136/eb-2015-102129 PMID: 25979629

Heimerl, A., Weitz, K., Baur, T., & André, E. (2022). Unraveling ML models of emotion with NOVA: Multi-level explainable AI for non-experts. *IEEE Transactions on Affective Computing*, 13(3), 1155–1167. DOI: 10.1109/TAFFC.2020.3043603

Heng, A., Abidin, A. Z. Z., Ng, C. J., Cheong, M. L., & Tamil, A. M. (2023). ChatGPT and clinical practice guidelines just a tap away. *The Medical Journal of Malaysia*, 78(1), 7. PMID: 36715184

Henrickson, L., & Meroño-Peñuela, A. (2022). The hermeneutics of computer-generated texts. *Configurations*, 30(2), 115–139. DOI: 10.1353/con.2022.0008

Henseler, J., Ringle, C. M., & Sarstedt, M. (2015). A new criterion for assessing discriminant validity in variance-based structural equation modeling. *Journal of the Academy of Marketing Science*, 43(1), 115–135. DOI: 10.1007/s11747-014-0403-8

Herlinawati, H., Marwa, M., Ismail, N., Liza, L. O., & Situmorang, D. D. B. (2024). The integration of 21st century skills in the curriculum of education. *Heliyon*, 10(15), e35148. DOI: 10.1016/j.heliyon.2024.e35148 PMID: 39170322

Herodotou, C., Hlosta, M., Boroowa, A., Rienties, B., Zdrahal, Z., & Mangafa, C. (2019). Empowering online teachers through predictive learning analytics. *British Journal of Educational Technology*, 50(6), 3064–3079. DOI: 10.1111/bjet.12853

Herring, M. C., Koehler, M. J., & Mishra, P. (Eds.). (2016). *Handbook of technological pedagogical content knowledge (TPACK) for educators* (Vol. 3, pp. 189–200). Routledge. DOI: 10.4324/9781315771328

He, S., Jiang, S., Zhu, R., & Hu, X. (2023). The influence of educational and emotional support on e-learning acceptance: An integration of social support theory and TAM. *Education and Information Technologies*, 28(9), 11145–11165. DOI: 10.1007/s10639-023-11648-1 PMID: 36818430

Hess, F. M. (2007). The case for educational entrepreneurship: Hard truths about risk, reform, and reinvention. *Phi Delta Kappan*, 89(1), 21–30. https://www.aei.org/wp-content/uploads/2011/10/20070913_PDKEntrepreneurship.pdf. DOI: 10.1177/003172170708900105

Hill, P. W., & Barber, M. (2014). *Preparing for a renaissance in assessment*. Pearson.

Hill-Yardin, E., Hutchinson, M. R., Laycock, R., & Spencer, S. J. (2023). A Chat(GPT) about the future of scientific publishing. *Brain, Behavior, and Immunity*, 110(2), 152–154. Advance online publication. DOI: 10.1016/j.bbi.2023.02.022 PMID: 36868432

Hinojo-Lucena, F.-J., Aznar-Díaz, I., Cáceres-Reche, M.-P., & Romero-Rodríguez, J.-M. (2019). Artificial intelligence in higher education: A bibliometric study on its impact in the scientific literature. *Education Sciences*, 9(1), 51. DOI: 10.3390/educsci9010051

Hinton, G. E., Osindero, S., & Teh, W. Y. (2006). A fast learning algorithm for deep belief nets. *Neural Computation*, 18(7), 1527–1554. DOI: 10.1162/neco.2006.18.7.1527 PMID: 16764513

Hmoud, M., Swaity, H., Hamad, N., Karram, O., & Daher, W. (2024). Higher education students' task motivation in the generative artificial intelligence context: The case of chatgpt. *Information (Basel)*, 15(1), 33. DOI: 10.3390/info15010033

Holmes, W., Anastopoulou, S., Schaumburg, H., & Mavrikis, M. (2018). *Technology-enhanced personalised learning: Untangling the evidence*. http://www.studie-personalisiertes-lernen.de/en/

Holmes, W., Bialik, M., & Fadel, C. (2019). Artificial intelligence in education: Promises and implications for teaching and learning. Center for Curriculum Redesign. https://curriculumredesign.org/wp-content/uploads/AI-in-Education-CCR-2019.pdf

Holmes, W., Bialik, M., & Fadel, C. (2019). *Artificial Intelligence in Education: Promises and Implications for Teaching and Learning*. Center for Curriculum Redesign. https://www.curriculumredesign.org/our-work/artificial-intelligence-in-education/

Holmes, W., Bialik, M., & Fadel, C. (2019). *Artificial intelligence in education: Promises and implications for teaching and learning*. Center for Curriculum Redesign. Retrieved from https://www.researchgate.net/publication/332180327_Artificial_Intelligence_in_Education_Promise_and_Implications_for_Teaching_and_Learning

Holmes, W., Persson, J., Chounta, I. A., Wasson, B., & Dimitrova, V. (2022). *Artificial intelligence and education: A critical view through the lens of human rights, democracy and the rule of law*. Council of Europe.

Holstein, K., & Doroudi, S. (2021). Equity and artificial intelligence in education: will" aied" amplify or alleviate inequities in education? arXiv preprint arXiv:2104.12920.

Holstein, K., McLaren, B. M., & Aleven, V. (2017, March). Intelligent tutors as teachers' aides: exploring teacher needs for real-time analytics in blended classrooms. In Proceedings of the seventh international learning analytics & knowledge conference (pp. 257-266).

Hong, L., Wan, Y.-y., Yang, W., Gong, Z., Hu, X.-y., & Ma, G. (2024). Two decades of academic service-learning in Chinese higher education: A review of research literature. *Applied Research in Quality of Life*, 19(5), 2171–2212. Advance online publication. DOI: 10.1007/s11482-024-10318-9

Hooda, M., Rana, C., Dahiya, O., Rizwan, A., & Hossain, M. S. (2022). Artificial intelligence for assessment and feedback to enhance student success in higher education. *Mathematical Problems in Engineering*, 2022(1), 5215722. DOI: 10.1155/2022/5215722

Hoppe, M., Westerberg, M., & Leffler, E. (2017). Educational approaches to entrepreneurship in higher education – A view from the Swedish horizon. *Education + Training*, 59(7/8), 751–765. DOI: 10.1108/ET-12-2016-0177

Horvath, J. C. (2024). [*Critical Problems Gen AI Poses for Learning*. https://hbsp.harvard.edu/inspiring-minds/the-limits-of-gen-ai-educators-in-higher-ed]. *Artificial Intelligence*, 3, •••.

Houwer, J., Barnes-Holmes, D., & Moors, A. (2013). What is learning? On the nature and merits of a functional definition of learning. *Psychonomic Bulletin & Review*, 20(4), 631–642. DOI: 10.3758/s13423-013-0386-3 PMID: 23359420

Hoy, W., & Miskel, C. G. (2013). *Educational administration: Theory, research, and practice* (9th ed.). McGraw-Hill Higher Education.

Hsu, H.-P., Mak, J., Werner, J., White-Taylor, J., Geiselhofer, M., Gorman, A., & Torrejon Capurro, C. (2024). Preliminary Study on Pre-Service Teachers' Applications and Perceptions of Generative Artificial Intelligence for Lesson Planning. *Journal of Technology and Teacher Education*, 32(3), 409–437.

Hsu, Y. C., & Ching, Y. H. (2023). Generative artificial intelligence in education, part one: The dynamic frontier. *TechTrends*, 67(4), 603–607. DOI: 10.1007/s11528-023-00863-9

Huang, Y. (2023). *The Future of Generative AI: How GenAI Would Change Human-Computer Co-creation in the Next 10 to 15 Years* CHI PLAY Companion '23: Companion Proceedings of the Annual Symposium on Computer-Human Interaction in Play.

Huang, A. Y., Lu, O. H., & Yang, S. J. (2023). Effects of artificial Intelligence–Enabled personalized recommendations on learners' learning engagement, motivation, and outcomes in a flipped classroom. *Computers & Education*, 194, 104684. DOI: 10.1016/j.compedu.2022.104684

Huang, F. L., Tortorelli, L. S., & Invernizzi, M. A. (2014). An investigation of factors associated with letter-sound knowledge at kindergarten entry. *Early Childhood Research Quarterly*, 29(2), 182–192. DOI: 10.1016/j.ecresq.2014.02.001

Huang, X., & Qiao, C. (2022). Enhancing computational thinking skills through artificial intelligence education at a STEAM high school. *Science & Education*, 33(2), 383–403. DOI: 10.1007/s11191-022-00392-6

Huang, Y. C., Backman, S. J., Backman, K. F., McGuire, F. A., & Moore, D. (2019). An investigation of motivation and experience in virtual learning environments: A self-determination theory. *Education and Information Technologies*, 24(1), 591–611. DOI: 10.1007/s10639-018-9784-5

Hu, X., Liu, Y., Huang, J., & Mu, S. (2022). The Effects of Different Patterns of Group Collaborative Learning on Fourth-Grade Students' Creative Thinking in a Digital Artificial Intelligence Course. *Sustainability (Basel)*, 14(19), 12674. DOI: 10.3390/su141912674

Hwang, G. J., & Chen, N. S. (2023). Exploring the potential of generative artificial intelligence in education: Applications, challenges, and future research directions. *Journal of Educational Technology & Society*, 26(2).

Hwang, G. J., Xie, H., Wah, B. W., & Gašević, D. (2020). Vision, challenges, roles and research issues of Artificial Intelligence in Education. *Computers and Education: Artificial Intelligence*, 1, 100001. Advance online publication. DOI: 10.1016/j.caeai.2020.100001

Ifinedo, P. (2017). Examining students' intention to continue using blogs for learning: Perspectives from technology acceptance, motivational, and social-cognitive frameworks. *Computers in Human Behavior*, 72, 189–199. DOI: 10.1016/j.chb.2016.12.049

Igbokwe, I. C. (2023). Application of artificial intelligence (AI) in educational management. *International Journal of Scientific and Research Publications*, 13(3), 300. https://www.ijsrp.org/research-paper-0323.php?rp=P13512782. DOI: 10.29322/IJSRP.13.03.2023.p13536

Ihde, D. (2010). *Embodied technics*.Automatic Press/vip.

Ilgun Dibek, M., Sahin Kursad, M., & Erdogan, T. (2024). Influence of artificial intelligence tools on higher order thinking skills: A meta-analysis. *Interactive Learning Environments*, •••, 1–23. DOI: 10.1080/10494820.2024.2402028

Ilić, M. P., Păun, D., Popović Šević, N., Hadžić, A., & Jianu, A. (2021). Needs and performance analysis for changes in higher education and implementation of artificial intelligence, machine learning, and extended reality. *Education Sciences*, 11(10), 568. Advance online publication. DOI: 10.3390/educsci11100568

Inie, N., Falk, J., & Tanimoto, S. (2023). Designing Participatory AI: Creative Professionals' Worries and Expectations about Generative AI *CHI Conference on Human Factors in Computing Systems*, Association for Computing Machinery, New York, NY, USA. DOI: 10.1145/3544549.3585657

Islam, I., & Islam, M. N. (2024). Exploring the opportunities and challenges of ChatGPT in academia. *Discover Education*, 3(1), 31. DOI: 10.1007/s44217-024-00114-w

Ivanović, M., Klašnja-Milićević, A., Paprzycki, M., Ganzha, M., Bădică, C., Bădică, A., & Jain, L. C. (2022). *Current trends in AI-based educational processes—an overview. Handbook on Intelligent Techniques in the Educational Process* (Vol. 1). Recent Advances and Case Studies.

Ivcevic, Z., & Grandinetti, M. (2024). Artificial intelligence as a tool for creativity. *Journal of Creativity*, 34(2), 100079. DOI: 10.1016/j.yjoc.2024.100079

Iyer, S. S. (2022). Application of Digital Technologies: Integrated Blockchain with Emerging Technologies. In *Handbook of Research on Supply Chain Resiliency, Efficiency, and Visibility in the Post-Pandemic Era* (pp. 267-294). IGI Global. DOI: DOI: 10.4018/978-1-7998-9506-0.ch014

Iyer, S. S., Malhotra, S., Reyes, F. E.Jr, Subramanian, R., Singh, R., & Anwar, S. (2024). Strategy For Business Recovery In Novo Cinemas. *Educational Administration: Theory and Practice*, 30(4), 7923–7942. DOI: 10.53555/kuey.v30i4.1621

Jacoby, B. (1996). *Service-Learning in Higher Education: Concepts and Practices*. Jossey-Bass.

Jaiswal, A., & Arun, C. J. (2021). Potential of Artificial Intelligence for transformation of the education system in India. *International Journal of Education and Development Using Information and Communication Technology*, 17(1), 142–158. https://eric.ed.gov/?id=EJ1285526

Jayadurga, D. R., & Rathika, M. S. (2023). *Significance and Impact of Artificial Intelligence and Immersive Technologies in the field of Education. International Journal of Recent Technology and Engineering*. IJRTE.

Johnson, S. R., & Stage, F. K. (2018). Academic engagement and student success: Do high-impact practices mean higher graduation rates? *The Journal of Higher Education*, 89(5), 753–781. DOI: 10.1080/00221546.2018.1441107

Jones, R., & Lee, S. (2023). Natural language processing for automated essay grading and feedback. *Educational Data Mining Journal*, 12(2), 89–104.

Jones, S. M., McGarrah, M. W., & Kahn, J. (2019). Social and emotional learning: A principled science of human development in context. *Educational Psychologist*, 54(3), 129–143. DOI: 10.1080/00461520.2019.1625776

Jones, S., & Latzko-Toth, G. (2017). Out from the PLATO cave: Uncovering the pre-Internet history of social computing. *Internet Histories*, 1(1-2), 60–69. DOI: 10.1080/24701475.2017.1307544

Joo, J., & Sang, Y. (2013). Exploring Koreans' smartphone usage: An integrated model of the technology acceptance model and uses and gratifications theory. *Computers in Human Behavior*, 29(6), 2512–2518. DOI: 10.1016/j.chb.2013.06.002

Jurayev, T. N. (2023). The use of mobile learning applications in higher education institutes. *Advances in Mobile Learning Educational Research*, 3(1), 610–620. DOI: 10.25082/AMLER.2023.01.010

Kabudi, T., Pappas, I., & Olsen, D. H. (2021). AI-enabled adaptive learning systems: A systematic mapping of the literature. *Computers and Education: Artificial Intelligence*, 2, 100017. DOI: 10.1016/j.caeai.2021.100017

Kadaruddin, K. (2023). Empowering education through Generative AI: Innovative instructional strategies for tomorrow's learners. *International Journal of Business, Law, and Education*, 4(2), 618–625. DOI: 10.56442/ijble.v4i2.215

Kaelbling, L. P., Littman, M. L., & Moore, A. W. (1996). Reinforcement Learning A Survey. *Journal of Artificial Intelligence Research*, 4, 237–285. https://www.cs.cmu.edu/~tom/10701_sp11/slides/Kaelbling.pdf. DOI: 10.1613/jair.301

Kamalov, F., Santandreu Calonge, D., & Gurrib, I. (2023). New era of artificial intelligence in education: Towards a sustainable multifaceted revolution. *Sustainability (Basel)*, 15(16), 12451. DOI: 10.3390/su151612451

Kampa, R. K. (2023). Combining technology readiness and acceptance model for investigating the acceptance of m-learning in higher education in India. *Asian Association of Open Universities Journal*, 18(2), 105–120. DOI: 10.1108/AAOUJ-10-2022-0149

Kannan, J., & Munday, P. (2018). New trends in second language learning and teaching through the lens of ICT, networked learning, and artificial intelligence.

Kaplan, A., & Haenlein, M. (2018). Siri Siri in my hand: Who's the fairest in the land? On the interpretations, illustrations, and implications of artificial intelligence. *Business Horizons*, 62(1), 15–25. DOI: 10.1016/j.bushor.2018.08.004

Karhunen, J., Raiko, T., & Cho, K. (2015). Unsupervised deep learning: A short review. *Advances in independent component analysis and learning machines*, 125-142.DOI: 10.1016/B978-0-12-802806-3.00007-5

Karimi, H., & Khawaja, S. (2023). The Impact of Artificial Intelligence on Higher Education in England. *Creative Education*, 14(12), 2405–2415. DOI: 10.4236/ce.2023.1412154

Kasneci, E., Seßler, K., Küchemann, S., Bannert, M., Dementieva, D., Fischer, F., & Kasneci, G. (2023). ChatGPT for good? On opportunities and challenges of large language models for education. *Learning and Individual Differences*, 103, 102274. DOI: 10.1016/j.lindif.2023.102274

Kasun, G. S., Liao, Y. C., Margulieux, L. E., & Woodall, M. (2024, June). Unexpected outcomes from an AI education course among education faculty: Toward making AI accessible with marginalized youth in urban Mexico. [). Frontiers Media SA.]. *Frontiers in Education*, 9, 1368604. DOI: 10.3389/feduc.2024.1368604

Kaswan, K. S., Dhatterwal, J. S., & Ojha, R. P. (2024). AI in personalized learning. In *Advances in Technological Innovations in Higher Education* (pp. 103–117). CRC Press. DOI: 10.1201/9781003376699-9

Kayyali, M. (2021). Positive Impact of High Technology on Higher Education.

Kayyali, M. (2020). Post COVID-19: New era for higher education systems. *International Journal of Applied Science and Engineering*, 8(2), 131–145. DOI: 10.30954/2322-0465.2.2020.6

Kayyali, M. (2023). Promoting entrepreneurship and innovation in higher education. *International Journal of Innovation and Entrepreneurship*, 2(1), 1–26. https://www.researchgate.net/publication/373923500_Promoting_Entrepreneurship_and_Innovation_in_Higher_Education

Kayyali, M. (2024). Future possibilities and challenges of AI in education. In *Transforming education with generative AI: Prompt engineering and synthetic content creation* (pp. 118–137). IGI Global. DOI: 10.4018/979-8-3693-1351-0.ch006

Kebritchi, M. (2024). The implications of AI in higher education. https://evolllution.com/the-implications-of-ai-in-higher-education

Kelly, A., Sullivan, M., & Strampel, K. (2023). Generative artificial intelligence: University student awareness, experience, and confidence in use across disciplines. *Journal of University Teaching & Learning Practice*, 20(6), 12. DOI: 10.53761/1.20.6.12

Kelly, S., Kaye, S. A., & Oviedo-Trespalacios, O. (2023). What factors contribute to the acceptance of artificial intelligence? A systematic review. *Telematics and Informatics*, 77, 101925. DOI: 10.1016/j.tele.2022.101925

Kembara, M. D., Rozak, R. W. A., & Hadian, V. A. (2019, Mart). Based lectures to improve students' 4C (communication, collaboration, critical thinking, and creativity) skills. *International Symposium on Social Sciences, Education, and Humanities (ISSEH 2018).* Atlantis Press. DOI: 10.2991/isseh-18.2019.6

Kemp, A., Palmer, E., & Strelan, P. (2019). A taxonomy of factors affecting attitudes towards educational technologies for use with technology acceptance models. *British Journal of Educational Technology*, 50(5), 2394–2413. DOI: 10.1111/bjet.12833

Keong, W. E. Y. (2022). Factors Influencing Adoption Intention Towards Chatbots as a Learning Tool. In The International Conference in Education (ICE), *Proceedings*; Faculty of Social Sciences and Humanities, UTM: Johor Bahru, Malaysia (pp. 96-99).

Ketelhut, D. J., Nelson, B. C., Clarke, J., & Dede, C. (2010). A multi-user virtual environment for building and assessing higher order inquiry skills in science. *British Journal of Educational Technology*, 41(1), 56–68. DOI: 10.1111/j.1467-8535.2009.01036.x

Kharbat, F. F., Alshawabkeh, A., & Woolsey, M. L. (2021). Identifying gaps in using artificial intelligence to support students with intellectual disabilities from education and health perspectives. *Aslib Journal of Information Management*, 73(1), 101–128. DOI: 10.1108/AJIM-02-2020-0054

Khare, K., Stewart, B., & Khare, A. (2018). Artificial intelligence and the student experience: An institutional perspective.

Khare, K., Stewart, B., & Khare, A. (2018). Artificial intelligence and the student experience: An institutional perspective. *IAFOR Journal of Education, 6*(3), 99–116. Retrieved from https://www.researchgate.net/publication/329366517_Artificial_Intelligence_and_the_Student_Experience_An_Institutional_Perspective

Khare, K., Stewart, B., & Khare, A. (2018). Artificial intelligence and the student experience: An institutional perspective. The International Academic Forum (IAFOR).

Khater, A. S., Zaaqoq, A. A., Wahdan, M. M., & Ashry, S. (2023). Knowledge and attitude of Ain Shams University Medical Students towards Artificial Intelligence and its application in Medical Education and Practice. *Educational Research and Innovation Journal*, 3(10), 29–42. DOI: 10.21608/erji.2023.306718

Khosravi, H., Sadiq, S., & Amer-Yahia, S. (2023). Data management of AI-powered education technologies: Challenges and opportunities. *Learning Letters*, 1, 2. Advance online publication. DOI: 10.59453/XLUD7002

Khosravi, H., Shum, S. B., Chen, G., Conati, C., Tsai, Y. S., Kay, J., & Gašević, D. (2022). Explainable artificial intelligence in education. *Computers and Education: Artificial Intelligence*, 3, 100074.

KIEMDE., S. M. A., & KORA, A. D. (2020, December). The challenges facing the development of AI in Africa. In *2020 IEEE International Conference on Advent Trends in Multidisciplinary Research and Innovation (ICATMRI)* (pp. 1–6). IEEE. https://doi.org/DOI: 10.1109/ICATMRI51801.2020.9398454

Kılınç, A. Ç., Polatcan, M., Savaş, G., & Er, E. (2024). How transformational leadership influences teachers' commitment and innovative practices: Understanding the moderating role of trust in principal. *Educational Management Administration & Leadership*, 52(2), 455–474. DOI: 10.1177/17411432221082803

Kim, G. M., & Lee, S. J. (2016). Korean Students' Intentions to Use Mobile-Assisted Language Learning: Applying the Technology Acceptance Model. *International Journal of Contents*, 12(3), 47–53. Advance online publication. DOI: 10.5392/IJoC.2016.12.3.047

Kim, J. (2024). Leading teachers' perspective on teacher-AI collaboration in education. *Education and Information Technologies*, 29(7), 8693–8724. DOI: 10.1007/s10639-023-12109-5

Kim, J., Merrill, K., Xu, K., & Sellnow, D. D. (2020). My teacher is a machine: Understanding students' perceptions of AI teaching assistants in online education. *International Journal of Human-Computer Interaction*, 36(20), 1902–1911. DOI: 10.1080/10447318.2020.1801227

Kindel, A. T., & Stevens, M. L. (2021). What is educational entrepreneurship? Strategic action, temporality, and the expansion of US higher education. *Theory and Society*, 50(3), 577–605. DOI: 10.1007/s11186-021-09443-3

Kirschner, P., & Van Merrienboer, J. J. (2008). *Ten steps to complex learning: A new approach to instruction and instructional design. In 21st century education: A reference handbook*. SAGE Publications Ltd.

Kitano, H., Asada, M., Kuniyoshi, Y., Noda, I., & Osawa, E. (1997).Robocup: The robot world cup initiative. In *Proceedings of the first international conference on Autonomous agents*, 340-347.DOI: 10.1145/267658.267738

Kitchenham, B., & Charters, S. (2007). *Guidelines for performing systematic literature reviews in software engineering* (Version 2.3). EBSE Technical Report, School of Computer Science and Mathematics, Keele University, and Department of Computer Science, University of Durham. Retrieved from https://www.researchgate.net/publication/302924724_Guidelines_for_performing_Systematic_Literature_Reviews_in_Software_Engineering

Kleij, F. M. V. D., Vermeulen, J. A., Schildkamp, K., & Eggen, T. J. H. M. (2015). Integrating data-based decision making, assessment for learning and diagnostic testing in formative assessment. *Assessment in Education: Principles, Policy & Practice*, 22(3), 324–343. DOI: 10.1080/0969594X.2014.999024

Kleiman, G. 2023, Teaching Students to Write with AI: The SPACE Framework Hamza Aoun, AI in Education https://media.licdn.com/dms/document/media/D4E1FAQFDyGd4zKH0LA/feedshare-document-pdf-analyzed/0/1718894249107?e=1729728000&v=beta&t=yOTdRvHrenhzJCDcJC4WCYhYMAlb7JAH-sgmluf-8O0

Koh, E., Zhang, L., Lee, A. V. Y., & Wang, H. (2024). Revolutionizing word clouds for teaching and learning with generative artificial intelligence: Cases from China and Singapore. *IEEE Transactions on Learning Technologies*, 17, 1416–1427. DOI: 10.1109/TLT.2024.3385009

Koichu, B., Schwarz, B. B., Heyd-Metzuyanim, E., Tabach, M., & Yarden, A. (2022). Design practices and principles for promoting dialogic argumentation via interdisciplinarity. *Learning, Culture and Social Interaction*, 37, 100657. https://doi.org/https://doi.org/10.1016/j.lcsi.2022.100657. DOI: 10.1016/j.lcsi.2022.100657

Kolluru, V., Mungara, S., & Chintakunta, A. N. (2018). Adaptive learning systems: Harnessing AI for customized educational experiences. [IJCSITY]. *International Journal of Computer Science and Information Technologies*, 6(1), 2. DOI: 10.5121/ijcsity.2018.6302

Konaklı, T., & Akdeniz, R. K. (2022). The emergence, reasons and results of resistance to change in teachers. *International Journal on Lifelong Education and Leadership*, 8(1), 1–19. DOI: 10.25233/ijlel.1107137

Kooli, C. (2023). Chatbots in education and research: A critical examination of ethical implications and solutions. *Sustainability (Basel)*, 15(7), 5614. DOI: 10.3390/su15075614

Koonce, B., & Koonce, B. (2021). EfficientNet. *Convolutional neural networks with swift for Tensorflow: image recognition and dataset categorization*, 109-123. 1913-1920.

Koos, S., & Wachsmann, S. (2023). Navigating the impact of ChatGPT/GPT4 on legal academic examinations: Challenges, opportunities and recommendations. *Media Iuris*, 6(2), 255–270. DOI: 10.20473/mi.v6i2.45270

Kordzadeh, N., & Ghasemaghaei, M. (2022). Algorithmic bias: Review, synthesis, and future research directions. *European Journal of Information Systems*, 31(3), 388–409. DOI: 10.1080/0960085X.2021.1927212

Koroteev, M. V. (2021). BERT: a review of applications in natural language processing and understanding. *arXiv preprint arXiv:2103*. https://doi.org//arXiv.2103.11943DOI: 10.48550

Kot, S. O., & Nykyporets, S. S. (2024). *Utilization of artificial intelligence in enhancing English language proficiency in tertiary education. Science and Education in the Third Millennium: Information Technology*. Education, Law, Psychology, Social Sphere, Management.

Krisshna, N. A., Deepak, V. K., Manikantan, K., & Ramachandran, S. (2014). Face recognition using transform domain feature extraction and PSO-based feature selection. *Applied Soft Computing*, 22, 141–161. DOI: 10.1016/j.asoc.2014.05.007

Kritikos, M., & Iphofen, R. (2023). A Human in the Loop Approach/Human Oversight. In Iphofen, R. (Ed.), *Ethical AI Surveillance in the Workplace* (Vol. 10, pp. 67–68). Emerald Publishing Limited., DOI: 10.1108/S2398-601820230000010028

Kromydas, T. (2017). Rethinking higher education and its relationship with social inequalities: Past knowledge, present state and future potential. *Palgrave Communications*, 3(1), 1–12. DOI: 10.1057/s41599-017-0001-8

Kucirkova, N., & Leaton Gray, S. (2023). Beyond Personalization: Embracing Democratic Learning Within Artificially Intelligent Systems. *Educational Theory*, 73(4), 469–489. DOI: 10.1111/edth.12590

Kuleto, V., Ilić, M., Dumangiu, M., Ranković, M., Martins, O. M., Păun, D., & Mihoreanu, L. (2021). Exploring opportunities and challenges of artificial intelligence and machine learning in higher education institutions. *Sustainability (Basel)*, 13(18), 10424. DOI: 10.3390/su131810424

Kulhavy, R. W. (1977). Feedback in written instruction. *Review of Educational Research*, 47(2), 211–232. DOI: 10.3102/00346543047002211

Kumar, A., & Silva, E. (2020). AI in education: Enhancing learning experiences through technology. *British Journal of Educational Technology*, 51(4), 1111–1130. DOI: 10.1111/bjet.12946

Kumar, A., Verma, S., & Kumar, P. (2023). Coalition formation games for load balancing in large-scale distributed systems. *IEEE Transactions on Parallel and Distributed Systems*, 34(5), 1567–1579.

Kumar, V. V. R., & Raman, R. (2022). *Student perceptions on Artificial Intelligence (AI) in higher education.2022 IEEE Integrated STEM Education Conference*. ISEC., DOI: 10.1109/ISEC54952.2022.10025165

Kurniawan, T. T. (2021). Development of 4C-Based Hots Assessment To Improve Critical Thinking Skills in Grade 6 Students of Kudus Elementary School. [Pendidikan Dan Pengajaran]. *JURNAL PAJAR*, 5(3), 675–683. DOI: 10.33578/pjr.v5i3.8319

Kwapinska, M. (2024). AI in education: Benefits, challenges, and use cases. Retrieved from- https://www.nomtek.com/blog/ai-in-education

Lacatus, M. L., & Staiculescu, M. (2016). Entrepreneurship in education. *International Conference Knowledge-Based Organization, 22*(2). https://doi.org/DOI: 10.1515/kbo-2016-0075

Lackéus, M. (2015). *Entrepreneurship in education: What, why, when, how*. OECD Publishing., Retrieved from https://www.oecd.org/cfe/leed/BGP_Entrepreneurship-in-Education.pdf

Lahiassi, J., Elwarraki, O., Aammou, S., & Jdidou, Y. (2024). Pedagogical Innovations in Personalized Learning. In *Fostering Pedagogical Innovation Through Effective Instructional Design* (pp. 329–341). IGI Global., DOI: 10.4018/979-8-3693-1206-3.ch015

Lang, J. M. (2021). *Small teaching: Everyday lessons from the science of learning*. John Wiley & Sons.

Lau, K. W., & Wu, Q. H. (2003). Online training of support vector classifier. *Pattern Recognition*, 36(8), 1913–1920. DOI: 10.1016/S0031-3203(03)00038-4

Law, L. (2024). Application of generative artificial intelligence (GenAI) in language teaching and learning: A scoping literature review. *Computers and Education Open*, 6, 100174. DOI: 10.1016/j.caeo.2024.100174

LearnDash Collaborator. (2018, November 14). *4 Ways Machine Learning Can Improve Online Education*. https://www.learndash.com/4-ways-machine-learning-can-improve-online-education/

Lee, S., & Choi, J. (2023). Dynamic content adaptation for resource-efficient cloud-based learning. *Educational Technology Research and Development*, 71(2), 789–805. PMID: 36533222

Lee, Y. J. (2020). The long-term effect of automated writing evaluation feedback on writing development. *English Teaching*, 75(1), 67–92. DOI: 10.15858/engtea.75.1.202003.67

Lepori, B. (2022). The heterogeneity of European Higher Education Institutions: A configurational approach. *Studies in Higher Education*, 47(9), 1827–1843. DOI: 10.1080/03075079.2021.1968368

Leslie, D., Burr, C., Aitken, M., Cowls, J., Katell, M., & Briggs, M. (2021). Artificial intelligence, human rights, democracy, and the rule of law: a primer. arXiv preprint arXiv:2104.04147.

Liang, J. K., Eccarius, T., & Lu, C. C. (2019). Investigating factors that affect the intention to use shared parking: A case study of Taipei City. *Transportation Research Part A, Policy and Practice*, 130, 799–812. DOI: 10.1016/j.tra.2019.10.006

Liang, W. (2020). *Development Trend and Thinking of Artificial Intelligence in Education. 2020 International Wireless Communications and Mobile Computing*. IWCMC., DOI: 10.1109/IWCMC48107.2020.9148078

Li, C., He, L., & Wong, I. A. (2021). Determinants predicting undergraduates' intention to adopt e-learning for studying english in chinese higher education context: A structural equation modelling approach. *Education and Information Technologies*, 26(4), 4221–4239. DOI: 10.1007/s10639-021-10462-x

Liesa-Orús, M., Latorre-Cosculluela, C., Sierra-Sánchez, V., & Vázquez-Toledo, S. (2023). Links between ease of use, perceived usefulness and attitudes towards technology in older people in university: A structural equation modelling approach. *Education and Information Technologies*, 28(3), 2419–2436. DOI: 10.1007/s10639-022-11292-1 PMID: 35996745

Li, F., He, Y., & Xue, Q. (2021). Progress, challenges and countermeasures of adaptive learning. *Journal of Educational Technology & Society*, 24(3), 238–255. https://www.jstor.org/stable/27032868

Li, J., & He, Y. (2023). Unpacking "Double Reduction" Policy in China: Ideas, Values, and Practices. *Beijing International Review of Education*, 5(3), 337–341. DOI: 10.1163/25902539-05030009

Li, L., & Gao, F. (2016). The effect of peer assessment on project performance of students at different learning levels. *Assessment & Evaluation in Higher Education*, 41(6), 885–900. DOI: 10.1080/02602938.2015.1048185

Lim, W. M., Gunasekara, A., Pallant, J. L., Pallant, J. I., & Pechenkina, E. (2023). Generative AI and the future of education: Ragnarök or reformation? A paradoxical perspective from management educators. *International Journal of Management Education*, 21(2), 100790. https://doi.org/https://doi.org/10.1016/j.ijme.2023.100790. DOI: 10.1016/j.ijme.2023.100790

Lin, P. H., & Chen, S. Y. (2020). Design and evaluation of a deep learning recommendation based augmented reality system for teaching programming and computational thinking. *IEEE Access : Practical Innovations, Open Solutions*, 8, 45689–45699. DOI: 10.1109/ACCESS.2020.2977679

Lin, Y., Luo, Q., & Qian, Y. (2023). Investigation of Artificial Intelligence algorithms in education. *Applied and Computational Engineering*, 16(1), 180–184. DOI: 10.54254/2755-2721/16/20230886

Lin, Y., & Yu, Z. (2023). Extending Technology Acceptance Model to higher-education students' use of digital academic reading tools on computers. *International Journal of Educational Technology in Higher Education*, 20(1), 34. DOI: 10.1186/s41239-023-00403-8

Liu, B. (2021). "Weak AI" is Likely to Never Become "Strong AI", So What is its Greatest Value for us? *Arxiv*. https://arxiv.org/pdf/2103.15294

Liu, J., Kong, X., Xia, F., Bai, X., Wang, L., Qing, Q., & Lee, I. (2018). Artificial intelligence in the 21st century. *IEEE Access : Practical Innovations, Open Solutions*, 6, 34403–34421. DOI: 10.1109/ACCESS.2018.2819688

Liu, Y., Li, Y., Yang, S., Ren, T., Li, H., Hogg, A., Shah, P., Li, J., Zhang, Y., & Chhetri, A. (2022). A hybrid and non-formal music education connecting China's local family communities and cultures with Nepal. [IJI]. *International Journal for Infonomics*, 15(1), 2088–2093. Advance online publication. DOI: 10.20533/iji.1742.4712.2022.0218

Liu, Z.. (2020). The role of perceived ease of use in the acceptance of AI writing tools among students. *Computers & Education*, 158, 103983. DOI: 10.1016/j.compedu.2020.103983

Li, X., & Patel, R. (2022). Reinforcement learning for optimal content sequencing in online courses. In *Proceedings of the ACM Conference on Learning at Scale* (pp. 267-276).

Li, X., Wang, S., Li, J., & Li, Z. (2024). A Study of Artificial Intelligence-Assisted Teaching on the Cultivation of Students' Creative Ability. *Applied Mathematics and Nonlinear Sciences*, 9(1), 1–18. DOI: 10.2478/amns.2023.2.01283

Lombard, M., Snyder-Duch, J., & Campanella Bracken, C. (2005). *Practical resources for assessing and reporting intercoder reliability in content analysis research projects*. Retrieved from https://www.researchgate.net/publication/242785900_Practical_Resources_for_Assessing_and_Reporting_Intercoder_Reliability_in_Content_Analysis_Research_Projects

Longhurst, R. (2009). Interviews: In-depth, semi-structured. In *International encyclopedia of human geography* (pp. 580–584). https://doi.org/DOI: 10.1016/B978-008044910-4.00458-2

López-Chila, R., Llerena-Izquierdo, J., Sumba-Nacipucha, N., & Cueva-Estrada, J. (2023). Artificial Intelligence in Higher Education: An Analysis of Existing Bibliometrics. *Education Sciences*, 14(1), 47. DOI: 10.3390/educsci14010047

Lorigo, L. M., & Govindaraju, V. (2006). Offline Arabic handwriting recognition: A survey. *IEEE Transactions on Pattern Analysis and Machine Intelligence*, 28(5), 712–724. DOI: 10.1109/TPAMI.2006.102 PMID: 16640258

Luan, H., Geczy, P., Lai, H., Gobert, J., Yang, S. J., Ogata, H., Baltes, J., Guerra, R., Li, P., & Tsai, C. C. (2020). Challenges and future directions of big data and artificial intelligence in education. *Frontiers in Psychology*, 11, 580820. DOI: 10.3389/fpsyg.2020.580820 PMID: 33192896

Luckin, R., & Holmes, W. (2016). Intelligence unleashed: An argument for AI in education. https://discovery.ucl.ac.uk/id/eprint/1475756/

Luckin, R., & Holmes, W. (2016). *Intelligence unleashed: An argument for AI in education*. Pearson.https://www.researchgate.net/publication/299561597_Intelligence_Unleashed_An_argument_for_AI_in_Education

Luckin, R., Holmes, W., Griffiths, M., & Forcier, L. B. (2016). Intelligence unleashed: An argument for AI in education. Pearson Education. https://www.pearson.com/content/dam/one-dot-com/one-dot-com/global/Files/about-pearson/innovation/open-ideas/Intelligence_Unleashed_Pearson.pdf

Luckin, R., Holmes, W., Griffiths, M., & Forcier, L. B. "Intelligence unleashed." *An argument for AI in Education 18* (2016). https://www.pearson.com/corporate/about-pearson/what-we-do/innovation/smarter-digital-tools/intelligence-unleashed.html

Luckin, R., Cukurova, M., Kent, C., & Du Boulay, B. (2022). Empowering educators to be AI-ready. *Computers and Education: Artificial Intelligence*, 3, 100076. DOI: 10.1016/j.caeai.2022.100076

Luckin, R., & Holmes, W. (2016). *Intelligence unleashed: An argument for AI in education*. Pearson.

Luna Scott, C. (2015). The futures of learning 2: What kind of learning for the 21st century?.

Luo, S. (2019). Research on the change of educational management in the era of artificial intelligence. In *Proceedings of the 2019 12th International Conference on Intelligent Computation Technology and Automation (ICICTA)*. https://doi.org/ DOI: 10.1109/ICICTA49267.2019.00101

Lynam, S., & Cachia, M. (2018). 2018 "Students' perceptions of the role of assessments at higher education,". *Assessment & Evaluation in Higher Education*, 43(2), 223–234. DOI: 10.1080/02602938.2017.1329928

Madi, J., Al Khasawneh, M., & Dandis, A. O. (2024). Visiting and revisiting destinations: Impact of augmented reality, content quality, perceived ease of use, perceived value and usefulness on E-WOM. *International Journal of Quality & Reliability Management*, 41(6), 1550–1571. DOI: 10.1108/IJQRM-10-2023-0314

Maghsudi, S., Lan, A., Xu, J., & van Der Schaar, M. (2021). Personalized education in the artificial intelligence era: What to expect next. *IEEE Signal Processing Magazine*, 38(3), 37–50. DOI: 10.1109/MSP.2021.3055032

Maguire, M., & Delahunt, B. (2017). Doing a thematic analysis: A practical, step-by-step guide for learning and teaching scholars. *All Ireland Journal of Teaching and Learning in Higher Education (AISHE-J), 9*(3). Retrieved from https://ojs.aishe.org/index.php/aishe-j/article/view/335

Malik, A., & Aslam, M. U. (May 2024). *Reimagining Teaching: Exploring Challenges of Generative AI Integration in Education.*https://www.researchgate.net/publication/380365121

Malik, G., Tayal, D. K., & Vij, S. (2018). An analysis of the role of artificial intelligence in education and teaching. In P. K. Sa, S. Sahni, B. B. Gupta, & S. P. Singh (Eds.), *Recent findings in intelligent computing techniques* (Advances in Intelligent Systems and Computing, Vol. 707, pp. 421–429). Springer Nature. https://doi.org/ DOI: 10.1007/978-981-10-8639-7_42

Malik, R., Shrama, A., Trivedi, S., & Mishra, R. (2021). Adoption of chatbots for learning among university students: Role of perceived convenience and enhanced performance. [iJET]. *International Journal of Emerging Technologies in Learning*, 16(18), 200–212. Retrieved August 10, 2024, from https://www.learntechlib.org/p/220124/. DOI: 10.3991/ijet.v16i18.24315

Man, T. W. Y. (2010). *Clarifying the domain of educational entrepreneurship: Implications for studying leadership, innovation and change.* The Hong Kong Institute of Education. Retrieved fromhttps://www.eduhk.hk/apclc/roundtable2010/paper/Clarifying%20Educational%20Entrepreneurship-Thomas%20Wing%20Yan%20MAN.pdf

Mandal, R., & Mete, J. (2023). Teachers' and students' perception towards integration of Artificial Intelligence in school curriculum: A survey. *International journal of multidisciplinary educational research, 127*(5), 95-103.

Manna, M. S., Balusamy, B., Sood, K., Chilamkurti, N., & George, I. R. (Eds.). (2022). Edutech Enabled Teaching: Challenges and Opportunities. DOI:DOI: 10.1201/9781003254942

Mao, J., Chen, B., & Liu, J. C. (2024). Generative artificial intelligence in education and its implications for assessment. *TechTrends*, 68(1), 58–66. DOI: 10.1007/s11528-023-00911-4

Maphoto, K. B., Sevnarayan, K., Mohale, N. E., Suliman, Z., Ntsopi, T. J., & Mokoena, D. (2024). Advancing students' academic excellence in distance education: Exploring the potential of generative AI integration to improve academic writing skills. *Open Praxis*, 16(2), 142–159. DOI: 10.55982/openpraxis.16.2.649

Marangunić, N., & Granić, A. (2015). Technology acceptance model: A literature review from 1986 to 2013. *Universal Access in the Information Society*, 14(1), 81–95. DOI: 10.1007/s10209-014-0348-1

Marantika, J. E. R. (2021). Metacognitive ability and autonomous learning strategy in improving learning outcomes. [EduLearn]. *Journal of Education and Learning*, 15(1), 88–96. https://eric.ed.gov/?id=EJ1299455

Marcelli, A., Parziale, A., & Santoro, A. (2012, September). Modeling handwriting style: a preliminary investigation. In *2012 International Conference on Frontiers in Handwriting Recognition* (pp. 411-416). IEEE. DOI: 10.1109/ICFHR.2012.234

Marcus, G., & Davi, E. (2019). *Rebooting AI: Building Artificial Intelligence we can trust. Vintage*. Pantheon Books.

Markauskaite, L., Marrone, R., Poquet, O., Knight, S., Martinez-Maldonado, R., Howard, S., & Siemens, G. (2022). Rethinking the entwinement between artificial intelligence and human learning: What capabilities do learners need for a world with AI? *Computers and Education: Artificial Intelligence*, 3, 100056. DOI: 10.1016/j.caeai.2022.100056

Marks, A., & AL-Ali, M. (2020). Digital transformation in higher education: A framework for maturity assessment. [IJACSA]. *International Journal of Advanced Computer Science and Applications*, 11(12), 504–513. DOI: 10.14569/IJACSA.2020.0111261

Marrone, R., Taddeo, V., & Hill, G. (2022). Creativity and artificial intelligence—A student perspective. *Journal of Intelligence*, 10(3), 65. DOI: 10.3390/jintelligence10030065 PMID: 36135606

Martinez, D., Malyska, N., Streilein, B., Caceres, R., Campbell, W., Dagli, C., Gadepally, V., Greenfeld, K., Hall, R., King, A., Lippmann, R., Miller, B., Reynolds, D., Richardson, F., Sahin, C., Tran, A., Trepagnier, P., & Zipkin, J. (2019). *Artifcial intelligence: Short history, present developments, and future outlook*. Massachusetts Institute of Technology.

Martin, K. (2019). Designing ethical algorithms. *MIS Quarterly Executive*, 18(5), 2. https://aisel.aisnet.org/misqe/vol18/iss2/5/

Marwan, A. (2020). Impact of artificial intelligence on education for employment:(learning and employability Framework).

Marzuki, W., Widiati, U., Rusdin, D., Darwin, , & Indrawati, I. (2023). The impact of AI writing tools on the content and organization of students' writing: EFL teachers' perspective. *Cogent Education*, 10(2), 2236469. DOI: 10.1080/2331186X.2023.2236469

Masino, S., & Niño-Zarazúa, M. (2016). What works to improve the quality of student learning in developing countries? *International Journal of Educational Development*, 48, 53–65. https://doi.org/https://doi.org/10.1016/j.ijedudev.2015.11.012. DOI: 10.1016/j.ijedudev.2015.11.012

Mateus, J. C., Cappello, G., Lugo, N., & Guerrero-Pico, M. (2024). Communication Educators Facing the Arrival of Generative Artificial Intelligence: Exploration in Mexico, Peru, and Spain. *Digital Education Review*, (45), 106–114. DOI: 10.1344/der.2024.45.106-114

McCalla, G. (2023). The history of artificial intelligence in education–the first quarter century. In *Handbook of artificial intelligence in education* (pp. 10–29). Edward Elgar Publishing. DOI: 10.4337/9781800375413.00010

McCarthy, J., Feigenbaum, E., & Lederberg, J. (1973). *Artificial Intelligence Project* (No. 4).Progress Report.

McCarthy, J., Minsky, M. L., Rochester, N., & Shannon, C. E. (1955). *A proposal for the Dartmouth summer research project on artificial intelligence*. Stanford University. Retrieved from http://www-formal.stanford.edu/jmc/history/dartmouth/dartmouth.html

McNatt, B. (2020). Service-learning: An experiment to increase interpersonal communication confidence and competence. *Education – Training*, 62(2), 129–144. DOI: 10.1108/ET-02-2019-0039

Mehdaoui, A. (2024). Unveiling barriers and challenges of AI technology integration in education: Assessing teachers' perceptions, readiness, and anticipated resistance. *Futurity Education*, 4(4), 95–103. DOI: 10.57125/FED.2024.12.25.06

Melas, C. D., Zampetakis, L. A., Dimopoulou, A., & Moustakis, V. (2011). Modeling the acceptance of clinical information systems among hospital medical staff: An extended TAM model. *Journal of Biomedical Informatics*, 44(4), 553–564. DOI: 10.1016/j.jbi.2011.01.009 PMID: 21292029

Mercader, C., & Gairín, J. (2020). University teachers' perception of barriers to the use of digital technologies: The importance of the academic discipline. *International Journal of Educational Technology in Higher Education*, 17(4), 1–14. DOI: 10.1186/s41239-020-0182-x

Merhi, M. I., & Meisami, A. (2024). Boosting Students' Engagement with Web-Based Assessment Platforms: A Self-Determination Theory Perspective. *AIS Transactions on Human-Computer Interaction*, 16(2), 216–236. DOI: 10.17705/1thci.00205

Messer, M., Brown, N. C., Kölling, M., & Shi, M. (2024). Automated grading and feedback tools for programming education: A systematic review. *ACM Transactions on Computing Education*, 24(1), 1–43. DOI: 10.1145/3636515

Miao, F., Holmes, W., Huang, R., & Zhang, H. (2021). *AI and education: A guidance for policymakers*. Unesco Publishing.

Miao, F., Zhang, Q., & Yan, J. (2023). Exploring the Effectiveness of Individualized Learning Trajectories in University Smart Sports Education Classrooms: A Design and Implementation Study. *Journal of Social Science Humanities and Literature*, 6(5), 67–73. DOI: 10.53469/jsshl.2023.06(05).10

Michel-Villarreal, R., Vilalta-Perdomo, E., Salinas-Navarro, D. E., Thierry-Aguilera, R., & Gerardou, F. S. (2023). Challenges and opportunities of generative AI for higher education as explained by ChatGPT. *Education Sciences*, 13(9), 856. DOI: 10.3390/educsci13090856

Mikalef, P., Lemmer, K., Schaefer, C., Ylinen, M., Fjørtoft, S. O., Torvatn, H. Y., Gupta, M., & Niehaves, B. (2023). Examining how AI capabilities can foster organizational performance in public organizations. *Government Information Quarterly*, 40(2), 101797. DOI: 10.1016/j.giq.2022.101797

Miles, D. T., & Robinson, R. E. (1969). *General planning framework for general teaching model*. Retrieved from https://www.homeofbob.com/pedagogy/plan/generalTeachingModel.html#:~:text=A%20general%20teaching%20model%20is,any%20length%20of%20instructional%20time

Miller, J., & Khera, O. (2010). Digital library adoption and the technology acceptance model: A cross-country analysis. *The Electronic Journal on Information Systems in Developing Countries*, 40(1), 1–19. DOI: 10.1002/j.1681-4835.2010.tb00288.x

Mishra, P., & Mehta, R. (2017). Educators What We Get Wrong About 21st-Century Learning: Results of a Survey. *Journal of Digital Learning in Teacher Education*, 33(1), 6–19. DOI: 10.1080/21532974.2016.1242392

Mislevy, R. J., Yan, D., Gobert, J., & Sao Pedro, M. (2020). Automated scoring in intelligent tutoring systems. In *Handbook of automated scoring* (pp. 403–422). Chapman and Hall/CRC. DOI: 10.1201/9781351264808-22

Modi, T. B. (2023). Artificial Intelligence Ethics and Fairness: A study to address bias and fairness issues in AI systems, and the ethical implications of AI applications. *Revista Review Index Journal of Multidisciplinary*, 3(2), 24–35. DOI: 10.31305/rrijm2023.v03.n02.004

Mohamed Hashim, M. A., Tlemsani, I., & Matthews, R. (2022). Higher education strategy in digital transformation. *Education and Information Technologies*, 27(3), 3171–3195. DOI: 10.1007/s10639-021-10739-1 PMID: 34539217

Mohammed, F. S., & Ozdamli, F. (2024). A Systematic Literature Review of Soft Skills in Information Technology Education. *Behavioral Sciences (Basel, Switzerland)*, 14(10), 894. DOI: 10.3390/bs14100894 PMID: 39457766

Mohd Rahim, N. I., & Iahad, A., N., Yusof, A. F., & A. Al-Sharafi, M. (. (2022). AI-based chatbots adoption model for higher-education institutions: A hybrid PLS-SEM-neural network modelling approach. *Sustainability*, 14(19), 12726. DOI: 10.3390/su141912726

Molefi, R. R., Ayanwale, M. A., Kurata, L., & Chere-Masopha, J. (2024). Do in-service teachers accept artificial intelligence-driven technology? The mediating role of school support and resources. *Computers and Education Open*, 6, 100191. DOI: 10.1016/j.caeo.2024.100191

Monat, J. P., & Gannon, T. F. (2018). Two professors' experience with competency-based education. *The Journal of Competency-Based Education*, 3(2), e01061. DOI: 10.1002/cbe2.1061

Montagner, I. S. (2019, October). An experience with peer assessment in the context of a Computer Systems course. In *2019 IEEE Frontiers in Education Conference (FIE)* (pp. 1-5). IEEE.

Morduchowicz, A., & Suasnábar, J. (2023). ChatGPT and Education: Op portunity, Challenge, or Threat? Retrieved from https://blogs.iadb.org/educacion/en/chatgpt-education/

Morreale, Sherwyn P., Joseph M. Valenzano, and Janessa A. Bauer. (2017). Why Communication Education Is Important: A Third Study on the Centrality of the Discipline's Content and Pedagogy. *Communication Education* 66: 402–22. https://doi.org/. 1265136. DOI: 10.1080/03634523.2016

Morze, N., Varchenko-Trotsenko, L., Terletska, T., & Smyrnova-Trybulska, E. (2021, March). Implementation of adaptive learning at higher education institutions by means of Moodle LMS. [). IOP Publishing.]. *Journal of Physics: Conference Series*, 1840(1), 012062. DOI: 10.1088/1742-6596/1840/1/012062

Moses, J. (2012). Macsyma: A personal history. *Journal of Symbolic Computation*, 47(2), 123–130. DOI: 10.1016/j.jsc.2010.08.018

Mosleh, S. M., Alsaadi, F. A., Alnaqbi, F. K., Alkhzaimi, M. A., Alnaqbi, S. W., & Alsereidi, W. M. (2024). Examining the association between emotional intelligence and chatbot utilization in education: A cross-sectional examination of undergraduate students in the UAE. *Heliyon*, 10(11), e31952. Advance online publication. DOI: 10.1016/j.heliyon.2024.e31952 PMID: 38868023

Mouta, A., Torrecilla-Sánchez, E. M., & Pinto-Llorente, A. M. (2024). Design of a future scenarios toolkit for an ethical implementation of artificial intelligence in education. *Education and Information Technologies*, 29(9), 10473–10498. DOI: 10.1007/s10639-023-12229-y

Muijsenberg, A. J., Houben-Wilke, S., Zeng, Y., Spruit, M. A., & Janssen, D. J. (2023). Methods to assess adults' learning styles and factors affecting learning in health education: A scoping review. *Patient Education and Counseling*, 107, 107588. DOI: 10.1016/j.pec.2022.107588 PMID: 36502561

Munien, C., & Viriri, S. (2021). Classification of hematoxylin and eosin-stained breast cancer histology microscopy images using transfer learning with EfficientNets. *Computational Intelligence and Neuroscience*, 2021(1), 5580914. DOI: 10.1155/2021/5580914 PMID: 33897774

Murdoch, B. (2021). Privacy and artificial intelligence: Challenges for protecting health information in a new era. *BMC Medical Ethics*, 22(1), 1–5. DOI: 10.1186/s12910-021-00687-3 PMID: 34525993

Murphy, R. F. (2019). *Artificial Intelligence Applications to Support K-12 Teachers and Teaching: A Review of Promising Applications, Opportunities, and Challenges. Perspective*. RAND Corporation.

Murtaza, M., Ahmed, Y., Shamsi, J. A., Sherwani, F., & Usman, M. (2022). AI-based personalized e-learning systems: Issues, challenges, and solutions. *IEEE Access : Practical Innovations, Open Solutions*, 10, 81323–81342. DOI: 10.1109/ACCESS.2022.3193938

Musoke, G. G., & Badru, M. (2018). Educational entrepreneurship (EE): Delineating and highlighting its domain, importance, and feasibility in Uganda's context. [Edu-Learn]. *Journal of Education and Learning*, 12(1), 126–136. https://www.researchgate.net/publication/324236127_Educational_Entrepreneurship_EE_Delineating_and_Highlighting_Its_Domain_Importance_and_Feasibility_in_Uganda's_Context

Myers, A. (2023). Provocations and possibilities: Stanford seminar examines the future of ChatGPT in education. Retrieved from https://acceleratelearning.stanford.edu/story/provocations-and-possibilitiesstanford-seminar-examines-the-future-of-chatgpt-in-education/]

Nagao, K., & Nagao, K. (2019). Artificial intelligence in education. *Artificial Intelligence Accelerates Human Learning: Discussion Data Analytics*, 1-17.

Nainggolan, O. T. P., Salim, D., Prasetiyo, A., & Marthien, V. A. (2020,). Integrating the Framework of 21st Century Learning (4C) into Creative Music Learning. *1st International Conference on Interdisciplinary Arts and Humanities*. https://doi.org/ DOI: 10.5220/0008562602340239

Nakashima, H. H., Mantovani, D., & Machado, C.Junior. (2024). Users' trust in black-box machine learning algorithms. *Revista de Gestão*, 31(2), 237–250. DOI: 10.1108/REGE-06-2022-0100

Namjoo, F., Liaghat, E., Shabaziasl, S., Modabernejad, Z., & Morshedi, H. (2023). Students Experience on Self-Study through AI. *AI and Tech in Behavioral and Social Sciences*, 1(3), 35–42. DOI: 10.61838/kman.aitech.1.3.6

Nanni, A. (2021). Educational entrepreneurship in an intensive English program in Thailand: A case study. *SAGE Open*, 11(1), 2158244021998694. Advance online publication. DOI: 10.1177/2158244021998694

Naqvi, A. (2020). *Artificial intelligence for audit, forensic accounting, and valuation: a strategic perspective*. John Wiley &Sons. DOI: 10.1002/9781119601906

Narciss, S. (2008). Feedback strategies for interactive learning tasks. *Handbook of research on educational communications and technology/Erlbaum.*

Naseer, F., Khalid, M. U., Ayub, N., Rasool, A., Abbas, T., & Afzal, M. W. (2024). Automated Assessment and Feedback in Higher Education Using Generative AI. In *Transforming Education With Generative AI: Prompt Engineering and Synthetic Content Creation* (pp. 433-461). IGI Global. DOI: DOI: 10.4018/979-8-3693-1351-0.ch021

Nawaz, N., Gomes, A. M., & Saldeen, M. A. (2020). Artificial intelligence (AI) applications for library services and resources in COVID-19 pandemic. *Journal of Critical Reviews*, 7(18), 1951–1955. https://www.researchgate.net/publication/342865777_Artificial_intelligence_AI_applications_for_library_services_and_resources_in_COVID-19_pandemic

NEA. (2010). Preparing 21st Century Students for a Global Society: An Educator's Guide to 'The Four Cs'. Washington DC, National Education Association. www.nea.org/ tools/52217. Htm

Neffati, O. S., Setiawan, R., Jayanthi, P., Vanithamani, S., Sharma, D. K., Regin, R., & Sengan, S. (2021). An educational tool for enhanced mobile e-Learning for technical higher education using mobile devices for augmented reality. *Microprocessors and Microsystems*, 83, 104030. Advance online publication. DOI: 10.1016/j.micpro.2021.104030

Neo, M. (2022). THE MERLIN PROJECT: MALAYSIAN STUDENTS'ACCEPTANCE OF AN AI CHATBOT IN THEIR LEARNING PROCESS. *Turkish Online Journal of Distance Education*, 23(3), 31–48. DOI: 10.17718/tojde.1137122

Newborn, M., & Newborn, M. (2003). *Deep Blue: an artificial intelligence milestone*. Springer Science & Business Media. DOI: 10.1007/978-0-387-21790-1

Newell, A., & Simon, H. (1956). The logic theory machine—A complex information processing system. *IEEE Transactions on Information Theory*, 2(3), 61–79. DOI: 10.1109/TIT.1956.1056797

Ng, D. T. K., Lee, M., Tan, R. J. Y., Hu, X., Downie, J. S., & Chu, S. K. W. (2023). A review of AI teaching and learning from 2000 to 2020. *Education and Information Technologies*, 28(7), 8445–8501. DOI: 10.1007/s10639-022-11491-w

Nguyen, N. (2023). Opportunities and challenges of AI in higher education. https://feedbackfruits.com/blog/opportunities-and-challenges-of-ai-in-higher-education

Nguyen, T. T., Thuan, H. T., & Nguyen, M. T. (2023). Artificial Intelligent (AI) in teaching and learning: A comprehensive review. ISTES BOOKS, 140-161.

Nguyen, A., Ngo, H. N., Hong, Y., Dang, B., & Nguyen, B. P. T. (2023). Ethical principles for artificial intelligence in education. *Education and Information Technologies*, 28(4), 4221–4241. DOI: 10.1007/s10639-022-11316-w PMID: 36254344

Nguyen, N. D. (2023). Exploring the role of AI in education. *London Journal of Social Sciences*, (6), 84–95. DOI: 10.31039/ljss.2023.6.108

Nikou, S. A., & Economides, A. A. (2016). The impact of paper-based, computer-based and mobile-based self-assessment on students' science motivation and achievement. *Computers in Human Behavior*, 55, 1241–1248. DOI: 10.1016/j.chb.2015.09.025

Noda, I., Suzuki, J. S., Matsubara, H., Asada, M., & Kitano, H. (1998). RoboCup-97: The first robot world cup soccer games and conferences. *AI Magazine*, 19(3), 49–49.

Novelli, C., Taddeo, M., & Floridi, L. (2023). Accountability in artificial intelligence: What it is and how it works. *AI & Society*, •••, 1–12. DOI: 10.1007/s00146-023-01635-y

Nowell, L. S., Norris, J. M., White, D. E., & Moules, N. J. (2017). Thematic analysis: Striving to meet the trustworthiness criteria. *International Journal of Qualitative Methods*, 16(1), 1609406917733847. Advance online publication. DOI: 10.1177/1609406917733847

Nuha, M. F. A. U., Muklason, A., & Agustiawan, Y. (2024). Enhancing Administrative Efficiency in Pondok Pesantren: Exploring the Acceptance of E-Santren App System for Administrative Tasks. *Procedia Computer Science*, 234, 795–804. DOI: 10.1016/j.procs.2024.03.096

Nye, B. D. (2015). Intelligent tutoring systems by and for the developing world: A review of trends and approaches for educational technology in a global context. *International Journal of Artificial Intelligence in Education*, 25(2), 177–203. DOI: 10.1007/s40593-014-0028-6

O'bannon, B. W., & Thomas, K. (2014). Teacher perceptions of using mobile phones in the classroom: Age matters! *Computers & Education*, 74, 15–25. DOI: 10.1016/j.compedu.2014.01.006

O'Connor, C., & Joffe, H. (2020). Intercoder reliability in qualitative research: Debates and practical guidelines. *International Journal of Qualitative Methods*, 19, 1–13. DOI: 10.1177/1609406919899220

Obaid, A. J., Bhushan, B., & Rajest, S. S. (Eds.). (2023). *Advanced applications of generative AI and natural language processing models*. IGI Global. DOI: 10.4018/979-8-3693-0502-7

Obenza, B. N., Salvahan, A., Rios, A. N., Solo, A., Alburo, R. A., & Gabila, R. J. (2023). University students' perception and use of ChatGPT: Generative Artificial Intelligence (AI) in higher education. *International Journal of Human-Computer Studies*, 5(12), 1–15. DOI: 10.5281/zenodo.10360697

OECD. (2018). Collaborative problem-solving. In The encyclopedia of social network analysis and mining, Vol. V. https://doi.org/DOI: 10.1007/978-1-4939-7131-2_100128

OECD. (2019). Future of Education and Skills 2030: A Series of Concept Notes. Paris: OECD Learning Compass. https://www.oecd.org/education/2030-project/teaching-and-learning/learning /learningcompass-2030/OECD_Learning_Compass_2030_Concept_Note_ Series.pdf

OECD/EU. (2019). Supporting entrepreneurship and innovation in higher education in Austria. OECD Skills Studies. OECD Publishing, Paris. https://doi.org/DOI: 10.1787/1c45127b-en

Ogunode, N. J., Idoko, G., & ThankGod, P. (2024). Artificial intelligence and implementation of educational administration and planning programme in Nigerian tertiary institutions. *International Journal of Academic Integrity and Curriculum Development, 1*(1), 41–47. Retrieved from https://academicajournal.com/IJAICD/article/view/13

Okonkwo, C. W., & Ade-Ibijola, A. O. (2021). Chatbots applications in education: A systematic review. *Computers & Education: Artificial Intelligence*, 2, 100033. DOI: 10.1016/j.caeai.2021.100033

Oktradiksa, A., Bhakti, C. P., Kurniawan, S. J., & Rahman, F. A. (2021, Ekim). Utilization artificial intelligence to improve creativity skills in society 5.0. *Journal of Physics: Conference Series*. IOP Publishing.

Oliveira, W., Hamari, J., Shi, L., Toda, A. M., Rodrigues, L., Palomino, P. T., & Isotani, S. (2023). Tailored gamification in education: A literature review and future agenda. *Education and Information Technologies*, 28(1), 373–406. DOI: 10.1007/s10639-022-11122-4

Open, A. I. (2023). ChatGPT: Optimizing Language Models for Dialogue Available at. https://openai.com/blog/chatgpt

Optimization and Scalability of Educational Platforms. (2023). *Integration of Artificial Intelligence and Cloud Computing*. MDPI Journal of Educational Technology and Society., DOI: 10.3390/educ-2023-01982.\

Oubibi, M., Zhou, Y., Oubibi, A., Fute, A., & Saleem, A. (2022). The challenges and opportunities for developing the use of data and artificial intelligence (AI) in North Africa: Case of Morocco. In *International Conference on Digital Technologies and Applications* (pp. 80–90). Cham: Springer International Publishing. https://doi.org/ DOI: 10.1007/978-3-031-02447-4_9

Ouyang, F., & Jiao, P. (2021). Artificial intelligence in education: The three paradigms. *Computers and Education: Artificial Intelligence*, 2, 100020. DOI: 10.1016/j.caeai.2021.100020

Ouyang, F., Wu, M., Zheng, L., Zhang, L., & Jiao, P. (2023). Integration of artificial intelligence performance prediction and learning analytics to improve student learning in online engineering course. *International Journal of Educational Technology in Higher Education*, 20(1), 4. DOI: 10.1186/s41239-022-00372-4 PMID: 36683653

Owan, V. J., Abang, K. B., Idika, D. O., Etta, E. O., & Bassey, B. A. (2023). Exploring the potential of artificial intelligence tools in educational measurement and assessment. *Eurasia Journal of Mathematics, Science and Technology Education*, 19(8), em2307. Advance online publication. DOI: 10.29333/ejmste/13428

Owoc, M. L., Sawicka, A., & Weichbroth, P. (2019, August). Artificial intelligence technologies in education: benefits, challenges and strategies of implementation. In *IFIP International Workshop on Artificial Intelligence for Knowledge Management* (pp. 37-58). Cham: Springer International Publishing.

Ozer, M., Kose, Y., Kucukkaya, G., Mukasheva, A., & Ciris, K. (2024). Adapting to the AI Disruption: Reshaping the IT Landscape and Educational Paradigms. arXiv preprint arXiv:2409.10541.

Ozturk, A. B., Bilgihan, A., Nusair, K., & Okumus, F. (2016). What keeps the mobile hotel booking users loyal? Investigating the roles of self-efficacy, compatibility, perceived ease of use, and perceived convenience. *International Journal of Information Management*, 36(6), 1350–1359. DOI: 10.1016/j.ijinfomgt.2016.04.005

Page, J., Bain, M., & Mukhlish, F. (2018). The risks of low level narrow artifcial intelligence. In 2018 IEEE international conference on intelligence and safety for robotics (ISR) (pp. 1-6). IEEE.

Palinkas, L. A., Horwitz, S. M., Green, C. A., Wisdom, J. P., Duan, N., & Hoagwood, K. (2013). Purposeful sampling for qualitative data collection and analysis in mixed method implementation research. *Administration and Policy in Mental Health*, 42(5), 533–544. DOI: 10.1007/s10488-013-0528-y PMID: 24193818

Pantelimon, F. V., Bologa, R., Toma, A., & Posedaru, B. S. (2021). The evolution of AI-driven educational systems during the COVID-19 pandemic. *Sustainability (Basel)*, 13(23), 13501. DOI: 10.3390/su132313501

Papamitsiou, Z., Lunde, M., Westermoen, J., & Giannakos, M. N. (2021). *"Supporting learners in a crisis context with smart self-assessment," in Radical Solutions for Education in a Crisis Context, Lecture Notes in Educational Technology*. Springer.

Park, E. S., & Park, M. S. (2020). Factors of the technology acceptance model for construction IT. *Applied Sciences (Basel, Switzerland)*, 10(22), 8299. DOI: 10.3390/app10228299

Park, J. S., Barber, R., Kirlik, A., & Karahalios, K. (2019). A slow algorithm improves users' assessments of the algorithm's accuracy. *Proceedings of the ACM on Human-Computer Interaction, 3*(CSCW), 1-15. DOI: 10.1145/3359204

Park, S. Y. (2009). An analysis of the technology acceptance model in understanding university students' behavioral intention to use e-learning. *Journal of Educational Technology & Society*, 12(3), 150–162. https://www.jstor.org/stable/jeductechsoci.12.3.150

Partnership for 21st Century Learning (P21). (2015). P21 framework definitions. http://www.p21.org/our-work/p21-framework

Pascale, B. (2023). 22. Time to Revisit Existing Student's Performance Evaluation Approach in Higher Education Sector in a New Era of ChatGPT — A Case Study. *Cogent Education*, 10(1), 2210461. Advance online publication. DOI: 10.1080/2331186X.2023.2210461

Passi, S., & Vorvoreanu, M. (2022). Overreliance on AI literature review. *Microsoft Research*. https://www.microsoft.com/en-us/research/uploads/prod/2022/06/Aether-Overreliance-on-AI-Review-Final-6.21.22.pdf

Patel, R., & Wong, S. (2023). 5G-enabled virtual and augmented reality in education: Opportunities and challenges. *Journal of Educational Technology Systems*, 52(1), 5–20.

Păvăloaia, V.-D., & Necula, S.-C. (2023). Artificial Intelligence as a Disruptive Technology—A Systematic Literature Review. *Electronics (Basel)*, 12(5), 1102. DOI: 10.3390/electronics12051102

Pavlik, J. V. (2023). Collaborating with ChatGPT: Considering the implications of generative artificial intelligence for journalism and media education. *Journalism & mass communication educator, 78*(1), 84-93. https://doi.org/. DOI: 10.1177/10776958221149577

Pearl, J. (1985). Bayesian networks: a model of self-activated memory for evidential reasoning. *In:Proceedings of the 7th conference of the cognitive science society*, 329–334.

Pearl, J. (1988). *Probabilistic reasoning in intelligent systems: networks of plausible inference*. Morgan Kaufmann.

Pedro, F., Subosa, M., Rivas, A., & Valverde, P. (2019). Artificial intelligence in education: Challenges and opportunities for sustainable development.

Peng, M. Y. P., Xu, Y., & Xu, C. (2023). Enhancing students' English language learning via M-learning: Integrating technology acceptance model and SOR model. *Heliyon*, 9(2), e13302. Advance online publication. DOI: 10.1016/j.heliyon.2023.e13302 PMID: 36755609

Pereira, D., Flores, M. A., & Niklasson, L. (2016). Assessment revisited: A review of research inAssessment and evaluation in higher education. *Assessment & Evaluation in Higher Education*, 41(7), 1008–1032. DOI: 10.1080/02602938.2015.1055233

Perera-Diltz, D. M., & Moe, J. L. (2014). Formative and summative assessment in online education. *Journal of Research in Innovative Teaching*, 7(1).

Perrotta, C., & Selwyn, N. (2019). Deep learning goes to school: Toward a relational understanding of AI in education. *Learning, Media and Technology*, 45(3), 251–264. DOI: 10.1080/17439884.2020.1686017

Pham, S. T., & Sampson, P. M. (2022). The development of artificial intelligence in education: A review in context. *Journal of Computer Assisted Learning*, 38(5), 1408–1421. DOI: 10.1111/jcal.12687

Pillai, S., Malik, M., & Mohd Rahim, N. (2023). AI in education: Challenges and opportunities for chatbot technology. *Journal of Computer Assisted Learning*, 39(2), 319–335. DOI: 10.1111/jcal.12776

Pinera, J. M. (2021). Adaptive Delivery as a Means to Increase Student Engagement and Learning Outcomes. https://digitalcommons.fiu.edu/etd/4727/

Pokrivcakova, S. (2019). Preparing teachers for the application of AI-powered technologies in foreign language education. *Journal of Language and Cultural Education*, 7(3), 135–153. DOI: 10.2478/jolace-2019-0025

Poole, A. H. (2021). *Promoting Diversity, Equity, and Inclusion in Library and Information Science through Community-Based Learning. Diversity, Divergence.* Dialogue.

Popenici, S. A., & Kerr, S. (2017). Exploring the impact of artificial intelligence on teaching and learning in higher education. *Research and Practice in Technology Enhanced Learning*, 12(1), 22. DOI: 10.1186/s41039-017-0062-8 PMID: 30595727

Prasad, A., Kumar, A. S., Sharma, P., Irawati, I. D., Chandrashekar, D. V., Musirin, I. B., & Abdullah, H. M. A. (2023). Artificial Intelligence in Computer Science: An Overview of Current Trends and Future Directions. *Advances in Artificial and Human Intelligence in the Modern Era*, 43-60.

Preiksaitis, C., & Rose, C. (2023). Opportunities, challenges, and future directions of generative artificial intelligence in medical education: Scoping review. *JMIR Medical Education*, 9, e48785. DOI: 10.2196/48785 PMID: 37862079

Professor Leslie Loble, A. M. 2024]Industry Professor, University of Technology Sydney (UTS), *Committee Hansard*, 20March 2024, p. 8

Proton, A. G. (2024). *What is GDPR, the EU's new data protection law?*https://gdpr.eu/what-is-gdpr/

Purnawirawan, O., Sudana, I. M., & Harlanu, M. (2019). Assessment of 4C softskills characteristics in learning productive graphic design subject for vocational. *Journal of Vocational Career Education*, 53-60.

Purwanto, E., Deviny, J., & Mutahar, A. M. (2020). The mediating role of trust in the relationship between corporate image, security, word of mouth and loyalty in M-banking using among the millennial generation in Indonesia. *Management & Marketing*, 15(2), 255–274. DOI: 10.2478/mmcks-2020-0016

Qadir, J. (2023). Engineering education in the era of ChatGPT: Promise and pitfalls of generative AI for education. In *2023 IEEE Global Engineering Education Conference (EDUCON)* (pp. 1-9). IEEE. DOI: 10.1109/EDUCON54358.2023.10125121

Quinn, S., Hogan, M., Dwyer, C., Finn, P., & Fogarty, E. (2020). Development and validation of the student-educator negotiated critical thinking dispositions scale (SENCTDS). *Thinking Skills and Creativity*, 38(4), 100710–100717. DOI: 10.1016/j.tsc.2020.100710

Rabaa'i, A. A. (2016). Extending the technology acceptance model (TAM) to assess students' behavioural intentions to adopt an e-learning system: The case of moodle as a learning tool. *Journal of emerging trends in engineering and applied sciences,* 7(1), 13-30.

Rafique, H., Almagrabi, A. C., Shamim, A., Anwar, F., & Bashir, A. K. (2020). Investigating the acceptance of mobile library applications with an extended technology acceptance model (TAM). *Computers & Education*, 145, 103732. Advance online publication. DOI: 10.1016/j.compedu.2019.103732

Ragheb, M. A., Tantawi, P., Farouk, N., & Hatata, A. (2022). Investigating the acceptance of applying chat-bot (Artificial intelligence) technology among higher education students in Egypt. *International Journal of Higher Education Management*, 8(2). Advance online publication. DOI: 10.24052/IJHEM/V08N02/ART-1

Rai, H. L., Saluja, N., & Pimplapure, A. (2024). Ethical and Social Impact of AI Driven Analysis for Students with Learning Disabilities Processes. *Journal of Electrical Systems*, 20(7s), 2704–2715.

Rajest, S. S., Singh, B., Obaid, A. J., Regin, R., & Chinnusamy, K. (Eds.). (2023). *Advances in artificial and human intelligence in the modern era*. IGI Global., DOI: 10.4018/979-8-3693-1301-5

Ramadevi, J., Sushama, C., Balaji, K., Talasila, V., Sindhwani, N., & Mukti, . (2023). AI enabled value-oriented collaborative learning: Centre for innovative education. *The Journal of High Technology Management Research*, 34(2), 100478. DOI: 10.1016/j.hitech.2023.100478

Randhawa, G. K., & Jackson, M (2020). The role of artificial intelligence in learning and professional development for healthcare professionals. Healthcare management forum, Rienties, B., Køhler Simonsen, H., & Herodotou, C. (2020). Defining the boundaries between artificial intelligence in education, computer-supported collaborative learning, educational data mining, and learning analytics: A need for coherence. Frontiers in Education, Schiff, D. (2021). Out of the laboratory and into the classroom: the future of artificial intelligence in education. *AI & Society*, 36(1), 331–348. PMID: 32836908

Rane, N., Choudhary, S., & Rane, J. (2023). Education 4.0 and 5.0: Integrating artificial intelligence (AI) for personalized and adaptive learning. *Available atSSRN* 4638365. DOI: 10.2139/ssrn.4638365

Reddy, E. V., Reddy, P., Sharma, B., Reddy, K., & Khan, M. G. (2023). Readiness and perception of pacific students to mobile phones for higher education. *Technology. Knowledge and Learning*, 28(3), 1113–1132. DOI: 10.1007/s10758-022-09595-w

Redmond, A. R. (2023). Combining Project-Based Learning and Service-Learning in Teaching Global Issues. In Butcher, C., Bhasin, T., Gordon, E., & Hallward, M. C. (Eds.), *The Palgrave Handbook of Teaching and Research in Political Science* (pp. 231–243). Springer International Publishing., DOI: 10.1007/978-3-031-42887-6_20

Regan, P. M., & Jesse, J. (2019). Ethical challenges of edtech, big data and personalized learning: Twenty-first century student sorting and tracking. *Ethics and Information Technology*, 21(3), 167–179. DOI: 10.1007/s10676-018-9492-2

Rejón-Guardia, F., & Vich-I-Martorell, G. A. (2020). Design and acceptance of chatbots for information automation in university classrooms. *In EDULEARN20 Proceedings* (pp. 2452-2462). IATED https://doi.org/DOI: 10.21125/edulearn.2020.0757

Rekha, K., Gopal, K., Satheeskumar, D., Anand, U. A., Doss, D. S. S., & Elayaperumal, S. (2024, May). Ai-Powered Personalized Learning System Design: Student Engagement and Performance Tracking System. In 2024 4th International Conference on Advance Computing and Innovative Technologies in Engineering (ICACITE) (pp. 1125-1130). IEEE.

Remian, D. (2019).Augmenting education: ethical considerations for incorporating artificial intelligence in education, 52.https://scholarworks.umb.edu/instruction_capstone/52

Renz, A., & Hilbig, R. (2020). Prerequisites for artificial intelligence in further education: Identification of drivers, barriers, and business models of educational technology companies. *International Journal of Educational Technology in Higher Education*, 17(1), 14. DOI: 10.1186/s41239-020-00193-3

Resch, K., & Schrittesser, I. (2023). Using the Service-Learning approach to bridge the gap between theory and practice in teacher education. *International Journal of Inclusive Education*, 27(10), 1118–1132. DOI: 10.1080/13603116.2021.1882053

Research Prospect. (2023). *Thematic analysis – A guide with examples.* Retrieved from https://www.researchprospect.com/thematic-analysis/

Resh, N., & Sabbagh, C. (2014). Sense of justice in school and civic attitudes. *Social Psychology of Education*, 17(1), 51–72. DOI: 10.1007/s11218-013-9240-8

Rieser, R. (2012). *Implementing inclusive education: a Commonwealth guide to implementing Article 24 of the UN Convention on the Rights of Persons with Disabilities.* Commonwealth Secretariat.

Rızvı, M. (2023). Investigating AI-Powered Tutoring Systems that Adapt to Individual Student Needs, Providing Personalized Guidance and Assessments. *The Eurasia Proceedings of Educational and Social Sciences*, 31, 67–73. DOI: 10.55549/epess.1381518

Rodriguez, C., Martinez, A., & Lee, J. (2024). A comprehensive Quality of Experience model for online learning platforms. *IEEE Access : Practical Innovations, Open Solutions*, 12, 34567–34580.

Rodríguez-Zurita, D., Jaya-Montalvo, M., Moreira-Arboleda, J., Raya-Diez, E., & Carrión-Mero, P. (2024). Sustainable development through service learning and community engagement in higher education: a systematic literature review. *International Journal of Sustainability in Higher Education, ahead-of-print*(ahead-of-print). https://doi.org/DOI: 10.1108/IJSHE-10-2023-0461

Rogers, R. (2017). The motivational pull of video game feedback, rules, and social interaction: Another self-determination theory approach. *Computers in Human Behavior*, 73, 446–450. DOI: 10.1016/j.chb.2017.03.048

Ronald, R. (2018). 'Generation rent'and intergenerational relations in the era of housing financialisation. *Critical Housing Analysis*, 5(2), 14–26. DOI: 10.13060/23362839.2018.5.2.439

Rosli, M. S., Saleh, N. S., Md. Ali, A., & Abu Bakar, S. (2022). Self-determination theory and online learning in university: Advancements, future direction and research gaps. *Sustainability*, 14(21). Advance online publication. DOI: 10.3390/su142114655

Rouabhi, S., Azerine, A., Tlemsani, R., Essaid, M., & Idoumghar, L. (2024). Conv-ViT fusion for improved handwritten Arabic character classification. *Signal, Image and Video Processing*, 18(S1), 1–18. DOI: 10.1007/s11760-024-03158-5

Rudolph, J., Tan, S., & Tan, S. (2023). ChatGPT: Bullshit spewer or the end of traditional assessments in higher education? *Journal of Applied Learning and Teaching*, 6(1), 342–363. DOI: 10.37074/jalt.2023.6.1.9

Ruiz-Rojas, L. I., Salvador-Ullauri, L., & Acosta-Vargas, P. (2024). Collaborative working and critical thinking: Adoption of generative artificial intelligence tools in higher education. *Sustainability (Basel)*, 16(13), 5367. DOI: 10.3390/su16135367

Rusmiyanto, R., Huriati, N., Fitriani, N., Tyas, N. K., Rofi'i, A., & Sari, M. N. (2023). The role of artificial intelligence (AI) in developing English language learner's communication skills. *Journal of Education*, 6(1), 750–757.

Russell, S. (2019). *Human compatible: Artificial Intelligence and the problem of control*. Penguin.

Saaida, M. B. (2023). AI-Driven transformations in higher education: Opportunities and challenges. *International Journal of Educational Research and Studies, 5*(1), 29-36. ISSN: 2664-6811

Saaida, M. B. (2023). AI-Driven transformations in higher education: Opportunities and challenges. *International Journal of Educational Research and Studies*, 5(1), 29–36.

Sabzalieva, E., & Valentini, A. (2023). *ChatGPT and artificial intelligence in higher education: Quick start guide*. UNESCO., https://www.iesalc.unesco.org/wp-content/uploads/2023/04/ChatGPT-and-Artificial-Intelligence-in-higher-education-Quick-Start-guide_EN_FINAL.pdf

Sadler, D. R. (1989). Formative assessment and the design of instructional systems. *Instructional Science*, 18(2), 119–144. DOI: 10.1007/BF00117714

Sadler, D. R. (2014). Beyond feedback: Developing student capability in complex appraisal. In *Approaches to assessment that enhance learning in higher education* (pp. 45–60). Routledge., DOI: 10.1080/02602930903541015

Saif, N., Khan, S. U., Shaheen, I., ALotaibi, F. A., Alnfiai, M. M., & Arif, M. (2024). Chat-GPT; validating Technology Acceptance Model (TAM) in education sector via ubiquitous learning mechanism. *Computers in Human Behavior*, 154, 108097. DOI: 10.1016/j.chb.2023.108097

Sajja, R., Sermet, Y., Cikmaz, M., Cwiertny, D., & Demir, I. (2024). Artificial intelligence-enabled intelligent assistant for personalized and adaptive learning in higher education. *Information (Basel)*, 15(10), 596. DOI: 10.3390/info15100596

Saleh, S. S., Nat, M., & Aqel, M. (2022). Sustainable adoption of e-learning from the TAM perspective. *Sustainability (Basel)*, 14(6), 3690. Advance online publication. DOI: 10.3390/su14063690

Salloum, S. A. (2024). AI Perils in Education: Exploring Ethical Concerns. *Artificial Intelligence in Education: The Power and Dangers of ChatGPT in the Classroom*, 669-675.

Salloum, S. A. (2024). AI perils in education: Exploring ethical concerns. In *Artificial Intelligence in Education: The Power and Dangers of ChatGPT in the Classroom* (pp. 669–675). Springer Nature Switzerland., DOI: 10.1007/978-3-031-52280-2_43

Saltman, K. J. (2022). *The alienation of fact: Digital educational privatization, AI, and the false promise of bodies and numbers*. MIT Press. DOI: 10.7551/mitpress/14387.001.0001

Samala, A. D., Rawas, S., Wang, T., Reed, J. M., Kim, J., Howard, N.-J., & Ertz, M. (2024). Unveiling the landscape of generative artificial intelligence in education: A comprehensive taxonomy of applications, challenges, and future prospects. *Education and Information Technologies*. Advance online publication. DOI: 10.1007/s10639-024-12936-0

Samuel, A. L. (1959). Some studies in machine learning using the game of checkers. *IBM Journal of Research and Development*, 3(3), 210–229. DOI: 10.1147/rd.33.0210

Sandhu, R., Channi, H. K., Ghai, D., Cheema, G. S., & Kaur, M. (2024). An Introduction to Generative AI Tools for Education 2030. *Integrating Generative AI in Education to Achieve Sustainable Development Goals*, 1-28. DOI: DOI: 10.4018/979-8-3693-2440-0.ch001

Sandor, C., & Sándor, C. (2023). The role of innovative technologies in learning a foreign language.

Sandu, N., & Gide, E. (2019, September). Adoption of AI-Chatbots to enhance student learning experience in higher education in India. In *2019 18th international conference on information technology based higher education and training (ITHET)* (pp. 1-5). IEEE.

Sanjari, M., Bahramnezhad, F., Khoshnavay Fomani, F., Shoghi, M., & Cheraghi, M. A. (2014). Ethical challenges of researchers in qualitative studies: The necessity to develop a specific guideline. *Journal of Medical Ethics and History of Medicine.* Retrieved from https://www.researchgate.net/publication/269712541_Ethical_challenges_of_researchers_in_qualitaive_studies_The_necessiy_to_develop_a_specific_guideline

Santiago, C. S.Jr, Embang, S. I., Conlu, M. T. N., Acanto, R. B., Lausa, S. M., Ambojia, K. W. P., Laput, E. Y., Aperocho, M. D. B., Malabag, B. A., & Balilo, B. B.Jr. (2023). Utilization of writing assistance tools in research in selected higher learning institutions in the philippines: A text mining analysis. *International Journal of Learning. Teaching and Educational Research*, 22(11), 259–284. DOI: 10.26803/ijlter.22.11.14

Santos, O. C. (2023). Beyond cognitive and affective issues: Designing smart learning environments for psychomotor personalized learning. In *Learning, Design, and Technology: An International Compendium of Theory, Research, Practice, and Policy* (pp. 3309–3332). Springer International Publishing., DOI: 10.1007/978-3-319-17461-7_8

Sarstedt, M., Hair, J. F.Jr, & Ringle, C. M. (2023). "PLS-SEM: Indeed a silver bullet"–retrospective observations and recent advances. *Journal of Marketing Theory and Practice*, 31(3), 261–275. DOI: 10.1080/10696679.2022.2056488

Sasahara, K., Chen, W., Peng, H., Ciampaglia, G. L., Flammini, A., & Menczer, F. (2021). Social influence and unfollowing accelerate the emergence of echo chambers. *Journal of Computational Social Science*, 4(1), 381–402. DOI: 10.1007/s42001-020-00084-7

Saxena, A. K., García, V., Amin, M. R., Salazar, J. M. R., & Dey, S. (2023). Structure, Objectives, and Operational Framework for Ethical Integration of Artificial Intelligence in Educational. *Sage Science Review of Educational Technology, 6*(1), 88-100. https://journals.sagescience.org/index.php/ssret/article/view/139

Saxena, D., & Cao, J. (2005). Generative Adversarial Networks (GANs): Challenges, Solutions, and Future Directions. *Arxiv*. https://arxiv.org/vc/arxiv/papers/2005/2005.00065v1.pdf

Scharpnick, M., & Monahan, A. (2023). *Building the Future of UX in a World of Generative AI.* https://media-publications.bcg.com/Building-the-Future-of-UX-in-a-World-of-Generative-AI.pdf

Schiff, D., Smith, K., & Peterson, J. L. (2006). What is educational entrepreneurship? In F. M. Hess (Ed.), *Educational entrepreneurship: Realities, challenges, possibilities*. Harvard Education Press. Retrieved from http://www.social-capital.net/docs/What_is_Educational_Entrepreneurship.pdf

Schiff, D. (2021). Out of the laboratory and into the classroom: The future of artificial intelligence in education. *AI & Society*, 36(1), 331–348. DOI: 10.1007/s00146-020-01033-8 PMID: 32836908

Schönberger, M. (2023). ChatGPT in higher education: the good, the bad, and the University.

Schwartz, A., & Meuers, A. (2024). Service-Learning: Empowering students to practice their civic character. https://www.character.org/service-learning

Schwartz, R., Schwartz, R., Vassilev, A., Greene, K., Perine, L., Burt, A., & Hall, P. (2022). *Towards a standard for identifying and managing bias in artificial intelligence* (Vol. 3, p. 00). US Department of Commerce, National Institute of Standards and Technology.

Seldon, A., Abidoye, O., & Metcalf, T. (2020). *The Fourth Education Revolution Reconsidered: Will Artificial Intelligence Enrich Or Diminish Humanity?* Legend Press Ltd.

Selwyn, N. (2021). *Should robots replace teachers? AI and the future of education.* Polity Press.

Selwyn, N. (2022). The future of AI and education: Some cautionary notes. *European Journal of Education*, 57(4), 620–631. DOI: 10.1111/ejed.12532

Sengar, S. S., Hasan, A. B., Kumar, S., & Carroll, F. (2024). Generative artificial intelligence: A systematic review and applications. *Multimedia Tools and Applications*. Advance online publication. DOI: 10.1007/s11042-024-20016-1

Seo, K., Tang, J., Roll, I., Fels, S., & Yoon, D. (2021). The impact of artificial intelligence on learner–instructor interaction in online learning. *International Journal of Educational Technology in Higher Education*, 18(54), 54. Advance online publication. DOI: 10.1186/s41239-021-00292-9 PMID: 34778540

Serpell, R., & Hatano, G. (1997). *Education, schooling, and literacy* (Vol. 2). Handbook of cross-cultural psychology.

ServiceMax. (n.d.). *Artificial Intelligence Scheduling*. https://www.servicemax.com/field-service-manual/artificial-intelligence-scheduling

Sethi, S. S., & Jain, K. (2024). AI technologies for social emotional learning: recent research and future directions. *Journal of Research in Innovative Teaching & Learning*. DOI: 10.1108/JRIT-03-2024-0073

Shafiq, M., & Gu, Z. (2022). Deep residual learning for image recognition: A survey. *Applied Sciences (Basel, Switzerland)*, 12(18), 8972. DOI: 10.3390/app12188972

Shahzad, M. F., Xu, S., & Javed, I. (2024). ChatGPT awareness, acceptance, and adoption in higher education: The role of trust as a cornerstone. *International Journal of Educational Technology in Higher Education*, 21(1), 46. DOI: 10.1186/s41239-024-00478-x

Shanta, S., & Wells, J. G. (2022). T/E design based learning: Assessing student critical thinking and problem solving abilities. *International Journal of Technology and Design Education*, 32(1), 267–285. DOI: 10.1007/s10798-020-09608-8

Sharma, D. M., Ramana, K. V., Jothilakshmi, R., Verma, R., Maheswari, B. U., & Boopathi, S. (2024). Integrating Generative AI Into K-12 Curriculums and Pedagogies in India: Opportunities and Challenges. *Facilitating Global Collaboration and Knowledge Sharing in Higher Education With Generative AI*, IGI Global, 133-161.

Sharma, S. K., & Wang, X. (2019). Collaborative distributed Q-learning for RACH congestion minimization in cellular IoT networks. *IEEE Communications Letters*, 23(4), 600–603. DOI: 10.1109/LCOMM.2019.2896929

Sheffler, P., Rodriguez, T. M., Cheung, C. S., & Wu, R. (2022). Cognitive and metacognitive, motivational, and resource considerations for learning new skills across the lifespan. *Wiley Interdisciplinary Reviews: Cognitive Science*, 13(2), e1585. DOI: 10.1002/wcs.1585 PMID: 34783458

Sheikh, H., Prins, C., & Schrijvers, E. (2023). Artificial intelligence: definition and background. In Mission, A. I. (Ed.), *The new system technology* (pp. 15–41). Springer International Publishing., DOI: 10.1007/978-3-031-21448-6_2

Shemshack, A., & Spector, J. M. (2020). A systematic literature review of personalized learning terms. *Smart Learning Environments*, 7(1), 33. DOI: 10.1186/s40561-020-00140-9

Shiohira, K. (2021). Understanding the Impact of Artificial Intelligence on Skills Development. [*UNESCO-UNEVOC International Centre for Technical and Vocational Education and Training*.]. *Education*, •••, 2030.

Shi, S. J., Li, J. W., & Zhang, R. (2024). A study on the impact of Generative Artificial Intelligence supported Situational Interactive Teaching on students' 'flow' experience and learning effectiveness—A case study of legal education in China. *Asia Pacific Journal of Education*, 44(1), 112–138. DOI: 10.1080/02188791.2024.2305161

Shmueli, G., & Koppius, O. R. (2011). Predictive analytics in information systems research. *Management Information Systems Quarterly*, 35(3), 553–572. DOI: 10.2307/23042796

Siddiqi, M. M. (2024). Future of Digital Education: Inclusive, Immersive, Equitable. *MediaSpace: DME Media Journal of Communication*, 5(01), 8–24. DOI: 10.53361/dmejc.v5i01.02

Sidiropoulos, D., & Anagnostopoulos, C. N. (2024).Applications, challenges and ethical issues of AI and ChatGPT in education. Retrieved from- https://arxiv.org/pdf/2402.07907

Singha, S., Singha, R., & Jasmine, E. (2024). Enhancing Language Teaching Materials Through Artificial Intelligence: Opportunities and Challenges. AI in Language Teaching, Learning, and Assessment, 22-42.

Sit, C., Srinivasan, R., Amlani, A., Muthuswamy, K., Azam, A., Monzon, L., & Poon, D. S. (2020). Attitudes and perceptions of UK medical students towards artificial intelligence and radiology: Amulticentre survey. *Insights Into Imaging*, 11(1), 14. Advance online publication. DOI: 10.1186/s13244-019-0830-7 PMID: 32025951

Slepankova, T. (2021). The long-term effects of AI chatbots in education. *British Journal of Educational Technology*, 52(5), 1602–1617. DOI: 10.1111/bjet.13098

Slimi, Z. (2023). The Impact of Artificial Intelligence on higher education: An empirical study. *European journal of educational sciences, 10*(1), 17-33.0p

Slimi, Z., & Carballido, B. V. (2023). Navigating the Ethical Challenges of Artificial Intelligence in Higher Education: An Analysis of Seven Global AI Ethics Policies. *TEM Journal, 12*(2).

Slimi, Z., & Carballido, B. V. (2023). Navigating the Ethical Challenges of Artificial Intelligence in Higher Education: An Analysis of Seven Global AI Ethics Policies. *TEM Journal, 12*(2). https://www.ceeol.com/search/article-detail?id=1122977

Slimi, Z., & Carballido, B. V. (2023). Navigating the ethical challenges of artificial intelligence in higher education: An analysis of seven global AI ethics policies. *TEM Journal, 12*(2). https://doi.org/DOI: 10.18421/TEM122-02

Smith, J., Johnson, A., & Brown, M. (2022). Machine learning approaches for personalized learning: A comprehensive review. *Journal of Educational Technology*, 45(3), 213–228.

Songkram, N., Chootongchai, S., Osuwan, H., Chuppunnarat, Y., & Songkram, N. (2023). Students' adoption towards behavioral intention of digital learning platform. *Education and Information Technologies*, 28(9), 11655–11677. DOI: 10.1007/s10639-023-11637-4 PMID: 36846495

Sousa, A. (2024). Multidisciplinary Perspectives on Artificial Intelligence and the Law. *Springer Nature*, 456. Advance online publication. DOI: 10.1007/978-3-031-41264-6

Southgate, E. (2020). Artificial intelligence, ethics, equity and higher education: A 'beginning-of-the-discussion' paper. National Centre for Student Equity in Higher Education, Curtin University, and the University of Newcastle.

Spector, J. M., & Ma, S. (2019). Inquiry and critical thinking skills for the next generation: From artificial intelligence back to human intelligence. *Smart Learning Environments*, 6(1), 1–11. DOI: 10.1186/s40561-019-0088-z

Srinivasa, K. G., Kurni, M., & Saritha, K. (2022). Harnessing the Power of AI to Education. In *Learning, teaching, and assessment methods for contemporary learners: pedagogy for the digital generation* (pp. 311–342). Springer Nature Singapore., DOI: 10.1007/978-981-19-6734-4_13

Stahl, B. C. (2021). *Artificial intelligence for a better future: an ecosystem perspective on the ethics of AI and emerging digital technologies*. Springer Nature. DOI: 10.1007/978-3-030-69978-9

StanfordUniversity. (2023). Cardinal Service: Engaging Students in Public Service. https://cardinalservice.stanford.edu

Strauss, A., & Corbin, J. M. (1990). *Basics of qualitative research: Grounded theory procedures and techniques*. SAGE Publications, Inc.

Strielkowski, W., Grebennikova, V., Lisovskiy, A., Rakhimova, G., & Vasileva, T. (2024). AI-driven adaptive learning for sustainable educational transformation. *Sustainable Development (Bradford)*, sd.3221. DOI: 10.1002/sd.3221

Stüber, J. (2018). Barriers of digital technologies in higher education: A teachers' perspective from a Swedish University. [Unpublished master's thesis]. Linnaeus University. https://www.diva-portal.org/smash/get/diva2:1201871/FULLTEXT01.pdf

Stuedahl, D. (2015). Future Orientation in Design, Participation and Learning no. 26, 2015, pp. DOI: . *Interaction Design and Architecture(s) Journal - IxD&A, 26*, 13.DOI: 10.55612/s-5002-026-009

Stupnisky, R. H., BrckaLorenz, A., Yuhas, B., & Guay, F. (2018). Faculty members' motivation for teaching and best practices: Testing a model based on self-determination theory across institution types. *Contemporary Educational Psychology*, 53, 15–26. DOI: 10.1016/j.cedpsych.2018.01.004

Su, J., & Yang, W. (2023). Unlocking the Power of ChatGPT: A Framework for Applying Generative AI in Education. *ECNU Review of Education*, 6(3), 355–366. DOI: 10.1177/20965311231168423

Šumak, B., Heričko, M., Pušnik, M., & Polančič, G. (2011). Factors affecting acceptance and use of Moodle: An empirical study based on TAM. *Informatica (Vilnius)*, 35(1), 91–100.

Sumakul, D. T. Y., Hamied, F. A., & Sukyadi, D. (2022, February). Students' perceptions of the use of AI in a writing class. *In 67th TEFLIN International Virtual Conference & the 9th ICOELT 2021* (TEFLIN ICOELT 2021) (pp. 52-57). Atlantis Press. https://doi.org/DOI: 10.2991/assehr.k.220201.009

Sun, H., Li, W., & Shen, B. (2017). Learning in physical education: A self-determination theory perspective. *Journal of Teaching in Physical Education*, 36(3), 277–291. DOI: 10.1123/jtpe.2017-0067

Suresh, A., Wighton, N. M., Sorensen, T. E., Palladino, T. C., & Pinto-Powell, R. C. (2022). A hybrid educational approach to service learning: Impact on student attitudes and readiness in working with medically underserved communities. *Medical Education Online*, 27(1), 2122106. Advance online publication. DOI: 10.1080/10872981.2022.2122106 PMID: 36120928

Sürücü, L., & Maslakçı, A. (2020). Validity and reliability in quantitative research. *Business & Management Studies: An International Journal, 8*(3), 2694–2726. Retrieved from https://www.researchgate.net/publication/344379869_Validity_and_Reliability_in_Quantitative_Research

Susanti, E., & Arista, A. (2019). Analisa tingkat pengetahuan guru terhadap kompetensi 4C. *Seminar Nasional Ilmu Sosial dan Teknologi (SNISTEK),* 2, 73-78.

Susilo, S. (2015). Curriculum of EFL Teacher Education and Indonesian Qualification Framework: A Blip of the Future Direction. The dynamics of the journal. *Science*, 15(1), 11–24.

Swiecki, Z., Khosravi, H., Chen, G., Martinez-Maldonado, R., Lodge, J. M., Milligan, S., Selwyn, N., & Gašević, D. (2022). Assessment in the age of artificial intelligence. *Computers and Education: Artificial Intelligence*, 3, 100075. Advance online publication. DOI: 10.1016/j.caeai.2022.100075

Syzdykbayeva, A., Baikulova, A., & Kerimbayeva, R. (2020). Introduction of artificial intelligence as the basis of modern online education on the example of higher education. In *2021 IEEE International Conference on Smart Information Systems and Technologies (SIST)* (pp. 1-8). IEEE.

Szegedy, C., Ioffe, S., Vanhoucke, V., & Alemi, A. (2017, February). Inception-v4, inception-resnet and the impact of residual connections on learning. *Proceedings of the AAAI Conference on Artificial Intelligence*, 31(1), •••. DOI: 10.1609/aaai.v31i1.11231

Taddeo, M., McCutcheon, T., & Floridi, L. (2019). Trusting artificial intelligence in cybersecurity is a double-edged sword. *Nature Machine Intelligence*, 1(12), 557–560. DOI: 10.1038/s42256-019-0109-1

Tahiru, F. (2021). AI in education: A systematic literature review. [JCIT]. *Journal of Cases on Information Technology*, 23(1), 1–20. DOI: 10.4018/JCIT.2021010101

Taneri, G. U. (2020). *Artificial intelligence & higher education: Towards customized teaching and learning and skills for an AI world of work.* University of California, Berkeley, Center for Studies in Higher Education. Retrieved from https://eric.ed.gov/?id=ED606654

Tang, L., & Su, Y. S. (2024). Ethical Implications and Principles of Using Artificial Intelligence Models in the Classroom: A Systematic Literature Review.

Tangen, S. (2002). Understanding the concept of productivity. In *Proceedings of the 7th Asia Pacific Industrial Engineering and Management Systems Conference (APIEMS2002), Taipei.* Retrieved from https://www.academia.edu/35502335/Understanding_the_concept_of_productivity?bulkDownload=thisPaper-topRelated-sameAuthor-citingThis-citedByThis-secondOrderCitations&from=cover_page

Tangen, S. (2005). Demystifying productivity and performance. *International Journal of Productivity and Performance Management*, 54(1), 34–46. DOI: 10.1108/17410400510571437

Tang, X., Zainal, S. R. B. M., & Li, Q. (2023). Multimedia use and its impact on the effectiveness of educators: A technology acceptance model perspective. *Humanities & Social Sciences Communications*, 10(1), 1–11. DOI: 10.1057/s41599-023-02458-4

Tan, K. (2013). A Framework for Assessment for Learning: Implications for Feedback Practices within and beyond the Gap. *International Scholarly Research Notices*, 2013(1), 640609.

Tan, K., Wong, L., & Ng, M. (2024). Edge computing for low-latency interactive learning applications. In *Proceedings of the IEEE International Conference on Edge Computing* (pp. 87-96).

Tao, D., Fu, P., Wang, Y., Zhang, T., & Qu, X. (2022). Key characteristics in designing massive open online courses (MOOCs) for user acceptance: An application of the extended technology acceptance model. *Interactive Learning Environments*, 30(5), 882–895. DOI: 10.1080/10494820.2019.1695214

Targ, S., Almeida, D., & Lyman, K. (2016). Resnet in resnet: Generalizing residual architectures. *arXiv preprint arXiv:1603.08029*.

Tariq, M. U. (Ed.). (2024). *AI-Driven Learning and Engagement in Higher Education*. IGI Global. DOI: 10.4018/979-8-3693-4074-5

Taylor, R. R., O'Dell, B., & Murphy, J. W. (2024). Human-centric AI: Philosophical and community-centric considerations. *AI & Society*, 39(5), 2417–2424. DOI: 10.1007/s00146-023-01694-1

Tenon, S. R., & Epler, P. (Eds.). (2020). *Evaluation of principles and best practices in personalized learning*. IGI Global. DOI: 10.4018/978-1-7998-4237-8

Thomas. (2020, August 17). *Natural language processing is changing these 5 industries.*https://fastdatascience.com/natural-language-processing-is-changing-these-5-industries/

Tijsma, G., Hilverda, F., Scheffelaar, A., Alders, S., Schoonmade, L., Blignaut, N., & Zweekhorst, M. (2020). Becoming productive 21 century citizens: A systematic review uncovering design principles for integrating community service learning into higher education courses. *Educational Research*, 62(4), 390–413. DOI: 10.1080/00131881.2020.1836987

Tong, A., Sainsbury, P., & Craig, J. (2007). Consolidated criteria for reporting qualitative research (COREQ): A 32-item checklist for interviews and focus groups. *International Journal for Quality in Health Care : Journal of the International Society for Quality in Health Care*, 19(6), 349–357. DOI: 10.1093/intqhc/mzm042 PMID: 17872937

Toprak-Yıldız, T. E. (2024). Natural Language Processing Applications in Language Assessment: The Use of Automated Speech Scoring. In *Fostering Foreign Language Teaching and Learning Environments With Contemporary Technologies* (pp. 216-234). IGI Global.

Torvinen, L. T. (2017). *The concept of orientation in teachers' thinking and practices in business education*. Institute of Education, University of London.

Trilling, B., & Fadel, C. (2009). *21st Century Skills: Learning for Life in Our Times*. John Wiley & Sons.

Triplett, W. J. (2023). Artificial intelligence in STEM education. *Cybersecurity and Innovative Technology Journal*, 1(1), 23–29. DOI: 10.53889/citj.v1i1.296

True Interaction. (n.d.). *AI and the Classroom: Machine Learning in Education*. True. https:/www.trueinteraction.com/ai-and-the-classroom-machine-learning-in-education/

TrustRadius. (2013-2024). *SchooLinks Competitors and Alternatives*. https://www.trustradius.com/products/schoolinks/competitors

Tucker, M. L., McCarthy, A. M., Hoxmeier, J. A., & Lenk, M. M. (1998). Community Service Learning Increases Communication Skills Across the Business Curriculum. *Business Communication Quarterly*, 61(2), 88–99. DOI: 10.1177/108056999806100211

Tuomi, I. (2020). The use of artificial intelligence (AI) in education. *Research for CULT Committee*. Retrieved from https://www.europarl.europa.eu/RegData/etudes/BRIE/2020/629222/IPOL_BRI(2020)629222_EN.pdf

Turek, M. (2017). *Explainable Artificial Intelligence (XAI) Program*. Defence Advanced Research Project Agency (DARPA).

U.S. Department of Education, Office of Educational Technology. (2023). *Artificial intelligence and the future of teaching and learning: Insights and recommendations.* Washington, DC: U.S. Department of Education. Retrieved from https://www2.ed.gov/documents/ai-report/ai-report.pdf

U.S. Department of Education. Office of Educational Technology, (2023). Artificial Intelligence and Future of Teaching and Learning: Insights and Recommendations, Washington, DC.

UBTech Robotics Pte. Ltd. (2012-2023). *AI Lab Solution.* https://www.ubtrobot.com/aiEducation/solutions/aiLabsInSchools?gad_source=1&gclid=Cj0KCQjwtZK1BhDuARIsAAy2VztQn4pEMQH18mgPXPxfH62EhavamQoIEwuDnSokJUxTvfPwul0caLsaAhvMEALw_wcB

Udeozor, C., Chan, P., Russo Abegão, F., & Glassey, J. (2023). Game-based assessment framework for virtual reality, augmented reality and digital game-based learning. *International Journal of Educational Technology in Higher Education*, 20(1), 36. DOI: 10.1186/s41239-023-00405-6 PMID: 36644670

Udvaros, J., & Forman, N. (2023). Artificial intelligence and Education 4.0. In *INTED2023 proceedings* (pp. 6309-6317). IATED. DOI: 10.21125/inted.2023.1670

Umali, J. N. D. (2024). Artificial Intelligence Technology Management of Teachers, Learners Motivation and Challenges Encountered. [IJMCER]. *Educational Research*, 6(3), 821–880. https://www.ijmcer.com/wp-content/uploads/2024/06/IJMCER_MM0630821880.pdf

Umar, A. M. A.-T., & Majeed, A. (2018). The impact of assessment for learning on students' achievement in English for specific purposes A case study of pre-medical students at khartoum university: Sudan. *English Language Teaching*, 11(2), 15–25. DOI: 10.5539/elt.v11n2p15

Umezuruike, C., & Ngugi, H. N. (2020). Imminent challenges of adoption of big data in educational systems in Sub-Saharan Africa nations. *International Journal of Recent Technology and Engineering*, 8(5), 4544–4550. DOI: 10.35940/ijrte.E6885.018520

UNCTAD. (n.d.). *Data Protection and Privacy Legislation Worldwide.* https://unctad.org/page/data-protection-and-privacy-legislation-worldwide

UNESCO. (2024a). AI competency framework for students. https://www.unesco.org/en/articles/ai-competency-framework-students

UNESCO. (2024b). AI competency framework for teachers. https://unesdoc.unesco.org/ark:/48223/pf0000391104

UNESCO. (2024c). Guidance for Generative AI in Education and Research. https://unesdoc.unesco.org/ark:/48223/pf0000386693

United Nations Educational, Scientific and Cultural Organization. (2019). *Artificial intelligence in education: Challenges and opportunities for sustainable development*. Paris, France: UNESCO. Retrieved from https://unesdoc.unesco.org/ark:/48223/pf0000366994

University of San Diego Senior College and University Commission. (2024). *43 Examples of Artificial Intelligence in Education*. https://onlinedegrees.sandiego.edu/artificial-intelligence-education/

Utomo, H. P., Bon, A. T., & Hendayun, M. (2017). Modeling of academic information system in higher education institution toward education 3.0: A literature review. *International Journal of Information and Education Technology (IJIET)*, 7(10), 738–742. DOI: 10.18178/ijiet.2017.7.10.964

Uzair, M., & Jamil, N. (2020, November). Effects of hidden layers on the efficiency of neural networks. In *2020 IEEE 23rd international multitopic conference (INMIC)* (pp. 1-6). IEEE. DOI: 10.1109/INMIC50486.2020.9318195

Vacalopoulou, A., Gardelli, V., Karafyllidis, T., Liwicki, F., Mokayed, H., Papaevripidou, M., . . . Katsouros, V. (2024). AI4EDU: An Innovative Conversational Ai Assistant For Teaching And Learning. In *INTED2024 Proceedings* (pp. 7119-7127). IATED.

Valenciano, J. de P., Uribe-Toril, J., & Ruiz-Real, J. L. (2019). Entrepreneurship and education in the 21st century: Analysis and trends in research. *Journal of Entrepreneurship Education*, 22(4). https://www.researchgate.net/publication/334825222_Entrepreneurship_and_Education_in_the_21st_Century_Analysis_and_Trends_in_Research

Van der Aalst, W. M. (2016). *Data science in action: Principles and ethics of big data*. Springer., DOI: 10.1007/978-3-662-49851-4_1

van der Vorst, T., & Jelicic, N. (2019). Artificial Intelligence in Education: Can AI bring the full potential of personalized learning to education?.

Van Dijk, J. A. G. M. (2017). Digital divide: Impact of access. The international encyclopedia of media effects, 1, 1-11.

Vanoye-García, A. Y., Menchaca-Torre, H. L., & López-Navarro, G. M. (2024). From Classroom to Community: Building Sustainability Competencies Through Service Learning in the Public Sector. 2024 IEEE Global Engineering Education Conference (EDUCON), Verger, A., Edwards Jr, D. B., & Altinyelken, H. K. (2014). Learning from all? The World Bank, aid agencies and the construction of hegemony in education for development. *Comparative Education*, 50(4), 381–399. DOI: 10.1080/03050068.2014.918713

Varier, D., Dumke, E. K., Abrams, L. M., Conklin, S. B., Barnes, J. S., & Hoover, N. R. (2017). Potential of one-to-one technologies in the classroom: Teachers and students weigh in. *Educational Technology Research and Development*, 65(4), 967–992. DOI: 10.1007/s11423-017-9509-2

Varshni, D., Thakral, K., Agarwal, L., Nijhawan, R., & Mittal, A. (2019, February). Pneumonia detection using CNN based feature extraction. In *2019 IEEE international conference on electrical, computer and communication technologies (ICECCT)* (pp. 1-7). IEEE. DOI: 10.1109/ICECCT.2019.8869364

Vattøy, K. D., Gamlem, S. M., & Rogne, W. M. (2021). Examining students' feedback engagement and assessment experiences: A mixed study. *Studies in Higher Education*, 46(11), 2325–2337. DOI: 10.1080/03075079.2020.1723523

Velagaleti, S. B., Choukaier, D., Nuthakki, R., Lamba, V., Sharma, V., & Rahul, S.Sesha Bhargavi Velagaleti. (2024). Empathetic Algorithms: The Role of AI in Understanding and Enhancing Human Emotional Intelligence. *Journal of Electrical Systems*, 20(3s), 2051–2060. DOI: 10.52783/jes.1806

Venkatesh, V., & Davis, F. D. (2000). A theoretical extension of the technology acceptance model: Four longitudinal field studies. *Management Science*, 46(2), 186–204. DOI: 10.1287/mnsc.46.2.186.11926

Venkatesh, V., Morris, M. G., Davis, G. B., & Davis, F. D. (2003). User acceptance of information technology: Toward a unified view. *Management Information Systems Quarterly*, 27(3), 425–478. DOI: 10.2307/30036540

Venkatesh, V., Thong, J. Y. L., & Xu, X. (2012). Consumer acceptance and use of information technology: Extending the unified theory of acceptance and use of technology. *Management Information Systems Quarterly*, 36(1), 157–178. DOI: 10.2307/41410412

Venkateswaran, P. S., Ayasrah, F. T. M., Nomula, V. K., Paramasivan, P., Anand, P., & Bogeshwaran, K. (2024). Applications of artificial intelligence tools in higher education. In *Data-Driven Decision Making for Long-Term Business Success* (pp. 124–136). IGI Global.

Verma, A., Kumar, Y., & Kohli, R. (2021). Study of AI techniques in quality educations: Challenges and recent progress. *SN Computer Science*, 2(4), 238. DOI: 10.1007/s42979-021-00635-3

Vincent, C. S. (2021). Critically Engaged Civic Learning: A Comprehensive Restructuring of Service-Learning Approaches. *Michigan Journal of Community Service Learning*, 27(2). Advance online publication. DOI: 10.3998/mjcsloa.3239521.0027.205

Voogt, J., & Roblin, N. P. (2012). A comparative analysis of international frameworks for 21st century competences: Implications for national curriculum policies. *Journal of Curriculum Studies*, 44(3), 299–321. DOI: 10.1080/00220272.2012.668938

Voorhees, E. (2016). The Service-Learning Scholar Model: Maximizing Impact by Improving Communication and Student Voice in Service Learning. *Undergraduate Journal of Service Learning & Community-Based Research*, 5, 1–13. DOI: 10.56421/ujslcbr.v5i0.239

Walter, Y. (2024). Embracing the future of Artificial Intelligence in the classroom: The relevance of AI literacy, prompt engineering, and critical thinking in modern education. *International Journal of Educational Technology in Higher Education*, 21(1), 15. Advance online publication. DOI: 10.1186/s41239-024-00448-3

Wang, J., & Liu, H. (2022). Cooperative game theory for fair network capacity allocation. *Computer Networks*, 185, 107731.

Wang, T., Yeh, R. K. J., Chen, C., & Tsydypov, Z. (2016). What drives electronic word-of-mouth on social networking sites? Perspectives of social capital and self-determination. *Telematics and Informatics*, 33(4), 1034–1047. DOI: 10.1016/j.tele.2016.03.005

Wang, Y., Liu, X., Zhang, Y., Sang, X., & Wang, M. (2020). The first model of family education on the delivery of bilingual British NCC digital literacy qualifications in Dalian, China — Engaging and motivating children. *Proceedings of the International Conference on Education in Mathematics, Science and Technology (ICEMST)*, Istanbul, Turkey, 21-24 March.

Ward, D., Loshbaugh, H. G., Gibbs, A. L., Henkel, T., Siering, G., Williamson, J., & Kayser, M. (2024). How Universities Can Move Forward With Generative AI in Teaching and Learning. *Change*, 56(1), 47–54. DOI: 10.1080/00091383.2024.2297635

Wasim, J., Youssef, M. H., Christodoulou, I., & Reinhardt, R. (2023). The path to entrepreneurship: The role of social networks in driving entrepreneurial learning and education. *Journal of Management Education*, 48(3), 459–493. DOI: 10.1177/10525629231219235

Watanabe, A. (2023). Exploring totalitarian elements of artificial intelligence in higher education with Hannah Arendt. [IJT]. *International Journal of Technoethics*, 14(1), 1–15. DOI: 10.4018/IJT.329239

Weishart, J. E. (2020). Democratizing education rights. *Wm. & Mary Bill Rts. J.*, 29, 1.

Weizenbaum, J. (1966). Eliza- A computer program for the study of natural language communication between man and machine. *Computational Linguistics*, 9(1), 36–45.

Wilkinson, S., Pullen, R., Rutledge, P., & Schmid, S. (2023). Digital Formative Assessments for Learning. DOI: 10.1039/9781839167942-00301

Williams, A. (2024). Delivering Effective Student Feedback in Higher Education: An Evaluation of the Challenges and Best Practice. *International Journal of Research in Education and Science*, 10(2), 473–501. https://eric.ed.gov/?id=EJ1426687. DOI: 10.46328/ijres.3404

Williamson, B. (2020). *Big data in education: The digital future of learning, policy, and practice*. Sage Publications.

Wilson, T. D. (2008). Activity theory in information seeking. *Annual Review of Information Science & Technology*, 42(1), 43. DOI: 10.1002/aris.2008.1440420111

Wise, A. F., Knight, S., & Shum, S. B. (2021). Collaborative learning analytics. International handbook of computer-supported collaborative learning, 425-443. DOI: 10.1007/978-3-030-65291-3_23

Wood, D., & Moss, S. H. (2024). Evaluating the impact of students' generative AI use in educational contexts. *Journal of Research in Innovative Teaching & Learning*. DOI: 10.1108/JRIT-06-2024-0151

Woolf, B. P., Lane, H. C., Chaudhri, V. K., & Kolodner, J. L. (2013). AI grand challenges for education. *AI Magazine*, 34(4), 6684. DOI: 10.1609/aimag.v34i4.2490

World Economic Forum. (2024). *From virtual tutors to accessible textbooks: 5 ways AI is transforming education*. https://www.weforum.org/agenda/2024/05/ways-ai-can-benefit-education/

Wu, R., & Yu, Z. (2024). Do AI chatbots improve students learning outcomes? Evidence from a meta-analysis. *British Journal of Educational Technology*, 55(1), 10–33. DOI: 10.1111/bjet.13334

Wu, Y., & Schunn, C. D. (2023). Passive, active, and constructive engagement with peer feedback: A revised model of learning from peer feedback. *Contemporary Educational Psychology*, 73, 102160. DOI: 10.1016/j.cedpsych.2023.102160

Wyatt-Smith, C., Klenowski, V., & Colbert, P. (2014). *"Assessment understood as enabling," in Designing Assessment for Quality Learning, 7e Enabling Power of Assessment*. Springer.

Xianhua, L. (2019). Research on the effect of artificial intelligence technology on English learning efficiency. In *Proceedings of the 12th International Conference on Intelligent Computation Technology and Automation (ICICTA)*. https://doi.org/ DOI: 10.1109/ICICTA49267.2019.00123

Xiao, Y., & Watson, M. (2017). Guidance on conducting a systematic literature review. *Journal of Planning Education and Research*, 37(1), 1–20. DOI: 10.1177/0739456X17723971

Xia, Q., Chiu, T. K., Lee, M., Sanusi, I. T., Dai, Y., & Chai, C. S. (2022). A self-determination theory (SDT) design approach for inclusive and diverse artificial intelligence (AI) education. *Computers & Education*, 189, 104582. Advance online publication. DOI: 10.1016/j.compedu.2022.104582

Xia, Q., Weng, X., Ouyang, F., Lin, T. J., & Chiu, T. K. (2024). A scoping review on how generative artificial intelligence transforms assessment in higher education. *International Journal of Educational Technology in Higher Education*, 21(1), 40. DOI: 10.1186/s41239-024-00468-z

Xu, F., Uszkoreit, H., Du, Y., Fan, W., Zhao, D., & Zhu, J. (2019). Explainable AI: A brief survey on history, research areas, approaches and challenges. In *Natural language processing and Chinese computing: 8th CCF international conference, NLPCC 2019, dunhuang, China, October 9–14, 2019, proceedings, part II 8*,563-574. Springer International Publishing. DOI: 10.1007/978-3-030-32236-6_51

Yadolahi Farsi, J., Modarresi, M., Motavaseli, M., & Salamzadeh, A. (2014). Institutional factors affecting academic entrepreneurship: The case of University of Tehran. *Economic Analysis*, 47(1–2), 139–159. https://core.ac.uk/download/pdf/33812235.pdf

Yan, Z. (2022). *Implementing a 21st century competency-based curriculum through lesson study: Teacher learning about cross-curricular and online pedagogy*. Routledge. https://orcid.org/0000-0001-9305-884X

Yang, S. J. H., Ogata, H., Matsui, T., & Chen, N.-S. (2021). Human-centered artificial intelligence in education: Seeing the invisible through the visible. *Computers and Education: Artificial Intelligence*, 2, 100008. DOI: 10.1016/j.caeai.2021.100008

Yan, W., Nakajima, T., & Sawada, R. (2024). Benefits and Challenges of Collaboration between Students and Conversational Generative Artificial Intelligence in Programming Learning: An Empirical Case Study. *Education Sciences*, 14(4), 433. DOI: 10.3390/educsci14040433

Yan, Z., & Brown, G. T. L. (2017). A cyclical self-assessment process: Towards a model of how students engage in self-assessment. *Assessment & Evaluation in Higher Education*, 42(8), 1247–1262. DOI: 10.1080/02602938.2016.1260091

Yan, Z., Brown, G. T. L., Lee, J. C.-K., & Qiu, X.-L. (2020). Student self-assessment: Why do they do it? *Educational Psychology*, 40(4), 509–532. DOI: 10.1080/01443410.2019.1672038

Ye, Y., Wang, J., & Weerasawainon, A. (2024). Enhancing the transformation leadership skill and capacities of educational leaders at all levels, from teachers to administrators. *Educational Administration: Theory and Practice, 30*(5), 6177–6181. Retrieved from https://kuey.net/index.php/kuey/article/view/3915

Ye, P., & Xu, X. (2023). A case study of interdisciplinary thematic learning curriculum to cultivate "4C skills". *Frontiers in Psychology*, 14, 1080811. DOI: 10.3389/fpsyg.2023.1080811 PMID: 36960001

Yildirim, Y., Arslan, E. A., Yildirim, K., & Bisen, I. (2021). Reimagining education with artificial intelligence. *Eurasian Journal of Higher Education*, 2(4), 32–46. DOI: 10.31039/ejohe.2021.4.52

Yilmaz, R., & Yilmaz, F. G. K. (2023). The effect of generative artificial intelligence (AI)-based tool use on students' computational thinking skills, programming self-efficacy and motivation. *Computers and Education: Artificial Intelligence*, 4, 100147. DOI: 10.1016/j.caeai.2023.100147

Yimer, Amedie, Muhie., Abeselom, Befekadu, Woldie. (2020). *Integration of Artificial Intelligence Technologies in Teaching and Learning in Higher Education.* 10(1):1-7.

Yin, R. K., & Moore, G. B. (1987). The use of advanced technologies in special education: Prospects from robotics, artificial intelligence, and computer simulation. *Journal of Learning Disabilities*, 20(1), 60–63. DOI: 10.1177/002221948702000111

Yousef, A. M. F., & Khatiry, A. R. (2023). Cognitive versus behavioral learning analytics dashboards for supporting learner's awareness, reflection, and learning process. *Interactive Learning Environments*, 31(9), 5460–5476. DOI: 10.1080/10494820.2021.2009881

Yu, H., Miao, C., Leung, C., & White, T. J. (2017). Towards AI-powered personalization in MOOC learning. npj Science of Learning, 2(1), 15.

Yu, P., Mulli, J., Syed, Z. A. S., & Umme, L. (Eds.). (2023). *Facilitating Global Collaboration and Knowledge Sharing in Higher Education with Generative AI*. IGI Global, ABD.

Yuen, K. F., Cai, L., Qi, G., & Wang, X. (2021). Factors influencing autonomous vehicle adoption: An application of the technology acceptance model and innovation diffusion theory. *Technology Analysis and Strategic Management*, 33(5), 505–519. DOI: 10.1080/09537325.2020.1826423

Yu, H., & Guo, Y. (2023, June). Generative artificial intelligence empowers educational reform: Current status, issues, and prospects. [). Frontiers Media SA.]. *Frontiers in Education*, 8, 1183162. DOI: 10.3389/feduc.2023.1183162

Yusof, M., Abdul-Samad, Z., Hassan, F., Darus, Z. M., Mohammad, M. F., & Zaharim, A. (2010). Academic entrepreneurship and innovation in higher education: An integrated framework for Malaysian universities. *Advanced Educational Technologies*. Retrieved from https://www.researchgate.net/publication/228410765_Academic_Entrepreneurship_and_Innovation_in_Higher_Education_An_Integrated_Framework_for_Malaysian_Universities

Yusuf, A., Pervin, N., & Roman-Gonzalez, M. (2024). Generative AI and the future of higher education: A threat to academic integrity or reformation? Evidence from multicultural perspectives. *International Journal of Educational Technology in Higher Education*, 21(1), 1–29. DOI: 10.1186/s41239-024-00453-6

Zainuri, A., & Huda, M. (2023). Empowering Cooperative Teamwork for Community Service Sustainability: Insights from Service Learning. *Sustainability (Basel)*, 15(5), 4551. DOI: 10.3390/su15054551

Zawacki-Richter, O., Marín, V. I., Bond, M., & Gouverneur, F. (2019). Systematic review of research on artificial intelligence applications in higher education–where are the educators? *International Journal of Educational Technology in Higher Education*, 16(1), 1–27. DOI: 10.1186/s41239-019-0171-0

Zdravkova, K. (2022). The potential of artificial intelligence for assistive technology in education. In Handbook on Intelligent Techniques in the Educational Process: Vol 1 Recent Advances and Case Studies (pp. 61-85). Cham: Springer International Publishing. DOI: 10.1007/978-3-031-04662-9_4

Zhai, C., Wibowo, S., & Li, L. D. (2024). The effects of over-reliance on AI dialogue systems on students' cognitive abilities: A systematic review. *Smart Learning Environments*, 11(1), 28. DOI: 10.1186/s40561-024-00316-7

Zhai, X., Chu, X., Chai, C. S., Jong, M. S. Y., Istenic, A., Spector, M., Liu, J.-B., Yuan, J., & Li, Y. (2021). A Review of Artificial Intelligence (AI) in Education from 2010 to 2020. *Complexity*, 2021(1), 8812542. DOI: 10.1155/2021/8812542

Zhang, F., Bazarevsky, V., Vakunov, A., Tkachenka, A., Sung, G., Chang, C. L., & Grundmann, M. (2020). Mediapipe hands: On-device real-time hand tracking. *arXiv preprint arXiv:2006.10214.*

Zhang, K., & Aslan, A. B. (2021). AI technologies for education: Recent research & future directions. *Computers and Education: Artificial Intelligence*, 2, 100025. DOI: 10.1016/j.caeai.2021.100025

Zhang, K., & Aslan, I. (2021). Ethical issues in AI-powered education systems: A comparative review. *Journal of Educational Technology & Society*, 24(4), 79–91. https://www.j-ets.net/ETS/journals/24_4/6.pdf

Zhang, L., & Patel, N. (2022). Impact of network conditions on remote learning: A study in rural communities. *Journal of Educational Technology & Society*, 25(3), 112–125.

Zhang, L., Ren, T., Xie, Y., Tian, Z., Tang, T., & Li, Y. (2022). Student Choirs and Virtual Social Practices by LivePBL: Linking Vocal Education with Project Based Learning. *Literacy Information and Computer Education Journal*, 13(1), 3860–3666. DOI: 10.20533/licej.2040.2589.2022.0482

Zhang, X.-H., Meng, L.-N., Liu, H.-H., Luo, R.-Z., Zhang, C.-M., Zhang, P.-P., & Liu, Y.-H. (2018). Role of academic self-efficacy in the relationship between self-directed learning readiness and problem-solving ability among nursing students. *Frontiers of Nursing*, 5(1), 75–81. DOI: 10.1515/fon-2018-0011

Zhang, Y., Chen, L., & Wang, K. (2023). Deep learning for adaptive learning path recommendation. In *Proceedings of the International Conference on Artificial Intelligence in Education* (pp. 178-189).

Zhao, F., Liu, G. Z., Zhou, J., & Yin, C. (2023). A learning analytics framework based on human-centered artificial intelligence for identifying the optimal learning strategy to intervene in learning behavior. *Journal of Educational Technology & Society*, 26(1), 132–146. https://www.jstor.org/stable/48707972

Zhou, P. (2024). Real time feedback and E-learning intelligent entertainment experience in computer English communication based on deep learning. *Entertainment Computing*, 100752, 100752. Advance online publication. DOI: 10.1016/j.entcom.2024.100752

Zhou, X., Xu, S., & Chen, C. (2022). AI-driven adaptive learning systems and their impact on student engagement. *Journal of Artificial Intelligence in Education*, 32(2), 289–312. DOI: 10.1007/s40593-022-00265-1

Zhou, Y., Ren, T., Chen, N., Li, J., Lu, K., Li, Y., Acharya, A., Shah, P., Hogg, A., & Liu, Y. (2023). Student virtual social practices between China and Nepal. *International Journal of Technology and Inclusive Education*, 12(1), 1802–1807. https://infonomics-society.org/wp-content/uploads/Student-Virtual-Social-Practices-between-China-and-Nepal.pdf. DOI: 10.20533/ijtie.2047.0533.2023.0223

Zhu, Y., & Newsam, S. (2017, September). Densenet for dense flow. In *2017 IEEE international conference on image processing (ICIP)* (pp. 790-794). IEEE. DOI: 10.1109/ICIP.2017.8296389

Zhu, X. (2015, March). Machine teaching: An inverse problem to machine learning and an approach toward optimal education. In *Proceedings of the AAAI conference on artificial intelligence*. DOI: 10.1609/aaai.v29i1.9761

Zimmerman, J., & Forlizzi, J. (2014). *Research Through Design in HCI*. Springer., DOI: 10.1007/978-1-4939-0378-8_8

Zirar, A., Ali, S. I., & Islam, N. (2023). Worker and workplace Artificial Intelligence (AI) coexistence: Emerging themes and research agenda. *Technovation*, 124, 102747. DOI: 10.1016/j.technovation.2023.102747

Zohuri, B., & Mossavar-Rahmani, F. (2024). Revolutionizing education: The dynamic synergy of personalized learning and artificial intelligence. *International Journal of Advanced Engineering and Management Research*, 9(1), 143–153. DOI: 10.51505/ijaemr.2024.9111

Zupanc, K., & Bosnic, Z. (2016). Advances in the field of automated essay evaluation. *Informatica (Vilnius)*, 39(4), 383–395.

About the Contributors

Eriona Cela is a distinguished academic and expert in European integration and negotiation, renowned for her contributions to education and public administration in Albania and beyond. Holding prominent positions within multiple institutions, she serves as a key figure at the Academy of European Integration and Negotiations (AIEN), the Albanian School of Public Administration (ASPA), and the Business Academy College. Dr. Cela's expertise is further recognized through her active involvement in various roles related to European Union policies and enlargement strategies. As a Jean Monnet Chair holder at the Institute of European Studies, University of Tirana, Dr. Cela has spearheaded significant projects such as the European Integration School 2023's eighth edition. Her work frequently appears in prestigious publications, including the European Journal of Arts, Humanities and Social Sciences, the European Journal of Contemporary Education, and the International Journal of Balkan Studies. She is also an Associate Editor for the International Journal of Risk and Contingency Management (IJRCM), an IGI Journal. She has also been engaged with the OSCE Academy in Bishkek, Vytautas Magnus University, and the Università degli Studi di Bari Aldo Moro, Dipartimento di Studi Umanistici, where she has furthered research and collaboration on a European scale. Dr. Cela's commitment to educational leadership is demonstrated through her involvement with Shkolla e Drejtorëve (CSL) and the AADF, where she focuses on developing future leaders and administrators. In recognition of her ongoing contributions to education and public administration, Dr. Cela has received numerous accolades and is frequently invited as a keynote speaker at various academic and policy-making webinars. Her work continues to influence the strategic development of education systems in Albania and serves as a benchmark for integrating European educational standards and practices in the region.

Narasimha Rao Vajjhala is working as the Dean of the Faculty of Engineering and Architecture at the University of New York Tirana, Albania. He had previously worked as the Chair of Computer Science and Software Engineering programs at the American University of Nigeria. He is a senior member of ACM and IEEE. He is the Editor-in-Chief (EiC) of the International Journal of Risk and Contingency Management (IJRCM). He is also a member of the Risk Management Society (RIMS), and the Project Management Institute (PMI). He has over 23 years of experience teaching programming and database-related courses at both graduate and undergraduate levels in Europe and Africa. He has also worked as a consultant in technology firms in Europe and has experience participating in EU-funded projects. He has completed a Doctorate in Information Systems and Technology (United States); holds a Master of Science in Computer Science and Applications (India), and a Master of Business Administration with a specialization in Information Systems (Switzerland).

Mathias Mbu Fonkam is a distinguished Associate Professor at the Penn State College of Information Sciences and Technology. With a rich background in computer science and systems engineering, Dr. Fonkam's academic and professional journey is marked by significant contributions to both academia and the software industry. Dr. Fonkam earned his Ph.D. in Computer Science from Cardiff University, where he also completed his Master of Science in Systems Engineering and Bachelor of Science with Honors in Computer Engineering. His scholarly work is complemented by industry certifications, including Sun Certified Programmer on the Java II Platform and multiple certifications from IBM's Cognitivelabs.ai in areas such as Data Science, Blockchain Technologies, and Cryptocurrencies. Professionally, Dr. Fonkam has an extensive record of academic leadership and innovation. Before his current role at Penn State University, he served as the Dean and Associate Professor at the American University of Nigeria (AUN). During his tenure, he played a pivotal role in establishing and leading the development of the University's open-source ERP system and its learning management system, CANVAS. His efforts in curriculum development and the implementation of graduate programs significantly advanced AUN's educational offerings. Dr. Fonkam's contributions extend beyond administrative leadership. He has been actively involved in the Nigerian academic community, participating in committees for the National Universities Commission (NUC) to develop new computing degree programs and accreditations. His international experience includes roles at Albany State University, St. Joseph's University, and as a visiting professor in Brazil, enhancing his global perspective on education in computer science and engineering. A prolific researcher and educator, Dr. Fonkam's interests span various aspects of computer science, including open-source software development, AI, data science, machine learning, and blockchain technology. His publications and conference presentations address a wide range of topics from systems dynamics to the application of ICTs in crisis management. Dr.

Mathias Mbu Fonkam is a dedicated educator and researcher whose work continues to influence the fields of information technology and computer science education, preparing the next generation of IT professionals and scholars.

***

Nirmal Acharya is a marketing expert and educator and serves as a Course Coordinator at the Australian International Institute of Higher Education. Nirmal is skilled in academic research and tools such as PLS-SEM, NVIVO, EndNote, SPSS, and MS Office Suite.

Omid Afsharpour is pursuing a Master of Finance at Iowa State University, where he passionately explores the intersections of corporate finance, entrepreneurship, and artificial intelligence. With a keen interest in innovative financial strategies, Omid aims to leverage AI to enhance decision-making processes within the finance sector. He is also fascinated by the potential of AI in education and entrepreneurship, seeking to explore how technology can drive growth and learning. Outside of his studies, he enjoys collaborating on projects that bridge technology and finance, aspiring to contribute to the future of the industry.

Mazhar Shamsi Ansary graduated with honors in Education from J.K. College in 2012 and completed his M.A. at Sidho Kanho Birsha University in 2014. He qualified for the National Eligibility Test (NET) in December 2016. Currently, he serves as an Assistant Professor in the Department of Education at Netaji Nagar College for Women, Kolkata. Dr. Ansary earned his Ph.D. in 2022 from Sidho Kanho Birsha University, focusing on the topic "Attitude of Postgraduate Students towards Mobile Learning in West Bengal and Jharkhand: A Comparative Study." Dr. Ansary has published over 20 research articles in respected national and international journals and edited volumes. He has also presented numerous papers at national and international conferences. His research interests include educational technology, peace education, women's education, minority education, sustainable development, and indigenous knowledge.

Santosh Kumar Behera is an Associate Professor in the Department of Education at Kazi Nazrul University, Paschim Bardhaman, West Bengal, India. He completed his undergraduate degree at Fakir Mohan University, Odisha, followed by an M.A. in Education at Vinaya Bhavana, Visva-Bharati (a Central University in India). Dr. Behera earned his Ph.D. from Visva-Bharati, with his research focused on "An Investigation into the Attitude of SC and ST Children of Southern Orissa towards Education." With over 14 years of teaching experience, including

12 years at the postgraduate level, Dr. Behera's research interests encompass SC and ST (Tribal) Education, Educational Technology, Philosophy of Education, Peace Education, Teacher Education, the Indian Knowledge System, Curriculum Studies, Higher Education, and Educational Measurement and Evaluation. He has contributed extensively to the field through articles and edited volumes. Dr. Behera serves as the Editor-in-Chief of EDUQUEST: An International Refereed Journal in Education (ISSN: 2277-3614) and the International Journal of Academic Research in Education and Related Fields.

Mustapha Bouakkaz is a Computer Science professor specializing in Artificial Intelligence (AI), cloud technologies, and education at Laghouat University, Algeria. With a Ph.D. co-supervised by the University of Lyon 2, he has over 15 years of experience in Java and Python, focusing on AI applications in education, digital intelligence, and biomedicine. Known for his research on AI-driven personalized learning and multilingual EFL tools, he contributes to international conferences, publishes in high-impact journals, and collaborates globally. Prof. Bouakkaz's teaching and research emphasize real-world applications, aiming to advance AI for societal benefit and lifelong learning.

Houda Boumediene is a scholar in the field of Applied Linguistics, holding a PhD and serving as a permanent lecturer (MCA) at the Department of English, University of Laghouat, Algeria. Her research interests focus on critical thinking, Integrating Content and Language in Higher Education (ICLHE), corpus analysis, artificial intelligence in education, and adaptive learning strategies. Dr. Boumediene's work in critical thinking emphasizes the development of analytical skills essential for academic and professional success. Her involvement in ICLHE reflects her dedication to innovative teaching methods that integrate language learning with subject matter content. Additionally, her research on corpus analysis provides valuable insights into language usage patterns, while her exploration of AI in education and adaptive learning strategies showcases her forward-thinking approach to leveraging technology for personalized learning.

Joy Cyprian is a Project Management Professional with over a decade of experience in diverse industries. He has expertise in strategic planning, risk management, and Agile methodologies. At Marwadi University, he developed innovative project frameworks that reduced project completion time by 50% and increased productivity by 25%, resulting in significant cost savings and enhanced stakeholder satisfaction. Skilled in data analytics, Joy optimizes resource allocation and decision-making accuracy, achieving a 40% improvement in project outcomes. His leadership in process improvement has streamlined operations, cutting overhead costs by 30% and raising customer satisfaction scores by 20%. He has also spearheaded IT integration projects that increased cross-departmental efficiency and data accuracy by 35%, as well as business service center optimizations that reduced response times by 45% and elevated service quality standards.

Nupur Gorai completed her M.A. in Education from the Department of Education at Kazi Nazrul University, Paschim Bardhaman, West Bengal, India. She is currently pursuing her B.Ed. at Saltora B.Ed. College in Bankura, West Bengal, India.

Miftachul Huda is a researcher at Faculty of Human Sciences, Universiti Pendidikan Sultan Idris Malaysia. His research interest includes the field of educational studies: moral, Islamic and multicultural education, learning theory, adaptive teaching and learning technology. He has been experienced in working on research for more than five years. Contributing several works, he is currently the member of the advisory editorial board in some international journals. Traveling in some countries with scholarly intent makes him extensive experience on his research expertise in international trend and issues. Thus, he commits to contributing his knowledge to the benefit of society through professional and social activities.

Shankar Subramanian Iyer has two and a half decades of experience in sales, marketing, business development, and CRM across various sectors including engineering, construction, mining, projects, finance, and education. Recently he has developed program and course curriculums, Quality Assurance for Business, Engineering, and Vocational Courses (KHDA), and assisting in their delivery after receiving approval from the sponsors (Dubai Municipality, Mohammed Bin Rashid Housing Establishment, Dubai Electrical and Water Authority, Dubai Road Transport Authority, Dubai Aluminium, Dubai Petroleum and Gas, and Academicians (EDEXCEL). Dr Shankar has also worked for QAD on TVET Approvals as an Internal Verifier and External Reviewer. His research interests include Blockchain in Education, Data Analysis, Big Data, Artificial Intelligence, Virtual Reality, and Augmented Reality.

Vishal Jain is Professor at Sharda University's Department of Computer Science and Engineering, with over 18 years of academic experience. He holds various degrees and has over 1900 research citations. Jain has authored over 150 research papers and edited over 60 books with various publishers. His research areas include machine learning, information retrieval, semantic web, ontology engineering, data mining, ad hoc networks, sensor networks, and network security. He has received awards from the Computer Society of India and BVICAM.

Aravindh K is currently conducting his studies at Vellore Institute of Technology, where he has established a strong foundation in computer science, with expertise in data structures and algorithms (DSA), database management, content creation, and public speaking. Actively engaged in various clubs and chapters throughout his academic journey, Aravindh demonstrates a commitment to personal and professional growth. His career goal is to become a data scientist and an effective communicator, continuously seeking new challenges to expand his skill set. Outside of academia, Aravindh enjoys reading, coding, and playing outdoor sports, which contribute to a well-rounded and fulfilling lifestyle.

Mustafa Kayyali has a Master's in Quality Management and Evaluation in Higher Education from Universitat Oberta de Catalunya, followed by a Ph.D. in Quality Management from Azteca University. As an entrepreneur, researcher, translator, and publisher, Mustafa is actively engaged in various aspects of the academic field. His areas of expertise include Management, Translation, Interpretation, and Academic Consulting, providing a comprehensive perspective on the industry. Throughout his career, Mustafa has made substantial contributions to academic literature, with over 20 published papers and 7 book chapters. Additionally, he has translated 5 books.

Madhavi Kilaru working as an Assistant Professor in the Department of Humanities & Sciences at VNR Vignana Jyothi Institute of Engineering & Technology, Hyderabad has about 17 years of teaching experience. She received her BA degree in Mathematics & Statistics with distinction and MBA degree in Marketing & HR with distinction from Andhra University, Visakhapatnam. She received Ph.D degree in Marketing from Andhra University, Visakhatnam AP state. She has published 25 research papers in refereed international journals and 30 research papers in the proceedings of various national and international conferences. She also published patents. Her areas of research include Supply chain Management, Human Resource Management, Consumer Behavior, Artificial Intelligent and Business Analytics. She is an active member CMOAI.

Yuanyuan Li is a Professor at the Music College of Capital Normal University in Beijing, China, specializing in vocal education and advancing music pedagogy for global citizenship education. During the COVID-19 pandemic, she co-founded the hybrid LivePBL (Linking Vocal Education through Project-Based Learning) project, collaborating with international teams to promote cultural and sustainable social development through music. LivePBL has been featured at major conferences, including the London International Conference on Education and QS Reimaging Education. Professor Li is a member of prestigious music associations and a judge for vocal competitions. Her students have won numerous awards, showcasing her effective teaching. She has led significant educational projects recognized by the Ministry of Education, including student-centred vocal teaching and nationwide cross-school online open courses on classical Chinese music.

Melissa Liow Li Sa is the Assistant Head of the School of Business and Management at PSB Academy. She holds a Bachelor of Business degree from the University of Technology Sydney (UTS), an MBA from the University of Wales (UOW), and a Ph.D. in Business from the International University of Malaya-Wales (IUMW). Dr. Liow has extensive experience teaching in the areas of Marketing, Human Resource Management, and Tourism and Hospitality Management. Her research interests focus on tourism entrepreneurship. In addition to her teaching and research responsibilities, Dr. Liow serves as the Program Leader for Hospitality and Tourism programs and as an Ex-Officio member of the Assessment Committee at PSB Academy.

Ying Liu is a lecturer at the London School of Science and Technology, UK, where he supports HE for disadvantaged communities. He holds a PhD from TU Delft, an MEd from Cambridge, and an MBA from Durham. A former advisor to China's Ministry of Education, Dr. Liu has held research fellowships at Cambridge, Edinburgh, and Aberdeen. He leads international education projects and founded LivePBL, a hybrid learning program shortlisted by European eLearning and QS Reimagine Education 2023.

Jayashree Mahanti is currently affiliated with the Department of Education at the Central University of Jharkhand, Ranchi, India. She previously served as a College Whole-Time Teacher at The Bhawanipur Education Society College in Kolkata, West Bengal. Dr. Mahanti earned her postgraduate degree in Education, graduating First Class First, from Sidho-Kanho-Birsha University, where she also completed her B.Ed. and Ph.D. She qualified for the UGC-NET JRF in 2016 and the WBCSC SET in 2018. An enthusiastic scholar, Dr. Mahanti has presented her research at numerous conferences and has published extensively in respected journals and edited volumes.

Indrajit Mahato holds an M A. in Education from Visva-Bharati University and is currently serving as a Visiting Lecturer at Mahatma Gandhi College in Lalpur, Purulia, West Bengal, India.

Mouad Malmous is a doctoral candidate in applied linguistics at the Faculty of Letters and Humanities Ben M'sik, Hassan II University of Casablanca. His research focuses on artificial intelligence, technology, writing, and automated feedback in language education. With over five years of teaching experience, he is dedicated to exploring innovative methodologies that support students' language development and critical thinking skills. His academic background includes teaching English for specific purposes, reading comprehension, and oral communication across multiple higher education institutions in Morocco.

Pınar Mıhcı Türker earned his undergraduate degree in Computer and Instructional Technologies Education from Gazi University in 2002, followed by a master's degree in the same field from Ankara University in 2009, and completed his doctorate at Gazi University in 2016. From 2002 to 2010, he served as an Information Technologies teacher with the Ministry of National Education. Since 2010, Dr. Turker has been a faculty member in the Department of Computer and Instructional Technologies Education at Aksaray University, advancing to the role of assistant professor in 2016 and achieving the rank of associate professor in Instructional Technologies in 2023. His research focuses on project-based learning, safe and responsible internet use, haptic and computational thinking, programming education, online learning, thinking skills, and artificial intelligence, with numerous publications in these areas.

Dibyanshu Mohanty is a researcher in Computer Science and Engineering at Sharda University. An emerging researcher interested in technology-driven platforms, he has gained practical experience as a student member in an apprenticeship, where he contributed to developing a competitive gaming event website. This platform provides a structured environment for players to participate in tournaments and receive guidance to enhance their skills. Dibyanshu utilized HTML, CSS, and JavaScript to create the website, demonstrating his proficiency in front-end development and dedication to fostering interactive, skill-based digital experiences.

Mücahit Ozturk is currently a faculty member in the Department of Instructional Technologies at Aksaray University. He completed his postgraduate studies in Instructional Technologies at Karadeniz Technical University. Dr. Ozturk teaches courses in computer programming, web programming, instructional design, and information technologies. His research interests include educational technologies, online learning, flipped learning, programming education, and self-regulated learning.

Rajasekhara Mouly Potluri is a Professor of Management/Marketing with thirty-three years of industry/teaching experience in around ten countries and is currently working as a Professor of Marketing at the Business School of Kazakh-British Technical University of Almaty, Kazakhstan. Dr. Raj holds a Ph.D. and M. Phil. in Management/Marketing from Shivaji University, an MBA (Marketing), and a Master of Commerce (Banking) from Andhra University, India. He has published and presented around a hundred and thirty research articles, books, book chapters, and case studies in renowned peer-reviewed journals indexed in Scopus, ABDC, SSCI, IEEE, KCI, and International Conferences and won more than twenty Best Research Paper Awards and Academic Service Excellence Awards. Prof. Raj has extensive teaching and research experience in multicultural and multi-ethnic environments in India, Ethiopia, Kazakhstan, South Korea, Nigeria, and the United Arab Emirates (Golden Visa Received). His research interests are Marketing, Islamic Marketing, CSR and Sustainability, HRM & OB, and Entrepreneurship. He has professional memberships in the Eurasian Business & Economics Society, International Islamic Marketing Association, Social Responsibility Research Network, International Society for Development & Sustainability, Emerald Literate Network, and Consumer Guidance Society of India.

Sarra Rouabhi was born in Oran, Algeria, in 1996. She earned her Bachelor's degree in Telecommunications from the University of Science and Technology of Oran Mohamed Boudiaf (USTO-MB) in 2017, followed by a Master's degree in Networks and Telecommunications from the same institution in 2019. Currently, she is pursuing a Ph.D. in the Department of Electronics, specializing in telecommunications. Her research interests include artificial intelligence, data processing, and deep learning.

Aidin Salamzadeh is the Vice Dean of the College of Management (University of Tehran) and an integrated researcher at CIICESI, Polytechnic of Porto (Portugal). His interests are startups, new venture creation, and entrepreneurship. Aidin serves as an associate editor for the Humanities and Social Sciences Communications (Nature.com); Journal of Enterprising Communities; Revista de Gestão; Innovation Management Review (Emerald), Entrepreneurial Business and Economics Review, Journal of Women's Entrepreneurship and Education, as well as The Bottom Line (Emerald). Besides, he is a reviewer in numerous distinguished international journals. Aidin is a member of the European SPES Forum (Belgium), the Asian Academy of Management (Malaysia), Ondokuz Mayis University (Turkey), and the Institute of Economic Sciences (Serbia). He co-founded the Innovation and Entrepreneurship Research Lab (London). In 2024, Stanford University listed him as the top 2% scientists.

Jeganathan Gomathi Sankar specializes in marketing and currently teaches at the BSSS Institute of Advanced Studies. He served as a research scholar at Pondicherry University, focusing on information diffusion, ICT, Marketing technology, AI, and Data Science. Dr. Sankar's research is published in journals indexed in Scopus and ABDC. Formerly a faculty member at Saveetha School of

Management, he contributed to marketing education. Dr. Beyond teaching, he is proficient in analytical tools such as SPSS, AMOS, STATA, PowerBI, and Python. He is a member of BSSS Institute of Advanced Studies.

Smitha Shivshankar is the Associate Academic Dean at the Australian International Institute of Higher Education. Her research interests center on data dissemination and cooperation in vehicular networks, particularly through the application of game theory. She has published extensively on topics including ad hoc networks, vehicular ad hoc networks, node contributions, control packets, packet forwarding, and asynchronous communication. Ms. Shivshankar is a recipient of the Australian Postgraduate Award, funded by the Australian Government, and was honored with the Telstra Award in 2012 for her solution to an industrial problem.

Brijendra Singh received his Ph.D. from VIT, Vellore, Tamil Nadu, India. He is currently an Associate Professor in the School of Computer Science and Engineering and Information Systems at VIT Vellore, Tamil Nadu, India. His research interests include health informatics, soft computing techniques, artificial intelligence, rough set theory, and knowledge representation.

Redouane Tlemsani is an accomplished academic and researcher, serving as an Associate Professor since 2017. Holding a Ph.D. in Data Sciences and Artificial Intelligence, he specializes in data processing and computer science. Affiliated with the University of Science and Technology of Oran (USTO) in Algeria, he conducts pioneering research in these fields. Alongside his research, he is a dedicated educator, sharing his expertise with students in computer science and software engineering at both the Engineering and LMD levels.

Alexey Vedishchev is an IT professional and educator with over 12 years of expertise in computer science education. He holds an MSc in Information Technology and Business from Altay State Technical University in Russia, where he also completed specialized training in information management for higher education. Since 2014, he has been an instructor at the American University of Nigeria, where he teaches various programming, database, and software development courses. His professional background includes roles in IT support and management at organizations like Russian Post and Quanteq LTD, focusing on product support, IT policy development, and infrastructure planning.

Said Zaidoune is a full-time professor at the Faculty of Letters and Humanities Ben M'sik, Hassan II University of Casablanca, specializing in Applied Linguistics and Citizenship in Education. In addition to his teaching, Prof. Zaidoune is an active member and consultant for several associations and NGOs in MoroccoHe has organized numerous workshops, seminars, and conferences on activism and community work, both nationally and internationally.

Ting Zhao is a Principal Lecturer and Scholar in Early Years Music Education at Beijing Youth and Politics Vocational College, China, with over a decade of experience. She also served as an Associate of the Overseas Chinese Bureau, promoting global cultural exchanges. Ms. Zhao's research interest is in innovative teaching methods, child development, and technology in music education. She co-founded LivePBL, a hybrid teaching platform praised for enhancing teacher education through real-world scenarios.

Mahnaz Zolfaghari is pursuing a Ph.D. in Curriculum and Instruction with a focus on Science Education at Indiana University Bloomington. Her research centers on the application of artificial intelligence in education, aiming to uncover its impact on educational practices and learning outcomes. Approaching her work as an educational entrepreneur, Mahnaz examines how AI can transform the educational landscape by enhancing student engagement and instructional strategies. This research builds on her year-long master's thesis in Educational Administration at the University of Tehran, where she began investigating the role of emerging technologies in education.

Index

Symbols

A

F

G

H

I

L

M

P

Q

R

S

T

U

V

W

www.ingramcontent.com/pod-product-compliance
Lightning Source LLC
LaVergne TN
LVHW080354011026
849161LV00009B/2301
9798369372203